LIBERALISM AND HEGEMONY:
DEBATING THE CANADIAN LIBERAL REVOLUTION

In 2000, Ian McKay, a highly respected historian at Queen's University, published an article in the *Canadian Historical Review* entitled 'The Liberal Order Framework: A Prospectus for a Reconnaissance of Canadian History.' Written to address a crisis in Canadian history, this detailed, programmatic, and well-argued article proposed that Canadian history should be mapped through a process of reconnaissance and that the Canadian state should be understood as a project of liberal rule in North America. McKay's essay prompted debate immediately upon publication. In *Liberalism and Hegemony*, some of Canada's finest historians continue this debate.

The essays collected here explore the possibilities and limits presented by 'The Liberal Order Framework' for various segments of Canadian history and discuss the paramount influence of liberalism throughout the nineteenth and twentieth centuries in the context of Aboriginal history, environmental history, the history of the family, the development of political thought and ideas, and municipal governance.

Like McKay's 'The Liberal Order Framework,' which is included in this volume along with his response to recent criticism, *Liberalism and Hegemony* is a fascinating foray into current historical thought and provides the historical community with a book that will act both as a reference and a guide for future research.

JEAN-FRANÇOIS CONSTANT is a PhD candidate in the Department of History at McGill University.

MICHEL DUCHARME is an assistant professor in the Department of History at the University of British Columbia.

Liberalism and Hegemony

Debating the Canadian Liberal Revolution

*Edited by Jean-François Constant
and Michel Ducharme*

UNIVERSITY OF TORONTO PRESS
Toronto Buffalo London

© University of Toronto Press Incorporated 2009
Toronto Buffalo London
www.utppublishing.com
Printed in Canada

ISBN 978-0-8020-9882-5 (cloth)
ISBN 978-0-8020-9589-3 (paper)

Printed on acid-free paper

Library and Archives Canada Cataloguing in Publication

Liberalism and hegemony : debating the Canadian liberal revolution /
edited by Jean-François Constant and Michel Ducharme.

Includes bibliographical references and index.
ISBN 978-0-8020-9882-5 (bound)   ISBN 978-0-8020-9589-3 (pbk.)

1. Liberalism – Canada.   2. Hegemony – Canada.   3. Canada –
Historiography.   4. Canada – Politics and government.   5. Canada –
History.   I. Ducharme, Michel, 1975–   II. Constant, Jean François, 1976–

FC176.L52 2009   971.0072   C2008-905828-3

University of Toronto Press acknowledges the financial assistance to its
publishing program of the Canada Council for the Arts and the Ontario
Arts Council.

University of Toronto Press acknowledges the financial support for its
publishing activities of the Government of Canada through the Book
Publishing Industry Development Program (BPIDP).

This book has been published with the help of a grant from the Canadian
Federation for the Humanities and Social Sciences, through the Aid to
Scholarly Publications Program, using funds provided by the Social Sciences
and Humanities Research Council of Canada.

Contents

Acknowledgments   vii

Introduction: A Project of Rule Called Canada – The Liberal Order
Framework and Historical Practice   3
MICHEL DUCHARME AND JEAN-FRANÇOIS CONSTANT

'The Liberal Order Framework: A Prospectus for a Reconnaissance of
Canadian History,' reproduction of *Canadian Historical Review* 81 (2000):
617–45   35
IAN McKAY

In Hope and Fear: Intellectual History, Liberalism, and the Liberal
Order Framework   64
JEFFREY L. McNAIRN

Canada as Counter-Revolution: The Loyalist Order Framework in
Canadian History, 1750–1840   98
JERRY BANNISTER

Rights Talk and the Liberal Order Framework   147
E.A. HEAMAN

After 'Canada': Liberalisms, Social Theory, and Historical
Analysis   176
BRUCE CURTIS

The Municipal Territory: A Product of the Liberal Order?   201
MICHÈLE DAGENAIS

The Nature of the Liberal Order: State Formation, Conservation, and the Government of Non-Humans in Canada   221
STÉPHANE CASTONGUAY AND DARIN KINSEY

Missing Canadians: Reclaiming the A-Liberal Past   246
R.W. SANDWELL

Women, Racialized People, and the Making of the Liberal Order in Northern North America   274
ADELE PERRY

A Persistent Antagonism: First Nations and the Liberal Order   298
ROBIN JARVIS BROWNLIE

'Variants of Liberalism' and the Liberal Order Framework in British Columbia   322
ROBERT McDONALD

Canada as a Long Liberal Revolution: On Writing the History of Actually Existing Canadian Liberalisms, 1840s–1940s   347
IAN McKAY

Contributors   453

Index   457

Acknowledgments

The essays collated in this book were first presented at the 'Liberal Order in Canadian History' symposium held at the McGill Institute for the Study of Canada in March 2006. The unshakable support of the Institute and its director, Antonia Maioni, towards the editors of this book made the organizing of the conference easy and agreeable. The Institute and the Department of History at McGill University, to which we are thankful, shared the financial burden of the event. *MENS: Revue d'histoire intellectuelle de l'Amérique française* also deserves our gratitude for the allotment of free advertising in its pages.

The responsibility for the success of the symposium, however, is mostly due to the people that helped organize it and who participated in the event. We can never thank Johanne Bilodeau and Linda Huddy enough for their constant, selfless efforts. The workers at Thomson House also deserve our thanks for their professionalism and hard work. The authors of the essays contained in this book aside, we are grateful to the following people for their participation in the conference: Jarrett Rudy, Denyse Baillargeon, Damien-Claude Bélanger, Desmond Morton, and Fernande Roy. More specifically, we thank Ian McKay, who gallantly accepted hearing the framework he put forth being analysed, scrutinized, and rigorously criticized by a dozen of his colleagues.

At the University of Toronto Press, Len Husband proved to be an enthusiastic and meticulous editor from the start. The anonymous readers also provided helpful critiques and suggestions. As for Frances Mundy and John St James, they deserve thanks for their fine editorial work. Finally, we thank the *Canadian Historical Review* for allowing us to reproduce the article that started the whole debate.

Jean-François Constant and Michel Ducharme

LIBERALISM AND HEGEMONY:
DEBATING THE CANADIAN LIBERAL REVOLUTION

Introduction: A Project of Rule Called Canada – The Liberal Order Framework and Historical Practice

MICHEL DUCHARME AND JEAN-FRANÇOIS CONSTANT[1]

In 2000 Ian McKay published a ground-breaking article in the *Canadian Historical Review* entitled 'The Liberal Order Framework: A Prospectus for a Reconnaissance of Canadian History.'[2] Following other historians, McKay suggests that Canadian history is currently going through a crisis. This crisis is not linked to any fundamental weakness in Canadian historiography, nor to a profound deficiency in the various scholarly approaches privileged by researchers working today. In fact, quite the opposite is true; it is actually the new-found richness and diversity of contemporary Canadian historiography that represents a real challenge within the discipline. The development of social and then cultural history since the 1960s led to the rediscovery of many different histories belonging to different groups of people once marginalized by traditional political historiography. Thanks to this important new wave of historical work, the past experiences of ordinary people, the working classes, women, and ethnic minorities are now understood in a more nuanced and comprehensive way. However, if the specialized monographs that now dominate the discipline have had the advantage of giving a voice back to those who have been silenced and excluded, the proliferation of these texts has also encouraged the fragmentation of the traditional discipline of history. It is this fracturing that McKay regrets and, further, the absence of any contemporary analytical framework that might allow us to study the broad contours of Canadian history since 1840 while still taking into account its diversity and complexity.

Though McKay deplores the fracturing of the historical discipline, he does not suggest that we should reject all the valuable work produced in the last forty years. Unlike Jack Granatstein and Michael Bliss,[3] McKay does not advocate a return to nationalist historical syntheses or to epic political narratives. He does not suggest that we should blindly celebrate Canada, or the political processes that led to its birth, nor that we should reject certain methodological approaches in favour of a return to more traditional models of political or social history. Rather, McKay believes that we should integrate the recent discoveries of social and cultural history into a new analytical framework inspired by the latest developments in Canadian intellectual, political, and legal history. He suggests that we should move towards a true reconnaissance, that we should revisit the history of Canada by studying what he calls 'the Canadian Liberal Revolution,'[4] a phrase he uses to describe the gradual deployment of a liberal order in the British colonies of North America, and later within the Canadian federation, between 1840 and 1940. In other words, McKay argues that we should approach Canada not as 'an essence we must defend or an empty homogeneous space we must possess,'[5] but rather as an ongoing 'project of liberal rule.'[6]

The originality of McKay's argument does not rest on the important status it grants to liberalism. His thesis can be integrated into the general development of Canadian and Québécois historiographies that have helped to illustrate the importance of liberal, capitalist, and modern principles in the development of Canada and Québec. McKay's argument accepts the conclusions of many other works which have demonstrated that Canadian economic and political elites have supported liberal economic principles since 1840.[7] It also links directly to other works that focus on state formation[8] and liberal social regulation.[9] McKay's thesis complements the work of historians and political scientists who have used an essentially political definition of liberalism, understood as British constitutionalism, to illustrate the Whig or Liberal roots of the political thought of Canada's elite.[10] If McKay's argument is original, it is because it allows us to leave behind the old debate in which Canadian historians have been forced to decide which historical perspective is the most important or valuable: social/cultural or political. By basing his argument simultaneously on new works in political, legal, and intellectual history *and* on new works in social and cultural history, McKay demonstrates that these perspectives are not necessarily contradictory, with each side studying the past in a different way. Rather, it is only by twinning these supposedly opposite approaches that we can come to a fuller understanding of Canadian history.

McKay's work advocates a movement beyond recent studies that are 'regional in range, monographic in strategy, and cautious about generalizing beyond tightly defined localities and 'cases.'[11] At the same time, he does not endorse a return to the epic narratives and teleological or Whiggish texts that present Canada's history as a kind of evolution 'from colony to nation.' Instead, he argues for the development of 'a third paradigm beyond the traditional nationalist and socio-cultural historical narratives.'[12] This third paradigm seeks to be more modest than the two preceding models. Even McKay suggests that his analytic framework should be interpreted as 'a contingent, partial, and (perhaps) somewhat risky attempt to derive a sense of general patterns from particular discrete sightings.'[13] This new model or paradigm, which McKay calls the liberal order framework, relies primarily on a study of the power relations that helped establish the liberal order in Canada between 1840 and 1940. More precisely, McKay suggests that historians must critically analyse the way in which these liberal principles came to be implanted on the Canadian territory in light of the theories of hegemony and passive revolution articulated by Antonio Gramsci. The liberal order framework also aims, in part, to clarify our understanding of the methods that the promoters of the liberal order used to impose their hegemony on Canada, as well as the many forms of resistance against which they had to struggle in order to realize their project.

Beyond its undeniable historiographic importance, the liberal order framework can also be seen as having a tremendous political potential. Although the political ramifications of McKay's argument are implicit in the article published in the *Canadian Historical Review*, they are quite explicit in his book *Rebels, Reds, Radicals: Rethinking Canada's Left History*, a work that revisits the same analytical framework.[14] In fact, even the simplest discussion of liberalism has always been a political act, both in Canada and elsewhere. Liberalism is, after all, one of the most influential ideologies of the nineteenth and twentieth centuries (and possibly the twenty-first century as well), and because of its power, liberalism has never left and, indeed, can never leave any intellectual or historian indifferent. The political, economic, social, and even moral implications of liberalism, both in the past and in the contemporary period, have been and still are too important not to have attracted the attention of historians, both in their roles as researchers and also as responsible citizens. McKay is no exception to this rule and he certainly does not hide from the political repercussions of his work. His paradigm openly contests the liberal presumptions on which Canada is built. It invites historians to discuss the violence that liberals used to establish, extend, and maintain the liberal order. It also aims to uncover the limitations that were imposed on Canada's emerging democracy in order to better protect the interests 'of a few liberal men, living in a few southern cities.'[15]

McKay's article is certainly one of the most ambitious and most important texts that the *Canadian Historical Review* has published in recent decades. It holds an essential position in Canadian historiography because it is one of the rare programmatic articles of this calibre. It is this desire to develop a more general understanding of Canadian history from 1840 to 1940 that explains why this one article holds such an important position in the country's historiography. Taking into account the wide interest this argument has attracted, continues to attract, and promises to attract in coming years within the academic community, in terms of both classroom discussion and higher-level research,[16] we believe the moment has come to discuss and debate the liberal order framework as well as its historiographic implications. Many Canadian and Québécois historians interested in liberalism and the liberal order were invited to share their reflections on McKay's argument during a symposium organized by the McGill Institute for the Study of Canada in March 2006. As the essays in this volume ably demonstrate, the meeting attracted a wide range of scholars from across the country and stimulated several passionate exchanges. Whether the historians who participated in this academic forum were supporters or critics of the analysis put forward by McKay, every one of them agreed that his argument was important enough to be discussed and debated at the highest level.

Liberalism and the Liberal Order

If contemporary Canadian and Québécois historians generally accept the idea that Canadian history between 1840 and 1940 was heavily influenced by liberalism, they continue to disagree on the nature and impact of liberalism in Canada. In this context, it is not so much the importance given to liberalism in McKay's paradigm that divides historians, but the very definition of liberalism he uses.

Defining Liberalism

In the beginning of his argument, McKay takes great care to underline the fact that the terms 'liberalism' and 'liberal order' are not synonyms.[17] Nevertheless, it is important to understand that the very particular model of liberal order that McKay seeks to uncover relies on a very particular definition of liberalism. As Jeffrey McNairn, Bruce Curtis, and Robert McDonald all note in their respective articles here, the definition of liberalism to which McKay refers is important because it colours almost every aspect of his discussion of the liberal order.

McKay borrows the definition of liberalism provided by Fernande Roy in her important book *Progrès, harmonie, liberté: Le libéralisme des milieux d'affaires francophones à Montréal au tournant du siècle*.[18] He presents liberalism as 'a totalizing philosophy'[19] founded on the principle of the primacy of the individual and the inviolability of certain individual rights. According to McKay, liberals grant to individuals the right to equality before the law and certain other civil liberties such as the freedom of expression, freedom of conscience, and freedom of work. His model places special emphasis on the sacred and unalienable liberal right to property, beginning immediately with the possession of the self. This right to property trumps all other rights within liberal philosophy because property is interpreted as 'the precondition of a liberal's identity.'[20]

No researcher can deny that the concept of 'the individual,' understood as an autonomous entity, informs the very foundation of any discussion of liberalism. It is equally undeniable that, despite its pretensions towards universality, liberalism has not always granted the status of individual to all human beings. McKay is correct to present the liberal individual as an intellectual construction or an 'abstract principle'[21] rather than a real person. In fact, between the middle of the nineteenth century and the middle of the twentieth, the very definition of an individual was based on a collective consideration of class, race, and gender. In this regard, liberalism is like any other contemporary ideology in that all ideologies rest on a fundamental abstraction from which a wide variety of political, legal, and social consequences are extrapolated. In this matter, liberalism is no different from fascism (based on an 'abstract principle' of the state), socialism (the society), nationalism (the nation), republicanism (the sovereign people), or conservatism (the social order), to name only the most well-known political ideologies.

By approaching the liberal individual as an abstract principle, the liberal order framework illustrates that there is a fundamental distinction within liberal thought between those who are considered as individuals and those who are not, between those who may take advantage of the rights provided by the liberal order and those who may not. Beyond that most basic distinction, there also exists in liberal thought a hierarchy of non-individuals divided by their race, their gender, and their class. The liberal order framework takes into account postcolonial studies that have drawn attention to the exclusive mechanisms that are inherent in liberalism.[22] One of the strengths of the framework is its ability to take into consideration this fundamental tension, which lies at the base of the liberal order, between those who are included and those who are excluded. In her article for this volume, Adele Perry demonstrates, confirming McKay's thesis, that the exclusion of women and Aboriginal peoples has been one result of the project of Canadian liberal order. However, Robin Jarvis Brownlie argues that the policies adopted by the Canadian government towards Aboriginal peoples are generally found to be in direct opposition to the liberal principles defined by McKay. Although Brownlie does recognize that the framework might be useful for studying the economic and political relations between non-Aboriginals and Aboriginals, she doubts that the framework allows us to adequately understand the other facets of this relationship, as well as the experiences of Aboriginals themselves.

The definition that McKay gives to liberal individualism has the advantage of being subtle enough to ensure that liberalism will not be conflated with other more radical forms of individualism such as libertarianism or individualist anarchism.[23] However, the relations that exist between individuals, groups with more restrictive memberships (such as families, races, classes, and genders), and society in general still need further clarification. For example, does the fact that the liberal order framework stresses the priority of the individual suggest that liberals have absolutely no interest whatsoever in the well-being of society? Most liberals would respond negatively to such a question. They would suggest that liberalism should not be interpreted as an apology for selfishness, even if it could become such a thing, but rather as a theory of sociability.[24] Liberals would argue as well that there is no opposition between individuals and society because society itself should be defined as a collection of these same individuals. In this model, social well-being is seen as the sum total of individual interests. Liberals could just as easily point to the fact that certain liberal thinkers, including John Stuart Mill, gave considerable thought to the problem of trying to find a balance between individual liberties and the common good.[25] The question here is not to determine whether liberal individualism and selfishness are or are not synonymous, but rather to point out that the relationship between the well-being of the individual and the well-being of the community (be that community restricted or enlarged) remains ambiguous in the analysis of the liberal order framework.

If no one can reasonably contest the fact that the primacy of the individual lies at the base of liberalism, the same can be said of the three fundamental liberal values that form the base of McKay's analysis. These are (1) equality before the law, (2) the enjoyment of certain civil liberties, and (3) the sacred right to private property. Although the liberal order framework does reference freedom and equality as fundamental values for liberalism, we must recognize, as E.A. Heaman and Jeffrey McNairn suggest, that these two values are not as well developed as property rights in McKay's analysis.[26] The reason for this is perhaps because, in the liberal order framework, the values of freedom and equality are considered subordinate to those of property rights. The framework's clear hierarchy of principles (property, freedom, equality) gives liberalism a certain economic bias, making it resemble the possessive individualism of C.B. Macpherson, to which McKay makes reference.[27] In this context, even if McKay calls on historians not to reduce liberalism to capitalism on one side and democracy on the other, his decision to base his definition of liberalism on something akin to possessive individualism does, despite the stated goal of the author, allow readers to combine liberalism and capitalism in order to better oppose them to a particular model of democracy.

Generally speaking, it is not the importance granted to these three fundamental values, but rather their hierarchal ranking within the framework that stimulates debate within the historical community. The framework's definition of liberalism is valuable when it is applied to questions of economic liberalism,[28] but one is often left to wonder why this definition of liberalism should prevail over Janet Ajzenstat's essentially political definition, which bases itself on British constitutionalism.[29] It is not that there is necessarily a major contradiction between these two modes; far from it.[30] Nevertheless, if the framework seeks to unify many different liberal perspectives within the same analytical model, the question of political liberty (which is not mentioned in McKay's list of liberal freedoms) should eventually be better developed. In the same way, it would be interesting if the religious principles that inform the base of John Locke's thought[31] or the ethical questions posed by Adam Smith and John Stuart Mill[32] could be integrated in a more obvious way within McKay's analysis in order to produce a model that might allow scholars to analyse liberalism in all its multiple shapes and forms. Conversely, it would be enlightening to see how these religious principles informed the practices of liberal men and women.

Beyond the debate over McKay's ranking of the liberal rights to property, liberty, and equality, the fact that he recognizes only these three fundamental principles promises to stimulate some discussion. The question here is, Do these particular values, considered in isolation, provide us with an adequate definition for the complexity of liberalism? Do we not need, for example, to stress the importance of reason as a fundamental element of liberalism? Is it not reason that allows individuals to know and understand their rights and to understand their limitations within the liberal model? And what about the importance of the rule of law?[33] In other words, are there not other fundamental principles beyond those three basic principles outlined by the framework that would allow us, as Robert McDonald suggests, following Stuart Hall, to think about the existence of not just one, but several 'variants of liberalism'?

As we have already seen, it is not so much the importance of liberalism within the construction of the new Canadian social order after 1840 that certain historians question. Rather, it is the definition of liberalism privileged by McKay. It is here that McNairn fears that the definitions given by the liberal order framework may direct the debate in a way that casts liberalism in a particularly unfavourable light. Despite such criticism, McKay's definition does have its advantages. For example, the framework allows us to reconfigure the study of Canadian history in terms of its broad theoretical principles rather than its political allegiances, which vary over time. Further, when the question of political liberty becomes better developed, this analytical framework will certainly allow us to study political and economic history by moving beyond the traditional distinction between political and economic liberalism. In this sense, the framework nuances the opposition between the Tories/Bleus/conservatives and the Grits/Rouges/liberals without limiting the ability of historians to add their own values to the three favoured by McKay. This would allow historians to better differentiate the many diverse currents of liberalism. Although McKay's definitions may be debatable, they have the added advantage of being flexible and non-restrictive. In fact, the framework clearly represents an interesting and promising point of departure in the effort to study the establishment of the liberal order in the British North American colonies from 1840 onward.

The Relationship between Liberalism and Conservatism

Questions surrounding the definition of liberalism are important, not just because they have a direct impact on how we understand the liberal order, but also because they provide some useful limitations for the discussion that may eventually help us address the issue of the relationship between liberalism and other contemporary ideologies such as conservatism and nationalism.

The integration of conservatism into the liberal order framework represents a challenge because conservatism certainly was not an individualistic ideology in the nineteenth century. Conservatism was not based on a defence of individual autonomy, but rather on the defence of a pre-existing social order and all the privileges that order entailed.[34] Certainly, since the close of the twentieth century, conservatives throughout the Anglo-American world, including Margaret Thatcher and Ronald Reagan, have defended and continue to defend neoliberal ideas that have been consensually termed 'conservative.' They can do this only because the existing social order is so clearly a liberal construction. This phenomenon confirms the general argument of the liberal order framework. However, it is important to note that the conservatives of the nineteenth century were not looking to defend a 'liberal' order. Instead they sought to defend the social order and privileges of the Old Regime.[35] This model of conservatism, based on a vision of society as an organic entity distinct and autonomous from individuals, could be associated with certain ideologies based on the 'society' or the 'community' rather than an ideology based on the 'individual.' It is this kind of logic that allowed Gad Horowitz in 1966 to establish a causal link between the presence of conservatism in Canada and the development of socialism. According to Horowitz, these were two ideologies based on the unity of society.[36]

In spite of this, conservatism does find itself associated with liberalism in the liberal order framework. If this is the case, it is because conservatism, like liberalism, was an ideology that defended private property and social inequalities. The fundamental opposition in the liberal order framework divides political ideologies that appear more socially egalitarian from those that defend private property and a basically anti-egalitarian social order. It is not so much the principle of individualism, freedom, or an openness to reform that provides the foundation for the liberal order framework, but rather the question of property and economic equality.

There is nothing surprising about this method of classifying conservatives and liberals. Since the end of the eighteenth century, British and
Canadian conservatives have accepted the political principles that
McKay defines as liberal, such as the respect of certain civil liberties,
equality before the law, and private property.[37] We could easily add the
rule of law to this list. In this context, despite all those elements that
obviously distinguish liberals and conservatives at the ideological level,
we must realize that these two groups agreed with each other sufficiently enough on certain principles to collaborate and work together
towards the establishment of a new social and political order after 1840.
Although they may not necessarily have understood the order they
were building in exactly the same way – liberals conceived of social
order beginning with the individual, while conservatives began with
the society – these two groups did find enough common ground to work
together. For instance, most conservatives and liberals upheld the superiority of British political institutions over American ones, promoted
industrialization and the development of railways, and agreed that
Métis and Aboriginal individual and collective rights should not
infringe on the political and territorial reorganizing and the economic
expansion of Western Canada.

One of the advantages of the liberal order framework is that it
encourages historians to move beyond the seemingly obvious contradictions between certain ideologies, such as liberalism and conservatism, and to discover that, oftentimes, the holders of these different
ideologies, who normally adapted them to fit their own contexts,
shared several common principles that allowed them to collaborate
with each other. As well, the liberal order framework invites us not
only to revisit liberalism, but also to look again at conservatism in order
to better understand how the conservatives could have participated in
the construction of a new liberal order. On this subject, historians can
follow Jerry Bannister's analysis, which interprets John Beverley Robinson's thought in light of the Lockean influences that are active in his
work. Also, we can turn to Jean-Marie Fecteau, who has demonstrated
how the establishment of the liberal order in Québec in the second half
of the nineteenth century could have gone hand in hand with the extension of the power of the Roman Catholic Church.[38]

Liberalism, Nationalism, and Religion

Conservatism is not the only ideology with which the creators of liberal
order had to compromise in their construction of this new social and

political model. Nationalism was another. Certainly, at the ideological level, liberalism would be just as different from nationalism as it is from conservatism because both conservatism and nationalism are based on abstract principles that are more collective than individualistic. From an ideological point of view, nationalism, with its emphasis on the collective rights of an entire nation, and liberalism, with its focus on the rights of the single individual, seem diametrically opposed. However, as was the case with the relationship between liberalism and conservatism in the Anglo-Saxon world, it often happens that liberal and nationalist arguments find themselves complementing rather than conflicting with each other.

It is, of course, quite difficult to reconcile the most intransigent forms of liberalism with certain types of nationalism. In the nineteenth century, for example, Lord Acton articulated just such a model of expressly antinationalist liberalism.[39] That being said, liberals have occasionally defended the national framework as essential to the full development of liberalism. This was the case with John Stuart Mill, who argued in *On Liberty* (1859) for the primacy of individual rights over collective rights while also asserting in *Considerations on Representative Government* (1863) that liberalism could only develop fully within the confines of a linguistically homogeneous nation. Conversely, supporters of a strictly nationalist doctrine, those who favour the 'strong' nationalism defined by Jean Leca,[40] can never grant recognition to even the basic concept of individuality. However, generally speaking, most nationalists, even those who support and articulate a strictly ethnic definition of the nation, still accept and support the principles of equality before the law, civil liberties, and private property. In this context, the presence of various nationalisms in Canada, beginning from the second half of the nineteenth century, never represented a true obstacle to the construction of the liberal order, especially when we take into consideration the fact that the majority of nationalists, both in Canada and in Québec, accepted the three fundamental liberal principles defined by McKay.

Given that a certain liberal order was progressively put in place after 1840 in Canada, it would be interesting to look back at the different types of nationalism that participated in the construction of Canada during this period and to study how these nationalisms – Canadian, French Canadian, and Québécois – contributed to and were influenced by the new liberal order. Beyond that, it might be wise to examine how French Canadian and later Québécois nationalisms could have developed within this new liberal order. Historians might want to ask why French Canadians as a group gave so little resistance to the expansion and deployment of this new order.[41] Although Jean-Marie Fecteau and Jarrett Rudy are interested in the question of the establishment of the liberal order in Québec, we still need to reconnect and reintegrate that Québec experience into the general experience of Canada as a whole.[42] Following up on Fecteau's argument, for example, it could be argued that the overwhelming presence and structuring power of the Catholic Church in the social domain might have allowed for a less individualistic understanding of liberalism to be implanted in the province, thus constructing a different – but still liberal – social order in Québec. As well, the transformation of a once pancanadian francophone nation[43] into a geographically limited Québécois nation, located within the territorial boundaries of the province, certainly merits further study relative to the evolution of the liberal order in Canada. Integrating Québec's history into the larger history of the establishment of the Canadian liberal order would allow us to better understand and situate the whole question of nationality within the analytic structure of the liberal order.

Moreover, studying the question of nationality within the liberal order framework also reinforces the necessity of exploring the religious dimension, and the specificity of religious experiences in Canada, both institutional and popular, in the creation of the liberal order. To pursue this line of argument with another example drawn from Québec, it should be noted that the historiography of religion in Québec has been concerned for some time now about the multifaceted nature by which the Catholic Church established and maintained its authority over the last three centuries.[44] The Church and Catholicism in general, especially at the local level, now appear less as a reactionary and conservative force than as an agent of change, the authority and social monitoring exercised by the Church being seen as a mode of transition from a pre-modern to a modern society.[45] This historiography has in turn led to significant reinterpretations of important aspects of Québec's history such as the Quiet Revolution.[46] While some historians of religion remain critical of the liberal order framework,[47] it can provide some common ground for comparative studies of religion in Canada that will address the religious dimensions of liberalism and its hegemonic possibilities and limits over time.

In the final analysis, perhaps the most important element of the liberal order framework is the invitation it offers to historians to re-evaluate the entire sphere of Canadian political culture between 1840 and 1940. There is still important work to be done. More scholarly effort must be put towards an examination of the essential roles played by identity markers such as nationalism and religion in the establishment of the liberal order.

The Liberal Order and the Question of Hegemony

By encouraging Canadian historians to accept the core arguments of his liberal order framework, McKay invited academics throughout the field to carry out a wide-ranging re-examination of Canadian history in order to discover exactly how the rise of the liberal order occurred and affected different aspects of society after 1840. It is in this context that Michèle Dagenais approaches the study of the establishment of Canadian municipal institutions from the beginning of the 1840s in her article for this collection. According to Dagenais, the creation of these municipal institutions, similar to the establishment of many educational institutions that also took place during this period,[48] was part of the expansion of the new liberal order within the context of Canadian state formation. In their work, Stéphane Castonguay and Darin Kinsey analyse the establishment of the liberal order from an environmental point of view. They argue that the social order put in place after 1840 affected not only the relationship between individuals, but also the relationship between those individuals and the world they inhabit.

McKay's invitation to historians is first and foremost an intellectual and historical challenge. In this context, many historians have interpreted McKay's 'reconnaissance' primarily as a call for another form of synthesis, one that would steer clear of drawing any teleological conclusions about Canada as a country, but which would rather emphasize the tensions that run through the whole historical experience of Canada as a project of liberal rule.[49] However, McKay's invitation did originate from a very particular intellectual perspective. By calling historians to undertake a 'reconnaissance' of Canadian history, McKay also encourages scholars to participate in an intellectual project inspired by the writings of Antonio Gramsci, especially his theory of hegemony.[50] If the meaning of the word 'reconnaissance' seemed ambiguous in McKay's initial essay, the true significance of the term becomes much clearer in *Rebels, Reds, Radicals*, where McKay explains that 'reconnaissance is a political act of research,' specifically designed 'to produce knowledge for a political purpose.'[51] In this context, the liberal order framework is not only a call to historians to reinterpret Canada's past, or even the concept of Canada itself, through the lens of the establishment of a hegemonic liberal order within the confines of Canadian territory, but also a direct suggestion to interpret the rise of this social order from an explicitly Gramscian perspective. More than liberalism itself, it is the overt Gramscian qualities of the liberal order framework that promise to fuel discussion and debate surrounding McKay's original article in years to come, not only within the field of history, but also beyond. Obviously, certain historians will accept and endorse the principle of hegemony, and others will argue against this model. In reality, many scholars would probably simply rather ignore the Gramscian elements of McKay's argument or suggest other alternatives that they feel might be better suited to an analysis of the establishment of the Canadian liberal order.

According to McKay, Gramsci understood that 'a given social group can only exercise leadership over others by going beyond its immediate corporate interests to take into account the interests of other groups and classes.'[52] McKay encourages Canadian historians to re-evaluate their field in light of these types of insights. When historians begin to reinterpret Canada's past in this way, McKay argues, they will discover that the fundamental compromises that have allowed Canada to exist and develop can not be explained or understood by referencing the supposed 'good will' of the promoters of the liberal order. These political compromises were not necessarily positive gestures deserving the kind of historiographic celebration we have witnessed in the past. Rather, from the Gramscian point of view, these compromises can be seen as strategic actions aimed at consolidating the position of strength held by supporters of the liberal order.

In this way, the liberal order framework attempts to illustrate the strategies and tactics used by promoters of the liberal order to destroy the pre-existing social order and to impose on the population – sometimes by way of force and sometimes by obtaining their consent – a new social structure based on private property, a new liberal order that, first and foremost, served the interests of its promoters. The framework also seeks to examine and evaluate 'the enormity of what the Canadian liberal order undertook – the replacement, often with a kind of revolutionary symbolic or actual violence, of antithetical traditions and forms that had functioned for centuries and even millennia with new conceptions of the human being and society.'[53]

The key question at this point in the discussion is clear: Does the concept of hegemony, as described by Gramsci and restated by McKay, provide scholars with the best analytical tool to study the rise of the liberal order in Canada while still taking into account the competing needs and claims of other communities such as women, Aboriginal peoples, or Québécois who might be considered marginal within the nation? Certain contributors to this volume, including Jerry Bannister, E.A. Heaman, and Ruth Sandwell, accept and reference the idea of hegemony without explicitly stating if they define the term in the same sense as the Gramscian model. Other scholars, such as Jeffrey McNairn and Robert McDonald, are more sceptical. McNairn openly worries about the possible effects a Gramscian analysis might have on Canadian intellectual history. He fears that the broad adaptation of hegemonic principles might shackle the entire question of liberalism within a very narrow and overly restrictive definition. From his point of view, Bruce Curtis suggests that Michel Foucault's concept of governmentality might be more helpful in the study of Canadian history than McKay's Gramscian analysis. In their essays, Dagenais, Castonguay, and Kinsey have all incorporated analytic models that are more relational or Foucauldian than Gramsci's hegemonic template. It is clear from the essays included in this collection that it is not so much the liberal nature of the social order framed in British North America after 1840 that needs a more extensive discussion among historians but the nature of Gramsci's theory of hegemony and its possible (or practical) application to the study of Canadian history.

In any case, the liberal order framework presents itself as an invitation to stimulate profound reflection and further research into Canadian history. As is the case with any argument, McKay's thesis must be explored in detail and its relevance and value must be continually tested and demonstrated. Jarrett Rudy's book on smoking and everyday liberalism provides an interesting example. Following the social rituals surrounding tobacco consumption, Rudy shows how the profoundly liberal underpinnings of these rituals 'served to normalize the exclusion of women from the definition of the liberal individual and to justify the subordination and exclusion of the poor and ethnic minorities.'[54] Although many of the scholars in this collection have chosen to integrate certain aspects of the framework into their analyses, others have approached McKay's argument more tentatively and they continue to remain somewhat doubtful about the significance of the framework's contribution to Canadian historiography.

Periodization

If the liberal order framework still remains at the developmental stage of its larger project, the basic contours of McKay's argument are well known and they follow along the path of the great moments of traditional political history. McKay's analysis covers the period from 1840 to 1940, and specifically defines the years between 1840 and 1900 as a phase of the 'Canadian Liberal Revolution.' During this time, promoters of the liberal order dismantled the pre-existing social order and imposed their alternative model. According to McKay, the entire political and social history of the mid-to-late nineteenth century can be described as 'the story of how the worldview of a few liberal men, living in a few southern cities, attained power over half a continent.'[55] During the years from 1900 to 1940, McKay argues, the 'Passive Revolution' phase of the liberal order took over and eventually adapted itself to the major challenges of the period, such as the Depression and the two world wars.

According to McKay, the Liberal Revolution was initiated by the failed rebellions of the Patriots in Lower Canada and the Radicals in Upper Canada in 1837–8. To support this interpretation, McKay references new historiographic models that present the 1837 rebellions as a confrontation between republicans and defenders of constitutional order. Obviously, this type of analysis is attractive to McKay because it provides him with a way of paralleling the opposition between two different understandings of the ideal society. On the one hand, the republicans resisted the earliest precursors of liberal order and promoted a certain kind of egalitarian society. On the other hand, the defenders of constitutional order defended a society based on private property. In that framework, the 'constitutionalists' were the earliest ancestors of the liberals and conservatives, and they would eventually build Canada according to the model of the liberal order framework.[56]

The dramatic transformations of political alliances that allowed the system of responsible government to function represent the next important phase of the liberal revolution. In McKay's formulation, this reorganization of political loyalties, especially the compromises that occurred from 1851 to 1854 and gave birth to the liberal-conservative party, can be easily interpreted as examples of a liberal hegemony in the making. According to the framework, the capacity of the Canadian political elite to negotiate a compromise during this period was directed by the twinned goals of conserving political power and continuing to develop the Canadian project according to their own interests. Here, the framework forces us to reconsider the role of the *Rouges* of Lower Canada, a group of politicians who appeared to be very critical towards the political and social order that was established after 1848. Until recently the *Rouges* have generally been depicted as the liberal heirs of the Patriots.[57] However, if we simultaneously accept both the new historiographic interpretations of the republicanism of the Lower Canadian Patriots and the Upper Canadian Radicals in the 1830s, as well as the core arguments of the liberal order framework, the combination may lead scholars to revisit and possibly reposition the *Rouges* within a republican framework rather than a liberal one. In other words, it remains to be seen whether these politicians should be understood as individuals who, despite their protests, still belonged to the hegemonic elite, or if they might be better interpreted as a group that formed part of the legal resistance to the establishment of the liberal order.

Along with other important historical events that helped construct the liberal order we must include Confederation, the development of the Canadian West, the National Policy, and the codification of civil and criminal law in Canada. To this list, it would probably be wise to add the development of the Maritime provinces and their subjugation to central Canada, as well as the changing status, throughout history and across Canadian geography, of certain categories of individuals (and non-individuals) such as women and Aboriginal peoples, not only from a judicial point of view, but also at a societal level. If McKay argues that it is difficult to determine the exact moment when the liberal order became hegemonic in Canada,[58] he does seem to take it for granted that this important conversion took place around the turn of the twentieth century. In fact, McKay no longer speaks of an active Liberal Revolution for the period after 1900, but rather of a passive Revolution during which the liberal order adapted itself and negotiated further compromises to maintain its hegemony within Canadian society. The period from 1900 to 1940 is therefore interpreted as a key transformative phase of the liberal order.[59] It remains to be determined exactly how the period that preceded 1840 differs from the period that followed it. On this topic, the essay that Bannister contributes to this collection, which focuses on the Loyalist order that preceded the liberal order, offers another possible interpretive track for historians to follow. Also, we will eventually need to know why McKay seems to think that the liberal order framework is not useful after 1940 when it is so clear that the liberal order survived and thrived after the Second World War. We must therefore pay close attention to the period following 1940 in order to better understand the evolution of the liberal order after 1945.

Who Is Liberal?

Clearly the liberal order framework presents the history of Canada as a process during which the liberal order is gradually established and transformed. The creation of this order was a difficult transformation that at times attacked the values, beliefs, and traditional customs of the population (when it was not attacking the people themselves) of the British North American colonies and eventually Canada. In this context, we must determine more precisely who the promoters of the liberal order were, a group McKay never names directly in his 2000 article. Were they the elites, the leading political class, the bourgeoisie? Were they all men? We also must determine exactly how and when an entire population, who eventually submitted to liberal hegemony, came to accept liberal principles.[60] On this topic, Ruth Sandwell calls into question the notion that liberal order was successfully imposed on the population during the nineteenth century. According to Sandwell, many people have lived for a very long time in a world that finds itself on the margins of liberal principles and economic policies, well beyond the turn of the twentieth century. These people would have passively resisted the type of changes that the elites, such as social reformers, sought to impose on their hygiene, security or civil norms, and so on.[61]

Conversely, Robert McDonald demonstrates that the majority of people living in British Columbia since the beginning of the twentieth century have come to share and understand liberal principles in different ways. McKay could easily integrate McDonald's analysis into his framework by citing his own application of Gramscian theory: 'Once a group, usually tied to a class, achieves hegemony, it works to make historical choices … seem to be just like natural phenomena, to which no sensible person can object. The language of the hegemonic group comes to seem like an ordinary common-sense way of describing reality.'[62] From his side, McDonald stresses that the loyalty British Columbians feel towards liberal principles does not imply that they have been forced to accept these principles against their will or by manipulation. Rather, he suggests that British Columbians have adopted these ideological principles voluntarily. They could do this because liberalism is not only an ideology of power but also an ideology of reform. On this point, McDonald is in agreement with Heaman. He argues that there are not one, but many definitions of liberalism and that certain versions of this discourse do reflect the values and aspirations of the masses. In fact, McDonald argues that the promoters of the framework still need to explain exactly how hegemony would actually function in the real world.

The discussion of liberal loyalty leads directly to the question of resistance to the liberal order, a subject that McKay finds particularly interesting.[63] While in the original article resistance to the liberal order seems to come mostly from groups that would seem more 'socialist,'[64] Heaman argues that this resistance could also come from the ultra-conservative elite. As well, traditionalists and other defenders of older social structures could also represent a challenge to the establishment of the liberal order. Perhaps this discussion of resistance might encourage historians to accept that opposition to liberal order can come just as much from groups and individuals who are traditionally associated with the maintenance of established order as it does from groups seeking to reverse or reform that order.

Conclusion

The liberal order framework certainly puts forth an argument that is both stimulating and promising. McKay's work is, first and foremost, an aggressive and original call to study the establishment of the liberal order in Canada in a way that responds to the challenges posed by the evolution of Canadian historiography during the last forty years. Rather than approaching the subject from the point of view of traditional ideology, McKay studies political history by focusing on certain fundamental principles such as property, liberty, and equality. This strategy allows us to move beyond traditional ideological categories. In this context, it is difficult not to notice that liberals and conservatives in Canada share these three principles and that may explain, at least in part, the relatively peaceful relationship between these two groups after 1850. However, certain historians continue to wish that the promoters of the liberal order framework might recognize more completely the versatility of liberalism, a single ideology that somehow manages to be reformist and conservative, radical and moderate, at the same time.

At another level, the liberal order framework illustrates that the principle of exclusion is a constituent component of the general analytical framework of Canadian history and not just an occasional contradiction or anomaly. Perry's article demonstrates this important facet of McKay's argument. The analysis of the liberal order framework also lends itself to political, social, and economic history. However, as Brownlie demonstrates, it still remains to be seen if the framework can be applied as directly to the study of culture.

A rigorous analysis and critique of the foundations of the liberal order framework, as well as its possibilities and its limitations, promises to inspire a whole new wave of research in Canadian and Québécois history. While we wait for the 'big books' that will help us '"think Canada" in a different way,'[65] this collection of essays is intended to stir debate about, and push forward the possibilities offered by, the liberal order framework.

Translated by Alexander MacLeod (St Mary's University)

NOTES

1 We would like to thank Michèle Dagenais, Robert McDonald, and Ian McKay for their comments on earlier versions of this text, as well as Alexander MacLeod for his translation. We also acknowledge the financial support of the Social Sciences and Humanities Research Council.

2 Ian McKay, 'The Liberal Order Framework: A Prospectus for a Reconnaissance of Canadian History,' *Canadian Historical Review* 81 (2000): 617–45. It is reproduced in this volume following this Introduction.

3 Michael Bliss, 'Privatizing the Mind: The Sundering of Canadian History, the Sundering of Canada,' *Journal of Canadian Studies* 26 (1992): 5–17; Jack Granatstein, *Who Killed Canadian History?* (Toronto: Harper Perennial, 1998). Other historians have also discussed this crisis.

4 McKay, 'Liberal Order Framework,' 632.

5 Ibid., 620.

6 Ibid., 627.

7 Fernande Roy, *Progrès, harmonie, liberté: Le libéralisme des milieux d'affaires francophones à Montréal au tournant du siècle* (Montreal: Boréal, 1988); Brian Young, *George-Étienne Cartier: Montreal bourgeois* (Montreal and Kingston: McGill-Queen's University Press, 1981); Young, *In Its Corporate Capacity: The Seminary of Montreal as a Business Institution, 1816–1876* (Montreal and Kingston: McGill-Queen's University Press, 1986); Young, *The Politics of Codification: The Lower Canadian Civil Code of 1866* (Montreal and Kingston:

McGill-Queen's University Press, 1994); Brian Young and John A. Dickinson, *A Short History of Quebec: A Socio-Economic Perspective* (Toronto: Copp Clark Pitman, 1988).

8 Allan Greer and Ian Radforth, eds., *Colonial Leviathan: State Formation in Mid-Nineteenth-Century Canada* (Toronto: University of Toronto Press, 1992); Bruce Curtis, *True Government by Choice Men? Inspection, Education and State Formation in Canada West* (Toronto: University of Toronto Press, 1992); Philip Corrigan and Bruce Curtis, 'Education, Inspection and State Formation: A Preliminary Statement,' Canadian Historical Association *Historical Papers*, 1985: 156–71; Bruce Curtis, *The Politics of Population: State Formation, Statistics, and the Census of Canada, 1840–1875* (Toronto: University of Toronto Press, 2001); Curtis, 'The Canada 'Blue Books' and the Administrative Capacity of the Canadian State, 1822–67,' *Canadian Historical Review* 74 (1993): 535–65; Michael J. Piva, 'Getting Hired: The Civil Service Act of 1857,' *Journal of the Canadian Historical Association* 3 (1992): 95–127; Piva, 'Debts, Salaries and Civil Service Reform in Pre-Confederation Canada,' *National History* 1 (1997): 127–37.

9 Jean-Marie Fecteau, *Un nouvel ordre des choses... la pauvreté, le crime, l'État au Québec, de la fin du XVIIIe siècle à 1840* (Outremont: VLB éditeur, 1989); Fecteau, *La liberté du pauvre: Sur la régulation du crime et de la pauvreté au XIXe siècle québécois* (Montreal: VLB éditeur, 2004); Jean-Marie Fecteau and Janice Harvey, eds., *La régulation sociale entre l'acteur et l'institution: Pour une problématique historique de l'interaction / Agency and Institutions in Social Regulation: Toward an Historical Understanding of Their Interaction* (Sainte-Foy: Les Presses de l'Université du Québec, 2005); Gilles Bourque, Jules Duchastel, and Jacques Beauchemin, *La société libérale duplessiste, 1944–1960* (Montréal: Presses de l'Université de Montréal, 1994). See also Alain-G. Gagnon and Michel Sarra-Bournet, eds., *Duplessis: Entre la grande noirceur et la société libérale* (Montreal: Québec/Amérique, 1997); James E. Moran, *Committed to the State Asylum: Insanity and Society in Nineteenth-Century Quebec and Ontario* (Montreal and Kingston: McGill-Queen's University Press, 2000); Nancy Christie and Michael Gauvreau, eds., *Mapping the Margins: The Family and Social Discipline in Canada, 1700–1975* (Montreal and Kingston: McGill-Queen's University Press, 2004).

10 See, in order of publication, Terry Cook, 'John Beverly Robinson and the Conservative Blueprint for the Upper Canadian Community,' *Ontario History* 64 (1972): 79; Rod Peerce, 'The Myth of Red Tory,' *Canadian Journal of Political and Social Theory* 1 (1977): 3–23; Peerce, 'The Anglo-Saxon Conservative Tradition,' *Canadian Journal of Political Science* 13 (1980): 3–32; Gordon T. Stewart, *The Origins of Canadian Politics: A Comparative Approach* (Vancou-

ver: UBC Press, 1986); Jane Errington, *The Lion, the Eagle, and Upper Canada: A Developing Colonial Ideology* (Montreal and Kingston: McGill-Queen's University Press, 1987); Janet Ajzenstat, *The Political Thought of Lord Durham* (Montreal and Kingston: McGill-Queen's University Press, 1988); Ajzenstat, *The Once and Future Canadian Democracy: An Essay in Political Thought* (Montreal and Kingston: McGill-Queen's University Press, 2003); Ajzenstat, *The Canadian Founding: John Locke and Parliament* (Montreal and Kingston: McGill-Queen's University Press, 2007); Michael McCulloch, 'The Death of Whiggery: Lower-Canadian British Constitutionalism and the *tentation de l'histoire parallèle*,' *Journal of the Canadian Historical Association* 2 (1991): 195–213; Paul Romney, *Getting It Wrong: How Canadians Forgot Their Past and Imperiled Confederation* (Toronto: University of Toronto Press, 1999); Michel Ducharme, 'Penser le Canada: La mise en place des assises intellectuelles de l'État canadien moderne (1838–1840),' *Revue d'histoire de l'Amérique française* 56 (2003): 357–86.

11 McKay, 'Liberal Order Framework,' 620.

12 Ibid.

13 Ibid., 637.

14 Ian McKay, *Rebels, Reds, Radicals: Rethinking Canada's Left History* (Toronto: Between the Lines, 2005).

15 Ibid., 57–8.

16 Certain authors have made direct reference to McKay's liberal order framework in their work. See, for example, in chronological order: Steven Maynard, 'The Maple Leaf (Gardens) Forever: Sex, Canadian Historians and National History,' *Journal of Canadian Studies* 36 (2001): 70–105; Ruth Sandwell, 'The Limits of Liberalism: The Liberal Reconnaissance and the History of the Family in Canada,' *Canadian Historical Review* 84 (2003): 423–50; Donica Belisle, 'Toward a Canadian Consumer History,' *Labour / Le Travail* 52 (2003): 181–206; Nancy Christie and Michael Gauvreau, 'Modalities of Social Authority: Suggesting an Interface for Religious and Social History,' *Histoire Sociale / Social History* 36 (2003): 1–30; Ducharme, 'Penser le Canada'; Philip Girard, 'Land Law, Liberalism, and the Agrarian Ideal: British North America, 1750–1920,' in *Despotic Dominion: Property Rights in British Settler Societies*, ed. John McLaren, A.R. Buck, and Nancy E. Wright (Vancouver: UBC Press, 2004): 120–43; Nancy Christie, 'Introduction: Family, Community, and the Rise of Liberal Society,' in *Mapping the Margins*, 3–26; Jarrett Rudy, *The Freedom to Smoke: Tobacco Consumption and Identity*, (Montreal and Kingston: McGill-Queen's University Press, 2005); Michael Gauvreau and Ollivier Hubert, 'Beyond Church History: Recent Developments in the History of Religion in Canada' and Nancy Christie, 'Carnal

Connection and Other Misdemeanors: Continuity and Change in Presbyte-
rian Church Courts, 1830–90,' both in *The Churches and Social Order in Nine-
teenth- and Twentieth-Century Canada*, ed. Michael Gauvreau and Ollivier
Hubert (Montreal and Kingston: McGill-Queen's University Press, 2006),
3–45 and 66–108; Joan Sangster, 'Archiving Feminist Histories: Women,
the 'Nation' and Metanarratives in Canadian Historical Writing,' *Women's
Studies International Forum* 29 (2006): 255–64; C. Wesley Biggs, with Stella
Stephanson, 'In Search of Gudrun Goodman: Reflections on Gender, 'Doing
History' and Memory,' *Canadian Historical Review* 87 (2006): 293–316; Jean-
François Constant, 'Beyond the City: Defining Metropolis in Canada and
Belgium in the Nineteenth Century,' in *Urban Europe in Comparative Perspective*, ed. Lars Nilsson (Stockholm: Stads-och kommunhistoriska institutet,
Studies in Urban History 31, 2007). It should be noted that some of these
authors remain critical of the liberal order framework.
17 McKay, 'Liberal Order Framework,' 623.
18 Roy, *Progrès, harmonie, liberté*, 45–58.
19 McKay, 'Liberal Order Framework,' 624.
20 Ibid., 627.
21 Ibid., 625.
22 In this regard, Uday Singh Metha has demonstrated that liberal values do
not necessarily exclude imperialism: *Liberalism and Empire: A Study in Nineteenth-Century British Liberal Thought* (Chicago: University of Chicago Press,
1999).
23 For several scholars, libertarians and individualist anarchists can be classified as radical liberals. While it is true that these groups do share common fundamental principles with classical liberals (such as individual
autonomy, personal liberty, and private property), nevertheless it is important to establish a clear distinction between libertarianism and individualist anarchism on the one hand and liberalism on the other, especially in
the case of the liberal order framework. In fact, the very establishment of
the liberal order that McKay studies actually relies on the sovereignty of
the state and monopoly capitalism, two things that the libertarians and the
individualist anarchists both rejected in the nineteenth century. For more
on libertarianism and individualist anarchism, see William Gary Kline,
The Individualist Anarchists: A Critique of Liberalism (Lanham, MD: University Press of America, 1987); Wendy McElroy, *The Debates of Liberty: An
Overview of Individualist Anarchism, 1881–1908* (Lanham, MD: Lexington
Books, 2003); William R. McKercher, *Freedom and Authority* (Montreal:
Black Rose Books, 1989); Jan Narveson, *The Libertarian Idea* (Philadelphia:
Temple University Press, 1988); Stephen L. Newman, *Liberalism at Wits'*

End: The Libertarian Revolt against the Modern State (Ithaca: Cornell University Press, 1984).

24 For example, John Locke believed that life in a society was unavoidable. On the one hand, man was created social in accordance with God's divine will. On the other, society provided the only means that would allow him to escape from a natural state in which he was continually at war with other individuals. See John Locke, 'The Second Treatise of Government' (1690), in *Two Treatises of Government*, ed. Peter Laslett, 15th ed. (Cambridge: Cambridge University Press, 2004), 282, 318–19. From his point of view, Montesquieu considered life in a society as an extension of natural law: Montesquieu, *De l'esprit des lois* (1748) (Paris: Garnier-Flammarion, 1979), vol. 1, 127. As for Adam Smith, he explicitly argued that an individual should take care 'of his own happiness, of that of his family, his friends, his country.' Adam Smith, *The Theory of Moral Sentiments* (1759) (New York: Augustus M. Kelley, 1866), 348.

25 John R. Fitzpatrick, *John Stuart Mill's Political Philosophy: Balancing Freedom and Collective Good* (London: Continuum, 2006); Leon H. Mayhew, *The Public Spirit: On the Origins of Liberal Thought: An Address to Library Associates, University of California, Davis* (Davis: Library Associates, 1984); Charles Robert McCann, *Individualism and the Social Order: The Social Element in Liberal Thought* (New York: Routledge, 2004); Avital Simhony and David Weinstein, eds., *The New Liberalism: Reconciling Liberty and Community* (Cambridge: Cambridge University Press, 2001).

26 For more on the fact that the principle of equality, in liberal thought, can go beyond the simple equality of rights, see Amy Gutman, *Liberal Equality* (Cambridge: Cambridge University Press, 1980). For more on the concept of freedom in liberalism, see David Spitz, *Essays in the Liberal Idea of Freedom* (Tucson: University of Arizona Press, 1964).

27 C.B. Macpherson, *The Political Theory of Possessive Individualism: Hobbes to Locke* (London: Oxford University Press, 1962), cited in McKay, 'Liberal Order Framework,' 623. For a discussion of Macpherson's work, see Joseph H. Carens, ed., *Democracy and Possessive Individualism: The Intellectual Legacy of C.B. Macpherson* (Albany: State University of New York Press, 1993). For a defence of Macpherson's work against his critics, see Jules Townshend, *C.B. Macpherson and the Problem of Liberal Democracy* (Edinburgh: Edinburgh University Press, 2000). For a study of the democratic political thought of Macpherson, see Peter Lindsay, *Creative Individualism: The Democratic Vision of C.B. Macpherson* (Albany: State University of New York, 1996).

28 For a definition and a history of economic liberalism, see also Pierre Rosan-

vallon, *Le libéralisme économique: Histoire de l'idée de marché* (Paris: Seuil, 1989 [1979]).

29 See, among others, Janet Ajzenstat, 'Modern Mixed Government: A Liberal Defence of Inequality,' *Canadian Journal of Political Science* 18 (1985): 119–34; Ajzenstat, *The Political Thought of Lord Durham*; Ajzenstat, 'Durham and Robinson: Political Faction and Moderation,' *Journal of Canadian Studies* 25 (1990): 24–38; Ajzenstat, *The Once and Future Canadian Democracy*; Janet Azjenstat and Peter J. Smith, eds., *Canada's Origins: Liberal, Tory, or Republican?* (Ottawa: Carleton University Press, 1995).

30 For a discussion of liberal philosophy in a broader context, see Georges Burdeau, *Le libéralisme* (Paris: Seuil, 1979); David Conway, *Classical Liberalism: The Unvanquished Ideal* (London: Macmillan, 1995); Ruth W. Grant, *John Locke's Liberalism* (Chicago: University of Chicago Press, 1987); John Gray, *Liberalism* (Milton Keynes: Open University Press, 1986); David Johnston, *The Idea of Liberal Theory: A Critique and Reconstruction* (Princeton: Princeton University Press, 1994); Alain Laurent, *La philosophie libérale: Histoire et actualité d'une tradition intellectuelle* (Paris: Les Belles Lettres, 2002); Pierre Manent, *Histoire intellectuelle du libéralisme: Dix leçons* (Paris: Calmann-Lévy, 1987); David John Manning, *Liberalism* (New York: St Martin's Press, 1976); André Vachet, *L'idéologie libérale, l'individu et sa propriété* (Paris: Éditions Anthropos, 1970).

31 For an analysis of the religious foundations of John Locke's thought, see John Dunn, *The Political Thought of John Locke: An Historical Account of the Argument of the 'Two Treatises of Government'* (Cambridge: Cambridge University Press, 1969). For an analysis of the role of faith in the thought of Thomas Hobbes, John Locke, and John Stuart Mill, see Eldon J. Eisenach, *Two Worlds of Liberalism: Religion and Politics in Hobbes, Locke, and Mill* (Chicago: University of Chicago Press, 1981).

32 Adam Smith was first interested in ethical questions in *The Theory of Moral Sentiments* (1759) before committing himself to economic concerns in *An Inquiry into the Nature and Causes of the Wealth of Nations* (1776). In the case of John Stuart Mill, his thought also rested on ethical considerations. For more on this subject, see Eldon Eisenach, ed., *Mill and the Moral Character of Liberalism* (University Park: Pennsylvania State University Press, 1998).

33 On the relationship between freedom and law as 'the expression of reason and freedom,' see Lucien Jaume, *La liberté et la loi: Les origines philosophiques du libéralisme* (Paris: Fayard, 2000), 17.

34 For the most important writings in the British conservative tradition, see Edmund Burke, *Selected Writings and Speeches*, ed. Peter J. Stanlis (Garden City: Anchor Books, 1963); Sir Robert Peel, *Memoirs by the Right Honourable*

Sir Robert Peel, Bart., M.P., &c, ed. Lord Mahon and the Right Honourable Edward Cardwell M.P. (London: John Murray, 1857); Benjamin Disraeli, *Selected Speeches of the late Right Honourable Earl of Beaconsfield*, ed. T.E. Kebbel (London: Longmans, Green, and Co., 1882); Disraeli, *Whigs and Whiggism: Political Writings*, ed. William Hutcheon (London: John Murray, 1913); Disraeli, *Sybil or The Two Nations* (1845) (Oxford: Oxford University Press, 1998); Robert Eccleshall, ed., *English Conservatism since the Restoration* (London: Unwin Hyman, 1990). For selected important studies of conservatism, see Russell Kirk, *The Conservative Mind from Burke to Santayana* (Chicago: Henry Regnery Co., 1953); Ian Gilmour, *Inside Right: A Study of Conservatism* (London: Hutchinson, 1977); Roger Scruton, *The Meaning of Conservatism* (Markham: Penguin Books, 1980); Arthur Aughey, Greta Jones, and W.T.M. Riches, *The Conservative Political Tradition in Britain and the United States* (Rutherford: Fairleigh Dickinson University Press, 1992); T.A. Jenkins, *Disraeli and Victorian Conservatism* (London: Macmillan, 1996).

35 For more on the survival of the Old Regime in the United Kingdom until 1832, see Jonathan C.D. Clark, *English Society, 1688–1832* (Cambridge: Cambridge University Press, 1985). In North America, social order was always less hierarchical than in Britain. Nevertheless, one thing is certain: colonial social order was not liberal before 1840.

36 Gad Horowitz, 'Conservatism, Liberalism, and Socialism in Canada: An Interpretation,' *Canadian Journal of Economics and Political Science* 32 (1966): 143–71. Horowitz's article has received several commentaries. See, for example, H.D. Forbes, 'Hartz-Horowitz at Twenty: Nationalism, Toryism and Socialism in Canada,' *Canadian Journal of Political Science* 20 (1987): 287–315; S.F. Wise, 'Liberal Consensus or Ideological Battleground: Some Reflections on the Hartz Thesis,' Canadian Historical Association *Historical Papers*, 1974: 1–14.

37 See Michel Ducharme, 'Aux fondements de l'État canadien: La liberté au Canada de 1776 à 1841' (PhD diss., McGill University, 2005), chaps. 2 and 5.

38 Fecteau, *La liberté du pauvre*, especially 265–329.

39 Lord Acton, 'Essay on Nationality' (1862), in *The History of Freedom and Other Essays* (London: MacMillan, 1907), 270–300. For a Canadian interpretation of this doctrine, see Pierre Elliott Trudeau, *Le fédéralisme et la société canadienne-française* (Montreal: HMH, 1967).

40 In 'Nationalisme et universalisme,' *Pouvoirs* 57 (1991): 33–42, Jean Leca defines a three-part typology for nationalism. According to this framework, supporters of the 'Ultra-faible' variant demand that a public space be reserved for the development and expression of a national culture without overtly calling for political sovereignty. Supporters of the 'minimale' vari-

ant demand political independence or the political unity of a nation defined
in ethnic terms. Individual rights are not necessarily antithetical to these
first two forms of nationalism. Lastly, the defenders of the 'forte' variant
believe that individuals must be subordinate to the nation.

41 Stéphane Kelly asked this question several years ago in *La petite loterie:
Comment la Couronne a obtenu la collaboration du Canada français après 1837*
(Montreal: Boréal, 1997).

42 Fecteau, *Un nouvel ordre des choses* and *La liberté du pauvre*; Rudy, *Freedom to
Smoke.*

43 On the pan-Canadian nationalism of Henri Bourassa and Lionel Groulx, see
André Laurendeau, 'Le nationalisme de Bourassa,' *L'Action nationale* 43
(1954): 9–56; Casey Morrow, *Henri Bourassa and French-Canadian Nationalism*
(Montreal: Harvest House, 1968); Joseph Levitt, ed., *Henri Bourassa on Imperialism and Bi-culturalism, 1900–1918* (Toronto: Copp Clark Publishing Co.,
1970), 101–59; Sylvie Lacombe, *La rencontre de deux peuples élus: Comparaison
des ambitions nationale et impériale au Canada entre 1896 et 1920* (Quebec: Les
Presses de l'Université Laval, 2002); Michel Bock, *Quand la nation débordait
les frontières. Les minorités françaises dans la pensée de Lionel Groulx* (Montreal:
Hurtubise HMH, 2004).

44 René Hardy, *Contrôle social et mutation de la culture religieuse au Québec, 1830–
1930* (Montreal: Boréal, 1999); Ollivier Hubert, *Sur la terre comme au ciel: La
gestion des rites par l'Église catholique au Québec, fin XVIIIe–mi-XIXe siècles*
(Sainte-Foy: Les Presses de l'Université Laval, 2000); Fecteau, *La liberté du
pauvre.*

45 Lucia Ferretti, *Entre voisins: La société paroissiale en milieu urbain: Saint-
Pierre-Apôtre de Montreal, 1848–1930* (Montreal: Boréal, 1992); Christine
Hudon, *Prêtres et fidèles dans le diocèse de Saint-Hyacinthe, 1820–1875* (Sillery:
Septentrion, 1996). To some extent, the refutation of the secularization thesis by historians of Protestantism can be seen as a similar historiographical
shift in English Canada. See, for example, Nancy Christie and Michael
Gauvreau, *A Full-Orbed Christianity: The Protestant Churches and Social Welfare in Canada, 1900–1940* (Montreal and Kingston: McGill-Queen's University Press, 1996).

46 See, for example, E.-Martin Meunier and Jean-Philippe Warren, *Sortir de la
'Grande Noirceur': L'horizon 'personnaliste' de la Révolution tranquille* (Sillery:
Septentrion, 2002); Louise Bienvenue, *Quand la jeunesse entre en scène:
L'Action catholique avant la Révolution tranquille* (Montreal: Boréal, 2003);
Lucie Piché, *Femmes et changement social au Québec: L'apport de la Jeunesse
ouvrière catholique féminine, 1931–1966* (Quebec: Les Presses de l'Université
Laval, 2003); Michael Gauvreau, *The Catholic Origins of Quebec's Quiet Revo-*

lution, 1931–1970 (Montreal and Kingston: McGill-Queen's University Press, 2005).

47 Michael Gauvreau and Ollivier Hubert thus fear that the liberal order framework's emphasis on 'economic individualism as the motor of socio-cultural change' will only 'legitimize a perception of Quebec as a foil to English Canada, because of the prominence of Catholic religious institutions.' Gauvreau and Hubert, 'Beyond Church History,' 8.

48 For more on the role played by schools in the development of liberal state formation, see Jean-Pierre Charland, *L'entreprise éducative au Québec, 1840–1900* (Saint-Nicolas: Les Presses de l'Université Laval, 2000), 53–89; Curtis, *True Government by Choice Men?*

49 This form of synthesis then raises the question of the style to be employed in putting it on paper. Namely, is it possible to write a synthesis of Canadian history that is not a narrative?

50 Gramsci's political thought can be found in English translation in his *Letters from Prison* (New York: Columbia University Press, 1994).

51 For the two definitions he gives for the word 'reconnaissance' and for more on McKay's Gramscian political project, see *Rebels, Reds, Radicals*, 83.

52 McKay, 'Liberal Order Framework,' 628. He specifies in *Rebels, Reds, Radicals*: 'Gramsci argued that, as the members of powerful social groups came together, they first had to sort out their often rival economic ('corporate') interests and work out an understanding among themselves ... Then, with their act more or less together, they had to take it on the road. They had to perform a politics that could draw in many other groups – even people with class interests completely opposed to themselves. This group had to secure its position of cultural and economic leadership through a combination of coercion and consent, in a never completely finalized, day-by-day process' (61).

53 McKay, 'Liberal Order Framework,' 630.

54 Rudy, *Freedom to Smoke*, 5.

55 McKay, *Rebels, Reds, Radicals*, 57–8.

56 On this subject, see Ducharme, 'Aux fondements de l'État canadien'; Allan Greer, 'Historical Roots of Canadian Democracy,' *Journal of Canadian Studies* 34 (1999): 7–26. On the republican ideology of the Patriots, see also Louis-Georges Harvey, *Le printemps de l'Amérique française: Américanité, anticolonialisme et républicanisme dans le discours politique québécois, 1805–1837* (Montreal: Boréal, 2005). For a 'Gramscian' perspective on the republicanism of the habitants of Lower Canada and their integration into the history of the rebellions, see Allan Greer, *The Patriots and the People: The Rebellion of 1837 in*

Rural Lower Canada (Toronto: University of Toronto Press, 1993). On the political principles of the Upper Canadian elite, see Cook, 'John Beverly Robinson and the Conservative Blueprint'; Stewart, *The Origins of Canadian Politics*; Ajzenstat, 'Durham and Robinson'; Ajzenstat, *The Once and Future Canadian Democracy*; Ajzenstat and Smith, eds., *Canada's Origins*; McCulloch, 'The Death of Whiggery'; as well as Bannister's analysis, in this collection, of the Lockean principles of John Beverley Robinson. From a practical point of view, several historians have demonstrated that the social repression that followed the rebellions permitted the establishment of a new social order. For more on this subject, see F. Murray Greenwood and Barry Wright, eds., *Canadian State Trials*, vol. 2, *Rebellion and Invasion in the Canadas, 1837–1839* (Toronto: The Osgoode Society for Canadian Legal History by University of Toronto Press, 2002).

57 Philippe Sylvain, 'Quelques aspects de l'antagonisme libéral-ultramontain au Canada français,' *Recherches Sociographiques* 8 (1967): 275–97; Sylvain, 'Un disciple canadien de Lamennais: Louis-Antoine Dessaulles,' *Cahiers des Dix* 34 (1969): 61–83; Sylvain, 'Quelques aspects de l'ultramontanisme canadien-français,' *Revue d'histoire de l'Amérique française* 25 (1971): 239–44; Jean-Paul Bernard, *Les Rouges : Libéralisme, nationalisme et anticléricalisme au milieu du XIXe siècle* (Montreal: Les Presses de l'Université du Québec, 1971); Yvan Lamonde, *Louis-Antoine Dessaulles, 1818–1895: Un seigneur libéral et anticlérical* (Saint-Laurent: Fides, 1994); Lamonde, *Histoire sociale des idées au Québec*, vol. 1, *1760–1896* (Montreal: Fides, 2000).

58 McKay, 'Liberal Order Framework,' 638.

59 Ian McKay, 'The Logic of the Canadian Passive Revolution: A Reconnaissance of the Transformation of Liberal Order, 1900–1950,' unpublished paper presented at the Liberal Order in Canadian History conference, McGill Institute for the Study of Canada, Montreal, 3 March 2006.

60 One way to look at it would be to reconcile the persistence of individual agency within a hegemonic liberal order by looking more specifically at the interactive aspect of power relations. For an example of such an approach, see Jean-Marie Fecteau and Janice Harvey, 'Des acteurs aux institutions: Dialectique historique de l'interaction et rapports de pouvoir,' in *La régulation sociale entre l'acteur et l'institution*, 3–15.

61 Beyond her contribution to this collection, see Sandwell, 'The Limits of Liberalism.'

62 McKay, *Rebels, Reds, Radicals*, 62.

63 See Ian McKay, *Reasoning Otherwise: Leftists and the People's Enlightenment in Canada, 1890–1920* (Toronto: Between the Lines, forthcoming, 2008).

64 Other authors are not as categorical as McKay in the way they oppose socialism and liberalism. For example, Monique Canto-Sperber suggests that the two ideologies can be reconciled: *Les règles de la liberté* (Paris: Plon, 2003).
65 McKay, 'Liberal Order Framework,' 621.

'The Liberal Order Framework:
A Prospectus for a Reconnaissance of
Canadian History'

IAN McKAY

What follows is a reproduction of Ian McKay's article from the *Canadian Historical Review* 81 (2000): 617–45.

The Liberal Order Framework:
A Prospectus for a Reconnaissance of Canadian History

IAN MCKAY

The present world of Canadian historians is at once proliferous and exhilarating, deprived and crisis-ridden. Proliferous: few humans could possibly absorb the yearly output of monographs, articles, theses, papers, and books through which hundreds of scholars pay homage to the ideals of detailed archival research, monographic thoroughness, and analytical objectivity. An ever-expanding literature, increasingly based on the specialized languages of social science and cultural studies, much of it written in the other official language, often hidden away in unpublished studies, and now ranging across many 'disciplines' and practices other than academic history, defies the most disciplined of readers. Exhilarating: one is over and over again reminded of the politico-ethical centrality of historical exploration, of the new knowledges, truths, and critiques that only detailed empirical research can generate. Deprived: most of all, of strategies of integration, whose feasibility seems to recede with each new addition to the sum of historical research. And crisis-ridden: there is a 'pre-millennial' atmosphere among Canadian historians, a sense that the field, like the country it seeks to understand, is in crisis.[1]

In this charged environment, calls for a return to centrally managed and well-disciplined nation-building political narratives have the paradoxical effect of inducing further fragmentation. Such 'traditionalist' interventions often miss the point that fears of irrelevance, incoherence, and balkanization are widely shared. Many historians in a variety of 'camps' are asking disturbing questions – if sometimes only in private conversations and correspondence. Why even have a field called history if it lacks internal coherence, if its distracted practitioners are too busy to attend seriously to each others' work, if many of their primary loyalties lie with other (sometimes ahistorical) theoretical and methodological traditions? Should we keep on producing historical monograph after monograph if neither we historians nor 'our audience' – a nebulous entity under conditions of postmodernity – will ever read more than a fraction of them? And why have a field of Canadian history if even the

---

1 It is telling that there are so few recent major works by Canadian historians of all persuasions on the political crisis of the past thirty years. For a critique of the historical assumptions in the existing literature on the crisis, see my 'After Canada: On Amnesia and Apocalypse in the Contemporary Crisis,' *Acadiensis* 28, 1 (1998): 76–97.

most powerful and far-reaching methodologies often treat Canada as a 'stage' on which relatively universal processes and formations interact? If Canada is more or less just a 'vacant lot,' one more (relatively minor) place where class, gender, race, ethnicity, sexual orientation, and so on, interact – as they do everywhere else on the planet – why not go to where the action really is, to the United States, to Europe, or 'global' analyses? What, besides narrow horizons, arbitrary and dated disciplinary boundaries, or sheer timidity, would hold us to this 'vacant lot'?

In our own thinly Canadianized 'History Wars North,'[2] we have dutifully followed our international mentors in demonizing the Other within our gates, all the better (perhaps) to keep our own more disabling fears of nihilism at bay. It is always the Other who threatens to destroy the Muse of History, by suffocating her in the airless corridors of the state or by dismembering him[3] in a postmodern orgy of self-indulgence, subjectivism, and cultural disorder. Such dualisms allow one both to describe a crisis and to exempt oneself from it. A panic-stricken polemical extravagance – the end is nigh! there is a corpse on the floor! – is paradoxically combined with the most complacent and removed sense of self-satisfaction.

The emergence of a substantial new Canadian political history in the past decade, centred on the themes of 'ideology,' 'state formation,' and 'law and order,' suggests a way out of this impasse. Drawing innovatively on international theory and historiography, these three streams have made a particularly strong contribution to the study of mid-nineteenth-century Canada. The new history of political thought, much of it written outside the discipline of history, has rediscovered Canada's nineteenth-century civic humanists, situated them imaginatively in a transatlantic debate centred on liberalism and communitarianism, and attempted to reperiodize Canadian history with respect to certain broad ideological

---

2 For the American prototype, see Edward T. Linenthal and Tom Engelhardt, *History Wars: The Enola Gay and Other Battles for the American Past* (New York: Metropolitan Books 1996). For an Australian intervention with a neo-Granatsteinian gothic title, see Keith Windschuttle, *The Killing of History: How Literary Critics and Social Theorists Are Murdering Our Past* (New York: Free Press 1996). For a thoughtful and moderate intervention on underlying issues in Anglo-American historical scholarship, see Thomas L. Haskell, *Objectivity Is Not Neutrality: Explanatory Schemes in History* (Baltimore and London: Johns Hopkins University Press 1998) – an excellent antidote to naïve realism and obscurantist theory-mongering in academic historical discourse.

3 After all, in a twenty-first-century context, there is no reason why Clio should be assigned a fixed gender identity.

patterns.[4] The new history of state formation, influenced to a greater extent by Marxist political economy and theories of the state, and also by such theorists as Gramsci and Foucault, has tracked the rise and consolidation of 'Colonial Leviathan' and focused on the fine grain of 'governmentality' as well as on the broader patterns of ideology.[5] The new history of Canadian law and order has probed not just the empirical history of jurisprudence, but reconstructed the form of law as a determinate abstraction, necessarily of a certain type and yet, at the same time, specific to its time and place.[6] If one were to pass from praising the

4 An informative collection based on the political-thought approach can be found in Janet Ajzenstat and Peter J. Smith, eds., *Canada's Origins: Liberal, Tory or Republican?* (Ottawa: Carleton University Press 1995). Among the important recent titles, see especially Jane Errington, *The Lion, the Eagle, and Upper Canada: A Developing Colonial Ideology* (Kingston and Montreal: McGill-Queen's University Press 1987); Paul Romney, *Getting It Wrong: How Canadians Forgot Their Past and Imperilled Confederation* (Toronto: University of Toronto Press 1999); Gordon Stewart, *The Origins of Canadian Politics: A Comparative Approach* (Vancouver: UBC Press 1986); Robert Vipond, *Liberty & Community: Canadian Federalism and the Failure of the Constitution* (Albany: State University of New York Press 1991).

5 Seminal titles here include Paul Craven, *'An Impartial Umpire': Industrial Relations and the Canadian State, 1900–1911* (Toronto: University of Toronto Press 1980); Bruce Curtis, *True Government by Choice Men? Inspection, Education, and State Formation in Canada West* (Toronto: University of Toronto Press 1992); Jean-Marie Fecteau, *Un nouvel ordre des choses: La pauvreté, le crime, l'État au Québec de la fin du XIXe siécle à 1840* (Montreal: VLB 1989); Alan Greer and Ian Radforth, eds., *Colonial Leviathan: State Formation in Mid-Nineteenth-Century Canada* (Toronto: University of Toronto Press 1992); and J.I. Little, *State and Society in Transition: The Politics of Institutional Reform in the Eastern Townships, 1838–1852* (Montreal and Kingston: McGill-Queen's University Press 1997). Some of the most important work from Atlantic Canada still remains unpublished: see Rusty Bittermann, 'Escheat! Rural Protest on Prince Edward Island, 1832–1842' (PhD thesis, University of New Brunswick 1991) and Daniel Samson, 'Industry and Improvement: State and Class Formations in Nova Scotia's Coal-Mining Countryside 1790–1864' (PhD thesis, Queen's University 1997). For interesting new international titles that might stimulate further Canadian work, see Gilbert M. Joseph and Daniel Nugent, eds., *Everyday Forms of State Formation: Revolution and the Negotiation of Rule in Modern Mexico* (Durham, NC: Duke University Press 1994), and James C. Scott, *Seeing Like a State: How Certain Schemes to Improve the Human Condition Have Failed* (New Haven: Yale University Press 1998). Graham Burchell, Colin Gordon, and Peter Miller, eds., *The Foucault Effect: Studies in Governmentality* (Chicago: University of Chicago Press 1991), has proved a stimulus to much recent work.

6 Among important recent titles, see Michael Boudreau, 'Crime and Society in a City of Order: Halifax, 1918–1935' (PhD thesis, Queen's University 1996); Desmond H. Brown, ed., *The Birth of a Criminal Code: The Evolution of Canada's Justice System* (Toronto: University of Toronto Press 1995); Philip Gerard and Jim Phillips, eds., *Essays in the History of Canadian Law, 3: Nova Scotia* (Toronto: The Osgoode Society for Canadian Legal History and University of Toronto Press 1990); Louis Knafla,

innovative and imaginative work associated with all three streams to a more critical observation, one might say that scholars in all three clusters have been unselfconsciously regional in range, monographic in strategy, and cautious about generalizing beyond tightly defined localities and 'cases'; many of them have proved remarkably resistant even to referring to the work of differently situated scholars on topics very close to their own.[7] This review article would like to take the risk of predicting that these themes, brought together in a new strategy of reconnaissance,[8] could provide us with a 'third paradigm' beyond the traditional nationalist and socio-cultural history narratives – a way of 'going beyond the fragments' in Canadian history writing. This prospectus is an early and inevitably flawed and partial reading of what this potential paradigm might hold for the writing of Canadian history in the twenty-first century.

The core argument is succinct: the category 'Canada' should henceforth denote a historically specific project of rule, rather than either an essence we must defend or an empty homogeneous space we must

ed., *Law and Justice in a New Land: Essays in Western Canadian Legal History* (Toronto: Carswell 1986); Peter Oliver, *'Terror to Evil-Doers': Prisons and Punishments in Nineteenth-Century Ontario* (Toronto: The Osgoode Society for Canadian Legal History and University of Toronto Press 1998); Steven Maynard, 'On the Case of the Case: The Emergence of the Homosexual as a Case History in Early-Twentieth-Century Ontario,' in Franca Iacovetta and Wendy Mitchinson, eds., *On the Case: Explorations in Social History* (Toronto: University of Toronto Press 1998), 65–87; Jim Phillips, Tina Loo, and Susan Lewthwaite, eds., *Essays in the History of Canadian Law, 5: Crime and Criminal Justice* (Toronto: The Osgoode Society for Canadian Legal History and University of Toronto Press 1994); Carolyn Strange and Tina Loo, *Making Good: Law and Moral Regulation in Canada, 1867–1939* (Toronto: University of Toronto Press 1997); John C. Weaver, *Crimes, Constables, and Courts: Order and Transgression in a Canadian City, 1816–1970* (Montreal and Kingston: McGill-Queen's University Press 1995); Brian Young, *The Politics of Codification: The Lower Canadian Civil Code of 1866* (Montreal and Kingston: The Osgoode Society for Canadian Legal History and McGill-Queen's University Press 1994).

7 One might point out that this failing is particularly glaring in the case of Ajzenstat and Smith, eds., *Canada's Origins*, wherein political theorists dissect what 'civic humanism' and 'liberalism' might mean without referring to the work of such historians as Fernande Roy, Jean-Marie Fecteau, Tina Loo, or the entire 'state-formation' school.

8 If we were to replace the scientist and positivist metaphor of 'synthesis,' in which all the subaltern identities lose themselves in a new compound, with antipalingenetic metaphors drawn from cognitive 'mapping' and 'reconnaissance,' we might have more interesting and useful conversations across the many barriers dividing historians. The 'modesty' of this prospectus may seem curiously mismatched to the high-powered polemics that characterize our millennial moment, within Canadian historiography as elsewhere, but any attempt to 'read into' a flourishing monographic literature an implicit general logic requires a sense of modesty.

possess. Canada-as-project can be analyzed through the study of the implantation and expansion over a heterogeneous terrain of a certain politico-economic logic – to wit, liberalism. A strategy of 'reconnaissance' will study those at the core of this project who articulated its values, and those 'insiders' or 'outsiders' who resisted and, to some extent at least, reshaped it.

Rather than beginning with the ambition of 'rethinking Canada' in one great social or political synthesis – a procedure that often takes for granted the very boundaries of the 'Canada' to be rethought – we could begin with the more modest goal of combining the new tools of social and cultural theory with more traditional political narratives and economic analyses. In this more problem-centred approach, to 'rethink' Canada does not mean to synthesize and integrate all Canadian experience into an account that, in the best of worlds, would be acceptable to everyone. It would entail, rather, probing the Canadian state's logical and historical conditions of possibility as a specific project in a particular time and place. Although this approach obviously shares a great deal with both the traditional nation-building and the newer socio-cultural schools, its development would require the elaboration of a new general paradigm distinct from either. Once we have abandoned synthesis as an unattainable goal, we can 'think Canada' in a different way.

We are missing a large library of big books that would help us do so. Where is our late-twentieth-century general interpretation, deeply informed by critical theory and enriched by a nuanced reading of a vast range of the primary and secondary sources, of 'French/English relations'? Or the substantial and sophisticated book, written with the historian's distinctive concern for the specific as well as the general, of the Quiet Revolution?[9] Or its counterpart, an equally 'big book' offering a general historical interpretation of Canadian regionalism, east and west? This questioning is not in any sense to minimize the political historians' achievements – in the writing of biographies and studies of specific trends, in the interpretation of federalism, and in writing subtle and interesting colony-to-nation and regional narratives – that many social and cultural historians have too easily cast aside; rather, it is to imagine a

---

9 This is not to detract from Kenneth McRoberts's classic *Quebec: Social Change and Political Crisis* (Toronto: McClelland & Stewart 1988), and similar titles from political science; but a general historical treatment of the Quiet Revolution would ask rather different questions and incorporate the cut-and-thrust of debates in its own way. It seems astonishing that Canadian cultural history, having long since accomplished the 'linguistic turn,' has yet to 'turn' to theorizing representations of the major language communities in Canada – a 'turn to language' that would obviously be of immense significance in Canada.

dialogue in which both camps add their insights to understanding Canada as a political and socially-specific solution to a series of historical problems. Nor does it mean jettisoning the outlook and achievements of social and economic history, particularly as it has indispensably reflected the insights of Marx into the complex logic of capitalism;[10] it is, rather, to imagine what would happen if the workaday adjective 'Canadian' – Canadian working-class history, Canadian women's history, Canadian gay and lesbian history – exerted the 'force of qualification' over that which it modifies. It is to imagine a way of doing history that locates the 'problem of Canada' within the history of power relations: to map, across northern North America, both the grids of power (penitentiaries and criminal codes, schools and legislatures) through which a given hegemonic 'social' was constructed and centred, and the forces of resistance capable, at certain times, of effecting far-reaching changes of the project itself. It is to imagine a Canada that, however 'solidly' if deceptively reified as a sovereign nation-state among nation-states, is nonetheless 'unsolidly' haunted by the insubstantiality of much of its 'sovereignty'[11] –

10 On Marxist attempts to write the 'general history of Canada,' see especially the often rich and suggestive work of Stanley Ryerson, *The Founding of Canada: Beginnings to 1815* (Toronto: Progress 1972), and *Unequal Union: Confederation and the Roots of Conflict in the Canadas, 1815–1873* (New York: International Publishers 1968). For interesting reflections on Ryerson's work, see Gregory S. Kealey, 'Stanley Bréhaut Ryerson: Canadian Revolutionary and Marxist Historian,' in *Workers and Canadian History* (Montreal and Kingston: McGill-Queen's University Press 1995), 48–100. Ryerson's general Marxist theorization of Canadian history has not been pursued by a subsequent generation of radical scholars: it would seem that, within major camps of Marxist scholarship – political economy (often in the journal *Studies in Political Economy*) and working-class history (exemplified by many of the historians associated with *Labour/Le travail*) – attempts to theorize Canada itself have been displaced by more monographic and 'case study' approaches.
11 And, for this reason, perhaps the most important of all the 'classic' Canadian historians for this approach was the heretical J.B. Brebner, whose sophisticated and brilliantly iconoclastic works – particularly *The Neutral Yankees of Nova Scotia: A Marginal Colony during the Revolutionary Years* (New York: Columbia University Press 1939) and *North Atlantic Triangle: The Interplay of Canada, the United States and Great Britain* (New York: Columbia University Press 1945) – are largely unexplored resources for contemporary historians. No doubt the reasons for Brebner's eviction from the Toronto-constructed canon are many. He worked intensively in a field far removed from the neo-Wagnerian myth-symbol complex Canadian nationalists have woven around the St Lawrence Valley, he became an American citizen, and his highly innovative micro-history did not sit well with the reigning environmentalism. One might also put forward the hypothesis that Brebner's sophisticated non-essentialist and non-nationalist treatment of a Canada not identical with the space of its present claim to sovereignty could only frighten and confuse those scholars schooled in the essentialist 'metropolitanism/continentalism' binaries of Toronto.

a Canada non-identical, in crucial respects, with itself, and non-reducible to some natural or supernatural agency or essence (such as the St Lawrence River, the Canadian Shield, or the workings of 'inevitability,' 'Fate,' and 'Providence'). On this new reading, Canada becomes less a self-evident and obvious unit, and more an arrestingly contradictory, complicated, and yet coherent process of liberal rule. It is to imagine a 'Canada' simultaneously as an *extensive* projection of liberal rule across a large territory and an *intensive* process of subjectification, whereby liberal assumptions are internalized and normalized within the dominion's subjects.

A liberal order is one that encourages and seeks to extend across time and space a belief in the epistemological and ontological primacy of the category 'individual.' It is important to make the analytical distinction between the liberal order as a principle of rule and the often partisan historical forms this principle has taken through 150 years of Canadian history. Canada as a project can be defined as an attempt to plant and nurture, in somewhat unlikely soil, the philosophical assumptions, and the related political and economic practices, of a liberal order. As Fernande Roy has remarked in her pathbreaking monograph on turn-of-the-twentieth-century Quebec, the term 'liberalism' simultaneously suffers from semantic overabundance and poverty; it is all too easily confounded with capitalism on the one hand and democracy on the other.[12] Liberalism begins when one accords a prior ontological and epistemological status to 'the individual' – the human being who is the 'proprietor' of him- or herself, and whose freedom should be limited only by voluntary obligations to others or to God, and by the rules necessary to obtain the equal freedom of other individuals.[13] In the sense brought to life by

12 Fernande Roy, *Progrès, harmonie, liberté: Le libéralisme des milieux d'affaires francophones de Montréal au tournant du siècle* (Montreal: Boréal 1988), 45–58. The discussion of the next two paragraphs is in all respects heavily dependent on Roy's discussion.

13 C.B. Macpherson, *The Political Theory of Possessive Individualism: Hobbes to Locke* (London: Oxford University Press 1962), 264. One should remark that it is a matter of debate among historians of political thought how much North American liberalism was centred on 'possessive individualism' as Macpherson defines it. One can retain the gist of Macpherson's definition and his emphasis on a material underpinning to individualism, without necessarily focusing on Lockean doctrines or according them originary status. See Élie Halévy, *The Growth of Philosophical Radicalism* (Boston: Beacon Press 1955), for the turn in liberal thought from natural rights towards utility, and David F. Ericson, *The Shaping of American Liberalism: The Debates over Ratification, Nullification and Slavery* (Chicago and London: University of Chicago Press 1993), for a stimulating point-by-point comparison of

Margaret Thatcher and theorized by many contemporary neo-liberals, it is the individual who truly exists, in a way 'society,' 'community,' and 'the cosmos' do not.[14] The state in particular lacks any finality of its own; it is the individual, whose rights are predicated on self-possession and property, whose purposes, knowledges, and practices truly exist, and whose 'interests' are 'obvious.' Roy suggests that 'liberalism' is best grasped as an ideology performing both a cognitive and a mobilizing function, which resolves antinomies by ranking three core elements: first 'Liberty,' which gives its name to the entire ideology (and from a basic affirmation of an individual's 'natural right' to liberty, we can move quickly to the claim that there exists a subset of liberties, encompassing 'free labour,' 'free trade,' a 'free press,' and so on); second, 'Equality,' which is always subordinated to the first principle of individualism, and interpreted in ways that render 'commonsensical' the particular inequalities stemming from the exercise of the individual's liberty; and, third, 'Property' – more exactly, the individual's right to hold property – which is in a sense even more 'fundamental' than 'liberty,' for if one's property in oneself is the precondition of one's liberty in the first place, the pursuit of property requires the further development of those characteristics that define one as a free-standing individual. In its classical, nineteenth-century form, liberalism entailed a hierarchy of principles, with formal equality at the bottom and property at the top. Conceptualized in this way, liberalism as a hierarchical ensemble of ideological principles can be distinguished from the historical forms it has assumed, and it can also be distinguished from the competing ideological formations alongside which it evolved and which it worked to envelope and 'include' – or to silence or even eliminate.

The liberalism that a liberal order sought to install as the structured and structuring principle of both public and private life is, in this reconnaissance of Canadian history, something more akin to a secular religion or a totalizing philosophy than to an easily manipulated set of political ideas; and, in this context, it is something more than one

republicanism and liberalism in a specific historical context. For an excellent Canadian discussion, see Colin D. Pearce, 'Egerton Ryerson's Canadian Liberalism,' in Ajzenstat and Smith, eds., *Canada's Origins*, chap. 8.

14 As Anthony Arblaster remarks in *The Rise and Decline of Western Liberalism* (Oxford: Basil Blackwell 1984), 15, liberalism 'involves attaching a higher moral value to the individual than to society, or to any collective group. In this way of thinking the individual comes before society in every sense. He is more real than society. In the quasi-historical theories of the social contract developed by Hobbes, Locke, Paine, and others, he is seen as existing before society temporally as well. Finally, his rights and demands come morally before those of society.'

bounded ideology among other ideologies. The 'individuals' at its conceptual nucleus are not to be confused with actual living beings. Rather, 'the individual' is an abstract principle of the entity each one of them might, if purified and rationalized, aspire to become. In the classical liberal model, hegemonic in Canada from the mid-nineteenth century to the 1940s, a true individual was he who was self-possessed – whose body and soul was his alone; only those human beings who met the criteria of true self-possession were 'true individuals.' It appears to be a paradox that mid-Victorian liberals in Canada sought to limit the right to vote for both women (on the grounds of gender) and adult men (on the grounds of property), that they imposed high property qualifications for such institutions as the Senate, and that they felt obliged to exclude from the franchise those from other races (notably the Chinese and Japanese, as well as unassimilated Amerindians) who, as deficient individuals, were not to be trusted with it.[15] Catholics, the largest denomination of Christians in northern North America, could not realistically be so excluded, but there remained a perceived tension between the demands of their faith and the claims of liberal individualism: they were, at least until the 1890s, in a sense probationary liberals.[16] Mid-nineteenth-century liberal discourse is also strikingly characterized by a hesitation to enfranchise even male adult workers and to extend to them the right to free association: uneducated, prisoners of their passions, prone to disrupt with their conspiracies and strikes the calculus of individual interest, and hence tendentially aliberal in their collectivism, workers

15 A fine study of 'legal liberalism' and discrimination on the grounds of race is James W. St. G. Walker, *'Race,' Rights and the Law in the Supreme Court of Canada: Historical Case Studies* (Waterloo: The Osgoode Society for Canadian Legal History and Wilfrid Laurier University Press 1997).

16 See Rainer Knopff, 'The Triumph of Liberalism in Canada: Laurier on Representation and Party Government,' in Ajzenstat and Smith, eds., *Canada's Origins*, chap. 7. An excellent account of mid-Victorian liberalism and the question of 'papal aggression' can be found in J.M.S. Careless, *Brown of The Globe*, 1: *The Voice of Upper Canada, 1818–1859* (Toronto: Macmillan 1959), 99–136. Much material of fascinating import can be found in J.R. Miller, *Equal Rights: The Jesuits' Estates Act Controversy* (Montreal and Kingston: McGill-Queen's University Press 1979). There is ample scope for Canadian historians armed with contemporary theories of nationalism, and following the lead of such historians as Linda Colley and Terence Ranger, to do important work on the ways in which Protestantism, British ethnicity, and imperialism fused into the image of the 'ideal Canadian individual' in the late-nineteenth and early twentieth centuries. For a sophisticated analysis that links the emergence of liberalism to theological politics, see Pierre Manent, *An Intellectual History of Liberalism*, trans. Rebecca Balinski (Princeton, NJ: Princeton University Press 1995). It may be suggested that the somewhat strained and inconclusive debate over 'secularization' would be sharpened and clarified if, on the basis of this and other studies, it could be transformed into a debate over 'liberalization.'

were often conceptualized as doubtful prospects for liberal individualism.[17] Women, tied as mothers or mothers-to-be by nature and society both to their bodies and to wider networks of family and kin, were also often excluded from individualism in this order;[18] and the same definitional rigour excluded Amerindians, many of them imprisoned in 'communism' and standing in the way of free-market 'development.'[19] Women, workers, ethnic minorities, and Amerindians all obviously have their own histories, which should not be lumped together into one homogeneous 'Canadian' synthesis; but their stories can all be related to each other by noting the consistency of a liberal model which tended to mark them all out as 'Other,' and which, in the nineteenth century, excluded them from the burdens and responsibilities of full individuality. There is a liberal-order 'bridge' connecting these autonomous subaltern histories of experience and struggle.

To rescue the rational kernel from the mystical 'Lockean' shell of Louis Hartz, famously associated with the thesis that American society was liberal from its inception,[20] one would say that, far from being already a 'consensus' viewpoint in northern North America, liberalism was, as late as the 1840s in the eastern British North American colonies, and the 1880s in the Prairie and Pacific West, a highly contentious and endangered program. Its adherents, who from the 1840s to the 1870s

17 For good Ontario overviews, see Jeremy Webber, 'Labour and the Law,' in Paul Craven, ed., *Labouring Lives: Work and Workers in Nineteenth-Century Ontario* (Toronto: University of Toronto Press for the Government of Ontario, 1995), 105–201; Eric Tucker, '"That Indefinite Area of Toleration": Criminal Conspiracy and Trade Unions in Ontario 1837–77,' *Labour/Le travail* 27 (1991): 15–54.

18 For an interesting distillation of the large literature on liberalism and patriarchy, see Mary Dietz, 'Context Is All: Feminism and Theories of Citizenship,' in Chantal Mouffe, ed., *Dimensions of Radical Democracy: Pluralism, Citizenship, Community* (London: Verso 1995), 63–85. She writes: 'The denial of citizenship to women is, of course, a historical but not a contemporary feature of liberalism. Nevertheless, it is worth noting that at least in early liberal thought, the ethical principles that distinguish liberalism – individual freedom and social equality – were not in practice (and often not in theory) extended to women, but solely to 'rational men,' whose 'rationality' was linked to the ownership of property' (82 n. 12). For a pathbreaking Canadian discussion, see Lykke de la Cour, Cecilia Morgan, and Mariana Valverde, 'Gender Regulation and State Formation in Nineteenth-Century Canada,' in Greer and Radforth, eds., *Colonial Leviathan*, 163–91. For a study of the subtle relationship between liberalism and the reform of married women's property law, see Lori Chambers, *Married Women and Property Law in Victorian Ontario* (Toronto: The Osgoode Society for Canadian Legal History and University of Toronto Press 1997).

19 Perhaps the most suggestive account from a liberal-order perspective is that of Sarah Carter, *Lost Harvests: Prairie Indian Reserve Farmers and Government Policy* (Montreal and Kingston: McGill-Queen's University Press 1990).

20 See Louis Hartz, *The Liberal Tradition in America: An Interpretation of American Political Thought since the Revolution* (New York: Harcourt, Brace & World 1955), chap. 1.

had won and consolidated hegemony within the Canadian and Maritime colonies, and in the federal state, nonetheless had to scramble to understand, control, and project into the future a liberal concept of their dominion. Liberal Canada was surrounded by 'exceptions' that defined the 'rule': and sovereign was he who decided on the exception – whose defence of the sovereignty of the core of liberal order required decisions to use force, cultural coercion, and other extraordinary but necessary measures against those spatially or conceptually on its periphery.[21] And one would also say that in contrast to the tendency of both Hartz and his 'civic humanist' critics to personify ideologies as agents in history, the Gramscian liberal-order research program would prefer to interpret ideological formations as being only relatively autonomous within social and economic formations. A distinguishing mark of the liberal-order framework would be the importance it attaches to the function of property, the *primum inter pares* in the trinity of liberal values, as the precondition of a liberal's identity. And one would also underline a difference in methodology. Arguments from the political-thought stream often seem both abstract and non-falsifiable because of their essentialism: more specifically, we are often launched on quixotic and somewhat ahistorical quests for the 'origins' of Canadian politics, on the assumption that they might prove to consist of a single idea set. The liberal-order strategy prescribes a more modest tactic of reconnaissance. It is conceded at the outset that, within the overall framework of the Canadian project of liberal order, a multitude of liberalisms share a definitional family resemblance, but not an essential identity. The realities of class, ethnicity, nation, regionality, gender, religion, and sexual orientation, which both Hartzians and their civic-humanist critics might treat as inessential, would be redescribed in this strategy as distinct, but also related categories of analysis. Such categories are distinct in that they emerge from their own levels of generality and are pertinent at their own levels of magnification, and can and should 'stand alone' in appropriate historical discussions. Yet they can also be illuminatingly related to each other. At a different level of magnification, a re/connaissance (a knowing again) of their interaction, and above all their general articulation with the project of Canada as a project of liberal rule, will lead us to a newly contextualized appreciation of (and eminently empirical propositions concerning) the many political and social realities a liberal order simultaneously preserved, cancelled, and transformed.[22]

21 For an important discussion, see John P. McCormick, *Carl Schmitt's Critique of Liberalism: Against Politics as Technology* (Cambridge: Cambridge University Press 1997), chap. 3.
22 One of the most valuable research projects illuminating this simultaneously conservative and revolutionary aspect of liberal order is that of Brian Young; of his

Placed beside mode-of-production Marxism, ready to 'expose' liberalism as an apology for emergent capitalist social relations, a liberal-order approach, although it comes from the same universe of interpretation and shares much the same drive to ideological critique, nonetheless suggests an alternative line of inquiry. Classical Marxist political economy and class analyses are fundamental to the understanding of the Canadian past, yet they have falteringly interpreted the rise of Canada itself. Their power has been greatest at the monographic, not the general, level where 'Canada' is often dissolved into 'the capitalist mode of production' or 'North America.' It has been empirically difficult, if not impossible, for Marxists to fortify a base-and-superstructure model with the argument that capital as such required a separate state in northern North America. Such a classical Marxist position is problematical in a colonial framework such as pertained through much of British North American and Canadian history, crowded as it is with liberal activists who, rather like communists in twentieth-century Third World countries, were the active 'superstructures' of a future base they earnestly struggled to build. They were determined to create in Canada, through tariffs, railway construction, a homegrown industrial transformation, and an expansive immigration policy, the material preconditions of a liberal society.[23] And classical Marxist exposures often have 'read off' class interest simply from class position. If Antonio Gramsci's theory of hegemony has taught us anything, it is to appreciate the extent to which a given social group can only exercise leadership over others by going beyond its immediate corporate interests to take into account the interests of other groups and classes. This group – in general, but not always, a social class – must secure its position of cultural leadership through a combination of coercion and consent, in a day-by-day process that is never finally completed, 'total,' or secure; it must also defend its claim to sovereignty against rival state projects. The 'historic bloc' that emerges from the transcendence of immediate corporate interests must engage in far-ranging compromises, both economic and cultural, with those subaltern groups necessary for its material survival; it must transcend, in a sense, its own temporality, by actively imagining as part of its

many studies, *In Its Corporate Capacity: The Seminary of Montreal as a Business Institution, 1816–1876* (Montreal and Kingston: McGill-Queen's University Press 1986) is a particularly engrossing account of the transition of one 'precapitalist' and 'seigneurial' institution to capitalist social relations.

23 See A.A. den Otter, *The Philosophy of Railways: The Transcontinental Railway Idea in British North America* (Toronto: University of Toronto Press 1997), for a fine discussion that imaginatively draws out the wider cultural purposes of railway construction in the liberal imagination.

project of rule the economic base most suited to its vision. (It is never denied, of course, that past economic structures set the material limits within which such strategies could be articulated and realized.) A liberal-order framework constructed on Gramscian lines would treat liberal politics not as something to be 'exposed,' and whose secret already lies in an underlying economic reality. Rather, politics is something to be 'explored,' a terrain in which people became aware of their interests and struggled, politically, to fight for them. In the case of the liberal order, the new framework had to be constructed against or alongside radically different ways of conceptualizing human beings and societies.[24] In contrast with classical Marxism, this neo-Marxist liberal-order framework would not necessarily privilege economic and class relations as the site, but rather as a crucial site, of liberal rule. At a certain level of magnification, it is as crucial to look at the power exerted by men over women, or by heterosexuals over homosexuals, as it is to attempt to trace all things back to class. Finally, it is an awkward fact that the nineteenth-century consolidation of the Canadian project required a massive extension of a relatively autonomous state, whose newly institutionalized capacities – in the census and in hospitals, in penitentiaries and insane asylums, the Criminal Code and the police, the tariff and the poorhouse – all bore witness to a dramatic new unleashing of institution building, a newly intense drive to master the chaos of life and liberalize social relations, often before the development of the 'fundamental classes' classical Marxists view as pivotal to capitalism.[25]

For many working in political theory, 'liberal' values are self-evidently good; the organizing binary is 'liberalism/illiberalism.'[26] At the close of

24 There was, of course, a lasting and deep mutual penetration of liberalism and capitalism after the mid-nineteenth century, but it is important to keep these categories analytically separate. And it is equally crucial to evade the temptations of overly emphatic social evolutionary accounts, for alternatives to liberal order were not 'fated' by evolution to disappear so much as liberals fought tenaciously and often against the odds to 'disappear' them, often in ways that changed the liberal project itself.
25 That such institution building fell far short of a twentieth-century conception of the state as 'general manager' of the economy is obvious, but a literature that stresses only this, or that merely critiques the individualist legacy of Victorian liberalism without asking what might have been (and still is) ideologically efficacious about it, is incomplete. See James Struthers, *No Fault of Their Own: Unemployment and the Canadian Welfare State, 1914–1941* (Toronto: University of Toronto Press 1983), for a superb discussion of the twentieth-century legacy of liberal individualist doctrines of 'less eligibility.'
26 A striking example can be found in Joseph H. Carens, ed., *Is Quebec Nationalism Just? Perspectives from English Canada* (Montreal and Kingston: McGill-Queen's University Press 1995), chap. 1.

the twentieth century, liberal assumptions have been so successfully and massively diffused through the population that it is difficult to see, let alone treat accurately and with scholarly empathy, the aliberal positions they have replaced. A liberal-order strategy of reconnaissance would attempt to do so, by treating 'liberty' and 'freedom' and (above all) 'the individual' as the contestable and historically relative terms of a particular and probably transient political program. A liberal-order reconnaissance would aim to see our present-day politics afresh, to make the familiar unfamiliar, to destabilize the conventional first-order apprehension of our own world. The presentist and hubristic catalogues of abnormalities, crimes, and mistakes that revisionist Canadian history has produced in such quantities – 'they were so misguided in the old days,' we say to ourselves, as we read of past racism and sexism – would give way to a more dispassionate and realistic analysis of the developmental logic, the socio-cultural structures, the non-accidental and general reasons for such phenomena. The paradoxical result might well be an appreciation of the enormity of what the Canadian liberal order undertook – the replacement, often with a kind of revolutionary symbolic or actual violence, of antithetical traditions and forms that had functioned for centuries and even millennia with new conceptions of the human being and society. It was no small matter to divorce 'man' from his surroundings, to make his economic and symbolic interests the centrepiece of political and social endeavour, to assert, with all the certainty of scientific political economy, that one could read the signs of his spiritual and material well-being from the data of the market. The construction of this 'individual' was a momentous and complex enterprise. It was not merely a weekend's work to wrench 'values' from the fabric of the cosmos, where, *inter alia*, Aristotle and the church fathers had found them, and to assert the 'individual's' right and duty to justify his own norms. It was not the work of an idle week to 'normalize' the laws of liberal political economy and society, with all their wrenching impact on the lives of settled communities and traditions, and to so consolidate the intellectual authority and prestige of those 'professionals' who commanded this language that their elevation within the state apparatus in the first quarter of the twentieth century would seem more the working out of an inevitability than the consequence of a political choice.[27] These

27 See J.L. Granatstein, *The Ottawa Men: The Civil Service Mandarins 1935–1957* (Toronto: Oxford University Press 1982); Doug Owram, *The Government Generation: Canadian Intellectuals and the State, 1900–1945* (Toronto: University of Toronto Press 1986); and Barry Ferguson, *Remaking Liberalism: The Intellectual Legacy of Adam Shortt, O.D. Skelton, W.C. Clark, and W.A. Mackintosh 1890–1925* (Montreal and Kingston: McGill-Queen's University Press 1993).

successive revolutions required a degree of inner certainty and ruthlessness; they required, one might even say, a liberal vanguard of 'free' and 'cultured' men willing to restrict 'democracy' (which many of them distrusted well into the twentieth century)[28] in the interests of safeguarding the true interests of 'individuals.' It would be easy for a contemporary mind, inescapably shaped by the liberal order, to miss what was startling, revolutionary, and endangered about the nucleus of liberalism when it first assumed its pedagogical role in northern North America, before its mid-century transition to a hegemonic ideology in the centre and its late-century transition to state hegemony from coast to coast. Judged in the light of a condescending posterity, these Canadian liberals can be defined by their limitations and timidity; but evaluated according to a different standard, one that pays attention to the demographic and cultural influence of forces arrayed against them and the totalizing force of their implicit vision, they can be realistically 're-viewed' as something more like revolutionaries. Compared to *ancien régime* societies, both in New France and in early mercantile British North America, in which honour was profoundly connected to rank – a principle of order connecting human beings to a vast, complicated, and dense social fabric[29] – a liberal order was a kind of revolutionary simplification. Compared with Amerindian societies, which saw humanity as positioned on a continuum in which animate and inanimate, human and animal, natural and supernatural were all interconnected – to the point that such contemporary categories themselves can only simplify the profoundly holistic Amerindian vision of the universe – the liberal vision saw individuals as

28 As Anthony Arblaster remarks, in the phrase 'liberal democracy,' the 'adjective "liberal" has the force of a qualification.' See Arblaster, *Liberalism*, 76–8. There is a good theoretical discussion in J.S. McClelland, *A History of Western Political Thought* (London and New York: Routledge 1996), 458–74, and a stimulating historical overview in Michael Bentley, *Politics without Democracy, 1815–1914: Perception and Preoccupation in British Government* (London: Fontana 1989). See also the important discussion in Paul Edward Gottfried, *After Liberalism: Mass Democracy in the Managerial State* (Princeton: Princeton University Press 1999), chap. 2, 'Liberalism vs. Democracy.' For an attempt to contextualize liberal critiques of democracy in the broader context of a debate with civic humanism, see Janet Ajzenstat, 'The Constitutionalism of Étienne Parent and Joseph Howe,' in Ajzenstat and Smith, eds., *Canada's Origins*, chap. 9, a treatment somewhat marred by an unconvincing attempt to associate enthusiasm for a one-party dictatorship with the civic humanism of Mackenzie and Papineau.
29 For illuminating discussions, see Dale Miquelon, *New France, 1701–1744: 'A Supplement to Europe'* (Toronto: McClelland & Stewart 1987), 227–58; and Edith I. Burley, *Servants of the Honourable Company: Work, Discipline and Conflict in the Hudson's Bay Company 1770–1879* (Toronto: Oxford University Press 1997), 19–63.

separate from, and acting upon, the natural world.[30] Out of a colonial population divided among a dozen-odd political entities, and substantially influenced by aliberal *ancien régime* cultures, emerged a small vanguard of true believers, fired by a utopian vision of progress, rationality, and individualism, who brilliantly adapted ideas and practices drawn from a North Atlantic triangle of liberal discourse to a highly heterogeneous and even unpromising early-nineteenth-century northern North American reality.

The book(s) we are missing on this theme of 'The Canadian Liberal Revolution' would necessarily dwell on seven arresting moments. First, the Rebellions of 1837, Lord Durham's Report, and the Act of Union of 1841 taken together as one moment could be interpreted as the high point and defeat of liberalism's civic humanist adversary;[31] and Lord Sydenham could be taken to be a liberal revolutionary, whose campaign of state violence and coercive institutional innovation was empowered not just by the British state but also by his Benthamite certainties.[32] Second, the 'historic compromise' of reconstructed Tories and 're-formed' radicals that British power did so much to effect was the necessary precondition of 'responsible government,' the formula for political compromise first tried out in Nova Scotia, which was so successfully generalized across colonies of markedly different economic and political circumstances.[33] Third, Confederation – interpreted more broadly and

30 I am drawing upon Georges E. Sioui, *For an Amerindian Autohistory* (Montreal and Kingston: McGill-Queen's University Press 1992), and Olive Patricia Dickason, *Canada's First Nations: A History of Founding Peoples from Earliest Times* (Toronto: McClelland & Stewart 1992), 79–83.

31 For the 'civic humanist' credentials of the Patriotes, see Louis-Georges Harvey, 'The First Distinct Society: French Canada, America, and the Constitution of 1791,' in Ajzenstat and Smith, eds., *Canada's Origins*, chap. 4.

32 See Ian Radforth, 'Sydenham and Utilitarian Reform,' in Greer and Radforth, *Colonial Leviathan*, 64–102; Janet Ajzenstat, *The Political Thought of Lord Durham* (Montreal and Kingston: McGill-Queen's University Press 1988); Phillip Buckner, *The Transition to Responsible Government: British Policy in British North America 1815–1850* (Westport, Conn.: Greenwood Press 1985).

33 That roughly the same kinds of liberal reform movements emerged in such a striking diversity of socioeconomic settings suggests the difficulty of explaining so pivotal an event as responsible government in straightforward 'mode-of-production' terms. See Peter Russell's important discussion of the elitist character and damaging long-term implications of the Confederation deal in *Constitutional Odyssey: Can Canadians Be a Sovereign People?* (Toronto: University of Toronto Press 1992); and Philip Resnick, *The Masks of Proteus: Canadian Reflections on the State* (Montreal and Kingston: McGill-Queen's University Press 1990), 54–70. After all, what could have been less marginal, less accidental, and more revealing of an underlying framework of political and economic values than the decision not to refer the scheme of Confederation to the votes of the people?

comprehensively than the political reorganization of 1864–7 to include the subsequent elaboration and stabilization of a federal system down to 1896 – could be seen not so much as the 'Birth of a Nation'[34] as the 'Consolidation of a General Liberal State Program'; here one would take on board Paul Romney's profoundly important questioning of the centralist 'Myth of Confederation' and see this extended moment as one that was more profoundly shaped by liberalism than is suggested in many conventional accounts. Fourth, the 'liberalization' of the West, first by the replacement of the paternalist Hudson's Bay Company with such new British colonies as Vancouver Island, and then by the Canadian state, and also through a massive extension of private property on the basis of the homestead acts and freehold tenure, would constitute an obvious theme of significance.[35] Fifth, the great historic compromise in the 1870s through which a National Policy of tariff protection designed to secure liberal objectives through the protection of industry was made palatable, first to a restive population largely dependent on primary production, and then to the Liberal Party, which after 1896, by inheriting and strengthening a policy it had once maligned, marginalized a once-powerful and pervasive radical critique of liberal political economy. Sixth, the 'liberalization' of Quebec, through patronage and, more crucially, strategic political compromises, which combined to neutralize and contain the civic humanist critique of liberalism and capitalism, given solidity – particularly in Quebec, but to a lesser degree in other provinces – by the Catholic Church. And, seventh, codification of a framework of civil and criminal law, culminating in the world novelty of the Criminal Code of Canada (1893), which solidified the liberal ideal of 'equality before the law' in a way that potentially made an abstract principle into a

34 The Fathers were convinced that they did not need to attain the approval of the mere human beings for the political order they were designing for individuals. The new federal government in Ottawa, although neither constituted from below by a sovereign people nor itself sovereign in most key respects, nonetheless consolidated much of the former British North America into that immense portion of the globe that Canada now claims. This exercise in liberal state formation was sold to French-speaking Lower Canadians as a divorce from Upper Canada that would guarantee their distinctive language and religious traditions; to Ontario anglophones as a divorce from the French Canadians and a measure that would open the West to Ontario farmers; and to British North Americans generally as a great measure to build a railway and thwart the expansion of the American democracy. See A.I. Silver, The French-Canadian Idea of Confederation, 1864–1900 (Toronto: University of Toronto Press 1982), and Ged Martin, Britain and the Origins of Canadian Confederation 1837–67 (Vancouver: UBC Press 1995).
35 Tina Loo, Making Law, Order, and Authority in British Columbia 1821–1871 (Toronto: University of Toronto Press 1994), which stands as one of the most exciting and provocative studies of the emergence of 'liberal legality.'

tangible reality for every adult Canadian. This ability to bring a liberal discourse on property and conduct into direct contact with every subject – there were legally, revealingly, and crucially, as yet no Canadian 'citizens'[36] – is as good an indication as any of a liberal project of Canada that, over sixty years, had achieved dominion-wide hegemony.

Another approach would be the systematic study of the obstacles to liberalism in northern North America, a method which, in itself, would serve to defamiliarize the ruling ideology. One can think of three sorts of major impediments, categorized according to how closely they were situated (both conceptually and, often, geographically) to the individualist nucleus of the project. First, there were those who were 'internal' to the project: not just 'republicans' and 'Tories' who had been 'persuaded' into liberalism in the 1840s, but also those who persistently confronted and were often influenced by different imperatives of liberalism in the United States.[37] Civic humanism was not so much a memory of the past as it was a cultural resource in the present: it did not die with William Lyon Mackenzie and A.A. Dorion, but persisted into the twentieth century, especially on the socialist left.[38] It would modify the strict reading of liberal order among subalterns. Labour historians have been hesitant to acknowledge the impact of liberalism on Canadian workers, who have given the Liberal Party far more support over time than the parties claiming to speak on their behalf.[39] The first women's movement in Canada suggests parallels. The elevation of women, even if in a separate sphere, was implicitly a collective goal requiring a collective

36 See William Kaplan, ed., Belonging: The Meaning and Future of Canadian Citizenship (Montreal and Kingston: McGill-Queen's University Press 1993), although this volume does not succeed in placing the concept of citizenship in an international or long-term perspective.

37 Vipond, Liberty & Community, brings David Mills, MP for Bothwell, and subsequently minister of justice under Laurier from 1897 to 1902, to life as a significant 'decentralizer' in Canada's constitutional history; Mills's liberalism, voiced eloquently in the London Advertiser, was very much influenced by the teachings of Thomas Cooley at the University of Michigan, one of the most important legal minds in the United States.

38 The history of 'citizenship' remains largely unwritten in Canada; one of the untapped primary resources for such an enterprise would be the organ of the country's first dominion-wide socialist movement, which was called Citizen and Country.

39 From the late-Victorian period to today, with only a few interruptions, Canadian workers have been successfully integrated as subordinates into the Canadian political project by the two mainstream liberal parties, a point radical and Marxist labour historiography has been reluctant to emphasize. But see Craig Heron's illuminating discussion in 'Labourism and the Canadian Working Class,' Labour/Le travail 13 (1984): 45–76. One of 'biggest' of the big books we are missing is a sophisticated and theoretically alert reconstruction of the liberal dimensions of agrarian revolt in Canada.

subject; and the first-wave feminists placed great strain on liberal definitions (implicit or explicit) of the 'individual,' whose family contexts and responsibilities they underlined, and whose sexual identity many of them came to question – a point not missed by the many ideologically consistent liberals who spoke against the enfranchisement of women from the 1880s on.[40] The social reforms with which feminism was closely allied, such as temperance, also caused many liberals great concern because these reforms tendentially interfered with the rights of free individuals and free enterprise.[41] It was characteristic of the workers' and women's movements that their political language was deeply marked by the liberalism they both implicitly and explicitly questioned.

Second, another category of opposition was that associated with francophone and Catholic Quebec,[42] ambiguously situated both 'within' the project (indeed, at its very geographical centre), yet culturally distanced from it by reasons of nationality and religion.[43] That the making of the liberal order in Quebec necessitated far-ranging compromises of liberal ideological principles can illuminate the more general issue of how the order was articulated to (and sought to incorporate) pre- and aliberal sociopolitical forms. That the British North America Act says so little about issues now taken to be fundamental, such as language rights, testifies to its profoundly liberal character; but that it says something about language at all, in section 133, later confirmed in the Manitoba Act, and something more about religious education, brings out the historic price liberals were willing to pay to achieve their dominion. In order to achieve a historic bloc that would allow them to convey liberal rule to as

40 Note in particular Stephen Leacock, 'The Woman Question,' in *Social Criticism: The Unsolved Riddle of Social Justice and Other Essays* (Toronto: University of Toronto Press 1996), 51–60, which turned to the 'law of supply and demand' for support for its argument against women's rights.

41 For a thoughtful discussion, see Brian Trainor, 'Towards a Genealogy of Temperance: Identity, Belief and Drink in Victorian Ontario' (MA thesis, Queen's University 1993).

42 Quebec shares with British Columbia the honour of having a sophisticated literature about the history of liberal politics. In addition to the works of Roy, Fecteau, and Young already mentioned, one should also note Jean-Paul Bernard, *Les Rouges: Libéralisme, nationalisme et anticléricalisme au milieu du XIXe siècle* (Montreal: Les Presses de l'Université du Québec 1971); Bernard L. Vigod, *Quebec before Duplessis: The Political Career of Louis-Alexandre Taschereau* (Montreal and Kingston: McGill-Queen's University Press 1986); and Gilles Bourque et Jules Duchastel, *Restons traditionnels et progressifs: Pour une nouvelle analyse du discours politique: Le cas du régime Duplessis au Québec* (Montreal: Les Éditions du Boréal 1988).

43 See Ronald Rudin, *Making History in Twentieth-Century Quebec* (Toronto: University of Toronto Press 1997), for an exploration of the ways in which Quebec historians have sought to 'normalize' their society's distinctiveness.

wide a population as possible, liberals were willing to compromise on the question of the separation of church and state and, to a point, on other sociocultural issues – but on the crucial condition that Catholic communitarianism be restricted as much as possible to Quebec (and even there subordinated in the hierarchy to a state liberalism that would remain, down to the 1950s, eminently 'classical').[44] The hegemonic incorporation of Quebec was indispensable to the achievement of liberal order and could only be achieved through carefully articulated politics of elite accommodation and cultural compromise, which have gone on to become misleadingly mythologized as defining features of Canada itself. What is misleading about this myth is that it overlooks the uncompromisingly liberal context within which such 'accommodations' and 'compromises' were made and which they were designed to preserve: these were less 'compromises' than 'bargains with liberal hegemony.'

Finally, there were, on the edges of a liberal dominion, other aliberal entities more completely external to its project of rule. Long-established and once militarily powerful, Aboriginals, the demographic majority in most of the territory eventually to be claimed by the liberal dominion, were people whose conceptions of property, politics, and the individual were scandalously not derived from the universe of Locke, Smith, Bentham, or Lord Durham. The containment of these alternative logics was an ideological imperative of the liberal order, without which it could not exist as a transcontinental project. A reconnaissance of this 'Other' would mean relativizing the Canadian/liberal claim to represent the rule of law; the Canadian project would be seen instead as a historically contingent formula for liberal order, in competition with older and long-established Aboriginal practices.[45] It would mean revisiting the history of prairie reservations and Native agricultural policy, which has already

44 For a sophisticated and convincing elaboration of this point, see Gilles Bourque, Jules Duchastel, et Jacques Beauchemin, *La société libérale duplessiste 1944–1960* (Montréal: Les Presses de l'Université de Montréal 1994). Catholics such as Laurier were 'defective individuals' in the mid-century liberal imagination because, trapped in medieval 'superstition,' and under the sway of a foreign pope, their 'free-standing' self-possession was imperfect. Laurier himself feared that his faith alone would bar him from the Liberal leadership. One might suggest that, on this issue, one finds an interesting difference between Canadian and American liberalisms. Despite intense Protestant misgivings on this issue, Catholics, who had as individuals been pivotal to the Canadian project since its inception, could be admitted even to the prime ministership in the 1890s – as witness John Thompson, not only a Catholic but a convert to Catholicism. The concept of 'Protestant hegemony' in Canadian history is in urgent need of re-examination.
45 For a fascinating illustration, see Hamar Foster, '"The Queen's Law Is Better Than Yours": International Homicide in Early British Columbia,' in Phillips, Loo, and Lewthwaite, eds., *Essays in the History of Canadian Law*, 5: 41–111.

been well explored and theorized, to ask what it tells us about the process of the Canadian liberal revolution in general. It would mean a revaluation of Ottawa's handling of the 'Indian Question' as not just a series of misunderstandings, premised on a distanced misreading of Native societies, but rather as a fulfilment of liberal norms, which required the subordination of alternatives. Canadian imperialism in the High Arctic and in the West was not incidentally related to the Canadian values articulated by the 'Ottawa men' of the nineteenth and early twentieth centuries. From Joseph Howe and John A. Macdonald down to the 1940s, there was a consistency of approach to Amerindian issues which invites theorization within a liberal-order research program.[46] It was perhaps in the residential schools that the full utopianism of a vanguard liberalism came to the fore, for within these Christian/liberal manufactories of individuals, pre-eminent laboratories of liberalism, First Nations children were 'forced to be free,' in the very particular liberal sense of 'free,' even at the cost of their lives.[47]

A liberal-order reconnaissance of Canadian history, which can be conveyed only partially and telegraphically here, entails seeing how far and how complexly this principle of liberal order functioned across the wide array of social formations and territories that ultimately cohered, from the 1860s to the 1890s, into the Dominion of Canada. It cannot, will never, and is in fact not designed to stand in for 'other' subaltern histories – the record of working-class struggle, the formation of the Quebec nation, emergence of first-wave feminism among women, and so on. A reconnaissance is not a synthesis. It is a contingent, partial, and (perhaps) somewhat risky attempt to derive a sense of general patterns from particular discrete sightings; its preferred tactic is to relate some of these autonomous histories to each other via bridging concepts and plausible correlations. A liberal-order framework, by beginning with the fact of the Canadian state project, might well be falsely accused of returning to a top-down, state-centric line of interpretation. The more accurate charge would be that this approach radically calls into question the 'top/bottom' binarism that has condemned so much historiographical debate in Canada to a wearisome and fractious sterility. From this

46 See E. Brian Titley, *A Narrow Vision: Duncan Campbell Scott and the Administration of Indian Affairs in Canada* (Vancouver: UBC Press 1986); Frank James Tester and Peter Kulchyski, *Tammarniit (Mistakes): Inuit Relocation in the Eastern Arctic, 1939–63* (Vancouver: UBC Press 1994).

47 On the residential schools, see J.R. Miller, *Shingwauk's Vision: A History of Native Residential Schools* (Toronto: University of Toronto Press 1996), and John S. Milloy, *A National Crime: The Canadian Government and the Residential School System 1879 to 1986* (Winnipeg: University of Manitoba Press 1999).

perspective, there is no 'top' and no 'bottom': there is a centre and a periphery, a liberal project and its 'resistors.'[48] One can read as much 'liberal ordering' into inheritance patterns, or the conception of the household as a 'private sphere' ruled by an authorized free-standing individual patriarch, or even in the location of a particular fence post, as one can into the National Policy. What connects the farmer's fence with Macdonald's tariff is a common respect for private property and the propertied individual as the foundation of a sociopolitical order ulti- mately defended by the state's legitimate violence. What it meant to succeed, to own things, to shine as a success in the eyes of one's parents,[49] to be a real man, to construct lines on maps and barriers around whole countries, to separate what's 'mine' from 'yours', 'ours' from 'theirs': with regard to these fundamental questions of property, the farmer's fence post and the prime minister's tariff policy share a com- mon universe of assumptions and values.

A central, and difficult, issue will be that of saying when the liberal order had attained hegemony – which, we remember from reading Gramsci, is never a once-and-for-all achievement of some (unverifiable) majority consensus, but a consistent (and verifiable) logic of rule. An equally challenging and interesting question for this project will be that of 'where.' Often imprisoned by the present-day Canadian nationalist myth-symbol complex, historians are inclined to write 'continuous na- tional histories,' a strategy that tends to eternalize the present-day map of Canada[50] and to attribute to the entire dominion patterns characteristic only of one of its parts. It would be more interesting to devise ways of mapping the spread of liberalism across both space and time, as it extended its grasp from a few nineteenth-century southern outposts to encompass, by the early twentieth century, a subcontinent. If the urban Maritimes and the St Lawrence Valley functioned as a sort of 'Piedmont' of liberal ordering, where the Canadian liberal formulae were first fully worked out, documenting and explaining the extension of these formu- lae from coast to coast to coast, in social and political conditions often bearing little resemblance to those of the 'liberal nucleus,' is the obvious

---

48 See Dante Germino, *Antonio Gramsci: Architect of a New Politics* (Baton Rouge and London: Louisiana State University Press 1990), 57–8, for a discussion of this Gramscian innovation in the language of Marxist politics.

49 For 'vulgar liberalism,' see Allan Smith, 'The Myth of the Self-Made Man in English Canada 1850–1914,' in *Canada: An American Nation? Essays on Continentalism, Identity, and the Canadian Frame of Mind* (Montreal and Kingston: McGill-Queen's University Press 1994), 324–58.

50 At least as this map has entered the popular imagination: the actual shape of the claims of Canadian sovereignty is quite different.

and necessary following step. Even so, even reading backwards from the 'end' of this process, one would want to avoid colouring the Canadian map a homogeneous liberal red: there would remain many places, and are to this day, where *de jure* liberal rule coexists with the *de facto* power of very different conceptions of the political and social world.[51]

A further challenge to confront a liberal-order framework as a new reconnaissance of Canadian history would be the related one of articulating the distinctiveness of the liberal order in Canada: that is, in trying to explain the country's existence in terms distinct from the essentialist generalizations of Laurentianism, frontierism, or the (now widely disputed) neo-Hartzian 'Tory touch' thesis.[52] Canada's 'origins' are typically sought in a river system, a rock formation, a mode of production, or the (highly debatable) ideological 'core' of its supposedly pivotal (Ontario Loyalist) settlers. Liberal-order arguments are admittedly not all that well suited to the Quest for Canadian Exceptionalism. Nonetheless, one anticipates they will develop a different, more modest explanation of Canada's separate North American existence, placing greater emphasis on the cumulative impact within a transatlantic liberal universe of marginal differences – 'adaptations,' to invoke social evolutionism for a moment – through which a universal ideology and general project of rule confronted, changed, and was changed over time by the particularities of its surroundings, most notably the strength of its opponents.

We know that principles of liberal governmentality and liberal political economy were directly imported from the colonial metropole. They also reflected, to an extent present-day historiography is only starting to recover, a dialogue with the republican founding principles and subsequent hegemonic liberalism of the United States. Against the environmentalism and naive nationalism of older interpretations of Canada's existence, against the 'Toronto School Syndrome,' the liberal-order reconnaissance would not look for a providential or natural something 'outside history' on which to secure the possibility of the 'Canadian' state project. It would rather explore the contingent and pragmatic reasons why one type of liberal state experiment might have been considered more efficient and less risky than another – why, for example, some quite astute liberal minds in Canada thought that '(Liberal) Freedom (Necessarily) Wore a Crown.'[53]

51 A fine monograph that could be read as an illuminating study of this pattern can be found in Ken Coates, *Best Left as Indians: Native-White Relations in the Yukon Territory 1840–1973* (Montreal and Kingston: McGill-Queen's University Press 1990).
52 See Gad Horowitz, 'Conservatism, Liberalism, and Socialism in Canada: An Interpretation,' in Ajzenstat and Smith, eds., *Canada's Origins*, chap. 2.
53 See John Farthing, *Freedom Wears a Crown* (Toronto: Kingswood House 1957).

In this sense, derivative as most liberal ideas were in Canadian history, they became cumulatively less so as they were adapted to the heterogeneous social and cultural terrain of northern North America. Thus the Canadian liberal order, inspired in many ways by its British prototype, and secondarily by its American competitor, was shaped and reshaped by the complexity of the pre-liberal and aliberal British North American worlds it had simultaneously to preserve, cancel, and transcend. Here, and not in any 'foundation' or 'essence,' is the complex logic of Canadian distinctiveness. It lies in the liberal imperative to harmonize older ways with its new, underlying conception of the world. As it expanded from its core in a few eastern centres to take ownership of a dominion encompassing a subcontinent, Canada as a liberal project of rule was shaped not only by its founding values but by the necessary and often difficult compromises that were required if such values were to become hegemonic – that is, durably install themselves in law, daily experience, personal conduct, and intellectual life.

From the beginning, this was an inescapably hybrid political project. In the mid-century making of Canada, the signs of 'bargaining with hegemony' were everywhere: a language of politics in which civic humanism, contractualism, and utilitarianism were woven together, often in the speeches of one and the same liberal activist; a 'mixed constitution' allowing for both monarchy and a measure of carefully controlled popular participation, a 'partial separation' between church and state that nonetheless left the Christian churches with a pivotal role in educating the young and 'civilizing' Amerindians, and a constitutional framework that left room, in a system of checks and balances, for local substates to flourish within a liberal dominion and under the sovereignty of the Crown. Such characteristics were not awkward compromises incidental to the liberal project of Canada, but indications of concessions that, in seemingly qualifying the liberal vision, also brought it down to Canadian earth – a specifically Canadian answer to such liberal challenges as political obligation, social cohesion, and economic development. Their cumulative impact was to give the Canadian liberal order its peculiar traditions and, one might say, its uncanny persistence.

Turn-of-the-century Canada represented, in many respects, the apex of the liberal project. With Laurier in power after 1896, the Catholic ultramontanes' communitarian critique of liberal order seemed to have been contained, if not silenced; with the Liberal Party's acceptance of the National Policy tariffs, a *modus vivendi* had been reached on the subject of the most corrosive single economic issue in Canadian politics. Across a wide political spectrum, Canadian political thinkers, even a French-Canadian nationalist like Henri Bourassa, saluted the brilliance of a classical liberalism inherited from Britain and developed afresh in northern North America. After years of disappointment, the West was being settled under the decisive policies of Clifford Sifton: as one would expect, the state left the key problems of accommodation to a strange and difficult terrain to the immigrant families themselves on their independent homesteads. Perhaps the *pièce de résistance* of the Canadian liberal order was to carve upon the map, in lines that majestically remind us of Euclidean geometry and panoptical state power, the perfect geometry of the Province of Saskatchewan: perhaps even more impressive, however, than this quadrilateral demonstration of panopticism was the molecular checkerboard of quarter-sections and individual properties contained within the new province's boundaries – a social ideology set down on the land and hence made part of everyday western experience.

Even the new immigrants in their 'sheepskin coats,' drawn to Canada through the free workings of an international labour market that operated just as liberal political economy said it would, could be 'Canadianized' (liberalized) in a generation. And when critics pointed out the anomalies in the pattern – a state-subsidized Canadian Pacific Railway enjoying monopoly privileges and enormous corporate and political power, or Ottawa's colonial policy of retaining control over crown land and mineral resources – they would be answered by other voices: such anomalies, often described as 'emergency measures,' indicated merely that Canada needed to return to its founding liberal principles.

In Winnipeg and in Saskatoon, one burned a lamp, in the early twentieth century, for the eternal truths of liberalism: no sense of the 'nucleus' of the twentieth-century liberal project could exclude one of its most powerful and prescient organic intellectuals, J.W. Dafoe of the *Manitoba Free Press*.[54] In the twentieth century that 'belonged to Canada,' racial minorities would long be excluded from the franchise, only a minority of adults could vote in federal and provincial elections (in Quebec, this restriction would persist until 1940), and there were, until the 1940s, subjects but not citizens. The magic of nationalism has converted this 'Canada' into a country like the one we now inhabit – but it was essentially a liberal empire, not a nation, and not a democratic state.

There is a textbook answer to explain a supposed transition from the nineteenth-century dominion to the multicultural liberal democratic nation state: Canada simply glided, slowly and surely, down Arthur

54 There is an interesting discussion of his 'crypto-liberalism' in David Laycock, *Populism and Democratic Thought in the Canadian Prairies 1910 to 1945* (Toronto: University of Toronto Press 1990).

Lower's *Most Famous Stream* of liberal democracy. More and more people were brought aboard the good ship, and the unsightly detritus of the past vanished into the distance. The liberal-order approach, centred on the Gramscian concept of 'passive revolution,' would undoubtedly offer a much bumpier and less pleasant ride.[55]

Liberal ideas and practices were undeniably rethought in the early twentieth century, by intellectuals such as John Watson and Mackenzie King, by Social Gospellers and Progressives – by a host of 'New Liberals' whose key insight was that the rights of the classically defined individual could no longer be the foundation of politics and social life. The requirements of society, that 'evolving social organism,' could only be safeguarded through a greatly expanded and much more activist state responsible for the general welfare of its citizens.[56] In much historical writing, the nineteenth-century liberal order is retrospectively abolished by such turn-of-the-century reformers; or else it is subdued in the second quarter of the twentieth century by the liberal order's first powerful 'opposition' outside itself, the socialist movement, which in Canada articulated a civic humanist argument for a postliberal democracy. Just as the first four decades of the nineteenth century can be mapped as ones in which, from a multitude of interests and identities,[57] a new project of liberal state formation eventually emerged to effect a historic compromise, so too might the first four decades of the twentieth century be mapped as ones in which a new democratic state formation slowly emerged which sought to redefine the meaning of the word 'Canada.'[58]

55 For the concept of passive revolution, see Antonio Gramsci, *Selections from the Prison Notebooks*, ed. and trans. Quintin Hoare and Geoffrey Nowell Smith (London: Lawrence & Wishart 1971), 207.
56 See Ramsay Cook, *The Regenerators: Social Criticism in Late Victorian Canada* (Toronto: University of Toronto Press 1985). For an interesting account of changing political ideals, see John English, *The Decline of Politics: The Conservatives and the Party System 1901-20* (1977; Toronto: University of Toronto Press 1993). The pioneering exploration of the concept of the 'new democracy' is James Naylor, *The New Democracy: Challenging the Social Order in Industrial Ontario 1914-25* (Toronto: University of Toronto Press 1991).
57 One might mention here the complex political character of Canadian regionalism, which has often paradoxically demanded not that 'Canada' cease to exist, but that the Canadian economy and political system operate 'fairly,' in a way that recognizes the distinctive interests of 'region.' Seemingly antithetical (the one centripetal, the other centrifugal), 'regionalism' and 'pan-Canadian nationalism' have historically been mutually dependent: often a Canadian regionalist is striving for the better, fairer integration of his or her region into the Canadian polity, yet in terms that are tendentially post-liberal.
58 There was logic, as well as poetry and 'popular-front politics,' in the appellation 'Mackenzie-Papineau' the left attached to the Canadian battalions that defended

It is an often-related narrative, and much of it captures a truth. Yet in many respects this 'new democracy' was contained: classical liberal assumptions did not disappear, and there was no 'institutional rupture' marginalizing either the Liberal Conservatives or the Liberals as continuing political formations. Another big book is waiting to be written on the ways the left program of new democracy was contained in the middle years of the twentieth century through a seemingly conciliatory, ultimately profoundly disintegrating, process of 'passive revolution' in which, unusually in world terms, Canadian liberalism vanquished its enemies within and without. The thesis of 'passive revolution' maintains that, confronted with a serious quasi-revolutionary challenge to its hegemony, the liberal state executed far-ranging changes in its social and political project to 'include' some of those previously excluded, with the *quid pro quo* that they divest themselves of the most radical aspects of their oppositional programs (such as demands for a comprehensive change in property relations or in the nature and function of political 'representation').

The crucial cases for examination in Canada would be that of the Co-operative Commonwealth Federation,[59] the Communist (subsequently Labor-Progressive) Party, and the left-led industrial unions. Substantial institutional concessions were made to this multi-voiced left, but only at the cost of 'editing' out their unacceptably aliberal elements. The 'passive revolution' imprisoned the left advocates of 'new democracy' in an ever-constricting iron cage of liberal pragmatism. The Canadian 'Keynes' revealingly lost, somewhere in his transatlantic passage, his quirky interest in the comprehensive socialization of investment along with his far-ranging schemes for regional development. What had once seemed a new democratic transformation of the locus of sovereignty in the 1940s – an event duly eternalized within the intertwined memories of social democracy and Canadian nationalism – proved deceptive. Since the 1950s the 'collective prince' has been not the people, but the market and the managerial state. Fiscal exuberance and a ballooning public debt did not change, but, in many respects, underwrote this reality. [60] It might be

democracy in republican Spain: socialists were reclaiming and legitimizing the civic humanist reading of Canadian history, and in particular the idea that the 'Canadian people' had a democratic legacy.

59 The historians who stress the CCF's essential moderation and mild 'social democracy' have often failed to register the sweeping character of the radical socialist transformation demanded in David Lewis and Frank Scott, *Make This Your Canada: A Review of CCF History and Policy* (Toronto: Central Canada Publishing Company 1943).

60 See James Struthers, *The Limits of Affluence: Welfare in Ontario 1920–1970* (Toronto: University of Toronto Press for the Government of Ontario 1994), for a careful

said that, if the collapse of the British Empire made the new Canadian democracy possible, the rise of the American Empire made it unlikely: postwar Americanization of popular culture and the economy was the ironic counterpart to the emergence of the 'new democratic nationality.'

An even more profound contradiction was that the new democracy never effected a political separation from the undemocratic liberal formulae from which it had descended. The new ideologues invested themselves completely in imperial state forms that, by design, had never explicitly articulated a doctrine of popular sovereignty. If the nineteenth-century dominion had never been the free state of a sovereign people, but was rather a locally managed dominion within a liberal empire, whose territorial claim rested fundamentally on the legacy of Britain's commercial might and armed violence in North America, the twentieth-century dominion, however much influenced by the Social Gospel, the 'new democracy,' the socialist ideals of the CCF and the Communist Party, and so on, nonetheless never decisively distanced itself from this imperial legacy. This was still, in many critical eyes, perhaps most decisively those of Québécois, the same old empire, with the same kinds of men in charge, revering the same distant queen, jockeying for the same threadbare colonial honours, flocking in their sunset years to the same anti-democratic Senate.

To abbreviate and anticipate what should some day be a long and more subtle discussion: the reconceived centre could not hold. It could not, without the old ideological resources of empire, or a new and more rigorous sense of its vocation, even become much of a hegemonic centre. An immensely powerful complex of liberal myths and symbols, amply sustained in a corporate guise by American multinationals and foundations, never went away in the days of the 'new democracy.' Since 1975, as the idea of new democracy and the 'Canada' it articulated has progressively faded from view, the country has rung, again and again, to manifestos of the 'true believers' of the doctrines of classical liberalism. After their brilliantly executed struggle for cultural hegemony, classical liberal

deromanticization of the partial transition to 'social citizenship.' See also C. David Naylor, *Private Practice, Public Payment: Canadian Medicine and the Politics of Health Insurance, 1911–1966* (Montreal and Kingston: McGill-Queen's University Press 1986); John R. Miron, *Housing in Postwar Canada: Demographic Change, Household Formation and Housing Demand* (Montreal and Kingston: McGill-Queen's University Press 1988); and John C. Bacher, *Keeping to the Marketplace: The Evolution of Canadian Housing Policy* (Montreal and Kingston: McGill-Queen's University Press 1993). The most suggestive and rigorous analysis of the capitalist entrapment of the welfare state remains Claus Offe, *Contradictions of the Welfare State* (Cambridge, Mass.: MIT Press 1985).

individualism rides high again, and what had once appeared a decisive 'transcendence of the classical liberal order of the nineteenth century' stands revealed as something more like an interregnum, a temporary moment of emergency social legislation.

Can Canada be reprogrammed a third time, along the lines of this undoubtedly massive shift away from the values of the new democracy, towards a restoration of the nineteenth-century paradigm? Notwithstanding the depth and tenacity of the liberal order in Canadian history, this refocus seems unlikely. Had we asked a Victorian liberal why one should support the project of Canada, the answer might well have entailed some version of 'Peace, Order, and good Government' – the benefits to all free-standing individuals of living in a stable British country, governed sensibly by a parliamentary monarchy, and anchored in a deep sense of the British Constitution and the Queen's law. If we asked a mid-twentieth-century Canadian the same question, we might well have heard a new democratic defence of national distinctiveness in terms of universal social programs, democratic inclusiveness and tolerance, east-west economic linkages, and international peacekeeping. How (or if) neo-liberals will attempt to 'Canadianize' themselves is an intriguing mystery. True believers in unfettered individualism and global markets, these exponents of the hegemonic ideology presently lack any persuasive justification for Canada in the reductionist market terms in which they seek to cast social and political questions. Most of the neo-liberals' grand economic objectives would, in fact, be better realized without a separate Canadian state in northern North America – and they know it.[61] Theirs is a brilliant definitional challenge that should arouse Canadian historians from their dogmatic slumbers, petty debates, and narrow horizons.

61 See Thomas J. Courchene with Colin R. Telmer, *From Heartland to North American Region State: The Social, Fiscal and Federal Evolution of Ontario. An Interpretive Essay.* Monograph Series on Public Policy (Toronto: University of Toronto, Faculty of Management 1998). The thesis of this much-honoured (if profoundly ahistorical) monograph is that Ontario is no longer the 'heartland' of a Canadian nation state, but is emerging as the 'premier economic region state within North America,' 2.

I would like to thank my History 873 class at Queen's University and audiences at McGill University and the Université du Québec à Montréal for responding to oral versions of this text.

In Hope and Fear: Intellectual History, Liberalism, and the Liberal Order Framework

JEFFREY L. MCNAIRN

I first read Ian McKay's 'The Liberal Order Framework' while preparing a job talk – a reconnaissance, if you will, of my past, current, and future research. My reaction was schizophrenic. On the one hand, the article took seriously the threats of irrelevance and fragmentation that many professional historians of Canada felt while moving beyond ineffectual hand-wringing and the stale binaries of political versus social history and nation versus 'limited' identities. On the other hand, the article made it clear that someone about to interview me – the job was at Queen's – had thought more seriously and creatively about my own period and research questions than I had.

My admiration for 'The Liberal Order Framework' as one of the most exciting developments in Canadian historiography remains undiminished. The article raises the debate to new theoretical levels and its insistence on Canada as a project or process rather than an event or geographic space and as 'essentially a liberal empire, not a nation' strikes me as both persuasive and powerful.[1] My unease, however, persists – now less about the trauma of the academic job market than the framework's implications for my own area of specialization. As an intellectual historian of the long nineteenth century, I continue to struggle with three related questions: How can intellectual history contribute to the liberal order framework? What are the implications for intellectual history of adopting such a framework? What is the relationship between liberalism and the liberal order?

My current answers are that while intellectual history and the liberal order framework have much to offer each other, the latter's implications for intellectual history are contradictory – liable to prompt and promote, but also to deter and distort. These implications repay the attention of non-intellectual historians as well, for they reveal some of the framework's more demanding aspects, many of which can be traced to its debt to the Italian interwar communist Antonio Gramsci. Of course, the fate of Canadian intellectual history was not among McKay's primary concerns. Nor can he be held responsible for how others take up his ideas. I am also cognizant of the fact that intellectual history embraces a number of different objects of study and research strategies.[2] For the most part, I have attempted to bracket my own preferences to speak about the relationship between the liberal order framework and intellectual history more generally. I have failed to bracket my hopes and fears.

The Hope

My admiration for Ian McKay's article is augmented by what I see as the six positive implications of the liberal order framework for Canadian intellectual history. Deliberately or not, the framework underscores trends evident in intellectual history elsewhere. Thus, it is also on these points that intellectual history has the most to offer those seeking to develop the framework further. First and most obviously, the framework centres the term 'liberal' rather than 'capitalism,' 'bourgeois democracy,' or 'modernity.' More immediately than such alternatives, 'liberal' denotes an outlook, an ideology or tradition of political thought, or certain arguments and assumptions; that is, it lies firmly, if not exclusively, within the realm of intellectual history. Indeed, McKay identifies recent scholarship on 'ideology' and 'the new history of political thought' as one of three trends leading to this reconnaissance.[3]

Second, McKay's conception of 'liberal' is a historicized one: it was once new, remained contested, and changed in content and influence over time. Unlike the often abstract principles of justice or the supposedly universal postulates of 'human nature' that still dominate rational-choice theory and much contemporary analytical philosophy and economics, the liberalism of the liberal order requires historical treatment. Instead of well-worn clichés about liberalism as a sort of anything-goes relativism or some extreme doctrine of *laissez-faire*, McKay rightly insists on its revolutionary character: its ambition to remake societies and the very subjectivity of individuals and its willingness, within limits, to use the state to do so.[4] Of course, intellectual historians need no reminder of the contingent and contested nature of liberalism. Indeed, the elegant essays of S.F. Wise and Carl Berger's compelling *A Sense of*

Power have long ensured that conservative, not enlightenment or liberal, ideas have been seen to dominate, even define, nineteenth-century
Canada.[5] Subsequently, J.G.A. Pocock's recovery of an Anglo-American language of civic humanism, designed to displace a liberal reading
of the past, has been extended to the Canadian context.[6] Indeed, intellectual historians have been so intent on studying liberalism's critics
that any framework premised on its rather rapid acceptance as 'common sense' is more radical than it may first appear.

Third, the liberal order framework not only enjoins a rapprochement
between intellectual and other forms of history, but it encourages an
expansive view of the topics and approaches of intellectual history
itself. While political, legal, and constitutional thought are among the
best-served topics in early Canadian history, the framework should
encourage work on a number of topics that have received more attention in other national contexts: the intellectual and cultural aspects of
the nineteenth-century 'market revolution,'[7] the religiosity of economic
ideas,[8] the creation of modern notions of the self,[9] ideas of social class
and wealth distribution,[10] attitudes towards risk, credit, and economic
failure,[11] and so on. The framework also prompts us to learn more about
how and by whom ideas were produced, circulated, and received.
Understanding how particular ideas of the individual and society
achieved the status of 'common sense' requires relating them to what
Gramsci called the 'material structure of ideology,' extending beyond
the press and publishing houses to 'everything which influences or is
able to influence public opinion, directly or indirectly ... libraries,
schools, associations and clubs of various kinds, even architecture and
the layout and names of streets.'[12] Some of the best intellectual history
does just that, connecting the study of thought to the history of reading
and the book, scholarly and intellectual networks, and popular mental-
ités or the public sphere.[13] Future work on the liberal order framework
can only benefit from engaging with this international literature – its
findings and the potential and pitfalls of its diverse methods – while
encouraging its greater application to the study of Canada's intellectual
past.

Fourth, by situating Canada in 'a transatlantic liberal universe,' the
framework reminds us of the issues at stake in northern North America; issues that give intellectual historians a reason to include the area in
their studies and that still resonate today.[14] Legislators, voters, and
newspaper readers confronted difficult questions about building and
maintaining a good and just society often in the midst of deep disagree-

ment about what constituted the good or the just. For instance, the pages of George Brown's *Globe* on church–state relations more than a century and a half ago never seemed so alive as during recent debates in Ontario about the relationship between sharia and provincial law in the adjudication of family disputes. McKay is surely right to insist on the connections between how this and other issues were addressed; to demand, for instance, 'a revaluation of Ottawa's handling of the 'Indian Question' as not just a series of misunderstandings, premised on a distanced misreading of Native societies,' but as attempted answers to a set of questions the premises of which informed how other issues, from franchise extension to tariff policy, were addressed.[15] The liberal order framework thus joins intellectual historians in insisting that public life in Canada was more than the localized, often petty, fence-post politics of power, patronage, and party.[16]

As the mid-nineteenth-century Toronto *Globe* also attests, British North Americans paid close attention to such issues outside their borders, whether it was the fate of the papal states in Italy or the rule of law in American slave states, not because politics was more mundane closer to home, but because questions about the role of organized religion in politics or the effects of dependence and violence on the administration of justice were of pressing local concern. Intellectual historians of the mid-nineteenth century have already demonstrated the importance of a trans-Atlantic perspective and the consequences for mutual understanding when British North Americans drew from different European traditions.[17] Hopefully, the popularity of the liberal order framework will encourage more such work attuned to the international dimensions of the central issues of power, authority, and the state that Canada-as-project raised.

Fifth, McKay holds out the possibility that 'marginal differences ... through which a universal ideology and general project of rule confronted, changed, and was changed over time by the particularities of its surroundings' might define something distinctively Canadian while eschewing claims of national exceptionalism.[18] There is certainly a literature on how national context shaped political thought from which to draw,[19] but the challenges of identifying such 'marginal differences' at the level of ideas in anything but the most impressionistic way are daunting. Moreover, such differences may lie within Canada and between non-national entities rather than between Canada and other 'national' contexts. A liberalism shaped by a North American as opposed to a European environment or one spread and nurtured by the

Scottish diaspora seem as likely as a distinctively 'Canadian' one. By offering his framework as an antidote to perceived problems in Canadian history, rather than in the discipline as a whole, McKay risks re-privileging the nation-state as the way we organize our knowledge and conversations when, in fact, 'Canada' may be of little relevance to the questions many intellectual (and other) historians ask.[20]

Of course, intellectual historians have long been implicated in the elusive search for a Canadian identity, but as McKay points out, 'we are often launched on quixotic and somewhat ahistorical quests for the 'origins' of Canadian politics, on the assumption that they might prove to consist of a single idea set.'[21] Searching for 'origins' or a distinctive 'political culture' too often assumes that the consensus revealed at some founding moment defines the 'real' Canada whose development can then be narrated in terms of progress or fall. The political demand that this particular definition be preserved or restored usually follows from such foundationalism.[22] We should attend, therefore, not only to how McKay has turned on its head George Grant's lament that 'the impossibility of conservatism in our era is the impossibility of Canada'[23] by substituting liberalism for conservatism, but also to his rejection of the nationalism on which such laments (and their celebratory twin) are based. While marginal differences may emerge from future scholarship, it would be unfortunate if the call to treat Canada as more than a 'vacant lot' – for a *Canadian* intellectual history rather than merely an intellectual history set in Canada – directed attention to issues of national identity where much has been done already and many of the roadblocks signed.[24]

Sixth, to effect a broad reconnaissance the liberal order framework rejects economic determinism and other crude forms of reductionism that expose or dismiss ideas as mere reflections of an economic base or the objective economic self-interest of particular individuals or social classes. Intellectual history is excluded from any framework that does not repudiate mechanical and deterministic approaches to meaning – there's no point studying ideas if ideas don't matter. In fact, McKay's criticism of 'mode-of-production Marxism' in this regard is more temperate than Gramsci's own dismissal of 'economism' or the absolute privileging of economic structures and causes as 'primitive infantilism' and 'doctrinaire pedantry.' Attempting to transcend the base-superstructure metaphor, Gramsci is emphatic that 'it is utterly false that peoples only allow themselves to be moved by considerations of self-interest.' For Gramsci 'there is no human activity from which every form of intellectual participation can be excluded: *homo faber* cannot be separated from *homo sapiens*. Each man ... carries on some form of intellectual activity, that is, he is a 'philosopher,' an artist, a man of taste, he participates in a particular conception of the world, has a conscious line of moral conduct, and therefore contributes to sustain a conception of the world or to modify it.' Following Gramsci, then, McKay insists that culture and politics must be accorded 'relatively autonomous' status.[25] Much depends, of course, on how relative and autonomous from what, but intellectual historians are at least invited to the discussion.

Any attempt to bridge sub-fields must also reject extreme forms of idealism. While McKay chides Louis 'Hartz and his 'civic humanist critics" for tending 'to personify ideologies as agents in history,' most intellectual historians do not refuse the reduction of meaning to experience only to cleave to the other, equally simplistic, extreme of asserting the absolute autonomy of meaning from experience. There is no unanimity among them on how to relate ideas to other forms of human behaviour, yet, perhaps because they have traditionally focused on one side of the representation-reality binary, intellectual historians have done much to explore their reciprocal relationship and to try to transcend the dichotomy altogether, just as any inclusive framework for Canadian history must.[26]

It is tempting to stop here, reading McKay's article as a skilful exercise in historiographic bridge-building and thereby to accept its own rather modest self-characterization as a 'framework,' 'prospectus,' and 'reconnaissance.' The bridges it builds are impressive. The framework offers important opportunities for Canadian intellectual historians, especially by prodding them further in the direction of developments elsewhere in their own field. It also gives other historians additional reasons to listen. That similar lists of the framework's positive implications could be made for other fields speaks to the scope of the article, the breadth of its reading, and the subtlety of its analysis. Yet, such a reading amounts to a 'reconnaissance lite,' skirting the framework's more challenging aspects. After all, no framework can be methodologically or politically innocent.[27]

The First Fear: Defining Liberalism

This first becomes evident in the bold and relatively straight-forward definition of 'liberal' offered for the liberal order framework. 'Liberalism begins,' McKay argues, 'when one accords a prior ontological and epistemological status to 'the individual." Following Fernande Roy's work on turn-of-the-twentieth-century Montreal, McKay defines liberalism as an 'ideology' with 'three core elements' – liberty, equality, and property – ranked to settle conflict among them. Thus, 'in its classical, nineteenth-century form, liberalism entailed a hierarchy of principles with formal equality at the bottom,' since it could not override inequalities that arose from and were justified by the exercise of individual liberty, 'and property at the top,' since liberty itself rested on owning oneself, especially one's labour.[28] Here I think intellectual historians will baulk.

First, however, it is important to acknowledge McKay's insistence that liberalism and the liberal order are not the same thing. The latter is 'a certain politico-economic logic' or 'a principle of rule' distinct from 'the often partisan historical forms this principle has taken,' 'more akin to a secular religion or totalizing philosophy than an easily manipulated set of political ideas'; and 'in this context, it is something more than one bounded ideology among other ideologies.' Yet, in the same pages, McKay also talks of the liberal order as, at least in part, 'a belief' or a set of 'philosophical assumptions' that have been 'brought to life' and 'theorized' by those 'who articulated its values.' Moreover, when defining the term liberal, McKay reverts to talking about liberal*ism* and 'a hierarchical ensemble of ideological principles,' albeit one that 'can be distinguished from the historical forms it has assumed.'[29] While distinct, liberalism and the liberal order are closely related. Otherwise, it is unclear where the 'liberal' in the liberal order comes from, unless it is arbitrary or somehow independent of people's thought.[30]

No one would dispute that the individual and his or her liberty, equal status, and property were important aspects of nineteenth-century thought. Numerous statements about the equality and rights of all 'British subjects' under the law or celebrating the political status and economic possibilities that accrued to property owners could be marshalled from across British North America, although not all from sources or in the service of causes we might wish to call 'liberal.' But why only these elements and why in this particular configuration? Would people even fully conscious of themselves as liberals recognize their beliefs as derived, no matter how distantly or creatively, from such a core?[31] How does such a definition shape the broader framework? Does it help us understand how people thought and argued in the past?

Other scholars using a similar method have arrived at different lists of liberalism's core principles.[32] For instance, John Gray includes individualism and equality (although he emphasizes their moral dimensions more than McKay), but adds that liberalism is also '*universalist*, affirming the moral unity of the human species ...; and *meliorist* in its affirmation of the corrigibility and improvability of all social institutions and political arrangements.' He makes no mention of property. Michael Freeden's list for 'the time-span stretching roughly from Locke to the early J.S. Mill' is less declarative: 'a fundamental belief in the rationality of man as an individual ...; a faith in the perfectibility of man which lent itself to conceptions of progress and development and hence to gradualist reform; the notion of empirical freedom both as condition for and as expression of rationality and justice; a concern with the interests of society as a whole rather than with advantages for particular individuals or groups, based on reasons irrelevant to the general interest; constitutional and institutional arrangements to ensure unfettered functioning of individuals within the framework of the law, with the concomitant of limited, responsible, and representative political power.' Over the longer term, Freeden deems natural rights doctrines that implied a view of society as artificial and contractual, 'the idea of private property as the concrete embodiment and expression of man's worth,' and liberalism's association 'with economic freedom and unrestrained competition, and with atomistic individualism' to have been 'transient' rather than constitutive elements of liberalism.[33]

The lists overlap considerably, but shifts in how we define 'liberal' affect how we characterize the liberal order. Gray's addition of universalism would bring us to emphasize liberalism's strategies of inclusion as well as exclusion. When combined with a meliorist commitment, it would prompt us to recall liberalism's links to humanitarian causes such as the abolition of slavery and the extension of moral concern and political power outward beyond the privileged few. Freeden's emphasis on specifically political concerns also reminds us that while liberty is included in McKay's definition of liberalism, it does little work in his liberal order. Liberalism as a political movement defined by its opposition to the concentration or arbitrary use of power by a state, church, or social class, to monopoly and unearned privilege, and to the legitimation of institutions, laws, and practices by traditions or sacred texts closed to critical scrutiny is remarkably absent. As E.A. Heaman points out in this volume, liberalism's connection to civil rights, religious toleration, and the critical use of reason as antidotes to what it opposed is thereby glossed over.[34] Such definitions of liberal do not transform historians into cheerleaders for *les lumières* against *l'infâme*. Nor do they deter us from studying how liberals betrayed their principles or how many of their 'reforms' tended to discipline in one sense even as they empowered in another. But they do require us to give greater attention to such topics and to balance our historical sense of what was lost with what was gained.

Limiting ourselves to the other elements of McKay's definition, are they sufficiently sensitive to the conceptual resources and plurality of liberalism? From the perspective of intellectual history, they can appear either too restrictive and thus exclude or distort much we might consider liberal or too abstract and inclusive and thus reveal little. Respecting the latter, setting out from core principles tells us little about the arguments and debates that shaped Canada-as-project or their relative import. The unwary might assume that key elements of the liberal order were championed primarily or even exclusively using arguments derived from McKay's liberal core and resisted with arguments derived from other, non-liberal cores. Yet, liberal arguments can usually be found with equal consistency on more than one side of a nineteenth-century debate, including in opposition to developments McKay associates with the liberal order. For instance, Upper Canadian reformers advanced what were arguably liberal arguments in favour of greater parental choice and local and ratepayer control over state-aided schools and thus against the more centralized and bureaucratic school system associated with Egerton Ryerson that serves as a prime example of Canadian institution-building.[35] Moreover, as Freeden argues about any set of core principles, 'these ideas by themselves tell us nothing about the nature of an ideology, just as an isolated piece of furniture conveys no sense of the room it stands in. The core exists within an idea-environment of adjacent and peripheral concepts, and this environment acts to colour and define the core.' For instance, 'the concept of liberty, by its mere appearance, tells us little; but if it is bordered on by the adjacent concepts of physical integrity and a notion of social atomism it will take on a completely different meaning than when bordered on, for example, by self-realization, mutuality and democracy.'[36] The context, not the core, matters.

McKay's inclusion of formal equality is the least troubling element of his definition, although many liberals assigned it greater status, adopted more substantive definitions of equality, or insisted that formal equality required a degree of resource equality to be meaningful.[37] Benjamin Constant, for instance, argued that 'the perfectibility of the human species is nothing other than the tendency toward equality ...

Equality alone conforms to the truth, that is to the respective relationships of things and men to each other.'[38] Competing schemes of colonial
emigration with different implications for equality were promoted to
create more consumers of British manufactured goods and producers
of food. Edward Gibbon Wakefield's plans were designed to recreate in
British North America the inequalities associated with labour's divorce
from capital as necessary for social and economic development, but
others sought the same end by means of the greater social equality that
came from reuniting labour with capital. The poor and dispossessed in
Britain who produced and consumed little could be transformed into
agrarian property-holders in colonial societies dominated by such petty
producers. A degree of inequality would persist, but the resulting colonial societies were far more egalitarian and therefore socially and politically democratic than Britain itself. In such a social context, nineteenth-
century liberalism – its celebration of independence and its desire to
equate individual economic success with virtue – seemed especially
plausible to contemporaries.[39]

McKay's emphasis on individualism also appears uncontroversial,
but we need to distinguish political and ethical individualism from
'ontological and epistemological' individualism.[40] The belief that individuals are politically and morally equal need not entail the claim that
individuals are asocial atoms whose needs and preferences are independent of society and who are somehow more real than the groups to
which they belong. Pegging liberalism to an atomistic view of the self
or an artificial view of society seems particularly problematic for the
'new liberalism' that developed in the second half of the nineteenth
century given its substantial debt to British idealism and evolutionary
biology.[41]

John Stuart Mill was certainly an individualist, but he valued an individuality that was profoundly social, created by and only possible in
the context of interactions with others: 'The social state is at once so natural, so necessary, and so habitual to man, that, except in some unusual
circumstances or by an effort of voluntary abstraction, he never conceives himself otherwise than as a member of a body.' This 'deeply-
rooted conception which every individual even now has of himself as a
social being' was 'the ultimate sanction of the greatest happiness morality.' With his liberal morality grounded in human beings' social nature,
Mill declared selfishness to be 'the principal cause which makes life
unsatisfactory' and repeatedly railed against the idea that what individuals owed to each other rested on their self-interest. There was no

'inherent necessity that any human being should be a selfish egotist, devoid of every feeling or care but those which centre in his own miserable individuality.'[42]

This was almost certainly the more common view in overwhelmingly Christian British North America than any celebration of the asocial individual or egoism. Thus, alongside Native residential schools as what McKay terms the 'pre-eminent laboratories of liberalism' stood the many voluntary associations individuals created and sustained by choice. Here they learned the 'voluntary abstraction' from the particular and powerful bonds of family, kin, community, rank, faith, and nationality required to relate to diverse 'others' as fellow human beings, moral equals, and rights-holders worthy of respect.[43]

Also problematic is the privileged place McKay accords to property. In support of private property as 'the *primum inter pares* in the trinity of liberal values,' he cites C.B. Macpherson's *The Political Theory of Possessive Individualism* (1962). While Macpherson's work continues to find support among liberalism's critics, it would be an understatement to say that its conclusions about early-modern English thought have been contested since its publication more than four decades ago.[44] As a number of historians have emphasized, Locke developed his theory to justify armed resistance to Charles II, not market relations. The notion of self-possession – individuals' right to their capacities – is not an exclusively liberal one either, but was taken up by radicals to support the claims of workers against capital. For many nineteenth-century readers, *Two Treatises of Government* (which was largely ignored at the time it was written) made Locke 'the father of modern socialism in England' rather than of liberalism.[45] In this volume, Jerry Bannister offers us an excellent example of how Lockean ideas could also be pressed into service by establishment Whigs. Finally, McKay's 'core' again seems ill suited to the 'new liberalism' that developed by the end of that century. In a book entitled *Liberalism* (1911), one of its principal theorists, L.T. Hobhouse, conceded that 'individualism, as ordinarily understood ... takes the rights of property for granted ... [but] we must not assume any of the rights of property as axiomatic. We must look at their actual working and consider how they affect the life of society.' Liberty and equality, not property, animated Hobhouse's liberalism.[46]

Of course, property still mattered, and not just to liberals, but the nature of property relations – how they were derived, their ethical and economic purpose, their extent and limits, and what they included, as in Locke's much debated formulation of property in 'Lives, Liberties and Estates' – varied tremendously. As Ruth Sandwell emphasizes in this volume, many emigrants to rural British North America participated in the economy as families rather than individuals, had fled the consequences of liberal economic development elsewhere, and strove to avoid wage-dependence. Yet, they were not thereby rendered hostile to the liberal message. Perhaps more than any other group in colonial society, they valued and were committed to maintaining the individual ownership of private property. They invested their labour, on and off the land, to acquire, improve, and, if possible, expand their property-holding across generations. Situated thus, they formed a large and sympathetic audience for key elements of political and economic liberalism. We should not be surprised that while wintering with his sister at Wolfville, Nova Scotia, in 1847–8 a British visitor found Adam Smith's *Wealth of Nations* among the small number of volumes in the local farmers' subscription library.[47]

Thus, while careful not to reduce liberalism to capitalism, McKay's treatment fits comfortably within a long tradition of Marxist critique: liberalism, despite its claim to universality, is irredeemably partial; ultimately little more than a rationalization for bourgeois values or market relations. McKay refers to liberalism as an ideology of 'the individual, whose rights are predicated on self-possession and property ... and whose "interests" are "obvious."' It justified material inequality, promoted 'free-market "development,"' and asserted 'with all the certainty of scientific political economy, that one could read the signs of his [the individual's] spiritual and material well-being from the data of the market.'[48] Thus, in 'Liberalism Defined,' a section of her already-published response to McKay, Sandwell turns to William Reddy, an expert on the history of the French cloth industry, instead of to a liberal thinker or an intellectual historian of liberalism. She quotes Reddy as asserting that liberalism began 'as an apologetics for merchant activities' whose synthesis was achieved by Adam Smith. Given what Smith said about merchants and their penchant for mistaking their own narrow interests for the common good, both statements cannot be true. As quoted by Sandwell, Reddy's depiction of Smith's 'full-blown liberal illusion' includes the propositions that the 'motive of gain was the mainspring of human behaviour' and that 'unregulated competition brought maximum progress' in a capitalist system that demanded that 'all elements of life [be reduced] to a single quantitative dimension.' Treated thus, liberalism can be dismissed as 'false' before proceeding to a discussion of its altogether baneful effects and the not-altogether-surprising resistance to such an unappealing set of propositions.[49]

There may be much in Smith to criticize, but our criticism ought to target what he wrote. It may, then, be worth insisting that Smith spoke rarely in terms of rights but emphasized the historical and environmental, rejected the social contract tradition, situated his work as an alternative to the egoism and individualism he disliked in Bernard Mandeville, insisted on the natural sociability of human beings, developed a complex psychology that gave ample room to vanity, delusion, and mutual sympathy as well as to personal ambition and *perceived* self-interest, did not justify unlimited accumulation, neither equated happiness with wealth nor reduced human needs to the material, and expressed considerable anxiety about the consequences of the economic changes he attempted to understand and, yes, to promote.[50] Of course, Smith (much less Locke) did not see himself as a liberal, but was elected one retroactively on the basis of particular interpretations of his work by later, self-consciously liberal thinkers or their critics. This retrospective construction and reconstruction has recently led philosopher Kwame Anthony Appiah to despair that a historical inquiry of 'what we now call the liberal tradition would look less like a body of ideas that developed through time and more like a collection of sources and interpretations of sources that we now find useful, looking backward.'[51] Ironically, while McKay claims civic humanism as a forerunner of Canadian socialism, a case can be made that it was precisely in the language of civic humanism deployed by Smith and others that 'commercial society' was first legitimated as well as criticized.[52]

Whatever Reddy's insights into capitalism and the social responses to it, the summary of his approach to liberalism presented by Sandwell as congruent with McKay's is an ideological construct to attack and blame rather than an attempt to understand what Smith thought or how his works were subsequently interpreted. Responding to just such a view of liberalism more generally, Richard Bellamy asserts that 'on the contrary, liberals were haunted by this ethos of egoistic, possessive individualism and strenuously battled against it. A more accurate version of the liberal idea would consist of a meritocratic society of self-reliant and responsible citizens, co-operating together in pursuit of individual, social, material, and moral improvement.'[53] Both McKay and Sandwell worry that liberalism has become so pervasive that scholars have difficulty treating the aliberal with empathy.[54] I worry that extending such empathy to liberals has proven no less difficult.

The Second Fear: (Mis)Using Definitions

If my first concern as an intellectual historian about the liberal order framework is its definition of liberal, my second is more methodological: how that definition and the framework more generally might influence the questions intellectual historians ask and how they try to answer them. By privileging unity within the realm of thought over diversity, suggesting particular methods, and relying on Gramsci's neo-Marxism, the liberal order framework imposes a substantial cost on intellectual history for its inclusion.

First, then, the framework privileges the unity of intellectual assumptions over the diversity of ideas; it directs our attention to a homogeneous liberalism and away from actual histories of political, social, economic, religious, scientific, and aesthetic thought. While McKay repeatedly acknowledges that liberalism assumed many 'historical forms,' what matters most to the framework is what they shared, not their diversity. Thus, a single 'order' or 'logic' is constructed to cover a disparate group of thinkers, polemicists, scholars, clerics, and other members of the intellectual elite as well as those who assimilated their ideas and values. Many were opponents or were unaware of each other. They addressed different problems in different periods and circumstances, used a variety of 'languages' or idioms, and drew in the nineteenth century alone from 'sources as diverse as natural rights doctrines, Whiggism, classical political economy, utilitarianism, evangelical Christianity, idealism, and evolutionary biology.'[55] Yet, reduced to so many forms of a single phenomenon, the liberal order framework licenses vague talk of liberalism in the singular or of a 'discourse of economic liberalism.'[56]

If we already know what they share and what connects them to the broader liberal order, why study liberalism's various manifestations? The only compelling reason seems to be to show how, under pressure from its opponents (and not the application of its own conceptual resources to new circumstances), liberalism was rethought in order to maintain its hegemony, that is, to maintain the dominance of its core assumptions.[57] The emphasis on what they share also means emphasizing the assumptions that define them all as 'liberal' rather than the ideas and debates they gave rise to. Thus, to the extent that intellectual history concerns itself with speech-acts in the past, it sits uncomfortably within the broader sweep of the liberal order framework. Moreover, by privileging the boundary between liberal and non-liberal over the boundaries within either, the focus on unity encourages a sort of zero-sum shell-game whereby historians debate whether an idea or value was 'really' liberal. Were liberal and republican ideas, to take two common examples in the literature, so distinct or could they find significant common ground in particular historical contexts? Perhaps, as D.J. Manning has argued, 'traditions of ideological writings do not have definable centres any more than they have fixed circumferences.'[58] In either case, fights over labels are rarely edifying or open to resolution.

By contrast, intellectual historians have worked hard to recover the complexity of authors and texts in their multiplicity, nuance, ambiguity, and contradiction even as they interpret them in light of the broader 'languages' or intellectual traditions within which they were written and read. The tendency of intellectual historians to emphasize particularity and contingency over unity is not a form of antiquarianism and it certainly has not prevented them from writing synthetic accounts of their own field.[59] Rather, the commitment stems from the conviction that ideas can only be understood fully and without anachronism if placed within the contexts of the particular problems, vocabularies, and circumstances in which they were articulated. Moreover, even fairly systematic thinkers were often promiscuous in their choice of argument and rhetoric in ways that wreck havoc with our desire to order the past into a few neat categories.[60] We miss much of the human agency and political intent of such eclecticism if we focus primarily on underlying unities and boundary-marking. Of course, intellectual historians do not thereby ignore webs of connection and continuity within their subject-matter, but are especially anxious to ensure that these have not been foisted on the past for narrative or political convenience.

This anxiety speaks to my second point of methodological concern: that the framework may inadvertently encourage intellectual historians to forget key methodological insights from their own field. Expectations of ideological coherence explain our surprise at learning that Locke was read as the father of socialism in the first half of the nineteenth century or that, as Gareth Stedman Jones has recently argued, radicals after the French Revolution drew inspiration for the idea that poverty could be eradicated from Adam Smith.[61] But such surprise will be less likely if intellectual historians frame their research in terms of the liberal order framework. For instance, only when he stopped equating economic thought with 'laissez-faire individualism' and 'classical' political economy, did Boyd Hilton rediscover an entire group of 'Christian Economists' and 'another model of free-trade individualism, one *not* based on classical economics or the prospects of growth, or the superiority of the industrial sector.'[62] Beginning with preconceived ideas of what should be there usually means missing what is.

As early as 1907, Lucien Febvre warned against how, in the words of Roger Chartier, 'such retrospective and classifying terms ... are not faithful to the lived psychological and intellectual experience of the time' and 'while pretending to identify former ways of thinking, in fact disguise them.'[63] Quentin Skinner is most responsible for extending this warning to the current generation of intellectual historians.[64] While not its author's intention, I fear that the attractiveness of the liberal order framework will send future intellectual historians searching for supporters and opponents of the assumptions it emphasizes. Asking whether a particular historical figure was a liberal in that sense transforms the framework's outline into a stable, uncontested yardstick. The intellectual historian's only task is then to measure how close that figure came to expressing or adhering to what now functions as an a priori definition of liberalism. The temptation will be great to proceed by extrapolating, if necessary, from a few scattered comments to a particular view of the individual or property (for our definition tells us that our subject must at least have assumed such views), to parcel him or her into a camp with others to whom the same assumptions have been attributed, and to ignore other aspects of their thought as immaterial to the task at hand. Finally, with the camps identified, particular statements from any of their members can be plucked almost indiscriminately to illustrate the features of the camp with little regard to the problems or interlocutors they addressed, the arguments and themes they emphasized or elided, and the terms they expressed themselves in. The definition takes on a life of its own at the expense of what actual people in the past actually thought.

But what if our intellectual historian of the liberal order confronts historical figures and texts that mix what are deemed liberal with other elements? And he or she surely will, for as McKay insists, hegemony is not a stable consensus. Given liberalism's struggle with the heterogeneous terrain of northern North America, the liberal order in Canada 'was an inescapably hybrid political project' such that a variety of elements 'were woven together, often in the speeches of one and the same liberal activist.'[65] If our intellectual historian successfully avoids the temptation to tidy up the mess by finding something 'behind' the statements to give them coherence or to criticize the figure for *their* failure to use *our* categories consistently, he or she will be tempted to label the diverse elements in terms of their relationship to the hegemonic order and its opponents, past and future; that is, as dominant, residual, and emergent. Of course, this merely re-packages and re-describes the elements of the speech in terms of the framework being investigated. It explains nothing.[66] (And, if the elements of the speech are so mixed, how do we determine that the activist was a liberal one?) It would, however, be a small step from such an exercise in re-description to the suggestion that the existence of these elements and their relationship to each other are *explained* by the 'rise' of the liberal order or the activist's temporal or socio-economic position in it. Such a shift from McKay's descriptive account to an explanatory one renders the entire exercise non-falsifiable and tautological. Setting out to test the liberal order framework, the intellectual historian ends by assuming its existence.

Third, the liberal order framework is dependent on the theoretical work of Antonio Gramsci. McKay provides us with one of the most arresting applications of Gramscian thought to the grand sweep of any country's history, but his reliance on Gramsci explains many of the most troubling aspects of the framework for intellectual historians. We don't need to insist, somewhat naively, that objectivity is neutrality[67] to see that the reconnaissance on offer is anything but 'lite' in the demands it makes on those whose subjects it would re-know. And yet, without Gramsci, there's no reconnaissance.

For instance, the framework's definition of liberal is best seen as 'not-socialism.' Whereas liberalism centres the individual, socialism is predicated on the social: a 'concept of species-being' and 'new conceptions of the sociality of human beings.' Equality is not limited to its formal aspects and 'a full program of human freedom entails conscious, rational control over economic and social forces' instead of a commitment to private property. Finally, whereas liberalism's relationship to democracy is problematic, 'democracy ... belongs to the left.' Such definitions ensure that liberalism and socialism (joined by liberalism's other opponents) are profoundly antagonistic world views rather than overlapping ones that shade into and draw creatively from each other. It is a view of liberalism borne in deep dismay at the rise of 'conservatism' (or neo-liberalism) in Western democracies after 1975, which McKay yokes tightly to the 'classical liberalism' of the early nineteenth century. The 'new liberalism' of the late nineteenth and much of the twentieth century becomes, in hindsight, an interregnum. From this perspective, liberalism has returned with a vengeance to its core principles of atomistic individualism, private property, and free markets. It is not coincidental, then, that the definition of that core is least attuned to the 'new liberalism' or that the only historical figure named as exemplifying its principles is Margaret Thatcher.[68]

McKay's debt to Gramsci also explains why the framework privileges unity over diversity in discussions of ideas, values, and assumptions. The many liberalisms can be lumped together precisely because they share a common failure to advance the fundamental reordering of social relations Gramsci sought. Indeed, the use of Gramsci explains why there is a liberal 'order' that connects liberalism as a set of ideas to events, practices, and institutions in the first place. The liberal order represents a particular 'historical bloc' or 'the necessary reciprocity between structure and superstructures.'[69] The concept allows McKay to escape reductionist accounts and to (re)connect an otherwise disparate historical literature, but it also determines what is fundamental rather than interesting historical detail. Referring to the debate between John A. Macdonald and Wilfrid Laurier about protective tariffs and continental union, McKay concludes that 'such debates were important. They were not fundamental.' It is a salutary warning to heed commonalities obscured by partisan debate, but the commonality is more 'fundamental' not because it determined the content of that debate or the particular policy outcome, but because neither Macdonald nor Laurier challenged 'capitalist priorities.'[70] Even so, what those priorities were and how best to advance them were not self-evident to contemporaries. They were the product of competing arguments and assumptions.

The framework's almost exclusive emphasis on the limits of liberalism, and thus how it positions the vast majority of the population as obstacles to it, can also be traced to Gramsci. McKay is at his most eloquent in reminding us how liberal assumptions were used to justify the exclusion or subordination of 'actual living beings' and policies that attempted to transform those beings into particular types of 'individuals,' often by starkly illiberal and undemocratic means.[71] Liberals frequently betrayed their ideals; the consequences were often frightful. Searching for patterns in those failures is among the framework's strengths; that it attributes them exclusively to contradictions in or the limits of liberalism itself rather than to the failure of liberals to be sufficiently liberal or to the particular uses to which liberal assumptions were put speaks to Gramsci's basic conviction that the liberal order can and should be transcended. The liberal order reflects the basic contradictions and injustices of capitalism which, by definition, no form of liberalism can overcome. The incentive to study the diversity of liberal opinion thus erodes further, since all are equally wanting and for much the same reason.[72] The framework thus situates all those who resisted that order as 'collectivist' models of 'living otherwise,' even at the risk of essentializing and romanticizing them.[73]

Two nineteenth-century examples reveal the consequences of this dynamic for intellectual history. As McKay notes, some of the 'maternal feminist' arguments made by the women's suffrage movement strained liberal notions of the individual, ensuring that there were 'many ideologically consistent liberals who spoke against the enfranchisement of women from the 1880s on.' That does not, however, mean we can simply ignore the fact that the movement articulated liberal arguments as well, ensuring that 'many ideologically consistent' liberals supported enfranchisement, as John Stuart Mill and Harriet Taylor did in Britain from the 1860s. In 'Why Women Need the Vote,' for instance, Toronto suffrage supporters made arguments based on the premise that 'women's special care is the home' and that 'a nation is but a larger home,' but they made others premised on equal citizenship: 'Because no race or class or sex can have its interest properly safeguarded in the Legislature of a country unless it is represented by direct suffrage ... Because women are taxed without being represented, and taxation without representation is tyranny. They have to obey the laws equally with men, and they ought to have a voice in deciding what those laws shall be.'[74] Advocates of female enfranchisement drew from a varied repertory of arguments and assumptions. Whatever the relative weight of liberal, anti-liberal, and non-liberal elements within that repertory, female suffrage stands as much as an example of the historical possibilities of liberalism as it does of its limits.

In fact, while McKay positions civic humanism and Catholic Quebec as fellow obstacles to liberalism, Allan Greer has argued that it was republicanism, following Jean-Jacques Rousseau, that most limited women's participation in the Patriot movement, and it would be hard to find a more uncompromising insistence on patriarchal authority than Bishop Louis-François Laflèche's *Quelques considérations sur les rapports de la société civile avec la religion et la famille* (Montreal, 1866). Laflèche condemned liberalism as a direct violation of the divine plan in which patriarchy figured prominently. Many nineteenth-century liberals actively participated in or failed to challenge the legal and social subordination of women and spoke in highly gendered terms, but their nineteenth-century critics seem even more hostile. Small wonder, then, that liberalism, more than civic humanism or ultramontane Catholicism, provided women with some of the conceptual and rhetorical resources with which they campaigned for political and civil rights.[75]

To take a second example, the liberal order would rightly draw our attention to the assumptions about the individual and property involved in the criminalization of Native potlatch ceremonies in 1884 at the behest of Christian missionaries who condemned these 'give aways' as a reckless and improvident squandering of resources, the very antithesis of their attempt to instil sobriety and industry. Yet, as Tina Loo has shown, the same assumptions led anthropologists and other British Columbians to defend the Native ceremonies as analogous to non-Native economic exchange or to the festivities and gift-giving associated with Christmas. Both positions understood Native cultural practices in terms of Christian and liberal assumptions, but shared assumptions led to opposite policy conclusions. Moreover, the difference, not just the shared assumptions, mattered. Native litigants, for instance, were able to thwart the policy's intentions by marshalling the latter arguments in state courts. While this underscores how the liberal order set the terms of the unequal contest, Native communities were also divided. Gah-uk-sta-lus / Jane Cook actively assisted in the legal suppression of the potlatch, informing a prominent state agent that 'there is no liberty in the potlatch, no choice whatever.' Other Native individuals used the law to challenge the hierarchical structures of authority within their own bands.[76]

Had there been no such evidence of internal division, the liberal order framework would emphasize the degree to which Native communities were obstacles to liberal assumptions. In light of such evidence, the framework would emphasize the liberal order's relentless and destructive power to remake subaltern groups who would still be portrayed as obstacles to its dominance. The framework's ability to accommodate opposite empirical outcomes is one of its great strengths for a reconnaissance of Canadian history, but it is thereby almost impervious to empirical testing. Hegemony is a powerful way to interpret the evidence of Native divisions over the legal suppression of the potlatch, but it is not the only one. Moreover, hegemony would remain the framework's interpretation regardless of how many Native individuals espoused liberal assumptions or what arguments they articulated and to what end or with what degree of conviction. Conversely, intellectual historians would probably begin with these very questions of scope, intellectual content, and authorial intent. Finally, if the liberal order framework enjoins us to explain the 'combination of coercion and consent'[77] that resulted in the apparently liberal assumptions of Native people like Jane Cook or first-wave feminists who claimed their rights as individuals, we also need to investigate the force and consent that led other Native individuals or women to implicitly or explicitly challenge liberal assumptions. Otherwise, the framework asks us to take sides in the internal divisions within these and other groups (just as it asks us to take sides in the debate between liberalism and its critics), to risk romanticizing Native 'communism' and other communitarian forms simply by virtue of the fact that they are not liberal,[78] and, no matter how dispassionate or sophisticated our analysis of hegemony, ultimately, to see Jane Cook as a victim of the liberal order and thereby 'less Native.' In the ultimate irony, Robin Jarvis Brownlie points out in this volume that some of these collectivist forms may have been the consequence of 'liberal' state policies rather than a pre-existing alternative to them.

While Gramsci's concept of hegemony is more hospitable to scholarship on ideological traditions than the classical Marxist explanation of 'false consciousness,' it was developed to answer the same basic question: why members of subaltern classes and groups failed to act on the interests and espouse the assumptions that, according to Marxist analysis, they should. That many of them did espouse liberal assumptions, often at some personal cost, and believed passionately that those assumptions and the ideas and practices they underwrote were in their or their community's best interests is not dismissed as of little theoretical or practical import, but can only be seen as yet more evidence of the power of the hegemonic process: the process of how a social class or group achieved and maintained dominance by 'going beyond its immediate corporate interests to take into account the interests of other groups and classes' in never-settled negotiations. Thus, culture and politics are 'a terrain in which people become aware of their interests and struggle, politically, to fight for them.'[79] Gramsci directed so much attention to this terrain precisely because he saw economic structures as setting only the objective conditions for socialist change. Such change could be actualized only when people became aware and critical of the liberal assumptions they had absorbed 'as an external political force, an element of cohesive force exercised by the ruling classes and therefore an element of subordination to an external hegemony' able to marshal impressive resources for coercion, 'corruption-fraud,' and, most insidious of all, manufacturing consent. Thus, 'ideologies are anything but arbitrary; they are historical facts which must be combated and their

nature as instruments of domination revealed, not for reasons of morality etc., but for reasons of political struggle: in order to make the governed intellectually independent of the governing, in order to destroy
one hegemony and create another.' This approach to ideology did not
apply to Marxism, since it alone understood the contradictions of capitalism and therefore was not 'an instrument of government of dominant groups in order to gain the consent of and exercise hegemony over
subaltern classes.'[80]

Thus, the liberal order framework divides societies essentially into
two groups, the dominant and the subaltern. Scholars and political
activists can know the fundamental interests of each independent of
what anyone belonging to either knew or said. With its own 'organic
intellectuals,' however, the dominant or governing class came to understand its interests and convinced, co-opted, or coerced others into
inhabiting the very mental world that maintained their dominance.
From such a theoretical perspective, liberals in British North America
could only be a small 'vanguard' geographically limited to 'a few nineteenth-century outposts' and opposed by the vast majority of the population.[81] Their liberal assumptions became 'common sense' for an
entire subcontinent despite the inherent limits and destructive consequences of those assumptions.

Hope and Fear Revisited

So, how should we assess the relationship between the liberal order
framework and intellectual history? It seems churlish to judge such an
expansive vision from the standpoint of a single sub-field. To insist on
the integrity of that field – the questions it asks and the methods it
favours – risks foregoing valuable opportunities to learn from and contribute to the more collaborative approach to the past promised by any
such reconnaissance. It also seems rash for a historian to focus on the
future – on the potential implications of the liberal order framework –
but its powerful antidote to the perceived malaise of professional Canadian history ensures it considerable influence. I remain, then, torn
between hope and fear; hope for dialogue and mutual questioning
between the liberal order framework and Canadian intellectual history
and fear for how the former may disfigure the latter.

The fear reflects my sense that the framework is nothing less than a
coherent and compelling attempt to re-conceive Canadian history in a
Gramscian mode. Some intellectual historians may share this perspec-

tive, but for good reason Gramsci has had far less influence on intellectual than cultural history. I suspect most intellectual historians will worry that it commits them to too much politically and methodologically; that a more empathetic, if still critical, eye is needed to understand liberalism – its possibilities as well as its limits. They will want to study arguments and debates as well as assumptions and commonalities and will fear that beginning from a particular definition of liberalism entangles them in avoidable substantive and methodological problems. The more pluralized view of liberalism that will result may still surprise us, perhaps in the ways it opposed as well as supported other developments associated with it by the liberal order framework. Most will also want to leave open the possibility that the self-understanding of individuals in the past has more to teach us than hegemony and resistance. They will thereby have to consider other explanations for how liberalism won an impressive, if never complete or uncontested, measure of popular assent and seek to explain the prevalence and diversity of non-liberal as much as liberal assumptions. Finally, some intellectual historians will worry that seeing the past in terms of dominant and subaltern groups is too binary and will wish to explore the extent to which the interests of any individual or group were 'socially constructed.' Gramsci offers us a powerful way to rethink Canadian history, but it is not the only route to steer between the 'economism' of mechanical explanations and an 'ideologism' that privileges individualistic and voluntarist accounts by ignoring structures.[82]

So, how should we proceed with the history of liberalism instead? We could do worse than heed for liberalism Ian McKay's call for 'nondeterminist narratives' of the history of Canadian socialism that adopt 'a less teleological and judgmental approach' than that of either its partisan supporters or detractors. Such a history 'would reconstruct a variety of Canadian' liberalisms as, 'in a sense a kind of experiment,' each grappling with the 'recurrent problems' it faced in its opposition to competing ways of seeing the world. Understanding the 'conjunctural specifics' of the many liberalisms in Canada's past may, as McKay hopes for a history of socialism, 'lead to a more optimistic conclusion.'[83]

NOTES

1 Ian McKay, 'The Liberal Order Framework: A Prospectus for a Reconnaissance of Canadian History,' *Canadian Historical Review* 81 (2000): 641. The

quotation continues that Canada is also 'not a democratic state,' a judgment that relies on a different definition of democracy than does my *The Capacity to Judge: Public Opinion and Deliberative Democracy in Upper Canada, 1791– 1854* (Toronto: University of Toronto Press, 2000). I would like to thank my colleague Andrew Jainchill for his thoughtful reading of an earlier draft of this essay and to dedicate this incarnation to Arthur Silver on the occasion of his retirement from the University of Toronto. He continues to teach me much about liberalism and history.

2 For one taxonomy, see Robert Darnton, 'Intellectual and Cultural History,' in *The Past before Us: Contemporary Historical Writing in the United States*, ed. Michael Kammen (Ithaca: Cornell University Press, 1980), 337–48 and its application to Canadian scholarship in Ramsay Cook, 'Canadian Intellectual History: What Has Been Done?' in *Les idées en mouvement: Perspectives en histoire intellectuelle et culturelle du Canada*, ed. Damien-Claude Bélanger, Sophie Coupal, and Michel Ducharme (Quebec: Les Presses de l'Université Laval, 2004), 15–27.

3 McKay, 'Liberal Order Framework,' 618.

4 Ibid., 630–2. His 'appreciation of the enormity of what the Canadian liberal order undertook' is the most positive-sounding thing McKay has to say about liberals. It reminds me of what Karl Marx and Friedrich Engels said about the bourgeoisie in their *Manifesto of the Communist Party* (1848).

5 S.F. Wise, *God's Peculiar Peoples: Essays on Political Culture in Nineteenth-Century Canada*, ed. A.B. McKillop and Paul Romney (Ottawa: Carleton University Press, 1993) and Carl Berger, *A Sense of Power: Studies in the Ideas of Canadian Imperialism, 1867–1914* (Toronto: University of Toronto Press, 1970).

6 Janet Ajzenstat and Peter J. Smith, eds., *Canada's Origins: Liberal, Tory, or Republican?* (Ottawa: Carleton University Press, 1995); Gordon Stewart, *The Origins of Canadian Politics* (Vancouver: University of British Columbia Press, 1986); David Milobar, 'The Origins of British-Quebec Merchant Ideology: New France, the British Atlantic and the Constitutional Periphery, 1720–70,' *Journal of Imperial and Commonwealth History* 24 (1996): 364–90.

7 Joyce Oldham Appleby, 'The Vexed Story of Capitalism Told by American Historians,' *Journal of the Early Republic* 21 (2001): 1–18; Melvyn Stokes and Stephen Conway, eds., *The Market Revolution in America: Social, Political, and Religious Expressions, 1800–1880* (Charlottesville: University Press of Virginia, 1996); Mark A. Noll, ed., *God and Mammon: Protestants, Money, and the Market, 1790–1860* (Oxford: Oxford University Press, 2002); and Scott C. Martin, ed., *Cultural Change and the Market Revolution in America, 1789–1860* (Lanham, MD: Rowman & Littlefield Publishers, Inc., 2005).

8 Besides works cited in note 7 above, see Boyd Hilton, *The Age of Atonement: The Influence of Evangelicalism on Social and Economic Thought, 1785–1865* (Oxford: Oxford University Press, 1988); A.M.C. Waterman, *Revolution, Economics & Religion: Christian Political Economy, 1798–1833* (Cambridge: Cambridge University Press, 1991); and G.R. Searle, *Morality and the Market in Victorian Britain* (Oxford: Oxford University Press, 1998).

9 Daniel Walker Howe, *Making the American Self: Jonathan Edwards to Abraham Lincoln* (Cambridge, MA: Harvard University Press, 1999); Jeffrey Sklansky, *The Soul's Economy: Market Society and Selfhood in American Thought, 1820–1920* (Chapel Hill: University of North Carolina Press, 2002); Patrick Joyce, *Democratic Subjects: The Self and the Social in Nineteenth-Century England* (Cambridge: Cambridge University Press, 1994); and Dror Wahrman, *The Making of the Modern Self: Identity and Culture in Eighteenth-Century England* (New Haven: Yale University Press, 2004).

10 On ideas of class, see Dror Wahrman, *Imagining the Middle Class: The Political Representation of Class in Britain, c. 1780–1840* (Cambridge: Cambridge University Press, 1995); Martin J. Burke, *The Conundrum of Class: Public Discourse on the Social Order in America* (Chicago: University of Chicago Press, 1995); and Sarah Maza, *The Myth of the French Bourgeoisie: An Essay on the Social Imaginary, 1750–1850* (Cambridge, MA: Harvard University Press, 2003). On economic inequality, see James L. Huston, *Securing the Fruits of Labor: The American Concept of Wealth Distribution, 1765–1900* (Baton Rouge: Louisiana State University Press, 1998); and Gareth Stedman Jones, *An End to Poverty? A Historical Debate* (New York: Columbia University Press, 2004).

11 Ann Fabian, *Card Sharps and Bucket Shops: Gambling in Nineteenth-Century America* (New York: Routledge, 1999); Bruce H. Mann, *Republic of Debtors: Bankruptcy in the Age of American Independence* (Cambridge, MA: Harvard University Press, 2002); Scott A. Sandage, *Born Losers: A History of Failure in America* (Cambridge, MA: Harvard University Press, 2005); Craig Muldrew, *The Economy of Obligation: The Culture of Credit and Social Relations in Early Modern England* (Basingstoke: Palgrave, 1998); and Margot C. Finn, *The Character of Credit: Personal Debt in English Culture, 1740–1914* (Cambridge: Cambridge University Press, 2003).

12 David Forgacs, ed., *The Antonio Gramsci Reader: Selected Writings, 1916–1935* (New York: New York University Press, 2000), 380–1.

13 For one example that combines traditional and innovative aspects of intellectual history to great effect, see Jonathan Rose, *The Intellectual History of the British Working Class* (New Haven: Yale University Press, 2001).

14 McKay, 'Liberal Order Framework,' 639.

15 Ibid., 637.
16 For this sort of political history at its best, see Scott W. See, 'Polling Crowds and Patronage: New Brunswick's 'Fighting Elections' of 1842–3,' *Canadian Historical Review* 72 (1991): 127–56, which notes the many speeches and editorials in both campaigns, but can see no reason to analyse their intellectual content.
17 Compare J.M.S. Careless, 'Mid-Victorian Liberalism in Central Canadian Newspapers, 1850–67,' *Canadian Historical Review* 31 (1950): 221–36 with Jacques Monet, 'French-Canadian Nationalism and the Challenge of Ultramontanism,' Canadian Historical Association *Historical Papers*, 1966: 41–55.
18 McKay, 'Liberal Order Framework,' 639.
19 See Roy Porter and Mikulas Teich, eds., *The Enlightenment in National Context* (Cambridge: Cambridge University Press, 1981) and Dario Castiglione and Iain Hampsher-Monk, eds., *The History of Political Thought in National Context* (Cambridge: Cambridge University Press, 2001). Did any differences between liberalism in Upper and Lower Canada correspond to differences often reputed to English and French liberalism (on which see L. Siedentop, 'Two Liberal Traditions,' in *The Idea of Freedom: Essays in Honour of Isaiah Berlin*, ed. Alan Ryan [Oxford: Oxford University Press, 1979], 153–74)?
20 This is only one place where the probing comments of one of the anonymous readers of this book were most helpful. For a recent example of the dangers of organizing our work around the nation-state, see Katherine Fierlbeck, *Political Thought in Canada: An Intellectual History* (Peterborough: Broadview Press, 2006), which returns to Gad Horowitz's suggestion of a 'tory touch' in Canadian political culture. McKay seems closer to Louis Hartz's original idea that Canada and the United States shared a common liberal universe. There is, therefore, much to learn from James T. Kloppenberg, 'From Hartz to Tocqueville: Shifting the Focus from Liberalism to Democracy in America,' in *The Democratic Experiment: New Directions in American Political History*, ed. Meg Jacobs, William J. Novak, and Julian E. Zelizer (Princeton: Princeton University Press, 2003), 350–80.
21 McKay, 'Liberal Order Framework,' 627.
22 Paul Romney, *Getting It Wrong: How Canadians Forgot Their Past and Imperilled Confederation* (Toronto: University of Toronto Press, 1999); Janet Ajzenstat et al., eds., *Canada's Founding Debates* (Toronto: Stoddart, 1999); Frederick Vaughan, *The Canadian Federalist Experiment: From Defiant Monarchy to Reluctant Republic* (Montreal and Kingston: McGill-Queen's University Press, 2003), Janet Ajzenstat, *The Canadian Founding: John Locke and Parliament* (Montreal and Kingston: McGill-Queen's University Press, 2007).

23 George Grant, *Lament for a Nation: The Defeat of Canadian Nationalism* (Montreal and Kingston: McGill-Queen's University Press, 2005 [1965]), 67.

24 McKay, 'Liberal Order Framework,' 618, 622. Intellectual historians have also alerted us to how nationalist assumptions can frame our work. See Ramsay Cook, 'La Survivance French-Canadian Style,' and 'La Survivance English-Canadian Style,' in *The Maple Leaf for Ever: Essays on Nationalism and Politics in Canada* (Toronto: Macmillan of Canada, 1971), 114–65. Other approaches to national identity that owe more to the history of ritual than ideas typically explore the contested construction of these sorts of foundational 'creation myths.' See, for instance, Robert Cupido, 'Appropriating the Past: Pageants, Politics, and the Diamond Jubilee of Confederation,' *Journal of the Canadian Historical Association* 8 (1988): 155–86.

25 McKay, 'Liberal Order Framework,' 627–8 and Forgacs, ed., *Antonio Gramsci Reader*, 190, 202, 214, 321. For my own critique of the concept of self-interest prevalent in certain types of political and economic history, see 'Why We Need, but Don't Have an Intellectual History of the British North American Economy,' in *Les idées en mouvement*, 143–73.

26 I rely here on Roger Chartier, 'Intellectual History or Sociocultural History? The French Trajectories,' in *Modern European Intellectual History: Reappraisals & New Perspectives*, ed. Dominick LaCapra and Steven L. Kaplan (Ithaca: Cornell University Press, 1982), 39–42, and John E. Toews, 'Intellectual History after the Linguistic Turn: The Autonomy of Meaning and the Irreducibility of Experience,' *American Historical Review* 92 (1987): 885–6. Martin Jay, *Songs of Experience: Modern American and European Variations on a Universal Theme* (Berkeley: University of California Press, 2005), 248–55 surveys the reaction to Toews.

27 Ian McKay, *Rebels, Reds, Radicals: Rethinking Canada's Left History* (Toronto: Between the Lines, 2005), 83: 'Reconnaissance is a political act of research ... to produce knowledge for a political purpose.' McKay is to be commended for making the politics of his historical program explicit. This essay explores the relationship between that particular vision and intellectual history. It does not address problems posed by any quest for synthesis, on which see Allan Megill, *Historical Knowledge, Historical Error: A Contemporary Guide to Practice* (Chicago: University of Chicago Press, 2007), 159–208.

28 McKay, 'Liberal Order Framework,' 623–4.

29 Ibid., 621, 623–5, 627. If the distinction only serves to emphasize that the liberal order framework encompasses institutions and practices as well as beliefs and values and that, as one subset of the latter, liberalism has varied tremendously over time while retaining a certain core or 'definitional family resemblance,' encompasses people who did not think of themselves as

liberals, and should not be confused with particular political movements or parties that have called themselves Liberal, intellectual historians have little cause for complaint.

30 Besides Roy, McKay cites C.B. Macpherson, *The Political Theory of Possessive Individualism: Hobbes to Locke* (Oxford: Oxford University Press, 1962) and Anthony Arblaster, *The Rise and Decline of Western Liberalism* (Oxford: Basil Blackwell, 1984) in the crucial paragraph. Both reflect on liberalism by discussing well-known intellectual and literary figures. Later, McKay himself speaks of 'the universe of Locke, Smith, Bentham, or Lord Durham' (636).

31 For a fine biographical case study, see Kenneth C. Dewar, *Charles Clarke: Pen and Ink Warrior* (Montreal and Kingston: McGill-Queen's University Press, 2002).

32 For more expansive versions of the core McKay identifies, see Stuart Hall, 'Variants of Liberalism,' in *Politics & Ideology,* ed. James Donald and Stuart Hall (Milton Keynes: Open University Press, 1986), 38–43 and Arblaster, *Rise and Decline of Western Liberalism*, 15–91.

33 John Gray, *Liberalism*, 2nd ed. (Minneapolis: University of Minnesota Press, 1995), xii and Michael Freeden, *The New Liberalism: An Ideology of Social Reform* (Oxford: Oxford University Press, 1978), 22–3.

34 On defining liberalism by what it opposed, see Eric Voegelin, 'Liberalism and Its History,' trans. Mary and Keith Algozin, *The Review of Politics* 36 (1974): 504–20.

35 Bruce Curtis, 'Preconditions of the Canadian State: Educational Reform and the Construction of a Public in Upper Canada, 1837–1846,' in *Historical Essays on Upper Canada: New Perspectives*, ed. J.K. Johnson and Bruce G. Wilson (Ottawa: Carleton University Press, 1989), 348–9.

36 Michael Freeden, *Liberalism Divided: A Study in British Political Thought, 1914–1939* (Oxford: Oxford University Press, 1986), 4–5. For a more thorough critique of isolating 'core' elements as a method, see W.H. Greenleaf, *The British Political Tradition*, vol. 2: *The Ideological Heritage* (London: Methuen & Co., 1983), 7–15 and D.J. Manning, *Liberalism* (London: J.M. Dent & Sons Ltd., 1976), 139–43.

37 See Richard B. Latner, 'Preserving 'the natural equality of rank and influence': Liberalism, Republicanism, and Equality of Condition in Jacksonian Politics,' in *The Culture of the Market: Historical Essays*, ed. Thomas L. Haskell and Richard F. Teichgraeber III (Cambridge: Cambridge University Press, 1993), 189–230 for the argument that distinctions between equality of opportunity and equality of condition can be overdrawn when applied to the past.

38 Constant quoted in Pierre Manent, *An Intellectual History of Liberalism*, Rebecca Balinski, trans. (Princeton: Princeton University Press, 1995), 84. I

have quoted thinkers such as Constant and John Stuart Mill in this section not because British North American examples cannot be found, but to avoid suspicion that I have chosen idiosyncratic figures who might not be accepted as 'real' liberals. I have also refrained from bolstering my argument by citing forms of liberalism more fully articulated in twentieth-century philosophy such as liberalism as pluralism associated with Isaiah Berlin, or the liberal defence of group and cultural rights associated with William Kymlicka, or liberalism as a political framework independent of any conception of the good associated with John Rawls.

39 See my 'The Malthusian Moment: British Travellers and the Vindication of Economic Liberalism in the Maritime Countryside,' in *Transatlantic Subjects: Ideas, Institutions and Social Experience in Post-Revolutionary British North America*, ed. Nancy Christie (Montreal and Kingston: McGill-Queen's University Press, 2008) 329–68.

40 McKay, 'Liberal Order Framework,' 624n14 quotes Arblaster, *Rise and Decline of Western Liberalism*, which points to the social contract tradition as evidence of liberalism's pre-social definition of the individual. Others Arblaster deems liberals, such as Adam Smith, were opponents of contractianism; John Dunn persuasively argued some time ago that John Locke's state of nature 'is not an asocial condition but an ahistorical condition. It is that state in which men are set by God. The state of nature is a topic for theological reflection, not for anthropological research'; and while Thomas Paine adopted a form of the social contract, later British radicals were far more likely to invoke 'the ancient constitution' than natural rights derived from outside a particular narrative of English history. See John Dunn, *The Political Thought of John Locke: An Historical Account of the Argument of the 'Two Treatises of Government'* (Cambridge: Cambridge University Press, 1969), 97; James A. Epstein, 'The Constitutionalist Idiom,' in *Radical Expression: Political Language, Ritual, and Symbol in England, 1790–1850* (New York: Oxford University Press, 1994), 3–28. For a similar conclusion about radicals and reformers in British North America, see my *The Capacity to Judge*, 23–62; Gregory Marquis, 'In Defense of Liberty: Seventeenth Century England and Nineteenth Century Maritime Political Culture,' *University of New Brunswick Law Journal* 42 (1993): 69–94; and, more generally, Heaman in this volume.

41 On which see Freeden, *New Liberalism*.

42 Mill quoted in Kwame Anthony Appiah, *The Ethics of Identity* (Princeton: Princeton University Press, 2005), 20–1, an account to which I am heavily indebted; but see also Katherine Smits, 'John Stuart Mill and the Social Construction of Identity,' *History of Political Thought* 25 (2004), 298–324.

43 McKay, 'Liberal Order Framework,' 637; McNairn, *Capacity to Judge*, 63–115, 418; and Appiah, *Ethics of Identity*, xv.

44 McKay, 'Liberal Order Framework,' 627, 623n13. For the politics of Macpherson's supporters, see J.G.A. Pocock, 'Authority and Property: The Question of Liberal Origins,' in *Virtue, Commerce, and History: Essays on Political Thought and History, Chiefly in the Eighteenth Century* (Cambridge: Cambridge University Press, 1985), 60. Given the fierce onslaught against Macpherson's interpretation of Locke (among others), McKay is well advised to deem it unnecessary to focus on him, but he retains Macpherson's view that the move from individualism to self-ownership to material property is central to liberalism.

45 James Tully, 'After the Macpherson Thesis' and 'The Framework of Natural Rights in Locke's Analysis of Property,' both in *An Approach to Political Philosophy: Locke in Contexts* (Cambridge: Cambridge University Press, 1993), 80, 84, 96–7.

46 Hobhouse, *Liberalism* (New York: Oxford University Press, 1964), 51–4. Indeed, any justification of private property based on its individual or social utility cannot thereby make property itself a core principle. While most liberals supported market mechanisms and individual property to achieve specific moral and other ends, they turned critical of both when those ends were not served.

47 Robert Playfair, *Recollections of a Visit to the United States and British Provinces of North America ...* (Edinburgh and London, 1856), 99. On emigrant families and landownership in the region, see Graeme Wynn, 'A Share of the Necessaries of Life: Remarks on Migration, Development, and Dependency in Atlantic Canada,' in *Beyond Anger and Longing: Community and Development in Atlantic Canada* (Fredericton: Acadiensis Press, 1988), 17–51; and for the variability of ideas about property, see Alan Ryan, *Property and Political Theory* (Oxford: Basil Blackwell, 1984) and John Brewer and Susan Staves, eds., *Early Modern Conceptions of Property* (London: Routledge, 1986).

48 McKay, 'Liberal Order Framework,' 624, 626, 630. Yet, Samuel Smiles, quoted in Richard Bellamy, *Liberalism and Modern Society: An Historical Argument* (Cambridge: Polity Press, 1982), 11, was emphatic in *Self-Help* (1859) that mere 'riches are no proof whatever of moral worth.'

49 Ruth Sandwell, 'The Limits of Liberalism: The Liberal Reconnaissance and the History of the Family in Canada,' *Canadian Historical Review* 84 (2003): 426–7, quoting William Reddy, *Money & Liberty in Modern Europe: A Critique of Historical Understanding* (Cambridge: Cambridge University Press, 1987), 87.

50 I rely here on the summary of scholarship on Smith provided by Jones, *An*

End To Poverty? 36–8, 46; but see also Donald Winch, 'Economic Liberalism as Ideology: The Appleby Version,' *Economic History Review* 38 (1985): 291–2 and his *Adam Smith's Politics: An Essay in Historiographic Revision* (Cambridge: Cambridge University Press, 1978) and *Riches and Poverty: An Intellectual History of Political Economy in Britain, 1750–1834* (Cambridge: Cambridge University Press, 1996); and Emma Rothchild, *Economic Sentiments: Adam Smith, Condorcet, and the Enlightenment* (Cambridge, MA: Harvard University Press, 2001).

51 Appiah, *Ethics of Identity*, ix–x.

52 Tully, 'After the Macpherson Thesis,' 90–1 and esp. Istvan Holt and Michael Ignatieff, eds., *Wealth & Virtue: The Shaping of Political Economy in the Scottish Enlightenment* (Cambridge: Cambridge University Press, 1983). In fairness, McKay, 'Liberal Order Framework,' 634, 642–3 links Canadian socialism and civic humanism primarily in political, rather than economic, terms.

53 Richard Bellamy, 'Introduction,' in *Victorian Liberalism: Nineteenth-Century Political Thought and Practice*, ed. Bellamy (London: Routledge, 1990), 2 and his *Liberalism and Modern Society*, 3, 9–35.

54 McKay, 'Liberal Order Framework,' 630 and Sandwell, 'Limits of Liberalism,' 424.

55 Bellamy, 'Introduction,' 2. For this line of criticism applied to C.B. Macpherson, see Tully, 'After the Macpherson thesis,' 76–7.

56 Sandwell, 'Limits of Liberalism,' 427. Likewise, Canada itself becomes a single, if hybrid, project rather than the outcome of multiple, potentially competing, ones. In less skilled hands, the framework risks becoming teleological: that whatever the obstacles or evaluation of the final destination, previous ideas and 'arresting moments' gain their meaning only in terms of that destination.

57 McKay, 'Liberal Order Framework,' 641–3. The relative weight in the article itself is revealing. The only substantive intellectual content is given to the core and comprises a single paragraph. For a rejection of the argument that late-nineteenth-century liberalism reinvented itself only in response to socialist and other 'external' pressures, see Freeden, *New Liberalism*, 12–13.

58 Manning, *Liberalism*, 62. For a nuanced study, see James T. Kloppenberg, 'The Virtues of Liberalism: Christianity, Republicanism, and Ethics in Early American Political Discourse,' *Journal of American History* 74 (June 1987): 9–33.

59 See, for instance, J.W. Burrow, *The Crisis of Reason: European Thought, 1848–1914* (New Haven: Yale University Press, 2000), one of three volumes already published in the Yale Intellectual History of the West.

60 McNairn, *Capacity to Judge*, 12–13.

61 Jones, *An End to Poverty?*
62 Hilton, *Age of Atonement*, vii–viii.
63 Chartier, 'Intellectual History or Sociocultural History?' 16.
64 I am heavily indebted in this and the next paragraph to Quentin Skinner, 'Meaning and Understanding in the History of Ideas,' *History and Theory* 8 (1969): 3–53, although I have simplified his analysis and adapted it to focus on assumptions more than ideas. My speculations about the future use of the liberal order framework are not entirely fanciful. See the characterization of C.B. Macperhson's approach as 'barometric' by Pocock, 'Authority and Property,' 59. For the important point that Skinner's concern with authorial intent does not preclude studying intellectual traditions, such as liberalism, where authors themselves consciously situated their work in relationship to such a tradition, see Freeden, *Liberalism Divided*, 6–7. For a critique of Skinner's article inspired by Gramsci, see Joseph V. Femia, 'An Historicist Critique of 'Revisionist' Methods for Studying the History of Ideas,' *History and Theory* 20 (1981): 112–34.
65 McKay, 'Liberal Order Framework,' 638, 640.
66 I borrow here from McKay's own criticism of the concept of 'working class culture' in 'Historians, Anthropology, and the Concept of Culture,' *Labour / Le Travailleur* 8/9 (1981/2): 223–5. To label an element as 'emergent' can also be teleological. To say, for instance, that someone in *ancien régime* New France whose thought included an element of the liberal order framework's definition of liberalism anticipated the rise of the liberal order in British North America cannot be a statement of what that person meant or was doing.
67 McKay, 'Liberal Order Framework,' 618 referring to Thomas Haskell's review of Peter Novick's *That Noble Dream* (1988). A consideration of the full range of evidence and argument prior to making a judgment, not neutrality or the lack of such a judgment, is at issue here.
68 McKay, 'Liberal Order Framework,' 623–4 and, more generally, 644–5; 'For a New Kind of History: A Reconnaissance of 100 years of Canadian Socialism,' *Labour / Le Travail* 46 (Fall 2000): 72; and *Rebels, Reds, Radicals*, 21–5, 27.
69 Forgacs, ed., *Antonio Gramsci Reader*, 192–3. For his own use of the term, see McKay, 'Liberal Order Framework,' 628.
70 McKay, *Rebels, Reds, Radicals*, 52, 58 and 'Liberal Order Framework,' 633. Thus, the National Policy as accepted by the Laurier Liberals is one of the seven 'arresting moments' of the liberal order and 'marginalized a once-powerful and pervasive critique of liberal political economy.' Yet, nothing was more closely associated with liberal political economy than free trade. This approach to the National Policy has considerable merit, but it effec-

tively sidelines intellectual history as did a similar analysis by Frank Underhill in 'The Development of National Political Parties in Canada,' *Canadian Historical Review* 16 (1935): 367–87.

71 McKay, 'Liberal Order Framework,' 625. The title of Sandwell's response in the *Canadian Historical Review*, 'Limits of Liberalism,' is perfectly clear.

72 See McKay, *Rebels, Reds, Radicals*, 78: 'The problem ... cannot be addressed in the language of individualism.'

73 McKay, 'Liberal Order Framework,' 625. It is not, however, clear that liberalism's critics have a better historical track record. The persistence of slavery in the nineteenth century and genocide in the twentieth, both based, in part, on the belief that human beings are not at some level equal individuals, but members of groups with their own moral and cultural standards, should caution against seeing liberalism only in terms of its failures and limits. See Appiah, *The Ethics of Identity*, esp. 143–6.

74 McKay, 'Liberal Order Framework,' 634–5. On the range of arguments marshalled by the suffrage movement, compare Carol Lee Bacchi, *Liberation Deferred? The Ideas of the English-Canadian Suffragists, 1877–1918* (Toronto: University of Toronto Press, 1983), in which 'Why Women Need the Vote' is reprinted, with Ernest R. Forbes, 'The Ideas of Carol Bacchi and the Suffragists of Halifax,' in *Challenging the Regional Stereotype: Essays on the Twentieth Century Maritimes* (Fredericton: Acadiensis Press, 1989), 90–9 and Veronica Strong-Boag, 'The Citizenship Debates: The 1885 Franchise Act,' in *Contesting Canadian Citizenship: Historical Readings*, ed. Robert Adamoski, Dorothy E. Chunn, and Robert Menzies (Peterborough: Broadview Press, 2002), esp. 77–80.

75 Allan Greer, *The Patriots and the People: The Rebellion of 1837 in Rural Lower Canada* (Toronto: University of Toronto Press, 1993), 189–218. For this line of argument, see Darrin M. McMahon, *Enemies of the Enlightenment: The French Counter-Enlightenment and the Making of Modernity* (Oxford: Oxford University Press, 2001), 136–7, 237. For McKay's own view of 'liberal feminism,' see *Rebels, Reds, Radicals*, 201–2.

76 Tina Loo, 'Dan Cranmer's Potlatch: Law as Coercion, Symbol, and Rhetoric in British Columbia, 1884–1951,' *Canadian Historical Review* 73 (1992): 125–65, quotation at 163. Mark D. Walters, "According to the Old Customs of Our Nation': Aboriginal Self-Government on the Credit River Mississauga Reserve, 1826–1842,' *Ottawa Law Review / Revue de droit d'Ottawa* 20 (1998–9): 1–45 provides fascinating evidence for a parallel analysis in the period before state policy turned as explicitly coercive. Paige Raibmon beautifully reveals how entangling the politics of authenticity were in *Authentic Indians: Episodes of Encounter from the Late-Nineteenth-Century Northwest Coast*

(Durham: Duke University Press, 2005). She also discusses the potlatch and Cook at 23–8.

77 McKay, 'Liberal Order Framework,' 628, 631 and 'For a New Kind of History,' 73 on how 'the liberal historic bloc has persistently penetrated, fractured and fragmented the territory of the dominated classes and groups.'

78 McKay, 'Liberal Order Framework,' 626. Likewise, some scholars have been attracted to nineteenth-century apologists for American slavery because of their critique of wage labour. McKay's claim ('For a New Kind of History,' 72) that 'Canadians are 'liberals by default': it is what they become when their socialist powers of resistance are worn down' seems to invert, rather than transcend, what he faults the nineteenth-century liberal vanguard for doing – assuming that everyone should be a liberal individual and therefore needing an explanation for and policies to address those who obviously weren't.

79 McKay, 'Liberal Order Framework,' 628–9.

80 Forgacs, ed., *Antonio Gramsci Reader*, 343–4, 261, 196. Thomas Bender, ed., *The Antislavery Debate: Capitalism and Abolitionism as a Problem in Historical Interpretation* (Berkeley: University of California Press, 1992) is a good place to explore the potentials and problems of 'hegemony' in concrete historical practice.

81 McKay, 'Liberal Order Framework,' 631, 638. There is something almost Creighton-esque in McKay's insistence in *Rebels, Reds, Radicals* (54) that Confederation was the product of a 'relatively small elite group of liberal British North Americans – not many more, when all is said and done, than a few dozen white men' intent on expanding from their narrow geographic base across an entire continent to construct a less democratic alternative to the United States. The incredible achievement of this small elite provides a model for what a socialist vanguard might achieve, just as the groups deemed obstacles to its project become proof of both the possibility and desirability of such a 'collectivist' alternative. See, *Rebels, Reds, Radicals*, 92.

82 Forgacs, ed., *Gramsci Reader*, 202.

83 McKay, 'For a New Kind of History,' 79.

Canada as Counter-Revolution: The Loyalist Order Framework in Canadian History, 1750–1840

JERRY BANNISTER[1]

As the 'Liberal Order' symposium demonstrated, chronology matters. We assembled at McGill University in March 2006 to discuss how Ian McKay's article has established a new paradigm for Canadian historians, and our panels progressed chronologically from the eighteenth century to the twentieth century. This is, of course, how our minds are supposed to work: as Kant explained, we are hardwired to think in terms of time, space, and cause. Following in this tradition, I had planned to present a conventional paper on how to relate the early modern period to the liberal order framework. I was going to contribute to the venerable tradition of complaining that my favourite patch of temporal ground – the eighteenth century – fits uneasily into McKay's ambitious reconnaissance. I was going to argue that the liberal order framework carries within it an implicit teleology that constrains historians to study the early modern past only insofar as it contributed to the eventual formation of the Canadian liberal project. I was going to point out the danger of adopting a myopic perspective that fails to take into account the full array of contingent events and contested decisions that created the politico-economic conditions in which the liberal order was born.

But I decided that McKay's article deserves better than simply a cranky complaint from another early modernist about how Canadian historians fail to appreciate the eighteenth century. I decided instead to offer an argument about how the origins (if we can use this term for such a process) of the liberal order reveal a central characteristic of that order itself. What I would like to argue is that if we are to take McKay seriously – that is, study Canada 'as a historically specific project of rule'[2] – then we have to understand Canada as not just a modern liberal order but also the product of an early modern loyalist order. This loyalist order preceded the apotheosis of liberalism and ensured that the nascent liberal order in British North America remained distinct from the American one.[3] I want to suggest that Canada is, at bottom, an experiment in counter-revolution fuelled as much by its imperial legacy and external relations as by its domestic imperatives. By 'counter-revolution,' I do not mean the type of internal counter-revolutionary process described by Crane Brinton in his classic theory of revolution. What happened in Canada after 1783 was not some sort of Thermidorian reaction, but rather a loyalist response that kept one polity (British North America) politically distinct from another (the United States).[4] Counter-revolution, in this sense, is distinct from the Marxist theory of passive revolution, which encompasses a more diffuse social phenomenon.[5] My paper examines aspects of British North America's development from roughly 1750 to 1840 and focuses on the 1838 treason trials in Upper Canada – the 'first arresting moment' in McKay's account of Canadian liberalism – as a case study of my loyalist thesis.

While my paper stresses the need to reconsider Canada's loyalist past, I reject the notion that British North America was an anti-liberal bastion. In a sense, as Seymour Martin Lipset asserted, the American Revolution led to the creation of two separate countries; however, I oppose Lipset's model of counter-revolution, which relies on the reductive dichotomy of Whig (United States) versus Tory (British North America) to explain the origins of Canada's political culture.[6] My argument, by contrast, is that Canada was both liberal and loyalist. McKay himself points out that a new reconnaissance of Canadian history should explore 'why, for example, some quite astute liberal minds in Canada thought that '(Liberal) Freedom (Necessarily) Wore a Crown.'"[7] Yet he subordinates these reasons as mere exceptions to the rule: for McKay, loyalism is a minor facet of liberal hybridization. But I would argue that it is as central to understanding British North America as liberalism itself.[8] Part of the problem in dealing with ambitious models in Canadian history, such as McKay's framework, is that historians tend to presume that one must be wholly in favour or wholly against a particular viewpoint. As Jeff McNairn and Elsbeth Heaman demonstrate in their incisive papers, it is indeed possible to agree with McKay on some points while disagreeing on others: one need not accept McKay's reconnaissance *in toto* for it to make a major contribution to historical inquiry.[9] Perhaps the most admirable trait of McKay's scholarship is his insistence on transcending the Manichean debates that have plagued

Canadian history. 'These debates,' McKay points out, 'will pay off richly only for those who have a deep psychological need to be absolutely in the right.'[10] I agree with McKay that Canada cannot be studied as an essence. By the same token, however, liberalism itself cannot be understood as an elemental or inviolable force that suddenly emerged, *ex nihilo*, in the mid-nineteenth century. For McKay, possessive individualism represents the only *sine qua non* of the liberal order, but loyalism was vital to the project of rule in British North America.

What I would like to suggest is that Canadian historians could benefit from borrowing a chapter from the history of the Atlantic world. In response to the remarkable wave of Atlantic scholarship, David Armitage has suggested that 'we are all Atlanticists now.'[11] Although historians continue to debate the nature and scope of Atlantic history, they generally agree on its basic premise: the need to place national and regional developments in a broader comparative context.[12] This is, in fact, nothing new: in his classic study of the making of the Atlantic world, J.H. Parry called the early modern period an *Age of Reconnaissance*. Like Ian McKay, Parry used the term *reconnaissance* to convey the highly tentative and contested nature of European expansion: the creation of empires was a multifaceted process, not a singular event.[13] But, unlike McKay, Parry placed as much emphasis on the clash of cultures – especially between Christians and Muslims – as he did on the internal development within the empires themselves. The process through which Europeans voyaged across the seas and forged empires (part of which, of course, would eventually constitute Canada) was rooted in a much larger history of negotiation and conflict. From this perspective, 1492 is not only the year of Columbus's voyage but also the culmination of the *Reconquista*, when Christian forces conquered the last Muslim region of the Iberian Peninsula.

For Canadian historians, this perspective has important ramifications. If we are to follow McKay and view Canada as a project of rule, then we have to recognize that for much of its history, that ruler was not a sovereign nation-state but rather two rival imperial states: England and France. One can no more study nineteenth-century Canada without considering 1760 than one can study twentieth-century Canada without considering 1867. As John Reid has argued, the history of early Canada should also be seen as Aboriginal history: Europeans did not begin to dominate most of the territory that became British North America until after the arrival of the Loyalists in the late eighteenth century.[14] Extra-national conflict and negotiation shaped Canadian history as much as the intra-national bargaining with hegemony that McKay places as the heart of his framework. As a number of scholars have demonstrated, the histories of British North America and New France cannot be understood apart from their larger Atlantic and imperial contexts.[15] If we are to follow McKay and see Canada as more than merely an empty homogenous space, then we must recognize that it cannot be divorced from its imperialist past. Imperial history, in this sense, differs considerably from Carl Berger's classic formulation of the political link between empire and Canadian nationalism.[16] It offers the opportunity, as Kathleen Wilson argues, 'to rethink the genealogies and historiographies of national belonging and exclusion.'[17] Viewed from this vantage point, state formation was never a purely domestic phenomenon.[18]

One drawback of McKay's liberal order framework is the relatively limited role it accords the Conquest. 'The central event in the history of Canada,' Ramsay Cook asserted, 'is the British Conquest of 1760.'[19] The Conquest cannot be understood as a discrete historical event, but Cook's emphasis on what he called the 'burden of Canadian history' is as prescient as ever.[20] In the case of Britain (as it was constituted in 1707), the ongoing struggle with Catholic Europe (particularly France) profoundly shaped its political culture. The powerful mix of Protestantism, militarism, and imperialism that shaped the emergent British national identity was, in turn, carried across the Atlantic in the eighteenth century. As McKay notes, there is a need to apply the insights of scholars of the formation of a Protestant British identity to the historical image of the 'ideal Canadian individual.'[21] To trace this process of identity formation, we need to situate nineteenth-century liberalism within the context of both support and resistance to the loyalist order. As Louis-Georges Harvey has argued, republicanism offered the political means to resist British rule in French Canada, feeding the struggle that culminated in the Rebellion of 1837 and its repressive aftermath.[22] This form of civic humanism may have been anti-liberal but, equally important, it was also anti-empire. Like liberalism, loyalism was the product of conflict and negotiation: British (later Canadian) rule was a contested process, not a passive event. Lord Durham's report, it must be remembered, was a testament to loyalism as much as to liberalism: for the British government, threats to the empire loomed as large as threats to private property.[23]

McKay invokes a rough chronology for the rise of the liberal order across a type of seven-act play that opens with the Rebellions of 1837.

At other points in his discussion, McKay refers to the 1840s as the starting point for the rise of the liberal order. This is a rather curious choice, since the Rebellion itself (if I may use the singular form) was deeply rooted in causes that stretched back to the mid-eighteenth century. But my argument here is not about the simple issue of establishing a correct temporal starting point: one can always (and usually quite lazily) complain that a historian needs to consider an earlier period. The first law of history is the law of selection, and we all have to begin somewhere. My point is that by starting with the mid-nineteenth century, McKay largely overlooks one of the most important aspects of what would become the liberal order: the perceived threat from France and, after 1775, the United States. Canada was counter-revolutionary in a political rather than an economic sense: the fault line separating British North America and the United States was loyalty, not liberalism.[24] As most schoolchildren learn from their textbooks, fear of American expansion contributed to the backroom negotiations that culminated in 1867; but these fears were neither recent nor alien to the political culture of British North America. On the contrary, these fears formed a central narrative in the Canadian story.

The Origins of the Loyalist Order

So where does the project-of-rule story start? It starts, I believe, in 1749. Historians continue to quarrel over the transformation of the British Empire and the origins of the American Revolution, but there appears to be a growing consensus that the real change in the empire began in the late 1740s with the reform movement that swept both domestic and imperial politics in England.[25] The end of salutary neglect and the tightening of imperial administration preceded (rather than followed, as historians had long assumed) the Seven Years War. The British government knew, like most people in North America, that the peace of 1748 was merely a temporary truce in the showdown for imperial supremacy. In 1749 they embarked on a momentous plan to expand their imperial presence in North America: first, their command over the lucrative cod fishery was strengthened through the establishment of an effective naval government in Newfoundland; second, they established an imperial outpost in Halifax to provide a strategic base for their North American operations. This was a departure from the historic patterns of British imperial governance: for the first time, a major settlement was planned and publicly funded to further essentially imperial rather than commercial goals. The British government made a heavy financial as well as political investment in this imperial venture, spending well over £500,000 on the founding of Halifax and even more on the larger naval and military operations to protect their Atlantic possessions.[26] This was a byproduct of the emergence of what John Brewer has called a 'fiscal military state,' which was much larger in size and scope than the 'colonial leviathan' that emerged a century later.[27]

For Canadian historians, the key question is not the imperial expansion per se but its long-term effects. In 1754 armed conflict erupted in Colonial America and spread to Nova Scotia. As Geoffrey Plank and, more recently, John Mack Faragher have explained, the expulsion of the Acadians can be understood only in the context of this imperial conflict.[28] Far from being a sideshow in the Canadian saga, the forced deportation of the Acadians was essential to the birth of the loyalist order in British America. With the removal of most of the French-speaking, Catholic people east of Quebec, the British had the opportunity to create a new colony dominated by English-speaking Protestants. The arrival of thousands of British immigrants in the 1760s, most from New England, marked the beginning of a demographic and political watershed. The Conquest of 1760 further transformed the face of British America, forcing imperial authorities to deal with the fact that thousands of French-speaking Catholics were now British subjects. The Quebec Act of 1774, which was designed to facilitate the integration of French Canada into the British Empire, fuelled Protestant resentment in the Thirteen Colonies, contributing to the crisis that erupted in New England the following year.[29]

With the arrival of tens of thousands of Loyalists after the outbreak of the Revolutionary War, the balance of power in British North America was forever altered. As John Reid has argued, by the end of the Loyalist migrations, the Native peoples of Nova Scotia had lost the strong negotiating position that they had long enjoyed. By the time of the Constitution Act of 1791, the British enjoyed the material power and sheer demographic presence to pursue a new phase of imperial expansion into Aboriginal lands.[30] The persecution and attempted subjugation of Aboriginal peoples in the nineteenth century that McKay discusses – a process that eventually culminated in a second British conquest (this one led by mounted police rather than British soldiers) – was made possible by this transformation in Imperial–Native relations.[31] As a number of scholars have pointed out, the arrival of the Loyalists engendered a series of myths that continues to shape Canadian history.[32] The Loyalist cause received widespread support in Britain, where the press portrayed American revolutionaries as wild savages.[33] Yet loyalty entailed more than simply anti-Americanism: it drew on the emergent British identity that encompassed specific conceptions of social order and monarchism.[34] The Loyalists were far from a homogenous group and, as David Bell reminds us, once they arrived in Nova Scotia (and, after 1784, New Brunswick) they were often not particularly 'loyal' in the narrow sense of local politics.[35] They brought a wide variety of backgrounds and political views that included a mixture of republican and monarchist doctrines, but they also had a broadly shared opposition to revolution. Most Loyalists opposed not the idea of America itself but the belief in revolution as an acceptable political choice. They were among the many thousands of colonial subjects who resented British policies in the 1760s and early 1770s but refused to support outright independence and a complete break with the Crown.[36] Despite the wide diversity of peoples and motivations caught up in the Loyalist migrations, a political fault line now separated American citizens from British subjects.[37] By the late eighteenth century, the presence of the colonial state in British North America could be characterized as 'dominance without hegemony,' though imperial conquest marked only the first phase in a longer politico-legal process.[38]

Equally important, the British Empire changed significantly after the American Revolution. The British government adopted counter-revolutionary policies to exert a tighter hold on its colonial possessions. As Eliga Gould points out, 'the second British Empire was at once more diverse and more authoritarian than the one George III had inherited twenty years before.'[39] The system of representative government established in most colonies in British North America was designed to keep democratic impulses in check. The Colonial Office circumscribed the powers of elected assemblies, and governors were expected to rely upon their executive and legislative councils, both of which were filled with unelected officials.[40] But the system never worked according to its design: colonial assemblies repeatedly contested the authority of the appointed councils; persistent public criticism of the governors' regimes created a divisive political climate; and efforts to curb political opposition damaged the legitimacy of local government.[41] The political debates across British North America represent what Lauren Benton has called the 'second discursive shift' that followed imperial conquest.[42] At the heart of the political disputes was the reformers' claim to the full rights of their fellow British subjects. As Lord Durham noted, 'The views of the great body of the Reformers appear to have been limited, according to their favourite expression, to the making the Colonial Constitution 'an exact transcript' of that of Great Britain.'[43] Yet the reformers who opposed imperial elites were themselves divided by factionalism, and during this period campaigns for specific legal and judicial reforms rarely succeeded.[44] Throughout the Atlantic colonies and the Canadas, the loyalist order influenced public opinion and the eventual development of what Jeffrey McNairn has called 'deliberative democracy.'[45]

In Newfoundland, for example, reformers drew upon the language of British justice to formulate their cases for constitutional change. William Carson, the island's most prominent political essayist, affirmed that 'all the rights and privileges, claimable by British subjects resident in Great Britain, are the rights and privileges of the people in Newfoundland.'[46] He used the appeal to British justice as a double-edged sword, raising the spectre of rebellion:

> There is not a colony belonging to Great Britain, in which the people do not feel a pride in being subjects to the King of England; in which they do not cherish sentiments of fond attachment to the Mother country, its constitution, customs and laws. But if they are doomed perpetually to experience from Governors, and other high officers, an insulting and contumelious disregard of their rights and privileges, *admiration will be converted into contempt, affection to animosity, and submission to revolt.*[47]

This form of threatening rhetoric never proved politically successful because it alienated the island's bourgeoisie. The fledgling reform movement, which consisted mainly of middle-class Catholics, failed to attract significant support from the mercantile and professional elites. In 1820 the reformers adopted a different strategy: they used a cause célèbre – the case involved actions against two surrogate magistrates for sentencing defendants to be whipped publicly for contempt of court – to challenge the entire legal system. Condemning the punishments as inhumane, they linked injustices committed by naval officers to the failure of the island's constitution and petitioned London to establish a local legislature.[48] This campaign achieved limited results; the British government abolished the surrogate courts but refused to grant an elected assembly.[49]

When the reform rhetoric shifted to the liberal issue of taxation, however, it revolutionized the island's political environment. In 1827 the British government announced new duties on imports into Newfoundland. While this threat united the fractious merchants and politicized the Chamber of Commerce, it also enabled the local press to transform concerns over the import duty into a cogent argument for legal reform. The editor of the pro-reform *Newfoundlander* argued: 'Such a tax on a Colony like ours, without representation, would be a direct violation of the pledge given by the Government to the Colonies after the American Revolutionary War.'[50] A series of letters and editorials followed denouncing 'taxation without representation.'[51] Based on the vociferous opposition to taxation, the island's reform movement transformed into a coalition that brought the Protestant and Catholic factions together in support of the campaign for a local legislature. Soon after the British government ceded representative government in 1832, a string of bitter sectarian disputes poisoned the island's public life.[52] To curtail the endemic political instability, in 1842 the British government combined the legislative council and elected assembly into a single amalgamated legislature; it would take another generation before the island achieved responsible government.[53] The reform coalition of 1827–32 engendered one of the few periods of political harmony in Newfoundland history.

By contrast, Nova Scotia was a model of constitutional reform. It never experienced the level of sectarian fervour and violence that marked other colonies. Led by Joseph Howe, the publisher of the *Novascotian*, the campaign against the ancien régime was effective, though it was not until 1848 that Nova Scotia became the first British colony to achieve responsible government.[54] The watershed in the colony's reform movement was the trial and acquittal of Howe for seditious libel in 1835. Historians consider it to be one of the most important cases in Canadian legal history because Howe's successful defence ostensibly secured the freedom of the press.[55] Barry Cahill has argued that *R. v. Howe* involved freedom of the press only indirectly; as a malicious prosecution, it was a political show trial designed to repress opposition to the ruling oligarchy.[56] Cahill focuses on its impact on legal procedure – he concludes that the case served to decriminalize libel in pre-Confederation Nova Scotia – yet it was equally important to the development of the language of Canadian liberalism.

Howe's defence was a masterful combination of sound legal reasoning and shrewd political oratory. In a six-hour speech studded with as many earthy quips as learned quotes, he expounded on the rampant corruption and injustices in the colony's legal system. He repeatedly singled out the judicial administration of local assessments, remarking that 'so unequal, arbitrary and oppressive have these taxes been, that there is scarcely a man in the town who has not at some time or other had to appeal against them.'[57] Howe explained his position through a personal anecdote:

> Last year I received a summons calling on me to pay my poor and county rates, amounting to about £4. I attended accordingly, where I saw a magistrate, the clerk and the collector, surrounded by several poor wretches who had been brought there on the same errand, and was accosted with, 'Oh! we suppose you have a check on the county and that is the reason you have not paid.' I answered, 'No, thank heaven, I have no check on the county, but when on the grand jury I observed that there were two classes, one who did and one who did not pay, and having been for six years among the former, I wanted if possible to get a berth among the latter.'[58]

He then turned serious:

> We may smile at these matters, but they are melancholy illustrations. Poor wretches are dragged down to their worships for non-payment, while they see their rich neighbours not paying at all, or not paying a fair proportion. If these men had done their duty things would not be in the state which they are; the community would not be thus excited; time would not be wasted with 'endless appeals'; the poor would not be taxed with summonses and suits, the Legislature would not have been tormented with investigations, or His Majesty's Council vainly employed in unraveling the maze; nor would the Governor, the moment he touched our shore, have been called to examine a system that might take its place in the black book among the 'robberies of charitable foundations,' and informed that an Augean Stable here awaited his purifying exertions. The same system of inequality and injustice, you will perceive, pervades all the taxes.[59]

Howe may have been a conservative reformer, but his political philosophy is at odds with the anti-liberal Toryism envisaged by Seymour Martin Lipset or the Hartz-Horowitz framework.[60]

When he ran for election the following year, Howe's stump speeches expounded a philosophy based on the concept of fiscal accountability. This time he invoked liberalism more explicitly:

> But, it may be asked, what are these *liberal opinions*? What are you all contending about? I will tell you. As respects this town, we ask for a system of

responsible government – such an administration of our municipal affairs as will give to the lower and middle classes that influence in society to which they are entitled, and *place all the officers who collect and expend the people's money under the people's control.*[61]

Howe eschewed abstract constitutionalist arguments in favour of a direct appeal to public justice because he knew that success depended upon building a broad base of political support within the loyalist order. This approach placed Howe within the mainstream of British political thought. His emphasis on taxation and the rooting out of corruption was in step with the broader trend in favour of greater rationalization in government.[62] It also accorded with the efforts of British authorities to reduce the costs of colonial administration.[63] Although Howe was periodically compared with Louis-Joseph Papineau and William Lyon Mackenzie, he never advocated a radical program or challenged the legitimacy of the Crown.

In Lower Canada, the reform movement appears at first glance to be outside the pale of British legal culture. Lord Durham identified the perceived roots of constitutional discord as a struggle not of political principles, but of races.[64] Historians have generally followed the conventional view that the political struggles in Lower Canada, which culminated in the Rebellion of 1837–8, were qualitatively different from the disputes in other British colonies.[65] Allan Greer has corrected this perspective by explaining that the events in Upper and Lower Canada constituted a single revolutionary crisis. Greer argues that the Patriot opposition in Lower Canada and their counterparts in Upper Canada adopted a similar approach towards colonial oligarchies: they both drew upon republican and democratic ideals to condemn the government as illegitimate.[66] Murray Greenwood and Barry Wright also juxtapose political and legal developments in the two Canadas. Citing the suppression of the press, they contend that disillusionment with the justice system fuelled incendiary debates and helped to precipitate the Rebellions.[67]

In many respects, the political crises of the 1820s–30s in the Canadas echoed the struggle of the 1760s–70s in the Thirteen Colonies. The Ninety-Two Resolutions – passed by the Lower Canada Assembly in 1834 and considered to be the cardinal statement of the Patriots' philosophy – affirmed that the colonial assembly had the same rights and privileges as the British parliament. Thus, the power to appropriate taxes belonged to the elected representatives:

Resolved, That the claims which have for many years been set up by the Executive Government to that control over and power of appropriating a great portion of the revenues levied in this province, which belong of right to this House, are contrary to the rights and to the constitution of the country; and that with regard to the said claims, this House persists in the declaration it has heretofore made.[68]

In the wake of the Resolutions, government became deadlocked in a battle between the Legislative Council and the Patriot-controlled Assembly, which refused to approve new budgets. In 1837 Lord John Russell announced that the British government would not alter the colony's system of government. Russell rejected calls to make the Legislative Council an elective body and, to cope with the financial crisis, proposed to authorize the executive to raise funds without the assembly's approval.[69] The Patriot press expressed outrage at this constitutional usurpation:

Russell may, therefore, order his *Deputy, Gosford, to plunder our public chest*. A second Falstaff, he may say to his worthy chum – 'Rob me the Exchequer, Hal!' – and his Deputy and chum may rob it accordingly: but even this will not legalize the plunder. Our rights must not be violated with impunity. A HOWL of indignation must be raised from one extremity of the Province to the other, against the ROBBERS, and against all those WHO PARTAKE OF THE PLUNDER.

HENCEFORTH, THERE MUST BE NO PEACE IN THE PROVINCE – *no quarter for the plunderers*. Agitate! *Agitate!!* Agitate!!! Destroy the Revenue; denounce the oppressors. Everything is lawful when the fundamental liberties are in danger. 'The guards die – they never surrender.'[70]

References to the American Revolution appeared repeatedly in the Patriot press, which recounted episodes such as the Stamp Act crisis of 1765.[71]

The controversy over colonial revenues also involved grievances over statute law. In 1823 the Lower Canada Assembly challenged the validity of the Quebec Revenues Act of 1774 – which authorized the Crown to raise internal revenues from customs duties – by arguing that it contravened the Declaratory Act of 1778.[72] The 1778 act had declared that the King and Parliament of Great Britain would not impose any duty, tax, or assessment payable in any British colony (except duties imposed to regulate commerce, which were to be allocated only for the internal government of the colony).[73] Upon considering the Assembly's report, the Crown's lawyers ruled that the Quebec Revenues Act did not contravene the Declaratory Act because the latter was a prospective law that did not apply to acts passed before 1778; repeal of the 1774 statute would require another act of Parliament.[74] At the heart of this ongoing dispute was the liberal principle that the elected representatives in each colony should have control over the appropriation of revenues raised through internal taxation.[75] After the Rebellion in Lower Canada had broken out, Joseph Howe admitted that the British government had acted correctly in dealing with the insurrection, since the 'rebels were allowed to appear by counsel in the bodies of the Houses of Parliament, there to state their opinions, to vindicate their acts, and to appeal to British justice and magnanimity.' But he added, 'It should be borne in mind, however, that *up to 1828 they were right* ... Up to that time the Canadians resorted to these modes of opposition they only did what a British population had a right to do; they had a right to stop the supplies, and I, as a colonist, would never relinquish that right.'[76] The dividing line for Howe was when the Patriots spurned what he saw as conciliatory efforts of the British government to reach an agreement on the issue of colonial revenues.[77] It was for Howe a question of loyalty, not liberalism.

In Upper Canada, historians have long drawn a line between the law-abiding moderates and the radical reformers led by William Lyon MacKenzie. Over the past decade Barry Wright and Paul Romney have argued that the opposition to the British government was, in fact, a just struggle fought over the principle of the rule of law.[78] Criticizing scholars who have suggested that the legal culture and jurisprudence of Upper Canada cannot be evaluated according to modernist notions of the rule of law,[79] Wright and Romney maintain that contemporary lawyers and judges knew that many aspects of the colony's legal regime were unjust and illegal.[80] Unfairly targeted by the Family Compact, William Lyon Mackenzie and his followers resisted oppression by appealing to democratic ideals.[81] The late Peter Oliver contested this view of law and politics in Upper Canada, claiming that the Tories were not only responsible for the building of Kingston Penitentiary, but they also led the effort to reform the criminal law of Upper Canada in 1833.[82]

As in Lower Canada and the other British colonies, the political struggle centred on the relationship between liberal and loyalist principles.[83] The reformers had lost the general election of 1836 and were anxious to regain their political support: Lord John Russell's announcement on appropriating revenues gave Mackenzie an opportunity to revive the campaign against the government. With the colony facing mounting economic difficulties, Mackenzie turned to the issue of taxes:

> Taxes! Your shops are taxed – your tea is prohibited from the cheapest market and you are forced into the dearest. If you want a cheap book, the custom house officer asks the invoice and demands £30 per £100 in taxes. If you buy oil in the States where it is cheap, the broad arrow of seizure is fixed upon the barrel, and a third of the spoil goes to F.B. Head! [the governor] Taxes! You pay £3,000 a year for M.P.P.'s to scourge and rob you by wholesale enactments. Ye pay the penalty of prohibition from free trade with all the world, through the Hudson, because your foreign task-masters exact heavy duties on American goods and exclude their grain and provisions. Taxes![84]

Designed as a direct appeal to property-holders, Mackenzie's populist language reflected his efforts to build a viable coalition. As Colin Read and Ronald Stagg point out, the reform movement was not a unified party but rather a shaky coalition of diverse political factions.[85] The public appearance of unity was crucial to the movement's political success. When the Toronto reformers drafted a public declaration in July 1837, they affirmed that they were 'sympathizing with our fellow citizens here and throughout the North American Colonies, who desire to obtain cheap, honest, and responsible government.' They also cited comments made in the British Parliament by Lord Brougham, a liberal Whig, criticizing the government's policy as contrary to 'the fundamental principle of the British constitution, that no part of the taxes levied on the people shall be applied to any purpose whatever, without the consent of the representatives in parliament.'[86] The protest against 'taxation without representation' was, in other words, part of the tradition of British justice.

The political battles that marked British North America before 1840 drew on a public culture that spanned the contested ideals of liberalism and loyalism. For most reformers, the problem was that colonial subjects did not enjoy the full rights and privileges of their compatriots living in England. And as British radicals pushed for even greater civil rights in the 1830s, the features of modern liberalism took shape. It is at this point – the cusp of revolution in 1837, which marked the 'first arresting moment' in Canadian liberalism – that we need to reconsider one of McKay's important questions: Why Canada? If the Rebellions of

1837 were parts of a broader revolutionary crisis that drew heavily on republicanism, why not study class formation or gender ideology across all of North America or the entire West? Aside from the practical answer – we make political decisions to keep our historical studies manageable in scope – there is, I think, a deeper issue at play here, one that explains the peculiarly Canadian nature of this problem. The crisis of 1837–8 involved not just ideologies and ideas but also allegiances. It cannot be understood outside of the international context of the perceived threat of the United States. For the defenders of the status quo, the Rebellion posed a serious problem: how could the government justify the suppression of rebels who did not fit the Burkean blueprint of an uneducated and unpropertied mob? The answer to this question strikes at the heart of the loyalist order and the project of rule that McKay has so usefully identified. It involves a reassessment of the role of Lockean principles in the legitimation of the state's power to execute those subjects who challenge its authority. The case study I would like to examine is the 1838 trial and execution of the Samuel Lount and Peter Matthews in Upper Canada.[87]

The First Arresting Moment Reconsidered

The treason trial of Lount and Matthews, presided over by Sir John Beverley Robinson, opened in Toronto in March 1838. During the previous session the provincial assembly had passed a package of emergency legislation, which included an act authorizing the suspension of habeas corpus, and the government had appointed a special commission to oversee the 'more effectual and impartial trial of persons charged with treason and treasonable practices.'[88] With the prisons full of suspected rebels, the commission faced a formidable task. The arrival of Sir George Arthur to replace Bond Head as lieutenant governor created further difficulties, but Robinson ensured that the commission commenced on time to consider the over one hundred people eventually indicted for treason.[89] For the charge to the grand jury on 8 March, he gave a prepared text that the local newspapers published in its entirety.[90]

On 26 March 1838 Lount and Matthews appeared before the chief justice for arraignment on the indictment of taking arms against the sovereign and levying war for the purpose of subverting the constitution and government. Their lawyer, Robert Baldwin, mysteriously advised them to plead guilty and, without an opportunity to hear their case, the court set sentencing for the 29th.[91] The prominent role of Lount and Matthews in the Rebellion was widely known. Lount had been one of the rebel leaders at Montgomery's tavern and had negoti- ated with the government emissaries, while Matthews had led a body of rebels in a skirmish with government forces at the Don River bridge.[92] On the morning of the 29th Robinson pronounced Lount and Matthews guilty of high treason and sentenced them to be executed on 12 April.[93] The Executive Council met on 31 March and again on 2 April to consider the case against the two prisoners, and concluded that there were no grounds for a pardon. The colonial government received a series of petitions that totalled over four thousand names – as well as a dramatic personal appeal by Mrs Lount to Governor Arthur – which the Council deliberated on 9 April. Nonetheless, the government fol- lowed its 'painful duty,' and on 12 April Lount and Matthews ascended the scaffold and dropped to their deaths.[94]

The colonial state faced an enormous challenge to legitimize its repression of the Rebellion. In his first report upon arriving in Toronto, Arthur informed the colonial secretary, Lord Glenelg, that 'public feel- ing is so conflicting – the large preponderating party looking to the Executive government to put down treason by energetic measures, and the party styling themselves Reformers hoping for the most lenient course.'[95] The new lieutenant governor soon received anonymous advice that 'the Chief Justice is at the head of what is called the Family Compact, which is as overbearing as it is wicked.'[96] Arthur also consid- ered a formal petition, signed by over seven hundred 'reformers,' which asked that 'severe punishments should not be inflicted upon the unfortunate persons' before the courts. While Arthur chided the reformers for their indiscretion, he admitted that his position was very difficult and, on the day Robinson sentenced Lount and Matthews, he appealed to the Colonial Office: 'How are the state prisoners to be dis- posed of?'[97]

The fate of the prisoners, particularly Lount and Matthews, became a contentious political issue. It had started after the arrests when an embellished report of Lount's confession, accompanied by editorial comments condemning the rebels, appeared in a government newspa- per.[98] Lount and Matthews attracted widespread sympathy throughout the province. Born in the United States, Samuel Lount first came to Upper Canada in 1811. After working as a blacksmith, woodsman, and a farmer, he was elected to the Provincial Assembly in 1834, becoming one of the most respected settlers in Simcoe County. Peter Matthews was the son of Loyalists, a veteran of the War of 1812, and a well-known and prosperous farmer; he was the reputed leader of the fifty men from Pickering who participated in the Rebellion. In addition to the lengthy petitions, which stressed that both men had large families, the plea of Mrs Lount for clemency raised the political stakes even further.[99] With the trial of Lount and Matthews now a focal point of the crisis, the authorities ordered the scaffold moved in front of the jail in order to heighten the hanging's political message. The execution's immediate impact was to fuel animosity towards the government.[100] After witnessing the execution, John Ryerson wrote to his brother: 'The general feeling is in total opposition to the execution of these men.'[101] Though the agitation eventually subsided, the trial and execution continued to be mentioned in the colonial press.[102] In his *Report on the Affairs of British North America* Lord Durham noted that the trial of Lount and Matthews had 'engaged a great share of the public sympathy' and had helped 'to spread a wide and serious irritation.' After speculating that the government might have purposely invited the Rebellion, Durham accused the dominant party of manipulating the judicial process 'in order to persecute or disable the whole body of their political opponents.'[103]

It is important, then, to ascertain the role of the Executive Council in the case of Lount and Matthews. After Robinson had formally reported the sentence passed on the 29th, Arthur convened the Council on 31 March to consider the situation.[104] He began the meeting by reviewing a despatch from Lord Glenelg dated 6 January. Arthur highlighted Glenelg's call for great circumspection before carrying into effect any capital sentences. The colonial secretary's argument for moderation stated clearly: 'I fear that the execution of such of the popular leaders as may be apprehended and convicted ... would have a strong tendency to embitter the spirit ... of their great body of followers.'[105] The government therefore faced an apparent obstacle to the planned execution of Lount and Matthews. Arthur then called Chief Justice Robinson into the meeting, briefed him on the Glenelg letter, and asked for an opinion on the necessity of executing those convicted of treason. Robinson replied that justice required that 'some examples should be made in the way of capital punishments.'[106] Questioned specifically on Lount and Matthews, he stated that he saw no grounds upon which to recommend a pardon or reprieve. Robinson explained that 'all the good to arise' from the death sentence would be lost in the delay caused by a pardon appeal to the queen. After requesting Robinson's attendance at the next Council meeting, Arthur turned to the attorney general, Christopher

Hagerman, who responded that although the number of executions should be limited, the Crown should carry out the death sentence on Lount and Matthews. To justify this position he claimed that Lount and Matthews were 'more peculiarly accountable' because they were not only among the most active rebels, but also 'not of a class liable or likely to be misled, or deluded by others.'[107] As propertied and respectable members of society, their involvement in the rebellion carried a special stigma and evidently a more serious threat to the regime.

On 2 April the attorney general presented the Executive Council with a full report on the cases of Lount and Matthews in which he repeated his earlier advice. In addition to an outline of their crimes the review stressed the social status of both Lount and Matthews. Hagerman noted that Lount had acquired a valuable property and Matthews was 'a yeoman, in affluent circumstances, and possessing very considerable influence among the people in his neighbourhood.'[108] During the meeting on the 2nd the Executive Council (with Robinson in attendance) formally advised Arthur that the death sentence on Lount and Matthews should be executed to provide the necessary public example. On 9 April the Council convened to discuss the case a final time. Following a review of the lengthy petitions for mercy, the Council reiterated that their duty to the public required the deaths of Lount and Matthews.[109] The propriety of the conduct of Arthur and Chief Justice Robinson represents a key aspect of the trial. Although his decisions contradicted Glenelg's advice, Arthur avoided informing London of his actions until after Lount and Matthews had been hanged. By presenting the Colonial Office with a *fait accompli*, he ensured that Glenelg could not interfere with the decision to execute the two men. Lord Glenelg later wrote in astonishment that he heard of the execution through the *public papers*.[110] In the meantime, Arthur fortified his despatch to Glenelg with all the possible materials justifying the execution. He argued that the disturbances in the colony were, like those in Lower Canada, of an essentially political character and, therefore, required strong measures. Arthur portrayed Lount and Matthews as prominent rebel leaders who had encouraged dissolute foreigners to attack the government. But he also conceded: 'There are some serious legal difficulties which hedge the movements of the Executive in on all sides. Something, perhaps, must be done that is abstractly wrong; but if this fence be broken through for a merciful purpose, I satisfy myself that Her Majesty's Government will relieve me from the responsibility of the damage.'[111] Apparent irregularities characterized the entire treason proceedings in Upper Canada, and the Colonial Office later tried to censure those involved.[112]

The trial and execution of Lount and Matthews reveal illiberal characteristics of the nascent liberal order. Chief Justice Robinson's active role in the Executive Council – in violation of imperial policy – meant that executive and judicial powers had essentially become one and the same thing. Robinson knew at the time (or should have known) that his actions were improper: he had already endured a furore in 1836 over his relationship with the previous lieutenant governor, Sir Francis Bond Head, and at one point even warned Head against meeting with judges too frequently.[113] Robinson's dealings with Arthur illustrate an anxiety over his relationship with the executive. After sending the despatch to Glenelg, Arthur broached with Robinson the question of the judge's role in government. Alarmed by such a potentially damaging issue, the chief justice sent Arthur a lengthy apologia. Blaming his earlier close relations with the executive on Sir Francis Head, Robinson affirmed, 'I desire no responsibility that does not belong to me.'[114] To placate his worried chief justice, Arthur replied that he never supposed that '*your* services had been unnecessarily called into activity in Executive matters.'[115] Though the matter soon subsided, their subsequent correspondence reveals a *modus operandi* whereby Robinson regularly dispensed advice on a wide range of issues before the government.

The circumstances surrounding the trial and execution of Lount and Matthews shed considerable light on the birth of the Canadian liberal order. Disregarding Glenelg's warning, the government's determination to hang Lount and Matthews made the case into a type of show trial.[116] From the perspective of English law, the politicized nature of the judicial proceedings was not particularly unusual: as a number of British historians have demonstrated, the administration of criminal law was characterized by discretion.[117] As Douglas Hay pointed out in his classic study of the relationship between property and authority, the administration of criminal law depended heavily on symbolism and rhetoric, which were expressed through the triad of majesty, justice, and mercy.[118] And, as E.P. Thompson noted, the criminal law was not a blunt weapon of class oppression but rather a carefully-calibrated instrument, attuned to social relations yet operating largely within the confines of the rule of law.[119] The trial of Lount and Matthews represented a critical opportunity for the colonial government to assert its authority in a volatile political climate: its justification of the executions would have to be carefully crafted. How did officials explain their actions to the public: aside from the terror of the scaffold, how did they try to persuade the populace to accept their policies? In his discussion of Gramsci's theory of hegemony, McKay emphasizes the extent to which a group can exercise leadership over others by going outside its immediate corporate interests to take into account the concerns of other groups and classes. How did this hegemonic process manifest itself in one of the most important court cases in Canadian history?

The Lockean Moment: Legitimizing the Colonial State

In the case of Lount and Matthews, the state's favoured rhetorical tools were the charge to the grand jury and the sentencing speech. These judicial procedures afforded the chance to deliver a secular sermon from the bench. Chief Justice Robinson ensured that both addresses were published in the local papers, and the texts circulated widely among the public.[120] Robinson told those assembled to hear the sentencing of Lount and Matthews that 'it may be of some public service ... if I use this occasion for expressing some reflections.'[121] As Kenneth McNaught has observed, the sentencing of Lount and Matthews afforded an ideal occasion for a political statement about issues of law and order.[122] Within the seemingly narrow confines of a judicial address, Robinson presented a forceful argument that drew on the central tenets of liberalism. What is interesting about the speech is the relative absence of two elements commonly associated with the legal culture of Upper Canada. First, the rule of law and British justice formed only minor parts of Robinson's judicial ideology: he relied on these rhetorical pillars only to stress, at the beginning and end of his address, that the law afforded him no choice but to pass the sentence of death. Second, though he utilized several biblical metaphors, Robinson's legal thought, as evidenced in these speeches, was not rooted in Protestant doctrines. He implicitly termed duty to God as duty to government and portrayed the press as the viper in the Garden of Eden, but he did not base his arguments on conventional religious principles.

Robinson's basic argument turned on the link between property and tacit consent. The chief justice expounded upon this theme in his charge to the grand jury. He described Upper Canada before the Rebellion as a place of universal peace, perfect security, and general contentment. Through public works and an unprejudiced justice system, the government had provided the inhabitants with 'every liberty and right which is consistent with human happiness' to enjoy the fruits of their labour.

The only possible sources of dissension were therefore the product of either bad passions or ill-constituted minds. Given the unrivalled economic prosperity of this fertile colony, Robinson concluded:

> I must confess myself to have been among the last, who could believe it possible, that those who were in enjoyment of such blessings could prevail upon themselves fatally to renounce them all, either for the gratification of some unaccountable resentment, or in the mad and guilty pursuit of such imaginary advantages as no form of Government did, or ever can confer.[123]

In other words, because the state promoted material security and a relatively high standard of living, there existed no legitimate grounds to oppose those in office.

Robinson refined and extended these views further in his sentencing of Lount and Matthews. His reasoning differed substantially from Arthur's report to the Colonial Office. References to prosperity formed the outer layer of a cogent socio-political argument modelled on the principles of John Locke's *Second Treatise of Government*.[124] Both Patrick Brode and Kenneth McNaught recognized similarities between Robinson's sentencing speech and Locke's ideas, but the connection went deeper than the use of well-known phrases.[125] Locke's ideas were, in fact, relatively prevalent in the political thought of the first wave of Loyalists, which included Robinson's own family.[126] An examination of the address reveals a systematic Lockean ideology that illustrates much about liberalism and the loyalist order. The issue that Robinson stressed first and then reiterated throughout the speech was the economic status of Lount and Matthews. This approach paralleled the attorney general's report on the case to the Executive Council. Robinson opened by noting that both prisoners had recently lived 'in the enjoyment of health and liberty, under circumstances as favourable, perhaps, as the condition of human nature permits.' Robinson emphasized the fact that the men were neither labourers nor tenants and had reached 'that middle station of life than which none is happier; you were your own masters.' Most important, the chief justice pointed out that Matthews and Lount had acquired *property*.[127] He clearly wanted to establish Lount and Matthews as full members of Upper Canadian society.

Robinson then moved into a discussion of the role of the state. The passage outlined the aims of government and asserted that those duties had been fully satisfied. 'You lived in a country where,' Robinson affirmed, 'every man who obeys the laws is secure in the protection of life, liberty, and property; under a form of government which has been the admiration of the world for ages.' As proof of this accomplishment, he referred to the province's use of trial by jury and a legal system that dispensed justice regardless of wealth. At the heart of this system rested the protection of property and thus the assurance that 'no man could deprive you, by force or by fraud, of the smallest portion of the fruits of your labour.' Robinson remarked that Lount and Matthews had served as jurors and had taken the oath of allegiance. He then shifted into a comparative description of the material conditions of less fortunate lands. Robinson pointed out that thousands in the British Empire were 'labouring in dangerous and sickly occupations, in dark and unwholesome mines ... gleaning in contentment a scanty subsistence, by far greater exertion than was necessary to place you, in this favoured country, in a state of comfort, and perhaps affluence.' Such were the blessings, he continued, 'which you have wantonly thrown away.' Robinson recounted the prisoners' unnatural rebellion designed 'to destroy the constitution which it was your bounden duty to maintain.' In addition to taking arms against the Crown, they had allegedly seduced others and corrupted their loyalty. Finally, Robinson underscored the fact that Lount and Matthews had attacked their countrymen and had undertaken to destroy their property.[128]

The connections between Robinson's address and John Locke's political philosophy are striking. Locke had argued that men united under a government in order to preserve 'their lives, liberties, and estates, which I call by the general name "property."'[129] Robinson's use of Locke's 'property' instead of Jefferson's 'pursuit of happiness' was not merely semantics, but part of a consistent argument.[130] For both Robinson and Locke, the core duty of government remained, as stated explicitly in the *Second Treatise*, 'the preservation of property.'[131] Immediately after discussing the ends of government, Robinson defined the role of the legal system as the protection of those aims. Similarly, Locke delineated three factors necessary to uphold the protection of property: a settled and known law, an indifferent and upright judge, and the power to support the execution of judicial sentences.[132] While Robinson may not have meant to take property rights as far as Locke had attempted, his specific and repeated references to the judiciary in terms of its *material* benefits (as opposed to, say, moral considerations) concurred with the principles of the *Second Treatise*. For Locke, property was a natural right preceding civil society and not created by it.[133] The emphasis Robinson placed on an impartial judiciary denoted more than a belief in the rule of law: rather than an end in itself, the law constituted a means to protect property and, as a corollary, the established socio-political order.

Locke had developed this argument into a social contract that men entered into when they united into a commonwealth. In return for the government's preservation of property, individuals relinquished to the government their right to dispense justice privately or to punish others. In addition, subjects had to surrender some personal autonomy to the state for the regulation of social needs through statute laws.[134] Though this appears democratic, Locke intended, as C.B. Macpherson explained, for only propertied men to control the legislative and the executive branches of government.[135] As a trust between the government and society, the contract dissolved when those in power acted contrary to the interests of the public good. Locke explained, 'Whenever the legislators endeavour to take away and destroy the property of the people, or to reduce them to slavery under arbitrary power, they put themselves in a state of war with the people who are thereupon absolved from any further obedience.'[136] Locke did not advocate revolution in the modern sense, but instead a type of just *coup d'état* directed by society's leading members and institutions.[137]

Robinson's sentencing speech framed the issue of rebellion in essentially the same manner. He cited the colony's material prosperity as evidence that the government had fulfilled its contractual obligation to protect property.[138] Robinson categorically denied the existence of tyranny, and thus the conditions of rebellion, as outlined by Locke. He pointed out that Lount and Matthews had used violence to force their political opinions upon others. In an effort to circumvent the political grievances associated with the Rebellion, Robinson concluded that Lount and Matthews had simply 'too long and unreservedly indulged in a feeling of envy and hatred towards your rulers.' He wanted to establish that not only had the government not breached any public trust, but Lount and Matthews had acted without any just cause. Robinson then added another important element to his condemnation of the rebels. To those such as Matthews and Lount who had persuaded themselves that 'a Republic, or any form of government, was preferable to a Monarchy,' Robinson proposed a liberal choice: emigration. In a remarkable passage in the sentencing speech, he pursued the point: 'It was open to you, if you were discontented with the Government that protected you, to sell your possessions here, and transfer yourselves to any other country whose laws and institutions you liked better than your own. *That* you could have done, without injuring others, without violating your oaths of allegiance, and without loading your consciences with crime.'[139] Locke had argued, in fact, that every man had a right of freedom of his person to leave a given country. However, as Robinson was also careful to include, Locke maintained that those who emigrated thereby relinquished their legal rights and could not hold property in their former country.[140]

The question of emigration bore directly upon the volatile political environment in Upper Canada. During 1837–9 thousands left the province for the United States. This movement included the rebel leaders who fled to America and, organized by Mackenzie, took part in the Patriot raids in December 1837.[141] Yet it also contained men, such as John Van Arnam, who preferred temporary banishment to what they considered illegal imprisonment. Van Arnam claimed in a petition that thousands of respectable and loyal subjects were now in exile.[142] In addition to those who feared further retribution, many moderates from both parties felt so disgusted with the colonial government that they chose to leave. In the wake of the treason trials, an editorial in the Toronto *Mirror* claimed: 'Our substantial farmers are leaving for what they call more liberal institutions, where they will have a voice in the selection of the men that will govern them.'[143] Some reformers even formed an Emigration Society, to found a colony in the Iowa territory, which reputedly attracted some of the province's wealthier inhabitants.[144]

Robinson's endorsement of emigration as an option for those who held dissenting political views propelled the judiciary into the heart of political controversy. The liberal choice of leaving British lands to join the *other* – the American republic – was presented as the means to secure freedom of conscience. This position implied, as D.J. MacMahon has noted, that those who criticized existing political arrangements were little better than criminals.[145] Robinson used the principles of a social contract to advance partisan aims, establishing an implicit but potent doctrine based on seemingly neutral propositions. Premised on the notion of tacit consent, this liberal logic contained three basic assertions: the purpose of government was to protect property; the inhabitants, that is, Lount and Matthews, had enjoyed property within the government's territory; they had thereby entered into a social contract and, therefore, accepted the government in power. Similarly, Locke had asserted in the *Second Treatise*: 'I say that every man that has any possessions or enjoyment of any part of the dominion of any government does thereby give his tacit consent and is as far forth obliged to obedience to the laws of that government, during such enjoyment, as anyone under it.'[146] Though Locke had also tried to qualify his theory of consent, Robinson's speech used the model in its basic form.

As a result, Robinson managed to reduce the many issues surrounding the Rebellion crisis to a liberal contract for property rights. The specific grievances raised by the reformers did not, according to this view, warrant consideration. Most important, Robinson's address circumvented a major problem that faced the Family Compact in its political battles. Since the ranks of the reformers and rebels were filled with propertied men whose social standing and, as with Lount and Matthews, previous loyalty could not be challenged, the elite could not resort to a Burkean condemnation of the rebels as a vile mob.[147] The notion of tacit consent and the right to emigrate gave Robinson the rhetorical means to repudiate political opposition: because the government had protected property, provided the concomitant need for an ordered legal system, and fostered material prosperity, there existed no legitimate grievances against the colonial state. Those who enjoyed property – Lount, Matthews, and the majority of rebels – had implicitly endorsed the government and, if they disagreed with its policies, their only recourse was emigration.

Rethinking the 'Tory Touch'

Judge Robinson's effort to legitimize the execution of Lount and Matthews goes a long way to explaining how liberalism was used to support state authority in a highly volatile political climate. Ian McKay calls the repression of the Rebellion the first arresting moment in the 'Canadian Liberal Revolution,' but I would propose counter-revolution as a more accurate description of this process. In the minds of Robinson and many others who remained loyal, 'revolution' had a specific sociopolitical meaning: the republic to the south. The liberal path that Robinson's successors followed may well have been revolutionary in its effects, but I would argue that it was successful precisely because it was framed in *counter*-revolutionary terms. In the wake of the Union of the Canadas, the transition to responsible government, and eventually Confederation itself, the spectre of the republic as a type of ideological *Doppelgänger* – or, as Stuart Pierson put it, a *Struwwelpeter* – continued to shadow the country's political culture.[148] This Other (if I may use such an unfashionable term) shaped the country's development as much as the many domestic Others that McKay examines.[149] It influenced patterns of state formation, particularly in the era of the National Policy and the battle to rule the West, as well as Canada's imperial relationship with Britain.[150] According to the *Cambridge Series for Schools and Training Colleges*, by the turn of the twentieth century the fear that Canada would drift away from Britain after 1867 had been put to rest, as Canadians enthusiastically supported the Boer War.[151] The First World War would demonstrate just how far many Canadians would go to support the loyalist ethos.[152]

In his critique of synthesis as a scholarly enterprise, McKay suggests ways to go beyond traditional nationalist narratives. In doing so, he provides a much-needed antidote not only to the tired debate over Jack Granatstein's mean-spirited polemic *Who Killed Canadian History*, but also to the larger discussion (and perennial hand-wringing) about the viability of Canadian history as a popular field of scholarly inquiry.[153] While the question of 'whither Canadian history' continues to occupy the nationalist intelligentsia, McKay's framework is a testament to the tremendous creative potential offered by Canadian history. As McKay himself is quick to point out, his prospectus is an early and partial reading of how the liberal order paradigm might reshape Canadian historiography. Nonetheless, McKay establishes clear parameters: 'Canada-as-project can be analyzed through the study of the implantation and expansion over a heterogeneous terrain of a certain politico-economic logic – to wit, liberalism.'[154] This leaves us with the question of how far we can stretch liberalism to cover the gamut of Canadian history. If taken to its logical extreme, the liberal order framework could itself become a sort of total ideology used to support the type of synthesis that McKay deplores. This raises two spectres: geographically homogenizing Canadian history as part of (North) American liberalism; and temporally collapsing several centuries into a single metanarrative of liberal rule. Confronting these problems brings us back to an old question: What is distinctive about Canadian history?

For a generation of scholars, the answer to this question was the so-called 'Tory touch.' As S.F. Wise noted in his address to the Canadian Historical Association in 1974, every Canadian historian had to come to grips with Louis Hartz's study *The Founding of New Societies*, which offered a popular paradigm for explaining North American history. In his general model of the societies spawned by European migration, Hartz had argued that Canada was a bourgeois fragment of the Old World, governed by largely the same liberal tradition that dominated the United States. The differences between English Canada and the

United States were, according to Hartz, merely the result of inherited Tory touches, which delayed the development of democracy in British North America.[155] In his critique of Hartz, Wise focused particularly on the notion that the elite of Upper Canada necessarily followed Lockean ideals; but he also offered a wide-ranging commentary on the state of Canadian history, which, of course, he assumed to be political history. Wise dismissed contemporary trends in Canadian history, especially the idea of 'limited identities,' and he doubted whether a new synthesis would emerge in the near future. But he had no doubt that Canadian historians needed to rescue the country's venerable conservative tradition from Hartz's fragment thesis and its notion of Lockean hegemony. For Wise, the collectivist nature of conservative thought in Upper Canada stood in stark contrast to the unmitigated individualism of American liberalism.[156]

Canadian history had, in fact, already outgrown the original Hartzian thesis. Hartz himself received a second intellectual life in English Canada through the scholarship of Gad Horowitz, who argued that Hartz underestimated the political and ideological differences between Canada and the United States.[157] Expanding upon Hartz's basic theory, Horowitz argued that the Tory touch had a profound impact on the development of Canadian political culture: unlike the United States, where socialist ideals never took hold in mainstream politics, the Canadian conservative tradition inherited from Britain facilitated the growth and dissemination of left-of-centre principles and politics. Horowitz summed up his argument with a type of rough syllogism: 'Canadian Conservatives are not American Republicans; Canadian socialists are not American socialists; Canadian Liberals are not American liberal Democrats.'[158] While Horowitz focused on the effects of Toryism in English Canada, Jacques Monet explored the rise of loyalism in Quebec. In *The Last Cannon Shot*, Monet explored the transformation of French-Canadian nationalism in the wake of the Rebellion of 1837.[159] He argued that Quebec successfully met the Durham Report's challenge to integrate with English Canada: the victory of La Fontaine's party facilitated acceptance of the Union and the transition to responsible government. Monet claimed that the development of a nationalism that embraced integration saved the collective identity of French Canada and paved the road to Confederation. Like Horowitz, Monet faced serious academic criticism, but his study underscored the importance of seeing loyalism as distinct from both liberalism and Britishness.[160]

As both English and French Canadian historians moved away from

political history after the 1970s, the scholarly discussion became ossified into a debate over ideological labelling. Following her revisionist
study of Lord Durham, Janet Ajzenstat systematically attacked the
Hartz-Horowitz framework.[161] Ajzenstat asserted that the men of the
Family Compact and the Château Clique should be understood not as
Tories but as oligarchs. She argued that the central theme in Canadian
political history is not the debate between liberals and Tories but rather
the struggle between traditional liberals and romantics who want to
ameliorate the inequities caused by classical liberalism.[162] As one of the
few scholars to bridge the divide between political science and history,
Ajzenstat has exerted significant influence; yet the tenacious Tory touch
still framed the terms of the analysis. Historians added civic republicanism to the discussion, but it merely served to expand the agenda of
the debate, not the terms of the debate itself. The intellectual Zeitgeist
of the 1990s is captured by the title of one collection: *Canada's Origins:
Liberal, Tory, or Republican?*[163] In a recent survey of Canadian political
thought, Katherine Fierlbeck points out the dangers of concentrating on
labels: 'While it may be fascinating to think about these nuances –
whether Egerton Ryerson was really a liberal, rather than a Tory;
whether Canadian political figures were more concerned with classical
virtues than with merely maintaining the prejudice of tradition; or
whether participatory democrats were in fact demonstrably distinct
from constitutional liberals – one risks fragmenting the history of Canadian political thought into an endless multitude of discrete "traditions."'[164] This problem is by no means unique to Canada: disputes
over political definitions also became something of a fetish for British
and American historians, toiling in the long shadows of J.G.A. Pocock
and Gordon Wood.[165] As Douglas Bradburn has pointed out, 'The
debate became a fight over jargon.'[166] Bradburn argues that Anglo-
American historians have now moved beyond this impasse, but Canadian historians face a seemingly stark choice: continue with the labelling approach, which fragments the political spectrum into quarrels
over semantics; or follow the liberal order framework, which raises the
danger of flattening history into a debate over liberalism. Recently,
Ajzenstat herself has addressed this problem by calling on scholars to
reconsider the impact of Lockean principles on the political formation
of Canada.[167]

While scholars continue to debate the merits of liberalism, loyalism
has received considerably less scholarly attention. Loyalism (as a political logic of Canada) should not be conflated with the Loyalists (the

actual people who fled the American Revolution). As J.M. Bumsted pointed out twenty years ago, 'there is a desperate need to be able to distinguish between the Loyalist reality and the Loyalist tradition.'[168] I would take this point further: there is a need to loosen loyalism from the grip of the Loyalist tradition. Loyalism was not the exclusive preserve of British Tories who used it to combat Lockean liberalism: it encompassed a wide range of peoples in Colonial America, such as Quakers, Mohawks, and African slaves, as well as most white colonists in the British Caribbean.[169] This mixture of peoples and cultures fuelled the development of a 'composite monarchy,' whereby loyalty to the Crown encompassed different political traditions.[170] The case of John Beverley Robinson demonstrates that it was perfectly possible to follow both Tory and Lockean principles. This is not to suggest that the British Loyalists themselves are not important to Canadian history: as leaders of what John Porter once called a 'charter group,' they helped to usher in the liberal order.[171] But it would be a mistake to view *loyalist* as merely a literal description for a particular party. Loyalty is both an idea and an act: citizens choose (either actively or passively) whether they will revolt, resist, or renounce the status quo. There is, of course, a vast grey area of ambiguous motives and meanings – the political attitudes of most people are rarely crystal clear even to themselves, let alone to a historian – but studying loyalism sheds valuable light on the alliances and antagonisms that feed the social organization of power.

Like liberalism, loyalism modified democracy by regulating the shifting boundaries of politically acceptable behaviour. But unlike liberalism, loyalism was a consequence of early modern imperialism – which, in the Canadian context, produced counter-revolution – not a by-product of modernity. Whereas liberalism fuelled the development of modern individualism, loyalism offered expedient means to restrict civil liberties in the interests of the state. Loyalism offers a key to understanding the seemingly illiberal nature of the liberal order.[172] Liberalism may have become hegemonic, as McKay insists, but it never existed in a pure form; rather, it adapted to the specific politico-economic conditions of its host society, mutating over time according to the changing currents of power. In other words, liberalism is a necessary rather than sufficient condition to explain Canada.

It is also important to distinguish between loyalism and reactionism. The loyalist order stood against republicanism, not liberalism: its core principle was the rejection of rebellion against the Crown as a justifiable means of pursuing a political goal. Canada's counter-revolution never rejected Lockean liberalism, nor was it 'an exercise in Burkean reaction,' as one commentator has suggested.[173] It embraced liberalism in much the same way as the American Revolution embraced republicanism. 'Loyalist,' as the *Oxford English Dictionary* reminds us, has a specific set of cultural meanings: fidelity to promises, oaths, or words of honour; allegiance to sovereign or lawful governments; and a commitment to lawfulness and legality.[174] What is interesting about loyalism is that its allegiance is to a sovereign rather than just a government: its basic principle is legality, not equality. The loyalist order in Canada was shaped by the relative absence of revolutionary myths and founding ideals. Both the American and French Revolutions represented a fundamental break with the past, a utopian moment when society could be cured from the disease of tyranny. Neither revolution lived up to its rhetoric, of course, but the consequent mythologies exerted a powerful and lasting influence on the rise of liberalism in France and the United States.[175] The lack of a revolutionary mythology in Canada meant that there was no foundational principle of natural justice – no *liberté, égalité, fraternité, ou la mort!* – to legitimize opposition to the laws of a sovereign state. As we have seen, the Jeffersonian notion of happiness was not part of the Lockean formulation used to justify the suppression of the Rebellion of 1837.

What Canada inherited instead of revolutionary doctrines was a loyalist ethos. This ethos manifested itself in section 91 of the British North America Act (now known as the Constitution Act, 1867), which laid out the powers of the Canadian Parliament: 'It shall be lawful for the Queen, by and with the Advice of the Senate and the House of Commons, to make Laws for the Peace, Order, and good Government of Canada, in relation to all Matters not coming within the Classes of Subjects by this Act assigned exclusively to the Legislatures of the Provinces.'[176] This power actually gave the Canadian federal state more authority than its American counterpart. The trinity of peace, order, and good government – known by the Orwellian acronym POGG – has been used to support a range of seemingly illiberal laws and regulations, from the War Measures Act to the establishment of wage and price controls.[177] The impact of POGG can be seen in the Constitution Act of 1982, which, as few Canadians seem to realize, begins with the preamble, 'Whereas Canada is founded upon principles that recognize the supremacy of God and the rule of law.'[178] The Charter of Rights and Freedoms establishes a series of negative freedoms subject only to reasonable limits prescribed by law, but it is no accident that the Constitution Act invokes the supremacy of law and God over ideals of natural justice, social equality, or even the pursuit of individual happiness.

Postscript: The Legacy of Counter-Revolution

At the end of his article, McKay addresses the apparent neo-liberal agenda to erase the political boundary between Canada and the United States. For neo-conservatives, as they are often known, this would be the natural political dénouement of the economic transformation wrought by the Free Trade Agreement. And yet, despite all the proclamations of Canada's imminent demise, it is still with us, with the full panoply of an unelected head of state, an ubiquitous RCMP, and plenty of royalist iconography supported by public funds.[179] We need to find ways to explain the *differences* as well as the similarities between and within the American and Canadian varieties of liberalism: in doing so, McKay's liberal order framework should be a starting point rather than a destination. Despite the popular conceit that all elected politicians are the same, it is important to distinguish between the liberalism of Jean Chrétien and that of Stephen Harper, for example, since such distinctions can mean the difference between joining the war in Iraq or staying out of American military ventures.[180]

As we continue to debate our national identity, echoes of the loyalist order can be heard in the ways we discuss our past and imagine our future. Canadians, we are told, are becoming increasingly different from Americans: while we have supposedly evolved into a tolerant, multicultural people led by a prudent government, they remain captive to reactionary ideologies and demagogic leaders.[181] The nationalist rhetoric may have changed from loyalism to multiculturalism, but the political framework remains rather similar to the era when English Canada was considered a British country.[182] As a recent issue of *The Walrus* demonstrates, English Canadian nationalism in the twenty-first century draws on three trends in liberal thought: a smug historical amnesia that reduces Canada's authoritarian past to a few isolated sins, such as the Chinese head tax; a virulent anti-Americanism that caricatures the United States as an evil beast; and a blind faith in a beneficently powerful central state.[183] This form of neo-nationalism is in many respects old political wine in a new cultural bottle. Mark Kingwell's vitriolic rant against the United States – which reeks of visceral revulsion towards Americans, who are castigated as followers of Mammon and Moloch – goes further than anything John Beverley Robinson would have written; but I suspect that Robinson would have liked its basic message.[184] Yet while such anti-Americanism has attracted significant scholarly attention in the United States, it remains a neglected aspect of Canadian historiography.[185] Liberalism explains much about our national culture, but it alone cannot account for the peculiar Canadian hegemony that McKay has so eloquently described. I am sure that to many of my colleagues, emphasizing the difference between a liberal and a loyalist order may seem like splitting temporal hairs, but I would contend that the devil is in the details. What has made (and may possibly unmake) Canada is its inherited legacy of counter-revolution.

NOTES

1 Earlier versions of this paper were presented to the history departments at the University of Manitoba, the University of New Brunswick, and Dalhousie University. I am indebted to many colleagues for their helpful suggestions: Margaret Conrad, Jack Crowley, Christopher Dummitt, Katherine Fierlbeck, David Frank, Allan Greer, Elsbeth Heaman, Krista Kesselring, Todd McCallum, Jeff McNairn, John Reid, Greg Smith, and Shirley Tillotson. I also thank Jean-François Constant and Michel Ducharme for their expert editorial work.

2 Ian McKay, 'The Liberal Order Framework: A Prospectus for a Reconnaissance of Canadian History,' *Canadian Historical Review* 81 (2000): 620.

3 McKay does not ignore international and imperial factors – he refers explicitly to the influence of the colonial metropole and the dialogue with American republicanism – but he focuses almost exclusively on domestic developments. See ibid., 639.

4 Crane Brinton, *The Anatomy of Revolution*, rev. ed. (New York: Vintage, 1965). My use of 'counter-revolution' is somewhat similar to the framework employed in Eliga Gould, 'Revolution and Counter-Revolution,' in *The British Atlantic World, 1500–1800*, ed. David Armitage and Michael Braddick (London: Palgrave Macmillan, 2002), 196–213; and Alan Taylor, 'The Late Loyalists: Northern Reflections of the Early American Republic,' *Journal of the Early Republic* 27 (2007): 1–34. But I disagree with Alan Taylor's argument that the arrival of the late Loyalists engendered a new liberalism that broke sharply with the counter-revolutionary political culture of the original Loyalists. My point is that British North America developed a counter-revolutionary liberalism that remained distinct from the republican liberalism of the United States.

5 See V.G. Kiernan, 'Revolution,' in *Dictionary of Marxist Thought*, ed. Tom Bottomore, 2nd ed. (Oxford: Blackwell, 1991), 476–80.

6 Following Gad Horowitz's ideological taxonomy, Lipset argues, 'The very organizing principles that framed these nations, the central cores around which institutions and events were to accommodate, were different. One was Whig and classically liberal or libertarian – doctrines that emphasize distrust of the state, egalitarianism, and populism – reinforced by a voluntaristic and congregational religious tradition. The other was Tory and conservative in the British and European sense – accepting of the need for a strong state, for respect for authority, for deference – and endorsed hierarchically organized religions that supported and were supported by the state.' See Seymour Martin Lipset, *Continental Divide: The Values and Institutions of the United States and Canada* (New York: Routledge, 1990), 2.

7 McKay, 'Liberal Order Framework,' 639. Here McKay is referring to John Farthing, *Freedom Wears a Crown* (Toronto: Kingswood House, 1957).

8 McKay, 'Liberal Order Framework,' 640.

9 See Jeffrey McNairn and Elsbeth Heaman in this volume.

10 Ian McKay, *Rebels, Reds, Radicals: Rethinking Canada's Left History* (Toronto: Between the Lines, 2005), 31.

11 David Armitage, 'Three Concepts of Atlantic History,' in *The British Atlantic World, 1500–1800*, 11.

12 On the debate over Atlantic history, see Peter Coclanis, '*Drang nach Osten*: Bernard Bailyn, the World Island, and the Idea of Atlantic History,' *Journal of World History* 13 (2002): 169–82; Bernard Bailyn, *Atlantic History: Concept and Contours* (Cambridge, MA: Harvard University Press, 2005); Linda Colley, 'The Sea Around Us,' *New York Review of Books* 53, 11 (22 June 2006): 43–5; Alison Games, 'Atlantic History: Definitions, Challenges, and Opportunities,' *American Historical Review* 111 (2006): 741–57. On the Canadian context, see Peter Pope, 'Comparisons: Atlantic Canada,' in *A Companion to Colonial America*, ed. Daniel Vickers (New York: Blackwell, 2003); Luca Codignola and John G. Reid, 'Forum: How Wide Is the Atlantic Ocean?' *Acadiensis* 34 (2005): 74–87.

13 J.H. Parry, *The Age of Reconnaissance: Discovery, Exploration, and Settlement, 1450–1650* (Berkeley: University of California Press, 1981).

14 John G. Reid, 'How Wide Is the Atlantic Ocean? Not Wide Enough!' *Acadiensis* 34 (2005): 84.

15 See, for example, Peter Pope, *Fish into Wine: The Newfoundland Plantation in the Seventeenth Century* (Chapel Hill: University of North Carolina Press, 2004); Stephen Hornsby, *British Atlantic, American Frontier: Spaces of Power in Early Modern British America* (Lebanon, NH: University Press of New

England, 2005); Kenneth Banks, *Chasing Empire Across the Sea: Communications and the State in the French Atlantic, 1713–1763* (Montreal and Kingston: McGill-Queen's University Press, 2002); N.E.S. Griffiths, *From Migrant to Acadian: A North American Border People, 1604–1755* (Montreal and Kingston: McGill-Queen's University Press, 2005).

16 Carl Berger, *The Sense of Power: Studies in the Ideas of Canadian Imperialism, 1867–1914* (Toronto: University of Toronto Press, 1970). On the development of the literature since Berger, see D.R. Owram, 'Canada and the Empire,' in *Oxford History of the British Empire*, vol. 5, *Historiography*, ed. Robin Winks (Oxford: Oxford University Press, 1999), 146–8. Owram offers this conclusion: 'The historiography of Empire in Canada, therefore, is in reality only partly about the Empire. It is instead the story of Canada and her main link to the wider world.'

17 Kathleen Wilson, 'Histories, Empires, Modernities,' in *A New Imperial History: Culture, Identity and Modernity in Britain and the Empire, 1660–1840*, ed. Kathleen Wilson (Cambridge: Cambridge University Press, 2004), 3.

18 See Michael Braddick, 'State Formation and Social Change in Early Modern England: A Problem Stated and Approaches Suggested,' *Social History* 16 (1991): 1–17; Braddick, *State Formation in Early Modern England, c. 1550–1700* (Cambridge: Cambridge University Press, 2000); John Brewer, 'The Eighteenth-Century British State: Contexts and Issues,' in *An Imperial State at War: Britain from 1689 to 1815*, ed. Lawrence Stone (New York: Routledge, 1994), 54; John Brewer and Eckhart Hellmuth, 'Introduction: Rethinking Leviathan,' in *Rethinking Leviathan: The Eighteenth-Century State in Britain and Germany*, ed. Brewer and Hellmuth (Oxford: Oxford University Press, 1999), 1–21.

19 Ramsay Cook, *Watching Quebec: Selected Essays* (Montreal and Kingston: McGill-Queen's University Press, 2005), 190.

20 On the historiography of the Conquest, see Serge Gagnon, *Quebec and Its Historians: The Twentieth Century*, trans. Jane Brierley (Montreal: Harvest House, 1985), chap. 1; Jocelyn Létourneau, *A History of the Future: Rewriting Memory and Identity in Quebec*, trans. Phyllis Aronoff and Howard Scott (Montreal: McGill Queen's University Press, 2004).

21 McKay, 'Liberal Order Framework,' 625n16. McKay's citation refers to Linda Colley's work on nationalism and imperialism in Britain (presumably her 1992 book *Britons*); but Colley's recent research underscores the degree to which Britishness was also rooted in political fear and cultural perception of threat. See *Captives: Britain, Empire, and the World, 1600–1850* (New York: Anchor Books, 2004).

22 Louis-Georges Harvey, *Le printemps de l'Amérique française: Américanité, anti-*

colonialisme et républicanisme dans le discours politique québécois, 1805–1837 (Montreal: Boréal, 2005), chap. 6.

23 For different perspectives on the importance of empire in Canadian history, see Gregory Kealey, 'The Empire Strikes Back: The Nineteenth-Century Origins of the Canadian Secret Service,' *Journal of the Canadian Historical Association* new ser. 10 (1999); Phillip Buckner, 'Was There a British Empire? The Oxford History of the British Empire from a Canadian Perspective,' *Acadiensis* 32 (2002): 110–28.

24 On the rise of individualism across Anglo-American culture, see Dror Wahrman, *The Making of the Modern Self: Identity and Culture in Eighteenth-Century England* (New Haven: Yale University Press, 2004).

25 Ian K. Steele, 'The Anointed, the Appointed, and the Elected: Governance of the British Empire, 1689–1784,' in *The Oxford History of the British Empire*, vol. 2, *The Eighteenth Century*, ed. P.J. Marshall (Oxford: Oxford University Press, 1998), 119–21; Doron Ben-Atar, 'The American Revolution,' in *The Oxford History of the British Empire*, vol. 5, 98–9; John G. Reid and Elizabeth Mancke, 'From Global Processes to Continental Strategies: The Emergence of British North America to 1783,' in *Canada and the British Empire*, ed. Phillip Buckner (Oxford: Oxford University Press, 2008), 22–41.

26 For overviews of this process of imperial expansion, see Stephen E. Patterson, '1744–1763: Colonial Wars and Aboriginal Peoples,' in *The Atlantic Region to Confederation: A History*, ed. Phillip Buckner and John Reid (Toronto: University of Toronto Press, 1994); Julian Gwyn, *Excessive Expectations: Maritime Commerce and the Economic Development of Nova Scotia, 1740–1870* (Montreal and Kingston: McGill-Queen's University Press, 1998), chap. 2; Elizabeth Mancke, 'Early Modern Imperial Governance and the Origins of Canadian Political Culture,' *Canadian Journal of Political Science* 32 (1999): 3–20.

27 John Brewer, *The Sinews of Power: War, Money, and the English State, 1688–1783* (London: Unwin Hyman, 1989); Allan Greer and Ian Radforth, eds., *Colonial Leviathan: State Formation in Mid-Nineteenth-Century Canada* (Toronto: University of Toronto Press, 1992).

28 Geoffrey Plank, *An Unsettled Conquest: The British Campaign against the Peoples of Acadia* (Philadelphia: University of Pennsylvania Press, 2001); John Mack Faragher, *A Great and Noble Scheme: The Tragic Story of the Expulsion of the French Acadians from Their American Homeland* (New York: Norton, 2005).

29 On the changes to the empire's legal systems after the Seven Years War, see Elizabeth Mancke, 'Colonial and Imperial Contexts,' in *The Supreme Court of Nova Scotia, 1754–2004*, ed. Philip Girard, Jim Phillips, and Barry Cahill (Toronto: University of Toronto Press for the Osgoode Society, 2004), 44–6.

30 John G. Reid, 'Pax Britannica *or* Pax Indigena? Planter Nova Scotia (1760–
    1782) and Competing Strategies of Pacification,' *Canadian Historical Review*
    85 (2004); John Reid et al., *The 'Conquest' of Acadia, 1710: Imperial, Colonial,
    and Aboriginal Constructions* (Toronto: University of Toronto Press, 2004);
    Emerson W. Baker and John G. Reid, 'Amerindian Power in the Early Mod-
    ern Northeast: A Reappraisal,' *William and Mary Quarterly* 3rd ser., 51
    (2004): 77–106.

31 On the conflict between the Canadian state and Aboriginal peoples, see
    Robin Jarvis Brownlie in this volume and *A Fatherly Eye: Indian Agents,
    Government Power, and Aboriginal Resistance in Ontario, 1918–1939* (Oxford:
    Oxford University Press, 2003). On the westward expansion of state
    authority and the role of liberalism, see Adele Perry, *On the Edge of Empire:
    Gender, Race, and the Making of British Columbia, 1849–1871* (Toronto: Uni-
    versity of Toronto Press, 2001); Tina Loo, *Making Law, Order, and Authority
    in British Columbia, 1821–1871* (Toronto: University of Toronto Press,
    1994).

32 Ann Gorman Condon, *The Loyalist Dream for New Brunswick: The Envy of the
    American States* (Fredericton: New Ireland Press, 1984); Neil MacKinnon,
    This Unfriendly Soil: The Loyalist Experience in Nova Scotia, 1783–1791 (Mont-
    real and Kingston: McGill-Queen's University Press, 1989); James W.
    Walker, *The Black Loyalists: The Search for a Promised Land in Nova Scotia and
    Sierra Leone*, 2nd ed. (Toronto: University of Toronto Press, 1992); L.F.S.
    Upton, *The United Empire Loyalists: Men and Myths* (Toronto: Copp Clark,
    1967); David Mills, *The Idea of Loyalty in Upper Canada, 1784–1850* (Montreal
    and Kingston: McGill-Queen's University Press, 1988); Norham James
    Knowles, *Inventing the Loyalists: The Ontario Loyalist Tradition and the Cre-
    ation of Usable Pasts* (Toronto: University of Toronto Press, 1997); Patricia
    Rogers, 'The Loyalist Experience in an Anglo-American Atlantic World,' in
    Planter Links: Community and Culture in Colonial Nova Scotia, ed. Margaret
    Conrad and Barry Moody (Fredericton: Acadiensis Press, 2001).

33 Eliga Gould, *The Persistence of Empire: British Political Culture in the Age of the
    American Revolution* (Chapel Hill: University of North Carolina Press, 2000),
    chap. 6.

34 Paul Langford, *A Polite and Commercial People: England, 1727–1783* (Oxford:
    Oxford University Press, 1989); Linda Colley, *Britons: Forging the Nation,
    1707–1837* (New Haven: Yale University Press, 1992); Kathleen Wilson, *The
    Sense of the People: Politics, Culture and Imperialism in England, 1715–1785*
    (Cambridge: Cambridge University Press, 1995); John Brewer, *The Pleasures
    of the Imagination: English Culture in the Eighteenth Century* (London: Harper-
    Collins, 1997).

35 David G. Bell, *Early Loyalist Saint John: The Origins of New Brunswick Politics, 1783–1786* (Fredericton: New Ireland Press, 1983).

36 On the role of power of loyalism in British American political culture, see Gordon Wood, *The Radicalism of the American Revolution* (New York: Random House, 1991), part I; Brendan McConville, *The King's Three Faces: The Rise and Fall of Royal America, 1688–1776* (Chapel Hill: University of North Carolina Press, 2007).

37 Elizabeth Mancke, *The Fault Lines of Empire: Political Differentiation in Massachusetts and Nova Scotia, 1760–1830* (New York: Routledge, 2004).

38 Ranajit Guha, *Dominance without Hegemony: History and Power in Colonial India* (Cambridge, MA: Harvard University Press, 1997).

39 Gould, *Persistence of Empire*, 210.

40 The best account of this period remains Phillip Buckner, *The Transition to Responsible Government: British Policy in British North America, 1815–1850* (Westport, CT: Greenwood Press, 1985), chap. 2.

41 Allan Greer, 'Historical Roots of Canadian Democracy,' *Journal of Canadian Studies* 34 (1999): 7–26.

42 As Benton argues in her persuasive revision of Guha's theory of 'dominance without hegemony,' this second discursive shift could produce novel judicial spaces, but it also tended to fuel hegemony. Benton defines hegemony as not merely the manufacturing of persuasion or consent, but as a process of constructs of conventions that become naturalized throughout a political community. She concludes, 'Procedure trumped justice; institutions outlived bandits,' a point that could be profitably applied to the Canadian context. See Lauren Benton, *Law and Colonial Cultures: Legal Regimes in World History, 1400–1900* (Cambridge: Cambridge University Press, 2002), 260.

43 *Lord Durham's Report on the Affairs of British North America*, vol. 2, ed. C.P. Lucas (Oxford: Clarendon Press, 1912 [1839]), 151.

44 On the lack of success of legal reform movements, see Robert Fraser, '"All the privileges which Englishmen possess": Order, Rights, and Constitutionalism in Upper Canada,' in *Provincial Justice: Upper Canadian Legal Portraits from the Dictionary of Canadian Biography*, ed. R. Fraser (Toronto: Osgoode Society, 1992), lxiii.

45 Jeffrey McNairn, *The Capacity to Judge: Public Opinion and Deliberative Democracy in Upper Canada, 1791–1854* (Toronto: University of Toronto Press, 2000).

46 William Carson, *Reasons for Colonizing the Island of Newfoundland, in a letter addressed to the inhabitants* (Greenock: William Scott, 1813), 25.

47 Ibid., 8; emphasis added.

48 Anon. *A Report of Certain Proceedings of the Inhabitants of the Town of Saint John, in the Island of Newfoundland, with the view to obtain a REFORM of the LAWS, more particularly in the mode of their administration, and an INDEPENDENT LEGISLATURE* (St John's: Printed by Lewis Ryan, 1821), iv, 10–11.

49 Jerry Bannister, *The Rule of the Admirals: Law, Custom, and Naval Government in Newfoundland, 1699–1832* (Toronto: University of Toronto Press for the Osgoode Society, 2003), chap. 8.

50 *Newfoundlander* (St John's), 21 November 1827.

51 See, for example, the letters and editorials in the *Public Ledger* (St John's), 25 December 1827 and 22 and 25 April 1828.

52 Linda Little, 'Collective Violence in Outport Newfoundland: A Case Study from the 1830s,' *Labour / Le Travail* 26 (1990): 7–35.

53 Patrick O'Flaherty, *Old Newfoundland: A History to 1843* (St John's: Long Beach Press, 1999), chap. 8.

54 J. Murray Beck, *Joseph Howe*, vol. 1, *Conservative Reformer, 1804–1848* (Montreal and Kingston: McGill-Queen's University Press, 1982), esp. chaps. 17–19.

55 Kenneth McNaught, 'Political Trials and the Canadian Political Tradition,' *University of Toronto Law Journal* 24 (1974): 149–64; J.M. Beck, "A Fool for a Client': The Trial of Joseph Howe,' in *The Acadiensis Reader*, vol. 1, *Atlantic Canada before Confederation*, ed. P.A. Buckner and David Frank, 2nd ed. (Fredericton: Acadiensis Press, 1990), 243–60; Wayne Hunt, ed., *The Proceedings of the Joseph Howe Symposium* (Sackville: Centre for Canadian Studies, 1983), 5–29, 117–34.

56 Barry Cahill, '*R. v. Howe* (1835) for Seditious Libel: A Tale of Twelve Magistrates,' in *Canadian State Trials*, vol. 1, *Law, Politics, and Security Measures, 1608–1837*, ed. F. Murray Greenwood and Barry Wright (Toronto: The Osgoode Society, 1996), 547–65.

57 *The Speeches and Public Letters of Joseph Howe*, vol. 1, ed. Joseph Chisolm (Halifax: Chronicle Publishing, 1909), 44.

58 Ibid., 45–6.

59 Ibid.

60 On the Hartz-Horowitz framework, see below, nn. 155–8.

61 *Speeches and Public Letters of Joseph Howe*, 1: 104; emphasis added.

62 Ian Radforth, 'Sydenham and Utilitarian Reform,' in *Colonial Leviathan*, ed. Greer and Radforth, 64–96; C.A. Bayly, *Imperial Meridian: The British Empire and the World, 1780–1830* (London: Longman, 1989), 195–209.

63 Phillip Buckner, 'The Colonial Office in British North America, 1801–50,' *Dictionary of Canadian Biography*, vol. 8 (Toronto: University of Toronto Press, 1985), xxx–xxxiv.

64 *Lord Durham's Report*, 2: 16. On the debates over Lord Durham's racial attitudes and political beliefs, see Janet Ajzenstat, *The Political Thought of Lord
Durham* (Montreal and Kingston: McGill-Queen's University Press, 1988),
and the special issue devoted to Durham in the *Journal of Canadian Studies*
25 (1990).

65 Ramsay Cook, *The Maple Leaf Forever* (Toronto: Macmillan, 1971).

66 Allan Greer, '1837–38: Rebellion Reconsidered,' *Canadian Historical Review*
76 (1995): 1–19.

67 F. Murray Greenwood and Barry Wright, 'Parliamentary Privilege and the
Repression of Dissent in the Canadas,' in *Canadian State Trials*, 1: 409–38.

68 Quoted from *Canadian History in Documents, 1763–1966*, ed. Michael Bliss
(Toronto: Ryerson Press, 1966), 28.

69 See Buckner, *Transition to Responsible Government*, chap. 5; Peter Burroughs,
The Canadian Crisis and British Colonial Policy, 1828–1841 (Toronto: Macmillan, 1979).

70 *Vindicator* (Montreal), 21 April 1837, as quoted in *Canadian History in Documents*, 33.

71 Greer emphasizes that the Patriots focused on events such as the Stamp Act
crisis, instead of Lexington or the Boston Tea Party, because they were not
yet prepared for armed rebellion. He quotes a speech made by Louis-
Joseph Papineau in June 1837: 'Let us examine what the Americans did,
under similar circumstances. Ten years before they took up arms, they
adopted the course which we are now about to recommend to you. They
abstained from taxed articles.' See Allan Greer, *The Patriots and the People:
The Rebellion of 1837 in Rural Lower Canada* (Toronto: University of Toronto
Press, 1993), 145–6.

72 14 Geo. III, c. 88 (1774).

73 18 Geo. III, c. 12 (1778).

74 'Law Officers' Opinion on the Validity of the Quebec Revenues Act, 13
November 1824,' in *Select Documents on the Constitutional History of the Brit-
ish Empire and Commonwealth*, vol. 3, *Imperial Reconstruction, 1763–1840*, ed.
Frederick Madden (Westport, CT: Greenwood Press, 1987), 530–1.

75 On internal versus external taxation, see Bernard Bailyn, *The Ideological Origins of the American Revolution*, 2nd ed. (Cambridge, MA: Harvard University Press, 1992), 209–21; on republicanism in British political discourse, see
John Belcham, 'Republicanism, Popular Constitutionalism and the Radical
Platform in Early Nineteenth-Century England,' *Social History* 6 (1981),
1–32.

76 *Speeches and Public Letters of Joseph Howe*, 1: 183; emphasis added.

77 Beck, *Joseph Howe*, 169–70.

78 Paul Romney, 'From the Types Riot to the Rebellion: Elite Ideology, Anti-Legal Sentiment, Political Violence, and the Rule of Law in Upper Canada,' *Ontario History* 79 (1987): 113–44; Romney, 'From Constitutionalism to Legalism: Trial by Jury, Responsible Government, and the Rule of Law in the Canadian Political Culture,' *Law and History Review* 7 (1989): 122–72; Barry Wright, 'The Ideological Dimensions of Law in Upper Canada: The Treason Proceedings of 1838,' *Criminal Justice History* (1989): 131–78; Wright, 'The Gourlay Affair: Seditious Libel and the Sedition Act in Upper Canada,' in *Canadian State Trials*, 1: 487–500.

79 David Howes, 'Property, God and Nature in the Thought of Sir John Beverley Robinson,' *McGill Law Journal* 30 (1985): 366–412; G. Blaine Baker, "So Elegant a Web': Providential Order and the Rule of Secular Law in Early Nineteenth-Century Upper Canada,' *University of Toronto Law Journal* 38 (1988): 184–205.

80 Paul Romney, 'Very Late Loyalist Fantasies: Nostalgic Tory History and the Rule of Law in Upper Canada,' in *Canadian Perspectives on Law and Society: Issues in Legal History*, ed. Wesley Pue and Barry Wright (Ottawa: Carleton University Press, 1988), 119–48; Wright, 'The Ideological Dimensions of Law in Upper Canada,' 131–78.

81 Paul Romney has gone so far as to term the opposition to Mackenzie a 'criminal conspiracy.' See Romney, 'Rebel as Magistrate: William Lyon Mackenzie and His Enemies,' in *Essays in the History of Canadian Law*, vol. 5, *Crime and Criminal Justice*, ed. Jim Phillips, Tina Loo, and Susan Lewthwaite (Toronto: Osgoode Society, 1994), 324–46.

82 Peter Oliver, *'Terror to Evil-Doers': Prisons and Punishment in Nineteenth-Century Ontario* (Toronto: Osgoode Society, 1998), chap. 3.

83 See Gerald M. Craig, *Upper Canada: The Formative Years, 1784–1841* (Toronto: McClelland & Stewart, 1963), chap. 10; Jane Errington, *The Lion, the Eagle, and Upper Canada: A Developing Colonial Ideology* (Montreal and Kingston: McGill-Queen's University Press, 1987).

84 *Constitution* (Toronto), 12 July 1837, as quoted in Colin Read and Ronald Stagg, eds., *The Rebellion of 1837 in Upper Canada* (Ottawa: Carleton University Press, 1988), 42.

85 Colin Read and Ronald Stagg, 'Introduction,' in *Rebellion of 1837*, xxv.

86 *Constitution* (Toronto), 2 August 1837, as quoted in Read and Stagg, eds., *Rebellion of 1837*, 61–2.

87 For recent analysis of the treason trials, which have received considerable scholarly attention, see F. Murray Greenwood and Barry Wright, 'Rebellion, Invasion, and the Crisis of the Colonial State in the Canadas, 1837–39,' Rainer Baehre, 'Trying the Rebels: Emergency Legislation and the Colonial

Executive's Overall Strategy in the Upper Canadian Rebellion,' and Paul
Romney and Barry Wright, 'The Toronto Treason Trials, March–May 1838,'
all in *Canadian State Trials*, vol. 2, *Rebellion and Invasion in the Canadas,
1837–39*, ed. F. Murray Greenwood and Barry Wright (Toronto: University
of Toronto Press for the Osgoode Society, 2002), 3–90.

88 Archives of Ontario, Colonial Office Papers, series 42 [hereafter CO/42],
vol. 446, MS 38, reel 66, Despatch from Arthur to Lord Glenelg, 23 April
1838.

89 Wright, 'The Ideological Dimensions of Law in Upper Canada,' 135.

90 *The Christian Guardian* (Toronto), 14 March 1838.

91 Judge Robinson kept voluminous notes on the proceedings, and they con-
tain the only direct report on the trial. See Archives of Ontario, Robinson
Papers, 'Calendered Papers' (1838), MS 4, reel 4 [hereafter Robinson
Papers].

92 Read and Stagg, 'Introduction,' in *Rebellion of 1837*, xix–xxxiii; Ronald
Stagg, 'Peter Matthews,' in *Provincial Justice*, 314–15.

93 At the sentencing, Baldwin objected that the indictment was too vague,
but he was too late: Robinson's report cites only a simple guilty verdict in
reply. See Robinson Papers, report on Special Commission, 29 March 1838.

94 CO/42/446, Executive Council Minutes, March–April 1838, despatch
from Arthur to Glenelg, 14 April 1838.

95 CO/42/446, Arthur to Glenelg, 29 March 1838.

96 Letter dated 27 March 1838, in *The Arthur Papers: Being the Canadian Papers
... of the Last Lieutenant-Governor of Upper Canada*, ed. C. Sanderson (Toronto: University of Toronto Press, 1957), vol. 1, 67 [hereafter Arthur
Papers].

97 The petition and Arthur's response are appended to his report to Glenelg,
see CO/42/446, Despatch from Arthur to Lord Glenelg, 23 April 1838.

98 *Patriot*, 19 January 1838, as quoted and discussed in J.C. Dent, *The Story of
the Upper Canadian Rebellion*, vol. 1 (Toronto: C. Blackett Robinson, 1885),
246–7.

99 Ronald J. Stagg, 'Samuel Lount,' and 'Peter Matthews,' in *Dictionary of
Canadian Biography Online*, see http://www.biographi.ca/ (accessed 17
November 2007).

100 Mackenzie later reported that ruffians around the scaffold had dragged
Lount's body about the jail-yard, shouting, 'This is how every damned
rebel deserves to be used!' See *The Caroline Almanack* (1840), printed in
Rebellion of 1837, 393.

101 John Ryerson to Egerton Ryerson, 12 April 1838, in *Egerton Ryerson: His
Life and Letters*, vol. 1, ed. C.B. Sissions (Toronto: Clarke, Irwin, 1937), 448.

102 For example, several months later a letter by Mrs Lount addressed to Chief Justice Robinson, which recounted Lount's 'martyrdom,' was published in the colonial press. See Greg Keilty, ed., *1837: Revolution in the Canadas, as Told by William Lyon Mackenzie* (Toronto: NC Press, 1974), 206–7; *Christian Guardian*, 27 June 1838.

103 *Lord Durham's Report*, 2: 165–6.

104 CO/42/447, Executive Council Minutes, Arthur to Glenelg, 14 April 1838.

105 CO/42/447, Despatch from Glenelg to Arthur, 30 January 1838.

106 Executive Council Minutes, 31 March 1838, as quoted in Read and Stagg, eds., *Rebellion of 1837*, 385.

107 CO/42/447, Arthur to Glenelg, 14 April 1838. See also the extracts of the Executive Council Minutes reprinted in Read and Stagg, eds., *Rebellion of 1837*, 386.

108 CO/42/447, Arthur to Glenelg, 14 April 1838, 'Report of the Attorney-general on the cases of Samuel Lount and Peter Matthews convicted of high treason.'

109 CO/42/447, Arthur to Glenelg, 14 April 1838, Executive Council Minutes. Robinson apparently did not attend this last meeting.

110 CO/42/446, Glenelg to Arthur, 22 May 1838.

111 CO/42/447, Arthur to Glenelg, 14 April 1838.

112 See Wright, 'The Ideological Dimensions of Law in Upper Canada,' 148, 157.

113 Patrick Brode, *Sir John Beverley Robinson: Bone and Sinew of the Compact* (Toronto: The Osgoode Society, 1984), 190–1. On the broader debate over Robinson's politico-legal role, see Kenneth McNaught, 'Political Trials and the Canadian Political Tradition,' in *Courts and Trials: A Multidisciplinary Approach*, ed. M. Friedland (Toronto: University of Toronto Press, 1975); Howes, 'Property, God and Nature'; G. Blaine Baker, '"So Elegant a Web"'; Paul Romney, 'From the Types Riot to the Rebellion: Elite Ideology, Anti-Legal Sentiment, Political Violence, and the Rule of Law in Upper Canada,' *Ontario History* 79 (1987); Romney, 'Very Late Loyalist Fantasies.'

114 Arthur Papers, Robinson to Arthur, 16 April 1838.

115 Arthur Papers, Arthur to Robinson, 17 April 1838; emphasis in original.

116 On this point, see Barry Wright, "Harshness and Forbearance': The Politics of Pardons and the Upper Canada Rebellion,' in *Qualities of Mercy: Justice, Punishment, and Discretion*, ed. Carolyn Strange (Vancouver: UBC Press, 1996), 77–98.

117 J.M. Beattie, *Crime and the Courts in England, 1660–1800* (Princeton: Princeton University Press, 1986); V.A.C. Gatrell, *The Hanging Tree: Execution and the English People, 1770–1868* (Oxford: Oxford University Press, 1994);

Peter King, *Crime, Justice, and Discretion in England, 1740–1820* (Oxford: Oxford University Press, 2000); J.M. Beattie, *Policing and Punishment in London, 1660–1750: Urban Crime and the Limits to Terror* (Oxford: Oxford University Press, 2001).

118 Douglas Hay, 'Property, Authority and the Criminal Law,' in Douglas Hay et al., *Albion's Fatal Tree: Crime and Society in Eighteenth-Century England* (New York: Pantheon, 1975). On the impact of Hay's work, see David Garland, *Punishment and Modern Society: A Study in Social Theory* (Oxford: Oxford University Press, 1990).

119 E.P. Thompson, *Whigs and Hunters: The Origins of the Black Act*, 2nd ed. (London: Penguin, 1977), 258–69; Thompson, *Customs in Common: Studies in Traditional Popular Culture* (New York: The New Press, 1991). On the application of Thompson's model in colonial legal cultures, see David Neal, *The Rule of Law in a Penal Colony: Law and Power in Early New South Wales* (Cambridge: Cambridge University Press, 1991).

120 See the *Christian Guardian*, 14 March, 4 April 1838; *Egerton Ryerson: His Life and Letters*, 1: 448.

121 Robinson Papers, MS 4, reel 4, Calendered Papers, 1838, 'Address of the Honourable Chief Justice; on passing sentence of death upon Samuel Lount and Peter Matthews.' See also *Christian Guardian*, 4 April 1838.

122 McNaught, 'Political Trials,' 143.

123 *Christian Guardian*, 14 March 1838.

124 On the influence of Locke on Anglo-American culture, see Gillian Brown, *The Consent of the Governed: The Lockean Legacy in Early American Culture* (Cambridge, MA: Harvard University Press, 2001); Lee Ward, *The Politics of Liberty in England and Revolutionary America* (Cambridge: Cambridge University Press, 2004).

125 Brode, *John Beverley Robinson*, 198; McNaught, 'Political Trials,' 141–3. To make his case for the 'essentially Lockean' character of Robinson's principles, McNaught lists a series of quotations that resemble the work of John Locke.

126 K.D. McRae, 'Louis Hartz's Concept of the Fragment Society and Its Application to Canada, *Études Canadiennes / Canadian Studies* 5 (1978): 21; David Bell, 'The Loyalist Tradition in Canada,' *Journal of Canadian Studies* 5 (1970): 22–5; Robert E. Saunders, 'Sir John Beverley Robinson,' *Dictionary of Canadian Biography Online*, see http://www.biographi.ca/ (accessed 17 November 2007).

127 Robinson Papers, 'Address of the Honourable Chief Justice.' See also *Christian Guardian*, 4 April 1838.

128 Robinson Papers, 'Address of the Honourable Chief Justice.'

129 John Locke, *Second Treatise of Government*, ed. T. Peardon (New York: Macmillan, 1986 [1690]), 70–1.

130 On the distinction between the Lockean and Jeffersonian formulae, see Akhil Reed Amar, *The Bill of Rights: Creation and Reconstruction* (New Haven: Yale University Press, 1998), 78–9. It must be remembered that Locke's definition of property was broader than its current liberal usage in Canada.

131 This point is reiterated throughout Locke's *Second Treatise*, in sections 97, 123, 124, and 138.

132 Locke, *Second Treatise*, 72–3.

133 McKay argues that the liberal order relies on a belief in the epistemological and ontological primacy of the category 'individual,' rather than property, though this distinction may break down when one considers that Locke's definition of property encompasses the individual. See McKay, 'Liberal Order Framework,' 623–4. On Locke's definition of property, see Thomas Peardon's introduction to the *Second Treatise*, xiii; and Matthew Kramer, *John Locke and the Origins of Private Property* (Cambridge: Cambridge University Press, 1997), chap. 4.

134 Locke, *Second Treatise*, 72–3.

135 C.B. Macpherson, *The Political Theory of Possessive Individualism: Hobbes to Locke* (Oxford: Oxford University Press, 1962), 256.

136 Locke, *Second Treatise*, 124.

137 Ibid., 127–8.

138 It is also important to note that, unlike Locke, Robinson believed that the approval of Upper Canadian legislators was desirable but not essential to the province's governance. On this point see Brode, *John Beverley Robinson*, 190.

139 Robinson Papers, 'Address of the Honourable Chief Justice.' See also *Christian Guardian*, 4 April 1838; emphasis in original.

140 Locke, *Second Treatise*, 107.

141 Craig, *Upper Canada*, 254; Read and Stagg, eds., *Rebellion of 1837*, xciii.

142 John Van Arnam to Sir George Arthur, 22 March 1838, as printed in Read and Stagg, eds., *Rebellion of 1837*, 416–17.

143 Quoted in the *Spectator* (Kingston), 18 May 1838.

144 William Ryerson to Egerton Ryerson, 4 May 1838, in *Egerton Ryerson*, 459–61.

145 D.J. MacMahon, 'Law and Public Authority: Sir John Beverley and the Purposes of the Criminal Law,' *University of Toronto Faculty of Law Review* 46 (1988): 409–22.

146 Locke, *Second Treatise*, 68.

147 Edmund Burke had singled out the lack of experience and poor quality of the leaders of Revolutionary France and concluded, 'The property of France does not govern it.' See *Reflections on the Revolution in France*, ed. Conor Cruise O'Brien (London: Penguin, 1968), 128, 141.

148 In his review of the *Historical Atlas of Canada*, Pierson commented, 'Often one gets the feeling that Canada needs the States as a kind of *Struwwelpeter*, an example of how not to behave.' See Stuart Pierson, *Hard-Headed and Big-Hearted: Writing Newfoundland*, ed. Stan Dragland (St John's: Pennywell Books, 2006), 64.

149 In making this claim, I am drawing on Lauren Benton's notion of legal culture. Paraphrasing Clifford Geertz, Benton argues that 'the global institutional order has its origins in the stories that people tell themselves about others.' See Benton, *Law and Colonial Cultures*, 263. On the decline of the concept of 'othering' in anthropology, see Robert Darnton's reminiscence, 'On Clifford Geertz: Fieldnotes from the Classroom,' *New York Review of Books* 54, 1 (11 January 2007).

150 On the other hand, there is a pressing need to reassess the influence of American pragmatism on Canada during this period. Canadian historians have tended mistakenly to portray pragmatism as a lack of political principles. On the origins and development of pragmatism, see Louis Menand, *The Metaphysical Club: A Story of Ideas in America* (New York: Farrar, Straus, and Giroux, 2001).

151 William Harrison Woodward, *A Short History of the Expansion of the British Empire, 1500–1902* (Cambridge: Cambridge University Press, 1911), 260–1.

152 The relative lack of direct public criticism of Britain's conduct of the war underscored how deeply loyalism had become ingrained in mainstream English Canada. On the construction of English Canadian war myths, see Jonathan Vance, *Death So Noble: Memory, Meaning, and the First World War* (Vancouver: UBC Press, 1997).

153 See J.L. Granatstein, *Who Killed Canadian History?* (Toronto: HarperCollins, 1998); A.B. Mckillop, 'Who Killed Canadian History? A View from the Trenches,' *Canadian Historical Review* 80 (June 1999): 269–300. It is a telling fact that the liveliest discussions on H-Canada almost always focus on the perceived problem of why Canadian history is unpopular. See the discussion logs at http://www.h-net.org/~canada.

154 McKay, 'Liberal Order Framework,' 621.

155 Louis Hartz, *The Liberal Tradition in America* (New York: Harcourt Brace, 1955); Louis Hartz, ed., *The Founding of New Societies* (New York: Harcourt Brace, 1964).

156 S.F. Wise, 'Liberal Consensus or Ideological Battleground: Some Reflec-

tions on the Hartz Thesis,' Canadian Historical Association *Historical Papers*, 1974: 1–14.

157 H.D. Forbes, 'Hartz-Horowitz at Twenty: Nationalism, Toryism, and Socialism in Canada and the United States,' *Canadian Journal of Political Science* 2 (1987): 287–315; Peter Smith, 'Civic Humanism vs. Liberalism: Fitting the Loyalists In,' *Journal of Canadian Studies* 26 (1991): 25–43; Janet Ajzenstat and Peter J. Smith, 'The 'Tory Touch' Thesis: Bad History, Poor Political Science,' in *Crosscurrents: Contemporary Political Issues*, ed. Mark Charlton and Paul Barker, 3rd ed. (Toronto: Nelson, 1988), 84–90.

158 Gad Horowitz, 'Conservatism, Liberalism, and Socialism in Canada: An Interpretation (1966),' in *The Development of Political Thought in Canada: An Anthology*, ed. Katherine Fierlbeck (Toronto: Broadview Press, 2005), 228. Horowitz's article, which is perhaps the most reprinted study in Canadian political science, originally appeared in 1966 in the *Canadian Journal of Political Science*.

159 Jacques Monet, *The Last Cannon Shot: A Study of French-Canadian Nationalism, 1837–1850* (Toronto: University of Toronto Press, 1969). For more recent studies of the relationship between French Canada and British imperialism, see H.V. Nelles, *The Art of Nation-Building: Pageantry and Spectacle at Quebec's Tercentenary* (Toronto: University of Toronto Press, 1999); Serge Courville, *Immigration, colonisation et propagande: Du rêve américain au rêve colonial* (Sainte-Foy: Éditions MultiMondes, 2002); Serge Courville, 'Part of the British Empire, Too: French Canada and Colonization Propaganda, in *Canada and the British World: Culture, Migration, and Identity*, ed. Phillip Buckner and R. Douglas Francis (Vancouver: University of British Columbia Press, 2006), 129–41.

160 As Carl Berger noted, historians of Quebec writing in English have tended to emphasize political accommodation rather than conflict. See Carl Berger, *The Writing of Canadian History: Aspects of English-Canadian Historical Writing since 1900*, 2nd ed. (Toronto: University of Toronto Press, 1986), 289.

161 Janet Ajzenstat, *The Political Thought of Lord Durham* (Montreal and Kingston: McGill-Queen's University Press, 1988).

162 Janet Ajzenstat, 'The Conservatism of the Canadian Founders,' in *After Liberalism: Essays in Search of Freedom, Virtue, and Order*, ed. William Gairdner (Toronto: Stoddart, 1998), 17–32; Peter J. Smith and Janet Ajzenstat, 'Canada's Origins: The New Debate,' *National History* 1 (1997): 113–26; Ajzenstat, *The Once and Future Canadian Democracy: An Essay in Political Thought* (Montreal and Kingston: McGill-Queen's University Press, 2003).

163 Janet Ajzenstat and P.J. Smith, eds., *Canada's Origins: Liberal, Tory, or Republican?* (Ottawa: Carleton University Press, 1995).

164 Katherine Fierlbeck, *Political Thought in Canada: An Intellectual History* (Toronto: Broadview Press, 2006), 91.

165 J.G.A. Pocock, *The Machiavellian Moment: Florentine Political Thought and the Atlantic Republican Tradition*, 2nd ed. (Princeton: Princeton University Press, 2003); Gordon S. Wood, *The Radicalism of the American Revolution* (New York: Knopf, 1992).

166 Douglas Bradburn, review of Lee Ward, *The Politics of Liberty in England and Revolutionary America* (Cambridge University Press, 2004), published online by H-Atlantic (May 2005), 4. See http://www.h-net.org/~atlantic/ (accessed 17 November 2007).

167 Janet Ajzenstat, *The Canadian Founding: John Locke and Parliament* (Montreal and Kingston: McGill-Queen's University Press, 2007); Katherine Fierlbeck, 'Canada: More Liberal than Tory?' *Literary Review of Canada* 15, 6 (2007): 6–7.

168 J.M. Bumsted, *Understanding the Loyalists* (Sackville: Mount Alison University Centre for Canadian Studies, 1986), 39.

169 Robert M. Calhoon, 'Loyalism and Neutrality,' in *The Blackwell Encyclopedia of the American Revolution*, ed. Jack P. Greene and J.R. Pole (Oxford: Blackwell, 1991), 247–59; Andrew Jackson O'Shaughnessy, *An Empire Divided: The American Revolution and the British Caribbean* (Philadelphia: University of Pennsylvania Press, 2000).

170 H.G. Koenigsberger, 'Composite States, Representative Institutions and the American Revolution,' *Historical Research: The Bulletin of the Institute of Historical Research* 62 (1989): 135–53; J.H. Elliott, 'A Europe of Composite Monarchies,' *Past and Present* 137 (1992): 48–71; P.J. Marshall, 'Empire and Authority in the Later Eighteenth Century,' *Journal of Imperial and Commonwealth History* 15 (1987): 105–22.

171 John Porter, *The Vertical Mosaic: An Analysis of Social Class and Power in Canada* (Toronto: University of Toronto Press, 1965); James Curtis and Richard Helmes-Hayes, eds., *The Vertical Mosaic Revisited* (Toronto: University of Toronto Press, 1998).

172 It is important to distinguish between illiberal politics, on the one hand, and antiliberalism as an intellectual tradition, on the other. I am referring to illiberal acts of governments that generally adhere to liberal principles, not the ideology of intellectuals opposed to liberalism. On antiliberalism, see Stephen Holmes, *The Anatomy of Antiliberalism* (Cambridge, MA: Harvard University Press, 1993).

173 Howard Doughty, 'Thought Across the 49th Parallel,' *The College Quarterly*

7 (2004): 1. Doughty refers to 'counter-revolutionary, tory Canada,' which he presents as the antithesis of Lockean liberalism.

174 *Oxford English Dictionary*, online version. See http://www.oed.com (accessed 17 November 2007).

175 For an extreme version of the counter-revolutionary hypothesis, see Larry E. Tise, *The American Counterrevolution: A Retreat from Liberty, 1783–1800* (Mechanicsburg, PA: Stackpole Books, 1999).

176 30 & 31 Vic., c. 3, s. 91 (1867).

177 According to an official Government of Canada website titled 'Canadians and Their Government: A Resource Guide,' POGG occupies a central place in our national culture: 'Indeed, the phrase "peace, order and good government" has become meaningful to Canadians and defines Canadian values in a way that is comparable to "liberté, égalité, fraternité" in France or "life, liberty and the pursuit of happiness" in the United States. It is a phrase that truly articulates the journey toward peaceful accommodation throughout Canada's evolution as a nation. This process, in itself, is reason enough to feel proud of Canada's accomplishments since before Confederation.' See http://www.canadianheritage.gc.ca/special/gouv-gov/section1/infobox1_e.cfm (accessed 17 November 2007). On the popular and legal meanings of POGG, see *Dictionary of Canadian Law*, ed. Daphne Dukelow and Betsy Nuse, 2nd ed. (Toronto: Carswell, 1995), 328; Gerald L. Gall, *The Canadian Legal System*, 4th ed. (Toronto: Carswell, 1995), chaps. 4–5; and 'Peace, Order and Good Government,' by A.A. McLellan (revised by Gerald Gall), in the online *Canadian Encyclopedia*, http://www.thecanadianencyclopedia.com (accessed 17 November 2007).

178 Preamble to part I of the Constitution Act, 1982.

179 On the development of the RCMP's cultural image, which represents perhaps the ultimate marriage of liberalism and loyalism, see Michael Dawson, *The Mountie from Dime Novel to Disney* (Toronto: Between the Lines, 1998).

180 I am not suggesting that such distinctions should be read solely along party lines: intra-party differences also deserve close scholarly attention. On this point, see Daniel Cere, 'Not Much New in Ignatieff's Vision of Liberalism,' *Globe and Mail*, web exclusive comment posted on 5 April 2006. See http://www.theglobeandmail.com (accessed 17 November 2007).

181 See Michael Adams, *Fire and Ice: The United States, Canada, and the Myth of Converging Values* (Toronto: Penguin, 2004). The best summary of the diverging-values thesis that I have seen in the English Canadian press is Doug Saunders, 'Why Canadians Are the New Americans,' *Globe and Mail*, 3 January 2004, F2.

182 On the decline of English Canada as a 'British Country,' see José Igartua, *The Other Quiet Revolution: National Identities in English Canada, 1945–71* (Vancouver: UBC Press, 2006).

183 See the June 2006 issue of *The Walrus* (vol. 3), which has this manifesto splashed across the front cover: 'NATIONAL DREAMS ... That Canada be united by a vigorous Ottawa; that we build great cities; that we recognize America for the rough beast that it is.' It contains nationalist articles by Roy Romanow, Alan Broadbent, and Mark Kingwell. Interestingly, the 'Features' section lists, under the heading 'National Dreams,' 'Three reports on the future of Canada and the United States.' The dream of Canada, it would seem, is inseparable from the nightmare of the American republic.

184 Mark Kingwell, 'On Life, Liberty, and the Pursuit of Upward Mobility,' *The Walrus* 3, 5 (2006): 64–72. According to Kingwell, 'The American dream is a zombie virus, consuming resources and citizens alike in an endless round of renewed desire and positional goods, obscuring the realities of class and race, erasing evidence of difference.' Under this ideological view, the world's problems are the result of Americanism, not liberalism: Canadians are thus exonerated, since our problems can be blamed on an alien virus rather than ourselves.

185 See the special forums devoted to anti-Americanism in both the *American Historical Review* 111, 4 (October 2006), and the *Journal of American History* 93, 2 (September 2006).

Rights Talk and the Liberal Order Framework

E.A. HEAMAN[1]

Ian McKay's article on the history of the liberal order in Canada has been attracting a great deal of attention since it appeared late in 2000.[2] It is an exciting article: it thinks big and suggests ways of pulling together a great deal of eclectic material in something like a master narrative, but one innocent of the Whiggish nationalist teleologies that have characterized most grand narratives in Canadian history. Students find it useful and provocative. It promises to revitalize political history in Canada and, in eschewing bloodless objectivity, to provoke exciting debates. In the spirit of praise, rather than criticism, therefore, I will make two general objections to the piece, regarding the discussion of liberties and the discussion of conservatism, with hopes of encouraging further debate and investigation. A more nuanced account of liberties, conservatism, and the connections between them, would suggest an alternative political tradition that was not quite submerged within hegemonic liberalism.

First, the article doesn't have much to say about liberty. The link between liberty and liberalism is more than nominal and does much to account for the political ideology's successes. Liberalism provided an important means for criticizing the forms of authority that preceded it: despotic and theocratic authority in particular. The origins of liberalism may lie in one phrase, 'the liberty of the subject.' If there is an early and key concept that gives shape and meaning to the subsequent development of liberalism as a political ideology, it is that phrase, as it appears in the title of the Habeas Corpus Act of 1679, entitled 'An Act for the better securing the liberty of the subject, and for prevention of imprisonments beyond the seas.' This act was aimed at preventing Crown officials from throwing people in prison almost interminably on grounds of very slight and vague insinuations of treason. In other words, political liberties such as habeas corpus are key to liberalism. Habeas corpus predates liberalism – existing at least since the twelfth century – but it was legally codified in 1679 and quickly became one of the foundation stones of legitimacy in Britain.[3] Before liberalism became hegemonic, and itself the means of rationalizing authority, its strength lay in its power as an instrument to criticize authority. Even in its hegemonic condition, the ways in which it constrains state powers are as important as the ways in which it empowers the state. We discard or undermine those constraints at our peril.

But if liberties are key to liberalism, they don't seem to be key to the liberal order as sketched out by Ian McKay in the article published in the *Canadian Historical Review*. McKay identifies the four most important constituents of liberalism as individualism, property, liberty, and equality. But further discussion of liberties is limited to a quick dismissive itemization – freedom of the press, freedom of labour, etc. – and an even more dismissive reference to the notion that 'Freedom wears a crown.' McKay has a good deal to say about individualism and property, which he considers the most important constituents of liberalism, while equality gets only slightly more attention than does liberty. In other words, McKay's liberalism doesn't include liberty in any serious way. Why might this be the case?

One reason might be political expediency. McKay is out to attack liberalism, but it's not clear that he wants to attack liberties. Perhaps he focuses on the darker side of liberalism because civil liberties remain vulnerable in the modern world. Indeed, given McKay's left-wing proclivities, given the fact that basic liberties like habeas corpus are endangered in a country very near ours and one that our current political masters apparently yearn to imitate, I suspect he's a fairly militant defender of civil liberties, and even of individual liberties.

But that's not a very interesting explanation and not a very respectful one to such a thoughtful scholar. I think there is a different explanation – namely, that liberties haven't been particularly central to the history of liberalism in Canada. It will be my contention that rights were, as McKay suggests, trumped by property and individualism in hegemonic liberal discourse, though I don't think that that is the end of the story. Rights talk remained an important feature of non-liberal discourse and was not the most useless tool for critics of liberal hegemony.

McKay's article dismisses rights quickly because rights, like equality, were marginal to modern liberalism, in comparison to the absolute centrality of property and individualism. The argument for the primacy of property doesn't originate with McKay, but has been one of the leading criticisms or explanations of liberalism for many years. McKay cites C.B. Macpherson's classic study of liberalism from Hobbes to Locke: according to Macpherson, Hobbes placed modern man in the marketplace, characterizing him as an owner of himself within a competitive market-oriented society, whereas Locke enshrined property as the major *raison d'être* of society: 'The great and chief end, therefore, of Mens uniting into Commonwealths, and putting themselves under Government, is the Preservation of their Property.'[4] Political historians have argued that liberties in the West survived precisely because they constituted a form of property. J.M. Hexter remarks: 'The spectrum of liberties was as varied as the rights of rule or authority that the lords of the land had. Liberties, that is to say, were treated as if they were property. Since property was one of the things that all who had it most ardently strove to keep, all through the West communities invested sizeable amounts of thought, energy and armed force in seeing to it that all their property, including their property in their liberties, was secure.'[5] And many others from David Hume to John Hall have insisted on the importance of merchants and commerce to the maintenance of civil liberties in general.

The argument is contestable – Jeffrey McNairn contests it in this collection – but I'm inclined to agree with McKay's argument for the primacy of property and individualism in modern liberalism and particularly in its hegemonic version. Once liberalism became hegemonic, it became all about justifying power in place rather than about instrumentalizing critiques of that power. And from that perspective, liberalism has shaded into conservatism, understanding conservatism to be a defence of the existing structures of authority (whether that authority be based on divine right, rational self-interest, or tradition). Liberalism has proved an extraordinarily successful apologist for existing structures of authority, so long as it could point to some aspect of individual rights and liberties as being represented in those structures of authority. By establishing hierarchies of rights according to something like the standard McKay lays out, liberalism was able to neglect some more radical elements of rights talk in favour of more conservative elements.

Many examples could be cited in favour of this line of reasoning. I'll cite only two, one drawn from the general literature of conservative liberalism and one from Canadian political discourse. They are two foundational texts for Canadian liberal conservatism. By liberal conservatism I refer to a discourse of liberalism, rooted in rights, but one that consciously styled itself in opposition to the more radical forms of liberalism in circulation. I'm using the phrase to postpone a more searching discussion of the relationship between liberalism and conservatism.

First, inevitably, Edmund Burke's *Reflections on the Revolution in France*. This is justly celebrated as one of the most important expressions of modern conservatism, albeit a conservatism rooted in liberal principles. Burke took on the task of explaining the difference between the Glorious Revolution of 1688 and the French Revolution of 1789. He sought to justify the one while condemning the other. According to Burke, there were some conditions under which populations might reasonably rise up against a tyrannous king, but those conditions were not in place in France, they could not be stated as any sort of systematic principle, and the act of interrupting legitimate descent of the kingship should be made as conservative as possible, with the least possible deviation from traditional forms and principles of succession.

Burke discussed property very explicitly, explaining precisely why large proprietors should have an influence in politics out of all proportion to their number or ability. The large proprietors, represented in the House of Lords, were, Burke argued, 'at the very worst, the ballast in the vessel of the commonwealth.' They saved it from being buffeted by rationalism. The ability of the vigorous few, the envy of the impoverished many – these had to be reined in from attacking or undermining property. Moreover, the best safeguard of property, large or small, was great masses of property: it formed 'a natural rampart about the lesser properties in all their gradations.'[6] The passage amounts to a defence of massive inequalities of wealth and enormous disproportions in political representation, on the grounds that this would best safeguard the existing form of authority. Property reinforced authority more effectively than other liberal principles; therefore, if a liberal order was to be maintained, it had to place property first. And, famously, John A. Macdonald, leader of the Liberal Conservative Party in Canada, took exactly this position at the Quebec conference in the lead-up to Confederation when he explained the reason for instituting an appointed upper house with a property qualification: 'The rights of the minority must be protected, and the rich are always fewer in number than the poor.'[7] Again, in 1870, as prime minister, arguing for a property qualification for voters, and against the notion that an education should suffice, Macdonald observed that 'the right of property ought to be respected, and it did not follow that a man because he had an education therefore was interested in the country; for there was no greater cause of disturbance than an ill-regulated intellect.'[8] Macdonald, in short, shared Burke's preference for property over brains or ability as the only reliable basis for good citizenship.

A second example, this one drawn from Canadian constitutional history: the 'Rivers and Streams' controversy of the 1880s. This is a notorious case for anyone interested in constitutional history: it established the precedent that the federal government could not veto provincial legislation that wasn't *ultra vires*. Given the centrality of property to liberal politics, it is no wonder that Macdonald thought he could win Rivers and Streams by invoking personal property rights over some sort of commons rights. Of course, the confrontation wasn't styled as such in the Commons – the Tories insisted that Peter McLaren was being despoiled of his property when the Ontario government forced him to permit rival lumbermen to float their logs down 'his' stream. In McLaren's favour was an 1849 law that declared unnavigable streams to be subject to private ownership, and McLaren also claimed that the improvements (which cost him $250,000) were only sufficient to let one man float his logs, not two or more. By this reasoning, according to the Tories, to let Boyd Caldwell use the stream at all was to despoil McLaren.[9] 'What property would be safe?' asked Macdonald, if this Ontario law were permitted to stand. 'What man would make an investment in this country? Would capitalists come to Canada if the rights of property were taken away, as was attempted under this Bill.'[10]

The Liberals said the same thing of federal disallowance, insisting that McLaren's attempt to control a navigable river fundamentally impeded the development of the province. This too was an argument from property – that of the province as a whole, and its interest in economic development. The Liberals argued from private property and private right as well: McLaren was forcing the local farmers and lumberers to sell their wood to him cheaply because they had no other way of getting it out. The Liberals also brought in the most venerable of Liberal arguments in favour of self-government and the rule of law, which, Laurier claimed, Macdonald was subverting by having 'two different ways of dealing, one for their friends and one for their enemies.'

Both Liberals and Tories invoked arguments from property rights, therefore, but property rights were much more central and important to the government's argument. Liberal spokesman Edward Blake observed, 'I am a friend to the preservation of the rights of property ...

but I believe in the subordination of those rights to the public good.'[11] Tory D'Alton McCarthy, by contrast, prioritized property rights over all others and went so far as to suggest that they alone could justify federal disallowance of provincial legislation. McCarthy was well aware of the contrast between this case and the federal government's refusal to exercise the veto when New Brunswick abolished separate schooling shortly after Confederation. Robert Vipond's account explains the distinctions but without paying particular attention to the centrality of property. But, according to McCarthy, the fact that property was involved in the Rivers and Streams case meant that the federal government could not but act:

> I do not intend to discuss the vexed question of the New Brunswick school law. It was, however, one of policy and not of vested rights. It was not discussed as destruction of property or of right, but as an improper exercise of legislative power in a matter on which men might well differ. The line is broadly and clearly drawn between a matter of that kind and this. If a private Bill had been allowed to pass the Local Legislature, and handing over one man's property to another, that would have been a good reason for vetoing the Bill.[12]

Alas for the government, the Judicial Committee of the Privy Council upheld Ontario's case.[13]

This is just one of many examples that could be provided whereby the Canadian government testified, in good Lockean form, that its most essential mission was the protection of property rights. So I'm not disposed to quarrel with McKay's contention that hegemonic liberalism was characterized by an obsession with property, and with individual autonomy which was also at issue in this case. One could multiply the examples – Jerry Bannister's paper in this collection provides another important one.

Studies that expose the historical trade-offs made between rights in general and property rights, or between individualism and collectivism, and that debunk the ways in which liberal ideologies and liberal techniques of hegemony were used to gain popular support for reactionary policies and structures have long been a staple of Canadian historiography and of history-writing more generally. Some of these debunkers have been Marxists. Others have been liberals, and here one might invoke Charles Beard's 1913 book *An Economic Interpretation of the Constitution of the United States* or Frank Underhill's comparable short pieces reflecting on political parties and liberalism in Canada, articles that insisted on the predominant role of businessmen in shaping Canadian policies.[14] It is in this vein that Thomas Frank, in *What's the Matter with Kansas?* undertakes to explain why this hardworking and impoverished heartland, once staunchly Democratic, now supports the Republican Party.[15] In the hands of such commentators, liberalism remains a powerful instrument for criticizing authority. They problematize the philosophy of self-interest at the heart of liberalism by revealing how a rhetoric of public spiritedness makes the interests of the many seem to coincide with the interests of the powerful few.

Still, there have been other ways of talking about rights. Even Karl Marx admitted something to that effect – that mostly the bourgeoisie, when it talked rights, meant property rights, individualism, and the like, rights designed to retrench bourgeois authority, but that nonetheless political emancipation, freedom of association, and freedom of the press were real accomplishments and improvements.[16]

In Canada there were other ways of talking about rights, even at the heyday of liberal hegemony. Some of them emanated from within liberalism, but others did not. And this is my second objection to McKay's article – that he joins too much in the tendency of recent historians to write conservatism out of Canadian history altogether. It's a tendency that began with Louis Hartz's theory that North America constituted a 'liberal fragment': formed in the image of Lockean liberalism, it could never overcome that decisive moment of origin. Even the Loyalists, though they were far to the right of the revolutionaries, nonetheless still subscribed to the basic tenets of Lockean liberalism.[17] Hartz's fairly simplistic account has been superseded by the 'Atlantic' interpretation of political history. Drawing on J.G.A. Pocock's argument that Machiavellian republicanism shaped American revolutionary discourse, historians have argued that, in Canada, political confrontations in the early nineteenth century were between liberals and republicanists, and that conservatism wasn't a serious feature of the debate.[18] McKay, rightly to my mind, criticizes this scholarship on the grounds that it doesn't root the ideologies in culture, economics, and social development but instead makes personalities of them. But a more grounded history of liberalism and republicanism would still be misleading because it would exaggerate the hold that liberalism had in nineteenth-century Canada.

Drawing on examples of rights talk, I'll suggest that there was a conservative discourse about rights and one that was quite seriously incompatible with liberalism in either its radical or its hegemonic forms. The rights-speak emanating from political authorities was, by and large, designed to prop up structures of power and authority throughout society. But there were other sources of rights talk in Canada. I'm not going to say a great deal about liberal critics of hegemonic liberalism, but I do want to signal their presence. The *Rouges* espoused a form of liberalism that was deeply concerned with universal human rights, rationally understood, that is to say, with liberal rights in the classic theoretical sense of the concept. These were tied up with property rights but weren't so wholly subordinated to property rights as when the ruling government talked of rights. Indeed, to no small degree the *rouges* inherited their talk of universal human rights from the rebels of the 1830s, who had grown frustrated by the British refusal to concede 'British' constitutional rights to Canadians and had begun openly to espouse republican views. Often, these views were grounded in abstract and universal human rights. Robert Nelson's Declaration of Independence of 1838 began by declaring 'That under the free government of Lower Canada, all citizens shall have the same rights' – even Aboriginal peoples. There could be no distinctions between citizens: all must have the same, universal rights, which were constructed on rational rather than historical grounds.

So I do not want to deny that there were liberal discourses of rights in Canada. But this sort of liberalism has, to my mind, been well studied previously by such scholars as Yvan Lamonde.[19] Michel Ducharme's recent dissertation nicely reviews the developing political polarization after 1828 in Upper and Lower Canada, inserting this discourse into recent Atlantic historiography that characterizes the polarization not as liberal versus conservative but, rather, as a confrontation between Lockean liberals and civic humanists drawing on a republican tradition inspired by Machiavelli and Rousseau.[20] Ducharme distinguishes between liberal and republican uses of the phrase or concept of liberty: liberal liberty was the classical variety, concerned with commercial rights and individualism, while republican liberty amounted to participation in the polis. That is to say, liberty and democracy were interchangeable. Whereas property trumped liberty in liberal discourse, democracy trumped liberty in republican discourse – leaving liberty itself something of an empty shell, to my mind.

Here, I'm going to look at something else – conservative discourses about rights. There existed a vibrant tradition of conservative rights talk in Canada, and at certain times and places it could serve as an important instrument for criticizing authority. As the liberals, in power, became apologists for the status quo, conservative opponents of liberalism became critics of that status quo and, by the same token, critics of the established authority. This reversal of positions can be traced back to the origins of liberalism. As the Whigs began to temper the radical universalist message of liberalism, by watering down the talk of rights, they made rights useful to conservatives. Conservatives could then use the language of liberty to defend people whom they felt liberalism was neglecting. Sometimes, as when they defended the wealthy and landed, conservatives provided only a modest variation on liberalism. But not infrequently conservatives took the part of people marginalized by liberal hegemony, including native people and the dependent poor, and tried to find ways of supporting them that were outside the liberal order. They were spectacularly unsuccessful on the whole and, as Jean-Marie Fecteau has shown, their efforts paradoxically entrenched liberalism all the more thoroughly in Quebec.[21] Nonetheless, I do want to draw attention to the history of conservative rights talk in Canada on the grounds that it reveals a more diverse cultural and political climate than McKay's short article might lead one to expect. Drawing on a range of key documents thrown up during moments of political controversy and crisis, during the 1760s, the 1830s, and the 1870s, I will seek to demonstrate that a continuous conservative discourse of rights predated hegemonic liberalism and continued to mount a serious challenge to it at the heyday of that hegemony. My object is not to identify a new group of conservative liberals or liberal conservatives but, rather, to identify some of the ways that people talked about rights within contexts and according to projects that are best understood as conservative. Liberals did not hold a monopoly on rights talk, and a whole spectrum of conservative positions was advanced under the banner of 'rights.'

When conservatives talked of rights, they didn't talk of abstract and universal human rights. Their rights weren't liberal rights but were, rather, collective, social, or historical rights, rights that were actually incompatible with hegemonic liberalism and that made the work of abstract and individualistic liberalism all the more difficult. One important source for this discourse was the concept of specifically *British* rights – the rights of Englishmen and British subjects. These were rooted in historical relations rather than abstract definitions, and indeed were developed quite precisely as a counterweight to abstract individual or human rights, that is to say, universal principles that, conservative political thinkers soon noticed, could be politically unsettling, not to say explosive. As Leo Strauss observed, in *Natural Right and History:* 'For the recognition of universal principles forces man to judge the established order, or what is actual here and now, in the light of the natural or rational order; and what is actual here and now is more likely than not to fall short of the universal and unchangeable norm.'[22] To the likes of Edmund Burke, the French Revolution epitomized all the dangers of the appeal to universal and abstract principles of human nature and human rights. This was a specifically eighteenth-century problem, created by the emergence of liberalism in the seventeenth. Apologists for established authority had to mediate between that concern and the powerful appeal of rights talk. They found, according to Strauss, 'a safe and solid middle ground between antisocial individualism and unnatural universality' in rights of 'local and temporal variety.' While the French Revolution made the problem particularly acute in the late eighteenth and early nineteenth centuries, other historians have observed that the rightward swing of the Whigs occurred long before the French Revolution. H.T. Dickinson remarked that both Whigs and Tories had moderated their positions by the early eighteenth century: while the Tories had abandoned divine right and hereditary succession, most Whigs 'preferred to defend the ancient constitution rather than the sovereignty of the people.'[23] That is to say, they abandoned abstract rights for historical ones. Many of these rights were spelled out ten years after the Habeas Corpus Act in the English Bill of Rights of 1689, including the rule of law, the right to a jury, the right to bear arms (if Protestant), a prohibition on excessive or cruel fines or punishments, and a series of parliamentary privileges and powers (such as free speech and control of taxation and armies). These were 'the known laws and statutes and freedom of this realm' that James II had broken.[24]

Abstract and historical rights were not inherently incompatible, but liberal-leaning and Tory-leaning commentators tended to prioritize them differently. Liberals, for the most part, privileged abstract rights over geographically, temporally, or socially restricted rights. As in Nelson's Declaration of Independence, equal rights came first, followed by more specific rights regarding bankruptcy legislation, property registration, and so forth. By contrast, conservative commentators insisted on the priority of historical rights, often on the grounds that rights couldn't reasonably be understood outside of history. According to the English jurist William Blackstone, author of the extremely influential *Commentaries on the Laws of England* (1765–9), English rights, like the English constitution generally, reflected a happy conjunction of natural order and historical development: natural rights had perished or been debased in every other country and remained 'in a peculiar and emphatical manner' only in England.[25]

Long before the French revolution, invoking the rights of the British subject had become a tradition in Canada. As early as 1764, British subjects settling in Montreal were beginning to agitate for what they saw as their rights as Englishmen. A manifesto of sorts appeared on a church door with a list of pointed questions for 'those in authority,' including: 'Whether or not they think a British subject, is visited with certain Rights & Privileges by the Magna Carta? Whether he forfeits those Rights by entering a Garrison Town?'[26] This was the beginning of a sustained campaign by Britons in Montreal demanding their rights and liberties as British subjects and criticizing the military rule of the conquered province. The merchants' protest against Governor James Murray and their remonstrances and petitions were filled with invocations of the trampled rights of Britons: a good example, perhaps, of the use of rights talk as a tool for criticizing arbitrary authority. Murray didn't see it that way, but instead denounced both the former soldiers and the 'set of free British merchants, as they are pleased to stile themselves,' who 'claim a sort of right to lord it over the vanquished.'[27] Interestingly, it was Murray rather than the leader of the merchants' party, the rapidly republicanizing Thomas Walker, who used the language of 'rights of Man' to denounce the beating and mutilation of Walker by soldiers – clearly the intention in this case was to refer not to a constitutional right but to the more basic human need for bodily integrity. This was not a specifically *British* right because similar protection of law would doubtless have been provided to foreign visitors to the province.

The vagueness of these purported 'British' rights, the lack of a written constitution or charter of rights, made the argument all the more useful, because the limits of loyalty could never be quite delineated. If the rights of British subjects included the right to political representation and to parliamentary institutions, then the colonials could fervently demand that their local legislatures be self-governing in the manner of the British parliament. Indeed, in the absence of an elected legislature, in 1764 the Grand Jury of Quebec insisted that the parallel with parliament be drawn with their body. As the Grand Jury was, its members claimed, the only representative body in the colony, its members, as Britons, should be consulted on any legislation to be passed.[28] Their claim that the Grand Jury fulfilled the representative function of the British legislature had little tradition behind it – but nonetheless the claim was made based on creative interpretation of tradition rather than an abstraction. Precisely because Canada was not Britain, and the historical and constitutional circumstances could not be identical, the argument for greater reform in the image of British precedent, to make Canada more like Britain and Canadian customs and liberties more like the British, was an always fertile source of inspiration. And while the Board of Trade, in response to the presentation, objected to the proceedings (as occurring in English and confounding the French members), it did concede that the king would 'give utmost attention and consideration to all proper representation from Canadians.' In effect, it recognized a right to representation, but preserved the power to determine what counted as 'proper' representation.[29]

The point I want to make here is that talk of the rights of the British subject were very quickly in full swing in Canada, used both to criticize authority and, in Murray's case, to defend it. But qua political rights these were very much historical British rights rather than liberal abstractions. The fact that they were historical meant that they were social not individual. They owed everything to the individual's relationship to place, neighbour, authority, and nothing to the abstract accoutrements of the human being. They were intended to enforce rather than erase political relationships based upon rank, which McKay signals as one of the important pre-liberal forms of organization. For the early British merchants settling in Montreal in particular, insistence upon the rights of British subjects was intended to ensure that the British-born dominated political institutions from which Catholics were to be excluded. The effect would have been nearly to abolish representation, with the few Protestants then resident composing the legislature (with a very small ratio of representation) and the many Catholics unrepresented by their peers. Thus, it bears repeating, the early introduction of purportedly liberal ideas like civil and political rights, in Canada, was put to deeply conservative uses.

The early British merchants thought that these rights, being historical rather than abstract, were their own private property rather than a property shared with 'the king's new subjects.' They were wrong. Precisely because they were historical, anyone with a history textbook in their hand and an oath of fealty to the British crown at their lips could claim to inherit them. Indeed, beginning in September 1765, a series of letters appeared in the Quebec *Gazette*, written by a French Canadian, that claimed full possession of the historic rights of British subjects, as descended from the Magna Carta. The author, in what amounted to a protest against the Stamp Act, held those historic rights up to standards of reason, public interest, and commerce, and found them lacking.[30] Once again, creative interpretation of the purported rights of British subjects could be put to all sorts of uses. Indeed, throughout the century or so after the Conquest, Canadians – French and English alike – turned 'the rights of the British subject' into a powerful argument in favour of constitutional reforms.

On the other hand, it wasn't clear to political commentators the extent to which these historical customs and rights could be transferred to peoples without history – namely Canada's Aboriginal population. Sidney Harring contrasts the 'liberal' treatment afforded white settlers and Native peoples: the term implied benevolence and paternalism, but in the former case this meant free lands and material support for settlement; in the latter case it meant 'minimal educational and social support, designed to speed up their assimilation.'[31] As I've argued elsewhere, Native people were seen to be outside the liberal public sphere, devoid of such qualifications as literacy, property, even reasoning power.[32] They did have contractual rights and they might also maintain some form of bodily human rights – protection against murder for example and perhaps starvation as well – but they weren't outfitted with the specifically British rights that the other ethnic groups could claim. Indeed, because their customs and habits weren't British, the Native peoples had no right to them: it wasn't abstract customs and habits that the British constitution protected but only specifically British ones. This was made explicit, for example, in the 1847 'Report on the Affairs of the Indians in Canada,' commissioned by Sir Charles Bagot. The opening pages explained that the Crown offered its paternal protection to Canadian Indians 'in compensation for the rights and independence which they have lost.' Likewise, the Commissioners recommended a program of education for 'the Indian youth' that 'must consist not merely of the training of the mind, but of a weaning from the habits and feelings of their ancestors, and the acquirements of the language, arts, and customs of civilized life.'[33] Thus, according to the reporters, Indians qua Indians had no rights and no legitimate customs, and couldn't have either until they had been educated up to the rightful practice of both these forms of British liberties. Advocates for aboriginal rights like Peter Jones, the Anishinabek leader and Methodist minister, responded to such diatribes by arguing that 'many of the Indians are sufficiently instructed in the knowledge of civil affairs to be able to use the rights of British subjects as judiciously as many of their white neighbours,' and he urged their emancipation.[34]

It cannot be denied that the arguments for British rights were probably most effective when deployed by those of British origin or descent, such as the Loyalists. As Bannister has shown, for the Loyalists the discourse of liberalism was a counter-revolutionary discourse. This was liberalism used not to check authority but to check popular sovereignty, a process, as we've seen, well established in British tradition almost from the moment of the Glorious Revolution. Bannister's paper focuses on property as the instrument of tacit consent: the government protected the property of Lount and Matthews and therefore rebellion was intolerable.

The same argument can be made with regard to rights talk – that it too was counter-revolutionary. Here is a passage from a slightly earlier document, dated 1825: '[T]he British nation is the most intellectual, and moral in Europe – The World's centre of arts, commerce and civilization. Here the light of freedom burns with the brightest radiance, and the rights and liberties of man are the best understood and most abundantly enjoyed; and here a lofty sense of independence is of universal growth.'[35] This sounds like it might be a manifesto by liberal reformers or republicans – in fact it comes from one of the most conservative documents that we have: Bishop Strachan's sermon on the death of Bishop Mountain – a manifesto in favour of an established Anglican clergy and something other than religious freedom. For Strachan, despite the references to 'rights and liberties of man,' those rights and liberties were British and historical rather than abstract and it was, he insisted, his object to see them fully established in the British colony. They were what we might call socially constructed rights: they functioned effectively only where an established church with control of education held sway:

> It is to religion that she owes her pre-eminence – it is this that throws a holy splendour round her head, makes her the hope of every land, and urges her to achieve the evangelization of mankind. Never without a religious establishment could she have soared so high above other nations – it is this that diffuses through her whole population, the most sublime and disinterested principles, which, refining the sentiments and elevating the affections, enable them to subdue the selfish passions and appetites, and to pant after the felicity of doing good.[36]

With its insistence on an absolute, rigorously defined, ostentatiously Christian public good and on a heavy-handed authority to uphold the much-admired liberties, this passage cannot be taken as liberalism in any simple or obvious way. If there was any such thing as Toryism in Canada, then surely John Strachan epitomized it, as S.F. Wise has argued based on a reading of his sermons.[37] And indeed, whereas William Lyon Mackenzie's draft constitution did not begin, like Nelson's Declaration, by insisting on universal human rights, it did begin with a long list of specific traditional and conservative 'liberties' dear to the heart of the Family Compact and that Mackenzie's ideal republic would abolish. There would be no established religion, no state encouragement for any religion, no clergy reserves, no priests in the legislature, and, clause number five, no exemptions from any law based upon 'tenure, estate, charter, degree, birth, or place.' Number six abolished hereditary privileges and honours, while number seven abolished their converse, slavery.[38] Whatever Mackenzie's debt to republicanism, it cannot be doubted that this was a confrontation between two liberalisms: one abstract, universal, and individualistic, and the other rooted in tradition, culture, and group rights.

Because appeals to British liberties were unimpeachably loyal, they were particularly useful to French Canadian politicians, both conservative and reform-minded. Whatever rights French Canadians had in Canada could only be understood as British rights. Thus, French Canadian reformers very frequently, especially in the early years, insisted on their rights as British subjects. In 1822, for example, Louis-Joseph Papineau denounced attempts to unite the Canadas by insisting on the rights of French Canadians, who, he proclaimed, 'are not foreigners in this the land of their birth; they claim rights as British subjects, in common with every other subject of His Majesty in these Colonies. These are their birth rights.'[39] From this perspective, Lord Durham's description of the French Canadians as a people with 'no history and no literature' was not comparable to the European refusal to recognize aboriginal history. Durham wanted to point out that the French Canadians read French rather than British or Canadian history and literature and, therefore, were at a remove from British or Canadian culture, as from French culture itself, so drastically changed by the Revolution. The argument is made explicit in the remainder of the paragraph:

They are a people with no history, and no literature. The literature of England is written in a language which is not theirs; and the only literature which their language renders familiar to them, is that of a nation from which they have been separated by eighty years of a foreign rule, and still more by those changes which the Revolution and its consequences have wrought in the whole political, moral and social state of France. [40]

The disconnect would have been all the greater if, indeed, French political discourse appealed to human rights, whereas British political discourse appealed to ethnic ones. Certainly, Laurier capitalized on this dichotomy in his famous speech of 1877 when he denounced European liberty, 'its history written in letters of blood,' and lauded the more moderate British variety. Yvan Lamonde describes Laurier's speech as marking the end point of the *rouge* tradition in Quebec. Henceforth, the oppositional stage would largely be left to the right-wing critics of liberalism. [41]

I'm especially interested in rights talk by churchmen, because the origins of liberalism lay in opposition to the power of the churches. Whether or not Britons in Canada were part of a liberal 'fragment,' the same cannot be said of the ultramontanes. They engaged in rights talk, but theirs was not a liberal discourse. Ultramontane leaders were openly hostile to the very concept of universal rights, seeing them as unwarrantable rationalism and independence of thought. [42] The ultramontanes were primarily concerned with the rights of collectivities, like the French Canadians, and of the Catholic Church itself, rights that dated back to specific promises made at the time of the Conquest. Thus, the Conquest simultaneously provided for a language of specific 'British' rights but also a specific set of 'Catholic' rights. One late-nineteenth-century textbook of Quebec history observed that when Canada became British, it was well understood that the inhabitants all became British subjects, complete with the right to practise their religion, preserve their possessions, and be governed by laws of their own making, even if they did suffer from other disqualifications such as the Test Act. [43]

Insistence on the Church's rights and liberties pervade the writings of ultramontanes in the late nineteenth century. One example is the circular letter denouncing liberalism signed by all the Quebec bishops in 1875. The 'liberal Catholic,' the bishops argued in that letter, 'invented pretended rights on behalf of a false liberty.' Meanwhile, true rights and liberties were threatened, like those of the Church: 'When the state invades the rights of the Church, and tramples under foot its most sacred privileges, as to-day happens in Italy, France and Switzerland, would it not be the height of derision to give to this same state the right to gag its victim?' [44] In short, they didn't see any contradiction between denouncing liberalism and defending liberties, liberties necessary to upholding the greater human goal of a Christian civilization, organized around the common good rather than around individualism.

Again, the Programme Catholique of 1871 isn't the place one would expect to find rights talk. These documents were anti-liberal manifestos, places where words and principles were carefully chosen. Again, the authors defended the liberties and rights not of individuals, but the collective rights of the Catholic Church: 'Thus it is with cause that the religious press complains that our laws on marriage, on education, on the erection of parishes, and on the registration of civil status are defective in so far as they diminish the rights of the Church, limit its liberty, hamper its administration, or are open to a hostile interpretation.' Ignace Bourget, the ultramontane bishop of Montreal, wrote to F.X.A. Trudel, the author of the Programme, in June 1871, that he supported it in principle for the sake of his beloved country which, he explained, would not be free unless the freedom of the Church was respected, with all its rights guaranteed and assured.[45]

In short, rights talk was as likely to be in the service of anti-liberals as of liberals. And those anti-liberals had as much influence as did the liberals in determining the development of the dominant political discourse. This wasn't simply liberal hegemony: it was serious resistance of a sort that the left might well envy. C.B. Macpherson identifies the root of liberal individualism, found in seventeenth-century political discourse, as follows: 'Its possessive quality is found in its conception of the individual as essentially the proprietor of his own person or capacities, owing nothing to society for them. The individual was seen neither as a moral whole, nor as a part of a larger social whole, but as an owner of himself.'[46] This simply doesn't describe the deeply religious perspectives put forward by the ultramontanes, for whom every individual was a moral whole, a soul, as well as a member of the Christian collectivity that determined the teleology of the human being. Humans weren't proprietors of themselves so much as authorized borrowers of capacities granted by and owed to God.

None of this is to disagree with Jean-Marie Fecteau's argument that, when it came to the construction of a liberal society, the ultramontanes were more Catholic than the pope. Fecteau sees remarkable parallels between the anti-statism of the Church and that of the late-nineteenth-century liberals, and notes that together they constructed a minimalist, liberal state in Quebec. Fecteau is interested in the extent to which the Catholics constructed a model of society that cohered with that of their arch-enemies. Given that, unlike McKay, Fecteau does organize his study around liberty rather than property, this would seem to be a damning indictment of my argument. The church, he observes, like the state, was pursuing hegemony and the result was moral regulation and authority. The Church, he insists, was more interested in truth and authority than in freedom, and some churchmen went so far as to describe even freedom of religion as a necessary evil.[47]

Fecteau's book amounts to a detailed description of the very limited sorts of freedom available in modern liberal democracy – and one could say the same of other Canadian historians working on state formation in Canada, in such books as *Colonial Leviathan*,[48] who convincingly argue that 'freedom' must always be understood to have quotations marks around it in modern liberal democracies. As McKay, among others, suggests, it was often violently imposed and violently resisted by communities clinging to their own moral and political sensibilities: to what E.P. Thompson called, in the context of the early modern bread riot, a 'moral economy.'[49] This leftist critique, whether inspired by Marx or by Foucault, has provided the best deconstruction of an aggressive and imperialistic liberalism that claims to monopolize 'freedom' in the modern world. Nonetheless, it has tended to overshadow the older critiques of liberalism even when it has tried to recapture them.

Take, for example, the classic liberal line of argument, developed by Hobbes and Locke in the seventeenth century, that life without the modern state was 'poor, nasty, brutish and short' and that the 'king of a large and fruitful territory' in America 'feeds, lodges, and is clad worse than a day-labourer in England.'[50] Long before, explorers to Canada, from André Thevet to Samuel de Champlain, observed of the peoples found along the St Lawrence that they were much freer than Europeans, enjoying freedom from religion, freedom from law, and freedom from authority, but that they were materially much worse off than Europeans and that there was a trade-off between well-being and freedom.[51] The ensuing debate about the 'noble savage' would seem somewhat removed from mainstream conservative political discourse. Few conservatives would prefer some sort of quintessential, aboriginal human freedom to the constraints and protections of liberal society.

And yet, precisely because Canada continued to have a western frontier that juxtaposed freedom and liberal society, that choice seemed to be, to some small degree, on offer. For conservative critics of liberalism, the contrast between the freedom of the frontier and liberal constraint nurtured the possibility of a fairly searching critique of the prevailing orthodoxy. The frontier was symbolically constituted as the antithesis of civilization, but it was also a place of alternative civilization where humans managed to rule themselves more or less effectively without liberal institutions. From that perspective, liberal institutions were an obvious threat and imposition. Examples can be found in some of the writings around the uprising at Red River in 1869–70: the Declaration of Rights issued by the rebels and the apologias on behalf of those rebels voiced by the bishop of St-Boniface, A.A. Taché. Taché provides an interesting counterpoint to Bannister's John Beverly Robinson: whereas the latter drew upon the relationship between rights and property to denounce rebellion, the former saw in it grounds for defending rebellion. Without revisiting the causes and content of the Red River Rebellion in any serious detail, I wish to focus on these texts in order to insist on the vitality of conservative rights talk as a political tradition. It could not, ultimately, withstand the hegemonic liberal state, but it could and did sustain a deep vein of resistance. And it is with this tradition in mind that we can, perhaps, make better sense of some of the linguistic peculiarities of these texts. Their positions were far from identical: Frits Pannekoek insists on the political distance between Riel and Taché.[52] Nonetheless, it is somewhat striking to see a certain shared hostility to liberal rule and a degree of solidarity for an uprising against that rule, at once radical and conservative. Ian Angus has recently argued that Riel was far too radical for Canadian political traditions and has become acceptable, even today, only to the extent that the Métis were 'recognized by Ottawa to be, or be willing to become, rights-bearing Englishmen, and thus he has been banished to the extent that the Métis claimed an original self-constitution.'[53] His arguments capture current political debates perfectly, but they miss the creative symbiosis between conservatism and radical alterity in the 1870s and 1880s.

According to Bishop Taché, their most direct link to Canadian and Catholic orthodoxy, the Métis rose up against the imposition of Canadian rule in the region because they feared being driven from the land by racist bigots from Canada who wanted to turn the prairies into another Ontario. Abstract human rights would have been little protection against this threat: recognition of their existing customs and rights, and material assistance in creating economic opportunities, were more likely to be useful to them and to guarantee their continued presence in the Assiniboine region. The Métis may well have learned ambivalence towards liberalism from Taché, who had voiced concern openly the previous year in a *Sketch of the North-West of America*, surveying the land, the resources, flora and fauna, inhabitants, and the political condition of the territory.

Taché described Rupert's Land as extraordinarily free: 'Excepting the difficulties to be met with in traveling, there is no country under the sun in which greater freedom is enjoyed, and this, notwithstanding the impression spread abroad that the [Hudson's Bay] Company holds the country in a half enslaved state.' As for the northern and western reaches of the Northwest Territories, 'The Home Government entirely disregard it; no established colony does or can exercise any authority in it; nobody in it has any rights or privileges; and the country is without law, without government, without administration, and without civil or legal jurisdiction.'[54] Remarkably, Taché seemed to think that this sort of freedom was preferable to the introduction of civil society. Presented with the classic Lockean choice between freedom and well-being, Taché preferred freedom. Similarly, in Red River itself, Taché predicted that the encroachment of civilization would probably improve the country, but only at the expense of the existing population, and he concluded, therefore, that 'we very much dread some of the promised changes.' Taché realized all too well that liberalism, whether concerned with property or with political rights, wouldn't adequately protect the Métis from the onslaught of colonization; that, as Tina Loo has observed for Aboriginal peoples in early British Columbia, the paternalism of the Hudson Bay Company's club law was, to some degree, better than an impersonal rule of law.[55] And of course Taché was quickly proved correct. In 1870, half of the members of the Manitoba legislature were Métis; by 1880, following a decade of immigration, much of it aggressively Protestant, Métis accounted for only four of the twenty-four members. The Métis were politically eclipsed and the legislature relaxed its concerns for their rights.

Taché revisited the origins of the liberal order, so to speak. His remarks seem drawn from outside mainstream, post-Hobbesian liberal discourse. Nonetheless, his writings and testimony were sprinkled with classic rights talk as well, as were the complaints of the provisional government. Taché passed on to the federal government the rebels' insistence on their rights as British subjects, rights that the rebels felt were being thwarted. Taché went so far as to dismiss the murder of Thomas Scott on the grounds that he wasn't the only British subject murdered in these parts; the Métis too were being murdered and no action was taken, no rule of law enforced. Taché demanded equal justice.[56]

What Taché said carefully and cautiously, the Métis rebels declared more directly. They chose the most natural and provocative format open to rebels who claimed to act with political authority: the revolutionary declaration. When Louis Riel's provisional government at Red

River issued a Declaration of the People of Rupert's Land and of the Northwest, complete with 'List of Rights,' it followed in the footsteps of Robert Nelson, as well as the American and French revolutionaries. But this declaration lacked the abstract liberalism of its predecessors. From this perspective, the differences between the title and the content of the document are striking. The Red River list of rights included demands for political representation and universal male suffrage, but the other demands were all particularly grounded – a railway line, for example, a steamship line, the use of both English and French in courts and legislature, and 'recognition of all rights, customs, and habits already acquired.'[57] These demands were neither liberal nor abstract nor individualistic. They were not unlike the sorts of demands for privileges being voiced by ultramontanes, and of course Catholicism was an important influence over many of the Métis, and especially over Louis Riel. They also, doubtless, owed something to the success that Aboriginal peoples of Canada had had over many years negotiating and petitioning not for abstract or even British rights but for recognition of particular local and ethnic rights to, say, exclusive hunting and fishing on the banks of a given river. These sorts of rights were not interchangeable: they invested people with privileges accrued over time. They more nearly resembled the insistence on privileges by rank that predated liberalism when confronted with a hegemonic liberalism that could not permit particularisms and local privileges and customs any longer. Small wonder that when the first emissary from Canada, Joseph-Alfred-Norbert Provencher (secretary to the newly named governor, William McDougall), was sent ahead to promise them respect for 'existing rights without reference to race or religion,' he was rebuffed.[58]

Rebels and bishop could voice shared language, shared concepts to criticize the established authority, using a discourse of traditional rights, descended on both sides from their British heritage and also from their traditional customs, customs that had some right to be perpetuated even in the face of an expanding liberal imperialism. In another publication, written in the aftermath of the rebellion of 1885, Taché stood his ground: the legitimate demands of the Métis were ignored, shrugged away with the remark 'I don't speak French.' He continued: 'On a oublié qu'étant les enfants du sol, ils avaient des droits particuliers. Si, au moins, on avait voulu se souvenir qu'étant le lien naturel, les intermédiaires les plus efficaces entre les sauvages et les blancs, leur concours était comme nécessaire.'[59] His earlier writings had also made the point that the Red River settlement had 'acquired certain rights; it possesses or occupies lands for which it has not always paid: it has cultivated them with its labor. True, – the labor has not always been great; but we speak of a child of the desert. It commands indulgence; it presumes to hope that here the foreigner shall not be preferred, that in the great and wise plans matured by the Mother Country and Canada – its eldest brother, its past history may not be entirely disregarded.'[60]

Taché was here trying to mediate between a Lockean argument from property – these people live on and own the land – and recognition that, by Locke's terms, these people didn't really have any title to the land at all. Locke justified the appropriation of North America from the Native peoples on the grounds that they hadn't invested labour in it and hadn't improved it for mankind as the Europeans would. For Locke, an 'Indian' owned not the land but his labour alone. His property consisted only in things that he had hunted or gathered – deer, fish, and the like; therein 'begins the property.' The rest was a commons. Anyone could extract property from the commons through their labour, without requiring consent from inhabitants. 'If such a consent as that was necessary, man had starved, notwithstanding the plenty God had given him.'[61]

There were, thus, two liberal theories of property: the one concerned with the commons, traditionally protected by the English common law, and the other concerned with private property owned by individuals. Both were dearly held 'rights of Englishmen' and both trumped any claims that the state might make to a given piece of property (even under the Royal Proclamation of 1763), because the state was constituted by and for the defence of property. And, of course, both these theories of property conflicted with and undermined Aboriginal arguments in favour of traditional, exclusive, group rights to territories and resources. Ultimately, the combination of private and commercial interests and the common-law doctrine came close to eradicating any notion of Aboriginal rights in the years shortly after Confederation.[62]

Nonetheless, for Taché and the Métis, there was also, clearly, a non-Lockean claim that continued the conservative rights talk: a right to their continued way of life on the land, hunting the buffalo as they always had done, and thus a right that existed in their customs and traditions as a people, perhaps even as an Aboriginal people. More strikingly, their position was, to some small degree, shared by the prime minister, John A. Macdonald, a man of deeply conservative leanings. As superintendant of indian affairs, in 1881 Macdonald advocated dedicated 'fishing grounds which should be kept for the exclusive use of the Indians,' only to be overruled by the officials of the Department of Marine and Fisheries.[63] And again, with regard to the uprising of 1870, Macdonald thought that the Métis had legitimate grounds for discontent, having their sovereignty transferred without their consent. He was temporarily so befuddled by the claims to rights as 'enfants du sol' as to admit that the Métis had some sort of Aboriginal title to the land that required extinguishment, a right that he quickly repudiated in subsequent negotiations.[64] Nonetheless, he wasn't so befuddled that he admitted to any but property rights in the Manitoba Act, excepting only those clauses of the British North America Act of 1867 that safeguarded any separate (i.e., Catholic) schools that existed in law and practice, a guarantee that had already been proved worthless in New Brunswick. The Métis, aided by the Catholic Church, mounted a conservative challenge to liberal hegemony in central Canada, but in the end they lost their struggle for recognition of their customs and habits. Taché's most important function, in the end, was to negotiate with the Canadian government for some slight mitigation of the full penalty of the law that Ontario Orangemen wanted to see carried out on Riel and his co-conspirators. Taché, like the ultramontanes described by Fecteau, ultimately eased the establishment of the liberal order on the prairies.

To conclude, McKay might be in danger of exaggerating the attachment to abstract individualism in Canada if he sees rights talk as being generally conducive to that abstract individualism. Rights talk in Canada was as likely to be expressed by peoples who were not liberal and might even be anti-liberal. McKay might respond that this is hegemony at work: evidence of liberal compromises effected in order to appear to accommodate non-liberal groups. Of Quebec in particular, McKay insists upon the 'uncompromisingly liberal context within which such "accommodations" and "compromises" were made and which they were designed to preserve: these were less "compromises" than "bargains with liberal hegemony."' I don't find the argument fully convincing. The anti-liberal discourse of rights was as deeply entrenched in Canadian history as the liberal discourse: its lineage was as venerable and it was constantly replenished from a variety of quarters, including Anglicans, ultramontanes, and Native peoples. These were not minor, fragmented episodes of disagreement with mainstream liberalism: these groups did as much as the liberals to bring meaning to such basic concepts as 'liberties' and 'rights.' At times, their collaboration, as in Manitoba in 1870, could prove explosive. Their insistence that these rights were historically grounded and communal rather than individual helped to shape the conception of Canada that emerged. McKay's use of Antonio Gramsci's theory of hegemony provides an excellent intellectual framework for explaining the coexistence of liberalism and conservatism in such a way as to privilege liberalism, but I would respectfully suggest that the case won't be closed until some techniques for evaluating comparative weights of influence and some hard evidence have been added to the story. We need to know more about why Canadian peoples signed up for particular projects that could be described as 'liberal' from one perspective, but as collectivist and historical from another perspective, and we further need to know more about the extent to which they found what they wanted in those projects. Without that evidence it cannot be clear just how hegemonic, that is to say, intensive, liberalism truly was, and McKay's remains merely an intriguing hypothesis.

Nevertheless, McKay is very probably correct to imply that, historically, there has not been much attachment to liberal human rights in Canada, in liberal or conservative circles. One final case in point: the history of rights talk was transformed after the Second World War when the United Nations came out with its Universal Declaration of Human Rights. This became the inspiration for later bills and charters of rights that are familiar to us, such as those of Diefenbaker and Trudeau. The Universal Declaration was written by a Canadian, by McGill professor John Humphrey. Remarkably, when the Declaration was presented for deliberation, Canadian delegates actually voted against it, until they were shamed into reversing their position by American and British pressure. According to William A. Schabas, 'There was simply no "human rights culture" within the Department of External Affairs' among such figures as Lester Pearson, Escott Reid, or George Ignatieff.[65] I would suggest that the ambivalence towards liberal rights in mainstream Canada is a very old tradition.

NOTES

1 I would like to say thanks to the students in my Canadian conservatism seminar: Philippe Boisvert, Guy-Philippe Bouchard, Olivier Lajoie, Jonathan Laxer, Sarah McNally, and Emily Kingsland.
2 Ian McKay, 'The Liberal Order Framework: A Prospectus for a Reconnaissance of Canadian History,' *Canadian Historical Review* 81 (2000): 617–45.
3 Helen A. Nutting, 'The Most Wholesome Law – The Habeas Corpus Act of 1679,' *American Historical Review* 65 (1960): 527–43.

4 C.B. Macpherson, *The Political Theory of Possessive Individualism: Hobbes to Locke* (Oxford: Clarendon Press, 1962), 197–8.
5 In the *Times Literary Supplement*, quoted by John Hall, *Powers and Liberties: The Causes and Consequences of the Rise of the West* (Harmondsworth: Penguin, 1985), 159.
6 Edmund Burke, *Reflections on the Revolution in France* (London, 1790) available online at: http://socserv.mcmaster.ca/econ/ugcm/3ll3/burke/revfrance.pdf, 43–4.
7 In Michael Bliss, *Right Honourable Men: The Descent of Canadian Politics from Macdonald to Mulroney* (Toronto: HarperCollins, 1994), 11.
8 *Hansard*, 29 March 1870, 747. The same line of argument can be found in Adam Smith and early American conservatives: Jeff Sklansky, *The Soul's Economy: Market Society and Selfhood in American Thought, 1820–1920* (Chapel Hill: University of North Carolina Press, 2002), 27–8.
9 *Hansard*, 14 April 1882, 886.
10 Robert Gregory Lamot, 'The Politics of the Judiciary: The S.C.C. and the J.C.P.C. in late 19th century Ontario' (MA thesis, Carleton University, 1998), 96.
11 Ibid., 100.
12 *Hansard*, 14 April 1882, 894.
13 The JCPC ignored the question of jurisdiction and based its judgment on the intention behind early Upper Canadian laws on river improvements. See Lamot, 'The Politics of the Judiciary' and also Robert Vipond, *Liberty and Community: Canadian Federalism and the Failure of the Constitution* (Albany: SUNY Press, 1991).
14 Frank Underhill, 'The Development of National Political Parties in Canada,' and 'Some Reflections on the Liberal Tradition in Canada,' both reprinted in *In Search of Canadian Liberalism* (Toronto: Macmillan, 1961).
15 Thomas Frank, *What's the Matter with Kansas? How Conservatives won the Heart of America* (New York: Metropolitan Books, 2004).
16 Ann Talbot, 'Marx and Democratic Rights,' *WSWS*, 24 December 2005, at http://www.wsws.org/articles/2005/dec2005/evan-d24.shtml.
17 Kenneth McRae, 'The Structure of Canadian History,' in Louis Hartz, *The Founding of New Societies* (New York: Harcourt, Brace & World, 1964), 219–74; Gad Horowitz, 'Conservatism, Liberalism and Socialism in Canada: An Interpretation,' *Canadian Journal of Economic and Political Science* 32 (1966), 143–71; and the essays in Janet Ajzenstat and Peter J. Smith, eds., *Canada's Origins: Liberal, Tory, or Republican?* (Ottawa: Carleton University Press, 1995).
18 Ajzenstat and Smith, eds., *Canada's Origins*.
19 Yvan Lamonde, *Histoire sociale des idées au Québec* (St-Laurent: Fides, 2000).

20 Michel Ducharme, 'Aux fondements de l'État canadien: La liberté au Canada de 1776 à 1841' (PhD diss., McGill University, 2005).
21 Jean-Marie Fecteau, *La liberté du pauvre: Crime et pauvreté au XIXe siècle québécois* (Montreal: VLB, 2004).
22 Leo Strauss, *Natural Right and History* (Chicago: University of Chicago Press, 1958), 13–14.
23 H.T. Dickinson, *Liberty and Property: Political Ideology in Eighteenth-Century Britain* (London: Methuen, 1977), 93.
24 Available online at http://www.yale.edu/lawweb/avalon/england.htm as part of the Yale University Avalon Project.
25 See the discussion in Lynn Hunt, *Inventing Human Rights: A History* (New York: W.W. Norton, 2007), 119; also Wilfrid Prest, 'Sir William Blackstone (1723–1780),' in *Oxford Dictionary of National Biography* (Oxford University Press, September 2004); online ed., October 2006, at http://www.oxforddnb.com/view/article/2536.
26 Ralph Burton, Governor of Montreal, to the Board of Trade, February 1764, Library and Archives of Canada (LAC), CO 42 1, 169–72.
27 James Murray to the Board of Trade, 24 April 1764, in LAC, CO 42, 1, 155–60.
28 LAC, CO 42, 1, 24.
29 LAC, C series, 42.5, 1–3.
30 E.A. Heaman, 'Constructing Ignorance: Epistemic and Military Failures in Britain and Canada during the Seven Years War,' in *Essays in Honour of Michael Bliss: Figuring the Social*, ed. E.A. Heaman, Alison Li, and Shelley McKellar (Toronto: University of Toronto Press, 2008), 93–118.
31 Sidney L. Harring, *White Man's Law: Native People in Nineteenth-Century Canadian Jurisprudence* (Toronto: University of Toronto Press, 1998), 12.
32 E.A. Heaman, *The Inglorious Arts of Peace: Exhibitions in Canadian Society during the Nineteenth Century* (Toronto: University of Toronto Press, 1999).
33 'Report on the Affairs of the Indians in Canada,' *Appendix to the Sixth Volume of the Journals of the Legislative Assembly of the Province of Canada* (1847), app. T.
34 Peter Jones, *History of the Ojebway Indians* (London: A.W. Bennett, 1861), 217–18.
35 John Strachan, *A Sermon, Preached at York, Upper Canada, third of July 1825, on the death of the late lord bishop of Quebec* (Kingston: J. Macfarlane, 1826), 16.
36 Ibid., 16–17.
37 S.F. Wise, 'God's Peculiar Peoples' and 'Sermon Literature and Canadian Intellectual History,' both in S.F. Wise, *God's Peculiar Peoples: Essays on Polit-*

ical Culture in Nineteenth-Century Canada, ed. A.B. McKillop and Paul Romney (Ottawa: Carleton University Press, 1993). Other essays insist on the importance of the conservative tradition in Canadian history and criticize Louis Hartz and his school for neglecting it.

38 H.D. Forbes, ed., *Canadian Political Thought* (Toronto: Oxford University Press, 1985), 38.

39 Arthur G. Doughty and Norah Story, eds., *Documents Relating to the Constitutional History of Canada, 1819–1828* (Ottawa: Patenaude, 1935), 145. The two-page document contains several further references to French Canadian rights and liberties, as do many other similarly representative documents.

40 Lord Durham, *Report on the Affairs of British North America*, ed. Sir C.P. Lucas (Oxford: Clarendon, 1912), vol. 2, 294–5.

41 This is not to deny the importance of a more mainstream, conservative liberalism in Quebec, especially concerning economics. See Fernande Roy, *Progrès, harmonie, liberté: Le libéralisme des milieux d'affaires francophones à Montréal au tournant du siècle* (Montreal: Boréal, 1988).

42 See, for example, the discussion in Lamonde, *Histoire sociale des idées au Québec*, 342–4.

43 Instituteur Catholique, *Grandes lignes de l'histoire du Canada à l'usage des écoles primaires* (Montréal, Toronto: D. & J. Sadlier, 1894).

44 This document and the next are available in Forbes, *Canadian Political Thought*, 93–106 and online at http://www2.marianopolis.edu/quebechistory/index.htm.

45 'Je m'attache à ce principe parce que j'y vois le salut de ma chère patrie, qui ne sera véritablement libre qu'en autant que la liberté de l'Église y sera respectée, avec tous les droits qui seront assurés et garantis.' Robert Rumilly, *Histoire de la province de Québec*, vol. 1, George-Étienne Cartier; at http://www2.marianopolis.edu/quebechistory/index.htm.

46 Macpherson, *The Political Theory of Possessive Individualism*, 3.

47 Fecteau, *La liberté du pauvre*, esp. 276–83 and conclusion.

48 Allan Greer and Ian Radforth, eds., *Colonial Leviathan: State Formation in Mid-Nineteenth-Century Canada* (Toronto: University of Toronto Press, 1992).

49 E.P. Thompson, 'The Moral Economy of the English Crowd in the Eighteenth Century' and 'The Moral Economy Reviewed,' in *Customs in Common* (London: Merlin Press, 1991), 184–351.

50 John Locke, *Two Treatises on Government*, ed. Peter Laslett (Cambridge: Cambridge University Press, 1963), 339.

51 See Olive P. Dickason, *The Myth of the Savage and the Beginnings of French Colonialism in the Americas* (Edmonton: University of Alberta Press, 1997) and Gordon M. Sayre, *Les Sauvages Américains: Representations of Native*

Americans in French and English Colonial Literature (Chapel Hill: University of North Carolina Press, 1997).

52 Frits Pannekoek, *A Snug Little Flock: The Social Origins of the Riel Resistance of 1869–70* (Winnipeg: Watson & Dwyer, 1991).

53 Ian Angus, 'Louis Riel and English-Canadian Political Thought,' *University of Toronto Quarterly* 74 (2005): 885.

54 A.A. Taché, *Sketch of the North-West of America*, trans D.E. Cameron (Montreal: J. Lovell, 1870), 63, 66 and passim for what follows.

55 Tina Loo, *Making Law, Order and Authority in British Columbia, 1821–1871* (Toronto: University of Toronto Press, 1994).

56 A.A. Taché, *Histoire et origine des troubles du N-Ouest, racontées sous serment par Sa Grandeur Mgr. L'archevêque de St-Boniface* [1874].

57 '1. Un corps législatif élu; 2. Une représentation auprès du gouvernement canadien; 3. L'affectation de terres publiques à la construction de routes et d'écoles; 4. Un statut de langues officielles de la législature et des cours de justice, tant pour les Anglais que pour les Français; 5. Un lien rattachant Winnipeg à la voie ferrée la plus proche; 6. Le développement de la navigation à vapeur entre le lac Supérieur et la Rivière-Rouge dans les cinq années suivantes; 7. Le droit de vote pour tous les hommes ayant plus de 21 ans; 8. La reconnaissance de tous les "droits, coutumes et habitudes" déjà acquis.'

58 Provencher told the Métis that the new government would not interfere with 'religious or private rights.' *Correspondence Relative to the Recent Disturbances in the Red River Settlement Presented to Both Houses of Parliament By Command of Her Majesty, August 1870* (London: William Clowes and Sons, 1870), 4. The same volume also has the declaration of rights, 76.

59 A.A. Taché, *La Situation nord-ouest* (Quebec: J.O. Filteau, 1885), 10.

60 Taché, *Sketch of the North-West*, 69.

61 Locke, *Two Treatises*, chap. 5, 'On Property,' passim; see also Ian Shapiro, *The Evolution of Rights in Liberal Theory* (Cambridge: Cambridge University Press, 1986), 92.

62 Douglas C. Harris, *Fish, Law, and Colonialism: The Legal Capture of Salmon in British Columbia* (Toronto: University of Toronto Press, 2001), 32–3, 76, and passim. There is a growing literature on Aboriginal 'rights' and laws as set forth by British statute law, common law, and Aboriginal traditions. See, *inter alia*, Harring, *White Man's Law* and Louis A. Knafla and Jonathan Swainger, eds., *Laws and Societies in the Canadian Prairie West, 1670–1940* (Vancouver: UBC Press, 2005). Knafla further notes the gap between doctrine and practice: 'Common law doctrines lived in the courts and not in the theatre of politics and empire.' 'Introduction: Laws and Societies in the Anglo-Canadian North-West Frontier and Prairie Provinces, 1670–1940,' 9.

63 Harris, *Fish, Law, and Colonialism*, 32.
64 See the discussion by Thomas Flanagan, who clearly thinks that Macdonald slipped up in the Manitoba Act: *Riel and the Rebellion: 1885 Reconsidered*, 2nd ed. (Toronto: University of Toronto Press, 2000).
65 Norman Hillmer, 'The Universal Declaration of Human Rights,' *Canadian Encyclopedia*, accessed from http://canadianencyclopedia.ca, 27 February 2006; William A. Schabas, 'Canada and the Adoption of the *Universal Declaration of Human Rights*,' *McGill Law Journal* 43 (1998): 441. George Egerton identifies libertarian dismay at the Canadian government's position: 'Entering the Age of Human Rights: Religion, Politics, and Canadian Liberalism, 1945–50,' *Canadian Historical Review* 85 (2004): 451–79.

After 'Canada': Liberalisms, Social Theory, and Historical Analysis

BRUCE CURTIS

Ian McKay's generally good-natured attempt to propose a 'liberal order framework' for a new 'reconnaissance' of Canadian history is striking for its breadth of coverage of the historical literature, for its attempt to integrate a wide range of class-, gender-, and race-focused articles and monographs in a Gramscian analytic framework, and particularly for its welcome encouragement for historians to move beyond the '"top/ bottom" binarism' that, he rightly remarks, 'has condemned so much historiographical debate in Canada to a wearisome and fractious sterility.'[1] McKay proposes to treat 'Canada' not as a given entity with essential characteristics, but as the contested result of a political project. Against a functionalist-Marxist account, he sees the state as implicated in the never-finished, always-unstable quest for political hegemony in a universe where individual liberty, equality, and private property rights are valued. The suggestion is that the framework may allow historians to bridge large-scale structures and individual experiences, political arrangements in Ottawa and farmers' fences in Saskatchewan, while attending to key moments in struggles for liberal hegemony. This bridging exercise would not be a synthesis, but a way of linking diverse practices at different levels of scale. Given the hysterical disciplinary 'crisis talk' lurking about in both Canadian historical and sociological debate, this well-modulated attempt to reorient historical research is especially congenial.[2]

And yet, despite his evident desire to move beyond them, McKay's proposals seem to me to remain thoroughly bounded by the rather narrow limits of a set of political-economic preconceptions. He has gone some way towards a post-Marxist understanding of historical analysis and seems often to wish to go further. He moves away from a base/

superstructure model, noting its empirical problems, for instance.[3] He proposes to study liberalism as a political 'ideology' in its own right, rather than dismissing it as ideology altogether, that is, as a bourgeois deviation. The Gramscian concept of 'revolution from above' makes it possible for him to study the political organization and initiatives of ruling classes or 'groups,' rather than looking for sources of social transformation only in a putative proletariat or alliance of subordinate classes. And McKay writes that his neo-Marxist framework will 'not *necessarily* privilege economic and class relations as *the site*, but rather as a *crucial site*, of liberal rule. At a certain level of magnification,' he continues, 'it is as *crucial* to look at the power exerted by men over women, or by heterosexuals over homosexuals, as it is to attempt to trace all things back to class.'[4]

The last statement might be read as an encouraging gesture away from economic determinism and towards drawing feminist and queer theory into historical work, but to me it seems mealy-mouthed. For one can freely continue to privilege economic determinism without 'necessarily' privileging it. And since 'crucial' means 'decisive for the resolution of a contest,' McKay in fact writes that we must indeed continue to attempt to trace all things back to class, that economic and class relations are the decisive subject of analysis, although at some scale, which is not specified, gendered and sexualized relations might be just as important. At least, if this is not what he intends to say, in the absence of any clear alternative conception of analytic holism, and no alternative conceptualization of scale (homology, for instance), the base/superstructure model remains in play.[5]

Indeed, I suspect the popularity of the proposed framework stems from the fact that it allows for a leftish Canadian 'history as usual.' This historiography is mildly revisionist in relation to the stories of 'Great Men and War' still trumpeted by some. Instead, it champions familiar underdogs: workers, women, Aboriginal peoples, immigrants, the poor, and perhaps gays and lesbians. It does so while maintaining the importance of familiar events: the Durham report, responsible government, Confederation, North-west expansion, the National Policy, the accommodation of Quebec, and the development of the Criminal Code. It will allow history teachers to continue on as they have done while they remain comfortably insulated from the developments of the last several decades in social theory: the 'turns' to language, to culture, to practice, to hermeneutics.

What is most promising in McKay's proposal is that historians should frame their work around the development of liberalism, or, as I would prefer, around a liberal mode of government. Yet I argue that three things are necessary – and largely lacking in McKay's account – to make such a project productive. First, we need a broad view of liberalism as a mode of government in which state sovereignty frames ongoing practices of the government of individual freedom. Government works in the liberal mode through the attribution of important degrees of autonomy, self-direction, and responsibility to individuals, groups, and to fictive individuals such as corporations. Michèle Dagenais's essay in this volume stresses the importance of municipal government reform in this regard. Self-governing individuals, in their relations with one another, with nature-made-property, with institutions, and with state sovereignty are the objects of liberal projects of government within the territorial boundaries of the state. Moreover, as a mode of government, liberalism contains internal tensions that we must study. Such tensions include those between its pretensions to universalism and its practices of exclusion and those between its claims to rule through reason and its reliance on violence. These tensions shape its development and point to its limitations.

Second, I think we need to attend closely to the everyday moments of the liberal mode of government. 'Violence is a means specific to the state,' Max Weber reminds us, but it is not the normal or most common means of the state. The everyday means are to be found in administration.[6] Alongside the exceptional moments, such as the 1837 Rebellion, the Riel Rebellion, or the War Measures Act, and alongside the brutal history of 'blood and fire,' which Ian McKay highlights in his concluding remarks, are the unexceptional moments: frequently bland, minor technical or organizational shifts, which nonetheless shape and extend the capacities of the state system, and set or shape the terms of practice across areas of social life.

In short, liberal state formation is also a history of administration. While liberal state administration works to mediate conflict and struggle among social groups and classes, it also works with and shapes an object peculiarly its own: population. The category 'population' itself is a category of sovereignty and of liberal state formation, for only sovereign authority can work the magic that makes every occupant of territory the equivalent of any other, and that determines the nature and limits of this equivalence. Liberal state formation is inextricably bound up with biopolitics, the determination and management of the elementary conditions of legitimate life and death.

Third, and relatedly, I argue, we need a post-structuralist practice of historiography and a reflexive practice of historiography. Post-structuralism is not a unitary social theory, but a theoretical and analytic move that begins with the recognition that we cannot 'read off' or deduce practices from the structural locations or structurally determined identities of agents. The popular equation, structural location – defines interest – constitutes identity – determines action, simply doesn't hold.[7] Such an observation is not a declaration that systematic patterns of wealth, power, authority, domination, brutality, or exploitation no longer exist, or that they no longer have any determining force. Rather, it is a recognition, as Jeff McNairn also stresses in this volume, that historical agents make meaning and that any given set of circumstances or events is susceptible to multiple interpretation. Industrial workers vote for Adolf Hitler or Margaret Thatcher; battered wives believe it's their own fault; French Canadian farmers think reading should be left to the priest, but some priests think there should be a democratic republic. Denouncing such interpretations as instances of false consciousness – as deviations from material interests – conflates political and scientific judgment. Attentive analysts who attempt to treat structures as if they were rules of practice learn that there are no rules that specify how the rules of practice will be practised. Indeed, if interpretation could not trump (class) interest, the concept 'hegemony' would itself be useless. A reflexive historiography, as a reflexive sociology, is one that interrogates the concepts and instruments that it uses.

Liberalism and the Work of Foucault

In what follows, I outline a more substantial conception of liberal government than that proposed in McKay's article and I describe some of the concepts developed by Michel Foucault that I find useful in research and analysis. I am not equating Foucault's work with post-structuralism; rather, its post-structuralist categories and analytic strategies are among those that I find useful. It is striking to me that there is no serious Foucault-work in McKay's framework, despite the preoccupation of the later Foucault and many writers inspired by his work with liberal modes of government. McKay's essay does contain a bit of Foucault-creep: we hear the words 'panoptic,' 'discourse,' and 'governmentality' once each, for instance. But its state conception remains firmly located in the state / civil society binary, despite Gramsci's own tendencies to see state hegemony as increasingly anchored in civil society. Gramsci's interest in the creation of the 'new man' of Fordism could certainly be extended by Foucault's analysis of the constitution of subjectivity.[8] As well, the absence, on the whole, in McKay's essay of a serious notion of discourse prevents us from examining the truth effects of statements independent of their putative veracity. Foucault's own use of 'discourse' is commonly misunderstood,[9] but without the concept we remain trapped in the science/ideology distinction where the historian may claim privilege as the arbiter of truth. I will return to Foucault later in this essay.

We need a richer and more nuanced portrayal of liberalism than the Thatcherite doctrine presented in the McKay essay. In this libertarian liberalism, sovereign individuals are all formally equal and equally interested first and foremost in property rights. 'Society' appears as an alien and mythical imposition. But the radical libertarian conception of the social is only possible as an attack on a highly socialized state. It is certainly anachronistic and perhaps also teleological to see Thatcherism as the goal of a Canadian 'liberal revolution' in the nineteenth century. Perhaps for one version of a Gramscian political economy, this view may make it possible to portray liberals as opposed to the social, and hence to re-appropriate the social for working-class struggle. Such a tactic is facilitated when liberalism is presented as having no internal dynamic, no inherent developmental tensions, and no conception of the public good.[10] Yet historically and currently, the libertarian dimensions of liberal discourses were and are opposed by many liberals. Other central preoccupations found in liberal discourses – with civilization, pacification, and security, especially – are absent from the essay's rendition of Thatcherism.

One thing we can usefully learn from the history of Continental and colonial liberalisms is that liberal theoreticians and political activists saw the existence of individual liberty, equality, and security as dependent on and as conditioned by forms of self, social structures, institutional arrangements, and collective political forms, including a sovereign state monopoly over the means of violence. They worked to reconstruct relations and practices in a thorough-going manner such that rational liberty could in fact exist. These multifaceted attempts involved projects of an infrastructural sort through which the social conditions of possibility for liberal subjectivities would be inscribed in the nature of things, in the everyday arrangements to which everyone would be subject, and which in consequence would have a formative influence. For example, people could not enjoy the 'rational freedom' at the heart of liberal conceptions in a world that was opaque, contradictory, confused, or illegible, in a world that was not conducive to rational comprehension and the calculation of personal interest. Writers such as Thomas Jefferson and Jeremy Bentham thus promoted a systematic and universal reform of weights and measures and of currency; Bentham a complete codification of law; Bentham and Mill 'education for all'; Bentham and Chadwick a 'preventive police'; and so on.[11] Conversely, the rational individual had to be equipped with the capacities necessary for rationality: to read, to write, to cipher, to plan, to master its momentary impulses, to defer to those most rational in society. The rational individual not only *could* do such things, but *did* do them, *wanted* to do them, something coded as 'a taste for liberty.'[12] Liberal political theorists and reformers from the outset sought to restructure the world and to colonize individual subjectivities.

Liberty and security were dependent upon what eighteenth- and early-nineteenth-century writers described as a 'well-ordered police': clean, well-lit streets; appropriately sited bridges; the orderly assize of bread; piped water and mains sewers; polite children and orderly families. These conditions are expansive across the liberal mode of government; now one would include social security numbers, bar codes, drivers' licences, photo identification, and so on. Rational liberty is antithetical to dissolute personal habits, to irregular sexual unions, to religious idolatry, to sloth and disease. The point is that a liberal political order demands a systematic organization of the social, of collective conditions of life, and of individual conduct in relation to those conditions. And while those nineteenth-century political struggles that were subsumed under the banner of liberalism aimed at a representative state (at least outside the colonial situation) and expert administration, liberal struggles equally targeted sexual relations, leisure-time activities, the location of cemeteries, the consumption of alcohol and tobacco, and so on. Such struggles issued from a wide variety of locations and did not inevitably lead to the creation of state institutions. If we appreciate that liberal political projects are communal projects, the historical contrast is not, then, as McKay frequently suggests, between liberal individualism and Aboriginal or Catholic or socialist collectivism, but rather between competing or antagonistic forms of collectivism and of individuality. Individuality, as Marx observed, is a form of social relation. Nor is the relation between individual conduct and social order best seen as one of 'magnification': rather, the two are inextricably intertwined and figure indifferently in liberal projects.

That liberalism as a mode of government demands communal forms implies that it contains conceptions of the common good. Neglecting the place of the 'public interest' or of the 'good of society' in liberalism prevents us from engaging with moments of universality in Canadian development – the public educational project or the struggle against epidemic disease, movements for citizenship rights, for instance. We need not be naive about these, nor assume that claims about universality are not partial political claims that serve as vehicles for forms of domination, but liberal discourse has consistently presented itself as a discourse of universality.

It may be noted that denying the existence of liberal conceptions of the collectivity aligns McKay's project for a 'liberal order framework' with a resurgent Quebec sovereigntist historiography. Such recent work on civic republicanism as L.-G. Harvey's *Printemps de l'Amérique française* attacks the 'myth of liberalism' and the 'myth of the defeat of 1837,' seeks to rehabilitate the Lower Canadian patriot republicanism of the 1830s by distancing it as completely as possible from 'liberalism,' and recasts Quebec's political struggles as New World republican struggles.[13] Here too liberalism is seen as a thoroughly individualistic doctrine that championed market relations and capitalist accumulation against the simple agrarian collectivism imputed to the republican patriot movement. Patriot republicanism is said to have found its theoretical and ethical roots in the literature of Rome and Athens, in which its classically educated leadership had been steeped, not in the writings of Hobbes and Locke imbibed by the liberals.

One obvious problem with such attempts to divorce liberalism from republicanism and a conception of the common good, and to equate it to a narrow individualism, in contrast to a 'civic humanist' tradition, is that the leading European intellectuals and activists who came to see themselves as liberals were classically educated, well versed in Greek and Roman history. Like their classically educated Lower Canadian contemporaries, for instance, the English liberals with whom I am most familiar learned to debate at university and continued to do so in groups such as the London Debating Society after they left.[14] They were often open admirers of republican democracy. As Biagini has shown, for example, John Stuart Mill, with other members of the English Radical circle (including George Grote, whose *History of Greece* the Radicals read avidly), thought that the 'luxuriant flowering of humanity in ancient Athens' meant that the city-republic held 'a position of extraordinary importance in world history.' The flowering in question was due to well-ordered democratic institutions that allowed for the mutual shaping of public opinion and the activities of public moralists. Mill emphasized that 'individual liberty could find its most perfect expression only when and where civic spirit was also exalted.'[15] As in classical republican doctrine, the liberal individual found completion in engagement in a public sphere where common interests were articulated. Nor was it only the more radical members of the younger generation of English liberals who related individual freedom to new collective institutions: James Mill's *Schools for All* is an earlier case in point and, in 1817, we find Bentham himself in his *Plan of Parliamentary Reform* arguing for annual parliaments, the secret ballot, and universal suffrage (including votes for women), while praising American institutions.[16] And the public schools, municipal councils, and registry offices promoted by the Durhamites and enacted by the Sydenham government in the British North American colonies were seen and promoted as collective institutions. Once again, the point is that liberal individualism was seen by liberal theorists and activists to depend upon and to promote forms of community.

If, up close, many influential real liberals look like republicans, the relationship between liberal political theory and capitalist accumulation is similarly messy. James Mill's foundational work on government insisted that the existence of 'society' depended upon the labour of the great mass of the people, but that labour could be justified only if government ensured that the civilizational effects of accumulation were extended downwards. Capitalist exploitation was necessary, but 'civilization' was a larger category, and men could be rational only if they were comfortable materially. The younger Mill has been described at times as a socialist in his concern with the redistribution of wealth, while we can read the French liberal sociologist Émile Durkheim insisting that there is no theoretical or social justification for the transmission of inherited wealth from one generation to the next: all surplus wealth accumulated by the individual once deceased should become the property of the state for the benefit of the community. The lines of descent towards 'third way' social democracy are reasonably clear. At another extreme, we do find libertarian liberals of Frederick von Hayek's stripe arguing that all unnecessary obstacles to the individual's free employment of his capacities for his own benefit should be removed, although, even in the libertarian account, there is room for arguments for social *minima* to enable individuals indeed to compete freely.[17]

Again, liberals have often been bitterly divided among themselves about the practical implications of their own political stances. In the case of the British North American 1830s, for instance, the internal oppositions among English Radicals over the colonial question worked to prevent them from developing an effective parliamentary politics. One faction, including the Lower Canadian Assembly's agent, J.A. Roebuck, argued that colonies were politically illegitimate, economically useless, and expensive and should be abandoned as quickly as possible. Another faction, including Charles Buller, rallied behind the Wakefieldian scheme of 'systematic colonization,' which saw the colonies as outlets for surplus English capital and population, and as venues for the extension of 'civilization.' The British American Land Company was one by-product of the latter position and its existence one grievance that propelled Lower Canada towards revolt.[18]

My point is that the argument for a 'liberal order framework' as an interpretive grid suffers from an oversimplified notion of liberalism, one that tends to assimilate it to domination in general, that misses its similarities with other competing political doctrines, that neglects its vision of community, and that does not treat it holistically. Tying a liberal project to a Gramscian notion of hegemony doesn't take us far unless we know which liberal project we are studying and unless we can identify concretely its proponents and opponents. I would suggest in any case that the proposition of a unitary, coherent liberal project is rather dubious, given the multiplicities of liberalisms that exist historically. While I appreciate McKay's move towards a non-essentialist conception of 'Canada,' suggesting that it is the result of a project of rule in the singular strikes me as far too neat. Instead, we need to attend to the messiness of multiple competing or antagonistic projects of rule, and of government, whose shifting articulations constitute more or less stable objects, such as 'the Canadian state.'

In stressing the complexity and variety of liberal doctrines and the practices they promote, I am not writing as liberalism's champion, nor forgetting what liberals have to answer for in the bloody work of 'civilization' and of enforcing their notions of freedom. Freedom's synonym, at times, was 'forcing government downwards,' an attempt to diffuse and render less visible state power. The doctrine of the Mills, père et fils, was practically often vicious and elitist; it justified the domination of India, the denigration of Hindu culture and letters, the sacrifice of anything not useful – poetry, for Mill père, at least, – to the narrow principle of utility.[19] Theirs was unambiguously a hegemonic doctrine that served to provide a theoretical justification for rule by men like themselves, men of the 'middling sort,' intellectuals, the financial and industrial bourgeoisie, reforming state servants. Others were to be ruled, workers and women, the colonized, 'coloured people' and 'mulattoes,' offered a bit of freedom here, a bit more there, subjected to relations of tutelage, trained, watched closely, and if, finally, they proved themselves prepared to accept the rule of reason, admitted to a sort of equality at some unspecified future date. Such was the neo-Platonism promoted by the younger Mill and his circle, and it is clear who the guardians were to be.

Yet the substance of liberalism is not exhausted by the interests or intentions of those who articulated it. Expressed interests and intentions and practical initiatives always have unintended consequences. As early-nineteenth-century English and Canadian liberals learned, for instance, encouraging people to read to be rational could just as easily lead them to question the established order, or to indulge in illicit pleasures.[20] Rather than focusing simply on the structural locations or class interests of 'liberals,' I suggest we need to attend to the internal dynamics, to the immanent logics, that may make it possible for us to understand how historically existing 'friends of liberty' could adopt thoroughly contradictory positions on events and practices in the name of one doctrine. At the same time, we need to attend to the ways in which unintended consequences result from consciously pursued projects for universalizing liberty.

One dynamic element in liberal theory and in the practices that stem from it is the tension between its universalistic anthropological premises and the principles of exclusion that exist alongside them. In both theory and practice, as Uday S. Mehta, among others, has shown[21] liberals proposed that human beings were possessed of a natural equality, but also argued that the practical right to liberty and self-determination was predicated on the cultivated capacity of the individual for reason and rational self-government. From the outset, those incapable of rational self-government – children, women, the insane, uneducated workers, the uncivilized – were excluded from liberal freedom, and liberals supported actively the principle and the practice of governing such people and groups illiberally. J.S. Mill's formula was that barbaric means were fitting for the government of barbarians. Mehta argues that British colonial rule justified often brutal domination through an active process of 'colonial infantilization' – that is, through the denial that the colonized possessed rationality and civilization – and through claims about the opacity and impenetrability of colonial social conditions that defied rational comprehension.[22]

The broad framework of liberal government, then, worked through a set of inclusions and exclusions, through the dominance of reason and reasonableness over ignorance and prejudice, through the demarcation of the civilized from the uncivilized, through the opposition between abstract equality and concrete inequality. Neither the lines of demarcation nor the substance of what is demarcated are given in advance. At the same time, for rational freedom to exist, the world had to be made intelligible to rational understanding; that is, invested in and subordinated to knowledge forms and practices that were amenable to critical and calculative rationality.[23] Liberal discourses and the practices they support thus also offer particular demarcations of the intelligible and the ineffable. It is the inherent tensions between particular ways of casting universality and particularity, protection and exploitation, reason and the unreasonable, that render liberal political discourses amenable to a broad range of incompatible projects and that constitute their immanent logic. It is such tensions that make it possible to think through the limits of liberalism.

The development of liberalism as a hegemonic mode of government could certainly provide an orienting framework for Canadian state formation. Yet such a framework would be ill served by seeing liberalism as a unitary 'ideology' aiming to destroy community in the interest of property and individual rights. There is no getting around the dynamics and inherent complexities of historical development; to engage them, we need adequate tools of analysis. I think that Michel Foucault's work, which also argued that liberalism is usefully approached as a mode of government, provides some useful analytic resources.[24]

Useful Bits of Foucault's Post-structuralism

Post-structuralist analysis has been slow to filter down into the practical work of anything like a majority of Canadian political and social historians. Three dimensions of the Foucauldian preoccupation with liberal governmentality seem to me to provide particularly rich resources for an engagement with the historical development of social conditions and practices: the analysis of technologies of power, totalizing/ individualizing initiatives, especially in relation to knowledge practices, and the 'governmentalization' of the state.

The elemental Foucauldian move towards looking at power in terms of technologies, whose articulation constitutes strategies or strategic ensembles, has much to recommend it. Looking at power in more technical and physical terms allows us to move beyond the class domination and ideology that limits most historical accounts of power, including neo-Marxist accounts. Starve people, control their ideas, or, ultimately, beat and kill them: these are the elements in the impoverished arsenal of earlier accounts of power. In the Foucauldian perspective, by contrast, power is seen to operate as the flow of force through relations, through networks in which individuals (and groups) are nodes. Power relations are constitutive and creative: the positivity of power is revealed through practices of incitement, stimulation, discipline, and specification. Power relations are not seen to work primarily through a repression/liberation binary; rather, power and pleasure intertwine. Power is not simply capacity, and not a possession monopolized by a social class. Power is relational and power relations are seen as characterized by reversibility. Major dominations appear as blockages in the flow of power relations, but such blockages are seen as inherently unstable. Methodologically, rather than beginning by positing major blockages of power in terms of class, gender, ethnic, colonial, or some other form of domination, and then proceeding to seek their traces empirically (which Jeffrey McNairn describes in this volume as the hunt for liberal ideas), one aims to reconstruct the ways in which major dominations result from particular kinds of articulations of forces.[25]

Foucault's initial model for the technology of power is the panopticon, but the limitations of thinking power largely in terms of the production of docile bodies and of subjectification as objectification led, first, to a consideration of the desiring subject and of the positive relations between power and pleasure, and then to the self-reflective subject made capable of self-fashioning and rational/ethical conduct. In his last formulations, Foucault pointed to four major technologies of power: of production, of signs and symbols, of domination, and of subjectification or the self. His late work focused on the last two of these, that is, on the technologies of domination that seek to subject individuals (or groups) to political ends, and on the technologies of the self, that is, those practices and devices through which individuals work on themselves in the pursuit of some end or other. The relation between the technologies of domination and the technologies of self is one late definition Foucault gave of the concept 'governmentality.' Here the questions asked are, How does domination work technically? How do individuals (I would add, and collectives) engage with domination? Through what technical means and practices, to what end?[26]

Writing in the France of the 1970s, Foucault was concerned to release the political imagination from the stranglehold of an economist Marxism that sought to relate every observable phenomenon to its functionality for capital.[27] What remains especially useful in this stance is its rejection of approaches that begin by positing the existence of some universal relation of domination or exploitation and that see the subsequent task of the analyst as one of documentation.

Yet one must also avoid the opposite tendency, visible in much of the Anglo-Australian 'governmentality school,' to neglect or ignore enduring and structurally rigid relations of domination and exploitation. Insisting on the reversibility of power relations in principle does not offer much analytic purchase on large-scale structures that are reversible only in the most extreme conditions (think, petroleum economy). Again, in state theory, the governmentality school usefully stresses that power is not simply a state monopoly. Yet in examining power as 'beyond the state' the state may be marginalized as a residual category or be reduced to an apparatus. Often in governmentality work little attention is paid to institutional arrangements and conduct is commonly seen as individual conduct. As well, some contributors express either disdain for or disinterest in the investigation of the working out of the relations between technologies and rationalities of government in practice. Analysts such as Nikolas Rose, while offering incisive analysis of the tensions in political thought, abjure concrete historical work and thus often reduce social change to change in thought itself.[28]

Nonetheless, one obvious way in which the notions of technologies of the self and of practices of subjectification can advance our understanding of liberal development is by taking us beyond Macpherson's useful, but historically specific, conception of the liberal 'possessive individual' on which McKay's essay relies.[29] The possessive individual of seventeenth-century political theory is not the possessive individual of nineteenth-, twentieth-, or twenty-first-century Canada. The former, recall, is the possessor of political will because he (and not she) is not subject to the will of others. For seventeenth-century thought, those who sold their labour power to others, those who were subject to patriarchal authority in the household, and perhaps those who engaged in commerce and thus depended on customers were not in possession of their own capacities and so were disqualified from autonomous political judgment. Their will was contained in the will of others, and hence property and patriarchal authority defined political will.

One of the lines of development of liberal discourse and of practice under liberalism is a re-conceptualization of the nature of self-possession, in which self-mastery through self-knowledge, through reason and rationality, rather than through property and authority, come to be defining characteristics. Reason and rationality are increasingly re-situated in such emerging discursive spaces as 'the Republic of Letters,' where reason has the potential to compensate for, if not simply to overcome, the effects of propertylessness. Empirically, practices in the 'republic of letters' are not contained within clear boundaries of class, race, gender, or region. And the exercise of reason and of rationality involves both techniques of domination and techniques and practices of the self.

In the working out of projects for the government of subjectivity in Canada the tensions are evident between domination over others and government of the self. These projects yield new interiorities, new boundaries between self and others, new bodily forms and new ways of being in the body, new contents and intensities in the internal life of the individual. What is at issue is not scale, in this matter, but homologous forms of practice. And it is not only and perhaps not primarily 'big' events in formal politics that change the world. Consider two examples: the campaign for school toilets and the debates over reading instruction in Canada West and Ontario.

In the first instance, school reformers campaigned actively and successfully against the 'squat culture' that prevailed in rural Canada West at least, and against the 'hygienic' problems generated by concentrating relatively large groups of children and teachers in close quarters for purposes of instruction. There were no school toilets at first, and indeed, some observers claimed that most farmhouses did not have privies. Children urinated and defecated in the school yard, and separate intervals or recesses for boys and girls were initiated in the 1840s so that boys and girls would not see each other engaged in acts of elimination. Yet, complained school inspectors, the order and good government in moral habits promoted by the school were being undermined by the sight of human excrement spread across the schoolyard. They agitated for the construction of privies and for separate privies for boys and girls. In the 1850s, the Education Office worked on privy design, both in an effort to deal with the technical problems associated with the centralization of excrement and to shape the acts of elimination themselves, in their timing, but also in their technical execution. Squat culture was eliminated, with consequences for the nature of embodiment.[30] Privies were designed with roofs that sloped down sharply towards the privy seat, for instance, in an effort to make boys sit to urinate.

As Norbert Elias has shown so forcefully, the privatization of the eliminatory functions is an important aspect of the 'civilizing process' that works in part through structuring the internal 'affective economy.' Moreover, Warwick Anderson demonstrates that some colonial projects were fixated on and fascinated with excrement. In the case of the Americans in the early-twentieth-century Philippines, practices of defecation marked the boundary between colonizer and colonized, with the former posited as the mouth and the latter the anus of the social body. And of course in its other manifestations, such as the movement for social sanitation or in bowel-cancer death rates, the politics of shit is a biopolitics.[31]

On the other hand, the problem and necessity of governing through pleasure are evident in debates over reading instruction in Canada West and Ontario. School administrators at mid-century adopted the position of the English Benthamites: reading should not stimulate the imagination or heighten fancy, but rather equip readers with 'useful knowledge' concerning the necessary physical and social structure of the universe. Once habituated to reading lessons in political economy, grammar, and the sciences, leavened with a bit of generic Christianity, administrators believed, readers would find pleasure in doing so, would do so freely, and would freely disdain dangerous or immoral literature and the frivolously misleading attractions of fiction. However, teachers and lesser administrators complained in increasing volume from the early 1850s that the Benthamite project did not work; students did not in fact take pleasure from heavily didactic and improving scientific tracts. What they wanted were stories, travel accounts, short and amusing pieces. These people agreed that readers had to be governed through 'taste' and through their capacity to experience pleasure and that such taste had to be developed and stimulated. Yet, in Foucauldian terms, in practice, the techniques of domination did not fit with actual techniques of the self. A major curriculum reform of the late 1860s in Ontario led to the introduction of more pleasurable books. Power and pleasure were not antithetical.[32]

We can advance our work by engaging with Foucault's understanding that liberal government and liberal domination work through the autonomous self-development of the individual; or, to put it differently, that domination under liberalism is a particular kind of articulation of techniques of government of others and of the government of the self.

Reason and rationality are obviously not essences, but historical social constructs. Still, the exercise of reason implies the freedom of an individual rendered capable of doing work on itself – in the simplest sense, of distancing itself from the immediacy of its experience, of critical reflection and self-reflection. It implies an individual able to master its passions and it also implies the construction of a particular hierarchy of the senses, in which those held closest to reason – sight and hearing – are privileged. Through what steps or stages, through what practices, at what moments, the self-reflecting individual comes to be a predicate and precondition of rule is a properly historical question. So is the matter of the contours of the diffusion (and blockage) of reason through the social and political body. Yet taking up Foucauldian and other post-structuralist analytic strategies of this sort gives us much more purchase on a far broader range of phenomena than that offered by neo-Gramscian concepts alone.

Although one may rightly be critical of Foucault's chronology and of some of his taxonomy of social-theoretical discourse, a second major Foucauldian contribution to the study of liberal government and state formation is his insistence upon the centrality of the novel knowledge/power relations that focused on population phenomena and that operated through the discourses of political economy. Having shown in his early work that the new disciplines of the 'classical age' contributed to the emergence of 'man' as an object of investigation and a subject of action, Foucault argued that a key political/intellectual shift in modern state formation came with the increasing 'discovery' by political theory that the world possesses its own intractable regularities. Foucault located this shift in the second half of the eighteenth century, as the science of police, with its dream of the detailed regulation of everything, gave way in the face of political economy. For the latter, the world of commerce and the market contains a structure of regularities of its own that is the product of the unintended consequences of the articulation of myriad diverse individual activities (the 'hidden hand').[33]

An intractable world has to be known to be governed, and seeking to govern that world gives rise to knowledge of new, seemingly intractable regularities. The new sciences of the eighteenth century – statistics and political economy especially – were articulated with and developed through the new state agencies of the early nineteenth century – health commissions, registry offices, inspectorates – to yield what has been called the 'flood' or the 'avalanche' of numbers. Individuals, events, and processes were torn from the particularities of their empirical existence and re-situated in new forms of abstraction. Of particular significance to Foucault is the notion of population: a notion that, paired with the analytic strategies of the emerging discipline of (what will later be called) demography, relocates the individual in relation to the collective in a two-fold sense. First, the notion of population depends on a radical equation of individuals; it effaces individual differences by constituting the individual indifferently as a member of a new collective. As I have argued elsewhere, on a large scale in the nineteenth century at least, only sovereign authority is capable practically of equating individuals.[34] Second, population creates the basis for a new register of difference, in and through which individuals can be categorized, classed, grouped, and assembled in keeping with some set of constructed characteristics.

  One of the obvious limitations of Foucault's own understanding of population in relation to state formation is the absence from his work of any robust concept of 'administration' and, indeed, of any systematic attention to the analysis of institutions. I argue that if we are to reconstruct the formation of the Canadian state, we need to attend to developing administrative capacities, technologies, and practices. At one level, population is an inescapably necessary theoretical construct for such an effort, because it constitutes one unifying object of secular government, one secular moment of political universality (more so and earlier than does 'citizenship,' for instance), in keeping with which liberal (and illiberal) government develops. At another level, attending to administration opens an alternative periodization of Canadian historical development, and enables us to chart state formation in a manner rather different than that suggested in the 'liberal order framework.'

  I read McKay's remarks about the 'great books that we need' as tending to identify the formation of the Canadian state with remarkable moments in the extension of state sovereignty. Yet alongside, underneath, and in parallel to great moments such as the Union of the Canadas or Confederation are a whole host of smaller moves and countermoves in the technologies of government and of administrative capacity. The rhythm of such moves is not identical to that of the epoch-making events identified by McKay. I have attempted to chart some of these in earlier work: the introduction of decimal currency; the long contested standardization of weights and measures; the development of the instrument of inspection; the continuing failure to create civil registration; moves for medical statistics; the modelling of the healthy body; the creation of uniform school curricula; the control of the Blue Book.[35]

Administration obviously has a material basis, but it is not exhausted by an examination of relations of production or class struggle. It is pre-occupied with ordering practices.[36]

The third element we can take from Foucault, I suggest, is his conception of the 'governmentalization' of the state. The concept depends on an expanded notion of government and on an engagement with liberal 'freedom.' Foucault argues that we need to think government as the 'conduct of conduct,' that is, in terms of all attempts wherever situated by some to structure the conduct of others. Government is seen not as action on individuals, but as action on action. As Foucault shows us, in Western political theory from the seventeenth century on, one frequently encounters homologous accounts of government: the good governor of the state, for instance, is first able to govern himself and to govern his own household.[37] Thinking government in these terms offers us two obvious advantages. First, the field of investigation is expanded dramatically, and second, we can seek commonalities across phenomena in terms of homologous practices and techniques rather than in conceptions of '(class or hegemonic) interest.' Of course, one must be attentive not to flatten the field of investigation in principle, so that all attempts to govern are seen as equivalent. And the fact that government is not conducted exclusively by 'the government' does not mean that governments do not govern. But homology (similarity with a difference) does not preclude hierarchy.

Again, for Foucault, government is axiomatically the government of 'freedom' (and, problematically, almost always conceived in terms of individuals). The removal of freedom to engage in alternate courses of conduct, to resist attempts to conduct conduct, replaces government by some other practice. Here we can notice that Foucault is true to the conventional conception of liberalism as the rational government of self and others. Where rational government of free individuals ceases – we recall Mill – we are dealing with barbarians and may or must do so barbarically.

Government as the conduct of conduct is not a monopoly of state. The technologies of domination are mobile and are not contained within the boundaries of an entity we can call putatively 'state.' Wal-Mart Stores, the world's largest corporation, is the second largest producer of information in the world, and is able not only to map the structure of individual purchases in each and every one of its stores at any given moment, but also to structure the display of merchandise to modify individual purchases. The governmentalization of the state, for Foucault and with much awkwardness, consists in the curiously ambiguous demarcation of the frontier of state and non-state. He goes so far as to suggest that what is specific to the modern state is its capacity to reproduce itself through the partial elimination of its own boundaries, that is, through the diffusion of governmental techniques throughout the social body. I think that Foucault is grappling with a problem inherent in the study of state formation and in the way social theory, broadly considered, attempts to engage with 'the state.' The problem is latent in Gramsci's attempts to conceptualize hegemony as state penetration of civil society in pursuit of consent, and in his analysis of the educative state, although his Bolshevism prevents him from a systematic engagement with it. The problem is equally evident in Mark Neocleous's repeated attempts to preserve the categories 'state' and 'civil society' while investigating the 'fabrication of social order' by the state, and in Pierre Bourdieu's arguments about the organization of the political field by the state.[38]

Simply put, if we inhabit state categories, if 'state intervention' effectively reconstructs civil society, then the state/non-state binary collapses. Although he is inconsistent and also loses his nerve in his governmentality essay, Foucault in fact presents us with an analytic strategy for dealing with this persistent problem: treat 'the state' nominalistically, as a descriptor for a particular condition of the political field, for a particular articulation of technologies, practices, and strategies of power and government. The history of state formation, in consequence, would become the conditional and conditioned history of theories, practices, technologies, and strategies, both in general and in the Canadian instance, in their particular articulations.

I think McKay's suggestion that we reject state essentialism takes us some way towards this position. Yet replacing the state/civil binary by such a new conception of holism would call into question the warrant for arguing both that the field of Canadian history is continuous with the formation of the Canadian state and that struggle over the state is a privileged object of historical investigation. My position is that we need to reject not only the top-down/bottom-up binary, but the state / civil society and the centre/periphery binaries that McKay uses to replace it. I argue that we would be much better off thinking in terms of histories of relations, practices, fields, figurations, games, tactics, and strategies in a much more abstract sense and letting the 'Canadian' in 'Canadian history' refer to a sense of the transient ways in which such things are territorialized at particular moments, de-territorialized at others. We study 'Canadian history' (or don't study it) because of certain contingencies.

NOTES

1 Ian McKay, 'The Liberal Order Framework: A Prospectus for a Reconnaissance of Canadian History,' *Canadian Historical Review* 81 (2000): 617–45, quotation at 637.

2 For sociology, Neil McLaughlin, 'Canada's Impossible Science: Historical and Institutional Origins of the Coming Crisis in Anglo-Canadian Sociology,' *Canadian Journal of Sociology* 30 (2005): 1–40, and the critical commentary that follows, 491ff. For history, Gérard Noiriel, *Sur la 'crise' de l'histoire* (Paris: Gallimard, 2005 [1996]); Timothy Stanley, 'Why I Killed Canadian History: Conditions for an Anti-Racist History in Canada,' *Histoire sociale / Social History* 33 (2000): 79–104.

3 But not its logical and conceptual problems. That is to say, he notices repeatedly that institutionalized state forms precede the existence of the fundamental class relations to which some Marxisms see them as responses: or at least they do so if our unit of analysis is 'Canada,' as I tried to suggest in 'Capitalist Development and Educational Reform: Comparative Material from England, Ireland and Upper Canada to 1850,' *Theory and Society* 13 (1984): 41–68. But he does not discuss more serious conceptual problems, such as the forced separation of culture from the material world, or the proposition that property relations can precede law.

4 McKay, 'Liberal Order Framework,' 629; emphasis added.

5 McKay does supplement the base/superstructure distinction, it is true, with a suggestion that we use the conception of centre/periphery from world systems theory, but nothing much is done with this distinction – which has its own difficulties – in the essay.

6 Max Weber, 'Politics as a Vocation,' in *From Max Weber: Essays in Sociology*, ed. H.H. Gerth and C.W. Mills (Oxford: Oxford University Press, 1958), 78.

7 Helpful is Frederick Cooper and Rogers Brubaker, 'Beyond 'Identity,'' *Theory and Society* 29 (2000): 1–47.

8 Carl Boggs, *The Two Revolutions: Gramsci and the Dilemmas of Western Marxism* (Boston: South End Press, 1984); Antonio Gramsci, 'Americanism and Fordism,' in *Selections from the Prison Notebooks*, ed. Quintin Hoare and Geoffrey Nowell Smith (New York: International Publishers, 1971), 279–318; Alan Hunt, 'Moral Regulation and Making-Up the New Person: Putting Gramsci to Work,' *Theoretical Criminology* 1 (1997): 275–301.

9 See R. Keith Sawyer, 'A Discourse on Discourse: An Archeological History of an Intellectual Concept,' *Cultural Studies* 16 (2002): 433–56; Trevor Purvis and Alan Hunt, 'Discourse, Ideology, Discourse, Ideology ...,' *British Journal of Sociology* 44 (1993): 473–99.

10 This view of liberalism sits uneasily with the growing literature on mixed monarchy, public opinion, and civic humanism, which includes Michel Ducharme's interesting reworking of Constant's contrast of ancient (Greek and Roman) and modern liberty, and Jeff McNairn's *Capacity to Judge*. See Michel Ducharme, 'Aux fondements de l'État canadien: La liberté au Canada de 1776 à 1841' (PhD diss., McGill University, 2005); Jeffrey L. McNairn, *The Capacity to Judge: Public Opinion and Deliberative Democracy in Upper Canada, 1791–1854* (Toronto: University of Toronto Press, 2000).

11 I discuss some of these initiatives in Bruce Curtis, 'From the Moral Thermometer to Money: Metrological Reform in pre-Confederation Canada,' *Social Studies in Science* 28 (1998): 547–70.

12 Melanie White and Alan Hunt, 'Citizenship: Care of the Self, Character and Personality,' *Citizenship Studies* 4 (2000): 93–116.

13 Louis-Georges Harvey, *Le printemps de l'Amérique française: Américanité, anti-colonialisme et républicanisme dans le discours politique québécois, 1805–1837* (Montreal: Boréal, 2004).

14 Debates in Lower Canadian classical colleges are seen as formative for republican discourse. See Marc-André Bernier, 'Patriotes et orateurs: De la classe de rhétorique à l'invention d'une parole rebelle,' *Voix et Images* 36 (2001): 498–515.

15 Eugenio F. Biagini, 'Liberalism and Direct Democracy: John Stuart Mill and the Model of Ancient Athens,' in *Citizenship and Community: Liberals, Radicals and Collective Identities in the British Isles, 1865–1931*, ed. E.F. Biagini (Cambridge: Cambridge University Press, 1996), 21–44, quotations at 32–3.

16 William Thomas, *The Philosophic Radicals: Nine Studies in Theory and Practice, 1817–41* (Oxford: Clarendon Press, 1979), chap. 1, 'Bentham and His Circle.'

17 Emile Durkheim, *Professional Ethics and Civic Morals* (London: Routledge, 1993); F.A. Hayek, *Economic Freedom and Representative Government*, Wincott Memorial Lecture (Westminster: The Institute of Economic Affairs, 1973); Hayek, *Law, Legislation and Liberty: A New Statement of the Liberal Principles of Justice and Political Economy*, vol. 2, *The Mirage of Social Justice* (Chicago: University of Chicago Press, 1976); James Mill, 'On Education,' in *Political Writings*, ed. Terrence Ball (Cambridge: Cambridge University Press, 1992), 139–94. I am not attempting to turn the elder Mill into a 'democrat'; his notion of government is thoroughly elitist and he supported class differences. The younger Mill is similar in many ways, but this is not the point.

18 For an account of the Wakefield plan, David A. Haury, *The Origins of the Liberal Party and Liberal Imperialism: The Career of Charles Buller, 1806–1848* (New York: Garland Publishing Inc., 1987); earlier, R. Wilmot-Horton, *An Outline of a Plan of Emigration to Upper Canada* (1823). For the divisions among the Radicals – all of whom had voted against Russell's Ten Resolutions, see Thomas, *The Philosophic Radicals*, 376–80.

19 On James Mill's analysis from his *History of British India*, see Thomas, *The Philosophic Radicals*.

20 Bruce Curtis, '"Littery Merrit," "Useful Knowledge," and the Organization of Township Libraries in Canada West, 1840–1860,' *Ontario History* 78 (1986): 284–312; Curtis, 'The Speller Expelled: Disciplining the Common Reader in Canada West,' *Canadian Review of Sociology and Anthropology* 22 (1985): 346–68; Richard Johnson, '"Really Useful Knowledge": Radical Working Class Culture,' in *Working Class Culture: Studies in History and Theory*, ed. J. Clarke et al., (London: Hutchinson, 1979).

21 Uday S. Mehta, 'Liberal Strategies of Exclusion,' in *Tensions of Empire: Colonial Cultures in a Bourgeois World*, ed. Frederick Cooper and Ann Laura Stoler (Berkeley: University of California Press, 1997), 59–86; see also Ducharme, 'Aux fondements de l'État' for a detailed discussion of the same point, and Bruce Curtis, 'Le redécoupage du Bas-Canada dans les années 1830: Un essai sur la "gouvernementalité" coloniale,' *Revue d'histoire de l'Amérique française* 58 (2004): 27–66.

22 See the description of the marketplace as it appeared to English travellers in Timothy Mitchell, *Colonizing Egypt* (Berkeley: University of California Press, 1988).

23 See, for instance, Bernard Cohn, *Colonialism and Its Forms of Knowledge: The British in India* (Princeton: Princeton University Press, 1996).

24 Michel Foucault, 'Naissance de la biopolitique,' in *Résumé des cours, 1970–1982* (Paris: Julliard, 1989).

25 The position is laid out in Michel Foucault, 'Truth and Power' and 'Two Lectures,' in *Power/Knowledge: Selected Interviews and Other Writings, 1972–1977*, ed. Colin Gordon (New York: Pantheon, 1980 [1976]), 109–33, 78–108.

26 Michel Foucault, 'Technologies of the Self,' in *Technologies of the Self: A Seminar with Michel Foucault*, ed. Luther H. Martin et al. (Amherst: University of Massachusetts Press, 1988), 16–49.

27 Michel Foucault, 'Méthodologie pour la connaissance du monde: Comment se débarrasser du marxisme,' in *Dits et écrits*, vol. 3, *1976–1979* (Paris: Gallimard, 1994 [1978]), 595–624.

28 For instance, Nikolas Rose, *Powers of Freedom: Reframing Political Thought* (Cambridge: Cambridge University Press, 1999), 140–1. Rose's attempt to

account for the decline of the social in 'advanced liberalism' rejects as erroneous would-be sociological claims that changes in government in liberal democracies are 'an inevitable response to a transformation of the conditions that made social government and the welfare state possible.' These claims are weak, he suggests, because many possible changes could have been made, only some were attended to, and choices were made among them. Social conditions of possibility do not determine the course of social development. Instead, Rose argues, 'government ... is a work of thought. And it was through thought, not through brute reality, that rationalities of social government began to crumble.' Without asking who it was that was thinking what in which conjuncture with what project, Rose's remaining determinants are rhetorical: 'Gradually, a new diagram of the relation between government, expertise and subjectivity *would* take shape ... It was not a matter of "freeing" an existing set of market relations from their social shackles, but of organizing all features of *one's* national policy to enable a market to exist, and to provide it what it needs to function. Social government *must be* restructured in the name of an economic logic' [my emphasis]. The complexity of state policy is rendered as a freely shifting set of beliefs. Who 'one' is and how 'one' could actually restructure social government are, presumably, sociological questions and so not of interest.

29 C.B. Macpherson, *The Political Theory of Possessive Individualism: From Hobbes to Locke* (Oxford: Oxford University Press, 1962).

30 For instance, 'An Australian study that sought to determine the best position for women to use when urinating had to be cancelled because Westerners could not squat for more than 30 seconds without tipping over. Furthermore, notes The Australian newspaper, one-third of the population is unable to squat.' Michael Kesterton, 'Social Studies,' *Globe and Mail*, 12 January 2005. On toilets in Canada West schools, see Bruce Curtis, *Building the Educational State: Canada West, 1836–1871* (London, ON, and Sussex, Eng.: Althouse Press and Falmer Press, 1988); Curtis, 'The Playground in Nineteenth-Century Ontario: History and Theory,' *Material History Bulletin* (1985): 21–31.

31 For the general issues, see Dominique Laporte, *History of Shit* (1978), trans. Nadia Benabid and Rudolphe el-Khoury (Cambridge, MA: MIT Press, 2000). Laporte argues that a key moment in the formation of the modern bourgeois order in France is the 1539 Ordinance of Villers-Cotterets that legislates, among other things, the principle 'to each his own shit.' Norbert Elias, *The Civilizing Process* (New York: Routledge, 1994); Warwick Anderson, 'Excremental Colonialism: Public Health and the Poetics of Pollution,' *Critical Inquiry* 21 (1995): 640–69.

32 See more generally Martyn Lyons, 'New Readers in the Nineteenth Century: Women, Children, Workers' and Reinhard Wittman, 'Was There a Reading Revolution at the End of the Eighteenth Century?' in *A History of Reading in the West*, ed. Guglielmo Cavallo and Roger Chartier, trans. Lydia G. Cochrane (Amherst: University of Massachusetts Press, 1999)', 313–44, 284–312. Also Bruce Curtis, 'Curricular Change and the Red Readers: History and Theory,' in *Reinterpreting Curriculum Research: Images & Arguments*, ed. R. Clarke, I. Goodson, and G. Milburn (London, ON, and Sussex, Eng.: Althouse Press and Falmer Press, 1989), 41–63; Curtis, "Littery Merrit,' Curtis, 'The Speller Expelled,' 346–68.

33 Michel Foucault, 'Governmentality,' in *Ideology and Consciousness* 6 (1979): 5–21; Foucault, 'The Politics of Health in the Eighteenth Century,' in *Power/Knowledge*, 166–82.

34 Bruce Curtis, 'Foucault on Governmentality and Population: The Impossible Discovery,' *Canadian Journal of Sociology* 27 (2002): 505–33.

35 Bruce Curtis, 'Administrative Infrastructure and Social Enquiry: Finding the Facts about Agriculture in Quebec, 1853-4,' *Journal of Social History* 32 (1998): 309–28; 'The Canada Blue Books and the Administrative Capacity of the Canadian State, 1822–1867,' *Canadian Historical Review* 74 (1993): 535–5; 'From the Moral Thermometer to Money: Metrological Reform in pre-Confederation Canada,' *Social Studies in Science* 28 (1998): 547–70; 'Mapping the Social: Jacob Keefer's Educational Tour, 1845,' *Journal of Canadian Studies* 28 (1993): 51–68; 'Official Documentary Systems and Colonial Governance: From Imperial Sovereignty to Colonial Autonomy in the Canadas, 1841–1867,' *Journal of Historical Sociology* 10 (1997): 389–417; *The Politics of Population: Statistics, State Formation, and the Census of Canada, 1840–1875* (Toronto: University of Toronto Press, 2001); 'Sanitary Medicine and the Social Body: The Case of National Civil Registration and Statistics in Canada, 1855–75,' *Canadian Bulletin of Medical History* 21 (2004): 73–101; 'Social Investment in Medical Forms: The 1866 Cholera Scare and Beyond,' *Canadian Historical Review* 81 (2000): 347–79; *True Government by Choice Men? Inspection, Education and State Formation in Canada West* (Toronto: University of Toronto Press, 1992).

36 I find Norbert Elias particularly helpful here; see 'The Retreat of Sociologists into the Present,' in *Modern German Sociology*, ed. V. Meyer et al. (New York: Columbia University Press, 1987), 150–72.

37 Foucault, 'Governmentality'; 'The Ethic of Care for the Self as a Practice of Freedom,' in *The Final Foucault*, ed. J. Bernauer and D. Rasmussen (Cambridge: MIT Press, 1991), 1–20; 'Morality and Practice of the Self,' in *The Use of Pleasure* (Harmondsworth: Penguin Books, 1985), 25–32; 'The Subject and

Power,' in *Michel Foucault: Beyond Structuralism and Hermeneutics*, ed. H.L. Dreyfus and P. Rabinow, 2nd ed. (Chicago: University of Chicago Press, 1983), 208–26.

38 Pierre Bourdieu, 'Rethinking the State: Genesis and Structure of the Bureaucratic Field,' in *State/Culture: State Formation after the Cultural Turn*, ed. George Steinmetz (Ithaca: Cornell University Press, 1999), 53–75; Mark Neocleous, *Administering Civil Society: Towards a Theory of State Power* (London: Macmillan, 1996); Neocleous, *Imagining the State* (Maidenhead: Open University Press, 2003). Also Bruce Curtis, 'Working Past the Great Abstraction: Abrams and Foucault on the State and Government,' *Les cahiers d'histoire* 17 (1997): 9–18.

The Municipal Territory:
A Product of the Liberal Order?

MICHÈLE DAGENAIS[1]

[I]t is with the deepest mortification that I find that the whole of the system for the establishment of local government has been omitted from the Bill, and that Her Majesty's Government and Parliament have contented themselves with the simple legislative re-union of the two Provinces, without providing any machinery by which they can be satisfactorily governed when united, or guarding against those evils which have been so severely felt from the absence of local government.[2]

These, among others, were the bitter words chosen by Lord Sydenham, in September 1840, to voice his profound disappointment to Colonial Secretary John Russell upon learning that the act recently adopted to unite the two Canadas contained no provision for the establishment of a municipal system, a measure he had himself recommended. Given his personal involvement in the matter, Sydenham was especially disconcerted by the British authorities' assent to the law. For while the idea of establishing a municipal regime, earlier put forth in Lord Durham's report, was not taken up by the British government in 1840, its establishment had nonetheless constituted part of the mandate given to Charles Edward Poulett Thomson (later Lord Sydenham) when he had been appointed governor general of British North America in September 1839;[3] hence Sydenham's resentment towards the Act of Union's silence on the matter. But why was the governor general so eager to see a municipal system installed in the colonies of British North America? What did the implementation of such a system imply? How was it susceptible of changing political life?

The following pages will consider the circumstances surrounding the creation of a municipal regime in the United Province of Canada, particularly in Canada East, and will attempt to carry out, as Ian McKay has recommended, a reconnaissance,[4] or re-reading, of this history in the context of the establishment of a liberal order. McKay's invitation is especially timely as it calls for a rethinking of political reforms undertaken in the wake of the emergence of a modern state in the 1840s and 1850s. Although McKay does not explicitly mention the implementation of a municipal regime in Canada during this period as part of the establishment of a liberal order, his invitation nonetheless suggests a need to revisit the creation of the municipal sphere. Such a reflection appears quite necessary in regards to this chapter of history, imprisoned as it is between a triumphant, Whiggish perception and more critical, though often overly mechanical, interpretations of the implementation of a municipal regime as an exercise in social control. Not to mention that this domain represented a chosen field of experimentation for liberal governance. Falling within the process of the establishment of the liberal order, conceived here as a 'specific project of rule,' the municipal sphere was shaped by the encounter, or confrontation, between the political designs of those who worked to create this new order and the realities on the field. Stemming from the 'specific project of rule' to which McKay refers, this important episode in the ongoing transformation of the exercise of power emerged out of the dynamic relationship between those who governed and those who were governed.[5]

The purpose of this paper, then, is to re-examine certain familiar developments surrounding the advent of a municipal system in the mid-nineteenth century in order to assess the role played by this level of government in the creation of a new liberal order that was reshaping Canadian society. Concomitant with the emergence of this broader political framework, there developed a specific system at the local level, one that was seen as both an essential component of the larger mode of governance and as a territory that would act as the outward expression of the overall project. As such, the creation of a new municipal body was part of a wider movement of political reorganization designed to better govern the Province of Canada, as well as to make it more governable. The municipalization of the local level took place in the wake of the 'étatisation ... des relations de pouvoir,' a process through which 'les relations de pouvoir ont été progressivement gouvernementalisées, c'est-à-dire élaborées, rationalisées et centralisées sous la forme ou sous la caution des institutions étatiques.'[6]

Because the objective of this chapter is to examine this element of a new 'project of rule,' conceived of here more as a project than as a readily imposed political form, Foucault's notion of 'governmentality' appears better suited than the theory of hegemony favoured by McKay in his article.[7] Indeed, this notion implies the analysis of power relations, rather than simply of power, by considering power not as a given but rather as an action, and by extension scrutinizing the 'techniques et procédures destinées à diriger la conduite des hommes.'[8] In fact, the municipalization that took place as of the mid-nineteenth century went well beyond the simple emergence of institutions at the local level. It was the result of a drive to objectify the local territory, or rather it carved out of this territory an object that might more readily be governed. Hence, the objective here is to piece together some of the operations through which the local realm was transformed into an abstract form, in this case the municipal territory, operations that also contributed to shaping this terrain, and by extension, the conditions in which people lived upon it.[9]

Historiographical Matters

Despite certain recommendations to this end, the formation of the municipal domain in Quebec and Canada remains insufficiently documented and theorized. In the 1990s Engin Isin invited reflection on this theme by publishing a monographic study of the intellectual roots of Canada's municipal system as well as a historiographical article reviewing existing studies on the subject, in which he pointed out their almost universally Whiggish conception of this history.[10] Isin criticizes these works for their tendency to take up uncritically the analyses contained in the studies published at the turn of the twentieth century, which portrayed the 'modern municipal government as the final and ultimate state where the principle of local self-government, after centuries of struggles and difficulties, had reached perfection.'[11] In this view, Britain's consent to laying the groundwork for a municipal system after repeated requests from the British North American colonies is understood as a step towards acquiring the autonomy necessary for the management of local affairs. These studies present the municipal regime episode as the prelude to Canada's long maturation 'from colony to nation,' to use Arthur Lower's oft-quoted turn of phrase.

In his own works Isin firmly criticizes this evolutionary interpretation of the history of local institutions. Tracing their intellectual origins, he demonstrates how their creation in fact contributed to the broader reorganization of the exercise of power that followed in the wake of the emergence of liberalism and the birth of the modern state. This fundamental transition, adds the author, was part of a historical process rooted in the sixteenth-century emergence of absolutist states. It was characterized by a shift in political sovereignty, formerly exercised in a more diffuse way, particularly on an urban scale, now appropriated by developing nation-states that ultimately benefited from this centralization of power. However, as of the nineteenth century, when liberalism 'became the main credo of state administration,' there occurred a devolution of power, notably through municipal institutions: 'Government through institutions was the pillar of a new conception of power: to govern meant that those invested with authority established laws, rules and regulations to direct and steer the actions or conduct of citizens of the State.'[12]

In contrast to this centralizing conception of politics proposed by Isin, who, while presenting a more theorized and complex vision, portrays the local scene as essentially reactive to reforms imposed by higher levels of government, other historians have scrutinized the municipal apparatus, focusing on its specific dynamics. Adopting an approach 'from the bottom up,' these scholars have formulated their critique primarily as a response to the 'state formation' current of Canadian historiography.[13] They concede that this current, which first appeared in the early 1990s, did have the merit of shedding light on the dynamics at play in the transformation of the role of the state in the mid-nineteenth century, interpreting it as the product not just of a political 'revolution,' but of a cultural one as well. Where they diverge, however, is with its exclusive focus on central powers. In their own studies, these historians have sought to demonstrate that the political changes accompanying the emergence of the modern state were not attributable only to reforms initiated by metropolitan and colonial elites. Instead, they argue, these changes were equally shaped by local dynamics, and were the result of demands expressed by the groups concerned, and especially by local elites. In his analysis of the influence of local communities on the formation of the modern state, for instance, Jack Little concludes that they played a determining role in the configuration of municipal institutions.[14]

Critics of the state formation current also focus on how the nature of the state's role was transformed. Defenders of this approach see in these transformations a major reorganization of power relations between institutions and society, through which the state appropriated a monopoly on violence and considerably increased its capacity to govern both people and territories. The critics, for their part, are hesitant to interpret these changes in such terms. Thus, Donald Fyson cautions against the tendency of certain historians to take up Durham's suggestion that there existed no proper local administrative structures before the 1840s and that the *ancien régime* state was at best anaemic. Demonstrating the central role played by parishes in local administration, Fyson maintains that the state was already displaying certain administrative capacities in the decades preceding 1830 to 1840: 'L'État est loin d'être absent des campagnes du Québec et du Bas-Canada; et la paroisse est l'un des cadres privilégiés par lequel l'État conceptualise cet espace en dehors des villes et organise ses structures en conséquence.'[15] In so doing, Fyson calls into question the state formation view that interprets the advent of modern Canada as a rupture, and instead perceives the changes under way in terms of transition. In sum, although studies such as those of Little and Fyson scrutinize local dynamics in order to bring out the complexity and diversity of political and social configurations on this scale, they do not put forth a more global interpretation that might explain how the interaction between local and central levels was transformed during the nineteenth century. Above all, they view the changes associated with the implementation of a new mode of governance in the wake of the 1837–8 Rebellions more in terms of continuity than as a watershed.

In a recent article, American political scientist Alan DiGaetano addresses the formation of the local state in nineteenth-century Great Britain and the United States, and attempts to reconcile approaches centred either on the state or on society. He calls for an 'integrated approach ... that combines structural (economic, social, and political context) and agency (political mobilization) levels of analysis into a comprehensive explanation of the rise and development of the modern local state in Britain and the United States.'[16] Although the author does bring a number of new factors to the analysis, in the end his interpretation is marked by a certain voluntarism and functionalism. He interprets the creation of the modern municipal system as the result of a two-fold process involving, first, a political mobilization in which pressure for a greater decentralization of power was exerted at the local level and, second, the appearance of new imperatives resulting from population growth, the expansion of the urban environment, and corresponding economic changes. DiGaetano essentially implies that a given situation can generate the structures needed to resolve the problems at hand. However, without denying the political influence of social groups or ignoring the socio-economic changes at play, it is clear that both sets of factors are largely contextual, and that while they heavily influenced the political configurations of the period, they cannot be seen as the explanation of, or grounds for, the creation of the municipal system.

A New Way of Governing People and Things

Rather than combining 'society – and state – centred theoretical approaches,'[17] and adding together all the various possible factors, it seems more instructive to reflect upon the advent of a municipal regime in the mid-nineteenth century through a more foundational and large-scale framework, one that accounts for the entire range of trans-formations in social and political relations in British North America, encompassing both state and society. It is necessary to think in terms of interconnections, of encounters, of relationships – relationships be-tween two 'entities' whose parameters were neither fixed nor definite, but fluid and continually redefined. Indeed, the establishment of a lib-eral order emerged precisely from a will, under constant pressure, to redefine the foundations of the socio-political structure, and thus, as Bruce Curtis argues in the present volume, the boundaries of diverse aspects of lived experiences:

> The broad framework of liberal government, then, worked through a set of inclusions and exclusions, through the dominance of reason and rea-sonableness over ignorance and prejudice, through the demarcation of the civilized from the uncivilized, through the opposition between abstract equality and concrete inequality. Neither the lines of demarcation nor the substance of what is demarcated are given in advance. At the same time, for rational freedom to exist, the world had to be made intelli-gible to rational understanding; that is, invested in and subordinated to knowledge forms and practices that were amenable to critical and calcula-tive rationality.[18]

What this entails, adds Curtis, is a questioning of the modalities through which power is exercised, something that must be approached in a dynamic and relational fashion. Thus, the installation of the liberal order as a 'project of rule' requires that we examine this manner of shaping the world not as a fixed program with predetermined objectives, but precisely as a *project*, taking into account its unfinished character, continually refined and reworked. Because it raises questions about the technologies of power, about the process through which domination is constructed both conceptually and concretely, an approach based on the idea of governmentality calls for a dynamic reflection on the exercise of power. Indeed, because the aim is to understand the liberal character of the reforms under way, and to shed light on the modalities through which the new political framework based on the principle of the liberty of subjects and their free adherence to the new regime functioned, it is important to problematize the question of how power was exercised. In this sense, a governmentality approach seems most appropriate as it challenges us to think in terms of means and practices, to investigate the concrete ways in which domination is exercised through configurations and circumstances that are equally fluid and changing. It allows us to move beyond a model that places power apriori in the hands of certain social groups by virtue of their class, gender or ethnicity.[19]

Hence, it is in this context, both conceptual and circumstantial, that Lord Sydenham's disappointment in the Act of Union can be read. Sydenham was convinced that the creation of a municipal regime was a necessary condition for political reform in the colonies, and he had made it one of his highest priorities. Though he was anxious to change the way local populations were administered, he nonetheless feared that the future members of the province's Legislative Assembly, soon to start sitting, would not share his view. As a result, he exercised the powers afforded to him by the Special Council to ensure the adoption of two ordinances through which he laid out the basis of a municipal system in Canada East.[20] Much like Durham and Commissioner Charles Buller, head of the investigation into the establishment of a municipal regime in Lower Canada, Sydenham was persuaded of the benefits of this measure, which he saw as essential for maintaining political stability. For him, the concentration of power within a single institution with no provisions for the diffusion of authority would exacerbate tensions and encourage opposition. All three were furthermore convinced that the lack of local institutions through which centrally held power could be diluted had been a primary cause of the Rebellions.[21]

Why were they so sure that municipal administrations possessed the virtues necessary for the maintenance of peace, order, and good government? In their eyes, these institutions were training grounds for political life, for the exercise of self-government. By entrusting local authorities with the management of issues at the local level, citizens could learn to set objectives and rely upon themselves to meet them. In other words, they could learn to govern their own conducts, thus acquiring experience in public life that could later be applied at other levels, notably when choosing elected representatives. Thus conceived, the municipal scene was a practice field, the suitability of which was bolstered by the fact that it allowed for a far more efficient and meaningful management of local issues than remote government authorities could offer. As a result, the displeasure that might easily arise from the way local issues were handled could be less readily projected to higher levels of government. As Sydenham eloquently asserted, 'Whatever uneasiness they (the people) may feel – whatever little improvement in their respective neighbourhoods may appear to be neglected, [the absence of municipal institutions] affords grounds for complaint against the executive. All is charged directly upon the Government, and a host of discontented spirits are ever ready to excite these feelings.'[22]

Municipal institutions appeared all the more important to Durham and Sydenham in their perceived capacity as liaisons between the local population and the central government. Duly elected municipal authorities enjoying the people's confidence were critical for keeping the government informed of developments at that level, to formulate local demands, and to maintain a link between the two levels of government.[23] In sum, these officials believed that the best way to neutralize possible popular opposition and stifle lurking inclinations to rebellion was to *diffuse* state power in a double sense. At one level, state power was to be devolved into all spheres of public life or, in other words, its presence and visibility increased. At another level, however, power was to be diluted by extending it to local groups, albeit within a framework defined according to a number of norms and laws, as power could clearly not be exercised in a disorderly, muddled, and unintelligible environment.[24]

The foundations of the municipal system were thus built upon the principle of self-government, one of the bases of liberalism, which McKay does not mention as such in his article. The municipal system also rests on two other principles, which he does identify, namely, liberty and the right to hold property.[25] Of these three principles, the third, property rights, is most crucial. Indeed, the territorialization of state power at the local level was grounded in landed property.[26] The cornerstone of municipal finances was property tax and its derivatives, business and water taxes. Moreover, the franchise was defined as a function of these three pillars of municipal taxation. In the first decades of the municipal regime, the right to vote and run in elections was limited to property owners. Suffrage rights were later extended to all taxpayers, such that tenants and landlords could vote as long as they paid their water, business, or property taxes in full.[27]

The Municipal Territory: An Essential Link in Liberal Governance

Government of the self, a sense of responsibility, and the diffusion of power thus constituted the cornerstones of the new mode of governance that was being elaborated in the British North American colonies. Based on liberal precepts, this system was seen as the legitimate successor to the structures deemed authoritarian and increasingly archaic that were in place up to the Rebellions. At the core of this process of fundamental transformation in the ways of governing people and things stood the municipal level, a territory that was both vital to the project and narrowly associated with the ongoing formation of the liberal state. In fact, the municipal system was born precisely as the way of governing was transformed, and whose new foundations rested on principles of individual responsibility and the consent of free political subjects, and on a set of laws, norms, and regulations designed to specify the modalities and conditions for participation in both political life and state activity.

It is striking to note the centrality of references to the establishment of the municipal regime in documents produced by colonial authorities during this period of transition in modes of governance, particularly in comparison to the minimal attention municipal issues receive today. What explains that institutions once seen as playing so fundamental a role as political training grounds[28] are now widely seen as inconsequential? Could it be that, over time, such institutions lost their significance to a central state whose sphere of action has continuously increased? This certainly provides part of the explanation. The answer probably also lies in the fact that areas of municipal jurisdiction primarily touched upon matters henceforth considered commonplace because they were associated with ordinary, material, in sum, everyday, life. Who would suggest that summertime street cleaning, snow removal in the winter, lighting, and firefighting constitute questions of great political import? Yet then, as now, these were crucial issues, essential to the proper organization of social and political life. It is clear that the creation of the conditions of collective existence, through the organization of road maintenance, water distribution, garbage removal, also played into the liberal order.[29] Indeed, the materiality of everyday life has and continues to shape conducts as much as have the norms designed to govern it, or what Foucault calls the conduct of conducts.[30]

All this can explain why the creation of a framework for managing such day-to-day issues engendered so much debate in the nineteenth century, as well as why it appeared so crucial to the proper functioning of political life. In fact, although the first ordinances adopted in the 1840s to define the municipal regime gave rather limited powers to local authorities, they nonetheless transformed several aspects of daily life. With the definition of procedures to oversee the construction and maintenance of streets, the establishment and upkeep of police forces, or the adoption of rules 'for providing for the establishment of and a reasonable allowance for the support of Parish and Township Schools,' the new political framework gradually took shape. The same was true of the power 'for raising, assessing, levying and appropriating such monies as may be required for carrying into effect all or any of the objects for which the said District Councils ... are hereby empowered to make by-laws.'[31] Through the interplay of these various measures, a new, local, reality was being integrated into the domain of the emerging state. It is in this context that the breadth of the laws passed between 1840 and 1855, which, in the words of legislators of the day, were aimed precisely at *incorporating* localities into the state, must be understood. At stake when Durham penned his report and Sydenham expressed his consternation was the attempt to transform the local sphere, urban or rural, into a territorial institution of the state. In sum, developing a municipal system at the local scale meant incorporating this level of governance into the broader state.

Among these issues, the question of territorializing cities found itself at the heart of reflections leading to the elaboration of municipal regimes in British North America, as well as in Great Britain and the United States.[32] Cities had historically developed certain administrative capacities, but these had waned with the advent of absolutist states in the sixteenth century, and this territory now had to be integrated and incorporated into a state realm being redefined by the liberal order. The allocation of powers to municipal administrations, however, would take place very gradually. Indeed, several decades went by between the first granting of a municipal charter in British North America, to Saint

John in 1785, and the extension of the same privilege to other cities such as Montreal, Quebec City, Toronto, and Kingston. Moreover, it was only in the 1840s that colonial authorities agreed to draw up permanent charters with a more extensive range of powers for these cities. In so doing, they sought not only to facilitate the management of urban territories, but also to make of them the laboratories of liberal governance. As Patrick Joyce has noted in his analysis of British cities, urban areas became sites for experimenting with new modes of governance and for displaying new norms, sites where the effort to order municipal realities along new lines was powerfully conveyed.[33]

This push to incorporate local territories into the larger state was accompanied by a second process, which, through the provisions laid out in the ordinances, defined the rules by which municipal institutions would operate and determined the frequency and length of their assemblies, the make-up of their electorate,[34] the electoral procedures to be followed, the eligibility of candidates, the number and capacities of municipal officials, and so on. The objective was essentially to regularize the diverse aspects of municipal politics. By describing a series of actions and practices and recording them in the ordinances and laws regarding municipalities, government authorities were able to make them into abstractions. Local political life was thus transformed into a measurable and reproducible object of governance. In other words, an entirely new sphere of politics was being instituted even as it was being normalized. Only in this way could a mode of governance be conceived that was at once founded upon the principle of liberty and that, instead of resulting in chaos, aimed to solidify the orderly and proper functioning of society. Herein lies the fundamental paradox of liberal governance, where the exercise of power is based on the principle of liberty, but where liberty is also used as a method of exercising this power, of subjugating individuals.[35]

To be sure, this process of incorporation was not always straightforward, and over time several modifications were brought to bear. Despite their determination, which shines through the title of the second ordinance of 1840, intended to 'provide for the better internal government of this Province,' colonial authorities were anxious about giving local populations the latitude needed to govern themselves. As the commissioners investigating municipal institutions suggested, 'The institutions by which the affairs of a country are to be regulated ought to be framed in accordance with the spirit of the people, their capacities for government, and the circumstances of their physical condition. To bestow upon a people modes of government greatly in advance of the general state of society is hardly less unwise than to cause institutions to linger in the rear of the public mind.'[36]

While the historiography has focused primarily on the overtly anti-francophone tone of this report, its full significance goes much further.[37] Beyond the contempt displayed by the authors, including the infamous Adam Thom, it is important to note the way in which the difficulties impeding the introduction of self-government at the local level were defined. More specifically, 'the obstacles to be encountered are the absence of education, popular inexperience, blind repugnance to taxation, and the absence of a wealthy and instructed class, interested in the prosperity of the many, and desirous of engaging gratuitously in the administration of local affairs.'[38] Without departing from the project of incorporating the local sphere into the liberal political space being created, this was one of the primary reasons why the colonial authorities would only grant the means for governing municipalities in a gradual way, as bespeak the multiple amendments introduced to the 1840 ordinance in 1845, 1847, and 1855.

These laws specified the powers attributed to the municipalities and intended for the implementation of conditions of collective existence at the local level. Municipalities were thus responsible for all matters in some way connected to daily life, including public works (thoroughfares, sidewalks, underground conduits, infrastructure, lighting), the management of nuisances and garbage, decency and morality, public health, or the layout of urban space (beautification, planning protection of different areas, maps and street plans). They were also expected to ensure security on their territory (police and fire brigades) and to take on various responsibilities associated with public welfare, such as the establishment of relief and shelters for the needy, assistance to fire victims, the opening of health offices, and so on. Municipalities had the power to adopt rules regarding all of these matters. They could also levy taxes and contributions to finance local improvement works, borrow, acquire property, and undertake expropriations in order to build new roads or construct new public spaces.[39]

These municipal laws remain to be analysed in detail in order to understand more subtly the shifting standards that defined, from one law to the next, such issues as the workings of local institutions, the holding of elections, the rules surrounding municipal council meetings, as well as the appointment of bureaucrats and their functions.

The New Mode of Governing Seen from the Local Scene

For the whole process to be meaningful, it needed the participation of the political subjects themselves. Yet there was considerable opposition, at least on the part of certain elites, during the first years of the creation of the municipal regime, with respect to the way the local level was being integrated into the state. Their reservations bore witness to the breadth of the changes the British authorities were attempting to introduce, changes that must also be examined in the light of what has been called the governmental revolution, which the historiography has not treated in reference to the municipal level.[40] What remains to be analysed is the significance of this opposition, too often dismissed as retrograde because of its unwillingness to adopt a framework deemed progressive. This interpretation has been put forth primarily by the Whig historiography, notorious for its celebration of the advent of municipal 'autonomy.'

Should the opposition of local populations in the face of the changes brought about by the establishment of a municipal regime in the middle of the nineteenth century not be seen instead as a refusal to accept a mode of governance that clashed with traditions and established practices? While this regime, inspired by a liberal conception of political life, certainly intended to replace an older one characterized by authoritarianism, its creation occurred through a process of normalization that evacuated established practices in order to replace them with a collection of norms dictated by municipal laws. What was lost in this transition? Certainly not a democratic or egalitarian system, but quite possibly a set of practices defined over time by the actions of the local community, a product of negotiations undertaken within these communities, as well as between them and local and colonial authorities. If the fact that they were written down in the form of laws made the new regulations more transparent, and in a sense more equitable, this does not conceal the obvious transfer of 'sovereignty' that resulted from this process.[41] Was it not precisely this sense of losing a measure of power that nurtured the opposition of local elites at the time that this new municipal regime was being established?

A rapid overview of certain reforms, such as those aiming to change road construction and maintenance practices, or those modifying territorial delineations with no regard for the existing boundaries according to which local communities had developed feelings of belonging and constructed part of their collective identity, would certainly point in this direction. And what of the opposition expressed to the new taxation system contained in the 1840 ordinance and subsequent laws? The nuanced perspective of Wendie Nelson's recent study of the establishment of a public schools system further reveals the complex ramifications of this opposition.[42] To see in this only a manifestation of a retrograde or a-liberal conception of community life is as simplistic as it is inaccurate. In the context of the *Guerre des éteignoirs* (Candle-snuffers' war), for instance, the rejection of the new tax was based in part on the burden felt by the population, but also on the fact that it corresponded to a loss of control over the school system at the local level. Not to mention that the use of taxation as a means of financing such government activities remained relatively novel in the British world of the mid-nineteenth century.[43] Indeed, the implementation of taxation policies presupposed the existence of a new relationship between ruling authorities and the populations, one based on the principles of liberty, trust, and legitimacy, conditions that were clearly lacking in the newly united Canadas, and that would take many years to achieve.

It remains to be examined how these relationships were developed, as well as how the new norms dictating political life were appropriated and, over time, modified. To date, too few studies have analysed these dynamics. Particular attention also needs to be paid to the nuances of how these issues played out in the very different contexts of urban and rural milieux, briefly discussed above. And yet although it was long in coming, this process of normalizing local political life would ultimately be successful. The fact that municipalities are now seen as common realities, fully integrated into everyday practices, eloquently attests to this. It can only be concluded that the establishment of the liberal order on the local scale, begun with efforts undertaken to municipalize local communities and incorporate them into the realm of the state, has been fully accomplished.

Ian McKay's invitation to revisit Canadian history in the context of the liberal order is important because the framework from which it is inspired is both renewed and stimulating. But if we are to fully grasp the way in which the liberal order took form, it is nonetheless necessary to further expand this framework, as the governing of people cannot be conceived separately or detached from the governing of things. Consubstantial to the formation of the liberal order during the middle of the nineteenth century, the territory, in a global as well as in a local and municipal sense, constituted both a prerequisite to its accomplishment and the terrain on which it was applied.

NOTES

1 I would like to express my warmest gratitude to Michel Ducharme for the generous and thought-provoking assistance he offered in the preparation and writing of this article. Thanks to Bruce Curtis who, with his insightful thoughts and questions, urged me to deepen my analysis of municipal political life. My thanks also go to Nicolas Kenny for translating this paper.

2 C. Poulett Thomson to John Russell, 16 September 1840, 'Correspondence and Other Papers Relating to Canada and to the Problem of Clergy Reserves 1840–1841,' in British Parliamentary Papers, Colonies/Canada, vol. 14 (Shannon: Irish University Press, 1968–72), 18.

3 'I was emphatically told,' continued Sydenham, 'that one of the most important principles to be kept in view in any measures for the future government of the Canadas was the establishment of a system of local government by representative bodies freely elected in the various cities, and rural districts.' Ibid., 19. For a biography of Charles Edward Poulett Thomson, made Baron Sydenham on 19 August 1840, see Philip Buckner's entry in the Dictionary of Canadian Biography, online at http:// www.biographi.ca/FR/ShowBio.asp ?BioId=37815&query =Thomson (accessed 20 February 2006). On the determining influence exercised by Lord Sydenham as governor of the colony, see Ian Radforth, 'Sydenham and Utilitarian Reform,' in Colonial Leviathan: State Formation in Mid-Nineteenth-Century Canada, ed. Allan Greer and Ian Radforth (Toronto: Toronto University Press, 1992), 64–102.

4 'a re/connaissance,' or as Ian McKay states, 'a knowing again.' 'The Liberal Order Framework: A Prospectus for a Reconnaissance of Canadian History,' Canadian Historical Review 81 (2000): 627.

5 This 'specific project of rule,' as conceived by Ian McKay, refers to the formation of modern Canada as a whole. Informed by a desire to depart from a reified vision of the political realm, this article takes up this concept by applying it to the municipal level. From this perspective, McKay's Canada, as well as the municipal domain, can be seen as 'a historically specific project of rule, rather than either an essence we must defend or an empty homogeneous space we must possess. Canada-as-project can be analyzed through the study of the implantation and expansion over a heterogeneous terrain of a certain politico-economic logic – to wit, liberalism. A strategy of 'reconnaissance' will study those at the core of this project who articulated its values, and those 'insiders' or 'outsiders' who resisted and, to some extent at least, reshaped it.' Ibid., 620–1.

6 Michel Foucault, 'Le sujet et le pouvoir,' in Dits et écrits 1954–1988, vol. 4, 1980–1988 (Paris: Gallimard, 1994), 241.

7 Michel Foucault, 'La gouvernementalité,' in *Dits et écrits 1954–1988*, vol. 3, *1976–1979* (Paris: Gallimard, 1994), 635–57. See also works that have used this framework to analyse the municipal and urban worlds, in particular the recent book by Patrick Joyce, *The Rule of Freedom: Liberalism and the Modern City* (London: Verso, 2003); as well as Engin F. Isin, *Cities without Citizens: Modernity of the City as a Corporation* (Montreal: Black Rose Books, 1992).

8 Michel Foucault, 'Du gouvernement des vivants,' in *Dits et écrits 1954–1988*, vol. 4, 125. On the notion of governmentality, highly appropriate for analysing the transformations taking place in methods of governing or, in other words, 'the mentality of government,' see Bruce Curtis, 'Le redécoupage du Bas-Canada dans les années 1830: Un essai sur la 'gouvernementalité' coloniale,' *Revue d'histoire de l'Amérique française* 58 (2004): 27–66.

9 Bruce Curtis has explained this in reference to a different context in 'La morale miasmatique: Le *Mémoire sur le choléra* de Joseph-Antoine Taché,' *Canadian Bulletin of Medical History / Bulletin canadien d'histoire de la médecine* 16 (1999): 322.

10 Isin, *Cities without Citizens*, and 'Rethinking the Origins of Canadian Municipal Government,' *Canadian Journal of Urban Research* 4 (1995): 73–92.

11 Isin, 'Rethinking the Origins,' 80. Early-twentieth-century scholars had, for instance, given the Municipal Corporations Act of 1849, which established a municipal regime in Canada West, the rather pompous title of 'Municipal Magna Carta.' Ibid., 77. To date, the only in-depth study of the origins of the municipal system remains J.H. Aitchison's 'The Development of Local Government in Upper Canada, 1783–1850' (PhD diss., University of Toronto, 1953). However, its focus is on Ontario exclusively.

12 Isin, *Cities without Citizens*, 56.

13 For a rapid overview of the 'state formation' historiography and the conception of the state it puts forth, see the introduction of Allan Greer and Ian Radforth's collection on the subject, considered a classic in the field. Greer and Radforth, 'Introduction,' in *Colonial Leviathan*, 3–16.

14 'Governor Sydenham did his best to ensure that democratic elements were minimized when he finally introduced municipal government, but community pressure would force the province to cede to a considerable degree of decentralization by mid-century.' J.I. Little, *State and Society in Transition: The Politics of Institutional Reform in the Eastern Townships, 1838–1852* (Montreal and Kingston: McGill-Queen's University Press, 1997), 14. See, by the same author, 'Colonization and Municipal Reform,' *Histoire sociale / Social History* 14, 27 (1981): 93–121.

15 Donald Fyson, 'La paroisse et l'administration étatique sous le Régime bri-

tannique (1764–1840),' in *Atlas historique du Québec: La paroisse*, ed. Serge Courville and Normand Séguin (Sainte-Foy: Les Presses de l'Université Laval, 2001), 39. For a more in-depth discussion on local administrative structures in the urban context, see Fyson, 'Les structures locales à Montréal au début du XIXe siècle,' *Cahiers d'histoire* 17 (1997): 55–75; Fyson, 'Jurys, participation civique et représentation au Québec et au Bas-Canada: Les grands jurys du district de Montréal (1764–1832),' *Revue d'histoire de l'Amérique française* 55 (2001): 85–120.

16 Alan DiGaetano, 'Creating the Public Domain: Nineteenth-Century Local State Formation in Britain and the United States,' *Urban Affairs Review* 41 (2006): 428.

17 Ibid., 430.

18 Bruce Curtis, 'After "Canada": Liberalisms, Social Theory, and Historical Analysis,' p. 186 above.

19 As Bruce Curtis suggests, 'Power is relational and power relations are seen as characterized by reversibility. ... Methodologically, rather than beginning by positing major blockages of power in terms of class, gender, ethnic, colonial, or some other form of domination, and then proceeding to seek their traces empirically ... one aims to reconstruct the ways in which major dominations result from particular kinds of articulations of forces.' Ibid., 187.

20 The two ordinances were adopted on 29 December 1840. The first, 'An Ordinance to prescribe and regulate the election and appointment of certain Officers in the several Parishes and Townships in this Province and to make other provisions for the local interests of the Inhabitants of these divisions of the Province' *(Ordinances of Lower Canada, 1841*, 4 Victoria c. 3.), It established all parishes and townships of 300 inhabitants or more as municipal corporations. The second, 'An Ordinance to provide for the better internal government of this Province, by the establishment of Local or Municipal Authorities therein' *(Ordinances of Lower Canada, 1841*, 4 Victoria c. 4), created a new territorial division on a regional scale. For further details, see Jacques L'Heureux, 'Les premières institutions municipales au Québec ou "machines à taxer,"' *Les Cahiers de droit* 20 (1979): 331–56.

21 As Sydenham argued, 'the opportunity I have of studying the state of the British North American provinces – of observing the social condition of the people, and the working of the constitutions under which they have been governed – has convinced me that the cause of nearly all the difficulty in the government of every one of them, is to be found in the absence of any well organized system of local government.' C. Poulett Thomson to John

Russell, 16 September 1840, 19. See also Lord Durham, *Lord Durham's Report on the Affairs of British North America*, vol. 2, ed. C.P. Lucas (Oxford: Clarendon Press, 1912), 113, 287.

22 Cited in Isin, *Cities without Citizens*, 132.

23 As Sydenham added, 'If I had to seek for information from any place from 10 to 150 miles from Quebec or Montreal, I possess no means whatever of obtaining it ... If the executive seeks to know the opinion of the people with regard to any improvement, there is no one to whom application can be made. In a word, every country district throughout the whole of the vast province of Lower Canada, is as completely cut off from any connection with the executive, as if it were on the other side of the Atlantic.' C. Poulett Thomson to John Russell, 16 September 1840, 20.

24 See Curtis, 'After "Canada."'

25 McKay, 'Liberal Order Framework,' 624.

26 One of the most important measures adopted during this period was in fact the abolition of the seigniorial regime in order to make more flexible the rules governing property ownership.

27 Jean-Pierre Collin and Michèle Dagenais, 'Évolution des enjeux politique locaux et des pratiques municipales dans l'île de Montréal, 1840–1950,' in *Enjeux et expressions de la vie politique municipale (XIIe–XXe siècles)*, ed. Denis Menjot and Jean-Luc Pinol (Paris: L'Harmattan, 1997), 202–3.

28 Charles Buller's assistant commissioners, William Kennedy and Adam Thom, expressed the same views when they wrote, 'The mass of the people ... have been denied the minor right ... of choosing municipal authorities, and thereby gradually acquiring a disciplined knowledge of their social duties in the school of practical citizenship.' 'Appendix C. Reports of the Commissioners of Inquiry into the Municipal Institutions of Lower Canada,' in *Lord Durham's Report*, 139.

29 For an illustration of the impact of municipal services on the conditions of collective existence, see Michèle Dagenais and Caroline Durand, 'Cleansing, Draining and Sanitizing the City: Conceptions and Uses of Water in the Montreal Region,' *Canadian Historical Review* 87 (2006): 621–51. See also Joyce, *Rule of Freedom*, esp. intro. and chap. 2.

30 'La conduite est à la fois l'acte de mener les autres ... et la manière de se comporter dans un champ plus ou moins ouvert de possibilités.' In this sense, the expression refers to the project of shaping the behaviour of individuals. Foucault, 'Le sujet et le pouvoir,' 237.

31 'An Ordinance to provide for the better internal government of this Province,' 4 Victoria c. 4, art. 37.

32 Engin Isin's study, *Cities without Citizens*, is devoted entirely to the origins

of the Canadian municipal system, which he analyses in the British and American contexts. On the origins of the British municipal system, see Derek Fraser, 'Municipal Reform in Historical Perspective,' in *Municipal Reform and the Industrial City*, ed. Derek Fraser (Leicester and New York: Leicester University Press and St Martin's Press, 1982), 2–14.

33 '[I]n the nineteenth century the city moved to the centre of the concerns of the governors about how the new society then emerging might be governed.' Joyce, *Rule of Freedom*, 8.

34 The important question of the municipal franchise would certainly merit additional attention, and the evolution of the norms defining who could vote remains to be traced. It is clear, however, that despite certain assurances to the contrary, colonial authorities had a very narrow conception of voting rights, in keeping with the widespread understandings of the day. As explained earlier in this chapter, the privilege to vote was granted only to persons owning land, the primary condition for being a free political subject. As Charles Buller eloquently put it upon delegating to the assistant commissioners the task of investigating the conditions necessary for establishing a municipal regime in Lower Canada, it was essential 'in such local management to give a voice to as large a number of people as can use the suffrage for the common advantage.' This comment alone could well be the object of extended analysis, not least because of the rich insinuations it contains, which merit further explanation, such as the idea of 'common advantage.' 'Appendix C,' in *Lord Durham's Report*, 136.

35 Here I am paraphrasing Patrick Joyce, who, in the introduction of his book, writes that it is important to see this liberty 'as something that is ruled *through*, freedom as a formula for exercising power, and freedom ... as a technique of rule.' *Rule of Freedom*, 1.

36 'Appendix C,' in *Lord Durham's Report*, 140.

37 On the British authorities' contempt for the local institutions in place and their refusal to recognize in them a form of local government, see Fyson, 'La paroisse et l'administration étatique,' 25–39.

38 'Appendix C,' in *Lord Durham's Report*, 143.

39 Jacques Léveillée and Marie-Odile Trépanier, 'Évolution relative à l'espace urbain au Québec,' in *Droit et société urbaine au Québec*, ed. Andrée Lajoie et al. (Montreal: Éditions Thémis, 1983), 27–8.

40 On the governmental revolution, seer Philip Corrigan and Derek Sayer, *The Great Arch: English State Formation as Cultural Revolution* (Oxford: Basic Blackwell Ltd, 1985).

41 On this aspect of the question, see *Colonial Leviathan*, esp. Allan Greer, 'The Birth of the Police,' 17–49.

42 Wendie Nelson, "Rage *Against* the Dying of the Light': Interpreting the Guerre des Éteignoirs,' *Canadian Historical Review* 81 (2000): 551–81.
43 On this specific question, see Martin Daunton, *Trusting Leviathan: The Politics of Taxation in Britain, 1799–1914* (Cambridge: Cambridge University Press, 2001), esp. chaps. 2 and 9.

The Nature of the Liberal Order: State Formation, Conservation, and the Government of Non-Humans in Canada

STÉPHANE CASTONGUAY AND DARIN KINSEY

In its attention to the processes of subjectification of the liberal ideology, Ian McKay's liberal order framework focuses the historian's gaze upon the human individual.[1] On the peripheries of that discerning view is the bio-geophysical environment, along with the biotic and abiotic elements that populate it, posed as seemingly indiscernible components of a static backdrop before which the constitution of the liberal subject has unfolded. This ontological posture eschews the findings in the humanities and social sciences that recognize the participation of non-humans in the construction of cultural and artifactual sets of human societies.[2]

Environmental history has been at the forefront of that venture, focusing its attention on the interactions between ecological processes, human actions, social changes, and power relations.[3] Like the liberal order framework, it seeks richer and more pertinent histories beyond those provided by narratives entrenched in the specificities of their case studies, or traditional accounts extolling a message of progress as a series of necessary steps towards predetermined goals of individual achievement. It also participates in the reinvigoration of political history by taking into account recent scholarship concerning ideology, state formation, and law and order. Environmental historians have analysed the marginalization of settlers, farmers, labourers, women, and Aboriginal peoples and the various ways in which they have resisted and subverted the omnipresent machinery of domination and, to a lesser extent, how the latter have co-opted them.[4] By exploring specifically the role of nature in the construction and representation of the Canadian nation and in the modernization of Canadian society, they have also contributed to our understanding of 'Canada as a project.'[5]

There remain, however, important differences in the two approaches.

Seemingly left out of the liberal order framework is any recognition of the social relationships with nature, let alone of the agency of non-human actors, which constitute the central tenets of environmental history. Where the focus of the liberal order framework leaves the environment to an indiscernible periphery of social changes, environmental historians see the dynamic interplay of nature and society. Thus, we need ask: can there be an environmental history of the liberal order?

This chapter explores potential answers to that question, particularly through the employ of current scholarship on state formation and governmentality, in order to better understand the ways in which non-human elements have become objects and means of power relations supporting the production and reproduction of the liberal order. Our purpose in examining the role of non-humans in the process of state formation, and with specific reference to the development of the administrative capacities of the state during a period of nascent conservationism in Quebec at the turn of the twentieth century, is to demonstrate how the environment should be considered an active and instrumental part of the liberal order. Far from being passive and neutral objects, non-human actors have participated in a process of acculturation of behaviours and values that were deliberately and systematically introduced by human actors of the liberal order. Our goal here is not to stress the polysemy of the liberal project, nor to identify those responsible for its production and reproduction, and even less to underline its contradictions. Nor do we wish to address the Gramscian agenda of the liberal order framework. Other contributions to this volume speak to these issues. Simply, our purpose is to direct the attention of proponents and critics of the hegemonic capabilities of the liberal order towards the contingencies of non-human actions in resisting its production or incapacitating its rejection. Like humans, non-human actors can be equally capable of subverting, contingently or purposefully, the liberal order.

Environmental History and the Reconnaissance of the Liberal Order in Canada

The heuristic value of the liberal order framework lies in its will to liberate the voices of dissent and to seriously consider the perspectives of those who rejected, voluntarily or not, the liberal construction of Canada.[6] But in granting such precedence to the individuals who articulated, internalized, resisted, or refashioned liberal values, the liberal order framework has relieved non-human entities of any historical role. This is, perhaps, merely an unintended consequence of the rejection of the traditional national narrative that reduced Canada to a collection of natural elements, such as the St Lawrence or the Canadian Shield.[7] While not named directly, one is led to believe that cod, beaver, grain, and other staples are a part of the elements of triumphal environmentalism responsible for the 'neo-Wagnerian myth-symbol complex Canadian nationalists have woven around the St Lawrence Valley.'[8] In that regard, it is understandable that in his framework McKay wishes to distance himself from narratives that have been construed as struggles against nature, be they celebration of pioneers who conquered the rugged land of the Canadian Shield, the Prairies, and the North, or exploration of the economic consequences of fisheries, fur trade, agriculture as well as timber, and mineral exploitation on the fashioning of the socio-economic system in Canada.

Environmental historians also reject such blatant environmental determinism. They do not merely look to understand the role played by staples and their influence upon modes of economic and social development, nor do they regard the land and its products as simple commodities to extract and consume, to buy and sell.[9] Rather, they reflect upon ecological transformations and interrelationships between the changing elements of society and the bio-geophysical context to reveal, among other things, how nature, construed and idealized by human beings, contributes to shaping social structures and cultural changes. Over the past thirty years, environmental history has sought to fully acknowledge the developments of scientific ecology and cease to treat human actors as if they were extricated from their environment. In so doing, this field of historical research has succeeded in fostering a better understanding of the interactions between social and ecological changes.

It is that environmental history perspective which reveals the anthropocentric bias of the liberal order framework, one that recognizes only the individual subject who has been invested the right to property, equality, and freedom. Such is not surprising, as this liberal individual is precisely the product of the European Enlightenment – a movement that took such great pains to disassociate nature from culture so that man, endowed with reason and master of his own destiny, could better control the elements of his environment. After all, human freedom became possible only when human beings envisioned ending all subjugation to natural forces and other external constraints.

We need only reference the heated debates that took place during the eighteenth and nineteenth centuries concerning the relationship between man and animal to see how the liberal individual emerged from the evanescence of nature. The European Enlightenment studied the natural world to master its function, to better manage it, and to guide it into the service of man. Reason, alone, permitted the conquest of nature, the ultimate condition for the emergence of civilization.[10] But this conquest was also intensely individualized, because the liberal subject had to struggle to resist his most basic instincts, which associated him with the animals from which he sought to distinguish himself.[11] Those individuals incapable of controlling their natural impulses were debased for having transgressed the boundaries separating man and animal.[12] As the anthropologist Mary Douglas notes, 'The contrast between man and not-man provides an analogy for the contrast between the member of the human community and the outsider.'[13] Therefore, the essential otherness of the liberal subject finds one of its strongest foundations in the negative portrayal of non-humans, which, by the contrast it provoked, reflected all that was particular and admirable in mankind. In that regard, non-humans were as much a part of the groups of those excluded from the liberal order as women, Natives, workers, and ethnic groups whose voices have since been recovered by social and cultural historians.[14]

Silenced by the liberal paradigm, non-human actors have, we suggest, their own history to rehabilitate, like those human beings whose exclusion was, as Adele Perry aptly describes it in this volume, intrinsically constitutive of the liberal order. Indeed, environmental historians have started the process of integrating and speaking for those biotic and abiotic inhabitants without a readily recognizable voice – everything from insects, worms, and fish to water and soil.[15] Similarly, they have shown how the appropriation and modification of landscapes formed a process that accompanied the subjugation of local populations, who found themselves muzzled because they did not comply with the values of progress and improvement as they manifested themselves in the transformation of the environment.[16] Exemplary of the new dialogue is the environmental historian's reinterpretation of the resettlement of the Americas. No longer an event marked solely by conquest by Europeans of indigenous peoples, but a larger process of biotic invasions including germs, plants, and animals, all of which acted in concert to suppress, control, and overcome parts of the indigenous flora and fauna.[17] That one wonders about the consciousness and will behind these acts of domination only reveals the supremacy accorded to human reason and a naive belief in its mighty power, while neglecting the fact that social changes may well result from the unintended consequences of human actions. It remains to be seen if, as objects and means of the liberal order, non-human actors did not also possess their own potential for subversion and resistance.

State Formation and the Government of Non-Human Actors: Towards the Bio-politics of Natural Elements

What a reconnaissance of the liberal order needs to recognize is that the construction of Canadian nature and the construction of liberal culture are part of the same ideological order. The domination and exclusion of human and non-human actors are both constitutive of the liberal order and materialize in landscapes and social structures. Social relationships with nature participate in a liberal order that, itself, instituted even more specific relationships with nature, notably by using elements of the environment to diffuse and inculcate liberal values of, say, property, equality, and freedom. Nature here refers both to discourses and representations – be they scientific, political, religious – and the bio-geophysical basis of environmental changes, whether they result from human actions or ecological dynamics.

The challenge for us, then, is how best to integrate non-human actors in the liberal order framework. One place to start is to consider the consequences of Crown land ownership on the definition and regulation of access to resources at a time when efforts were directed at implementing a rational and efficient exploitation of natural resources.[18] Because the state thus appears to be a central actor in fashioning new social relationships to nature, it seems appropriate to articulate our reflection around the extension of its administrative capacities, provided that one does not treat the state as the sole actor and that one emphasizes the constructed character of the State. In that regard, a state formation approach seems appropriate, especially since it forms, along with ideology as well as law and order, one of the three recent strands of the renewal of Canadian political history upon which McKay builds his liberal order framework.[19] Not that liberal ideology, or law and order, are irrelevant to our purpose of clarifying the role of nature in the liberal order. Quite the contrary. As our case studies will demonstrate, regulations under the liberal state and diffusion of the liberal ideology of improvement both played a role in defining social relationships to nature and turning nature into property.[20] Yet, a state formation approach has more to offer for the integration of environmental history and the liberal order framework. It provides us with analytical tools to attend to the production of a liberal order as an on-going process that rests on power relations best understood not simply as acts of domination exercised by one social group over another (or others), but as a *dispositif*. Since the latter refers to a cluster of relations composed of 'man and things' that the modern form of liberal government seeks to improve, it enables us to acknowledge the role of non-human actors in the productive relations of the liberal order.[21] Furthermore, as discussed by Bruce Curtis and Michèle Dagenais in this volume, a study of liberal governmentality highlights the process through which domination and self-governance of individuals and populations were made possible by their being abstracted and formatted into objects of knowledge and power. Since that process of knowledge formation equally applies to human and non-human objects, a state formation approach informed by governmentality studies appears key for a reconnaissance of the nature of the liberal order.

Two aspects of the process of state formation, in particular, are of interest to analyse the administration of nature and social relationships to the environment as the project of rules accompanied the production of the liberal order: the state as an agent of articulation and inculcation of values projected by the liberal order and the support of science in extending the liberal administrative capacities of the state. Far from limiting itself to the growth of government institutions, state formation engaged in the diffusion and inculcation of a system of norms and values. This process would be accomplished not just by the force of the government institutions that would promote it, but also through the internalization of these norms and values by targeted populations. The cultural revolution that accompanied the transformation of government during the eighteenth century rested precisely on the norms and values of the elite liberal, who would use the state as a vehicle to generalize the adhesion to abstract forms of property and individualism as well as all other behaviour appropriate to the *embourgeoisement* of society.[22]

Building on this approach, historians have drawn upon the work of Michel Foucault to show how the modern liberal state became an agent of moral regulation through the extension of its administrative capacities.[23] This extension was made possible in part due to the scientific knowledge that the state generated and mobilized from the end of the eighteenth century in order to resolve the dilemmas posed by liberalism, such as how to govern less, following liberal principles, but control more, all in accordance with the principles of security and sovereignty.[24] Practices of governmentality provided solutions to the dilemma, first through the discipline of the human body, and then through the government of populations.[25] Herein, to this bio-power exercised over individuals succeeded a bio-politics, a 'manner ... of rationalizing the problems posed to the practice of government by phenomena belonging to a population: health, hygiene, birth, longevity, and race.'[26] Statistics, public health, psychiatry, education were domains wherein the state science formulated tools to define and master the behaviour of individuals, and to govern the conduct of populations in a manner coherent with liberal principles. As it shaped human beings into populations for their government, abstractly and concretely, science equipped the state with tools to formulate social programs and policies. These also enabled a liberal government of populations by leaving the individual a margin of freedom and the values attendant to the exercise of liberty. State science thus contributed to the establishment of the liberal order as it informed state activities and mechanisms used to imprint norms and values and teach individuals how to govern themselves.

Yet, not unlike the liberal order framework, studies of the rise of liberal governmentality have also tended to limit our understanding of state science by focusing on instruments applied to the government of human conduct and a bio-politics exclusively concerned with human populations.[27] While these studies privilege common domains of governmental activities such as education and health, the extension of administrative capacities also targeted non-human actors to imprint moral progress in areas other than those taken up by social policies.[28]

The British and French movements for the prevention of the cruelty towards animals at the beginning of the nineteenth century provide a revealing illustration. This movement sought foremost to avoid the debasement of man by cruel and degrading acts towards sentient beings and constituted above all, a form of social instruction, 'a problem relating to humanity, and not to nature.'[29] The prohibition of cruel treatment towards animals was directed generally only towards domesticated animals, those closest to man, and it reprimanded only displays of cruelty in public that could corrupt the sensibility of man. Here, animals became a tool to inculcate liberal behaviour in the population and prevent degrading spectacles that could encourage similar reprehensible acts towards other humans.[30]

The government of conduct and the process of state formation also rested on state science that expanded the notion of population to include humans and non-humans, consequently co-producing natural and social orders.[31] Scientific forestry as developed in Prussia and Saxony at the end of the eighteenth century illustrates how state science equally fashioned the environment and the function of the latter – manipulated, tamed, and framed – in the government of individuals and populations. Originally developed within the realm of cameralism, forestry sought to provide constant revenue for the public treasury; operations of selective cuts maintaining a balance with the natural regeneration of the forest ensured a constant production of commercial wood and prevented the premature exhaustion of timber resources. Prussian state forestry based the commercial exploitation of the forest on the manipulation of the forest environment that was composed of communities of animals, plants, and humans.[32] Protecting the forest also meant expropriating rural landholders, eliminating pasturage, or banishing peasants from forestry resources they counted on for food, building, and energy. The forest scientifically managed by the state foresters began giving access to its resources to multiple users who would adopt a new code of conduct for the use of the forest. Thus, trappers, hunters, and gleaners who did not adopt the new modes of operation in the scientifically managed forest became poachers and illegal interlopers. Through the simplification of the forest habitat, forestry as state science aimed at regulating not only the economic exploitation of a natural resource – the trees – but also those human and non-human inhabitants that lived in and that made up the forest landscape.[33]

As a state science, Prussian forestry intervened simultaneously in the environment and in society by designing the forest as an entity equally composed of humans and non- humans and acting upon it accordingly. Such intervention was not simply limited to defining and enclosing space in order to establish a new social and natural order. As a technology of power, the scientific activities of the government enabled the state to manipulate the environment and enlist non-human actors for the expressed purpose of inculcating into its human subjects moral values, attitudes, and behaviours. But, as James Scott reminds us, a century after the implementation of the scientific forest, Germany had unwittingly created a 'dead forest.' Provoked in large part by the simplification of the forest environment into an intensive monoculture, the disruption of ecological processes involving the nutrient cycle and interactions between plants, animals and fungi caused a production loss and a drop in timber quality, thereby defeating the purpose of scientific forestry.[34]

These experiences of liberal governance in early-nineteenth-century Europe highlight processes wherein state science and populations of human and non-human actors intermingled to produce a landscape of self-government. The next sections briefly present two case studies of the conservationist movement in Quebec at the turn of the twentieth century whereby forests and aquatic landscapes – partly produced by the state, partly by the self-governed populations of humans and non-humans that inhabited them – bore the imprint of liberal values. Species were introduced and reproduced to shape human relationships to society and nature over publicly owned but privately leased territories. The liberal order materialized in a landscape transformed for the self-government of human and non-human actors, notably through their participation in subsistence and commercial activities.

Seeding Liberal Values in the Forests of Quebec

Often identified as the precursor of contemporary environmentalism, the conservation movement of the late-nineteenth and early-twentieth centuries found its purpose in the encouragement of wise use of natural resources (timber, fish, wildlife, soil, water, and minerals) so as to avoid their exhaustion, while at the same time attempting to assure an equitable access among different interests and from one generation to the next. The historiography of the North American conservation movement has sufficiently demonstrated how these objectives were attained through a process of state appropriation of resources and a gradual integration of a coordinated policy of management guided by scientists under the employ of the state.[35] More recently, it has shown also how humans subverted the domination of the ideal of a conservationist elite.[36]

In Quebec, as elsewhere in North America, the conservation movement grew out of a debate over the best method of addressing the exploitation of forestry resources in the late nineteenth century. Rapid growth and construction, along with the diffusion of the railroad, provided favourable conditions for the steady decline of forest reserves in the United States. This decline was accompanied by enormous anxiety among those who feared a shortage of the basic materials needed to assure unchecked prosperity and brought about correspondingly diverse solutions to the problems of forest exploitation.[37] Some recommended restricting forestry development to special reserves, while others supported restricted access to the forest itself.[38]

Basic to these two seemingly divergent approaches were issues of property and of improvement of land and woodlots, with conservationists at the same time putting forward the need for applying the principles of a scientific forestry with a corresponding program of managed reforestation. By basing itself on a whole collection of social and cultural realities, the idea of reforestation would ultimately go far beyond the technical and ecological realms. It was not so much the forest resources that were to be regenerated, as it was the actual seeding and cultivation of new attitudes among the rural population, especially the one in charge of settling new territories. Reforestation initiatives and publications by individuals and government scientists served to educate rural populations and, consequently, stressed small-scale projects such as the cultivation of woodlands on farms.

During the late nineteenth century, as settlement efforts were undertaken to populate the western and northern areas of Quebec, conservationists adapted the reforestation movement by speaking of it not only as a solution to deforestation of large tracks of forest by the timber industry, but as a method of reconstructing a landscape stripped by rapid and careless settlement and by destructive land clearing, voluntary or not, of the wooded areas around farms. The ardent reforestation propagandist Henri-Gustave Joly de Lotbinière denounced the kind of clearing formerly undertaken in the parishes and called for farmers to plant trees on their land in order to avoid a shortage of firewood and disturbance of agro-climatic conditions.[39] Preoccupied by the disappearance of the forests in the older parishes, he founded the *Société pour le reboisement de la Province de Québec* in 1872, with the goal of sensitizing the population, especially farmers, about the necessity of conservation and the means to 'somehow restore our ruined forests.'[40] Another proponent of reforestation and member of that association, Jean-Charles Chapais, spoke out against the voracious appetite for new land by settlers and called for them to temper their destructive clearing practices. In his *Guide illustré du sylviculteur canadien*, he called upon the settler, so often blamed for the felling of the forest, whether by negligence in his use of fire or by blind land clearing, to cease his injurious practices of deforestation, and instead engage himself in beneficial reforestation.[41] Chapais counselled the settler to think of his children and throw himself immediately into the planting and husbanding of a woodlot on their farm. Not only would the woodlot provide the settler and his family with firewood and construction material, its surplus could also be sold to supplement his family income.

Here was the model of liberal conduct that the settler should adopt. Rather than engaging in ruinous and unprofitable cutting of the forest, the liberal French Canadian settler was encouraged to maintain a renewable woodlot that would generate a stable income, thereby giving his family security against unforeseen events. While remaining safe from misfortune, the settler and his family could devote themselves to further improvement of their land. This wise cultivation would bring an end to the constant search for food and other basic necessities thereby permitting activities that could be channelled into the elevation of the spirit and of individual tastes. More basically, the settler would cease subsistence practices to participate in the market economy by selling the products of his land.

Founded on the idea that the eventual disappearance of the forest should be prevented, the rhetoric surrounding reforestation and the overall protection of the forest gave value to one type of relationship, wherein nature was cast as property. The settler-farmer was to improve the land on his property and the landscape in his county, not just for himself, but for those who would inherit it; otherwise he risked entering into a pitiful cycle of misery and poverty. And, of course, the upkeep of his woodland would teach him to better respect the property of others as well. The cultivation of the reforestation ideal among the settlers, with its common ideals of respect for trees and property, brought another issue to the forefront – the reservation of forestry concessions to the timber industry.

In the aftermath of the Second American Forestry Congress held in Montreal in 1882, the commissioner of Crown lands of the Province of Quebec, William Lynch,[42] created a vast forest reserve near the tributaries of the Outaouais River[43] to guarantee timber merchants a constant supply of pine. At the same time, he sought to exclude from these territories the settler – whom he regarded as little more than an agent of destruction and waste and, most significantly, the main cause of fire. For conservationists, the issue of fire was a convenient one. Rather than having to account for popular revolt ignited by the exclusion of settlers from the timber reserve, they used the issue to denounce the irresponsible character of settlers whose neglect often caused brush fires and destroyed the resources on a territory privately leased to timber interests.[44]

Facing limitations on their public access to timber resources by a system of private control of public forest territory, settlers simply cut wood illegally, sometimes engaging in setting fires out of resentment.[45] Despite the abolition of the forest reserves in 1888, antagonism between the settlers and timber merchants continued. If settlers and timbers were to form a landscape coherent with the policy and interests of the provincial government and supporting industry, they would have to do so outside a territory of licensed timber cutters. They were encouraged to participate in economic activities based on forest exploitation, but on agricultural lands classified for their exclusive use.[46] At issue here was the separation of agricultural and forestry lands to enable the timber industry to re-conquer forests lost to settlement.[47]

Scientific forestry acted as a lever to classify Crown lands and to extend control over the landscape to the Department of Land and Forests. Between 1905 and 1907 the Department created large forest reserves in Gaspésie, Rimouski, Saguenay, Labrador, Saint-Maurice and, Chaudière, solely for the future use of timber companies. In 1911 it set aside smaller reserves for the exclusive use of settlers.[48] Under the supervision of forest wardens, these township reserves were intended to ensure wood for heating and construction.[49] The ministry hoped to stimulate the interest of the settlers in protecting the forest by their gaining a direct knowledge of forestry and to promote an understanding of the forest as property, albeit a common one.[50] The Department of Lands and Forests also engaged in a reforestation program in these townships, to ensure a steady supply of trees for settlers, although the tree species it selected for that purpose – the white spruce – was specifically meant for growing a pulp forest.[51]

These new forest reserves ultimately succeeded in ending the opposition between timber interests and the settlement movement. A new discourse described the nascent pulp and paper industry as 'the natural auxiliary' of settlement because 'it gave to the settler the means to make money with the waste timber that he would have otherwise been obliged to burn in order to clean up his land.'[52] Thus, scientific activities of the Department of Lands and Forests altered the relationship between settlers and the forest. It also shaped the values and the attitudes of the settlers towards the forest, perceived as a productive landscape and a model of common property. At the same time, reforestation ceased being only a responsibility for settlers – who had been propagandized into maintaining their own woodlot – and now became the responsibility of the state. In that regard, the reforestation of township reserves called for a specific material construction of the landscape, essentially composed of white spruce, which enabled settlers to participate actively in commercial transactions with the pulp and paper industry, and to respect the integrity of the vast domains leased to the lumber industry.

Improving Aquatic Habitats and Their Users

The efforts of conservationists and the provincial government to promote good stewardship over Crown lands manifested themselves not only in the cultural and ecological changes of the forests of Quebec. Agents of civil society and state authorities also sought to bring order and value to aquatic ecosystems. They assembled freshwater lakes, rivers, and streams into a new cultural space called a sport fishery and generated valuable and iconic mythologies of landscape that were diffused far beyond the province's wilderness into the drawing rooms of the elite from London, to Boston, to New York, and Philadelphia.[53] As in the case of forestry, conservation of the aquatic wilderness became a process by which the liberal order redefined the boundaries between nature and culture, as well as those between humans and non-humans, for the common good.

Pivotal to these changes were the fish and game clubs that had beseiged the aquatic wilderness well before the provincial government.[54] Pressed to protect fish resources over a vast territory but lacking the necessary means to do so, the provincial government leased large tracts of well-watered lands to anglers for their fishing pursuits. This placed vast territorial holdings under leasehold tenure in the hands of fish and game clubs that acted as 'wise stewards' for the improvement of natural resources situated on Crown lands. Between 1870 and 1914, more than five hundred of these clubs were created.[55] Wealthy and influential clubs like the Roberval and the Triton clubs came to exercise great control over large tracts of land, and spent vast sums of money in Quebec's wilderness areas, sometimes for the enjoyment of a mere few hundred people, thereby turning fish and game resources into the property of an urban elite. Furthermore, through their activities and investments these clubs enticed cultural changes in far-reaching communities where they created work and injected currency into local economies, seeking to emancipate residents from their subsistence practices rather than seeing them implicated in unsustainable activities.

Starting with the adoption of the Act for the Protection of Fisheries in Lower Canada in 1855, the provincial government legislated for the protection of fishery resources. Guardians and wardens of clubs became deputized agents of state authority in implementing laws and regulations that, conservation advocates argued, aimed at ensuring an equal access to fish, during their own time and for future generations.[56]

State agents and private wardens employed by clubs used all methods of coercion to tackle poaching, including public humiliation, fines, and jail time.[57]

Compared to the angler, an essentially good agent of 'fair play,' who came during the spring and took one fish at a time with rod and line, those who continued to catch fish in freshwater environments through the use of such outlawed methods as nets, harpoons, weirs, and traps were cast as poachers who flaunted state authority by continuing to harvest fish in large quantities.[58] For conservation advocates, poaching amounted to a social ill that illustrated rural ignorance and a lack of individual self-control and demonstrated wastefulness. The poacher was a person who selfishly acted against his own better interest and the good of his community by 'destroying' fish in all seasons, even taking them through the ice in winter.[59] This irresponsible behaviour also infringed on the leisure and liberty of those who adhered to club rules and regulations and paid their dues to extol nature's bounty.

For Aboriginal peoples and rural populations, however, the liberal policy encouraging the development of a sport fishery and the improvement of the aquatic landscape by anglers led to an increasing marginalization from freshwater fisheries. Some turned to the courts for redress or delivered petitions to parliament, but to little avail.[60] Mostly, common people simply ignored the laws – setting up systems to avoid wardens or threatening them into submission. Consequently, some proponents of conservation opted for a permissive approach to accommodate local subsistence practices, which they considered to have a less detrimental impact on the resources.[61]

By the end of the nineteenth century, Aboriginal peoples and rural populations had abandoned many of their own fishing traditions in order to mimic the habits of the elite anglers. By doing so they facilitated the transformation of the ubiquitous fly rod and creel from symbols of the elite into a necessary and accessible tool for a broader element of society that participated in the production of the liberal order.[62] Governmental promotion of the fishery, in conjunction with the opening up of new areas by the railroad, the broader availability of cheaper angling equipment, and the publication of popular angling literature that promoted more readily accessible species like perch, walleye, and bass, supported these changes. In exchange, new participants in the conservation of fish resources obtained public fishing reserves 'in which the residents [...] may freely fish for their subsistence and that of their family.'[63] Much like the forest reserves in the townships, the fishing reserves were created to address the issue of a growing dissatisfaction by local anglers who, having increasingly been deprived of access to fishing, opposed the system of privately controlled fishing leases and its attendant elite privileges. These reserves, however, were few and of little consequence for the existing system.

The legal marginalization of individuals who did not respect the property rights of tenure holders – and who persevered in adopting malevolent attitudes toward the replenishing capacity of fishing resources – and the co-optation of those who did had an ecological parallel. With a new understanding as to the exhaustibility of resources, proponents of conservation and state agents engaged in pisciculture – the cultivation of fish through the science of artificial fecundation.[64] By 1889 the federal Department of Marine and Fisheries had twelve hatcheries in various provinces, all largely intended for the conservation of salmon.[65] In 1915 it transferred its six federal hatcheries in Quebec to provincial control in a federal handover of jurisdiction concerning inland waters. Almost immediately, the provincial government adapted the new hatchery system to the amelioration of its sport fishery by importing species popular with anglers from around the world, such as rainbow trout from the watersheds west of the Rocky Mountains, and brown trout from Europe.[66]

In much the same way that elite anglers and nineteenth-century agents of the liberal order had deeply modified human cultures engaged in fishing activities, the plan to improve the aquatic landscape brought along a new cultural space that comprised communities of fish and sportsmen, some deemed desirable and others not. Fish and game clubs and the provincial Department of Lands and Forests expended great scientific energy in efforts to propagate and broadly distribute the valuable salmon and trout. As Natives and rural people confronted a system that conservation advocates believed was in their own best interest, fish that had been so culturally important for them, such as sturgeon and eel, became classified as less valuable.[67]

The sport fishery may have been built around anglers whose interactions with the natural world were based upon codes of conducts among a coterie of a two-hundred-year- old elitist tradition, but these activities were also taking place within dynamic ecosystems where fish species, possessing their own codes – albeit genetic – resulting from hundreds of millions of years of evolution lived and adapted, independent of human influence.[68] Despite consistent efforts, the use of hatcheries, the development of protective laws, and the privileging of anglers, Atlantic salmon runs continued to decline and even disappear.[69] Furthermore, the use of fish ladders intended to give migratory salmon a chance to negotiate dams were less useful for other migratory species like eel and sturgeon, which lacked the biological advantage of being able to make powerful leaps.[70] The disinterest in conserving migratory species of little value to anglers was one factor in their eventual decline all along the St Lawrence.[71] At the same time, many of the non-indigenous fish like rainbow and brown trout, thrived and fashioned ecological systems that reinforced the cultural orders of the elite anglers.

Conclusion

The history of conservation efforts in late-nineteenth-century Quebec has illustrated how the co-construction of nature and society can characterize the production of a liberal order. Whether fashioned directly by state science or indirectly, through the carefully guided actions of its citizens via accepted codes of conduct, the environment bore the imprint of a dominant culture in which non-human and human actors alike participated. Inculcated with a set of liberal values aimed at the protection of habitats as well as the stewardship and regeneration of biotic and abiotic elements they considered valuable economic resources, populations have governed themselves according to these values.

By exploring scientific discourses and practices that produced social relationships to nature as well as hybrid populations, environmental history can bring to light the mechanisms of subjectification of a liberal order taking shape in the landscape itself. Furthermore, by giving a role to non-human actors – however they were eventually manipulated by human beings and subsequently humanized – it can reveal the moral frame that has nourished the representations of nature and interventions upon it. By doing so, environmental history provides an interpretation of the processes of state formation and social regulation distinct from current socio-political historical studies, as state science enacted upon a broader terrain than that inhabited by humans alone. If the fashioning of a social reality was a product of state formation, with the social sciences participating, the latter did so in conjunction with natural sciences that moulded a natural reality, part human artifice and part ecological fact.[72]

Still, it remained that non-humans raised specific problems and issues for the art of liberal governance. For one thing, the variability and diversity of life made non-humans difficult to handle for the state seeking, above all, to make them pliable enough to fit into its schemes of sovereignty and security. Moreover, changes in the regime of scientific knowledge further perturbed ancient natural orders upon which novel social orders were being constructed. Trees uprooted from accompanying ecosystems and transplanted into ordered landscapes either became subject to disease, refused to grow, or formed new habitats. Exotic game fishes seeded into foreign aquatic habitats failed to replicate, devastated indigenous species, or became acclimatized. In these, and many other ways, non-humans rendered the production of a liberal order in constant need of being thought anew.

If environmental history can broaden our understanding of the production of the liberal order, the application of the latter to environmental history has equally useful implications. The liberal order framework offers environmental historians working on the nineteenth century a greater understanding of governments and members of civil society, whether in Canada, Great Britain, or the United States, that manipulated the environment and the culture that shaped the landscape. Moreover, the liberal order framework shows that there was a great, common moral imperative to be found among modern liberal states. For too long environmental historians have worked within the isolation of their own national identities, searching to identify specific causes for particular interactions with the environment that the liberal order framework has revealed to be common to a Western ideology. Perhaps, most interestingly, the liberal order framework offers environmental historians a better way to understand the paradox of the conservation movement: a paradox because so-called conservation practices often went beyond conserving, and became improving – whether through the creation of new habitats, the acculturation of human populations, the acclimatization of non-humans, or even creation of new forms of life itself – all of which remain firmly rooted in liberal principles.

NOTES

The authors thank Jean-François Constant and Michel Ducharme for their organization of the 'Liberal Order in Canadian History' symposium and for the edition of its proceedings. Their invitation, insistence, and enduring support have made our participation and this chapter possible.

238 Stéphane Castonguay and Darin Kinsey

1 Ian McKay, 'The Liberal Order Framework: A Prospectus for a Reconnaissance of Canadian History,' *Canadian Historical Review* 81 (2000): 624.
2 See among others, Harriet Ritvo, 'Animal Planet,' *Environmental History* 9 (2004): 204–20; Bruno Latour, *Nous n'avons jamais été modernes* (Paris: La Découverte, 2001); Richard White, *The Organic Machine* (New York: Hill and Wang, 1995); Edmund Russell, 'Evolutionary History: Prospectus for a New Field,' *Environmental History* 8 (2003): 204–28; Robert Delort, *Les animaux ont une histoire* (Paris: Les Éditions du Seuil, 1984); Julie Cruikshank, *Do Glaciers Listen? Local Knowledge, Colonial Encounters, and Social Imagination* (Vancouver: UBC Press, 2005).
3 For recent surveys of the field, see J.R. McNeill, 'Observations on the Nature and Culture of Environmental History,' *History and Theory* 42 (2003): 5–43 and the special issue of *Environment and History* 10 (2004): 379–536. Recent surveys of Canadian environmental history are provided by Graeme Wynn and M. Evenden, "54:40 or Fight': Writing within and across Borders in North American Environmental History,' in *Nature's End: History and the Environment*, ed. Paul Warde and Sverker Sörlin (London: Palgrave, forthcoming, 2008) and, for Quebec, S. Castonguay, 'Society, Territory and Ecology in Québec: A Historiographic Review,' in S. Castonguay, R. Judd, and S.J. Pyne, *Positioning Québec in Global Environmental History* (Quebec: Nota Bene, 2007), 11–86. See also Alan MacEachern and M. Evenden, 'Special issue on Canada,' *Environmental History* 12 (2007): 755–1019.
4 Theodore Binnema, *Common and Contested Ground: A Human and Environmental History of the Northwestern Plains* (Norman: University of Oklahoma Press, 2001); Bill Parenteau, 'A 'Very Determined Opposition to the Law': Conservation, Angling Leases, and Social Conflict in the Canadian Atlantic Salmon Fishery, 1867–1914,' *Environmental History* 9 (2004): 436–63; Parenteau, '"Care, Control and Supervision": Native People in the Canadian Atlantic Salmon Fishery, 1867–1900,' *Canadian Historical Review* 79 (1998): 1–35; Tina Loo, 'Making a Modern Wilderness: Wildlife Management in Canada, 1900–1950,' *Canadian Historical Review* 82 (2001): 91–121; Loo, 'People in the Way: Modernity, Environment, and Society on the Arrow Lakes,' *BC Studies* 142/143 (2004): 43–77; Loo, 'Of Moose and Men: Hunting for Masculinities in the Far West,' *Western Historical Quarterly* 32 (2001): 296–319; Alan MacEachern, *Natural Selection: National Parks in Atlantic Canada, 1935–1970* (Montreal and Kingston: McGill-Queen's University Press, 2001).
5 McKay, 'Liberal Order Framework,' 621 for the citation. See also Suzanne Zeller, *Inventing Canada: Early Victorian Science and the Idea of a Transcontinental Nation* (Toronto: University of Toronto Press, 1987); Stéphane Castonguay, 'Naturalizing Federalism: Insect Outbreaks and the Centralization of

Entomological Research in Canada, 1884–1914,' *Canadian Historical Review* 85 (2004): 1–34.

6 McKay, 'Liberal Order Framework,' 620–1.

7 Ibid., 624.

8 Ibid., 622n11.

9 Wynn and D. Evenden, '"54:40 or Fight."'

10 Max Horkheimer and Theodor W. Adorno, 'Le concept d'"Aufklärung,"' in *La dialectique de la raison: Fragments philosophiques* (Paris: Gallimard, 1974), 21–57; Stephen Toulmin, *Cosmopolis: The Hidden Agenda of Modernity* (Chicago: University of Chicago Press, 1990).

11 Anita Guerrini, *Experimenting with Humans and Animals* (Baltimore: Johns Hopkins University Press, 2003), 70–92; Harriet Ritvo, *The Animal Estate: The English and Other Creatures in the Victorian Age* (Cambridge: Oxford University Press, 1987).

12 Keith Thomas, *Man and the Natural World: Changing Attitudes in England, 1500–1800* (New York: Oxford University Press, 1993).

13 Mary Douglas, 'Self-evidence,' in *Implicit Meanings: Selected Essays in Anthropology*, 2nd ed. (New York: Routledge, 1999), 262.

14 Chad Gaffield and Pam Gaffield, 'Introduction,' in *Consuming Canada: Readings in Environmental History*, ed. Chad Gaffield and Pam Gaffield (Toronto: Copp Clark Ltd, 1995), 4–5.

15 Donald Worster, 'A Long Cold View of History,' *American Scholar* 74 (2005): 57–66; Castonguay, 'Naturalizing Federalism,' 1n3; Darin Kinsey, "Seeding the Water as the Earth': The Epicenter and Peripheries of a Western *Aquacultural Revolution*,' *Environmental History* 11 (2006): 527–66; Marc Cioc, *The Rhine an Eco-Biography 1815–2000* (Seattle: University of Washington Press, 2002); Steven Stoll, *Larding the Lean Earth: Soil and Society in Nineteenth-Century America* (New York: Hill and Wang, 2002).

16 Colin Coates, *The Metamorphoses of Landscape and Community in Early Quebec* (Montreal and Kingston: McGill-Queen's University Press, 2000); Loo, 'People in the Way'; John Sandlos, *Hunters at the Margin: Native People and Wildlife Conservation in the Northwest Territories* (Vancouver: UBC Press, 2007); Mark Spence, *Dispossessing the Wilderness: Indian Removal and the Making of the National Parks* (New York: Oxford University Press, 1999).

17 Alfred W. Crosby, *Columbian Exchange: Biological and Cultural Consequences of 1492* (Westport, CT: Greenwood Press, 1972); William H. McNeil, *The Global Condition: Conquerors, Catastrophes, and Community* (Princeton: Princeton University Press, 2001); Elinor G.K. Melville, *A Plague of Sheep: Environmental Consequences of the Conquest of Mexico* (Cambridge: Cambridge University Press, 1994); Virginia DeJohn Anderson, *Creatures of Empire: How*

Domestic Animals Transformed Early America (Oxford: Oxford University Press, 2004).

18 H.V. Nelles, *The Politics of Development: Forests, Mines & Hydro-Electric Power in Ontario, 1849–1941* (Toronto: Macmillan, 1974).

19 McKay, 'Liberal Order Framework,' 621.

20 William Cronon, *Changes in the Land: Indians, Colonists, and the Ecology of New England* (New York: Hill and Wang, 1983).

21 Michel Foucault, 'Le jeu de Michel Foucault,' in *Dits et Écrits*, vol. 3, *1976–1979* (Paris: Gallimard, 1984), 298–301.

22 Philip Abrams, 'Notes on the Difficulty of Studying the State,' *Journal of Historical Sociology* 1 (1998): 58–89; Philip Corrigan and Derek Sawyer, *The Great Arch: English State Formation as Cultural Revolution* (Oxford: Blackwell, 1991). The connection between the process described here and the liberal order is remarkable, even if these authors are curiously absent from the works cited in McKay's article.

23 Bruce Curtis, 'Révolution gouvernementale et savoir politique au Canada-Uni,' *Sociologie et société* 24 (1992): 169–79; Curtis, *The Politics of Population: State Formation, Statistics, and the Census of Canada, 1840–1875* (Toronto: University of Toronto Press, 2000); see also Jean-Marie Fecteau, *Un nouvel ordre des choses ... La pauvreté, le crime, l'État au Québec, de la fin du 18e siècle à 1840* (Montreal: VLB éditeur, 1989); and *La liberté du pauvre: Sur la régulation du crime et de la pauvreté au XIXe siècle québécois* (Montreal: VLB éditeur, 2004). Corrigan and Sawyer's *The Great Arch* has inspired the Canadian historians whose works were published in Allan Greer and Ian Radforth, eds., *Colonial Leviathan: State Formation in Mid-Nineteenth-Century Canada* (Toronto: University of Toronto Press, 1992); see p. 10.

24 That question, central to the later thought of Michel Foucault, should encourage us to properly assess the relevance of the works of the French philosopher for the reconnaissance of the liberal order. See his *Sécurité, territoire, population* (Paris: Seuil Gallimard, 2004).

25 Among others, by Foucault, *Sécurité, territoire, population*, 91–118.

26 Michel Foucault, *Naissance de la biopolitique* (Paris: Seuil, 2004), 323.

27 Bruce Curtis, *True Government by Choice Men? Inspection, Education, and State Formation in Canada West* (Toronto: University of Toronto Press, 1992); Ian Hacking, 'Biopower and the Avalanche of Printed Numbers,' *Humanities in Society* 5 (1982): 279–95; Rémi Lenoir, 'Savoirs et sciences d'état: Généalogie et démographie,' *Actes de la recherche en sciences sociales* 133 (2000): 96–7; François Delaporte, *Le savoir de la maladie: Essai sur le choléra de 1832 à Paris* (Paris: Presses universitaires de France, 1990); Thomas Osborne, 'Security and Vitality: Drains, Liberalism and Power in the Nineteenth Century,' in

Foucault and Political Reason: Liberalism, Neo-Liberalism, and Rationalities of Government, ed. Andrew Barry, Thomas Osborne, and Nikolas Rose (Chicago: University of Chicago Press, 1996), 99–121; Ian Hacking, 'How Should We Do the History of Statistics?' in *The Foucault Effect: Studies in Governmentality*, ed. Graham Burchell, Colin Gordon, and Peter Miller (Chicago: University of Chicago Press, 1991), 181–96; Matthew G. Hannah, *Governmentality and the Mastery of Territory in Nineteenth-Century America* (New York: Cambridge University Press, 2000). In addition to Foucault, see Didier Fassin and Dominique Memmi, eds., *Le gouvernement des corps*, (Paris: École des hautes études en sciences sociales, 2004), 24.

28 See, by contrast, James C. Scott, *Seeing Like a State: How Certain Schemes to Improve the Human Condition Have Failed* (New Haven: Yale University Press, 1998); Bruce Braun, 'Producing Vertical Territory: Geology and Governmentality in Late Victorian Canada,' *Ecumene* 7 (2000): 7–46; Patrick Carroll, *Science, Culture, and Modern State Formation* (Berkeley: University of California Press, 2006).

29 Luc Ferry, 'L'héritage du cartésianisme et l'approche française de la nature: Le cas du droit des animaux,' in *Les sentiments de la nature*, ed. Dominique Bourg (Paris: Éditions la Découverte, 1993), 215–26.

30 Brian Harrison, 'Animals and the State in Nineteenth-Century England,' *English Historical Review* 58 (1973): 786–820; Maurice Agulhon, 'Le sang des bêtes: Le problème de la protection des animaux en France au XIXe siècle,' *Romantisme* 31 (1981): 81–109. See also Ferry, 'L'héritage du cartésianisme.'

31 Sheila Jasanoff, ed., *States of Knowledge: The Co-Production of Science and Social Order* (New York: Routledge, 2004).

32 Henry E. Lowood, 'The Calculating Forester: Quantification, Cameral Science, and the Emergence of Scientific Forestry Management in Germany,' in *The Quantifying Spirit in the 18th Century*, ed. J.L. Heilbron and R.E. Reider (Berkeley: University of California Press, 1990), 315–42.

33 A description of this process can be found in Scott, *Seeing Like a State*, 20–1.

34 Ibid., 20.

35 On the conservation movement in the United States, see the classic account of Samuel P. Hays, *Conservation and the Gospel of Efficiency* (Cambridge: Harvard University Press, 1959), and in Canada, Michel Girard, *L'écologisme retrouvé: Essor et déclin de la Commission de la conservation du Canada* (Ottawa: Les Presses de l'Université d'Ottawa, 1994) and Janet Foster, *Working for Wildlife: The Beginning of Preservation in Canada* (Toronto: University of Toronto Press, 1978).

36 Karl Jacoby, *Crimes against Nature: Squatters, Poachers, and the Hidden History*

of American Conservation (Berkeley: University of California Press, 2001); Richard W. Judd, *Common Lands, Common People: The Origins of Conservation in Northern New England* (Cambridge: Harvard University Press, 1997); Louis S. Warren, *The Hunter's Game: Poachers and Conservationists in Twentieth-Century America* (New Haven: Yale University Press, 1997).

37 William Cronon, *Nature's Metropolis: Chicago and the Great West* (New York: Norton, 1991), 148–206, describes the effect of industry and construction on the forests of Michigan and Wisconsin.

38 Stéphane Castonguay, 'Foresterie scientifique et reforestation : L'État et la production d'une 'forêt à pâte' au Québec,' *Revue d'histoire de l'Amérique française* 60 (2006): 61–93.

39 On Joly de Lotbinière, see Marcel Hamelin 'Joly de Lotbinière, sir Henri-Gustave,' in *Dictionary of Canadian Biography*, vol. 13 (Sainte-Foy: Les Presses de l'Université Laval), 518–25; Henry-Gustave Joly de Lotbinière, 'Rapport sur la sylviculture et les forêts du Canada,' *Documents de la Session*, 9, 8 (1878): 2–20.

40 Anonymous, 'Le reboisement,' *La Gazette des campagnes*, 20 March 1873, 183–4.

41 Jean-Charles Chapais, *Le guide illustré du sylviculteur canadien* (Montreal: Eusèbe Senécal & Fils éditeur, 1883).

42 *Proceedings of the American Forestry Congress at Its Sessions Held at Cincinnati, Ohio, in April 1882 and at Montreal, Canada, in August, 1882* (Washington: Printed for the Society, 1883). On the organization of the congress and its impact on the politics of forestry in Canada, see R. Peter Gillis and T.R. Roach, *Lost Initiatives: Canada's Forest Industries, Forest Policy and Forest Conservation* (New York: Greenwood Press, 1986), 31–49, as well as Kenneth Johnstone, *Forêts et tourments: 75 ans d'histoire du Service fédéral des forêts 1899–1974* (Ottawa: Forests Canada, 1991); Patrick Blanchet, *Feux de forêt. L'histoire d'une guerre* (Montreal: Trait d'Union, 2003), 39–41.

43 *Statuts de la province de Québec*, 46 Vic. (1883) cc. 9 & 10, 'Acte pour amender de nouveau le chapitre 23 des statuts refondus du Canada concernant la vente et l'administration des bois croissant sur les terres publiques' and 'Acte pour pourvoir d'une manière plus efficace aux moyens de prévenir les feux de forêts.'

44 *Statuts de la province de Québec*, 51–52 Vic. (1895) c. 15, 'Acte relatif à la vente et l'administration des terres publiques, aux bois et aux mines, ainsi qu'au défrichement des terres et à la protection des forêts.' On the creation of reserves for wildlife protection, see Paul-Louis Martin, *La chasse au Québec*, new enlarged ed. (Montreal: Boréal, 1990), 135–9; *Statuts de la province de*

Québec, 58 Vic. (1895) cc. 22 & 23. On the reserves, see also Yves Hébert, 'Conservation, culture et identité: La création du Parc des Laurentides et du Parc de la Montagne Tremblante, 1894–1938,' in *Changing Parks: The History, Future, and Cultural Context of Parks and Heritage Landscapes*, ed. John S. Marsh and Bruce W. Hodgins (Toronto: Natural Heritage / Natural History, 1998), 140–59.

45 On the opposition between forestry interests and the colonization movement, see Bruce W. Hodgins, Jamie Benidickson, and Peter Gillis, 'The Ontario and Quebec Experiment in Forest Reserves 1883–1930,' *Journal of Forest History* 26 (1982): 20–33.

46 *L'administration libérale. Discours prononcé par l'hon. M. Lomer Gouin, ministre de la colonisation et des travaux publics, à l'Assemblée législative de Québec le 24 mars 1904* (N.P., 1904), 83.

47 Castonguay, 'Foresterie scientifique et reforestation.'

48 'The Forest Reserves of the Province of Quebec,' *Canadian Forestry Journal* 3 (1907): 68; *Statuts de la province de Québec*, 6 Ed. VII (1906) cc. 17, 'Loi établissant une réserve de forêt, de chasse et de pêche dans la Gaspésie.'

49 *Statuts de la province de Québec*, Geo. V (2e session) (1911), c. 17, 'Loi amendant les Statuts refondus, 1909, relativement à la création des réserves forestières cantonales.' In 1913 Quebec had fifteen reserves, mainly situated in the region of Lac Saint-Jean and on the South Shore of the St Lawrence: 'Quebec Forestry Notes,' *Canadian Forestry Journal* 9 (1913): 138.

50 'Forestry in Quebec,' *Canadian Forestry Journal* 9 (1913): 167.

51 Castonguay, 'Foresterie scientique et reforestation.'

52 *Rapport de la Commission de la colonisation de la province de Québec* (Quebec: Charles Pageau, 1904), 85.

53 Darin Kinsey, 'Fashioning a Freshwater Eden: Elite Anglers, Fish Culture, and State Development of Quebec's 'Sport' Fishery' (PhD diss., Université du Québec à Trois-Rivières, 2008).

54 On the early origins of the fish and game clubs in Quebec, see Darcy Ingram, 'Nature's Improvement: Wildlife, Conservation, and Conflict in Quebec, 1850–1914' (PhD diss., McGill University, 2007).

55 *The Fish and Game Clubs of the Province of Quebec. What they Mean to the Province. What Privileges they Enjoy* (Quebec: Minister of Colonization, Mines and Fisheries, 1914). For a detailed discussion of the rise of the club movement see Martin, *La chasse au Québec*.

56 *Rapport Annuel du Département de la Marine et des Pêcheries. Documents de la Session (No. 12)* (Ottawa: Hunter, Rose et Lemieux, 1869).

57 Parenteau, 'A "Very Determined Opposition to the Law."'

58 This juxtaposition between the good 'angler' and the 'evil' poacher is well
enunciated in Richard Nettle, *The Salmon Fisheries of the St. Lawrence and its
Tributaries* (Montreal: Printed by John Lovell, 1857).

59 For a study of the conservation elite's viewpoint of poachers, see Jacoby,
Crimes against Nature. In some cases residents were matter of fact about
their 'illegal' activities, even speaking to journalists about them. See 'Two
Winter Harvests: How the Ice-Crop and Fishing Out of Season Enable the
Hardy Countryman to Increase His Income During the Dull Season,' *Canadian Life and Resources* 6, 3 (1908): 16–17.

60 See, for example, the petition sent by the Montagnais at Moisie in 1861 to
Ottawa quoted in Brian Stewart, *A Life on the Line: Commander Pierre-Étienne
Fortin and His Times* (Ottawa: Carleton University Press, 1997), 143.

61 The different philosophies are readily seen in the reports of Hector Caron,
who took over as superintendent of hunting and fisheries after the death of
Louis-Zepherin Joncas in 1903. Caron would write a long argument against
what he saw as the extremist position of many conservationists on pages
161–3 in the *Rapport Général du Ministre de la Colonisation, des Mines et des
Pêcheries de la province de Québec*, in 1914: 'Je viens de parler de préservation,
permettez-moi, Monsieur le Ministre, de vous dire qu'un grand nombre de
gens, je dirai même de sportsmen, se font illusion sur ces termes, protection
ou conservation de notre gibier et de notre poisson, et ils s'imaginent rendre un bien grand service en prêchant qu'il faut, sans merci, punir un pauvre colon qui aura tué soit un chevreuil ou un lièvre en temps prohibé, ou
encore, pour avoir pris quelques dorés ou achigans n'ayant pas tout à fait la
longueur exigée.'

62 On this struggle between hard-line conservationists and those with a more
realistic outlook, see chap. 9, 'Our Rivers Taken from Us,' in Stewart, *A Life
on the Line*.

63 'An Act to amend and consolidate the laws relating to fisheries,' *Statutes of
Quebec*, 1888, 51–52 Vic. c. 17, s. 4.

64 For a discussion of the development of pisciculture in general, see Kinsey,
'Seeding the Water as the Earth.'

65 On the development of Canadian pisciculture, see William Knight, 'Samuel
Wilmot, Fish Culture, and Recreational Fisheries in Late-19th-Century
Ontario,' *Scientia Canadensis* 30 (2007): 75–90.

66 For information on Canadian hatchery operations see the *Forty-Ninth
Annual Report of the Fisheries Branch*, Department of the Naval Service, 1915–
16 (Ottawa, 1916), esp. app. 16, 'Report on Fish Breeding by J.A. Rodd,
Superintendent of Fish Culture'; *Rapport Général du Ministre de la Colonisation, des Mines, et des Pêcheries de la province de Québec, 1916*, Documents de la

Session, no. 7, 130. Quebec already had some control over its inland fisheries since 1882, but this was limited to riparian rights and the right to control fishing licenses. See the *Supreme Court Digest of Cases, 1875–1903*, articles 'Riparian Rights' and 'Fishery Licenses,' 1260. The superintendent of fisheries and game, Hector Caron, stated: 'Il convient de noter que les alevinières sont plutôt une charge pour notre budget, puisque tout avantageuses qu'elles puissent être à un autre point de vue, elles ne rapportent que relativement peu au Trésor.' It should be noted that there had been a visible disinterest in conservation work since the beginning of Caron's tenure in 1905. When Caron finally came to realize there was a problem with species degradation in Quebec, he came to the conclusion that conservation could better be achieved through economic pressure than public sentiment.

67 Kinsey, 'Fashioning a Freshwater Eden.'

68 John A. Long, *The Rise of the Fishes: 500 Million Years of Fish Evolution* (Baltimore: Johns Hopkins University Press, 1995); on the elitist pretensions of anglers, see Colleen J. Sheehey, 'American Angling: Urbanism and the Rise of the Rod and Reel,' in *Hard at Play: Leisure in America, 1840–1940*, ed. Kathryn Grover (Amherst: University of Massachusetts Press, 1992), 77–92.

69 Yolande Allard, 'Le saumon dans la rivière Saint-François: Un choix de société,' *Journal of Eastern Townships Studies / Revue d'Études des Cantons de l'Est* 5 (1994): 3–19.

70 The creation of laws that benefited some species over others could be seen as a form of 'speciesism' in the sense coined by British psychologist Richard D. Ryder. See the influential text to which Ryder made important contributions: Stanley Godlovitch, Roslind Godlovitch, and John Harris, eds., *Animals, Men and Morals: An Inquiry into the Maltreatment of Non-Humans* (New York: Taplinger Publishing Co., 1971).

71 Geoffrey J. Eales, *The Eel Fisheries of Eastern Canada* (Ottawa: Fisheries Research Board of Canada, 1968); M. Castonguay, P.V. Hodson, C.M. Couillard, M.J. Eckersley, J.-D. Dutil and G. Verreault, 'Why Is Recruitment of the American Eel, Anguilla Rostrata, Declining in the St. Lawrence River and Gulf?' *Canadian Journal of Fisheries and Aquatic Sciences* 51 (1994): 479–88.

72 On hybrid landscapes, see Matthew Booker, 'Real Estate and Refuge: An Environmental History of San Francisco Bay's Tidal Wetlands, 1846–1972' (PhD diss., Stanford University, 2005).

Missing Canadians:
Reclaiming the A-Liberal Past

R.W. SANDWELL

Introduction: Defining the Problem

Like Jerry Bannister, who decided not to argue in his essay in this collection that 'the liberal order carries within it an implicit teleology that constrains historians to study the ... past only insofar as it contributes to the eventual formation of the Canadian liberal project,' I too am going to resist this 'cranky complaint.'[1] Unlike Professor Bannister, however, I will resist it because I believe that one of the most valuable contributions of the Liberal Order Framework as a way of understanding Canadian history may turn out to be its potential to disrupt and de-naturalize that persistent master narrative that has, until recently, tended to measure the progress of the Canadian peoples – however historians evaluate it – within the hegemonic terms of liberalism. For even though many historians have formally eschewed the motif of 'progress to modernity' for some time now, there is still a residual tendency to write about the progress of individuals (or, alternatively, their 'failure' to progress) in terms of naturalized, essentialized liberal ideologies, practices, and epistemologies. Within this naturalized liberal discourse freedom, equality, justice, property, and increased material acquisitions are assumed to be the goals of all individuals as they work towards further inclusion in the world of rational citizenship. Simply by naming the Liberal Order Framework – whatever it is precisely – as a historically contingent set of ideological changes, McKay offers historians a clearly articulated theoretical foundation from which we can see not only the varieties of liberalism, but those forms of behaviour and belief that preceded and coexisted with it. McKay has given us at the very least the ontological space (if not quite the permission) to see who lies outside the liberal order, and even beyond those various coherent resistances and oppositions to liberalisms that he has articulated.[2]

This chapter is concerned with using the terms of the Liberal Order Framework to clarify and refine a dialogue already begun among historians about those who both fell outside the new liberal order and organized forms of resistance to it. It draws attention to those who, if only for a while, frustrated the zeal of reformers wanting to make Canadian society a cleaner, safer, more decent, polite, well managed, and more 'civilized' place. It is concerned with establishing the grounds upon which we can claim a meaningful historical space for those who (as we know from twenty years of historical research into those who were 'making good')[3] sometimes drove reformers to distraction with their refusal or inability either to regulate their behaviour or to reconstruct their subjectivity in accordance with the rules of the new citizenship of the liberal order, persisting instead in their disorganized, dirty, impolite, intemperate, irregular, patriarchal, improvident, irrational, criminal, or just plain feckless behaviours, even in the face of constant harassment from their 'betters.' This chapter is concerned to make an ontological space to talk about others who, by clinging to ways of life seen by some as outmoded, or insufficiently egalitarian, or too tradition-bound, or too 'ethnic,' or too attached to outmoded beliefs, excited reformers' pity, their scorn, and sometimes their compassion. It is concerned with establishing the need to further interrogate the world views and behaviours of those who, throughout the nineteenth and even twentieth centuries, constituted an ever-shrinking portion of the population who, for a variety of reasons, had less exposure to, or were slower to take up, the new forms of knowledge, identity, and power that distinguished the liberal order from other ways of being, and being in society. It is concerned, in short, with drawing more attention to, problematizing, and giving meaning to the experiences and world views of those who demonstrated a degree of immunity, in myriad ways and for a wide variety of reasons, to the hegemonic forces of colonialism, governmentality, and liberalism.[4] After defining liberalism, this chapter will provide some general arguments to support my contention that a-liberal ideologies continued to influence Canadians throughout the nineteenth and twentieth centuries. I will then go on to briefly review three subject areas where evidence of a-liberalism has already made a significant impact on Canadian historiography. I will conclude with a temperate plea to historians to continue to look beyond the Liberal Order Framework to include a wider range of peoples and behaviours within the purview of Canadian history.

Defining Liberalism

McKay defines the liberal order as 'one that encourages and seeks to extend across time and space a belief in the epistemological and onto-logical primacy of the category "individual."'[5] William Reddy situates the term a little more firmly in European history, arguing that the idea of the primacy of the individual and his freedom, justice, and equality were related to some specific economic and political changes in the late eighteenth and nineteenth centuries that created a new way for society to imagine itself. While liberal political/economic ideology began as an 'apologetics for merchant activities' in the attempt 'to win social ac-ceptance for commercial profit and interest on debt,'[6] liberal economic theory soon appeared as a much larger set of precepts, identities, and disciplinary practices related to the growth of the modern state. Reddy argues that liberalism was accepted as an ideology on the part of the newly emerging ruling classes long before most people understood or accommodated the rights, privileges, and disciplinary practices of mod-ern citizenship. The cluster of values and beliefs about the individual and society that constituted liberalism – or the 'liberal illusion' as Reddy terms it[7] – are as follows: '1) the unlimited and easy substitutability of money for any other object of desire and therefore 2) the universality of the underlying desire for "advantage" or gain; 3) the political neutrality of money exchanges, and therefore 4) the compatibility of free trade with human liberty.'[8] Reddy explores how Europeans gradually began to incorporate this 'illusion' into their lives and, in the process, came to see social relationships exclusively in terms relating to commodities and exchanges, even though 'they continued to involve so much more – loy-alty, deference, faith, fear, hostility.'[9] The disciplinary complex of the lib-eral state and the structures of power on which it relies 'work' through the individual's search for rational citizenship. The individual's rational search for freedom, equality, and wealth that constitutes the heart of liberal ideology have replaced (for example) faith-based communi-ties where inherited inequality and special entitlements are sustained by more or less institutionalized patterns of deference and violence (in-cluding threats of violence).

It is not surprising that the dominant historical narrative in Canada documents the rise of liberalism – through, for example, studies of the rights (and wrongs) of the labouring classes, women's increasing polit-ical and economic freedom, colonialism and its impact on the growth of the Canadian nation-state, and the inequities of racism and various forms of sexism, and a broad range of cultural studies exploring the growth and shaping of individual identities – for, as McKay has argued, liberal beliefs are so deeply embedded in our own contemporary consciousness that they function as 'something more akin to a secular religion or a totalizing philosophy than to an easily manipulated set of political ideas.'[10] It is the very pervasiveness of the liberal project, its 'taken-for-granted-ness,' that helps to explain why the massive transition in social values, structures of power, and daily practices that eventually resulted in something resembling a coherent liberal order has been strangely invisible to most contemporary Canadians (hasn't everyone, always, 'really' wanted individual freedom and equality so that they could maximize their own self-interest?). For liberalism, as McKay suggests, is our doxa, the essential world view that determines, albeit unconsciously, just who and what *matters* (in this case, liberty, equality, and justice and those individuals who aspire to them) on the basis of common-sense criteria that seem so natural that they do not require explanation.[11] Here, as Bruce Curtis argues at some length in this collection, lies its power to shape our lives, inside and out.[12]

As a number of authors argue in these pages, while the Liberal Order Framework as outlined by McKay offers a fascinating opportunity to consciously revision Canada as a project of liberal rule, some important questions remain about how the overall framework of analysis will work in practice. As Robert McDonald, E.A. Heaman, and Jerry Bannister argue, McKay's liberalism needs to include the more varied, fragmented, contested, distinct, and multiple kinds of liberalism that have constituted the 'Canadian' experience from the eighteenth century to the present. It needs to provide more nuanced approaches both to liberalism as a project of rule and to the differences between liberalism and its counterpoint articulated by McKay: the vast and varied Left in Canada. And, as Bruce Curtis reminds us, the modern state in Canada was not only shaped from the outside, as it were, by new structures and relations; it was also shaped by the creation of a new kind of subjectivity, where nascent rational citizens learned to desire both the freedoms and the disciplinary practices involved in governmentality.

While historians in this collection contest the exact terms of liberalism, all would, I think, agree that whatever it was, it was not monolithic: some people quickly warmed to liberalism's fire, including school promoters, certain kinds of political reformers, many of the emergent professionals, and those involved in generally 'improving' society to ensure its safe and rational functioning. Others, as McKay argues, responded to the changes attendant on the growth of liberalism with a very different social vision, with clearly articulated alternatives that reacted perhaps most vehemently against the coercive individualism and anti-communitarianism of liberalism. Bob McDonald argues here that the 'rebels, reds, and radicals' of British Columbia did not, however, provide an alternative to liberalism per se, but only to one narrow (if 'classic') definition of it. Their clearly articulated political goals, their 'rights talk,' their coherent social vision, their confidence in their own ability to turn individual or collective action into social change, marks them as a particular, new kind of liberal individual. And like other people engaged with the new liberal order, they have left behind particularly detailed and coherent written accounts of their beliefs and behaviours that provide historians with evidence about their clearly articulated, carefully reasoned, ways of knowing and being.

Drawing on the work of a variety of historians in Canada and elsewhere, this essay posits that a third group or kind of people existed in the nineteenth and twentieth century: those whose lives intersected only intermittently, or marginally, or not at all with the new liberal project. The word 'group' is a difficult one to use in this context, for one of the most notable characteristics of those living outside of the Liberal Order Framework is certainly their general reluctance to identify with any coherent, clearly defined set of political beliefs, or to sign on to any particular program for or against specific social, economic, or ideological change. Indeed, their identity as a group accrues to them only from the outside, as it were; it is a collectivity applied by outsiders in general, and historians in particular, to a kind of people who, whatever else they did and believed, shared a disinclination, or failure, or reluctance, to adhere to the foundations of liberal ideology outlined above by William Reddy and here, once again, by Ian McKay: the liberal order framework is 'one that encourages and seeks to extend across time and space a belief in the epistemological and ontological primacy of the category "individual."'[13]

Is There Anyone Outside?[14]

Was there anyone outside the Liberal Order Framework in eighteenth-, nineteenth-, or twentieth-century Canada? Was there anyone whose life involved, if only in part or from time to time, other ideological frameworks, and other ways of knowing the world than those provided by liberal ideology? What evidence is there to support their existence?

Without disputing the existence of various forms and types of liberalism in Canada, historians generally do make the (usually tacit) assumption that a-liberal peoples and kinds of behaviour also existed from the eighteenth to the twentieth centuries. This is suggested by the truism that, if liberalism was, at some point in Canadian history a nascent and complex new phenomenon (a premise accepted by most of the contributors to this collection), it must have replaced other ways of being, behaving, and knowing the world. If it was adopted and absorbed gradually (as, again, a number of historians in this collection have suggested), then there must have been other ways of life that co-existed with it. By asserting the historical contingency of liberalism, McKay has declared the existence of people who had other ways of being and doing that *necessarily* – speaking logically and teleologically – *must have* preceded and/or coexisted with the new Liberal Order.

In addition to their tacit assumption that other ideologies existed before and along with liberal ideology, historians have for some time been providing us with clear and abundant evidence that a-liberal people and a-liberal kinds of behaviour persisted and even played a significant role in Canada, even as liberalism increased its hegemonic hold. Over the last thirty years, historians have presented us with a long line of Canadians who were exhorted by reformers to be good liberal subjects and citizens, presumably because they were not. They were badgered about being cleaner, more organized, better money managers, to have more regular habits, and to be 'better' (i.e., more rational and organized) mothers, to speak English, to attend school more regularly and for longer, to participate more actively in their communities, to drink, smoke, and gamble less, to get to work on time, to get some job training, to stop dancing, to be more polite, and to go to bed early. In an important sense, we know so much about the hegemonic disciplinary framework of the modern state that historians have recently been documenting precisely because the emerging, liberal middle classes were hectoring those who were not – or not yet – conforming enough to its disciplinary framework.

While it might be argued that Canadian historians have done a better job of exploring how these a-liberal practices, beliefs, ideologies, and structures of meaning looked from the vantage point of middle-class reformers, or 'the state' – from the outside, or above – than from inside or below,[15] recent historiography has left little doubt that there was a profound struggle in the nineteenth and twentieth centuries about what made a good society, how people should live in it, and who deserved to do so. Within the contours of our history, this struggle (as McKay so persuasively argues) has been worked out as the struggle of the Liberal Order Framework to replace or supplant forms of knowing and being that did *not* conform to it.

In an important sense, of course, there is no need to remind anyone, particularly historians, that there have been other ways of being and knowing in societies of the past. People, and groups of people, throughout history did not always or only know, live by, or work out their lives within the liberal freedoms and disciplinary practices identified with the 'modern' world. They were different from us, and the Liberal Order Framework that permeates the present provides us with only one more measure of understanding these differences. Peasants, pastoralists, hunters and gatherers – most people throughout most of human history, in other words – meet this description. Their lives differed significantly from those within the Liberal Order in a number of important ways including their behaviour, their subjectivity, their views on the place of the individual in society, their understanding of what 'society' is, their relation to their local environments, and their experience of authority, discipline, and power.

The most obvious identifiable a-liberal kind of society with which non–North American historians have been consistently obliged to deal is the peasant. It is worth contemplating here the relationship of this kind of society to the Liberal Order Framework. Historians have found it difficult to ignore peasant cultures, peasant economics, and peasant practices in Europe, Russia, and Asia because these peoples created particular problems to 'modernizing' societies. From the nineteenth century onwards the governing state found peasants difficult to ignore, at least in part, precisely because varied peasant societies were increasingly identified by nascent state bureaucracies (above all in Stalinist Russia) as posing very particular obstacles to the growth and functioning of a modern state, and of the modern, liberal individuals needed to populate it.[16]

The pronounced differences between peasants and others who were more amenable to the Liberal Order in the modernizing world have been explained in different ways. In the parlance of political economists, peasants were a problem for the state because they existed *outside of* political economy; their continued adherence to the household (rather than the nation-state) as the organizing principle for their economic activities isolated them from, and therefore made them relatively immune to, the economic and disciplinary relations of power germane to the nation-state, whether communist, fascist, or capitalist.[17] Social and political theorists, for their part, had considerable difficulty labelling peasants coherently within the terms of any ideological framework, and hence identified them, in Teodore Shanin's words, as 'the awkward class.'[18] Linked to capitalist forms of labour only intermittently, antagonistic to the regulation, the high levels of taxation, and the 'tutelary complex' of newly forged states,[19] peasants could not be predictably relied upon to seek common cause with those on either the Left or the Right, though they did both from time to time. And if they could not be relied upon to identify with either the Right or the Left, in many cases they could not be forced to either; whether it was their economic self-reliance, or their rigid adherence to an alternative system of social regulation rooted in the family and religion, or a stubborn refusal to 'modernize,' or their unwillingness to take the risks needed to change, many peasant societies successfully insulated themselves from liberal forms of power and identity well into the twentieth century.[20]

If peasants have been widely identified as living outside of liberalism's disciplinary structures and freedoms, they have provided some cultural historians with a different platform for analysis. Some have examined peasants within a semiotic turn, examining them as a discursive, sentimentalized foil by which urban societies in the twentieth century could examine themselves.[21] Ian McKay examined the folk culture of Nova Scotia, a culture analogous in some ways to those of peasant Europe, arguing that The Folk have never really existed 'as a self defined group or as an externally defined population; they existed in the mind of the interpreters.'[22]

Other historians have explored the different-ness of peasant societies in yet another way, using microhistorical evidence to explore them from the vantage point of the 'practices of everyday life.' As Schatzki argues, 'Practice theorists conceive of practices as embodied, materially mediated arrays of human activity centrally organized around shared practical understanding.'[23] Historians such as James Lehning and Giovanni Levi argue that it is at the level of the everyday that the most significant differences between peasants and others are manifested, and it is only at the microscopic level that normative structures, meaningful activity, and the complex webs of identity, power, and meaning can be observed.[24] The focus is on a methodology that can explore the ways in which the fluid minutiae of daily practice worked themselves out within shared structures of meaning that existed outside of, or alongside, such hegemonic forces as liberalism.

Giovanni Levi has argued that the rich and multilayered minutiae of historical experience revealed in microhistorical studies have not only contributed to our understanding of the varied complexities of societies in the past, but have helped to disrupt simplistic ideological perspectives that chart social change as a 'regular progression through a uniform and predictable series of stages' in which individuals respond to social and economic structures in a way that seemed to be 'given, natural and inevitable.'[25] For the microhistorian does not see change as originating in large structures imposed in a general way and evaluated in terms appropriate to an implied centre, but rather in the 'minute and endless strategies and choices operating within the interstices of contradictory normative systems.'[26] It is in their day-to-day practices that people make 'innumerable and infinitesimal transformations of and within the dominant cultural economy in order to adapt it to their own interests and their own rules.'[27] It is only at the level of microhistorical research that these practices, and the strategies they contain, become visible. Microhistory, in other words, can give us a very different kind of history than that written from the vantage point of the state, of a particular class, race or gender, or the winners in the progression to liberalism, even as it documents the minute intersections of the state, liberalism, and everyday experience. For the microhistorical gaze provides a scale of observation that leads us to see the limits, extents, and variations within ideologies like liberalism, and the alternative ideologies and practices that might have preceded and coexisted with it.[28]

Eschewing what they perceive as the nihilism of poststructuralism, some microhistorical, practice-oriented theorists have located emancipatory potential not only in the lives of peasants (though they initially provided a model), or in the lives of people in the past, but in the everyday *generally*; for the everyday, they argue, offers a place to experience, observe, and respond against the hegemonic, alienating, homogenizing, and reifying forces that constitute, in Reddy's words, 'the liberal illusion.'[29] Precisely because the knowledges and experiences of everyday life, as Michael Gardiner argues, may be dismissed as 'something that is "left over" and hence of little consequence in relation to such "superior" pursuits as politics, the arts or science,' the everyday is where it may still be possible for people to spend time away from the direct naming, surveillance, and examination that increasingly constitutes our lives in the workplace and in the public gaze; 'it is the place where routine praxis occurs and concrete bodily and intersubjective needs are formulated and met. It cannot simply be transcended by ideological fiat.' Indeed, some theorists argue that what is repressed in liberalism is 'precisely the "force of the prosaic," the counter-authenticity, if you will, of the texture and rhythm of our daily lives and decisions, the myriad of minute and careful adjustments that we are ready to offer in the interests of a habitable world.' If we are 'progressively under the thumb of a bureaucratic, functionalist logic ... [t]he result is a homogenization of the concrete particularities of the everyday life-world, an "emptying out" of the richness and complexity of daily experience ... This prevents us from grasping the qualitative features of the real; we remain blind to the nature of "difference" or "otherness."'[30] The discovery of the everyday and the search for the richer and deeper humanity that it seems to contain may provide, if not the seeds of resistance, then at least the creation of a tiny space outside of the hegemonic individualism, the conformity, and the numbing standardization of governmentality that characterized life for so many in the Liberal Order Framework. Other historiographies, and other disciplines, in sum, have managed to find ways of recognizing or claiming peoples, or parts of people's lives, that do not participate in the values, beliefs, practices, or hegemonic spaces of modernity that we recognize as liberal.

Canadian Historians Dealing with Difference

A class of peasants has not been part of Canadian historians' cosmology, notwithstanding some heated discussions about the role of the *habitants* in what is now Quebec.[31] Without this highly visible 'exception' to liberal modernity, how have Canadian historians dealt with those people who do not conform to the tenets of liberalism – those who, like the immigrants from peasant Russia or the Ukraine, seemed to refuse, if only for a generation, personal 'improvement' in the terms offered by the Liberal Order;[32] or who, like so many mothers in the nineteenth and early twentieth centuries, did not actively seek out personal equality or freedom for themselves, and seem instead to have subordinated their 'interests' to a patriarchal definition of the collective good of their families;[33] or those who, like a majority of farmers in the later nineteenth-century Canada, could have made more money on their investments in almost any other line of work, but chose *not* to maximize their self-interest and continued with farming;[34] or the members of First Nations who continue to hunt, fish, and trap for their own use in northern British Columbia;[35] or those members of the lumpen proletariat who did not participate in any clearly articulated political movement, in spite of their unequal status;[36] or those who identified themselves more as members of a particular religious community than as citizens of the modern Canadian state?[37]

The short answer is that peoples who are marginal to the terms and progress of liberalism, when they are studied at all, tend to be studied as discrete, marginalized groups, organized by ethnicity, gender, religious community, occupation, or income level. It is ironic that in spite of the intentions of the historians studying them, those on the margins of the liberal gaze are still, in a sense, homogenized, reified, and unified (in spite of the vast differences that might distinguish one 'marginalized' group from another) within the collective gaze of their liberal critics, past and present. Indeed, Todd McCallum has argued that a defining characteristic of marginal people generally is their tendency to appear exclusively through someone else's eyes, perhaps a bureaucrat or reformer, but *without* 'histories of their own lives told in their own terms.' Within this framework, marginalized people are 'sensationalized, sentimentalized or trivialized' and, as a result, obscured within the historical record.[38] As I have argued elsewhere, liberal ideology structures the world in particularly rigid and polarized ways:

> [W]ithin the liberal gaze, whatever is not 'about us' seems to be about what is the opposite of us – a package of predictable characters and characteristics especially designed to tell us who we are by defining what we are not, or what we are no longer. The strength of liberal hegemony can, perhaps, be measured most precisely in this – in the apparent impossibility of constructing a convincing description or analysis of behaviours or beliefs that are different from our own liberal ones.[39]

And nested in the problem of 'othering' is a curious conundrum. Canadian historians, in spite of their recent successes at including more, and more kinds, of people within 'our' history, still sometimes conflate liberalism with humanity itself. This is most clearly seen in historians' treatment of that majority of people in the late nineteenth century who did not involve themselves in organized politics, those who did not vote, who did not as adults work for wages, who did not express their individual hopes, beliefs, convictions, and aspirations through writing – those women, most notably, and some men who did not express their individual identities in liberal ways commensurate with their roles as individuals within the modern state or capitalist relations. Evidence that many people simply did not behave in a way that corresponds to liberal theory has, strangely, at times been interpreted as if there were a problem with the particular historical actors rather than with the theory or prevalence of liberalism itself. To the extent that people do not act in accordance with the rules of justice, equality, and freedom – the wife, for example, who agreed not to work for wages because she accepted her husband's authority over her – the assumption too often is made that such variations, or deviations, could only be manifestations of the strong *external* factors that must be inhibiting 'normal' (aka 'liberal') responses: their behaviour tends, in other words, to be interpreted by historians as ipso facto evidence of their oppression. Underdevelopment, racism, gender inequality, and insufficient education are called upon by historians to explain the 'failure' of those who, because they do not maximize their own self-interest, can be neither good liberal citizens nor true individuals. What needs to be explained, these historians suggest, is why such people did not want to accumulate capital, or maximize in a variety of other ways their own self-interest. Too often we are left with the paradoxical conclusion that marginalized peoples can be best understood by exclusive reference to the Liberal Order that defines their marginalization, rather than (as Giovanni Levi would urge) in terms of the beliefs, behaviours, and naturalized systems of power that frame their lives on a day-to-day basis.[40]

Both the problems and promise of recognizing worlds outside of liberalism's hegemonic hold can be seen with particular clarity in a few areas of Canadian history. One of the most politically significant concerns Aboriginal history. 'Race' or ethnicity stands alone, albeit in a curious way, within the lexicon of Canadian difference as a category of analysis that seems to leave space for the recognition of worlds outside of the Liberal Order. Indeed, in the minds of many history students, 'race' is a category of analysis that is emblematic of the issues of identity and power that give 'difference' its critical edge.[41] This is arguably one of the few places in contemporary Canadian historiography where it is possible to make an explicit, legitimate claim, however tentative, for a way of being that differs from that imposed by liberalism, the modern state, capitalism, or governmentality.

The exceptionalism of Aboriginal peoples has come to the attention of Canadian historians over the last few years as both history and politics, and both are heavily dependent on historical interpretations of the 'different-ness' of First Nations' history. First Nations are making their historical case for land rights in part by claiming a historical identity outside of the Liberal Order Framework.[42] In the process, Aboriginal historians and First Nations peoples have been revealing some key links between liberal identity, citizenship, and human rights within contemporary Canada. They have also been demonstrating the difficulties of negotiating a way of life, and representing that way of life, that is different from liberalism and its primitivist opposite or 'other.' British Columbia Supreme Court Chief Justice Allan McEachern nicely summarized the paradoxes and problems of racialized identity outside of liberal values and rights in his Delgamuukw decision of 1991. Explaining why the Gitksan and Witsuwit'en had no legitimate claim to their hereditary lands, he pointed out that while they were traditionally 'a primitive people without any form of writing, horses, or wheeled wagons,' they had lost touch with (and thus any legal rights attendant on) their true 'nativeness'; for 'witness after witness admitted participation in the wage or cash economy.'[43] As Robin Ridington summarizes, 'For McEachern, such participation negated the plaintiffs' claims "for ownership and jurisdiction over the territory and for aboriginal rights in the territory." In his eyes, the plaintiffs had failed the pizza test.'[44] McEachern's decision was overturned some years later, but not before historians had done considerable soul-searching about the power of historical representation and the political as well as cultural meanings of difference.[45]

The Liberal Order Framework provides an important point of entry for understanding precisely the kinds of difference that 'Aboriginal' refers to: those behaviours and beliefs that cannot be easily reconciled with liberal economic theory, or liberal subjectivities, or governmentality. And in this sense, First Nations peoples function as our peasant equivalents, providing us at best with detailed examples of cultures, politics, and economies that are different from our own, and at worst providing us with an essentialized, primitivist foil for understanding our own liberal modernity. While there is considerable debate about the extent to which First Nations have been, and continue to be, colonized in Canada, about the nature and extent of changes within their varied cultures and societies, and even more about the existence of 'primitivism' within the historiography, there is also a growing recognition within the field and across Canada that this racialized group has indeed been acting in accordance with a set of historical principles, or beliefs, or hierarchies, or political constraints, that are in some senses different from and outside of those attributed to the rest of non-racialized Canadians.[46] 'Race,' particularly as it is applied to First Nations populations, is now widely believed to provide a legitimate explanation of how and why a particular group of people can be outside the Liberal Order Framework, exempt from or at least marginal to the 'normal' and 'normalizing' terms of the liberal discourse.[47]

Important work has already begun elsewhere in Canada that documents the 'marginalized' lives of a-liberal, *non-racialized* people living outside of, or alongside, the newly emerging liberal order. Some of it is beginning to examine such people on their own terms, and from 'the inside.' The rest of this chapter will briefly summarize two further areas where historians have had some considerable success documenting 'other,' non-racialized, ways of being: the family and rural Canada.

As I have argued elsewhere in considerable detail with regard to the history of the family, historians of Canada have already provided overwhelming evidence that the family acted as a social and cultural institution that, in some key ways, existed alongside of, rather than within, liberalism in the nineteenth and twentieth centuries.[48] For in spite of continued attempts within the Liberal Order to replace a familial structure of power with the ideals of equality and justice of liberal individualism, many households (and not only of the working classes) continued to be defined by rigid though not necessarily uncomfortable, hierarchies of gender and age.[49] This is not to situate the family in a private sphere outside of liberalism or change; instead, women and the families in which they lived, in all their various and changing forms and formations, had a complicated, varied, and often intimate relationship with liberalism and the rise of the modern state. Over the past twenty-five years, historians have not only succeeded in documenting the persistence of distinctive a-liberal characteristics within the modern Canadian family and household, but they have convincingly demonstrated that the family changed in some significant ways in negotiation with new economic and political realities. Historians have argued convincingly that the family was often at the centre of the struggle between an emerging liberal order and older cultures and economies rooted in the family.[50] The transitions to the new liberal world were often worked out, and perhaps most painfully, in the homes of the nation. In spite of its role as both a key player in the formation of the modern state and as a leading competitor to the modern state in the field of hegemonic values, the family continues to be marginalized, reified, and trivialized in Canadian history because of its marginal relationship to the Liberal Order Framework.

The history of rural Canada arguably provides another detailed, if largely unnoticed, exploration of alternative political economies and cultures that continued alongside of new liberal beliefs and practices in the nineteenth and twentieth centuries. Recent research into rural Canada has documented a considerable dissonance between rural behaviours and liberalism.[51] While Canadians often assume a line of progress from self-sufficiency and pioneer farming, through the development of staples and local markets for goods, through to the self-realized commercial farmer, and ending up with inevitable urbanization and rural depopulation, a wide variety of microhistorical studies challenges the rigid model that constructs nineteenth- and twentieth-century Canada exclusively as an expanding liberal space. Legal studies are also confirming the anomalous relationship of rural societies, cultures, and economies to the growth of liberalism in urban areas, well into the twentieth century.[52] Liberalism was, in a general sort of way, increasingly making itself felt in rural Canada, manifesting itself with particular clarity in educational, agricultural, and rural political reforms of the late nineteenth and early twentieth centuries. Nevertheless, it is possible to articulate patterns in rural Canada that suggest that something *else* was also going on within rural societies as liberalism was slowly gaining its hegemonic hold.[53] My purpose here is not to prove that rural Canada contained spaces where liberalism was ignored, or held at bay, or resisted. Instead, I would like to argue that there is sufficient evidence to suggest the need for more research into the worlds that existed outside, and alongside, the liberal order in rural Canada.

For evidence is abundant that for those living in rural Canada, the march of progress towards modern liberal ways of being was by no means uniform, one-directional, or always consistent with liberal ideology. While liberal economic theory assumes that individuals want to maximize their own self-interest, and posits that they will do so by participating in a system of commodification and exchange (labour or goods) that will best allow them to do so, the evidence is not at all clear that most Canadian rural dwellers were doing either in any consistent fashion in the later nineteenth and early twentieth centuries. And if they were trying to create a life as profit-maximizing, commodity-producing, self-interested individuals, many were having little success. Most significantly for our understanding of non-urban Canada, microhistorical studies indicate that many rural communities were not supported exclusively by agricultural production. Many 'farmers' simply did not grow or sell enough produce to support themselves through commercial agriculture, owing to the exigencies of environment, the vagaries of international trade, and the impact of low population densities within rural Canada. Evidence from the microhistories suggests instead that occupational plurality – often referred to as off-farm work – was not an exception in Canada, nor was it necessarily a sign of failure within a rural household. Evidence is growing that most families survived on the work of all household members, who engaged in a variety of waged work, commercial sales, and hunting and gathering activities organized around a loosely defined 'family farm.' The lively subsistence versus the market debate polarized market and non-market activities, liberal and illiberal formations, but did little to explain how both could exist within the same rural household, or even, indeed, within the same person.[54]

The prevalence of occupational plurality in rural Canada points up another key difference between the triumph of liberalism and the evidence from microhistories: the continued importance of the household to the political economy and society of rural Canada. This is not to suggest that rural households were always backward-looking, or reluctant to change in response to market activities or other exigencies of the modern world. The subsistence versus the markets debate has been upstaged, to some extent, by more complex interpretations that refuse such polarized models of difference and change. Rural families were seldom either *only* market driven or subsistence based. Instead, old economic and social formations often coexisted in volatile and variable relation to capitalized international market-oriented activities aimed at mobilizing the products of the farm, the forest, the ocean, the mine, and the factory. This combination created in Canada several distinctive and environmentally driven patterns of occupational plurality, of mobility, and of social and familial relations.[55] Characterized by these complex and household-based patterns, rural societies throughout Canada differed from each other in their particular combination of household-based and other work by which they were supported, but more significantly from the liberal wage-based, commodity-driven, and individualistic political economy usually associated with modern urban society. A major task for historians, it seems to me, is to try to see and understand the continuation of a-liberal beliefs and practices even after liberalism had created substantial changes in many areas of life.[56]

If rural families continued to be characterized, at least in part, by older 'a-liberal' forms, including subsistence activities – non-waged forms of labour organized, according to hierarchies of age and gender[57] – the family was not a single, coherent entity that stayed the same during the late nineteenth and early twentieth centuries. Families adapted to the particularities of land, environment, changing technologies, and government policies, creating new patterns of rural work, sociability, and family life. A good example of a hybrid pattern of liberal/a-liberal rural family life is provided by the prairie wheat farm. As Harriet Friedmann has argued, the typical wheat farm of early-twentieth-century North America was premised on the 'traditional' (a-liberal) farm labour of women and children, who received no cash payment for their work. It was also completely dependent on both the modern, capitalist systems of international trade and the innovations in farm technology that allowed the nuclear family to provide sufficient 'hands' for most stages of wheat production. It was this combination of 'new' systems and 'old' social organization that raised Canadian wheat production to international prominence. This mix proved itself to be remarkably dynamic, forcing down the international price of wheat and driving out more capitalized and wage-dependent agricultural production throughout the world, from the late nineteenth century onward. By 1935 'the vast majority of commercial wheat producers throughout the world market were organized through household rather than wage labour,' and enterprises producing wheat 'through capitalist relations were supplanted by enterprises producing wheat through kinship relations.'[58]

In Canada, the profit-maximizing farmer was widely believed to have replaced the peasant farmer typical of Europe by the mid-nineteenth century. Nevertheless, occupational plurality, intermittent and poorly paid wage labour, and the predominance of small, often unsuccessful family farms, have emerged in the historical record as a cluster of definitive rural characteristics well into the twentieth century. These patterns are difficult to explain within the Liberal Order Framework of social and economic change in Canada. Fortunately, a number of historians are taking a different tack in understanding the intermittent refusal of rural populations to conform to the tenets of liberalism. Historians such as Hal Baron, Daniel Samson, Kenneth Sylvester, Christopher Clarkson, Royden Loewen, and Bruce Curtis, for example, have argued that evaluations of rural society have been uncritically engaged in the same liberal discourse that constructed rural populations as urban *manquées*: those who, because of outdated social relations, retarded economic relations, and immature political systems, were unable to fully transform themselves into the modern economic men demanded by liberal, urban, and industrial society.[59] Rather than trying to explain rural populations in terms of their failure *vis-à-vis* liberal master narratives, past and present, they are finding ways to see and understand the different behaviours, values, and beliefs that seem to have characterized life for many people in rural Canada.

Conclusion

Within a liberal discourse that understands rational self-interest, equality, justice, and liberty as the mainsprings of human nature and progress, it is precisely the a-liberal aspects of First Nations groups, families, and rural societies that have been difficult to see, and even harder to understand. In practice, those parts of the political economy and culture of Aboriginal peoples, other rural populations, and family life having little to do with markets, or rational self-interest, or improvement, or equality, tend to appear (when they do at all) as awkward exceptions hovering uneasily on the edges of historical significance. Difficult to reconcile with our liberal concerns, they are marginalia in any grand narrative of Canadian history.

To phrase the problem that this chapter has sought to address in another way, while Canadian historians are doing a good job of identifying the terms of the colonial and the almost indistinguishable liberal project as seen from the point of view of colonizers and reformers, we need to know more about the beliefs and practices of those who, according to contemporary reformers and other independent evidence available to historians, were refusing, or ignoring, or were oblivious or somehow immune to (in historians' parlance) the hegemonic disciplinary project of liberalism. This essay has urged historians to take up Ian McKay's call for a Reconnaissance of Liberalism in order to create a space where we can start to find answers to such questions as, If the liberal order was new or uncommon in Canada in the nineteenth century, what preceded it? As liberalism became more common, and more widely accepted in various ways, how did those who were 'left behind' understand the changes happening to their neighbours, their communities, and their families? What made them immune, or immune in some ways, to liberalism? On what terms were differences perceived between the new liberal ways and what they replaced? Did the varied peoples of Canada understand the changes that historians have identified as 'liberalism' or 'governmentality' or 'colonialism' as the coherent package that historians now project back onto the past, and if not, within what kinds of categories of experience did they understand them? And what kind of evidence is there – outside of the obvious logical and teleological kind – to support the existence of something 'else' – some other core values, beliefs, and epistemologies – at work in people's lives in the late nineteenth and twentieth centuries?

If Canadian historians interested in the Liberal Order Framework aspire to more than 'seeing like a state,' they need to do more than examine just that liberal world that was the focus of the ever-widening gaze of the Canadian liberal state.[60] Historians need to take seriously as historical subjects those who existed outside of, or alongside, the new liberal order, even as the changes associated with modernity/governmentality/liberalism were increasingly affecting more people, and more parts of people's lives. We need, in summary, to find out more about more of these missing Canadians.

NOTES

1 Jerry Bannister, 'Canada as Counter-Revolution: The Loyalist Order Framework in Canadian History, 1750–1840,' 98 above.
2 Ian McKay, *Rebels, Reds, Radicals: Rethinking Canada's Left History* (Toronto: Between the Lines, 2005).
3 Many historians have been writing about this process in the last twenty years, and the best summary of their works is in Carolyn Strange and Tina Loo, *Making Good: Law and Moral Regulation in Canada, 1867–1939* (Toronto: University of Toronto Press, 1997).
4 For the purposes of this essay, the terms modernity, governmentality, colonialism will all be used to denote that range of practices, beliefs, and epistemologies identified with the implementation of the new Liberal Order, and defined in more detail in the next section.'
5 Ian McKay 'The Liberal Order Framework: A Prospectus for a Reconnaissance of Canadian History,' *Canadian Historical Review* 81 (2000): 623.
6 William M. Reddy, *Money and Liberty in Modern Europe: A Critique of Human Understanding* (Cambridge: Cambridge University Press, 1987), 87.
7 I will return to the 'illusory' nature of liberal ideology later in the chapter.
8 Reddy, *Money and Liberty,* 87.
9 William Reddy, *The Rise of Market Culture: The Textile Trade in French Society 1750–1900* (Cambridge: Cambridge University Press, 1984), 3.
10 McKay, 'The Liberal Order Framework,' 624.
11 Pierre Bourdieu, *Outline of a Theory of Practice* (Cambridge: Cambridge University Press, 1977).
12 Not, of course, that Curtis would identify the hegemonic and discursive

power at work as 'the Liberal Order Framework'; for, as he puts it, 'a liberal order framework as an interpretive grid suffers from an oversimplified notion of liberalism, one that tends to assimilate it to domination in general, that misses its similarities with other competing political doctrines, that neglects its vision of community, and that does not treat it holistically.' Bruce Curtis, 'After "Canada": Liberalisms, Social Theory, and Historical Analysis,' 184.

13 McKay 'The Liberal Order,' 623.

14 An earlier version of this chapter, delivered to the symposium on the Liberal Order Framework at McGill University in March 2006, did not contain an explicit discussion of the existence of the worlds outside of the Liberal Order. Instead, the paper focused almost exclusively on specific evidence relating to the a-liberal characteristics of nineteenth-century rural Canada. During the question-and-answer period, it became clear that the learned audience needed more evidence that a world outside 'The Liberal Order' existed at all, hence the change in emphasis in this chapter.

15 For a more detailed discussion of this point, see R.W. Sandwell, 'The Limits of Liberalism: The Liberal Reconnaissance and the History of the Family in Canada,' *Canadian Historical Review* 84 (2003): 423–50.

16 See Moshe Lewin, for example, 'Rural Society in Twentieth Century Russia: An Introduction,' *Social History* 9 (1984): 171–80.

17 For example, peasants have not been willing to commodify all of their capacity for labour; their participation in commodity circuits has always been partial or episodic, and has consequently limited the power of either employers or the state over their lives. In the late nineteenth century, thanks to the advent of heavy industry, accumulating Euro-American capital stopped needing to commodify all available labour power and became more selective. Sometimes it imported special categories (e.g., Chinese for the Canadian Pacific Railway), sometimes it left peasantries intact. In many parts of the world rural people in the twentieth century suddenly became an over-population, a bureaucratic nuisance. Canada peculiarly welcomed many of them. And in Canada they were able to live somewhat on their own terms by working episodically for international capital while owning their own, often marginal, lands.

18 Teodor Shanin, *The Awkward Class: Political Sociology of Peasantry in a Developing Society, Russia, 1910–1925* (Oxford: Clarendon Press, 1972).

19 See Jacques Donzelot, *The Policing of Families* (London: Pantheon, 1979 [1977]), especially the chapter on the Tutelary Complex, where he outlines the differences that families encountered with the rise of the modern state. For a discussion of the effect of the liberal public education system on the

French peasantry, see James Lehning, *Peasant and French: Cultural Contact in Rural France during the Nineteenth Century* (Cambridge: Cambridge University Press, 1995), 130–56.

20 See, for example, Eric R. Wolf, *Peasant Wars of the Twentieth Century* (Norman: University of Oklahoma Press, 1999); James C. Scott, *Weapons of the Weak: Everyday Forms of Peasant Resistance* (New Haven: Yale University Press, 1985).

21 For a discussion of French peasants as cultural construction, see Eugen Joseph Weber, *Peasants into Frenchmen: The Modernization of Rural France, 1870–1914* (Stanford: Stanford University Press, 1976), and a response in Lehning, *Peasant and French*.

22 Ian McKay, *The Quest of the Folk: Antimodernism and Cultural Selection in Twentieth-Century Nova Scotia* (Montreal and Kingston: McGill-Queen's University Press, 1994), 21.

23 Theodore R. Schatzki, 'Introduction: Practice Theory' in *The Practice Turn in Contemporary Theory*, ed. Theodore R. Schatzki, Karin Knorr Cetina, and Eike von Savigny (London and New York: Routledge, 2001), 2. For an overview of the practices-of-everyday-life school, see Michael E. Gardiner, ed., *Critiques of Everyday Life* (London and New York: Routledge, 2001).

24 Giovanni Levi, 'On Microhistory,' in *New Perspectives on Historical Writing*, ed. Peter Burke (University Park: Pennsylvania State University Press, 1991).

25 Ibid., 94.

26 Ibid., 107.

27 Michel de Certeau, *The Practice of Everyday Life* (Berkeley: University of California Press, 1984), xiv.

28 This difference in scale and focus is at the root of the difference between my conclusions and Bob McDonald's, in this collection, about the 'liberal' nature of British Columbia in the late nineteenth and twentieth centuries. My microhistorical study of a rural community, Saltspring Island, in the late nineteenth century (*Contesting Rural Space: Land Policy and Practices of Resettlement on Saltspring Island, 1859–1891* [Montreal and Kingston: McGill-Queen's University Press, 2005]) revealed a population that was profoundly a-liberal in several key respects: most of the self-identified 'farmer' families on the island sold no produce, and had very little cleared land. The political economy on the island was based instead on the usually unwaged labour of all household members, and organized according to kinship, gender, and age, combined with intermittent, seasonal waged labour by men in the nearby resource industries. A rich and benign natural environment and a lax and generous land-granting system inhibited the commodification of

both labour and land. An accessible and bountiful environment and almost free land allowed families not only to survive on the self-provisioning activities of hunting, gathering, and fishing, but also, in the process, to insulate themselves from many of the disciplinary practices of liberalism, particularly waged labour, commodity sales, taxes, and landlords, all related to the failed commodification of labour and land on the island. The population quarrelled and drank to excess, resulting in high levels of personal violence and 'unrest' that was not infrequently focused on a variety of government officials and religious personnel who attempted to encourage a reconstituted, rational, and respectable subjectivity onto them in the classroom, the saloon, or on their farms. Generally apathetic and a-political, the male portion of the 'community' came together to express their political will for the last time in 1885, in order to not only oust the members of their current municipal government, but to insist that the provincial government revoke their municipal charter altogether. Bob McDonald has argued convincingly that there were many people in British Columbia – and perhaps in greater numbers than elsewhere – involved with diverse forms of liberalism expressed in volatile political activity concerning issues of liberty, equality, and justice for individuals and groups. The presence of people in British Columbia, like those on Saltspring Island, who did *not* act as if they subscribed to this liberal ideology does not disprove his argument; it simply suggests that there was more going on – and perhaps particularly for women, and for both sexes in rural areas – than can be explained or described exclusively within the terms of the expanded and varied Liberal Order Framework he outlines.

29 Reddy, *Money and Liberty,* 87.
30 Gardiner, 'Introduction,' in *Critiques of Everyday Life,* 11, 13. Michael Andre Bernstein, *Bitter Carnival: Ressentiment and the Abject Hero* (Princeton: Princeton University Press, 1992), 182.
31 For a discussion of 'peasants' in Canadian historiography see R.W. Sandwell, 'Rural Reconstruction: Towards a New Synthesis in Canadian History,' *Histoire Sociale/Social History* 27, 53 (1994): 1–32, and 'Peasants on the Coast?: A Problematique of Rural British Columbia,' in *Canadian Papers in Rural History,* ed. Donald Akenson (Ganonoque: Langdale Press, 1996), vol. 10, 275–303.
32 See, for example, J.L. Black, *The Peasant Kingdom: Canada in the 19th Century Russian Imagination* (Manotick: Penumbra Press, 2001); Royden Loewen, *Family, Church and Market: A Mennonite Community in the Old and the New Worlds, 1850–1930* (Toronto: University of Toronto Press, 1993).
33 For a review of the literature on the a-liberal aspects of the family in the

nineteenth and twentieth centuries, see Sandwell, 'The Limits of Liberalism.'

34 For a review of the literature on rural history in Canada, see Sandwell, 'Rural Reconstruction,' 1–32.

35 For a discussion of the salvage paradigm in First Nations history, see Marcia Crosby, 'The Construction of the Imaginary Indian,' in *Vancouver Anthology: The Institutional Politics of Art*, ed. Stan Douglas (Vancouver: Talonbooks, 1991). For just one example of recent histories documenting the persistence of First Nations lifeways in the late twentieth century, see E. Richard Atleo Umeek, *Tsawalk: A Nuu-chah-nulth Worldview* (Vancouver: UBC Press, 2004).

36 For a review of the historiographic discord between the master narrative of Canadian history and the history of the very poor, see Todd McCallum 'The Great Depression's First History? The Vancouver Archives of Major J.S. Matthews and the Writing of Hobo History,' *Canadian Historical Review* 87 (2006): 79–108.

37 See, for example, Royden Loewen, 'Ethnic Farmers and the "Outside" World: Mennonites in Manitoba and Nebraska, 1874–1900,' *Journal of the Canadian Historical Association* 1 (1990): 195–213; Larry Hannant, 'Explosion on the Kettle Valley Line: The Assassination of Peter "the Lordly" Verigin,' at http://www.canadianmysteries.ca/sites/verigin/indexen.html.

38 McCallum, 'The Great Depression's First History?' 92.

39 Sandwell, 'The Limits of Liberalism.' As I went on to argue, 'The emphasis on representations of marginality not only obscures a wide range of a-liberal behaviours, but it also distorts them in some systematic ways. As Loo and Strange's *Making Good* nicely summarizes, marginalized groups in Canadian history, largely invisible to earlier generations of historians, have now burst onto the historical stage. Unfortunately, they all seem to be playing the same role. The socially dysfunctional, criminals, non-English or Scottish ethnic groups, and recently arrived immigrants, when seen through the lens of reformers' liberal values and beliefs, all seem to exhibit the same characteristics as families of the urban poor, women, Aboriginal peoples, and the vast majority of rural people both male and female, young and old. They are all defined by poverty, degrees of filth, irregular habits, and a problematic, intermittent relation to the formal market economy, particularly to money and waged work. The sheer volume of people defined so coherently by their marginalization confirms that the term "marginal" does not refer to relative numbers of people. Instead, it documents the distance between popular a-liberal behaviours and the liberal values of those seeking to establish their hegemonic vision. "The marginal" have not only been made visible, they

have been transformed into a "homogenous Canadian synthesis" by their alienation from the new liberal order' (447).

40 For a full discussion of this aspect of marginalization, see McKay, *The Quest of the Folk*, 3–42. See also R.W. Sandwell's review of Annie York and Andrea Laforet, *Spuzzum: Fraser Canyon Histories 1808–1939* (Vancouver: UBC Press, 1998) in the *Canadian Historical Review* 82 (2001), 357–60.

41 As I have argued in 'The Limits of Liberalism,' gender has not benefited from this kind of revision. In spite of key theoretical insights about gender, women, politics, and the family, there is a noticeable tendency in women's history in Canada to naturalize liberalism, to assume that the only reasons that women did not behave as men was because their true nature was oppressed by hegemonic sexism. Ibid., 443–7.

42 Tina Loo and Jo-Anne Fiske have both argued that First Nations people also, at times, made arguments that explicitly appealed to the liberal sensitivites of Whites in British Columbia in order to gain legitimacy for their points of view. See Tina Loo, 'Dan Cranmer's Potlatch: Law as Coercion, Symbol, and Rhetoric in British Columbia, 1884–1951,' *Canadian Historical Review* 73, 2 (1992): 125–65; Jo-Anne Fiske, 'Carrier Women and the Politics of Mothering,' in Veronica Strong-Boag and Anita Clair Fellman, eds., *Rethinking Canada: The Promise of Women's History*, 3rd ed. (Toronto: University of Toronto Press, 1997), 359–74.

43 Allan McEachern, 1991 *Delgamuukw v. A.G. Reasons for Judgment of the Honourable Justice Allan McEachern* (Vancouver: Queen's Printer, 1991), 25, 56.

44 Robin Ridington, 'Re-creation in Canadian First Nations Literatures: "When you sing it now, just like new,"' *Anthropologica* 43, 2 (2001): 221–30, citing McEachern, 1991 *Delgamuukw v. A.G*, 297.

45 See, for example, Robin Fisher, 'Matter for Reflection: BC Studies and British Columbia History,' *BC Studies* 100, 4 (1993): 59–77. For an illuminating discussion of the ways in which different kinds of liberalism influenced Aboriginal policies in the nineteenth century, see R. Cole Harris, *Making Native Space: Colonialism, Resistance and Reserves in British Columbia* (Vancouver: UBC Press, 2002), esp. chapters 1–3.

46 For an overview of these and related issues about First Nations epistemologies and cosmologies, see Julie Cruishank's *Do Glaciers Listen?: Local Knowledge, Colonial Encounters and Social Imagination* (Vancouver: UBC Press, 2005) and Cole Harris's review, 'Do Glaciers Really Listen?' *BC Studies* 148 (2005/6): 103–6.

47 But as Jean-Jacques Simard reminds us, it is not possible to deconstruct the Primitive Aboriginal without deconstructing the other end of the modern-

ization dichotomy. For both Natives *and* Whites are 'fabled creatures,' formed as 'simultaneous and symbiotic creations of the discourse of modernization and progress.' '[T]he Invented Indian cannot be understood by itself, in its own terms: this is but one side of a coin whose other side bears the unearthly features of the Invented White Man ... The much-favored modern definition of the White man as a materialist, morally delinquent, environmentally estranged, socially alienated creature is a historical emergent, one that cannot make sense without reference to the opposite traits of the true Indian.' Jean-Jacques Simard, 'White Ghosts, Red Shadows: The Reduction of North American Natives,' in *The Invented Indian: Cultural Fictions and Government Policies*, ed. James A. Clifton (New Brunswick, NJ: Transaction Publishers, 1990), 333, 353–4.

It is, I believe, only by deconstructing the other side of this polarized paradigm of a liberal modernity, that historians will be able to reach beyond the rigid terms of this bipolar hegemonic liberal discourse. This is not to dispute the importance of 'race' in nineteenth- and twentieth-century Canada, or to challenge the existence of structural inequalities along the axis of racialization. It is simply to suggest that our understanding of non-Native Canadians has also been compromised by forcing a broad spectrum of human motives, behaviours, and activities into binary oppositions polarized by 'race.'

48 Sandwell, 'The Limits of Liberalism.' There have been long discussions about the differences and similarities between the terms 'family' and 'household,' none of which seem particularly useful here. My purpose is to distinguish between the new formations of the modern liberal society, particularly the state and the workplace, and the older social formation of the family/household. The terms will be used interchangeably here. For a review of the debate about the terms, see for example the essays in Richard Wilk, ed., *The Household Economy: Reconsidering the Domestic Mode of Production* (Boulder: Westview Press, 1989); Joan Smith and Emmanuel Wallerstein, *Creating and Transforming Households: The Constraints of the World Economy* (Cambridge: Cambridge University Press, 1992); Michael Anderson, *Approaches to the History of the Western Family, 1500–1914* (London: Macmillan, 1980); and Peter Laslett, *The World We Have Lost* (London: Methuen, 1971).

49 For a review of the literature on this topic, see Sandwell, 'The Limits of Liberalism.'

50 A number of historians have pointed out that the emerging state used the family as an institution that worked to protect capitalism from the most destructive and anti-social aspects of itself. See, for example, the excellent twentieth-century study by Nancy Christie, *Engendering the State: Family,*

Work, and Welfare in Canada (Toronto: University of Toronto Press, 2000); and the nineteenth-century focus of Christopher Clarkson, 'Property Law and Family Regulation in Pacific British North America, 1862–1873,' *Histoire Sociale / Social History* 30, 60 (1997): 386–416.

51 For a review of rural history in Canada, and a discussion of the dissonance between microhistory and the master narrative, see Sandwell, 'Rural Reconstruction.'

52 See, for example, Phillip Girard, 'Land Law, Liberalism and the Agrarian Ideal: British North America, 1750–1920,' in *Depotic Dominion: Property Rights in British Settler Societies*, ed. John McLaren, A.R. Buck, and Nancy E. Wright (Kingston and Montreal: McGill-Queen's University Press, 2005), 120–43.

53 A number of authors do an excellent job of conveying the different kind of ideology – different from 'old ways' in the country of origin, and different from the usual liberalizing ideology that characterized urban North America – in rural Canada in the nineteenth and twentieth centuries. See Girard, 'Land Law, Liberalism and the Agrarian Ideal'; James Murton, *Creating a Modern Countryside: Liberalism and Re-settlement in British Columbia* (Vancouver: UBC Press, 2007); Rod Bantjes, *Improved Earth: Prairie Space as Modern Artefact, 1869–1944* (Toronto: University of Toronto Press, 2005); Royden Loewen, *Diaspora in the Countryside: Two Mennonite Communities and Mid-Twentieth Century Rural Disjuncture* (Toronto: University of Toronto Press, 2006)

54 For the American 'subsistence vs. the market' debate that has provided the context for the more specifically pre-industrial American debate, see R.E. Mutch, 'Yeoman and Merchant in Pre-Industrial America: Eighteenth Century Massachusetts as a Case Study,' *Societas* 7 (1977): 279–302; M. Merril '"Cash Is Good to Eat": Self-Sufficiency and Exchange in the Rural Economy of the United States,' *Radical History Review* 7 (1975): 42–71; J. Lemon, 'Early Americans and Their Social Environment,' *Journal of Historical Geography* 6 (1980): 115–31; W. Rothenberg, *From Market Places to a Market Economy: The Transformation of Rural Massachusetts, 1750–1850* (Chicago: University of Chicago Press, 1992); C. Shamus, 'How Self-Sufficient Was Early America?' *Journal of Interdisciplinary History* 13 (1982): 247–72. This argument has not been fully articulated in the Canadian context, but when it has appeared it has tended to fall, implicitly, along ethnic lines, appearing as the difference between Québec and Ontario. Within the Québec context, to which the debate has so far been largely limited, it took on a distinctly nationalistic tone, with Fernand Ouellet suggesting that the *habitants* of Québec were unable, essentially owing to racial character flaws, to participate in a market

economy, with the result that the Québec economy stagnated in the early nineteenth century. Paquette and Wallot were among those arguing that the economy did not stagnate until later in the century, and attempt to prove the participation of the *habitant* in commercial agriculture. See Fernand Ouellet, *Economy, Class and Nation in Quebec: Interpretive Essays* (Toronto: Copp Clark, 1991); *Évolution et éclatement du monde rural: Structures, fonctionnement et évolution différentielle des sociétés rurales françaises et québécoises, XVIIe–XXe siècles*, published under the direction of Joseph Goy and Jean-Pierre Wallot and collected by Rolande Bonnain (Montreal: Les Presses de l'Université de Montréal, 1986); Gilles Paquet and Jean-Pierre Wallot, *Patronage et pouvoir dans le Bas-Canada, 1794–1812* (Montreal: Les Presses de l'Université de Montréal, 1973). The work of Allan Greer, like that of Gérard Bouchard, has had a different focus. They question the assumptions that inform the theory of the linear transformation from subsistence farming to the commercial market economy, and argue for a thorough understanding of the household economy in an analysis of the complexities of pre-industrial life. Gérard Bouchard, 'Sur un démarrage raté: Industrie laitière et co-intégration au Saguenay, 1880-1940,' *Recherches Sociographiques* 45 (1991): 73–100, and *Quelques arpents d'Amérique: Population, économie, famille au Saguenay, 1838–1971* (Montreal: Boréal, 1996); Allan Greer, *Peasant, Lord, and Merchant: Rural Society in Three Quebec Parishes, 1740–1840,* (Toronto: University of Toronto Press, 1985). Ronald Rudin, in 'Revisionism and the Search for a Normal Society: A Critique of Recent Quebec Historical Writing,' *Canadian Historical Review* 73 (1992): 30–61, accepts the modernization paradigm for English Canada, but questions its applicability to Québec's distinctive culture and economy. For western Canadian analyses, see Kenneth Sylvester, *The Limits of Rural Capitalism: Family, Culture, and Markets in Montcalm, Manitoba, 1870–1940* (Toronto: University of Toronto Press, 2001), and Loewen, *Family, Church and Market.*

55 This is not to say that the history of Canada is environmentally determined, but the climate and the land have, however, set some strict boundaries to the kinds of relationship between land and human beings that are possible in Canada as in the rest of the world, as historians from Harold Innis onward have been well aware. In Canada, occupational plurality has been a long-standing response to the harsh climate and poor soils that characterize so much of the country. For an interesting overview of the North American model of rural change – and one that is politically provocative for its refusal to create Quebec as an exceptional society – see Gérard Bouchard, 'Family Reproduction in New Rural Areas: Outline of a North American Model,' *Canadian Historical Review* 75 (1994): 475–510.

56 Sandwell, 'The Limits of Liberalism.'

57 Ibid.

58 Harriet Friedmann, 'World Market, State and Family Farm: Social Bases of Household Production in the Era of Wage Labour,' *Comparative Studies in Society and History* 20 (1978): 547–8. Marjorie Griffin Cohen notes the importance of unwaged women's work in supporting the staples trade in wheat by maintaining the farm through unprofitable times: *Women's Work, Markets, and Economic Development in Nineteenth-Century Ontario* (Toronto: University of Toronto Press, 1988).

59 Hal S. Barron, *Those Who Stayed Behind: Rural Society in Nineteenth-Century New England* (Cambridge: Cambridge University Press, 1984); Bruce Curtis, 'Preconditions of the Canadian State: Educational Reform and the Construction of a Public in Upper Canada, 1837–1846,' *Studies in Political Economy* 10 (1983); Daniel Samson, 'Industry and Improvement: State and Class Formations in Nova Scotia's Coal-Mining Countryside, 1790–1864' (PhD diss., Queen's University, 1997); see also Sylvester, *The Limits of Rural Capitalism* and Loewen, *Diaspora in the Countryside*.

60 James C. Scott, *Seeing Like a State: How Certain Schemes to Improve the Human Condition Have Failed* (New Haven: Yale University Press, 1998).

Women, Racialized People, and the Making of the Liberal Order in Northern North America

ADELE PERRY[1]

Ian McKay's liberal order framework offers something that historians sorely need – a way to think about the state outside of the existing conventions of English Canadian historiography. Most notably, it provides a vantage point that sidesteps the presumed and radically unhelpful dichotomy between social and political history. McKay is not the first to chart this course – the contributors to Ian Radforth and Allan Greer's collection *Colonial Leviathan*, Bruce Curtis's *The Politics of Population*, and Jean-Marie Fecteau's *Un nouvel ordre des choses* all query the gap between the allegedly political and the allegedly social.[2] And much of what passes as new social and cultural history revisits traditional historiography's themes, archives, and methods, including the colonial states of British North America or the moral reform movements of early-twentieth-century urban Canada.[3] But McKay shifts the ground by showing us in a humbly programmatic way that three decades of sustained research into Canadian social history has provided us with the tools to imagine a history of politics that is neither drenched in one form of nationalism or another nor tied to a one-way track that begins at colony and comes to a grinding halt at nation. My contribution to the discussion provoked by McKay's timely intervention is to read the liberal order framework through the doubled vision of feminist and postcolonial scholarship.

From this vantage point, the liberal order framework is simultaneously enormously promising and in need of recasting. Recent work highlighting the possibilities of thinking outside the nation suggests that McKay's call to think of 'Canada-as-project'[4] should be taken to its logical conclusion, and that is to question whether historians need the rubric of the nation at all or, at least, if we need to think more critically and carefully about how and when we invoke it as a historical category. Historians have cleaved to the nation since the discipline first developed in the nineteenth century. It is time that Canadian historians joined a wider dialogue raising questions about the intellectual and political costs of invariably tying our work to the nation and the enormous potential of imagining a different set of connections and frameworks.[5] As Allan Greer has recently argued, analysing the variety of societies that have existed on northern North American soil within the global frame they existed in holds the potential to enrich the project of Canadian historians rather than compromise it.[6]

But I do not think this is the best opportunity to press the point about nations and their limits. My usage of 'northern North America' instead of Canada, unless referring to the specific state formation of the Canadian nation forged in 1867 and expanded thereafter, should register this point loudly enough. My central intention is to address where gender and race fit in the liberal order framework. McKay's original formulation registers the particular place of women and Indigenous peoples within the liberal order in northern North America, noting that 'Liberal Canada was surrounded by "exceptions" that defined the "rule."'[7] I would like to push and re-situate this line of argument. Globally and locally the liberal order project was predicated on the privatization of women and the relegation of non-Western peoples to various states of reduced humanity, savagery, unfreedom, or containment. Thus, imperialism and patriarchy were not complications of or exceptions to the liberal order: they were necessary to its very production. To put it another way, it is by privatizing women and assuming and sometimes legislating the reduced humanity of non-Western peoples that the liberal subject was defined and redefined.

This was not an uncomplicated process. The years that McKay rightly registers as the heyday of Canada's liberal order – roughly the middle of the nineteenth century through to the Second World War – were ambiguous ones for gendered and racialized exclusions. The juridical exclusion of women from formal political subjecthood in British North America, the creation of a specified and intensely regulated subject 'Chinese' within Canadian immigration policy and the codification of the 'Status Indian' begun in 1876 suggest that raced and gendered parameters were being solidified and hardened. Yet early in that time frame chattel slavery was abolished. As the nineteenth century wore on the conditions of industrial wage-labour and geographic mobility allowed increasing numbers of people to live outside the ambit of patriarchal and heterosexual family formation. Women demonstrated themselves remarkably successful at challenging some of the signature ways in which we were denied full humanity within the liberal state. We might see these years as the fragile and contradictory beginning of the period of late-modernity so incisively analysed by political theorist Wendy Brown. Brown argues that liberalism's exclusionary character persists even as the divisions of labour and activity it is premised upon unravel because exclusions of race, gender, and sexuality structure 'the *terms* of liberal discourse that configure and organize liberal jurisprudence, public policy, and popular consciousness.' 'To the extent that the attributes of liberal personhood and liberal justice are established by excluding certain beings and certain domains of activity from their purview,' she explains, 'liberalism cannot fulfill its universalist vision but persistently reproduces the exclusions of Humanist man.'[8]

This paper proceeds in two parts. First, I offer a summary of feminist and postcolonial critiques of liberal theory and try to highlight their particular purchase in North America during the last half of the nineteenth century and the first half of the twentieth. Second, I add to McKay's list of the 'large library of big books we are missing' by suggesting some of the ways we might begin to better map the racialized and gendered character of the liberal order with an analysis of the regulation of Indigenous peoples, racialization of migrant people of colour, property ownership, and voting. This discussion is not limited to the formal mechanisms of state activity, but it does highlight them. The state is not the sine qua non of history, but its brittle laws, rules, and orders did symbolize and help to constitute a world implicitly or explicitly ordered along the belief that white men were genuine political and economic subjects and that women and racialized people were not so, only potentially so, or at best provisionally and partially so.

Colonialism, Patriarchy, and Thinking the Liberal Order

It is no accident that liberalism – as both a political theory and a clarion call of political reform – developed in the seventeenth and eighteenth centuries just as European authority over much of the globe was being established and the trade in enslaved Africans reached its height. How did liberal thinkers resolve the contradictions between claims to individuality and equality, upon which all liberalism(s) were in some way premised, and the presence of systematic and highly racialized inequality? Philosopher Charles Mills argues that they did so via the 'racial contract,' namely, the belief that white peoples had more and different rights than non-white peoples, a contract codified in the Indian laws, slave codes, and colonial native acts of the seventeenth, eighteenth, and nineteenth centuries.[9]

I suspect that Mills's argument does not pay sufficient heed to how porous, adaptable, and unstable liberalism could be, including around race. But it does prompt us to consider how racial inequality plays a structural rather than incidental role in liberal theory and, in the process, suggests how it might do so in the kind of praxis that concerns McKay and his work on Canada's liberal order project. The rights-bearing individual subject was articulated in critique of systems of rank and ascribed status and in explicit or implicit comparison with the perceived partial, flawed, or conditional humanity of people from Africa, Asia, the Americas, and the Antipodes. Liberalism's claims could, as E.A. Heaman points out elsewhere in this volume, be put in service of demands for colonized and enslaved peoples the world over, as they were when the Métis mounted armed resistance against Canadian expansion in 1869–70 and 1885. The Métis were not alone in finding that their demand for the full fruits of individual and national subjecthood prompted a political response that delivered the opposite. Catherine Hall has shown how the painful interface between British humanitarians and freed Blacks in Jamaica ultimately produced a sharpened racial politics and imaginary.[10] Farther north and west, Louis Riel's attempts to have the Métis included within visions of freeborn Englishmen – and perhaps, more significantly, his efforts to bend these ideas to local practices like customary land tenure and local identities such as Métis – consigned him, in Ian Angus's understated phrase, to 'the alternatives of madness or military defeat.'[11]

The liberal subject was coded male as well as European. In her classic feminist interpretation of women in modern American and British political thought, Carole Pateman argues that 'civil freedom depends on patriarchal right.'[12] Men, in other words, secure their rights as individuals via the explicit – and essentially unnegotiable – unfreedom of women enacted through and codified by the marriage contract. Pateman's account is a powerful one that remains influential. Yet recent scholarship has proposed a more nuanced reading of classical liberal theory's conceptions of women, gender, and the body.[13] One significant line of critique concerns reproduction and childcare, and where they fit in both classical liberal theory and feminist critiques of it. How can a body that potentially or actually contains and nourishes another be reconciled to a liberal world view premised on the inviolable and singular subject? How have liberal thinkers, asks Ingrid Makus, managed or failed to manage to account for society's need to raise children without consigning women wholesale to the work of childcare?[14] These critiques highlight not only the shortcomings of Pateman's formulation, but the genuine difficulties of reconciling childbearing and rearing with liberalism's foundational promises. From this perspective, it is no surprise that first-wave feminists in Canada turned so often to maternalist rhetoric that attempted to capitalize on the particularities of womanhood, and more so motherhood, in their bids to challenge women's exclusion from the hallmarks of the liberal polities – the vote, the right to hold political office, and to own property and claim wages.[15]

There are other reasons to complicate Pateman's thesis. In *States of Injury*, Wendy Brown argues that *The Sexual Contract* ignores the wide varieties of liberalism and is especially unable to account for the contemporary world, where the marriage contract is not mandatory either in theory or in practice. It is not that Brown disagrees with Pateman about the outcome of women's place in liberal polities: her query is with *The Sexual Contract*'s account of how we got from here to there. Brown explains that liberalism's promises are eternally deferred to women not because of the sexual contract, but because 'the constitutive terms of liberal political discourse depend upon their implicit opposition to a subject and set of activities marked "feminine," and at the same time obscure both this dependence and this opposition.' Equality/difference, liberty/necessity, autonomy/dependence, rights/needs, individual/family, self-interest/selflessness, public/private, contract/consent all help to produce a masculinist liberal order, even while women work for wages, exercise a degree of choice around marriage and heterosexuality, vote, and are told that their opportunities and powers are equal.[16]

The deceptive and pervasive liberal politics so aptly analysed by Brown was not fully formed in northern North America during the years discussed by McKay. In these years cruelly overt racial and gendered exclusions and inequities existed alongside more subtle and oblique ones. Blatant or not, these exclusions operated within wider social circumstances that could render them problematic if not inoperable, yet could not always be anticipated. In British North America plebeian men could vote sometimes but not always. In late-nineteenth-century Ontario women might attend medical school but be prevented from actually becoming accredited as doctors.[17] After 1876, Indigenous people in Canada might be allowed to become citizens but only on

terms that ensured that virtually none could or would. No wonder
Velma Demerson, the young white woman incarcerated for living with
Harry Yip in 1939 under an Ontario statute criminalizing young women
for being 'incorrigible' and later stripped of her citizenship for marrying
Yip, was so perplexed about the parameters of her choices.[18] Demerson
and Yip lived in an economic, cultural, and social world that made possible, outside of the convention of marriage, a relationship between a
woman provisionally coded as White and a man definitively coded as
Chinese, but could also punish them harshly for doing so. No wonder
the law had to struggle so hard to justify racialized practices without naming them as such. Thus, when Viola Desmond's challenged
Jim Crow segregation in 1940s Nova Scotia the case was argued without actually naming race or Desmond's blackness in court.[19] For women
and people of colour, liberal order Canada was a place where signs
could easily be read for wonders, and where things were not always
what they seemed, not all of the time.

These exclusions and the confusion and pain they produced were not
incidental to the liberal order or curious holdovers from older social
models. Uday Singh Mehta argues convincingly that the exclusionary
basis of liberalism derives from its 'theoretical core,' not because the
'ideals are theoretically disingenuous or concretely impractical, but
rather because behind the capacities ascribed to all human beings there
exist a thicker set of social credentials that constitute the real bases of
political inclusion.'[20] Social histories of northern North America in the
nineteenth and twentieth centuries have made clear where those social
credentials lay: in axes of class, gender, race, and ethnicity. How, I want
to ask, did these social credentials work to produce some people as more
secure liberal subjects than others? Examining instances of law, policy,
and legislation between the middle of the nineteenth century and the
Second World War suggests some of the ways that we might write the
history of the liberal order in northern North America that takes fuller
account of the exclusions that lay in the bones of the liberal body.

Making Indians

In northern North America Indigenous peoples provided the central
script against which liberal, autonomous subjects could imagine and
construct themselves as distinct from both the alleged 'old world' of
France and Britain and the Indigenous peoples upon whose land they
undeniably stood. From the outset of settlement Indigenous North

Americans were denied the rights of autonomy and citizenship given
to settlers and, more particularly, settler men. Aboriginal people's subjecthood was at best *potential* and infrequently actual. That the 1857
'An Act to encourage the Gradual Civilization of the Indian Tribes of
the Canada' laid out the mechanism by which Indigenous men could
be enfranchised demonstrates that, in effect, they were not, and makes
clear that women could never be.[21] On the Pacific coast, the possibility
of Indigenous people pre-empting land was removed in 1866 by a law
that specifically excluded 'Aboriginies of this Colony or the territories
neighbouring thereto.'[22]

It is revealing that the distinct and subject status of Indigenous
peoples became more codified as the liberal order project extended its
claims and influence. The 1876 Indian Act was a watershed. This
sweeping piece of legislation tied together the piecemeal laws and policies of British North America and anchored them to the newly formed
Canadian state. In a few brief pages 'Indians' were made. This was a
document of nineteenth-century race classification par excellence,
working to fix and stabilize race as an idea and apply it to some bodies
and not others. It rejected the simple blood-quantum of earlier pieces of
legislation and instead, as Renisa Mawani explains, 'linked blood with
real property and citizenship.'[23] Patriarchy was made through race and
vice versa. 'Status Indians' were defined as those with a secure kin relationship to an 'Indian' man in descending order from their proximity to
him: '*First.* Any male person of Indian blood reputed to belong to a particular band; *Secondly.* Any child of such a person; *Thirdly.* Any woman
who is or was lawfully married to such a person.'[24] It is a clear attempt
to impose practices of patriarchal descent and lineage on Indigenous
peoples, who reckoned kinship and lived gender in a variety of ways. It
is also very much a document of moral, gendered, and sexual regulation, where reproduction, marriage, and kinship are the tools through
which race is negotiated. The Indian Act mandated that Aboriginal
women would lose their status as 'Indians' if they married non-status
men, as would any children they bore with them. Conversely, non-
Aboriginal women who had the temerity to marry across the citizenship line – and there were always some, even though they could not be
imagined in the minds of those who wrote the statute – became status
Indians in the eyes of the law.[25]

That this was a distinctly patriarchal flavour of non-citizenship is
made clear by the enormously complex process whereby a status Indian
could become enfranchised and thus a full member of Canada's liberal

order. A status Indian man or unmarried woman over twenty-one years of age could exchange their status as Indians for that of citizen if they became a physician, a barrister, a notary public, or a Christian minister. Otherwise enfranchisement could occur if a status Indian's band was willing and the superintendent-general was convinced that 'the applicant is an Indian who, from the degree of civilization to which he or she has attained, and the character for integrity, morality and sobriety which he or she bears' was *qualified* for the rights that the liberal project claimed were universal, inherent, and uncontestable.[26]

That fewer than five hundred status Indians opted and qualified for enfranchisement between 1857 and 1940 makes clear that this was citizenship almost permanently denied.[27] Attempts to make enfranchisement easier were protested by settlers, who saw in the expansion of Indigenous citizenship rights the abrogation of their own. The government of John A. Macdonald tried to loosen requirements for enfranchisement, but the government that followed rejected this path, its spokesman remarking, 'It is a derogation to the dignity of the people and an insult to free white people in the country to place them on a level with pagan and barbarian Indians.'[28] The Indian Act allowed the Canadian state to restrict the numbers of people able to claim privileges and benefits from the state, a goal of colonial regimes the world over.[29] It also provided, as that Liberal member of parliament so candidly implied, a way for male settlers to define themselves as citizens and full members of the liberal project. The Indian Act did not, of course, function in a vacuum, but rather existed at the symbolic and real centre of a range of overlapping controls placed on Aboriginal peoples by the Canadian state, sometimes via missionary churches. Such controls reached their apogee with what historian Jim Miller calls the 'policy of the Bible and the plough,' which developed revealingly in step with the liberal order. The reserve system, farm labour programs, and residential schooling system were the most central components of this unabashedly illiberal order, aided by more episodic controls including the pass system that controlled Indigenous movement in the prairies from 1880s to the 1920s.[30] As Robin Jarvis Brownlie argues elsewhere in this collection, the Canadian state has worked hard to keep Indigenous peoples outside of the liberal project, including by mandating an explicitly illiberal form of economic collectivization. It was not simply that the liberal order had yet to be extended to Indigenous peoples in northern North America; their exclusion was categorical, and a condition that anchored and animated the inclusion of male settlers.

Making Citizens

The liberal order was racialized in other ways as well. Discourses, definitions, and practices of race and nation also worked to determine which settlers could access the privileges of the liberal order and on what terms. The late eighteenth and early nineteenth centuries were ambiguous ones of practices and codes of race in northern North America and elsewhere. They witnessed the expansion and consolidation of European imperialism alongside the flowering of democratic critique and unprecedented challenge to one of the most egregious forms of racialized inequality – the slavery of people of African origin in the Americas. Canada's liberal order was forged in this contradictory climate. Upper Canada's historic rejection of chattel slavery in 1793 and Canada West's emergence as the terminus for the Underground Railroad helped to position anti-slavery as a cornerstone of English Canadian identity, the decidedly mixed experience of African-Canadians notwithstanding.[31] It remains one today, a cherished counterpoint to what is discursively positioned as the archetypal racism of the United States.

As Sherene Razack argues, English Canadians' belief in their history as unstained by racial division is an absence that speaks to presence and forecloses discussion at the same time.[32] We can see this kind of chimeric and deceptive work of gender and racial divisions within liberal societies developing in northern North America between the 1840s and the Second World War. As Constance Backhouse writes, '"Race" does not appear as a recognizable legal category of classification between 1900 and 1950.'[33] Yet race was shot through the law, albeit unevenly. The province of British Columbia enacted over one hundred pieces of legislation discriminating against Asians between 1872 and 1922.[34]

With the important exception of the baroque regulation of Indigenous peoples, this was not a seamless racist order. Patterns of segregation were variable and regional. Separate schooling for Black children was legally codified in Ontario and Nova Scotia from the middle of the nineteenth until the middle of twentieth century.[35] Efforts to codify separate schooling for Chinese children in Victoria were less successful. It was apparently neutral public-health legislation that buttressed the construction of Chinatowns across twentieth-century Canada. But, as Kay Anderson has argued, Chinatown was more an idea than a strictly legal practice.[36] So too the segregation of work places, movie theatres, swimming pools, beer parlours, and neighbourhoods was enacted and maintained via customary, extra-legal, and at times distinctly sneaky means. The spaces of segregation shifted, as did the groups segregated – Jews in 1930s Toronto, Chinese in British Columbia, Blacks in Nova Scotia, Eastern Europeans in the prairies. Often, no law codified these practices, but until provinces began passing irregular laws preventing racial discrimination in the 1930s, none prevented them either.[37] Robert Campbell's study of Vancouver's beer parlours points out that while the laws regulating public drinking were putatively egalitarian, notions of decency were inextricably bound up with highly racialized ideas of appropriate and inappropriate behaviour.[38]

The way that notions of race and nation conditioned claims to Canada's liberal order became clear in times of crisis. The poverty and dislocation that came with the Depression of the 1930s prompted a wave of radical activity, one that palpably threatened the Canadian state. This was not, of course, a crisis primarily about ideas of nation: it was a crisis of faith in capitalism and its ability to provide the best methods of government. Yet this crisis was negotiated through irreparably racialized and gendered terms. Take, for instance, the phalanx of desperate personal letters written to R.B. Bennett, the wealthy and pompous Conservative prime minister from 1930 to 1935. Cut through the threats of revolution, requests for winter boots, and proclamations of political loyalty were the politics of race, nation, and loyalty: references to United Empire Loyalist lineage, claims to being 'Loyal English,' diatribes against the 'Chinese' and foreigners 'who can neither read nor write English.'[39] When a well-meaning clergyman in Vancouver sought to describe the mobile homeless men who filled his city, he could only do so in the language of the wider empire – they lived in jungles and were equivalent to the 'untouchables' of India.[40]

In 1935, an archetypal clash of mutually unintelligible visions of an appropriate political order occurred when Bennett and his cabinet met with eight representatives of the thousands of radical men who had travelled eastward from Vancouver under the banner of the On-to-Ottawa Trek. Both sides attempted to mobilize definitions of manly loyalty in their effort to discredit the other. Bennett asked the strike leaders their age, if they were married, where they were born, and challenged Arthur 'Slim' Evans's claim to have been born in Toronto. Bennett linked their births in England, Scotland, Newfoundland, and Denmark with criminality, making reference to Evans having served jail time. 'With the exception of one of you, who has a record that we will not discuss, you were born outside of Canada,' the prime minister charged. Evans responded by escalating the language of nation and loyalty to that of race and savagery and telling Bennett that he was 'not fit to be the premier of a Hottentot village.' Those who had led the general strike a generation earlier in Winnipeg worked to appropriate the language of loyal British manhood for their own ends.[41] The leaders of the On-to-Ottawa Trek were less trustful of the politics of nation and empire, but were fully willing to use their claims to national membership, and more particularly wartime service, to defend themselves. They expressed their umbrage at the injustice of men who had served in France being called 'foreigners.' After Bennett threatened to remove Jack Cosgrove and ordered him to sit down, Cosgrove retorted, 'I fought in the war as a boy fifteen years old. I have the interests of this country as much at heart as you have.' Even a belligerent and didactic prime minister could not argue with this. 'That is good enough,' replied Bennett.[42] But, of course, it wasn't, not in the larger sense. The Trek was crushed at Regina, and the radical vision of Canada that it represented would take decades to recover.

The politics of race and nation that bubbled through political life were rendered blunt in the federal immigration policy that governed admission to and, in effect, citizenship within Canada during the heyday of the liberal order. The birth of formal immigration policy was also the birth of overt racial exclusion. Once the construction of the Canadian Pacific Railway was essentially completed and the labour of Chinese men was less required by big business, the Royal Commission on Chinese Immigration was called and began to canvas racial thinking on North America's Pacific coast. The report it produced was a revealing and often bizarre compilation of experience, opinion, and conjecture, the economic focus of which has been overstated by historians. However much they made divergent arguments, the people who spoke before or wrote to the commission seemed to have shared the bedrock opinion that 'Chinese' people were a distinct race whose capacity for full membership in the Canadian nation fell somewhere between limited and non-existent.[43] This was put into legislative form with the Chinese Immigration Act of 1885, which set limits on how many Chinese could be brought on each vessel and imposed a head tax of fifty dollars on 'every person of chinese origin' entering Canada, with the exception of tourists, representatives of state, or professionals.[44] It was, of course, only the beginning: the head tax was raised until it reached an intentionally prohibitive five hundred dollars, and in 1923 a new Chinese Immigration Act banned Chinese immigration altogether. It remained in force until 1947.[45]

It is no accident that both the exclusion of Chinese people and the hyper-regulation of Indigenous peoples coincided so neatly with the consolidation of the Canadian nation or, in McKay's framework, the liberal order. Nations are always produced to some extent by their exteriors, and Canada found different if both serviceable ones in Chinese and Aboriginal peoples. In the American context Lisa Lowe has argued convincingly that the discourse of exclusion obfuscates a more complicated experience of Asian people's relationship to the nation. Immigration policy, she argues, walked and continues to walk a fine line between political demands for a racially homogeneous nation and capitalist requirements for cheap labour. The result was not exclusion per se but a highly strategic and limited inclusion cloaked in the simpler language of absence and ban.[46] So too Chinese people would continue to be part of Canada's liberal order, simply on terms that impoverished them, diminished their numbers, and ultimately compromised their ability to participate in and make claims against the places they lived and worked.

Elsewhere, the demands of formal liberal discourse and the exigencies of Canada's continued place in the British Empire ensured that the racialization of Canada's liberal order via immigration policy would be piecemeal and at times deceptive. Political pressure from Japan, the British Empire, and the United States would ensure that people of Japanese, South Asian, and African-American origin would have their movement to Canada limited and controlled by a more complicated and obtuse legislation. The revealingly titled Gentleman's Agreement of 1907 that limited Japanese immigration, the Continuous Passage Act of 1908 that mandated that people must come to Canada from the Indian subcontinent via the essentially impossible direct passage, the use of 1910's Immigration Act provision that the state could exclude 'any race deemed unsuited to the climate or requirements of Canada' all worked to limit the possibilities of non-White migration to Canada.[47] Yet, as the *Komagata Maru* incident made clear, these were never stable vehicles of inclusion and exclusion. Radhika Viyas Mongia has shown how the Canadian passport proved itself an unreliable method of controlling the movements of British subjects with roots in the Indian subcontinent.[48] It was the highly malleable and much used tool of deportation that immigration officials found the most reliable method of constituting modern Canada.[49] This liberal order and the nation that defined it would find its own unique ways of rendering some people outsiders and, in the process, making itself.

Laws of the Land

The liberal order that developed in northern North America in the last half of the nineteenth and the first half of the twentieth century defined itself through an unstable and at times deceptive version of the racial contract. This went alongside a local rendition of the sexual contract whereby men's status as individuals was secured through the privatization of women as wives. The Royal Proclamation of 1763 claimed a substantial part of northern North America as part of the British Empire and laid out key components of a colonial but dialogic relationship between First Nations and the British crown. Part of this regime change would involve the imposition of British laws, including those relating to property and marriage. That the allegedly illiberal *ancien régime* of New France offered married women greater property rights than did British North America or Canada calls into question overtly teleological and implicitly ethnocentric ideas about the spread of liberal individualism, an irony that Québécois feminists have long been aware of. In New France under the Coutume de Paris and in Quebec after 1774 all the property obtained by a couple after their marriage was their 'joint' property, although it was administered by husbands alone.

The English common law made married women non-existent as legal actors, unable to manage real estate, to contract, to sue or be sued, or to claim wages. In 1900 Clara Brett Martin, Canada's first woman lawyer, wrote: 'This notion of the unity of husband and wife ... meaning thereby the suspicion of the wife and the lordship of the husband, seems to have been particularly agreeable to the whole race of English jurists, tickling their grim humor and gratifying their very limited sense of the fitness of things.'[50] Here Martin registers the centrality of a narrowly defined patriarchy to the British legal culture of northern North America. Property law concerned feminists from the mid-nineteenth century onwards because it had enormous implications for women's economic security and agency, and also because it symbolized Pateman's sexual contract in no uncertain terms – wives were essentially excluded from the base promises and principles of the liberal contract, namely, the right to own property.

But the liberal order politics of northern North America also unsettled these rigid structures and reworked them in important if ultimately partial ways. After 1851 the law of married women's property began to change, in part in response to liberal ideas questioning 'all forms of hierarchical organization,' including those between men and women and adults and children.[51] As Bettina Bradbury has argued, the redefinition of women's autonomy was inseparable from the process by which white, settler-colonies claimed themselves to be as advanced, white and civilized as the British themselves.[52] It was also about the economic and ideological preconditions for patriarchy shifting in measurable ways. The increasing number of women, especially young ones, able to support themselves through wage-work and live outside of family homes in the late nineteenth and early twentieth century suggests some real limits to the sexual contract through marriage.[53] The declining birth rate likewise indicates that the conditions and politics of motherhood were a shifting ground. For the most part, first-wave feminists in Canada displayed a remarkable faith in heterosexual marriage and the privatized family: they reserved their critique for the workings of male licence and authority within marriage and family rather than for the institutions themselves. But within this framework they were able to press the point that property law disempowered married women to the detriment of women, children, and, they would argue, the family itself.

Under the pressure of persuasive feminist critique and increased possibilities for female financial autonomy, patriarchy in marriage was, in Bradbury's apt term, 're-landscaped' in the latter half of the nineteenth century. Wives were gradually given new legal power if they had any property of their own, but men's control over their bodies and labour power remained.[54] That men continued to secure their subjectivity via exclusive rights to land ownership was reaffirmed with the 1872 Dominion Lands Act. This mandated that only a select and elaborately constituted category of women – widows, divorcees, and separated or deserted wives with dependent children under eighteen – could apply for homesteads.[55] Thus, the patriarchal contract that underwrote property law was doubly encoded on the new territories north and west of the Great Lakes.[56] The liberal subject continued to be defined through wives' lack of economic autonomy, and this would motivate feminist activism from the 1920s struggle for a dower law on the prairies to the 1980s effort to reform marriage and divorce laws.[57] The family, as Ruth Sandwell has argued elsewhere and in this volume, is a realm where the liberal principles of individualism and industry did not rule supreme.[58] It is also an institution that demonstrates how the liberal order was premised on the exclusion of women, albeit in complex and shifting terms.

Votes for Whom?

Along with the right to control one's body and possess property, the right to participate in formal electoral politics is a hallmark of liberal subjecthood, and one that has a revealingly partial history in northern North America. In the eighteenth and early nineteenth century property-owning women occasionally availed themselves of the possibility of voting in Britain's North American colonies, usually for local governments. Such practices came under attack as reformers demanding a new voice for colonial citizens increasingly associated femininity and the family with the 'old' world of monarchy, despotism, and corruption that they wished to separate themselves from. When the French Canadian rebels of Lower Canada exclaimed, 'The Queen is a whore' and the critics of British administration in Upper Canada lambasted the 'family compact' they both borrowed the language of gender and morality to articulate their critique of the British Empire and their place in it.[59]

As reformers argued for the extension of political rights to the settler-citizen they also defined legitimate political authority as necessarily male. In 1834 the Lower Canadian legislature disenfranchised women of all ranks as part of a wider campaign waged against electoral corruption. Prince Edward Island followed suit in that year, as did New Brunswick in 1843, the Union of the Canadas in 1849, and Nova Scotia in 1851.[60] Women were thus categorically evicted from the central terms of the liberal order as it was taking shape. Yet Bradbury's fine study of women voters in the Montreal by-election of 1823 reminds us that the history of women and voting in the era of the liberal order is a complicated one. In 1873 the city of Victoria, British Columbia, gave propertied widows and spinsters the municipal vote, and the 1880s witnessed a string of jurisdictions, including Ontario and Manitoba, granting women the right to vote and be elected to local governments, especially school boards.[61]

Seen from this perspective, the time that women were juridically barred from the franchise is one critical component in a wider history of interlocking exclusions that defined the liberal order project. The exclusion of those who did not own property or enough of it, a category into which the vast bulk of women and 'status Indians' necessarily fell, would survive the challenges of liberalism remarkably intact into the closing years of the nineteenth century.[62] Prison inmates and residents of lunatic asylums and state-funded charitable institutions were disenfranchised federally in 1898 and remained so until at least 1920. So too were those whose occupations were deemed too proximate to the mechanics of the provincial state – judges, tax and customs officials, and a wide swath of civil servants, including those who worked for the post office, as teachers in British Columbia, or in Nova Scotia's lighthouses.[63]

These seemingly picayune exclusions all speak to the liberal order project's investment in a highly particular imagined political subject, one who was literally male during certain legislative moments. At other points it was more indirectly anchored to the attributes associated with masculinity, most notably independence and property ownership. As the exclusions on the basis of religion that littered the statute books of British North America[64] were removed, the liberal order's political subject was increasingly constructed in overtly racial terms. This went well beyond the routine specification that voters needed to be subjects of the British empire, citizens of Canada, or have been 'landed' for a specified period of time. In 1854 Nova Scotia specified that 'Indians' could not vote. In 1863 the colony of British Columbia barred Chinese and Indians from voting. Even when and where Indigenous people could vote, their legal status as 'Indians' could, in practice, strip them of the right to vote and be elected. John Brant's election to the Upper Canada Assembly in 1831 was subsequently nullified on the grounds that he did not and could never meet the property requirements for voting or office as an 'Indian' who did not hold land in 'fee simple.'[65]

That Brant stood for and was elected to office reminds us that it is not that these exclusions from the liberal polity were not contested; they were. In 1885 the Canadian House of Commons had an extensive debate about who could and should vote in Canada, and the conclusion was a remarkable distillation of the liberal order's political subject, now deliberately defined to exclude all women, most Indigenous peoples, and all Chinese people.[66] Ontario, Manitoba, and British Columbia entirely or in effect excluded people of Indigenous origins until 1885.[67] British Columbia was the only province where the franchise was not regulated by a property qualification, and where non-white settlers were denied the provincial vote by law. This province disenfranchised the 'Chinese' in 1874, the 'Japanese' in 1895, 'Hindus' in 1907, and 'Dukhobors' in 1931.[68] It is tough sledding to reconcile this history of variable but escalating racial exclusion with the conventional narrative of increasing access and equality.

The new nation forged in the crucible of the liberal order project would be one where settler men would gain their constituent status through the layered exclusion of women, Indigenous people, and racialized migrants. That these exclusions were constituent does not mean that they were stable. Women's exclusion from formal politics would be criticized with special efficacy only a few decades after it was formalized. Suffragists proved adept at reading the liberal order and reworking its claims and inconsistencies to argue for women's right to political participation. They made unabashedly liberal rights-claims rooted in a belief in women's inherent equality. Often suffragists found trading in liberalism's tensions around women, reproduction, and the body more useful. In anchoring their (ultimately successful) demand that women be admitted into the liberal polity on the sticky and distinctly illiberal contention that women's experience of mothering gave them unique political claims, suffragists called one of the liberal order's many bluffs. Suffragists also turned the tensions produced by the imbrications of different kinds of exclusion to the advantage of an imagined female subject explicitly coded as white and Canadian-born. Thus, suffragists contrasted the dubious 'foreigner' with electoral privileges with the virtuous 'Canadian' woman who was denied the right to vote.[69]

The gradual and partial inclusion of women and racialized peoples would be as piecemeal and revealing as were their exclusions. Provinces began passing legislation allowing women to vote in 1916. Federally, it would be ties to the state and Empire that would leverage women's partial re-admission to the liberal pact of modern nationhood. The Military Voters Act of 1917 gave the vote to women nurses serving in the war; later that year the Wartime Elections Act extended the franchise to wives, widows, mothers, sisters, and daughters of those who served in the Canadian or British military. In 1918 the Women's Franchise Act gave the vote to women who were British subjects aged twenty-one and over. Women would not vote in Quebec until 1940. It would be wartime service that would constitute the necessary stuff for Chinese, Japanese, Indigenous, and South Asian men who had served in the Second World War to be enfranchised in 1945. Other Chinese Canadians would wait another two years, and those of Japanese origin another three years, to receive the root promises of the liberal order. Inuit peoples would not vote until 1950, and status Indians would remain voteless until 1960. It seems telling that it is only as the liberal order came to be undone in the years following the Second World War that women, people of Asian origin, and Aboriginal peoples would conclusively receive the right to vote at the provincial and federal levels.

These various exclusions and partial and strategic inclusions and the points at which they were done and undone suggest some of the ways that women and people of colour fit within northern North America's liberal order project. McKay noted this in his initial formulation, arguing that women, Indigenous peoples, and the Québécois are telling reminders of the liberal order's inability to incorporate everything and everyone in its midst – to quote McKay, 'entities' 'on the edges of a liberal dominion.'[70] My point in this chapter has been to expand on this point and, to some extent, to shift it from the periphery to the centre of the analysis. Liberal theory was anchored in the privatization of women and relegation of non-Western peoples to a different space of humanity and political life. In northern North America during the heyday of the liberal order these ideas clearly were refracted through policies regulating Indigenous peoples, laws, policies and practices of race and nation, and the politics of property ownership and suffrage. Reading history through the optic provided by the marginal and disempowered leverages new perspectives on old chapters of history. As Jennifer Morgan writes, remembering that enslaved Sally Hemings held the candle while her master and unacknowledged partner Thomas Jefferson wrote the American Declaration of Independence radically changes how we see that document and the history that surrounds it.[71]

Yet history, and more particularly modern Canadian history, often gives us complicated scenarios where inequalities and oppression appear alongside proclamations of their absence and genuine possibilities for social change. Wendy Brown is wise to point out that contemporary liberal political cultures function to secure the exclusion of women and people of colour in complicated and at times obtuse ways, ways that can and do slip too easily below our critical radar and are part of liberalism's very functioning. In the last half of the nineteenth century and the first half of the twentieth structures of patriarchy, colonialism, and racism were simultaneously and sometimes contradictorily challenged, reaffirmed, and reincorporated in British North America and Canada. We need to better acknowledge the pervasively gendered and racialized character of the liberal order and understand that it rarely functioned in straightforward terms. Then, perhaps, the liberal order and those who stood at its margins will come more fully into historians' views.

NOTES

1 Canada Research Chair in Western Canadian Social History, Department of History, University of Manitoba. This research was undertaken, in part, thanks to funding from the Canada Research Chairs Program, and I thank them for that. The arguments here were developed in hallway conversations at St John's College, and I would especially like to acknowledge the engage-

ment of Robin Jarvis Brownlie, Ryan Eyford, Barry Ferguson, Esyllt Jones, Kurt Korneski, and Gerry Friesen. At times like this it helps to have a live-in political theorist, and I appreciate the help Peter Ives gave me. Thanks also go to the editors of and contributors to this volume, and especially to 'Reader Two' for upping my game.

2 Jean-Marie Fecteau, *Un nouvel ordre des choses: La pauvreté, le crime, l'État au Québec, de la fin du XVIIIe siècle à 1840* (Montreal: VLB éditeur, 1989); Bruce Curtis, *The Politics of Population: State Formation, Statistics, and the Census of Canada, 1840–1875* (Toronto: University of Toronto Press, 2001); Allan Greer and Ian Radforth, eds., *Colonial Leviathan: State Formation in Mid-Nineteenth-Century Canada* (Toronto: University of Toronto Press, 1992).

3 Here I include my own *On the Edge of Empire: Gender, Race, and the Making of British Columbia, 1849–1871* (Toronto: University of Toronto Press, 2001), but see also Jerry Bannister, *The Rule of the Admirals: Naval Government in Newfoundland, 1699–1832* (Toronto: University of Toronto Press, 2003). On reform movements see, for instance, Mariana Valverde, *The Age of Light, Soap and Water: Moral Reform in English Canada, 1885–1920* (Toronto: McClelland and Stewart, 1992) and Mary Louise Adams, *The Trouble with Normal: Post-War Youth and the Making of Heterosexuality* (Toronto: University of Toronto Press, 1997).

4 Ian McKay, 'The Liberal Order Framework: A Prospectus for a Reconnaissance of Canadian History,' *Canadian Historical Review* 81 (2000): 621.

5 See, for instance, Antoinette Burton, ed., *After the Imperial Turn: Thinking with and through the Nation* (Chapel Hill: Duke University Press, 2003); Burton, 'Who Needs the Nation? Interrogating "British" History,' in *Cultures of Empire: A Reader*, ed. Catherine Hall (Manchester: Manchester University Press, 2000); Patricia Limerick, 'Going West and Ending Up Global,' *Western Historical Quarterly* 32 (2001): 5–24; Ann Laura Stoler, 'Tense and Tender Ties: The Politics of Comparison in North American History and (Post) Colonial Studies,' *Journal of American History* 88 (2001): 829–65. In Canada, this point is best made by work on migration, including Marlene Epp, *Women without Men: Mennonite Refugees of the Second World War* (Toronto: University of Toronto Press, 2000) and Royden Loewen, *Family, Church and Market: A Mennonite Community in the Old and the New Worlds, 1850–1930* (Urbana: University of Illinois Press and University of Toronto Press, 1993); Bruno Ramirez, *On the Move: French-Canadian and Italian Migrants in the North Atlantic Economy, 1860–1914* (Toronto: McClelland and Stewart, 1991).

6 Allan Greer, 'Canadian History Is So Boring ...,' *National Post*, 20 August 2005.

7 McKay, 'Liberal Order Framework,' 627.

8 Wendy Brown, 'Liberalism's Family Values,' in *States of Injury: Power and Freedom in Late Modernity* (Princeton: Princeton University Press, 1995), 152, 164. My debt to Brown's argument should be amply clear from this paper.
9 Charles W. Mills, *The Racial Contract* (Ithaca: Cornell University Press, 1999).
10 Catherine Hall, *Civilizing Subjects: Metropole and Colony in the English Imagination, 1830–1867* (Chicago: University of Chicago Press, 2002).
11 Ian Angus, 'Louis Riel and English-Canadian Political Thought,' *University of Toronto Quarterly* 74 (2005): 886.
12 Carole Pateman, *The Sexual Contract* (Stanford: Stanford University Press, 1988), 219.
13 See Joanne Boucher, 'Male Power and Contact Theory: Hobbes and Locke in Carole Pateman's *The Sexual Contract*,' *Canadian Journal of Political Science* 36 (2003): 23–38; Joanne H. Wright, 'Going Against the Grain: Hobbes's Case for Original Maternal Dominion,' *Journal of Women's History* 14 (2002): 123–48.
14 Ingrid Makus, *Women, Politics, and Reproduction: The Liberal Legacy* (Toronto: University of Toronto Press, 1996); Lealle Ruhl, 'Dilemmas of the Will: Uncertainty, Reproduction, and the Rhetoric of Control,' *Signs* 27 (2002): 641–62.
15 First-wave feminism in Canada awaits its revisionist historian. Mariana Valverde's work suggests some of the ways it might go. See her 'When the Mother of the Race Is Free: Race, Reproduction, and Sexuality in First-Wave Feminism,' in *Gender Conflicts: New Essays in Women's History,* ed. Franca Iacovetta and Mariana Valverde (Toronto: University of Toronto Press, 1992); and her '"Racial Poison": Drink, Male Vice, and Degeneration in First Wave Feminism,' in *Women's Suffrage in the British Empire: Citizenship, Nation and Race,* ed. Ian Christopher Fletcher, Laura E. Nym Mayhall, and Philippa Levine (New York: Routledge, 2000). The rich Australian historiography is suggestive on the connections between liberalism, citizenship, race, motherhood, and first-wave feminism and might suggest useful starting points for historians of women in North America as well. See, especially, Marilyn Lake, 'Marriage as Bondage: The Anomaly of the Citizen Wife,' *Australian Historical Studies* 112 (1999): 116–29; Lake, 'Childbearers as Rights-Bearers: Feminist Discourse on the Rights of Aboriginal and Non-Aboriginal Mothers in Australia, 1920–50,' *Women's History Review* 8 (1999): 347–63.
16 Brown, 'Liberalism's Family Values,' 152.
17 Veronica Strong-Boag, 'Canada's Women Doctors: Feminism Constrained,' in *A Not Unreasonable Claim: Women and Reform in Canada, 1880s-1920s,* ed. Linda Kealey (Toronto: The Women's Press, 1976).
18 Velma Demerson, *Incorrigible* (Waterloo: Wilfrid Laurier University Press,

2004). For the wider context, see Joan Sangster, *Regulating Girls and Women: Sexuality, Family, and the Law in Ontario, 1920–1960* (Toronto: Oxford University Press, 2001).

19 Constance Backhouse, *Colour-Coded: A Legal History of Racism in Canada, 1900–1950* (Toronto: University of Toronto Press, 1999).

20 Uday Singh Mehta, *Liberalism and Empire: A Study in Nineteenth-Century British Liberal Thought* (Chicago: University of Chicago Press, 1999), 48–9.

21 See Olive Dickason, *Canada's First Nations: A History of Founding Peoples from Earliest Times*, 2nd ed. (Toronto: Oxford University Press, 1997), 225.

22 Quoted in Paul Tennant, *Aboriginal People and Politics: The Indian Land Question in British Columbia, 1849–1989* (Vancouver: UBC Press, 1990), 41.

23 Renisa Mawani, 'In Between and Out of Place: Mixed-Race Identity, Liquor and the Law in British Columbia, 1850–1913,' in *Race, Space, and the Law: Unmapping a White Settler Society*, ed. Sherene Razack (Toronto: Between the Lines, 2002), 56.

24 The Indian Act, 1876, *Statutes of Canada*, 39 Vict., c. 18, s. 3. The implications for Aboriginal women were and continue to be enormous. See Audrey Huntley and Fay Blaney, *Bill C-31: Its Impact, Implications, and Recommendations for Change in British Columbia: Final Report* (Vancouver: Aboriginal Women's Action Network, 1999).

25 See Dara Culhane Speck's discussion of becoming status via marriage to a status Indian man in *The Pleasure of the Crown: Anthropology, Law and First Nations* (Vancouver: UBC Press, 1998) 25n4.

26 The Indian Act, 1876, s. 86.

27 Dickason, *Canada's First Nations*, 225.

28 David Mills, cited in Dickason, *Canada's First Nations*, 264n52.

29 On this process elsewhere, see Ann Laura Stoler, 'Rethinking Colonial Categories: European Communities and the Boundaries of Rule,' *Comparative Studies in Society and History* 31 (1989): 134–61; Stoler, 'Sexual Affronts and Racial Frontiers: European Identities and Cultural Politics of Exclusion in Colonial Southeast Asia,' *Comparative Studies in Society and History* 34 (1992): 514–51.

30 See here J.R. Miller, *Skyscrapers Hide the Heavens: A History of Indian-White Relations in Canada*, rev. ed. (Toronto: University of Toronto Press, 1989), chap. 11.

31 Maureen Elgersman Lee, *Unyielding Spirits: Black Women and Slavery in Early Canada and Jamaica* (New York: Garland, 1999).

32 Sherene H. Razack, *Dark Threats and White Knights: The Somalia Affair, Peacekeeping, and the New Imperialism* (Toronto: University of Toronto Press, 2004).

33 Backhouse, *Colour-Coded*, 11.

34 Timothy Stanley, 'Schooling, White Supremacy, and the Formation of a Chinese Merchant Public in British Columbia,' in *Making Western Canada: Essays on European Colonization and Settlement*, ed. Catherine Cavanaugh and Jeremy Mouat (Toronto: Garamound, 1996), 219.
35 Backhouse, *Colour-Coded*, 250–1.
36 Kay J. Anderson, *Vancouver's Chinatown: Racial Discourse in Canada, 1875–1980* (Montreal and Kingston: McGill-Queen's University Press, 1995).
37 Backhouse, *Colour-Coded*, 197. The first comprehensive human-rights legislation was in Saskatchewan, 1947. See also ibid., 250–1.
38 Robert A. Campbell, *Sit Down and Drink Your Beer: Regulating Vancouver's Beer Parlours, 1925–1954* (Vancouver: UBC Press, 2001), 86.
39 See L.M. Grayson and Michael Bliss, eds., *The Wretched of Canada: Letters to R.B. Bennett, 1930–1935* (Toronto: University of Toronto Press, 1971), 44, 97, 18.
40 Andrew Roddan, *Canada's Untouchables: The Story of the Man without a Home* (Vancouver: Clark and Stuary, 1932).
41 Chad Reimer, 'War, Nationhood, and the Working-Class Entitlement: The Counterhegemonic Challenge of the 1919 Winnipeg General Strike,' *Prairie Forum* 18 (1993): 219–237.
42 See transcript of the meeting in 'The Interview between the Delegation of Strikers and the Prime Minister and His Cabinet,' in *Ronald Liversedge: Recollections of the On to Ottawa Trek*, ed. Victor Hoar (Toronto: McClelland and Stewart, 1972), 205, 210, 211. The context is dealt with in Bill Waiser, *All Hell Can't Stop Us: The On-to-Ottawa Trek and the Regina Riot* (Calgary: Fitzhenry and Whiteside, 2003).
43 *Report of the Royal Commission on Chinese Immigration: Report and Evidence* (Ottawa: The Commission, 1885; repr. New York: Arno Press, 1978). The places at which this royal commission gathered evidence – San Francisco, Victoria, and Portland – remind us of the need to look beyond and across national borders.
44 Chinese Immigration Act, 1885, c. 71; at http://www.asian.ca/law/cia1885.htm(accessed 19 November 2007).
45 Chinese Immigration Act, 1923, 13–14 Geo. V, c. 38 accessed at http://www.asian.ca/law/cia1923.htm (accessed 19 November 2007).
46 Lisa Lowe, Immigrant Acts: On Asian American Cultural Politics (Durham: Duke University Press, 1996), esp. chap. 1.
47 Sunera Thobani, 'Closing the Nation's Doors to Immigrant Women: The Restructuring of Canadian Immigration Policy,' *Atlantis* 24 (2000): 16–26; Agnes Calliste, 'Canada's Immigration Policy and Domestics from the Caribbean: The Second Domestic Scheme,' in *Race, Class and Gender: Bonds*

and Barriers, ed. Jesse Vorst et al. (Toronto: Garamound Press and Society for Socialist Studies, 1989).

48 Radhika Viyas Mongia, 'Race, Nationality, Mobility: A History of the Passport,' in *After the Imperial Turn*. Also see Enakshi Dua, 'Racializing Imperial Canada: Indian Women and the Making of Ethnic Communities,' in *Sisters or Strangers? Immigrant, Ethnic, and Racialized Women in Canada's History*, ed. Marlene Epp, Franca Iacovetta, and Frances Swyripa (Toronto: University of Toronto Press, 2004).

49 See Barbara Roberts, *Whence They Came: Deportation from Canada, 1900–1935* (Ottawa: University of Ottawa Press, 1997). Migrant labour programs perform the same work in the present. See Nandita Sharma, *Home Economics: Nationalism and the Making of Migrant Workers in Canada* (Toronto: University of Toronto Press, 2006).

50 Quoted in Constance Backhouse, 'Married Women's Property Law in Nineteenth-Century Canada,' *Law and History Review* 6 (1988): 212–13.

51 Christopher A. Clarkson, 'Property Law and Family Regulation in Pacific British North America, 1862–1873,' *Histoire Sociale / Social History* 30, 60 (1997): 414.

52 Bettina Bradbury, 'Colonial Comparisons: Rethinking Marriage, Civilization and Nation in Nineteenth-Century White Settler Societies,' in *Rediscovering the British World*, ed. Doug Francis and Phillip Buckner (Calgary: University of Calgary Press, 2006).

53 See Carolyn Strange, *Toronto's Girl Problem: The Perils and Pleasures of the City, 1880–1930* (Toronto: University of Toronto Press, 1995).

54 Bradbury, 'Colonial Comparisons,' 149.

55 Dominion Lands Act, 1872, *Statutes of Canada*, 35 Vict., c. 23, s. 33.

56 Catherine Cavanaugh, 'The Limitations of Pioneering Partnership: The Alberta Campaign for Homestead Dower, 1909–1925,' in *Making Western Canada*; Kathryn McPherson, 'Was the "Frontier" Good for Women?: Historical Approaches to Women and Agricultural Settlement in the Prairie West, 1870–1925,' *Atlantis* 25 (2000): 75–86.

57 Constance Backhouse, *Petticoats and Prejudice: Women and Law in Nineteenth-Century Canada* (Toronto: The Osgoode Society, 1991), 177–9.

58 Ruth Sandwell, 'The Limits of Liberalism: The Liberal Reconnaissance and the History of the Family in Canada,' *Canadian Historical Review* 84 (2003): 423–50.

59 'L'Acte pour régler la manière de procéder sur les contestations relatives aux élections des Membres pour servir dans la Chambre d'Assemblée et pour révoquer certains Actes y mentionnés,' 4 W IV, c. 28, 1834; quoted in Bettina Bradbury, 'Women at the Hustings: Gender, Citizenship, and the Montreal

By-Elections of 1832,' in *Rethinking Canada: The Promise of Women's History*, 5th ed., ed. Mona Gleason and Adele Perry (Toronto: Oxford Canada, 2006), 94n64.

60 Veronica Strong-Boag, 'The Citizenship Debates: The 1885 Franchise Act,' in *Contesting Canadian Citizenship: Historical Readings*, ed. R. Adamoski, D.E. Chunn, and R. Menzies (Peterborough: Broadview Press, 2002).

61 Ibid., 73.

62 See Minister of Public Works and Government Services Canada, *A History of the Vote in Canada* (Ottawa: Canadian Government Publishing, 1997), table 2.1, 46. I thank 'Reader Two' for drawing my attention to this volume.

63 Ibid., 53–4, table 2.2, 47.

64 Ibid., 10, 24.

65 Ibid., 71–2; Dickason, *Canada's First Nations*, 471n7.

66 Strong-Boag, 'The Citizenship Debates,' 71–3.

67 Minister of Public Works, *A History of the Vote in Canada*, table 2.2, 47.

68 See Jean Barman, *The West beyond the West: A History of British Columbia* (Toronto: University of Toronto Press, 1991), 142; Stanley, 'Schooling.' There is a good list available at http://www.elections.bc.ca/general/history.html.

69 Carol Lee Bacchi, *Liberation Deferred? The Ideas of the English-Canadian Suffragists, 1877–1918* (Toronto: University of Toronto Press, 1983), 50–5.

70 McKay, 'Liberal Order Framework,' 636.

71 Jennifer L. Morgan, *Labouring Women: Reproduction and Gender in New World Slavery* (Philadelphia: University of Pennsylvania Press, 2004), epilogue.

A Persistent Antagonism: First Nations and the Liberal Order

ROBIN JARVIS BROWNLIE

Ian McKay's reconnaissance of the liberal order framework clearly offers a useful perspective on many aspects of Canadian history. The concept has some obvious utility for explaining the ways that Canadian governments have handled Aboriginal peoples and also, more generally, Aboriginal experiences under colonialism as practised in Canada. Conversely, the investigation of First Nations experience has something relevant to offer liberal order analysis, given McKay's emphasis on studying the ways that opposition reshaped liberalism into a distinctly Canadian form. Though First Nations people have lost and suffered a great deal in their interactions with Canada and its predecessor colonies, they have inflicted some important defeats as well. They have done so in part by blocking liberal order initiatives and in part by selectively deploying liberal rhetoric about rights and justice, infused with their own understandings of such concepts, to win at least some battles in the long war over property, law, jurisdiction, and authority. While First Nations people had difficulty modifying liberal initiatives before the 1960s, in the late twentieth century many decades of political work paid off in their successful entrenchment of distinct, collective rights in the repatriated Canadian constitution. This was no small achievement, given the long-standing liberal agenda of absorbing Aboriginal peoples seamlessly into the Euro-Canadian public, ensuring a homogeneous population endowed with uniform, *individual* equal rights. Thus, Aboriginal peoples have played a role in forcing the liberal order in Canada to accept much greater cultural pluralism than it envisioned. They have also confronted it with competing definitions of rights and insisted on the maintenance of multiple legal regimes – the Indian Act, treaties, and distinct Aboriginal constitutional rights – that contradict its universalistic claims.

One way to apply the liberal order framework to Native-newcomer relations is to investigate the long contestation between First Nations people and government over self-determination and assimilation. The colonial policy of assimilating First Nations people, first developed in the mid-nineteenth century, was clearly a liberal initiative that sought to turn culturally distinct, communally oriented opponents into individualistic, private-property-owning liberal subjects. Since its inception, this initiative has met broad-based resistance fought in the fields of culture, education, law, and politics. Indeed, historian John Milloy has argued that the adoption of the assimilation policy fundamentally transformed relations between First Nations in Upper Canada and the government officials and missionaries who worked with them. While this trio had previously formed a partnership to help First Nations adapt to white settlement, Aboriginal leaders had clearly envisioned continuing self-determination and the revitalization of their own traditions and communities. This partnership began to break down with the first steps towards liberal order initiatives. In 1846 Upper Canada introduced a policy of subdividing reserves that met strong resistance from Aboriginal leaders, who immediately perceived the measure as a move toward dissolving their remaining land base. The clash of visions became even more evident with the commencement of the assimilation policy, initially embodied in the Gradual Civilization Act of 1857 passed by the united colony of Canada. Aboriginal leaders attacked the new law and denounced its intentions.

> [The chiefs] wanted education and agricultural and resource development but would not participate in a system designed, as an Oneida petition said, to 'separate our people.' Civilization, which they might define as the revitalization of their traditional culture within an agricultural context, they would have; Assimilation, the total abandonment of their culture, they would not. The policy of civilization, particularly as it was now centred on enfranchisement, was destined to founder upon the rocks of tribal nationalism.[1]

What ensued was a new antagonism between the two sides, the chiefs rejecting the enfranchisement policy, missionaries and government officials retaliating with increasingly coercive measures. Thus, the advance of the liberal order can be directly linked with the beginnings of an extended political and cultural conflict between the state and First Nations.

Within Canadian Indian policy, the liberalization process that began in the mid-nineteenth century was and remains remarkably incomplete, even ineffective in some respects. There are at least three major reasons for the limited success of liberalization with respect to government Aboriginal policy and institutions. First, many, though not all, First Nations people have strongly opposed key liberal initiatives. Second, Christian churches had a significant influence on government policies until at least the mid-twentieth century, and their paternalistic tendencies acted as a brake on the more laissez-faire forms of liberalism and even, in the case of Catholics, on the cultural homogenization typical of liberal approaches. Third, the eighteenth-century imperial emphasis on protecting Aboriginal people has never ceased to influence government planning and decision-making. While there have been countervailing tendencies as well, the protective habit has effectively hampered attempts to remove protectionist laws and other measures that contradict liberal notions of equality, free commerce, individual freedom of choice, and possessive individualism.

Liberalization within government Indian policy consisted of a campaign to insinuate liberal principles into the pre-existing network of laws, practices, and institutions by which Britain administered First Nations people. The fundamental policies, consisting of treaties, reserves, Christianization, and 'civilization' (Europeanization), were already in place by the beginning of the nineteenth century. Though they were unevenly and differentially applied across British North America – on the east and west coasts, for example, virtually no land-surrender treaties were signed – they were well developed in Upper Canada, the colony whose structures and principles were adopted by the federal state after 1867. These basic policies and institutions, developed by the Tory officials of the eighteenth- and nineteenth-century British Empire, received new elements and elaborations, but remained structurally unchanged for the next two centuries.

The first liberal modifications took place in the 1820s and 1830s through the influence of the liberal humanitarians. These liberals, particularly those associated with the Aborigines Protection Society, lobbied successfully for a policy of 'civilization' that would stave off the extinction of Indigenous peoples by teaching them farming and Christianity.[2] Reserves were considered suitable for this process, providing insulation from the vices and potential impositions of incoming white settlers until First Peoples were sufficiently acculturated to deal with them. This period also saw the development of protective legislation, designed to secure reserve lands and protect Aboriginal fisheries.[3]

Though these laws were poorly enforced,[4] they established the principle of legal protection that has remained a feature of the Indian Act ever since. By the 1850s, however, there was widespread disillusionment with the reserves among officials, missionaries, and other segments of colonial society. Isolation was now seen as a hindrance to Europeanization, and the perceived solution was assimilation or absorption.[5] This was the context in which the major liberal component of Canadian Indian policy, enfranchisement, was inserted into law and practice. The long battle between First Nations people and government over enfranchisement neatly encapsulates the determined and largely successful Aboriginal resistance to key aspects of the liberal order.

If one contemplates the period from the 1840s to the 1880s, in which McKay identifies the rise of the liberal order, it is clear that there were competing ideologies at work within Indian policy. On the one hand, separate treatment and institutions were clearly in evidence; on the other hand, there was a visible effort to establish processes that would facilitate the eventual dismantling of separate Indian status and rights. During this period, the system of treaties and reserves was being expanded from the southern Great Lakes all the way to the Rocky Mountains, following the old imperial land protocols that had been formalized in the Royal Proclamation of 1763. The two Canadas created legislation that treated 'Indians' as a distinct group and the federal government followed suit after Confederation. A regime of distinct status and treatment for First Nations people was thus continued and institutionalized, administered by the Department of Indian Affairs and codified in the consolidated Indian Act of 1876, which established distinct laws, rights, and disabilities for First Nations people. The treaties did, of course, extend the private property regime throughout much of northern North America, an accomplishment that was far from incidental. But they also extended the reserves, those anomalous property arrangements that remained outside the new colonial cultural geography – an 'uneasy limbo,' as Irene Spry has described it, 'part way between the old institutions of shared resources and the new institutions of private personal property.' Reserves were 'neither fully a matter of common property nor fully a matter of individual private property,'[6] and Aboriginal determination to preserve these remaining lands has thwarted privatization efforts ever since.

At the same time, a major innovation in Indian policy occurred in this period that seems obviously related to the rise of the liberal order, namely, the establishment of the enfranchisement policy. Designed to complete the assimilation of First Nations people, the policy allowed individuals with Indian status to renounce that status in exchange for basic citizenship rights and up to fifty acres of private property taken out of their erstwhile reserve. The intention was to create liberal individuals out of 'Indians' by removing them from their Aboriginal communities, endowing them with private property, and making them formally equal to all other Canadians. It is true, as John Milloy has noted, that this measure actually created the categorical distinctions for 'Indians' that it was ostensibly supposed to help remove.[7] Nevertheless, the goal was to terminate such distinctions, dissolve the reserves, and abolish treaty entitlements by eliminating the group who could claim them. The enfranchisement provision, first introduced in 1857 by the united colony of Canada, was adopted by the federal government shortly after Confederation in its first Indian act, the Enfranchisement Act of 1869, and remained on the books until 1985.[8]

Another important factor in Aboriginal–state relations was Christianity and the Christian churches. From the origins of contact, converting Aboriginal people to Christianity was one of the primary modes of colonization and a key strategy for obtaining Aboriginal consent to the colonial process. The nineteenth-century policies of civilization and assimilation relied heavily on missionary work for their accomplishment. The emphasis on Christianization remained central to government Aboriginal policy until well into the twentieth century and was particularly important during the 1840–80 period, which saw a highly active missionary engagement by the Roman Catholic Church and several of the Protestant denominations.[9] For their part, the churches saw themselves as saving First Nations people not only from themselves but also from the negative effects of the newcomer society. They and other humanitarian allies spoke in Aboriginal people's defence, decisively shaped Upper Canada's Indian policy in the 1820s and 1830s, and frequently intervened in Aboriginal affairs for many decades afterwards.

Christian agendas had some overlap with liberalism; for example, both tended to emphasize equality, though with quite different premises and purposes. The churches were also vigorously assimilationist, and worked in concert with government from the early nineteenth century until at least the middle of the twentieth to eradicate Aboriginal cultures, partly through persuasion and example, but also through a legal assault on Aboriginal governments, spiritual practices, medical practitioners, and ceremonies.[10] At the same time, their fundamental belief in equality before God set them apart from other philosophical tendencies of the newcomer society. The churches tended to resist the turn towards biological racism and social Darwinism in the mid-nineteenth century and to oppose the resulting dismissal of the goal of equality for colonized peoples. As Sarah Carter has noted, their consistent advocacy for Aboriginal peoples played a significant role: 'Missionaries were genuinely concerned for the welfare of the people they worked among; they took action to preserve and defend Aboriginal communities, and even challenged the dominant idea of the late nineteenth century that Aboriginal people were doomed to extinction. Many were important advocates, spokesmen, and mediators at a time when government officials refused to pay attention to Aboriginal spokespeople.'[11] Churches and missionaries maintained a belief in Aboriginal potential for cultural and political equality long after such beliefs were effectively abandoned by the general Canadian population and by most Department of Indian Affairs officials. This mattered because of Christianity's importance to government officials: throughout the nineteenth century and much of the twentieth, Christianization of Aboriginal people was at least as important to government officials as any liberal objective, and so the churches had a major influence on policy.

In this regard, it is important to consider the relationship of residential schools to the advance of the liberal order. Ian McKay suggests that residential schools represent 'Christian/liberal manufactories of individuals, pre-eminent laboratories of liberalism, [in which] First Nations children were "forced to be free," in the very particular liberal sense of "free," even at the cost of their lives.'[12] One could perhaps argue that alienating children from their families was partly designed to advance individualism, though its primary purpose was to prevent the transmission of Aboriginal cultures. But overall residential schools were only marginally touched by liberalism. Instead, the schools illustrate one of the ways that Christian churches refracted liberal intentions into religious goals. Residential schools were a Christian missionizing tool from the beginning, and remained so throughout their existence.[13] Although the federal government largely funded these institutions from the 1880s on and viewed them as the principal vehicle for assimilation, they were run by the churches and were always designed first and foremost to fulfil the churches' goals. Among these, conversion to a particular Christian denomination was uppermost. It is true that there were also efforts to inculcate a peculiarly Western work ethic in the children, but while this concept can be linked to liberalism, it is certainly not unique to it. The residential schools were intended to impose the values and norms of Euro-Christian society, but, again, liberal notions were not prominent in the ideas and behaviours they actually promoted. Discipline, regimentation, and Christian conversion were the main themes. Liberal notions such as freedom and individualization were difficult to perceive in their practices, while a vision of equality was at best a distant, long-range goal.

One of the most important factors in determining government policy has been a fundamental paternalism towards First Nations. The ideological source of this paternalism is an interesting question. The monarchical, Tory tradition that reigned during the founding of the Indian Affairs system was profoundly paternalistic; so were the Christian churches that missionized First Nations people. At the same time, liberal philosophy has also had an element of paternalism in its approach to colonized people. Many of its most prominent nineteenth-century thinkers were colonial bureaucrats and/or ardent proponents of empire and the subjugation of colonized peoples. John Stuart Mill, for example, worked for twenty-five years as an official of the East India Company and explicitly opposed self-rule for colonized peoples, prescribing instead a 'vigorous despotism.'[14]

It seems to me that, over time, the Indian Affairs system became a complex amalgam of liberal and Tory precepts. Its enfranchisement and assimilation policies embodied liberal ideals of individualization, homogenization, and formal equality, as well as the hope of converting Indian reserves to taxable, commodified private property. Yet overall the Indian Act and actual administrative practice were predominantly products of another mode of thinking, colonial paternalism. This paternalism saw not individuals, but a collective group collectively unfit to rule themselves, make their own contracts, or vote. In some sense this paternalism can be seen as a convergence of the old Tory paternalism and liberal notions of a necessary colonial despotism: both agreed on the need to run the affairs of colonized peoples who were allegedly unable to do so themselves. Some Christian missionaries shared this view. But the different models of paternalism diverged in some respects, particularly in the amount of interference that was appropriate to protect Indigenous people from the effects of resettlement and from the capitalist economy itself. Liberal paternalism favoured political control over colonized peoples, in large part as a means of protecting the colonizers' economic interests, but liberals were leery of other economic intervention, especially assistance. The protective aspects of the Indian Act are certainly at odds with liberal models of commerce, property, and economics. The old Tory model, on the other hand, was built on an imperial diplomatic tradition in which Britain had explicitly positioned itself as a father in relation to First Nations and had consequently been more or less forced to conform to some Aboriginal ideas about the paternal role, specifically the responsibility to provide sustenance and protection.[15] Thus, Indian department policy and practice exhibited competing streams of thought – on the one hand, a rhetoric of ensuring Aboriginal self-support and constant attempts to avoid and minimize assistance; on the other hand, acceptance of the need for some practical aid and also the extension of medical care long before the general population received it. The Indian department's grudgingly accepted mandate to provide minimal relief for destitute Aboriginal people clearly conformed to an older Tory model of relations and also to Aboriginal expectations of generosity from those in power.[16]

First Nations People and the Liberal Order

First Nations people were not automatically opposed to all aspects of liberalism, nor have they simply rejected all the political and cultural ideas imported from Europe. In order to comprehend their relationship to the ideas of the liberal order, it is important to compare liberal principles with the central principles of Aboriginal systems of thought. This can only be done at a high level of generalization, given the diversity of Aboriginal peoples in Canada, but some meaningful observations are possible. On one hand, certain tenets of liberalism found parallels in Aboriginal societies, most notably the ideal of freedom, including personal liberty, free speech, and freedom of belief. The principle of equality also found its parallel in the egalitarianism of most Aboriginal societies, with the exception of the hierarchical societies on the west coast. At the same time, the similarities should not be overstated. Importantly, Aboriginal societies have defined and practised these ideals differently and according to varying underlying principles. For example, many of them are said to have a strict principle of non-interference, according to which it is wrong to interfere 'in any way with the rights, privileges and activities of another person,' even if only to state one's own opinion of what a person ought to do.[17] This principle is part of the ideal of personal freedom in such societies, and it is distinctly different from Western and Christian ideas about personal interaction.

One should also be careful about assuming that individualism was inherently antithetical to Aboriginal belief systems. The extent of collectivism or communitarianism in these societies has probably been exaggerated. Despite a lot of current talk about Aboriginal cultures being focused on community harmony and collective well-being, it is clear that the rights and importance of individuals were also safeguarded. Cree/Métis scholar Emma LaRocque explains attitudes towards individuals in this way:

> In anthropological fact individuals were highly regarded in Native societies, and their safety and dignity was, as a rule, not sacrificed for the collectivity. The vision quest with its emphasis on individual dreams, the daring culture of the coup among the Plains, the competitive haranguing traditions of important leaders in the potlatch system, and the independent Métis are among the many examples of individuality expressed within Aboriginal cultures.[18]

One could add that the emphasis on non-interference and personal freedom presumed wide latitude for individual choice and decision-making. In circumstances where anyone could end up surviving alone for extended periods, maximum autonomy and resourcefulness had to be taught to all members. In storytelling, a central communications strategy of these societies, listeners were allowed to draw their own conclusions from stories.[19] In short, both the circumstances of existence and the fundamental principles of coexistence required considerable respect for the individual and her or his freedom of action.

All of this being said, what individualism existed in Aboriginal societies clearly took forms that differed radically from the possessive individualism of the British liberal tradition. As Theodore Binnema has pointed out, though individualism had a strong presence in many ways and existed in tension with collectivism, overall the primacy of the group remained clear.[20] Possessiveness and acquisitiveness were strongly censured in most groups, again excepting west coast societies – though even here wealth was continually redistributed. Aboriginal societies also placed particular emphasis on relationships, understanding each member of society in terms of her or his relationships with others.[21] C.B. Macpherson has analysed the possessive individualism at the heart of liberal thought, identifying in particular its 'conception of the individual as essentially the proprietor of his own person or capacities, owing nothing to society for them. The individual was seen neither as a moral whole, nor as part of a larger social whole, but as an owner of himself.'[22] In this atomizing vision, society is limited to a materialist, market model in which no one has responsibilities or mutual obligations. Indeed, no one's freedom should be constrained except to the minimal extent necessary to secure the same freedom for others: 'Society becomes a lot of free equal individuals related to each other as proprietors of their own capacities and of what they have acquired by their exercise. Society consists of relations of exchange between proprietors. Political society becomes a calculated device for the protection of this property and for the maintenance of an orderly relation of exchange.'[23]

Such ideas about the individual and society are profoundly at odds with the principles of Aboriginal societies. Inupiat/Inuvialuit legal scholar Gordon Christie writes these words about Aboriginal community, and belief systems, and their difference from the vision of Western communitarian critical theorists:

> At the heart of Aboriginal belief systems are senses of responsibility demanding that Aboriginal peoples resist being reconceived, either as liberal moral agents or as free-floating, self-creating, boundary-less beings. While Aboriginal people may feel comfortable with the communitarian leanings of the critical theorist's vision (for individuals in Aboriginal societies are seen as interwoven into intricate webs of relationships, the self being defined in its relation to others), nevertheless individuals are conceptualized in Aboriginal societies as *nodes* in these webs, as relatively *fixed and determined beings* connected by strands of the web. The identity of these individuals (and the various communities they collectively comprise) is provided by the responsibilities they have, which work to weave the web of which they are parts. There are, quite simply, things the individual *must* do, responsibilities to family, clan and community that *must* be respected and that *must* lead to action. Responsibilities act to define a core of the identity of the individual, just as the existence of a society centred around responsibilities defines the identity of Aboriginal communities.[24]

One of the ways in which liberalism threatens Aboriginal cultures is by undermining the central beliefs that underpin this system and thus affecting identity and community. Christie describes how the moral education provided in Aboriginal communities centres on 'building a core sense of responsibility' that is 'an integral part of one's sense of personal identity.' Liberalism threatens this vital centre of the belief system because of its limited view of community and its tendency to negate mutual responsibility: 'The introduction of liberalism threatens to undercut this carefully balanced existence, for it suggests to the individual that the community has no inherent value, that others only have value in relation to one's own self-examined beliefs and that one has no inherent responsibilities to any being other than oneself.'[25] As long as Aboriginal people remained committed to the type of community model that Christie has described, they did not qualify as 'true' or 'self-possessed' individuals in liberal thinking, and were therefore not worthy of citizenship and equality.

In responding to the liberal order, Aboriginal people have had to defend their own beliefs, structures, and social and legal regimes. For them, it would normally have been difficult, if not impossible, to distinguish between the liberal order and other imported systems of thought and practice with which it is intertwined, especially colonization and capitalism. Attempts to introduce individual ownership of private property, for example, have been a consistent theme of government policies since 1846 and bear an obvious relation to liberalism, but they are also simply another means by which Euro-Canadians have sought more access to Aboriginal lands. Aboriginal objections to such policies have demonstrated a recognition of their twin goals: the change in property relations, which both sides assumed would include further land alienation as well as privatization, and the social impact of atomization on the community. One chief's observation that the Gradual Civilization Act was an attempt to 'break them to pieces' neatly summarized both these effects.[26] Possessive individualism proposed other losses as well, tending to subvert the sharing practices and systems of intra-familial duties and responsibilities that had always helped secure survival. Such displacement of survival networks was particularly damaging under conditions of simultaneous land and resource dispossession.

Another new ideological proposition for Aboriginal people to navigate was the liberal notion of equality. Some of them, including men such as Peter Jones, adopted an accommodationist approach that sought equality within the new society. But Jones's efforts to acquire land titles and equal rights for his Mississauga people revealed the colonizers' unwillingness to place them on an equal footing.[27] Colonized peoples were excluded from liberal equality on the grounds of culture and of their claimed irrationality.[28] The assimilation policy was designed to withhold equal rights and citizenship from First Nations people until they had abandoned their own cultural values; at this point, they would be rewarded with enfranchisement. Indian department head Lawrence Oliphant described the plan in 1854, writing that 'the prospect of one day sharing upon equal terms in those rights and liberties which the whole community now enjoy would operate as the highest stimulant to exertion, which could be held out to young Indians.'[29]

Notions of equal rights have not only excluded First Nations people and other colonized groups, but have often worked directly against them. One function of the liberal 'equal rights' position has been to open all of Canada's resources to non-Aboriginal people and undermine treaty protections through which First Nations people had endeavoured to retain control of the resources vital to their existence. This position has been used continuously to oppose Aboriginal rights on the grounds that they violate equality rights and therefore discriminate against non-Aboriginal people.[30] Thus, First Nations people have had to counter the notion of equal rights with their own constructions of treaty and Aboriginal rights.

Treaties may be seen as a central feature of Aboriginal responses to these various pressures. In negotiating treaties that alienated parts of their territory, First Nations people insisted upon reserves and other treaty terms as bulwarks against total subjection and dispossession, attempting to institutionalize Indigenous forms of property in defence against European private property. Subsequently, they worked for decades to try to enforce treaty provisions. This project was unsuccessful in many ways. For example, the rights to plant and animal resources that Aboriginal treaty signatories attempted to entrench in treaties were ignored by non-Aboriginal settlers and systematically abrogated by Canadian governments.[31] More insidiously, Canadian governments assumed the power to define the legalities of reserve-land ownership, and did so in ways that overthrew Aboriginal regimes of land and resource use. Reserves are *not* an Indigenous form of property-holding, thanks to the structures and legalities imposed on them by government. But despite these failures, which First Nations people could not prevent, it is clear that one of their intentions in negotiating treaties was to preserve Aboriginal forms of property rights.

In general, it can be said that Aboriginal people adopted two basic strategies for responding to liberal order initiatives: rejecting liberalism outright and trying to use its precepts as tools to fight colonization. In rejecting liberalism, one approach was to seek allies among representatives of non-liberal streams of Western thought, who were more sympathetic to their interests. For example, in the nineteenth century the Anishinabek and Haudenosaunee who had been engulfed by the colony of Upper Canada worked to maintain their connections to Family Compact Tories who embodied the British imperial tradition of treaty-making and limited pragmatic recognition of Aboriginal title.[32] In many parts of the continent the Christian message was initially embraced because its missionaries were seen as potential allies in the struggle against colonization and dispossession.[33] In nineteenth-century Upper Canada, the Anishinabek and Haudenosaunee heard much more about equality from missionaries, especially the Methodists, than from proponents of liberalism. Conversion to Christianity offered a religious rhetoric of equality before God, as well as a route to Western education, church support, and a far-flung Christian public that was interested in hearing from Native converts and potentially supportive of Aboriginal causes. For these reasons, those who argued for racial equality found more opportunity in Christian principles than in liberal ones.

Non-liberal elements of the existing Indian Affairs structure have also been useful to Aboriginal people fighting for distinct rights and trying to retain or regain lands. During the twentieth century, the courts began to enforce Aboriginal rights when they had been recorded in treaties or in the statute book – for example, the Royal Proclamation of 1763, a product of Tory, monarchical thinking.[34] The Indian Act and constitutional federal responsibility for Indian Affairs have also become problematic but useful tools for the maintenance of distinct status and rights. As Anishinabe scholar Dale Turner points out in his recent book *This Is Not a Peace Pipe: Towards a Critical Indigenous Philosophy*, both the Indian Act and the federal government's fiduciary role have been simultaneously oppressive and enabling: 'It cannot be overemphasized that the *Indian Act*, and its enforcer the Department of Indian Affairs, have always had a stranglehold over Indians ... Ironically, though, the *Indian Act*, while clearly a colonial policy, also prevents the federal government from stealing Indian lands.' Similarly, 'The "trust" relationship between Indians and the federal government has undoubtedly been oppressive to Indians, but it has also provided a way for Indians to seek political and legal recognition of the rights they believe they possess.'[35] Meanwhile, the people themselves chafed at elements of the Indian Act but also made use of it and the geographical separation of reserves to pursue their own goal of maintaining themselves as distinctive communities and peoples. Over time, they also made parts of the Indian Act into tools of resistance. Despite its serious flaws, the Indian Act entrenches certain prized Aboriginal rights, such as tax exemption for those living on reserves and other financial protections. These elements of the act, of course, are another contradiction to liberal principles of equal citizenship rights and responsibilities. The federal government has worked diligently for decades to try to impose taxation on all First Nations people, and this is a continuing area of confrontation.[36]

Especially in the twentieth century, another central tactic has been to advance liberal arguments to counter the often racialized restrictions that the state has placed on First Nations people. Strategic deployment of liberal equality arguments resulted in the repeal of discriminatory laws concerning alcohol as well as the repeal of section 12 (1)(b) of the Indian Act, which had deprived many women of Indian status when they married non-status men.[37] Anishinabe people in south-central Ontario in the 1920s and 1930s advanced rights arguments in response to non-Aboriginal appropriation of fish and game through commercial fisheries, sport hunting, and encroachment on trapping territories. Although these arguments expressed Aboriginal understandings of entitlement based on prior occupation and kin-based inheritance, as well as treaties, they used the language of rights and sometimes even borrowed European concepts such as the injustice of taxation without representation.[38] Minority rights arguments were also invoked to obtain the affirmation and entrenchment of 'existing Aboriginal rights' in section 35 of the 1982 Charter of Rights and Freedoms.

Although First Nations people have made some accommodations with the liberal order, liberal arguments and their underlying tenets remain problematic and limiting. Liberalism has dominated public debate and enabled the oppressed to make arguments for their equality, while liberals have been prominent among the thinkers who have tried to make philosophical and constitutional space for Aboriginal aspirations. Yet Dale Turner argues that even sympathetic non-Aboriginal thinkers such as Alan Cairns and Will Kymlicka have developed liberal justifications for Aboriginal rights that Aboriginal people must ultimately reject. In Turner's view, although Cairns and Kymlicka offer systematic arguments in favour of Aboriginal rights as 'part of a larger account of political justice,'[39] they also severely circumscribe the scope of those rights by assuming or asserting the supremacy of Canadian sovereignty and law. These approaches dismiss Aboriginal people's nationhood, preclude their sovereignty, and justify the overthrow of their legal regimes. In the end, Turner calls for the deployment of Aboriginal world views and epistemologies to produce a workable theory and practice of Aboriginal rights, instead of the current approach in which liberal ideas drawn from the European tradition set the terms of debate.[40]

The Liberal Order and Government Policy towards Aboriginal Peoples

While First Nations people have experienced the liberal order as a powerful force, an analysis of Aboriginal–government relations over the past 150 years or so suggests the degree of accommodation the liberal order has itself been forced to accept. Most of the major structures and institutions that shape the relationship between First Nations peoples and Canadian governments contradict liberal principles. Reserves, treaties, the Indian Act, and federal responsibility for Aboriginal health and education all set Aboriginal people apart, perpetuate their distinctiveness, and create unwanted federal obligations. All these institutions maintain separate arrangements, status, and rights for First Nations people that differ from those of non-Aboriginal people, contradicting the liberal model of equality and, in the case of reserves, steadfastly refusing the private-property regime that lies at the foundation of liberalism.

The federal government has played a major role in blocking its own efforts at liberalizing First Nations. It has, for instance, implemented a kind of economic collectivization for the people that has become ossified in the Indian Act and has undoubtedly now influenced Aboriginal people's own sense of their cultural forms of ownership. As Emma LaRocque has pointed out, 'Native "collectivity" was in many ways invented through the creation of reserves and a legalized collective identity via the Indian Act.'[41] Federal efforts to undermine that government-constructed collectivity have focused primarily on extracting individuals from it, rather than dismantling the structures themselves. Thus, in effect, the Department of Indian Affairs has pursued *both* the liberal goal of individualizing First Nations people and simultaneously the construction of forms of legal collective ownership that bear no real relation to First Nations practices, but have still hampered the individualization of land and resources. For many years it imposed wardship status on the people and withheld citizenship, proffering the potential for citizenship to those who had become fully individualized and liberalized. The goal was to assimilate and absorb First Nations people, but the chosen methods had the opposite effect, creating a separate Indian status that combined with physical segregation to help preserve Aboriginal identities and communities.

Reserves embody a distinct form of property regime, in which the federal government legally owns the land and holds it in trust for a collective group, the 'band' or First Nation for whose use it is designated.

Many of the other legal arrangements concerning various types of ownership and transfer of such land are unique compared to the laws governing land ownership for everyone else. Reserve land can only be held
by band members and can be sold to outsiders only by agreement of all
the adult members, through a legal surrender to the Crown. Perhaps
most important, from the government's perspective, it is non-taxable
and so is income earned by its residents. Although successive federal
governments throughout most of the nineteenth and twentieth centuries persuaded First Nations groups to part with enormous quantities of
reserve land via surrenders, they were unable to abolish the actual institution of the non-taxable, collectively held Indian reserve. Yet Indian
reserves should not be confused with Indigenous property regimes. The
latter varied a good deal from one group to another, from systems of
substantial chiefly authority over land on the west coast to strongly
egalitarian models in the subarctic and the eastern woodlands. But they
had certain features in common that distinguish them from the reserve
land regime, including vastly larger areas of land per person, considerable flexibility in land use and residence patterns, and relationships to
territory based on kinship. Thus, while there were elements of collec-
tiveness in Aboriginal approaches to territory, their Indigenous systems
had little in common with the colonial reserve system.

Indian treaties are another colonial institution that has no obvious
parallel elsewhere in Canada. First Nations are the only groups in Canada that have treaty relations with government laying out the rights
and obligations of each party. From a liberal perspective, it is anomalous that one group should have rights and entitlements that other
groups do not have. From First Nations perspectives, however, the treaties have always been valued *because* they represented a special relationship with Canada or the Crown. Many groups understood the
treaties they signed as being primarily focused on establishing peace
and friendship with the British Crown, in preparation for the influx of
non-Aboriginal people.[42] Even those Aboriginal groups that did view
the treaties as alienating land considered these agreements acceptable
solely because of the special relationship they created with the Crown,
in which the loss of the land would be offset by government aid and
bounty.[43] By contrast, for much of Canada's history, governments have
viewed treaties mainly as real estate deals that effected large-scale land
transfers without the resort to military force. Their provisions were
selectively fulfilled, courts were reluctant to enforce them, and in 1969
the Trudeau government overtly expressed the need to find ways that

the treaties could be 'equitably ended.'[44] Only the powerful outcry of First Nations against this approach, combined with the 1973 Calder decision affirming the existence of Aboriginal title, forced the federal government to take treaties more seriously.

Another important area of dispute has been the enfranchisement policy, for many years the primary means by which the Canadian government sought to dismantle all these non-liberal institutions and shed its unwelcome responsibility for Aboriginal people. The history of enfranchisement demonstrates the effectiveness of Aboriginal resistance, exercised both by individual rejection of the process and by band councils that withheld the permission that was required for individual enfranchisement under the original policy. The procedure introduced in 1857 aroused major objections in part because it awarded each enfranchisee a parcel of reserve land to hold as private property. Thus, each time a person or family became enfranchised, their home reserve would shrink. The architects of the plan envisioned the eventual disappearance of both 'Indians' and reserves, but these objectives were foiled by the widespread refusal to undergo enfranchisement.

In the early twentieth century, the government introduced two new measures designed to circumvent this long-term resistance. First, in 1918, it added a new, simplified procedure to the Indian Act that struck people off the band list without subtracting any reserve land. Henceforth, the reserve land base was protected from erosion through enfranchisements – a significant victory for First Nations concerned with retaining their land.[45] In 1920 the federal government added another new provision to the Indian Act permitting it to impose enfranchisement on individuals without their consent. This sparked vociferous objections from Aboriginal leaders, who were able to have the provision removed upon the return of the Liberal Party to power in 1923.[46] Although it was reinstated in the 1930s, it does not appear to have been used, presumably because the government believed that Aboriginal opposition was too strong. The 1918 amendment did increase the number of people who relinquished Indian status for citizenship; about 2400 people became enfranchised between 1918 and 1939.[47] This, however, represented only about 2 per cent of the status Indian population, and subsequent years did not witness much greater success for the policy. By 1985 the government was ready to abandon its failed enfranchisement policy, and removed the procedure from the Indian Act. Thus ended a major liberal innovation, a casualty of Aboriginal resistance to the liberal order.

Conclusion

The advance of liberal ideas of private property, acquisitive individualism, and homogenizing equality has not offered First Nations people much of value, considering what they stood to lose in the process – their land, their social cohesion, their cultural identity. Not surprisingly, then, the history of First Nations people's interaction with the liberal order is by and large a story of persistent antagonism. The keystones of liberal ideology have posed direct contradictions to Aboriginal world views as well as real threats to their well-being. Most obviously, the radical appropriation of land accomplished through the extension of the private-property regime across Aboriginal territories was a devastating material loss for First Nations, one they fought in a variety of ways. Hardly less damage was done through the erosion of kinship networks and community solidarity initiated by the introduction of the cash economy, residential schools, and the ideology of individualism.[48] And the doctrine of equality has been mobilized right up to the present to argue against Aboriginal and treaty rights, which are claimed to be a form of discrimination against non-Natives. It is true that Aboriginal people have adopted the vocabulary of rights as part of their self-defence strategy. But despite the current tendency to associate rights talk with liberalism, historian E.A. Heaman has demonstrated persuasively that it is considerably older than liberalism and has taken many forms.[49]

For practical and existential reasons, then, liberalization initiatives have encountered Aboriginal resistance from the beginning. Not all Aboriginal people have waged such resistance; cultural accommodation has been another important tactic to cope with colonization, and Aboriginal individuals at various times have embraced different levels of assimilation. Some First Nations people chose enfranchisement, largely for financial reasons, and accepted types of equality that were predicated on the erasure of cultural difference.[50] At the same time, many other First Nations people have sought separate identities, group rights, and distinct property regimes that stood in direct contradiction to a homogenizing liberalism. They have fought the extension of the private-property regime, particularly the attempt to impose this regime on the reserves, those tiny remnants of the ancestral domain. The attack on Aboriginal cultures and sovereignty, often justified by liberalism's universalizing equality rhetoric, has been met with the assertion, in various forms, of a 'parallel path' or 'two-row wampum' model. Through this approach, First Nations groups long sought to remain allies and friends of immigrant peoples and governments, but also to retain their sovereign, self-governing status.[51] From the first signing of treaties to the present, there has been a consistent movement to assert and protect collective Aboriginal and treaty rights, including distinct harvesting rights buttressed by an Aboriginal belief that game animals belonged to First Nations, while settlers were to live off their domestic animals.[52] Such rights pose a fundamental contradiction to *two* classical liberal principles: the insistence on individualism, especially the construction of rights as properties of individuals, and the belief in an undifferentiated, universalizing equality that is, in practice, intolerant of difference.

The state's inability to eliminate reserves stands as one of the most visible failures of the liberal order, alongside its inability to eliminate First Nations themselves as distinct peoples. In the political realm the liberal order has been somewhat more successful, having managed to impose its own laws and principles, subjugate Aboriginal nations, and assert a Canadian sovereignty and Crown title to all land within Canada's borders, 'surrendered' or not, that most non-Aboriginal Canadians do not question. Nevertheless, it is clear that Canadian governments pursuing liberal agendas have had to make a long series of concessions and compromises, or 'bargains with Aboriginal persistence,' to adapt McKay's phrase.[53] They have had to live within a framework of law and practice with respect to Aboriginal peoples that pre-dated the rise of liberalism. Treaties, the rules of the Royal Proclamation, and the honour of the Crown are some of the central principles of Indian policy laid down long before the Canadian liberal democracy was founded. In part, these created an essentially constitutional framework that proved impossible to alter, though it could be, and was, selectively ignored. At the same time, Aboriginal negotiators from 1763 to the present have constantly reiterated principles of coexistence and reciprocity that their eastern and Great Lakes counterparts had hammered out with Tory empire-builders and representatives of the British monarchy in the seventeenth and eighteenth centuries. Even after liberalism had become largely hegemonic, it was unable to transform the legal and constitutional structure of Canada into a fully liberal regime. The goal of abolishing the Indian Act, and all the other colonial, non-liberal institutions, has remained elusive. At considerable cost to themselves, and with great perseverance, many First Nations people have pursued their own aliberal vision to preserve their communities and values. In the process, they have helped shape the Canadian liberal democracy into the distinct, negotiated, hybrid form it takes today.

NOTES

I would like to thank the Social Sciences and Humanities Research Council of Canada for its support for the research on which this chapter is based. I am also grateful to its two anonymous reviewers for their useful comments and insights.

1 John Milloy, 'The Early Indian Acts: Development Strategy and Constitutional Change,' in *As Long as the Sun Shines and Water Flows: A Reader in Canadian Native Studies*, ed. Ian A.L. Getty and Antoine S. Lussier (Vancouver: UBC Press, 1983), 58–60. The whole paragraph is based on this article.
2 John Milloy, 'Protection, Civilization, Assimilation: An Outline History of Canada's Indian Policy,' in *As Long as the Sun Shines*, 40–1.
3 Milloy, 'Protection, Civilization, Assimilation,' 41.
4 See, for example, Sidney L. Harring, *White Man's Law: Native People in Nineteenth-Century Canadian Jurisprudence* (Toronto: University of Toronto Press, 1998).
5 Milloy, 'Protection, Civilization, Assimilation,' 42.
6 Irene Spry, 'The Tragedy of the Loss of the Commons in Western Canada,' in *As Long as the Sun Shines*, 222.
7 Milloy, 'Protection, Civilization, Assimilation,' 42.
8 For more information on enfranchisement, see R.J. Brownlie, '"A better citizen than lots of white men": First Nations Enfranchisement, an Ontario Case Study, 1918–1940,' *Canadian Historical Review* 87 (2006): 29–52.
9 See, for example, John Webster Grant, *Moon of Wintertime: Missionaries and the Indians of Canada in Encounter since 1534* (Toronto: University of Toronto Press, 1984); Carol Higham, *Noble, Wretched, and Redeemable: Protestant Missionaries to the Indians in Canada and the United States, 1820–1900* (Calgary: University of Calgary Press, 2000); Raymond Huel, *Proclaiming the Gospel to the Indians and the Metis* (Edmonton: University of Alberta Press, 1996); Martha McCarthy, *From the Great River to the Ends of the Earth: Oblate Missions to the Dene, 1847–1921* (Edmonton: University of Alberta Press, 1995).
10 Milloy, 'The Early Indian Acts,' 58–63; Katherine Pettipas, *Severing the Ties That Bind: Government Repression of Indigenous Religious Ceremonies on the Prairies* (Winnipeg: University of Manitoba Press, 1994); Douglas Cole and Ira Chaikin, *An Iron Hand upon the People: The Law against the Potlatch on the Northwest Coast* (Vancouver: Douglas and McIntyre, Ltd, 1990).
11 Sarah Carter, *Aboriginal People and Colonizers of Western Canada to 1900* (Toronto: University of Toronto Press, 1999), 76.

12 Ian McKay, 'The Liberal Order Framework: A Prospectus for a Reconnaissance of Canadian History,' *Canadian Historical Review* 81 (2000): 637.
13 See J.R. Miller, *Shingwauk's Vision: A History of Native Residential Schools* (Toronto: University of Toronto Press, 1996).
14 See John Stuart Mill, 'Of the Government of Dependencies by a Free State,' in *Considerations on Representative Government* (New York: Harper and Brothers, 1862), chap. 18.
15 See John L. Tobias, 'The Treaty Rights Movement in Saskatchewan,' in *1885 and After: Native Society in Transition*, ed. F. Laurie Barron and James B. Waldram (Regina: Canadian Plains Research Centre, 1986), 248, and also Paul Williams, 'The Chain' (LLM thesis, York University, 1981).
16 Support for impoverished Aboriginal people also conformed to statements made by government officials at many treaty negotiations, though it is not clear that Department of Indian Affairs officials considered such statements binding, or were even aware of them after a certain point in time. See Arthur J. Ray, J.R. Miller, and Frank Tough, *Bounty and Benevolence: A History of Saskatchewan Treaties* (Montreal: McGill-Queen's University Press, 2000); R.J. Brownlie, *A Fatherly Eye: Indian Agents, Government Power, and Aboriginal Resistance in Ontario, 1918–1939* (Don Mills: Oxford University Press, 2003); Treaty 7 Elders and Tribal Council with Walter Hildebrandt, Sarah Carter, and Dorothy First Rider, *The True Spirit and Original Intent of Treaty 7* (Montreal and Kingston: McGill-Queen's University Press, 1996).
17 Speech of Mohawk psychologist Dr Clare Brant, quoted in Rupert Ross, *Dancing with a Ghost: Exploring Indian Reality* (Markham, ON: Octopus Books, 1992), 12. See also Ross's second book, *Returning to the Teachings: Exploring Aboriginal Justice* (Toronto, London: Penguin, 1996).
18 Emma LaRocque, 'Re-examining Culturally Appropriate Models in Criminal Justice Applications,' in *Aboriginal and Treaty Rights in Canada: Essays on Law, Equality, and Respect for Difference*, ed. Michael Asch (Vancouver: UBC Press, 1997), 83.
19 See, for example, Basil Johnston, *Ojibway Heritage: The Ceremonies, Rituals, Songs, Dances, Prayers and Legends of the Ojibway* (Toronto: McClelland & Stewart, 1976), 8.
20 Theodore Binnema, *Common and Contested Ground: A Human and Environmental History of the Northwestern Plains* (Toronto: University of Toronto Press, 2004), 12.
21 See, e.g., Betty Bastien, *Blackfoot Ways of Knowing: The Worldview of the Siksikaitsitapi* (Calgary: University of Calgary Press, 2004), 77, 82, 84–6, 88, 100, 102, 106, 111–13, 119–21. See also Gordon Christie, below.
22 C.B. Macpherson, *The Political Theory of Possessive Individualism, Hobbes to Locke* (London: Oxford University Press, 1962), 3.

23 Ibid.
24 Gordon Christie, 'Law, Theory, and Aboriginal Peoples,' *Indigenous Law Journal* 2 (2003): 110–11; emphasis in original.
25 Ibid., 109.
26 Milloy, 'Early Indian Acts,' 59.
27 Donald Smith's biography of Peter Jones illustrates Jones's repeated efforts in this direction and his inability to obtain satisfaction from a series of government officials. Donald B. Smith, *Sacred Feathers: The Reverend Peter Jones (Kahkewaquonaby) and the Mississsauga Indians* (Toronto: University of Toronto Press, 1987).
28 Uday S. Mehta, 'Liberal Strategies of Exclusion,' in *Tensions of Empire: Colonial Cultures in a Bourgeois World*, ed. F. Cooper and A.L. Stoler (Berkeley: University of California Press, 1997), 70.
29 Milloy 'Early Indian Acts,' 61.
30 The most prominent proponent of this view is Tom Flanagan, particularly in his book *First Nations? Second Thoughts* (Montreal and Kingston: McGill-Queen's University Press, 2000). Melvin Smith takes the same line in his *Our Home or Native Land? What Governments' Aboriginal Policy Is Doing to Canada* (Toronto: Stoddart, 1996). But many members of the general public display a similar commitment to equality as a system in which everyone has exactly the same rights. See, for example, Scott Sheffield's analysis of public submissions to the Special Joint Committee of the Senate and House of Commons in the wake of the Second World War, in *The Red Man's on the Warpath: The Image of the 'Indian' and the Second World War* (Vancouver: UBC Press, 2004), 148–75.
31 See, for example, Frank Tough, 'Ontario's Appropriation of Indian Hunting: Provincial Conservation Policies vs. Aboriginal and Treaty Rights, ca. 1892–1930' (Ontario Native Affairs Secretariat, 1991).
32 See Anthony J. Hall, *The American Empire and the Fourth World: The Bowl with One Spoon*, vol. 1 (Montreal and Kingston: McGill-Queen's University Press, 2003).
33 See, for example, Clarence R. Bolt, 'The Conversion of the Port Simpson Tsimshian: Indian Control or Missionary Manipulation?' in *Out of the Background: Readings on Canadian Native History*, ed. Robin Fisher and Ken Coates (Mississauga, ON: Copp Clark Pitman, 1988).
34 The Royal Proclamation declared all lands within certain boundaries that had not been surrendered to the king to be reserved for Indians. It also laid down a set of rules for the transfer of land from First Nations to Europeans within British territory, requiring a formal surrender agreed to by a majority of adult males at a pre-announced meeting for this specific purpose. Only the Crown could take such a surrender, ensuring that no one else could pur-

chase Aboriginal land. Although these rules were not followed everywhere in Canada (they were ignored in the Atlantic provinces and British Columbia), they had and still have the force of law.

35 Dale Turner, *This Is Not a Peace Pipe: Towards a Critical Indigenous Philosophy* (Toronto: University of Toronto Press, 2006), 18, 14.

36 Two recent court cases include *Benoit v. Canada* and *Canada v. Schilling*. In the first case, Gordon Benoit went to court asserting that verbal assurances to Treaty 8 signatories during negotiations included a promise of perpetual exemption from taxation. Although he won at the trial-court level, the decision was overturned on appeal. In the second case, Rachel Schilling of Ontario convinced a Federal Court judge that her income earned off-reserve should be tax-exempt under section 87(1)(b) of the Indian Act, but the decision was overturned on appeal, and when she then appealed to the Supreme Court of Canada, the court decided not to hear the case. See Melanie Wells, 'Benoit v. Canada – Treaty 8 Promise Respecting Taxation,' *Aboriginal Times*, September 2003 (accessed from http://www.aboriginaltimes.com/taxation/treaty%208%20taxation/view on 4 August 2006) and Paul Barnsley, 'Taxation Ruling Riles Canadians,' *Windspeaker* (Edmonton), April 2002 (accessed from http://www.ammsa.com/windspeaker/topnews_April_2002.html on 4 August 2006).

37 See, for example, *Enough Is Enough: Aboriginal Women Speak Out*, as told to Janet Silman (Toronto: Women's Press, 1987).

38 See R.J. Brownlie, '"Nothing left for me or any other Indian": The Georgian Bay Anishinabek and Inter-War Articulations of Aboriginal Rights,' *Ontario History* 96 (2004): 116–42.

39 Turner, *This Is Not a Peace Pipe*, 5.

40 Ibid., 38–70.

41 LaRocque, 'Re-examining Culturally Appropriate Models,' 87.

42 See Treaty 7 Elders et al., *The True Spirit and Original Intent of Treaty 7*, and Harold Cardinal and Walter Hildebrand, eds., *Treaty Elders of Saskatchewan: Our Dream Is That Our People Will One Day Be Clearly Recognized as Nations* (Calgary: University of Calgary Press, 2000).

43 See, for example, J.R. Miller, *Lethal Legacy: Current Native Controversies in Canada* (Toronto: McClelland & Stewart, 2004), 144–5.

44 Canada, 'Statement of the Government of Canada on Indian Policy, 1969,' quoted in Turner, *This Is Not a Peace Pipe*, 138.

45 The old procedure remained on the books, but an examination of enfranchisement case files for the period 1918–40 shows that it had been abandoned in favour of the new form of enfranchisement. See Brownlie, '"A better citizen."'

46 See E. Brian Titley, *Duncan Campbell Scott and the Administration of Indian Affairs in Canada* (Vancouver: UBC Press, 1986), 51, 114–16; P.S. Schmalz, *The Ojibwa of Southern Ontario* (Toronto: University of Toronto Press, 1991), 231.

47 This figure is derived from the annual reports of the Department of Indian Affairs between 1918 and 1939.

48 On the introduction of the cash economy, see Rosemary Brown, 'The Exploitation of the Oil and Gas Frontier: Its Impact on Lubicon Lake Cree Women,' in *Women of the First Nations: Power, Wisdom, and Strength*, ed. Christine Miller and Patricia Chuchryk, with Maria Smallface Marule, Brenda Manyfingers, and Cheryl Deering (Winnipeg: University of Manitoba Press, 1996). On residential schools, see J.R. Miller, *Shingwauk's Vision: A History of Native Residential Schools* (Toronto: University of Toronto Press, 1996) and John S. Milloy, *A National Crime: The Canadian Government and the Residential School System, 1879 to 1986* (Winnipeg: University of Manitoba Press, 1999).

49 E.A. Heaman, 'Rights Talk and the Liberal Order Framework,' in this volume.

50 On enfranchisement and assimilation, see R.J. Brownlie, '"Living the same as the white people": Mohawk and Anishinabe Women's Labour in Southern Ontario in the 1920s and 30s,' *Labour / Le Travail* 61 (2008): 41–68, and '"A better citizen."'

51 See John Borrows, 'Wampum at Niagara: The Royal Proclamation, Canadian Legal History, and Self-Government,' in *Aboriginal and Treaty Rights in Canada: Essays on Law, Equality, and Respect for Difference*, ed. Michael Asch (Vancouver: UBC Press, 1997).

52 The belief that game animals and fish were a resource set aside exclusively for First Nations people has been asserted in widely separated parts of Canada, including British Columbia, Alberta, Saskatchewan, and Ontario. In the latter three cases, treaties were and are viewed as guarantors of this arrangement. See Treaty 7 Elders et al., *The True Spirit and Original Intent of Treaty 7*; Sharon Venne, 'Understanding Treaty 6: An Indigenous Perspective,' in *Aboriginal and Treaty Rights in Canada*, 192, 196; Brownlie, *A Fatherly Eye*, chap. 4.

53 McKay, 'Liberal Order Framework,' 636.

'Variants of Liberalism' and the Liberal Order Framework in British Columbia

ROBERT McDONALD[1]

Ian McKay's argument that a 'reconnaissance' of Canada's 'liberal order' offers a fruitful way to explore Canadian history has generated considerable interest among scholars, and was the subject of a one-day symposium at McGill University in March 2006. First developed in the December 2000 issue of the *Canadian Historical Review*,[2] McKay's thesis presents both a provocative framework for understanding the political and institutional development of Canada – what he calls a historically specific liberal project of rule – and a strategy for exploring Canadian history as a process of governance rather than as a story of events, people, or periods. Especially exciting is the possibility that the liberal order thesis will help renew the field of Canadian political history, a field that was pushed to the margins of historical enquiry by first social, and then cultural, history, but which, as McKay suggests, is being revitalized by the 'emergence of a substantial new Canadian political history ... centred on the themes of "ideology," "state formation," and "law and order."'[3]

Broadly speaking, Liberal Order conference participants approached Ian McKay's argument from two perspectives. McKay himself sought to put flesh on the skeletal framework of his liberal order thesis by exploring the transformation of the liberal order in a crucial period of Canadian history, the first half of the twentieth century. Confronted by challenges to its hegemony, the liberal order, McKay argues, 'executed far-ranging changes that, in selectively attempting to satisfy popular demands "by small doses, legally in a reformist manner" worked to destabilize and discredit subaltern counter-hegemonic strategies.'[4] The argument is compelling especially for the 1930s when the liberal principles upon which Canada's system of governance had been constructed

– individualism and private property in particular – were challenged by economic dislocation and a vigorous and growing socialist critique. The essay is informed by Gramsci's concept of hegemony, which McKay defines as a process by which 'a given social group can ... exercise leadership over others' only by taking 'into account the interests of other groups or classes,' carried out 'through a combination of coercion and consent.'[5] It explores the contribution of hegemony to our understanding of how the general population continued to accept a society organized and governed on the basis of liberal principles even when fundamental change seemed attractive and necessary. While 'liberalism' and 'hegemony' together constitute the intellectual foundation of McKay's argument, it is Gramsci's concept of hegemony that provides the analytical method of his neo-Marxist liberal order framework, and liberalism the subject.

Unfortunately, conference presenters offered no clear vision of how hegemony works in practice. In particular, the question of who or what is the driving force in maintaining a hegemonic system of governance remains to be explored. McKay's definition of hegemony, quoted above, refers to 'a given social group,' a group that is in general, but not always, a social class. In his 'Logic of the Canadian Passive Revolution' paper he defined a 'passive-revolution reconnaissance of Canadian history from 1900 to 1950' as one that 'emphasizes the imposition of and resistance to a state-generated program continuous with the liberal revolution of the nineteenth century.'[6] But what group or portion of society controlled 'the imposition' referred to here? In other words, who controlled and directed the liberal order? Was it a set of identifiable people or some more abstract force? McKay's language seems to support Jeffrey McNairn's observation in his chapter here that the former's debt to Gramsci accounts for the framework's 'almost exclusive emphasis on the limits of liberalism and how it positions the vast majority of the population as obstacles to it.'[7] A fuller discussion of how Canada's liberal order came into being, and whether, once established, a society founded upon broadly shared liberal values is best explained by Gramsci's theory of hegemony, remains open to debate.

More comprehensive was discussion of the place of liberalism in the liberal order thesis. McKay makes clear that 'liberal' and 'liberal order' are related but not synonymous. He also understands 'liberal' to consist of three core elements – liberty (marked by the primacy of individual liberty), property (meaning privately held property), and equality. Of these, he principally emphasizes acquisitive individualism and property. Several conference discussants suggested that McKay's definition of liberalism is too narrow and overlooks the vibrant, changing, and pluralistic nature of liberalism as both an ideology and a source of political action. Indeed, Jeff McNairn argues – I think correctly – that 'shifts in how we define "liberal" effect how we characterize the liberal order.'[8] Thus, for example, an emphasis on the universalist aspects of liberalism or the liberal discourse on human rights and civil liberties might reveal important sources of opposition to the hegemonic tendencies of the liberal project of rule.[9] The concept of 'liberty' in particular appears to have been dynamic, its meaning contested and altered by the changing contexts of the nineteenth and twentieth centuries.[10] Yet, as Elsbeth Heaman notes, 'McKay's liberalism doesn't include liberty in any serious way.'[11]

My response to Ian McKay's engaging hypothesis also focuses on the relationship of liberalism to Canada's liberal order, which I propose to explore within the context of a regional setting. What, I ask, can we learn about the liberal order in Canada by reflecting upon the role of liberalism in the political culture of the province of British Columbia? My approach starts with the assumption that a regional perspective can enrich a project that is fundamentally national and international in scope. A regional approach may be particularly appropriate for British Columbia because, while McKay's framework suggests that Canadian liberalism 'extended its grasp from a few nineteenth-century southern outposts [in central Canada] to encompass ... a subcontinent' – though admittedly 'within a transatlantic liberal universe' – BC's early history is one of very limited connection to Canada, and of strong connections to Britain.[12] In other words, I am suggesting that a regional approach centred on British Columbia may invite us to think about the geographic assumptions of McKay's liberal order thesis. In addition, my approach takes up McKay's assertion that one way to understand liberal order rule in Canada is to explore politics as 'a terrain in which people became aware of their interests and struggled, politically, to fight for them.'[13] Finally, I believe, as Bruce Curtis does in his contribution to this volume, that there is no single, coherent form of liberalism. Rather, liberalism is characterized by a complex variety of doctrines and procedures, and the multiplicities of liberalisms must be taken into account in any assessment of how liberal order rule operated. Thus, for example, if we accept the premise that liberalism consisted of separate strands within a single tradition, does the unitary quality of liberalism in McKay's liberal order framework thesis adequately explain a liberal order such as that in British Columbia which was characterized by a pervasive liberalism that had both popular and elitist elements and was marked by substantial internal conflict?

Particularly useful here is Michael Freeden's argument that 'ideologies may be seen as a set of concentric circles with a core cluster of concepts and ideas, an adjacent band and a peripheral one.' Freeden, like McKay, identifies the three core ideas of liberalism as liberty, property, and equality, though he adds that 'rationality, a belief in rational change, a commitment to legality and constitutionality, and a concern for the general good' also constitute 'core components observable in all varieties of liberalism.' These core values exist 'within an idea-environment of adjacent and peripheral concepts, and this environment acts to colour and define the core.' For Britain between the wars, he argues, adjacent values such as individuality, private property, and security were associated with and defined centrist liberalism, whereas for left liberals 'private property was severely restricted by social needs and communal priorities.' Centrist liberals 'wanted individual development on lines of efficiency and productivity,' while left liberals were more concerned with 'the universal improvement ... of social conditions, and ... an extension of the assault on property.' Shared core values remained central to both strands of liberalism, however. This identification of a complex relationship between core and adjacent values is useful because it offers a way to understand, in Freeden's words, 'the existence of more than one liberal variant.'[14]

My analysis starts with the assertion that British Columbia was, broadly speaking, a liberal society in which the majority of citizens chose to accept a liberal order of rule. 'Majority' of course does not mean 'all,' and in the nineteenth century especially it excludes the conservative elite from the colonial period who continued to participate in public life after British Columbia entered Confederation; Aboriginal peoples (who made up over half of BC's population until the mid-1880s but were a rapidly diminishing proportion thereafter); most of the Asian workforce; and what Ruth Sandwell has called the 'missing Canadians' – people on society's economic and social margins.[15]

Whether women were also 'missing' from the emerging liberal order in nineteenth-century Canada is a complicated question. Sandwell argues that denial to women of the basic rights of citizenship placed them outside of the liberal order; they were 'a-liberal.'[16] The paternalistic structure of power within the nineteenth-century family, and the gendered distribution of rights, is beyond dispute, but the meaning of liberalism for women may be more complex than Sandwell's argument suggests. One can speculate that women embraced many of the tenets of liberalism, such as the rule of law and the right to own property, even though patriarchy limited access to those rights. Concerning property, for example, Peter Baskerville's study of women and investment in Victoria and Hamilton shows that 'land markets in both cities were becoming ... increasingly feminized during the later years of the nineteenth century,' and that 'many women paid extremely close attention to the management and disposition of their financial assets.'[17] This analysis indicates that middle-class women did not shy away from engaging in property matters when given the chance.[18] In addition, in British Columbia as elsewhere in Canada, women fought to expand their civic rights by marshalling liberal arguments to reform the franchise.[19] In other words, defining women as being outside the ambit of liberalism may overlook the fact that, while the distribution of rights within a patriarchal social system was highly gendered in favour of men, many women shared the same commitment to (if not the same ownership of) individual rights and property as men.

The argument here, then, is that while not all settlers who came to British Columbia could be accommodated within the liberal tent, liberalism constituted BC society's broad ideological foundation, a base that crossed class lines.[20] McKay would agree with this conclusion. Less clear is how we should understand how liberal dominance came about. If we think of liberalism as an ideology with strong popular roots within Anglo-Canadian culture – as argued in this paper for British Columbia – and not just as the ideology of an identifiable leadership group or elite – as McKay's analysis suggests – liberalism emerges both as a source of power and as a source of resistance to power. In other words, in a provincial society where liberal ideas have remained – as Stuart Hall observes for Britain – 'an essential component in the bedrock common-sense wisdom' of the political culture, resistance to liberal order rule came significantly from within liberalism itself. My response to Ian McKay's essay, in other words, has led me to the conclusion that a fuller appreciation of the complex nature of liberalism – what sociologist Stuart Hall calls the 'variants of liberalism'[21] – is necessary if we are to explore further the implications of McKay's liberal order thesis for our understanding of modern British Columbian, and Canadian, history. More specifically, it has led me to believe that, while liberalism was hegemonic in British Columbia – if 'hegemonic' is defined in a non-theoretical way to mean 'dominant' – a Gramscian hegemonic approach may not be the only, or best, way to explain power relations within such a liberal-oriented society.

My thinking about the relationship between liberalism and political culture in British Columbia for the first century after Confederation is shaped substantially by writing about nineteenth-and twentieth-century Britain in the fields of both political history and intellectual history. This British writing provides a framework – a hypothesis of sorts – for thinking about the political culture of a provincial, British-dominated settler society at the western end of the Dominion of Canada. While the relevance of British politics to an understanding of political thought in British Columbia might seem questionable, the model presented here for thinking about the role of liberalism within the liberal order in British Columbia is premised upon the fact that Anglo-Canadian and British immigration had given a strongly British hue to the region's political culture. Institutions such as the law, the monarchy, and parliamentary democracy are obvious connections, but so too are values such as patriotism, compromise, and gradualism. Norbert MacDonald gave us a sense of this British influence when noting that early-twentieth-century Vancouver, 'with a third of its population from Britain ... had a style and ambience quite unlike that of Seattle. The prevalence of British accents among its store clerks, schoolteachers, and policemen was but one indication of that role, as were the number of British papers in newsstands, the abundance of Tudor houses, and the popularity of flower gardens.'[22] The British orientation of provincial politics is suggested in the ethnic make-up of the Eighteenth Legislature, which sat from 1933 to 1937 and marked the introduction to BC politics of a new left-of-centre party called the Co-operative Commonwealth Federation, or CCF. Of forty-eight members elected, 37 per cent were British-born – including all but one of the seven CCFers. Over 90 per cent claimed British ethnic roots.[23] As Margaret Ormsby noted in 1958, one hundred years after the gold rush the name 'British Columbia' still suggested more aptly than any other 'the sentiment and the outlook' of the people who lived in Canada's far west.[24]

A useful way to think about liberalism in Canada and British Columbia is through a comparison with other western countries founded at least partially upon liberal values. For instance, Richard Bellamy in a study of *Liberalism and Modern Society* notes that whereas in Britain and France liberalism emerged in the nineteenth century in an evolutionary manner that allowed liberalism to be taken for granted, and that masked 'the comparative hegemony of bourgeois interests,' in Germany and Italy liberal social structures had to be created, and thus became the object of attention and contention. In Italy, asserts Bellamy, 'liberalism became associated with the narrow economic interests of the privileged classes,' while in Germany the state 'remained dominated by pre-industrial elites, notably the Prussian Junkers.'[25] By contrast, in Britain liberalism articulated the key concepts of what has come to be recognized as 'bourgeois society.' Indeed, the history of liberalism in Britain and France also reveals important differences: the French Revolution was a radical liberal one that forced liberalism upon governing elites and structures, whereas in Britain liberalism evolved slowly, with governing elites and structures becoming more liberal and generally more in tune with the sentiments of the lower classes over time.[26] Though 'its different strands have been articulated to different social strata at different times,' Stuart Hall asserts, liberalism 'clearly helped to shape and form English political "common sense."'[27] British popular liberalism – a form of liberalism embraced voluntarily by British working people – differed from European standards of radicalism by being 'relatively restrained' and 'religiously inspired.'[28] In fact, as Euginio Biagini and Alastair Reid assert, from their inception 'the traditions of British popular radicalism had ... been predominantly legalistic and constitutional.'[29] The popular and classical strands of liberalism jointly contributed to 'the complicated processes by which the hegemony of liberal conceptions was achieved.'[30] Liberal ideas, then, assumed a 'taken for granted' quality in Britain – and, I would argue, Canada and British Columbia – that contrasted with the ideological effects of liberalism in Germany and Italy, at least up to the Second World War.

Recent historical writing on British political history adds depth to the insight that liberalism held a common-sense status in Victorian Britain. It does so in part by identifying the phenomenon of popular liberalism that was linked to but separate from classical liberalism, the latter of which emphasized individualism, property, lower taxes, and limited government and became the ideology of the Victorian middle class. But an older belief that Victorian liberalism was simply a bourgeois ideology has for some time given way to an understanding that 'the elements of liberal ideology did not have any absolutely fixed class identity or connotation.'[31] The term 'popular liberalism' is used to refer to both rank-and-file members of the British Liberal Party (as well as a wider group hostile to local Liberal Party organizations) and a broader range of people who supported radical democracy (most directly those associated with the Chartist movement of the 1840s) and resisted monopolies and elites. Popular liberalism thus refers to the values and outlook of artisans, unorganized workers, and small shopkeepers who sought 'the continuation of older and genuinely plebeian traditions,'[32] traditions that included the civic humanist ideals of civic duty and public spiritedness. William Gladstone is a central figure in this analysis, portrayed now as a man who grew more radical with age,[33] a man who 'was able to square the circle of making classical liberalism viable in a mass democracy.'[34] Gladstone's brand of popular liberalism was widely and enthusiastically supported by Britain's working class, a support that was common to the radical tradition in English and Scottish politics.[35] While his leadership exhibited hegemonic qualities, it also stands out for giving direction to the broadly shared popular liberalism of mid-to-late Victorian England.

A key insight in the literature on popular liberalism is the observation that at its core, popular liberalism was the liberalism of local communities. Euginio Biagini, a major contributor to this rethinking of Victorian liberalism, argues that 'nineteenth century [English] liberalism – and especially its *popular* manifestation – was a "community ideology,"' an ideology that, for instance, took Gladstonian liberalism in a far more collectivist direction than was once understood.[36] For both popular radicals and intellectual liberals such as John Stuart Mill, individual liberty had meaning 'only within the collective identity provided by local self-governing units.'[37] In other words, localism and community went hand-in-hand with a strong commitment to democracy, liberty, and especially independence, the latter an important component of artisanal culture. Both could lead to responses such as the creation of cooperatives that, while collectivist, were not statist or socialist and were compatible with a belief in the fundamental liberal principle of individualism. McKay's association of liberalism with an unmediated form of 'acquisitive individualism'[38] does not leave open the possibility of community collectivism within popular liberalism.

Late Victorian and Edwardian liberalism also generated another strand, known as 'new liberalism,' that was far more deliberately collectivist than popular liberalism but remained faithful to core liberal values. Influenced by intellectuals such as John Stuart Mill and T.H. Green, new liberalism illustrates Stuart Hall's observation that liberalism did not survive 'by holding fast to every concept and shibboleth of the past, for that would have guaranteed its irrelevance to the modern world.'[39] Arguing for 'much greater state intervention, especially in the fields of welfare and redistributive justice,' than would either classical liberals or popular liberals, Green asserted that it was the new duty of the state 'to create those conditions in which self-fulfilment of individuals could occur.'[40] Names such as L.T. Hobhouse, John Maynard Keynes, and Sir William Beveridge are associated with the advancement of the new liberalism in Britain, as are Mackenzie King, the League for Social Reconstruction, and Leonard Marsh in Canada.

In British literature the twentieth-century rise of the Labour Party and the separation of the British Liberal Party from its working-class supporters has been interpreted as a fundamental break between liberalism and socialism, but another reading of the history of the centre/left in Britain emphasizes continuity rather than change and the persistence of liberalism as a key part of the evolving left tradition in British politics. Indeed, Biagini and Reid maintain that in Britain 'the central demands of progressive popular politics remained largely those of radical liberalism well into the twentieth century: for open government and the rule of law, for freedom from intervention both at home and abroad, and for individual liberty and community-centred democracy.'[41] Stuart Hall, emphasizing liberalism's 'remarkable fluidity,' suggests that 'the transformation of old liberalism into the new liberalism produced a hybrid ideological formation: neither "pure" liberalism nor radical socialism but what we recognize today as "social democracy."'[42] From this perspective, the Labour Party can be interpreted as 'a dynamic recomposition of popular radicalism.'[43] Michael Freeden argues that in interwar Britain, when socialism seemed pitted against liberalism, there existed more than one variant of liberalism, with liberalism shading off into socialism, 'or for that matter, socialism into conservatism.'[44] Jon Lawrence adds that British working-class politics 'was far more complex' than categories such as 'socialist,' 'lib/lab,' or 'labourist' would suggest.[45]

If new variants of liberalism obviously led to the left – with 'left' defined by demands for an active state and an increasing focus on issues related to equality and the inequitable influence of class – recent British political writing makes clear that both classical liberalism and popular liberalism could also move to the right. That the transformation of liberalism at the popular level could lead to the right becomes important for British Columbia history when we ask questions like, Why did working-class voters substantially support W.A.C. Bennett's Social Credit government in the 1950s and 1960s, or why did many working people find Preston Manning's Reform Party so attractive in the 1990s?[46] British writers suggest that an important part of the heritage of popular radicalism in the nineteenth century was reaction to 'the infringement of popular liberty and democracy' that accompanied the top-down, elitist, and paternalistic policies of new liberals and socialists alike. In his overview of society and the state in twentieth-century Britain, José Harris insists that the conversion of state intervention met considerable resistance from workers whose heritage of popular plebeian traditions led them to resent 'red tape' and other manifestations of official interference. In the words of Biagini and Reid, workers felt that such matters 'ought to be left to the self-organization of working people.'[47] What is presented by this group of authors is a portrait of political culture in twentieth-century Britain that ranged from social democracy on the left to lib-lab reformist and eventually neo-liberal conservatism on the right, all of which fell 'within the limit or circumference of the liberal circle of thought' (Hall's words).[48]

Several insights emerge from this discussion of recent scholarship on British political culture: (1) that liberalism constituted more than a static set of core values; rather, it comprised a number of variants defined by concepts and ideas that were adjacent to the core principles of liberty, property, and equality; (2) that liberalism was not the ideology of the bourgeoisie alone, or of a limited group in society, but in its various forms constituted a form of 'common sense' that was shared broadly in some form by working- and middle-class Britons; (3) that popular liberalism, an important component of liberalism in Britain, had the capacity to evolve in both a collectivist – or ideologically left – direction as well as in an anti-statist, anti-bureaucratic direction to the right; and (4) that the boundary between liberalism and socialism is better understood as a continuum, with a substantial measure of overlapping political territory, than as a sharply differentiated ideological divide. To say that these insights can be applied to British Columbia is to engage necessarily in a highly speculative form of enquiry, yet my reading of British Columbia's past suggests that scholarship on British liberalism offers a potentially fruitful way to enhance our understanding of BC political history and to reflect on Ian McKay's liberal order thesis. Indeed, the fact that British Columbia was (and remains) a highly materialistic and capitalist society that was newer, more open, and less class-bound than British society during the age of industry suggests that liberalism in its various forms was even more likely to form the 'common sense' foundation of political culture in this western Canadian province than it did in Britain.

To think about these ideas in a regional context, let's start with the thirty years or so after British Columbia entered Confederation in 1871. Colonization continued apace as newcomers 'resettled' the province at the expense of the original inhabitants. Reserves were laid out, taking land from Native peoples and creating property for settlers.[49] Legislators established three instruments of social regulation: a system of public schools, an insane asylum, and a penitentiary. They also argued for the professionalization of the judiciary – and an end to the employment of judges untrained in law – on the grounds that expansion of the market economy required a system of codified and formalistic law, especially civil law, that would increase the predictability of legal decisions.[50] In addition, the government of the eighties and nineties, whose members included or reflected the interests of leading landholders and capitalists, amended the Land Act to facilitate the growth of the forest sector and encourage the sale of Crown land. Robert Cail has shown that a list of those who bought land during a brief period from 1888 to 1891, when the government decided to sell Crown land at fire-sale prices, 'read(s) like a *Who's Who* of the province.'[51] In other words, legislators created policies from which they themselves derived the largest benefit. They also equated their own 'private interests' with the public good. For instance, coal-mine owner Robert Dunsmuir was a member of the Legislative Assembly in 1883 when the provincial government, which he supported, agreed to cede to the Dominion of Canada 1.9 million acres of land on Vancouver Island – including all timber and mineral rights associated with the land – in return for federal willingness to bonus the land back to a private syndicate that would build a seventy-five-mile railway from Esquimalt to Nanaimo. Dunsmuir headed the syndicate that received the railway contract, and the land.[52] Here, surely, is evidence of the process by which a property-based liberal order of rule was established in British Columbia.

Yet, a history of early settlement also illustrates the influence among settlers of more popular and radical liberal values, and thus suggests that the creation of a liberal order in British Columbia had plebeian as well as elite roots. In Vancouver in the 1890s liberalism informed the challenge of small business people and skilled tradesmen to the political influence of the monopolistic Canadian Pacific Railway. Local people shared a common ideology as producers, believing that labour was the source of wealth and that employers and workers together created wealth. In opposition to the 'producing classes' stood the 'capitalists' and 'monopolists.' For workers this liberal belief in individualism and private property was mediated by the collectivist heritage of artisans who drew from their own work experience and the principles of moral economy to emphasize the concept of 'fairness' in labour relations and to urge the collective ownership of 'the so-called natural monopolies such as transit, power and water.'[53] Indeed, the history of Vancouver during its early years as a city was one of conflicting visions of how society should be organized: one rooted in the culture of local communities and marked by small-scale production, face-to-face contact, opposition to monopolies, and Gladstonian politics; the other reflecting the interests of large property holders and corporations. Both conceptions of society were substantially informed by liberalism: one a popular variant, the other classical.[54]

The dialogue within nineteenth-century liberalism in British Columbia also found expression on the coalfields of Vancouver Island, where skilled miners challenged the power and wealth of BC's leading monopolist, the coal mining capitalist and railway builder Robert Dunsmuir. Local citizens from Nanaimo and the surrounding area petitioned the provincial government and wrote letters to the *Nanaimo Free Press* challenging the award of an 'empire of land' to the syndicate that was to build the Esquimalt and Nanaimo Railway.[55] In addition, the submission of the Nanaimo Lodge of the Knights of Labor to the Royal Commission on Chinese Immigration in 1884 expressed a critique of corporate power that reflected the values of popular liberalism. In it miners argued that the monopolization of resources by wealthy employers left 'no hope of a number of small, independent companies being formed to work our mines, and (of) a healthy competition arising.' Rather than themselves becoming owners, miners would remain forever in the subordinate position of employees to capitalists like Dunsmuir.[56] Indeed, John Belshaw has shown that over the twenty years after 1880, of 324 miners in the Nanaimo area at the outset 60 per cent had left mining to open shops, run boarding houses, purchase and operate boats, or become farmers. In so doing they expressed 'expectations of self-improvement' and, it seems, a desire to own property.[57] In 1890 a left-of-centre critique of British Columbia's liberal order began its distinguished history within BC politics when two Labour candidates and a Farmer candidate backed by the local Miners' and Mine Labourers' Protective Association were elected to the provincial legislature in the home territory of the miners, in and around Nanaimo.[58]

This oppositional culture developed along two trajectories, one populist, which emerged from nineteenth-century popular and radical politics, and the other socialist, mainly evident after 1900. In the context of British Columbia, both can be explained substantially, though not wholly, as variants of liberalism. Of these, the link is more obvious for populism. Some years ago political scientist David Elkins observed that 'populist ideas about the goodness and wisdom of ordinary people' characterized British Columbia.[59] While a complex subject, North American populism can be understood through two broad approaches. The first is suggested by Margaret Canovan, who defines populism not as a specific movement but as an 'ethos' or 'syndrome,' of which the central premise is that 'virtue resides in the simple people.'[60] As argued by Elkins, in British Columbia the 'syndrome' is distinguished by values that are 'at the core of all populist outlooks ... a suspicion of "experts" and a concomitant trust in "ordinary people" and common sense,' an orientation that can manifest itself 'in ideological form as campaign rhetoric and legislative debate but also in styles of conduct and habits of thought.'[61] It is this cultural expression of a set of broadly shared values and 'ways of seeing' that is mainly referred to when political scientists speak of the populist dimension of BC political culture.[62]

The second approach shares with the first the view that populism is a form of challenge by 'the people' to elites, but insists that to be populist it must take some organizational form, such as a political movement or political party. In that sense populism is more organizationally concrete than an 'ethos,' a political discourse, or a political leadership style. David Laycock, for instance, in an important study of *Populism and Democratic Thought in the Canadian Prairies, 1910 to 1945*, rejects the first approach, arguing that it too easily leads to an acceptance of 'folksy appeal(s) to the "average guy," or some allegedly general will' that 'ignores the mass-organizational requirement of populist experience.'[63] Canadian writing on populism, especially studies of farm movements and the emergence of third parties on the Canadian prairies, characteristically emphasize agrarian populism's organizational history. In British Columbia the 1952 provincial election, at which a fringe movement called Social Credit emerged first as a minority government, and then as a governing party in office for thirty-seven of the next forty years, is the most notable and most studied expression of organizational populism in the coast province's history.[64]

The second approach may be more analytically rigorous than the first, but it may also – in modern societies based on liberal principles, such as the United States, Britain, and Canada – overlook the underlying ideological character of populism. In particular, it may overlook the intellectual foundation of British Columbia populism in popular British liberalism, a liberalism rooted in the culture of local communities and marked by small-scale production and face-to-face contact. It is a liberalism that found expression among the ordinary people of nineteenth-century British Columbia; that linked working people with farmers and small business people in their support for William Aberhart when he led Alberta's Social Credit movement to victory in the Alberta provincial election of 1935;[65] and that explains why the farmer premier of British Columbia, John Oliver, having wrapped himself in the mantle of 'the people,' was able in 1924 to defeat the challenge of a new Vancouver-based party headed by British Columbia's leading industrialist, A.D. McRae, the latter supported by Vancouver's most prestigious and powerful families.[66]

Popular liberalism may also explain why so many British Columbians voted for the newly created CCF in the 1933 provincial election. The leadership of the new party was strongly socialist, but what about the majority of supporters? Gordon Hak offers useful insights on this subject in a comparative study of left politics in two small resource-based communities, Port Alberni and Prince George, from 1911 to 1933.[67] Hak's conclusion is unambiguous: in the main, he asserts, 'small businessmen, often with working-class roots, carried the torch for leftist organizations in the years from 1911 to 1933 ... In an environment where small businessmen and skilled workers could play a leading role in social and political affairs, the ideal of an egalitarian society based on community improvement and self-improvement continued to have resonance.' In such an environment, where localism shaped both identity and politics, 'socialists and labourists offered a view of society that was not easily distinguishable from that desired by farmers and the petit bourgeoisie. In small-town British Columbia these people came together to develop communities and forge political organizations. They became activists in the CCF,'[68] and twenty years later many formed the core of the movement that came to power under the banner of Social Credit.

Following this line of thinking, perhaps we need to reassess as well our understanding of the important election of 1952 when the upstart Social Credit party formed a government that held uninterrupted power for twenty years and presided over what David Mitchell has called 'the rise of British Columbia.'[69] The post-war expansion and consolidation of corporate power, especially in the forest industry, and the impulse for modernization of social and government services generated a wave of support for the two parties that best expressed populist ideals, the CCF and Social Credit. Scholars have mainly emphasized the election's organizational form, and thus interpret it as a product of historical influences specific to the late 1940s and early 1950s. For instance, Gordon Hak draws on the work of Ernest Laclau to suggest that a populist movement like that in British Columbia in 1952 'starts in times of crisis, when the ideology of the people is articulated in a popular-democratic antagonism against the ideology of the dominant bloc.' Thus, the crisis in 1952 can be understood as a response to the shock of high modernity, bringing with it a consolidation of capital and a challenge to the 'sense of community and way of life' of ordinary British Columbians.[70] Hak's analysis is convincing, to a point, but I wonder if what we are seeing here is not in fact a challenge to those in charge of British Columbia's capitalist order whose ideology was that of economic (or classical) liberalism – now moderated by the state interventionist and reformist ideas of the new liberalism – by those whose world view was rooted in the assumptions of popular liberalism? In other words, does the 'populist moment' of the 1952 election not require an understanding of both the political stress caused by the post-war rush to modernity *and* the continuous tradition of popular liberalism in BC politics?

Expressions of populism in these examples emphasize the values of localism, independence, and community that fit Canovan's definition of populism, but are perhaps better understood as a variant of popular liberalism. In that sense British Columbia populism was part of what Michael Freeden has referred to as the time-honoured liberal approach to 'restricting the abusive power of monopolies.'[71] In other words, is the populism that has been viewed as a distinctive part of British Columbia's political culture, including what scholars have called left and right populism, not best understood within the framework of Stuart Hall's 'variants of liberalism?'[72] I think it is. Here is a good example of real resistance to the liberal order from within liberalism itself.

British Columbia's second oppositional tradition, that of socialism, challenges both the idea that liberalism formed the 'common sense' foundation of the province's political culture and the suggestion that resistance to the province's governing forces came substantially from among the different variants of liberalism, including populism. Indeed, there is considerable evidence to support the argument that opposition to the economic, social, and institutional concentration of power that characterized liberal order rule in British Columbia came primarily from socialists who privileged equality over individualism and argued that social justice could be achieved only when capitalism had given way to the social ownership of production. British Columbia has a rich socialist tradition that emerged from nineteenth-century popular radicalism and blossomed in the mining camps of Vancouver Island and the southern interior, and in working-class Vancouver.[73] This heritage contributed to the emergence of the left-of-centre Co-operative Commonwealth Federation as the province's official opposition in 1933 and the subsequent polarization of provincial politics along left/right lines up to the present day. Reflecting the political influence of socialists in British Columbia politics, BC socialists wrote the most radical sections of the CCF Manifesto at Regina in 1933, boldly asserting in the opening paragraph and final sentence, 'We aim to replace the capitalist system, with its inherent injustice and inhumanity, by a social order from which the domination and exploitation of one class by another will be eliminated ... No CCF government will rest content until it has eradicated capitalism and put into operation the full programme of socialized planning which will lead to the establishment in Canada of the cooperative commonwealth.'[74] Socialism found champions in radical Members of the Legislative Assembly Dorothy Steeves (North Vancouver, 1934–45), Wallis Lefeaux (Vancouver Centre, 1941–5), and Scottish-born coal miner Sam Guthrie (Newcastle, 1920–4 and Cowichan-Newcastle, 1937–49), who throughout his legislative career called for the eradication of capitalism and its replacement by socialism.[75] The major presence of the left in the political culture of British Columbia remains one of BC's distinguishing features.

But what exactly are we to make of this left political tradition? British scholars have observed that political identities were often much more centrist than labels and language might suggest. Furthermore, individuals frequently shifted between supposedly discrete ideological positions such as socialist or labourist, or, 'more revealingly, behaved as though they were completely ignorant' of such categories.[76] One wonders, for example, if this explains how James H. McVety, the machinist and prominent turn-of-the-century labour man who for several years wrote for the *Western Clarion*, the organ of the Socialist Labour Party, and who boasted in 1916 that he had voted socialist for the past fifteen years, could be the same person who as a reformer helped create the province's first Workmen's Compensation Act, who served for many years on both the Vancouver Board of Trade and the Vancouver Hospital Board, and who spent much of his career looking for 'practical' solutions to unemployment?[77] Or what about Victor Midgley and W.A. Pritchard, two declared socialists from the pre-war years who actively supported the One Big Union at the end of the war but found themselves in the mid-1930s, now members of the newly formed CCF, supporting the reform-minded Rev. Robert Connell, a moderate leftist and first leader of the CCF in British Columbia, against the party's doctrinaire socialists?[78] The question, raised above, concerning whether the large number of voters who supported CCF candidates in the 1933 election embraced a populist or a socialist critique of the political order in depression-ridden British Columbia is also critically important here.

The increasing support for state initiatives that would make possible 'a fuller realisation of individual liberty' by the removal of barriers to self-development – key concepts in what is referred to as the new liberalism[79] – also influenced social and political thought in British Columbia as it did in Canada at the national level in the 1930s and 1940s, and ushered in new programs in the fields of unemployment insurance, family allowance, and economic management that underpinned the emerging welfare state. The CCF was very much influenced by both new liberal ideas and the statist ideas of Fabian socialism. The extent to which CCF policies owed their inspiration to socialist thinking, and the extent owed to new liberal ideas, remains a complex issue that awaits fuller exploration, but there can be no doubt that left liberalism was a key part of the mix. One consequence was a division within the CCF between left populism, on the one hand, and statism, whether of new liberal or socialist inspiration, on the other, and this division may explain why the left populist supporters of the CCF so easily switched allegiance to the right populist Social Credit party as their second choice in the 1952 election, an exception in British Columbia's electoral history in that it was run according to an alternative (preferential) voting system and not the normal first-past-the-post system. It was the statist elements within the CCF – including people who enthusiastically embraced policies calling for planning, the use of experts, and expansion of the state's role in delivering social services – that triumphed when the CCF united with the labour movement to form the New Democratic Party (NDP) in 1961. The NDP has continued to function as a left-of-centre social democratic party, though much more in the tradition of new liberalism rather than that of the earlier popular liberalism.[80]

Perhaps what this discussion of socialism in British Columbia suggests is that we need to shift our gaze away from the leaders of the left and ask what a left-of-centre vote meant for ordinary people. The answer, I think, is to be found in an understanding of the complex history of liberalism in British Columbia, and in particular the capacity of both popular liberalism and new liberalism to illuminate and challenge the hegemonic tendencies of the province's liberal capitalist order. The conjunction on the left of populism and new liberal ideas, the latter from sources such as the League for Social Reconstruction, is instructive here, and returns us to the observations of British historians about the fluidity and imprecise meaning of terms such as 'socialist,' 'social democrat,' 'progressive,' or 'populist.' The point is underlined by Walter Young in his history of the CCF when noting that, once established, the party focused on monopoly capitalism rather than capitalism as such and emphasized values that were entirely consistent with both populism and popular liberalism, values such as localism, community, individual initiative, and democracy.[81] The shared outlook of these different strands of radical thought is striking and suggests that perhaps historians and political scientists have stressed the differences between them at the cost of understanding their broadly based and common foundation in liberalism.

The main insight to be drawn from this speculative discussion is that, for a province where liberalism was a pervasive part of the region's political culture,[82] resistance to the hegemonic tendencies of the province's liberal order is perhaps best understood as part of a dialogue within the liberal family of values and beliefs. This conclusion agrees with McKay's analysis of the fundamental role of liberalism in shaping modern Canadian society but questions whether Gramscian theory best explains how the liberal order has functioned in British Columbia. Based on my understanding of McKay's argument, what he is saying is that Canada's liberal order was put in place by a limited strata/group/elite of influential people – what he refers to in his book *Rebels, Reds, Radicals* as a 'few liberal men'[83] – and that the process advanced outward from a small part of central Canada to the nation as a whole. The regional focus of this paper challenges the transnational assumption of the McKay thesis and gives new urgency to questions about how a process of hegemony worked in practice. In particular, the argument presented here suggests that liberalism emerged in British Columbia through both popular and elite avenues of influence, that is, from above *and* below. I would conclude, then, that while McKay's provocative thesis on liberal order rule in Canada has already stimulated an important discussion about the place of liberalism within the country's political culture, further work is required if we are to understand how a hegemonic system of governance might have functioned in a region where several variants of liberalism came together to form the area's political 'common sense,' and where the dominant liberalism had emerged from diverse roots.

NOTES

1 I would like to thank Matthew Jackson for his assistance in researching published literature on liberalism, especially writing on nineteenth-century British liberalism and popular politics, and Michel Ducharme for his insightful editorial suggestions.
2 Ian McKay, 'The Liberal Order Framework: A Prospectus for a Reconnaissance of Canadian History,' *Canadian Historical Review* 81, 4 (2000): 617–45. His thesis is also presented in his *Rebels, Reds, Radicals: Rethinking Canada's Left History* (Toronto: Between the Lines, 2005).
3 McKay, 'Liberal Order Framework,' 618.
4 Ian McKay, 'The Logic of the Canadian Passive Revolution: A Reconnaissance of the Transformation of the Liberal Order, 1900–1950,' unpublished paper presented to the Liberal Order in Canadian History Conference, McGill University, 3 March 2006, 3.
5 McKay, 'Liberal Order Framework,' 628. Anne Showstack Sassoon describes Gramsci's concept of hegemony as follows: 'The organizing principle of a society in which one class rules over others not just through force but by maintaining the allegiance of the mass of the population. This allegiance is obtained both through reforms and compromises in which the interests of different groups are taken into account, and also through influencing the way people think ... The state in the modern period could only be understood as force plus consent.' Anne Showstack Sassoon, 'Hegemony,' in *The Blackwell Dictionary of Twentieth-Century Social Thought*, ed. William Outhwaite and Tom Bottomore (Oxford: Blackwell, 1993), 265.
6 McKay, 'Logic of the Canadian Passive Revolution,' 9.
7 Jeffrey L. McNairn, 'In Hope and Fear: Intellectual History, Liberalism, and the Liberal Order Framework,' 81 above. Also supporting McNairn's conclusion that McKay sees the liberals who controlled the liberal order as a small portion of society is McKay's statement in *Rebels, Reds, Radicals* (57–8) that 'Canadian political and social history of the nineteenth century is in large measure the story of how the worldview of a few liberal men ... attained power over half a continent.'

8 McNairn, 'In Hope and Fear,' 71.
9 Ibid., 71–2 and his observation that 'liberalism more than civic humanism or ultramontane Catholicism, provided women with some of the conceptual and rhetorical resources with which they campaigned for political and civil rights' 82–3. Also see Elsbeth Heaman, 'Rights Talk and the Liberal Order Framework,' 148 above.
10 In his study of liberalism in interwar Britain, Michael Freeden suggests that 'the single concept of liberty should be broken down into a multiplicity of "liberties."' See Michael Freeden, *Liberalism Divided: A Study in British Political Thought 1914–1939* (Oxford: Clarendon Press, 1986), 274.
11 Heaman, 'Rights Talk and the Liberal Order Framework,' 148.
12 McKay, 'Liberal Order Framework,' 638–9.
13 Ibid., 629.
14 Quotations in the preceding paragraph are from Freeden, *Liberalism Divided*, 4–6 (including n2) and 257.
15 R.W. Sandwell, 'Missing Canadians: Reclaiming the A-Liberal Past.'
16 Ruth Sandwell, 'The Limits of Liberalism: The Liberal Reconnaissance and the History of the Family in Canada,' *Canadian Historical Review* 84, 3 (2003): 429–33, 444–5.
17 Peter Baskerville, 'Women and Investment in Late-Nineteenth-Century Urban Canada: Victoria and Hamilton, 1880–1901,' *Canadian Historical Review* 80, 2 (1999): 198, 200.
18 Chris Clarkson, *Domestic Reforms: Political Visions and Family Regulation in British Columbia, 1862–1940* (Vancouver: UBC Press, 2007).
19 Linda Louise Hale, 'The British Columbia Woman Suffrage Movement, 1890–1917' (MA thesis, University of British Columbia, 1977), 60–2.
20 For instance, Philip Resnick has observed that individualism, 'and with it conflicting rather than overarching communal values, is the dominant characteristic of BC's inhabitants.' See Philip Resnick, *The Politics of Resentment: British Columbia Regionalism and Canadian Unity* (Vancouver: UBC Press, 2000), 19.
21 Stuart Hall, 'Variants of Liberalism,' in *Politics and Ideology,* ed. James Donald and Stuart Hall (Milton Keynes: Open University Press, 1986), 34–69.
22 The importance of British influences in British Columbia are suggested by a number of authors including Jean Barman, *The West beyond the West: History of British Columbia*, rev. ed. (Toronto: University of Toronto Press, 1996), 358–9; Barman, *Growing Up British in British Columbia: Boys in Private School* (Vancouver: UBC Press, 1984); Norbert MacDonald, 'Population Growth and Change in Seattle and Vancouver, 1880–1960,' in *Historical Essays on British Columbia*, ed. J. Friesen and H.K. Ralston, Carleton Library no. 96 (Toronto:

McClelland and Stewart, 1976), 201–27; and Cole Harris, *The Resettlement of British Columbia: Essays on Colonialism and Geographical Change* (Vancouver: UBC Press, 1997), 262–4, 272. Quotation from Norbert MacDonald, *Distant Neighbors: A Comparative History of Seattle and Vancouver* (Lincoln: University of Nebraska Press, 1987), 60.

23 John Douglas Belshaw, 'The Eighteenth Legislature of British Columbia: A Collective Biography,' unpublished History honours thesis, University of British Columbia, 1979, 17, 23.

24 Margaret A. Ormsby, *British Columbia: A History* (Toronto: Macmillan, 1958), 495. Similarly, David Elkins, writing in the 1980s, concluded that British Columbia is perceived to be 'fairly homogeneous. It is believed to be a very British place.' David Elkins, 'British Columbia as a State of Mind,' in *Two Political Worlds: Parties and Voting in British Columbia*, ed. Donald Blake (Vancouver: UBC Press, 1985), 52.

25 Richard Bellamy, *Liberalism and Modern Society: An Historical Argument* (University Park: Pennsylvania State University Press, 1992), 5–6, 159.

26 Personal contribution from Matthew Jackson, 31 August 2006.

27 Hall, 'Variants of Liberalism,' 68.

28 Robert Leach, *British Political Ideologies*, 2nd ed. (London: Prentice Hall, Harvester Wheatsheaf, 1996), 79.

29 Euginio F. Biagini and Alastair J. Reid, 'Currents of Radicalism, 1850–1914,' in *Currents of Radicalism: Popular Radicalism, Organised Labour and Party Politics in Britain, 1850–1914*, ed. Biagini and Reid (Cambridge: Cambridge University Press, 1991), 11.

30 Hall, 'Variants of Liberalism,' 67–8.

31 Ibid., 57, 63.

32 Euginio F. Biagini, *Liberty, Retrenchment and Reform: Popular Liberalism in the Age of Gladstone, 1860–1880* (Cambridge: Cambridge University Press, 1992), 6, 9.

33 Leach, *British Political Ideologies*, 83.

34 Biagini, *Liberty, Retrenchment and Reform*, 4.

35 Robert Kelley, *The TransAtlantic Persuasion: The Liberal-Democratic Mind in the Age of Gladstone* (New York: Alfred A. Knopf, 1969), chaps. 5 and 6.

36 Euginio Biagini, 'Liberalism and Direct Democracy: John Stuart Mill and the Model of Ancient Athens,' in *Citizenship and Community: Liberals, Radicals and Collective Identities in the British Isles, 1865–1931*, ed. Euginio F. Biagini (Cambridge: Cambridge University Press, 1996), 18, 21.

37 Biagini and Reid, 'Currents of Radicalism,' 9. Also see McNairn, 'In Hope and Fear,' 73.

38 McKay, *Rebels, Reds, Radicals*, 69.

39 Hall, 'Variants of Liberalism,' 65.
40 Ibid., 64–5. For Mill, Green, and the 'New Liberalism,' see Bellamy, *Liberalism and Modern Society*, 1–47; Leach, *British Political Ideologies*, chap. 4; and John Gray, *Liberalism*, 2nd ed. (Buckingham: Open University Press, 1995).
41 Biagini and Reid, 'Currents of Radicalism,' 5.
42 Hall, 'Variants of Liberalism,' 66. Also see Leach, *British Political Ideologies*, 96, 145, 155; Biagini, *Liberty, Retrenchment and Reform*, 9; and Michael Freeden, *The New Liberalism: An Ideology of Social Reform* (Oxford: Clarendon Press, 1986 [1978]), 145–9.
43 Alastair J. Reid, 'Old Unionism Reconsidered: The Radicalism of Robert Knight, 1870–1900,' in *Currents of Radicalism*, 243.
44 Freeden, *Liberalism Divided*, 6. Also see McNairn, 'In Hope and Fear,' 80.
45 Jon Lawrence, 'Popular Politics and the Limitations of Party: Wolverhampton, 1867–1900,' in *Currents of Radicalism*, 82–3.
46 Blake, *Two Political Worlds*, 82. One can speculate that the same generalization applies to Social Credit under Bill Bennett in the 1970s and 1980s and the Reform Party under Preston Manning in the early 1990s.
47 José Harris, 'Society and the State in Twentieth-Century Britain,' in *The Cambridge Social History of Britain 1750–1950*, vol. 3, ed. F.L.M. Thompson (Cambridge: Cambridge University Press, 1990), 70, 91, 116–17; Leach, *British Political Ideologies*, 57, 141; and Biagini and Reid, 'Currents of Radicalism,' 11.
48 I am here adopting and broadening a phrase that Stuart Hall used specifically to refer to 'new liberal ideas.' 'Variants of Liberalism,' 65.
49 Harris, *The Resettlement of British Columbia* and *Making Native Space: Colonialism, Resistance, and Reserves in British Columbia* (Vancouver: UBC Press, 2002).
50 Hamar Foster, 'The Struggle for the Supreme Court: Law and Politics in British Columbia, 1871–1885,' in *Law and Justice in a New Land: Essays in Western Canadian Legal History*, ed. Louis A. Knafla (Toronto: Carswell, 1986), 167–213 and Adrian Stephen Clark, 'For Better Administration of Justice: County Reform in Late-Nineteenth-Century British Columbia,' MA thesis, University of British Columbia, 1992, 39, 53, and passim. For the expansion of civil law in the colonial period see Tina Loo, *Making Law, Order, and Authority in British Columbia, 1821–1871* (Toronto: University of Toronto Press, 1994).
51 Robert E. Cail, *Land, Man, and the Law: The Disposal of Crown Lands in British Columbia, 1871–1913* (Vancouver: UBC Press, 1974), 28–31, 45–6.
52 Ibid., 138–9.
53 Mark Leier, *Red Flags and Red Tape: The Making of a Labour Bureaucracy* (Tor-

onto: University of Toronto Press, 1995), 93. Also see Craig Heron, 'Labourism and the Canadian Working Class,' *Labour/LeTravail* 13 (1984): 45–76.

54 Robert A.J. McDonald, *Making Vancouver: Class, Status, and Social Boundaries, 1863–1913* (Vancouver: UBC Press, 1996), chap. 3; and Leier, *Red Flags and Red Tape*, chap. 4.

55 Letter to the editor by 'Fortis Est Veritas,' *Nanaimo Free Press*, 25 October 1883 and by 'Fair Play,' ibid., 20 October 1883. My thanks to J. Bryan Cuthill for these references.

56 Canada, Royal Commission on Chinese Immigration, *Report* (Ottawa: Queen's Printers, 1885), 156–7.

57 John Douglas Belshaw, 'The British Collier in British Columbia: Another Archetype Reconsidered,' *Labour/LeTravail* 34 (1994): 21–2.

58 Miners Thomas Forster and Joseph Keith were elected for the ridings of Nanaimo and Nanaimo City respectively. The Miners' and Mine Labourers' Protective Association also endorsed the successful 'farmers' candidate' for the Nanaimo area, Colin McKenzie.

59 Elkins, 'British Columbia as a State of Mind,' 57.

60 Margaret Canovan, *Populism* (New York: Harcourt Brace, 1981), 7, 135. Also see Peter Wiles, 'A Syndrome, Not a Doctrine: Some Elementary Theses on Populism,' in *Populism: Its Meanings and National Characteristics*, ed. G. Ionescu and E. Gellner (London: Weidenfeld and Nicolson, 1969), 169.

61 Elkins, 'British Columbia as a State of Mind,' 62–3.

62 Ibid., 63–4, 68 and Blake, ed., *Two Political Worlds*, 82–4. Recent British writing also includes frequent references to 'populism' as a characteristic of nineteenth-century popular politics in Britain. For example, British writers speak of the 'populism' of John Stuart Mill; 'populist Conservatism'; the populism and radicalism of Gladstone; and the 'populist socialism' of the Independent Labour Party. See Biagini, 'Liberalism and Direct Democracy,' 28, 39 (for Mill); Leach, *British Political Ideologies*, 83 (for Gladstone) and 155 (for the ILP); and Lawrence, 'Popular Politics and the Limitations of Party,' 75 (for Conservatives). For an extensive discussion of populism in British political culture up to the First World War, including references to populism across Britain's whole political and social spectrum, see Patrick Joyce, *Visions of the People: Industrial England and the Question of Class, 1848–1914* (Cambridge: Cambridge University Press, 1991), esp. 10–13, 35, 55–6, 67, and 73–8. For an argument that nineteenth-century populism and liberalism were fundamentally opposed (rather than being part of a popular radical culture, as is argued in this chapter), see Christopher Lasch, *The True and Only Heaven: Progress and Its Critics* (New York: Norton, 1991), chap. 5, 'The Populist Campaign against "Improvement."'

63 David Laycock, *Populism and Democratic Thought in the Canadian Prairies, 1910 to 1945* (Toronto: University of Toronto Press, 1990), 15.
64 Gordon Hak, 'Populism and the 1952 Social Credit Breakthrough in British Columbia,' *Canadian Historical Review* 85, 2 (2004): 277–96.
65 Alvin Finkel, *The Social Credit Phenomenon in Alberta* (Toronto: University of Toronto Press, 1989), 37–8.
66 Robert A.J. McDonald, 'Sir Charles Hibbert Tupper and the Political Culture of British Columbia, 1903–1924,' *BC Studies* 149 (Spring 2006): 82–5.
67 Gordon Hak, 'The Socialist and Labourist Impulse in Small-Town British Columbia: Port Alberni and Prince George, 1911–33,' *Canadian Historical Review* 70, 4 (1989): 519–42.
68 Ibid., 521–2.
69 David J. Mitchell, *W.A.C. Bennett and the Rise of British Columbia* (Vancouver: Douglas and McIntyre, 1983).
70 Hak, 'Populism and the 1952 Social Credit Breakthrough,' 289. On high modernity in post-war British Columbia see Tina Loo, 'People in the Way: Modernity, Environment, and Society on the Arrow Lakes,' *BC Studies* 142/143 (Summer/Autumn 2004): 161–96 and Arn Keeling and Robert McDonald, 'The Profligate Province: Roderick Haig-Brown and the Modernizing of British Columbia,' *Journal of Canadian Studies* 36, 3 (2001): 7–23.
71 Freeden, *Liberalism Divided*, 189.
72 The connection between populism and liberalism is also suggested in Elkins, 'British Columbia as a State of Mind,' 61–2. On left and right populism see ibid., 62–73; John Richards and Larry Pratt, *Prairie Capitalism* (Toronto: McClelland and Stewart, 1979), 20–3; and Walter Young, 'Political Parties,' in *The Reins of Power: Governing British Columbia*, ed. J. Terence Morley et al. (Vancouver: Douglas and McIntyre, 1983), 108–11.
73 For the history of socialism in the early years of the century in British Columbia, see Martin Robin, *Radical Politics and Canadian Labour* (Kingston: Queen's University Press, 1968); Dorothy G. Steeves, *The Compassionate Rebel: Ernest Winch and the Growth of Socialism in Western Canada* (Vancouver: J.J. Douglas, 1960); and Allen Seager, 'Socialists and Workers: The Western Canadian Coal Miners, 1900–1921,' *Labour/LeTravail* 16 (Fall 1985): 23–59.
74 For the CCF Manifesto see Gregory Baum, *Catholics and Canadian Socialism: Political Thought in the Thirties and Forties* (Toronto: James Lorimer, 1980), 17 and 8–40.
75 For Guthrie, see the *Victoria Times*, 6 December 1923, 16 and 16 November 1937, 10 and the *Victoria Colonist*, 21 November 1939, 3. Guthrie was elected in the riding of Newcastle for the FLP in 1920 and Cowichan-Newcastle for the CCF in 1937, 1941, and 1945.

346   Robert McDonald

76 Biagini and Reid, *Currents of Radicalism*, 82–3. Robert Leach also emphasizes the fuzziness of political categories in twentieth-century British politics. For instance, he suggests that it 'could be argued that the dividing line between New Liberalism and Fabian socialism or labourism was always a thin one,' and asserts that British socialism 'substantially grew out of radical liberalism.' Leach, *British Political Ideologies*, 96, 145. Writing about interwar Britain, Michael Freeden concludes that 'some major socialist thinkers – Laski, Tawney and, to a lesser extent, Cole – were at times within the left-liberal tradition in all senses save that of self-awareness.' Freeden, *Liberalism Divided*, 14, 178–9.

77 Robin, *Radical Politics and Canadian Labour*, 96, 116, 127, 136, 149, 172; *Vancouver World*, 3 March 1916, 11 and 6 April 1916, 10; *Vancouver Sun*, 5 January 1943, 1, 4; *Vancouver Province*, 5 January 1943, 1, 4; and City of Vancouver Archives, Clippings file, 11 September 1921.

78 Robin, *Radical Politics and Canadian Labour*, chaps. 8–12 and Dorothy June Roberts, 'Doctrine and Disunity in the British Columbia Section of the C.C.F., 1932–1956' (MA thesis, University of Victoria, 1966), 32–48. Also see Steeves, *The Compassionate Rebel*, 79, 107–12.

79 Leach, *British Political Ideologies*, 91.

80 As suggested above, liberalism has shaped the ideological character of BC's CCF and New Democratic parties much more extensively than socialism, though analysts have a tendency to stress the socialist side of their history. For an evaluation of the NDP government of David Barrett (1972–5) that emphasizes its failure to implement socialist policies, see Philip Resnick, 'Social Democracy in Power: The Case of British Columbia,' *BC Studies* 34 (Summer 1977): 3–20.

81 Walter D. Young, *The Anatomy of a Party: The National CCF 1932–61* (Toronto: University of Toronto Press, 1969), 61–72, 107, 130, and 194.

82 This paper focuses on the first century after Confederation when British Columbia's non-Aboriginal population was overwhelmingly of European, and especially British, origin. Other peoples have substantially diversified the province's ethnic base since the implementation of new immigration policies in Canada in the 1970s. Thus, the question of how immigrants from non-liberal societies adapted to liberalism in British Columbia is of major importance to our understanding of British Columbia's political culture, and indeed to our discussion of the relevance of McKay's liberal order thesis, for the more recent period of the province's history. This question awaits future study.

83 McKay, *Rebels, Reds, Radicals*, 57.

Canada as a Long Liberal Revolution: On Writing the History of Actually Existing Canadian Liberalisms, 1840s–1940s

IAN MCKAY[1]

1. The Framework Revisited

Why does Canada exist and what does it mean? It is a question that has exercised many fine scholarly minds for generations. Many estimable figures of the nineteenth and early twentieth centuries would have looked to providence and visualized Canada as 'God's Dominion,' the expansive and civilizing manifestation of Britishness and Protestantism (or, in the major rival formulation, of the *mission civilisatrice* of Frenchness and Catholicism). More secular scholars, particularly in the interwar period, would look to the natural world, hoping to find, in the patterns of coastlines and fishing banks, rivers and rocks, trade routes and staple trades, extra-historical 'natural' indications of the country's true essence. A post-1945 contingent of historians, discreetly building on nineteenth-century concepts of 'racial compacts' and also arguably relying on a form of providentialism, developed a third approach, in which Canada exists because it is a tolerant and multicultural beacon of Enlightenment values – in essence, a 'Peaceable Kingdom' of reason, harmony, and ethnic accommodation in an often unenlightened world. Common to all three 'transcendental' approaches, and pervasively present in most historiography, at least outside Québec, has been an unspoken but potent belief in the inevitability and goodness of Canada.[2]

Deeply respecting the work of these past schools of interpretation, scholars who work within the liberal order framework nonetheless start off with rather different questions in mind. If we assume that Canada is a state in northern North America consolidated some time in the mid-nineteenth century, and if we seek non-providential and non-teleologi-

cal approaches to researching it, we might well want to look at the strategies and tactics, motivations and ideals, and the underlying values and
discursive frameworks of the people instrumental in constructing it as a
political project. Within this liberal order framework, the 'problem of
Canada' is that of explaining how a political project conceived in the
second quarter of the nineteenth century, and initially focused on just a
few colonies – in world terms, tiny British territories with small populations and relatively minor economic assets – could have come to construct the second-largest country in the world. Moreover, in contrast to
the (explicit or implicit) providentialism of the first three approaches,
often tightly aligned with the nationalisms that shape textbooks and
televised docudramas alike, this different framework would assume
neither the inevitability nor the goodness of Canada.

In essence, especially if it is set against the backdrop of approximately
20,000 years of human life in northern North America, the moment of
'Canada' was a revolution – that is, a permanent, fundamental, socio-
economic, and political reordering of the world. Canada was a project
of rule – indeed, a 'Dominion' – that entailed the installation of a specifically mid-nineteenth-century British liberal paradigm within which
fundamental problems of human existence were represented and provisionally resolved within distinct but related political, legal, economic,
social, and cultural frameworks. The Problem of Canada – that is, how
one nation-state could have emerged from such an extraordinarily heterogeneous set of societies, encompassing both the kin-ordered social
formations that predominated in most of the territory *and* the various
'neo-Europes,' feudal, mercantile, and agrarian-capitalist, that made up
the remainder – can best be tackled by looking, first, at the interests,
practices, and ideas of those who initiated this project of state formation; second, at those who either resisted or welcomed this project, and
thereby partially reshaped it; and third, at the ways in which this dynamic was managed over the longer term by major institutions within
the state and civil society, which acquired their own interests and traditions within it. More specifically, the framework argues that, if we look
at many of the most prominent Canadian and British initiators of the
project, we find that they came to share a powerful political rationality.
They were, in a specifically nineteenth-century British imperial sense,
liberals.

In brief, the Liberal Order Framework proposes that 'Canada' from
the 1840s to the 1940s can be usefully defined as a project of liberal rule.
One interesting answer to the question, Why does Canada exist and

what does it mean? is to propose that Canada came into being as an extended colonial experiment in British liberal forms of rule in northern North America. Drawing not upon transcendent concepts of God, Nation, Nature, Culture, Race, or Enlightenment, but rather upon more concrete, non-metaphysical, open-ended, and historically specific (in a Gramscian word, 'immanent') styles of inquiry, this approach to the Problem of Canada argues that Canada was the instantiation in nineteenth-century northern North America of a transnational (and more specifically British liberal) approach to perennial problems of politics, economy, and society. Or, to put this another way, if we ask what it was that made it possible to 'imagine Canada' in the 1840s, and then to project this 'imagined community' across a vast expanse of northern North America, the liberal order framework tentatively answers that the precondition, implicit philosophy, and concrete practice of this community was none other than transatlantic mid-nineteenth-century liberalism.[3] Noticing the emergence of a vast transcontinental dominion from the 1840s to the 1940s – or, to be more exact, from the Act of Union in 1841 to Confederation with Newfoundland in 1949 – the liberal order framework theorizes that this 'Canada' can be understood, not as a self-evident thing, nor as a Dominion into which 'we' stumbled absent-mindedly, nor as a mere happenstance or 'miracle' that defies all logico-historical understanding, but rather as a *project of rule* – a project necessarily conditioned by its rulers' core understandings of and practical interventions in economic, social, and political life.[4]

What was the emergent rationality at the heart of this expansive liberal order, which, according to the framework, provided the theory for the revolution that was first consolidated in a few southern zones, and then incrementally pushed north and west across the subcontinent? Liberalism is one of the most slippery words in the lexicon of politics. Any attempt to formulate a definition for all the ages is doomed in advance, confounded by evidence that many liberals disavow principles others hold to be utterly essential to their world view.[5] The search for a permanent 'gold standard' of universal liberal values can be profoundly ahistorical. Yet, conversely, simply using the term without defining it leads to endless frustration and confusion. We confront a challenge very characteristic of historical work – that of trying to find a workable and sensible definition that can enable useful conversations and shared insights. It is a question, not of boiling an immensely rich and complicated body of political thought down to a simplistic formula, but of elaborating a definition appropriate to a particular context

– in this case, that of the Dominion of Canada from the 1840s to the 1940s.

One important answer to the puzzle of Canada, according to the liberal order framework, lies in the category that lies at the heart of an entire paradigm: 'the individual.' The 'individual' was both a foundational category of analysis and a vivid ideal. The term was significant not so much as an empirical description of living human beings, but rather as a more abstract term denoting the idealized free-standing entity each person, if suitably purified, rationalized, and 'improved' within the state and civil society, might ultimately become. A true individual was he who was self-possessed – whose body and soul were not owned by or strictly dependent upon another person or upon the external natural world.[6] It was its central commitment to this 'individual' that made the liberal project revolutionary – that is, one geared to (rapidly or gradually) overturning patterns of economic and social relations that had persisted for centuries.[7]

In an important sense, there is absolutely nothing novel about the liberal order framework. Much of it merely rehearses and summarizes well-known evidence about Canadian history from the 1840s to the 1940s. First, there is the obvious fact that, quite unusually in the world of global politics, two self-avowedly liberal parties – the Liberal Conservatives (later Progressive Conservatives and now just the Conservatives) and the Liberal Party (earlier the Reformers) – have monopolized government at the federal level since Confederation, the latter much longer than the former. At the provincial level, although there are some fascinating exceptions, a rather similar pattern of liberal dominance can be discerned. The same two parties have enjoyed considerable and enduring success at that level as well.[8] Second, the governments associated with these two liberal parties have generally vested much of the responsibility for the production, transportation, and distribution of material goods with free-standing individual proprietors (and subsequently with corporations interpreted in law and society as individuals). Such governments have conventionally tried to create a propitious environment for their prosperity and have listened closely to their views. Third, the creation of social programs at both levels was designed to stimulate individualism and discourage adult dependence upon the state – in large part through the application of the principle of 'less eligibility,' whereby relief of poverty was so designed that it would not lure the able-bodied from regular employment.[9] Fourth, we find a pervasive assumption of improvement, which vested in individuals the right and indeed the responsibility to 'master' the natural world by 'individualizing' their surroundings in manageable 'properties.'[10] Fifth, the individual was defined according to racial, ethnic, gender, sexual, and class criteria – so that the rigorous application of the 'rights of the individual' meant a consistent denial of equal treatment to those human beings who, whether by legal definition or social convention, were excluded.

In this sense, the liberal order framework, far from representing any sort of new 'master narrative,' merely seeks to provide helpful reminders that many seemingly unrelated events from the 1840s to the 1940s, across a wide spectrum of people and places, can be connected to each other if we remember that they all took place within a liberal dominion organically linked to the British Empire. The framework provides productive ways of bringing these and other topics together, without making any claim that they can all be comprehensively explained by this context. And it mildly observes that, as both other places and post-1940s developments have revealed, many of these happenings were not actually the only ways people might have organized social and political relations. Rather, they were choices, made with various degrees of lucidity and self-awareness, sometimes the result of intensive and sustained reflections on the structures of the system (here we think of Lord Durham and Mackenzie King), and sometimes simply ad hoc responses to the practical problems of everyday life arising within the context of a particular social and political formation.

Yet in addition to simply providing a handy checklist of such conceivably linked phenomena, the liberal order framework tries to grasp what was *necessarily* at work in order for them to make their appearance. To reference terms so powerfully developed by William Sewell, the framework seeks to grasp the decisive relocations of the precepts of liberal order from one sphere to the next – transpositions through which they were subtly modified in each new context, without altogether losing their identity and coherence. It shares with him the conviction that events can 'transform or reconfigure social relations,' that different eras had 'varying forms of life and different social dynamics,' that 'what entities exist in the social world, how they operate, and what they mean change fundamentally over time.' It also agrees with his observation that 'every important form of social relations is potentially subject to change: not only ideas, institutions, and identities, but tools, forms of shelter, sex, gods, climate, diseases, cultivated plants, and languages,' and that social life 'is fundamentally constituted ... by humanly constructed practices, conventions, and beliefs that shape all aspects of social life, from agriculture and procreation to poetry and religion.' It understands that 'temporal heterogeneity' implies 'causal heterogeneity' – that is, 'the consequences of a given act are not intrinsic in the act but rather will depend on the nature of the social world within which it takes place.' Rather than attempting to discover and apply *'general causal laws,* laws implicitly or explicitly assumed to be independent of time and place' – in this case, the supposedly invariant, universal, and transcendental rules of liberal order – the framework assumes 'that the social logics governing past social worlds varied fundamentally, and therefore that their logics must be discovered and puzzled out by the researcher.' And this in turn mandates an attentiveness to *historical contextualization,* for we 'cannot know what an act or an utterance means and what its consequences might be without knowing the semantics, the technologies, the conventions – in brief, the logics – that characterize the world in which the action takes place.'[11]

Thus, the liberal order framework does not privilege economic, political, social, cultural, or intellectual history, as these fields have been generally demarcated in the academy. Nor does it naively assume that 'liberals' can be taken as the iconic spokesmen for 'liberty' (a concept long predating liberalism) nor the standard-bearers of the world's enlightenment.[12] If the liberal interlocutors of the framework tend to refer back to a curiously static and stable set of revered iconic figures, calling to mind the true believers of rival twentieth-century secular religions, they do so with different motivations and questions than those of the framework itself.[13] (The 'John Stuart Mill' so reverently and selectively called forth in liberal memory is a very different figure from the 'John Stuart Mill' of the liberal order framework, in that the latter notices, alongside his passionate if often vague proclamations on liberty, his developmentalist and equivocal endorsement of slavery, his well-developed suspicion of democracy, and his passionate preoccupations with the civilizing mission of the British Empire).[14] Within the myth-symbol complex of true liberal belief, very well-represented in this volume, the 'idea of liberty' itself drives history forward: from its first genesis in Europe, then to North America and then the rest of the world, as an expansive project of human liberation from tribalism, superstition, and despotism. Conversely, within the liberal order framework, such statements are mainly of interest as primary evidence of liberalism's extraordinarily powerful presence in the academy and in everyday life. Fascinating as it is to comprehend the theories of Bentham, Locke, Mill, and the unjustly-neglected Spencer, to name perhaps the liberal Canadians' most revered guides to true political belief in the nineteenth century, we cannot mistake their theories for reality, nor imagine that the transposition of their ideas into northern North America from the 1840s to the 1940s proceeded without incident, complication, or systematic revision. *Actually existing liberalism* – to adapt an expression from Rudolf Bahro[15] – should not be evaded by flights into high theory. What the liberal order framework demands is not generic and perpetually unresolvable debates about 'liberalism-in-general' and 'potential-if-undocumentable-intellectual influences,' but determinate (and inherently testable) abstractions about 'liberty-on-the-ground,' that is, as a political framework put to work in the specific historical context of Canada as a political project of rule in North America.

Oddly enough, this stance means taking *much more seriously* than is conventionally the case the Canadian liberals themselves – as coherent and rigorous proponents of a continent-wide transformation of society, inheritors of a great intellectual tradition which they then articulated to the vast heterogeneous terrain they sought to understand and to transform. It means a new appreciation of the great theorists and activists, the 'organic intellectuals,'[16] of Canadian liberal order – Lords Durham and Sydenham, Joseph Howe and Robert Baldwin, George Brown and David Mills, Goldwin Smith and Duncan Campbell Scott, R.B. Bennett and the brilliant Arthur Meighen, Duff Pattulo and Angus L. Macdonald, Mitch Hepburn and Maurice Duplessis, and perhaps above all William Lyon Mackenzie King, to name but a few – as the new order's often insightful and imaginative militants. And it also suggests a heightened awareness of the 'everyday activists,' the countless businessmen who diffused the gospels of individualism and improvement through advertising, and the thousands of journalists who, day in and day out, authored everyday liberal perceptions of the social world.[17] In such ways great and small, the once inchoate colonies and territories of British North America were reshaped into the disciplined and hierarchical state necessary for the transformation, at once cultural, political, and economic, of an entire subcontinent.

In a carefully historicized discussion focused on that mid-nineteenth-century 'classical liberalism' that attained tremendous influence throughout the North Atlantic world precisely in the same decades of the consolidation of the Canadian project of rule, J.S. McClelland suggests that 'at its most intellectually coherent,' the doctrine can be summarized as a structure of three interlocking and dependent 'economies' (that is, in his interpretation, well-organized and self-regulating sys-tems). First, in the 'moral economy' of liberalism, one found a unifying assumption that 'individually chosen paths to human happiness can be harmonized with each other.' (And so, Daniel T. Rodgers would add, the 'age of laissez-faire' was in fact 'no mere retrospective construction of its critics,' and it is simplistic to conflate it with government passiv-ity, for '[w]hatever else laissez-faire meant, it meant devolving primary responsibility for economic well-being from politics to markets, from considerations of state to myriad private desires.')[18] Second, in the 'political economy' of liberalism, government ought to reflect the sum of opinion already formed, but not meddle in the formation of new opinion, which should change through mechanisms of its own. (And so, as Jürgen Habermas so famously urged, a liberal order, rather than encouraging a freewheeling 'public sphere' or the proliferation of a diversity of 'public spheres,' worked indirectly to reshape public opin-ion and encourage it to greater degrees of homogeneity).[19] Finally, with respect to 'international economy,' liberals were united in a critique of mercantilism, which 'artificially maintained an improper trading advantage and ... retarded domestic economic growth,' and were in favour of the emergence of a world economy made up of relatively au-tonomous nations, each of them a vital interlocking part in a harmoni-ous order. Liberals expected the world 'to improve gradually rather than to become perfect,' yet – since the 'basis of the liberal faith in the future was undoubtedly economic' – they found in the emergent world of industrial capitalism and in the division of labour a basis for their optimistic belief that the human world would gradually attain rational harmonies that fulfilled their aspirations.[20]

McClelland's formulation of the doctrine is a helpful and sympathetic one, which usefully goes beyond the existing binaries to suggest new ways of connecting liberal themes. In the specific context of this research – that of the period of liberal revolution in Canada from the 1840s to the 1940s – it seems prudent to adopt McClelland's minimalist definitional strategy, rather than ones that enumerate lengthy shopping lists of pre-dispositions and concepts, many of them shared by some 'liberals' but not by others.[21] Such definitional economy is by no means a recipe for reductionism. It does not entail, for instance, any 'cutting down to size' of the idea of liberty, which classical liberals arguably interpreted in ways strikingly different than democrats, socialists, or anarchists (to cite just three other major traditions that adopted and developed the con-cept). What it does enable are meaningful hypotheses, susceptible to rigorous empirical testing. In actually existing Canadian liberalism, it seems judicious to reserve the term 'liberal' for those whose words and deeds drew upon these three paramount 'economies.' Or, in a more down-to-earth sense, we might think of three paramount values suggested by these 'economies': the formal equality of adult male individuals before the law, the liberty of some individuals to certain carefully delimited rights and freedoms, and finally their freedom to acquire and defend private property.[22] In both McClelland's more abstract, and this more down-to-earth, version of liberal ideology, the 'individual' links the three 'economies.' In this framework, the 'individual' – an 'abstraction' in one sense, but one that over time corresponded to actually discernible human beings – was a free-standing adult male. He was formally the equal of other such males – not owned by, or directly dependent upon them, capable of freely signing contracts, and to be formally treated as the equal of any other individual in a court of law. His enjoyment of important rights and freedoms (freedom of religion, expression, association, and so on) was carefully regulated to minimize any real or apprehended challenge to social order and private property. His social and political identity was safeguarded by the legal and political recognition of his right, under the terms of 'British Justice,' to conduct his business without 'interference' from the state.

One empirical observation about the Dominion from the 1840s to the 1940s that emerges from the consistent application of this 'triune' definition of liberalism is that these values seem often to have been placed in a hierarchy – with property rights implicitly or explicitly taking precedence over equality and freedom.[23] The liberal order framework would be disconfirmed as an interpretation of Canadian history from 1840 to 1940 if it could be generally shown that the Canadian state in its federal, provincial, or municipal manifestations, or the organic intellectuals and activists who justified its existence and were instrumental in developing its policies, demonstrated consistent indifference or hostility to these core values or argued against their interrelation from the 1840s to the 1940s. It is a framework vulnerable in general and in specifics to empirical challenge – which is, in my estimation, one of its considerable strengths. The hypothesis that this classical liberalism provided both an institutional and cultural framework for the Canadian project is not a prescription for reducing everything to a uniform shade of liberal grey. The restricted freedom of expression allowed within a liberal order made it possible to use the tradition creatively – even to argue, in some instances successfully, for the eradication of some individuals' property rights, in the name of the greater good of the project as a whole and the triune formula more specifically.[24] What the framework maintains is that, overall, from the 1840s to 1940s, there was an empirically verifiable tendency to shape the state and civil society according to the precepts of liberal order, without presupposing that there was a predetermined outcome to the many debates about how best to interpret and implement these precepts.[25] If we may regard the 'triune formula' of liberty, equality, and property as a useful benchmark for classical liberalism, it must be always remembered that in particular contexts this formula was articulated and managed in quite different ways.

More specifically, we might note five leading traits of the classical liberal order in Canada:

(1) An economic base made up of competing profit-seeking entities, no one of which can determine general levels of supply or demand, but all of which function in a marketplace not directly managed by a state authority. (The achievement of such a free marketplace was nonetheless a conscious state achievement, closely associated with the 1840s.) Relatedly, throughout society, a pervasive cult of the propertied individual – the self-made man whose business prowess, tastes in architecture, intellectual preferences, and so on are the stuff of song and legend, dime novels and magazine profiles;[26]

(2) A relatively small state whose functions are largely restricted to maintaining law and order, accelerating the process of capitalist accumulation, educating the young (with various degrees of compulsion), and providing some services to the 'social residuum,' that is, those non-individuals unable, through no fault of their own, to provide for themselves – as distinct from the able-bodied adult males who should be encouraged to enter the labour market under the rule of 'less eligibility';[27]

(3) A political system that allowed for a measure of free debate and democratic deliberation for some, but that excluded most adults, on grounds of race, ethnicity, class, or gender, from participation in the formal political process;

(4) A system of law that safeguarded the individual's civil and political liberties, most obviously through the common law, and a constitution that also made some provision for the collective rights of religious minorities;

(5) Relatedly, a strong attachment to the 'British constitution' – the guarantor of the rights of 'free-born Englishmen,' the 'organic' continuity linking British North Americans and Canadians to the world's

greatest and most civilizing power – and to exemplary heroes who stood for the 'Most Famous Stream' of British liberty.[28]

Although the words 'Canada' and 'revolution' are rarely brought together, liberal order *was* revolutionary, especially if we consider it in the temporal context of the human habitation of North America. It consolidated and extended ways of conceiving humanity and its environment that were radically different from any existing previously. The preconditions of this revolution were, perhaps, five-fold: first, the generation of economic surpluses – in Atlantic and Central Canada, and to a point in British Columbia – that made it possible to conceive of a new state project aiming at further economic growth; second, a social and political transformation in Britain that, thanks to the Empire's transformative conquests of 1710 and 1759, were imported into, and at times magnified within, the British North America itself; third, a massive transatlantic movement of population, part of the 'great global land rush' that ushered a host of new 'neo-Europes' into being and initiated a vast demographic transformation in northern North America; fourth, a diplomatic accommodation, down to 1930 fairly fragile, between the two North Atlantic superpowers, Britain and the United States, by virtue of which a semi-autonomous Canadian state project was permitted to take shape, on condition that it did not fundamentally challenge more powerful imperial interests; fifth, and finally, a 'historic compromise,' enforced from above through a hegemonic strategy combining coercion, consent, and corruption, by which leftists of various descriptions – PEI Escheaters, Lower Canadian Patriotes, Pictou Radicals, Canada East Rouges, Upper Canadian Clear Grits, assorted Republican admirers of American democracy, among many others – could be brought into working relationships with their old Tory enemies, who themselves had built formidable political and social networks organically linked to the various colonial states and to the Empire itself. Without these five preconditions, the liberal order would not have been installed in its first nuclei, the small British colonies hugging what is now the Canada/U.S. border. Nor would it have been able to consolidate the wider and more inclusive state forms, beginning in 1841, that expanded step by step over radically different social and political formations – notably the kin-ordered social formations associated with the indigenous nations, the feudal relations associated with New France, and the pre-liberal patriarchal coastal enclaves linked with venerable North Atlantic merchant empires in fur, fish, and timber.

Thus, as a first modest step towards a rethinking of Canada-as-project, the liberal order framework suggests the usefulness of the concept of the long 'Liberal Revolution' from c. 1840 to c. 1950. And of the five preconditions of this long revolution, it draws particular attention to the fifth – the historic compromise and passive revolution (i.e., as we shall explore in detail later on, a combination of conservative restoration and revolutionary transformation) of 1841–8. It was only with the defeat of the radical democrats in 1837–8 and the imposition of a new form of rule under Lords Durham and Sydenham that the liberal revolution could move from utopian dream to an emergent reality.[29] Both Lords must figure as the unheralded fathers of Confederation – Durham because, as recent revisionist work has proposed, he worked so strenuously to shore up executive authority and to 'liberalize' French Canadian civil society, even at the cost of its unlamented future assimilation and dissolution,[30] and Sydenham because, through the imaginative and disciplined application of state terror and the ruthless transformation of the traditional rules of patronage and preferment under which an older oligarchy had flourished for generations, he effected a historic compromise between left and right and transformed Durham's abstract model into a functioning reality.[31] Throughout the project's southern nuclei, the new Durham-Sydenham vanguard formula of utilitarianism, executive power, and individual enterprise brought together Tories and democrats, old enemies who gradually found new ways of negotiating their differences. It was thanks to this fledgling historical bloc that, through the 1840s and 1850s, initially inchoate liberal organisms could gradually attain the discipline, hierarchy, and historical will necessary for any project of state formation. They could become the standard-bearers of liberalism, more and more capable of theorizing a body of law and crafting forms of legitimate violence through which the vast northern reaches of the continent could be brought 'to order,' that is, made 'legible' and 'coherent' for the liberal vanguard itself. As Gerald Craig so perceptively remarks: 'In the political realm moderate men were at last gaining at the expense of extremists, and would soon help to release and quicken the constructive energies of the population.'[32] He here aptly distils the underlying logic of the 1840s: that of the slow, painful, and intricate convergence of pre-existing political formations, the upshot in part of coercion (the official terror of 1837–40), in part of consensus (the gradual diffusion of new forms of rule attractive to subaltern individuals and groups), and in part of corruption (the conscious use of the state to multiply the numbers of people who had a material attachment to it).[33]

If democrats and Tories had disputed the very definition of a legitimate state in the 1830s, by the 1850s such debates had been transformed, through a complex process of restoration and revolution, into ones that focused on the detailed functioning of a liberal order – and not on its underlying constitutional or moral legitimacy.[34] Across all of British North America, old enemies fused into the new parties, which presented two dialects (sometimes easily distinguishable from each other, and oftentimes not) of the same language of liberalism – those, that is, of the Liberal Conservatives and of the (increasingly conservative) Liberals respectively. Without such multifaceted and energetic leadership, the liberal revolution would have been unthinkable in so heterogeneous and massive a territory.[35] It was in the two decades following the 1840s that the project of Canada took shape. It did so on the basis of this 'revolution from above,' one that simultaneously *restored* the power of the executive (and through it the prestige of the Empire itself), *revolutionized* the terms under which some elements of imperial power were essentially contracted out to its local representatives, and *pacified* elements tendentially disposed to mount democratic movements of critique and resistance. Only in this way could the Province of Canada gradually acquire the decisive status of the nucleus of the emergent liberal Dominion – as suggested by the new country's very title and confirmed by its increasingly coherent state institutions.[36]

Empirically, this periodization captures the fundamental processes through which an expanding Canadian state system came to occupy the second largest land mass of any country in the world – a process of territorial aggrandizement that commenced in 1841, with the union of the Canadas; underwent a series of major westward expansions, via Confederation with British Columbia, the purchase of much of the Hudson's Bay Company's vast empire, the extensions of transcontinental railways, the Indian Act and the Criminal Code, the organization of new western provinces, and the acquisition of territories in the Arctic; and culminated in the entry of Newfoundland in 1949 under the aegis of the 'new liberalism' and the welfare state. Thus the period 1840s–1940s has, on this reading, a unity. It encompasses the years of Canada's expansion – in essence, the acquisition of a vast land-based empire, made possible with the (at times grudging) mutual consent of Great Britain and the United States.[37]

The liberal order framework thus provides us with a 'bridging concept' that allows us to connect (but without reducing, homogenizing, or minimizing) the various distinct moments of the project of Canada in the era of its most rapid territorial expansion. In the Liberal Era, 'Canada' evolved out of a diversity of forms – merchant empires, semi-feudal agrarian settlements, autonomous native societies, crown colonies, and frontier zones lacking any one authoritative source of legitimate violence – into the second largest country in the world, with a comprehensive criminal code, an intricate system of federal and provincial parliaments, a (national and transnational) network of communications media, and so on. The logic and coherence of the Liberal Era resides in a sustained and coherent political *and* cultural project, from the 1840s to the 1940s, through which activists and institutions struggled to organize and render coherent – or even 'legible' in rational terms, from the perspective of the distance-managing apparatuses of the modern state[38] – a strikingly heterogeneous terrain in northern North America.

This claim is easily misunderstood. It does not come down to a reductionist proposition that, from 1840 to 1950, 'the Canadians' were in some way all 'liberals' in any sophisticated or thoroughgoing sense, or indeed in any sense. It is extremely hazardous to generalize about 'the Canadians' of this period as though they were a sovereign or distinct people, or as if evidence garnered from particular places can yield insight into their supposedly unitary ideological or cultural 'essence.' It is even hazardous, *pace* many political scientists, to write with certainty about the supposed 'Fathers' and 'Founders' of Confederation.[39] Empirically, 'the Canadians' – that is, in the long period before the invention of Canadian citizenship in the 1940s, those subjects of the British Crown normally found on territories presided over by the Canadian state – constituted an untidy array of peoples and nations, religions and ethnicities. They did not share a unifying national myth-symbol complex.[40] They spoke dozens of different languages. They lived in widely dispersed areas, settled at different times by different peoples with different objectives. Attempts to transform their heterogeneity into unity by focusing on underlying geographical patterns have proved empirically unconvincing. So, too, have neo-Hartzian attempts that have tried to correlate 'Canadianness' with an original ideological essence – say, a 'Tory fragment.'[41] What most of these many 'Canadians' *did* necessarily share, whether they wanted to or not, was an experience of an emergent continent-wide project of liberal rule. The liberal order framework allows us to grasp the project of Canada, not as the outcome of a 'consensus,' but rather as the conflictual hegemonic culmination of a particular and well-documented political project.

In the Liberal Era, an elite, initially quite small, dispersed, and divided within itself on religious, economic, and social grounds, transcended its immediate narrow interests and, with considerable assistance from Westminster and a cadre of British intellectuals, developed a cohesive economic, social, and political program that it gradually projected into the far reaches of a massive subcontinent. The territory now claimed by Canada has been settled for many thousands of years, only a small fraction of which are accounted for by the years of European colonization. Many of the nations and societies present in northern North America before 1840 were plainly non-liberal in their conceptions of property, politics, and the individual. If, when they gazed north and west, the first Canadian state-builders could barely make out the figures of the Natives – who were, in this *precise sense* only, spatially 'marginal' at the outset of the Canadian project[42] – such colonizers also quite quickly grasped how essential the First Nations' eventual effective marginalization would be to the project of Canada. Realized through a variety of programs, the 'liquidation of the Natives as a class,' so to speak, was the explicitly acknowledged precondition of a transcontinental liberal order. Contrary to transcendental nationalist myth-symbol complexes, whether of the religious, natural, or multiculturalist varieties, actually existing liberalism in Canada was not the outcome of a harmonious pact among the peoples. It was largely the outcome of British colonization, as it worked upon and with pre-existing social and political formations and as it was championed and developed by an aggressive and self-confident local elite. That the country was (and in many respects still is) a 'white settlers' dominion,' whose predominant political, legal, and religious systems were imposed on its indigenous inhabitants, is an underlying assumption of the liberal order framework. It is in this sense that those First Nations forcefully marginalized from positions of political and economic power, from the 1840s in central Canada, from the 1880s on the West Coast, and from the 1920s in the High Arctic, were always and everywhere *central* figures in the project of rule in some of its most important moments, such as unreciprocal treaty negotiations and the development of reservations, pass laws, and residential schools, all integral aspects of a sustained liberal project designed over decades to simultaneously 'individualize' *and* marginalize the indigenous peoples. A reconnaissance of the liberal revolution thus demands full attention not only to the vanguard exponents of its values but to the responses of the many peoples they sought to control and reshape and in some instances effectively to destroy.

If indigenous peoples were, after the 1840s, clearly among the (actually or potentially) ruled, who (at the other extreme) were the rulers? The 'owners of the means of production,' might be one (traditional Marxist) answer; the 'British Crown and its agents,' might be another response from those focused on both the conquests of 1710 and 1759 and the constitutional realities of 1867;[43] 'the middle class,' might be the increasingly interesting response from those attentive to the local prestige and cultural influence of middlemost professionals;[44] the 'ruling parties,' conventional historians of the 1940s and 1950s might remark; the ever-more-sophisticated 'administrative state,' their successors in the 1970s and 1980s might add.[45] All of these answers have opened up highly productive lines of inquiry. None seems adequate in itself.

The liberal 'rulers' of the project of Canada – those with the documented capacity to write statutes, direct state institutions, craft tariff rates, write authoritative editorials, and crush rebellions – both transcended the 'objective' determinations of their social and economic base and yet also had to pay heed to them. They were single-minded in their pursuit of improvement, but of many minds when it came to important questions, such as tariff protection, the provision of patronage, the precise terms under which the transcontinental railways should be built, and so on. Even on such a basic issue as the definitional identity of the individual – whether, for example, women or people of colour or Aboriginals could be considered full rights-bearing 'individuals' – there could be fierce disagreement, as *some* of those who enjoyed at best liminal status as individuals under classical liberalism acquired certain rights and privileges (thus, with Quebec's adoption of women's suffrage in 1940, most women of European descent could finally vote in federal and provincial elections, whereas racially segregated schools and racially exclusive franchises still eliminated other large groups from effective participation). Against the upwards-and-onwards tendency of liberal historians to use the gradual and hesitant expansion of the category 'individual' to demonstrate the inevitability and goodness of Canada, one might note the marked cultural, spatial, and economic *unevenness* of the advent of such an expanded concept of rights – as exemplified by the retention and even strengthening (in the 1940s) of racially restrictive provisions for the franchise, segregated schools, state-orchestrated forced migrations of indigenous peoples,[46] and so on. What is perhaps more striking than the hesitant and partial extension of the political community to incorporate some of the hitherto excluded, was the undiminished confidence of those at the centre of the project that they were themselves entitled to draw and re-draw the lines of effective citizenship – a concept that, in Canada down to the late 1940s and beyond, remained revealingly undertheorized and undeveloped.

2. Hegemony, Historical Bloc, Passive Revolution

Perceptive liberal critics, Jeff McNairn among them, rightly observe that this framework has been developed in dialogue with the thought of Antonio Gramsci, which has been received in so many different ways since extensive selections from the *Prison Notebooks* were published in the English-speaking world in the 1970s. The metaphor of dialogue is important: for rather than 'Gramscianism' setting the agenda and supplying the concepts at the outset, with 'Canadian history' merely offering up raw materials for theory, the liberal order framework emerged in response to perceived deficiencies – empirical, logical, and ethico-political – within prevailing interpretations of Canadian history itself. Moreover, since the 1970s, the very meaning of 'Gramsci' has shifted, as his work has been read more and more intensively and rigorously, an undertaking revolutionized by the publication of critical editions of the *Prison Notebooks*.[47] What had earlier been a somewhat eclectic 'hunting for gems' in Gramsci, to supply the appearance of sophistication and polish to often bleakly pedestrian formulations, or to provide a few uplifting quotations from a sanctified figure, has been superseded by a far more sustained engagement with his writings.

Core to that work, and to the liberal order framework, is the concept of hegemony. It is easy to supply relatively 'simple' definitions of the term. Roger Simon's introduction to *Gramsci's Political Thought*, still a very useful starting-point for those beginning their exploration of Gramsci's work, defines it as that 'combination of coercion and persuasion' used by a ruling class and its representatives in the exercise of power over subordinate classes. Hegemony 'is the organisation of consent.' Gramsci, he notes, typically uses the word *direzione* (leadership, direction) interchangeably with *egemonia* (hegemony), and in contrast to *dominazione* (domination). A hegemonic class, or a fraction thereof, is 'one which gains the consent of other classes and social forces through creating and maintaining a system of alliances by means of political and ideological struggle.' Yet, once attained, hegemony cannot be taken for granted; it has to be 'continually fought for afresh.'[48] For Denis Forgacs, editor of the deservedly much-consulted *Gramsci Reader*, Gramsci's concept of 'hegemony' has three major meanings. One, associated with his writings before his imprisonment in 1926, means 'leadership of a class alliance,' such as proletarian leadership of an alliance with the peasantry and other exploited groups. Here hegemony is 'necessarily rooted in an economically dominant, or potentially dominant, mode of production and in one of the "fundamental" social classes (bourgeoisie or proletariat), but it is defined precisely by an expansion beyond economic class interest into the sphere of political direction through a system of class alliances.' After 1926, observes Forgacs, Gramsci extended the concept in two ways. 'First, it is applied not just to situations of proletarian leadership but also to the rule of other classes at other periods of history. Secondly, it is qualitatively modified: hegemony comes to mean "cultural, moral and ideological" leadership over allied and subordinate groups. Hegemony in this sense ... is identified with the formation of a new ideological "terrain," with political, cultural and moral leadership and with consent.'[49] As Simon Gunn remarks, Gramscian hegemony always implied more than 'ideology' or 'social control'; rather, it involved 'the construction of a whole lived reality such that the existing political, economic and social structures would be taken for granted by the mass of the people, seen as "common sense."'[50] Peter Ives, who has especially focused on Gramsci's linguistics, remarks that 'consent does not mean individually based agreement, as portrayed by naïve and much simplified liberalism. On the contrary, consent like coercion is created, and the process of its production cannot be characterized by an absence of coercion and constraint.'[51] As Leo Panitch and Sam Gindin remark, hegemony is a 'variable quality of rule,' with a shifting balance between coercion and consent according to the demands of the national and international conjuncture.[52] Although cultural-studies interpretations of Gramsci prevalent in the 1980s and 1990s stressed his writings on intellectuals and the world of ideas, Gramsci emphasized that 'though hegemony is ethical-political, it must also be economic.'[53] As Adam David Morton suggests, no less than through *ideas* and in the *institutions* that promulgate them, hegemony is constituted by '*material capabilities*.'[54]

Hegemony, in other words, denotes a complex process – the always provisional, up-to-be-renegotiated, situated project of rule whereby some definitions of reality were enshrined in law and custom, and others marginalized – although not necessarily forever. Hegemony is not a 'thing' but a process and a struggle. Kate Crehen has suggestively commented that 'hegemony,' rather than attaining a thing-like status, is more accurately thought of as the naming of a problem – that is, 'how the power relations underpinning various forms of inequality are produced and reproduced.'[55] Jonathan Joseph, in a powerful critical-realist analysis of the concept, remarks that hegemony is best conceived as a process of 'trying to conserve or transform social structures or relations, within very specific limitations.'[56] It is characteristic of hegemony, argues Robert Cox, that relations of dominance are obscured 'by achieving an appearance of acquiescence ... as if it were the natural order of things.'[57] In a fully realized hegemony, citizens govern themselves, without necessarily entering into conflict with the state, even if, on another level of analysis, that state is actively pursuing strategies that undermine their long-term viability as producers or even puts their lives in danger (as in the case of neoliberal states, among them Canada, that resist implementing global responses to a humanity-threatening environmental crisis).

Even at this rudimentary level of the most basic concepts, one can see how the faithful copying-out of 'one' definition of hegemony from the *Prison Notebooks* might oversimplify a much richer and evolving concept from Gramsci's work. In the 1970s and 1980s, the North American tendency was to popularize Gramsci's concept by assimilating it to structural-functionalist concepts of social control, so that an essentialized 'hegemony' came to be equated with a top-down, static, and near-total pattern of domination. Conversely, 'hegemony' was taken as a recipe for 'consensus versions of history,' which implied once-and-for-all periods of ideological consolidation. (And echoes of both these misreadings can be found in this collection, when we encounter scholars who take it as evidence against the liberal order framework that liberalism was always staunchly contested, in various ways; or that it was never 'total'; or that it was interpreted differently by different strata, and so on and so forth – all positions perfectly in harmony with Gramsci's concept of hegemony as an unfolding historical process in the *Prison Notebooks*.) Many critics of Gramscian hegemony – who focus on its supposed elitism, institutional focus, emphasis on integration, narrow national boundaries, and incipient authoritarianism – fail to hit their target, because they have in essence relied upon very abbreviated definitions that do not do justice to the complexity and subtlety of his writings, which moreover they do not seem to have read at all attentively.[58] They characteristically proceed by seeing in Gramsci's descriptions of actually existing hegemonies prescriptions for the left as it struggles for socialism – and overlook Gramsci's explicit insistence that the philosophy of praxis (his term for Marxism) will function very differently in its quest for hegemony than its bourgeois counterparts. One senses the ramifications of some of these oversimplified oppositions in polemical responses to the liberal order framework that, almost with a sense of nostalgia for the liberal certainties of the Cold War, attack it as though it were simply another version of paleo-Marxism. What is often being polemically pilloried is a 1970s/1980s version of 'Gramsci' who was pervasively misinterpreted in North America as the theorist and even celebrator of state dominance, achieved through 'social control' or through a permanent binding consensus.

Such polemics adopt an oversimplified view of Gramsci's project of 'absolute historicism,' his distinctive view of historical method. Against metaphysical and speculative liberalism, which he associated particularly with Benedetto Croce, Gramsci posits a form of research in which philosophy, history, and politics are essentially equated. In this form of thought, an integral philosophy of praxis would hold itself to a higher empirical and ethical standard than its competitors, because it would reflexively incorporate not only a drive to truth and exactitude, but also a critical appreciation of its own preconditions – as itself a historical product of particular social dynamics, and immanent within them as 'an element of the contradiction.'[59] (It is entirely in the spirit of Gramsci, then, to demand empirical rigour, clarity with respect to interpretive criteria, and a specification of the exact ways in which arguments can be tested and modified.) In general, the most promising and responsible twenty-first-century readings of the *Prison Notebooks* construe hegemony not as a 'general social theory,' but as a *historical method* – one that loses much of its interest and meaning when it is abbreviated and condensed into a general *sociological abstraction*. In this sense, while one can well understand the need for easily summarized and repeatable 'definitions' of this and other terms, doing so in ways which make them timeless and transcendent is a betrayal of Gramsci's profoundly historicist and realist conception of the philosophy of praxis.

The privileged terrain of this historical method, for Gramsci, was the Italian *Risorgimento* – that ambiguous and contradictory process whereby the peninsula was unified under a particular state project in the mid-nineteenth century. Gramsci's study of the *Risorgimento* suggests the power of the theory of hegemony to provide a reconnaissance of three moments in the rise of liberalism: (a) the economic-corporate (the direct expression of material interests); (b) the political moment of the struggle for hegemony (to impose a new 'conception of the world' with its appropriate 'norms of conduct'); and (c) the moment of state power, 'when the existing economic, political and ideological structures are transformed by the victorious class and its allies.'[60]

Hegemony, in this more up-to-date critical reading, makes sense only within an 'eventful' concept of temporality, which assumes (to cite William Sewell) that 'what has happened at an earlier point in time will affect the possible outcomes of a sequence of events occurring at a later point in time.'[61] It is at odds with attempts to discover general causal laws applicable across broad and heterogeneous stretches of time and space, and seeks rather to uncover historically determinate patterns: why *this* Risorgimento or *this* Confederation necessarily acquired these *particular* characteristics, and not others. It denotes, not a 'thing' nor even a 'relationship' (whether of coercion or consent), but a *historical process*. More than encapsulating a specific model, 'hegemony' condenses a powerful realist narrative about the emergence, consolidation, and potentially the fall of a ruling group – for instance, the liberals who came to dominate politics in both Italy and Canada in the mid-nineteenth century.[62] In short, much as one admires their polemical ardour, many critics of Gramsci in this volume and elsewhere are writing period pieces, from the good old days of the 1980s and 1990s when irrationalist and anti-realist positions proliferated within the mainstream 'liberal' arts and sciences, and when a naively transcribed version of Parsonian social control theory, sometimes adorned with the most fashionable nominalist flourishes, passed itself off as the latest word in social theory.

Thus, the 'logic of hegemony' is not inherently top-down, state-centric, institutionalist, nationally parochial, or totalizing. Such readings grasp and dehistoricize possible moments of a specific hegemonic process. They convert the real-world *eventfulness* of hegemony into the abstract *functionality* of social control theory. What *is* and *is not* required for a given hegemonic project, whether those of rulers or the counter projects of subalterns, is a question resolvable only through the empirical and logical reconstruction of a given economy and society, and cannot be decided abstractly and in advance. If we look at a project at one moment in its history – say, that of the moderate liberals in 1830s Italy or Canada respectively – we could quite realistically describe their position as non-hegemonic. Yet as that project emerges from its social and economic setting, as its proponents acquire the linguistic and political skills necessary to broaden its appeal, as they attain access to some levers of state power and sharpen their understanding of how best to use them, as they attain an appropriate level of philosophical and practical sophistication – at some culminating point in this process, when they have achieved a recognized position of leadership within the state, we could then realistically describe their position as hegemonic. Hegemony was not an 'it' they could seize and hold at a precise moment; it rather denotes this entire process, renewed day by day and year by year, and illuminated only through critical and empirical investigation.[63] There are many 'Gramscis,' but it is this critical-realist Gramsci, the radical democratic historian of Italian unification, that one would recommend to Canadian historians.

Liberal hegemony in Canada from 1840 to 1950 was a process of state formation and consolidation, combining consent, coercion, and corruption, whereby the party of liberal order attained a position of leadership within Canada and a secure if subordinate place within the international world. They were able to do so because they formed a *historical bloc* – not merely a short-term alliance of social forces, but a dynamic trans-generational unity of theory and practice specifically attuned to the national-popular currents shaping the concept and diffusion of 'Canada.'

The historical bloc[64] is the 'party' (in the broadest sense of the term) that undertakes the long-term project of hegemony through an intensive and extended pedagogical relationship with the 'people.' Thus, in contrast with traditional Marxism, which argued for the functional priority of the (economic) structure over the (ideological) superstructure, Gramsci argues that, working on the basis of a successfully established hegemony, a historical bloc is able to incorporate and transcend this dualism, through its understanding and, within structural limits, harmonization of contending social forces, so that the particular agenda and outlook of a given social group can plausibly be represented as *generic* and *human* interests. And, again in contrast to traditional Marxism, this concept entails a wholesale reworking of the concept of the state, which is no longer construed as a parasitical encrustation or the repressive apparatus of government, a mere body of bureaucrats and armed men functioning as the 'executive committee of the bourgeoisie,' but rather an integral part of the 'private sphere' of civil society. It is only within this integral state organically linked to civil society that can one find the 'exchange of individual elements between the rulers and ruled, leaders ... and led,' leading to a sense of a 'shared life.'[65] Of special 'pedagogical' significance here is the law, which is simultaneously one of the key instruments through which private property and other

core elements of liberal order were imposed upon subalterns and colonized peoples, yet at the same time articulated a complex discourse
of 'rights' through which such human *objects* of liberal order could
become, within limits, its agents and *subjects* – through an internalization of its precepts that, far from a 'top-down' process of brainwashing
or social control, in many cases constituted common-sense languages of
'popular liberalism' as dialects of resistance and subaltern assertion
and 'legal activism' as a pragmatic and tangible mode of subaltern
assertion and resistance. As intensive and prolonged debates over all
aspects of law suggest, the link between a realized hegemony and the
historical bloc charged with its implementation is neither a one-to-one
relationship of functional dependence nor a static 'reflection' of underlying socio-economic patterns. Rather, it is within a historical bloc that
the functionality of the economic order is metabolized into a political
ideal, a lived historicity, and a national (and imperial) myth-symbol
complex – so that, when this 'national-popular' formation is finally
realized, to question 'property' is tantamount to questioning 'the people.' Contesting social forces – often the 'fundamental classes,' but
under conditions of postmodernity, many other social groups as well –
will continually attempt to shift a specific historical bloc in pursuit of
their own agendas, but unless and until the entire order enters a deep-
seated, 'organic' crisis, such programs are more likely to constitute
incremental alterations in the historic equilibria of coercion/consent/
corruption than fundamental transformations of it. Typically such historical blocs form at the national level, but (especially at times of global
socio-economic revolution) they necessarily, as they shape and reshape
the state, must also address 'the international,' especially since a historical bloc successful within the boundaries of its nation-state will seek to
project itself outwards, to secure its position against rival historical
blocs. Moreover, under conditions of capitalist modernity, within the
state/civil society complex there will be elements closely identified
with *transnational* social forces, which will be concerned to harmonize
the historical bloc as a national phenomenon with their understanding
of the necessary future of the world order.

A further instance of reading Gramsci too simplistically and polemically, and one of special significance in the era of globalization, can be
found in those critiques (here echoed to some degree by Bruce Curtis)
which argue that he was, above all, a theorist resolutely focused on patterns contained within the borders of nation-states – Italy in particular.
They then suggest that this 'national focus' renders redundant any

attempt to 'globalize Gramsci.'[66] Yet, once again, this reading seems far too simple. It clashes with Gramsci's own insistence that 'every relationship of "hegemony" is necessarily an educational relationship and occurs not only within a nation, between the various forces that comprise it, but in the entire international and world field, between complexes of national and continental civilisations.'[67] If the first moment of hegemony lies within the specific social relations of production, and the second in the state/civil society complex of a particular country, the third and arguably decisive moment of hegemony comes with the constitution of a world order. As Adam David Morton argues, in a pathbreaking recent contribution to the literature, 'Hegemony ... can operate at two levels: by constructing a historical bloc and establishing social cohesion *within* a form of state as well as by expanding a mode of production *internationally* to protect hegemony through the level of world order.'[68] Rather than a problematic exclusively focused on national social formations, Gramsci's is one that apprehends nation-states as nodes within a transnational hegemonic system.[69] If for many pragmatic and political reasons it still makes sense to begin with the 'national' as our point of departure, this is best interpreted 'as *nodal* rather than *dominant* in relation to "the international."'[70]

Gramsci's intense internationalism is most in evidence with his analysis of *passive revolution*, which emerges in his work as a key concept to explain Italy's difficult nineteenth-century transition to capitalist modernity. In some respects, as his North American readers know very well, Gramsci is obsessed with the specifics of the Italian case – to the point of losing even the most keen students in a forest of specific and often arcane details about Italian culture and history. Yet the minutiae should not conceal the underlying logic of his theme of passive revolution, which seeks an explanation of patterns of spatial differentiation and state formation in a territory subject to interventions by external powers. Gramsci is in pursuit of the 'conditioning circumstances of Italian state formation in relation to the wider emerging European statessystem.'[71]

Powerful classes in an economically backward country seek to mirror the wealth and power of advanced countries through state-led development strategies, which typically combine primitive accumulation (the active dispossession of peasants and other producers of their land and other means of production) with import substitution, whether indirectly (through tariffs, subsidies, and bonuses) or directly (through state ownership). To achieve such 'combined and uneven development,' to use Trotsky's expression, they must first achieve hegemony within the state (even generating new state structures, where a unitary state capable of undertaking such a program is missing) and within civil society (creating a new common sense favouring their economic, political, and cultural objectives). Passive revolution hence calls for an *active* state – but it also requires the incorporation of producers within the system, not as agents of its revolutionary transformation, as was more the case in the heartlands of capitalism, but rather as its subaltern and mainly quiescent supporters. It rests upon a minimal hegemony, a relatively narrow consensus with respect to the pursuit of particular modernizing policies – not upon the hegemony of a new 'people-nation' in an ongoing democratic revolution. The key to passive revolution is that leadership passes from local social groups to the state, which itself must theorize and act upon *both* the 'national' and 'international' levels. Thus, although discrete passive revolutions can legitimately be analysed within the confines of a particular nation-state, they arise 'as differentiated *outcomes* or *moments* of an historically integrated process,' elements of a 'cumulative process of historically linked state formation moments within the world market order of capitalism and the international states-system.'[72] Because 'the international' is a constitutive moment of state formation itself, furnishing the global socio-economic context within which any new state form must emerge *and* the political-ethical content of the project the new state form is committed to realize, any analysis of passive revolutions that confines itself to a particular country is bound to be a partial one.[73]

Once it has reshaped civil society and the state, a passive revolutionary historical bloc can settle into a pattern of *trasformismo* – Gramsci even suggested that the 'entire State life of Italy from 1848 onwards' could be so characterized[74] – through which attempts to establish alternative hegemonies are absorbed and radical leaders co-opted. Yet such a normalization of the new patterns of hegemony should not conceal the unusual and crisis-laden moments of passive revolution themselves – ones in which both global and domestic pressures combine to force organic intellectuals to recalibrate politics and society in programs that simultaneously revolutionize politics and society, restore and fortify pre-existing social relationships, and generate a hegemonic 'common sense,' most notably authoritative historical narratives of nationhood and identity, through which such far-reaching transformations are normalized – in today's language, becoming the 'new normal.'

With its hegemony thus re-secured, the dominant class can then construct a new 'historical bloc' to integrate a variety of different groups within the renovated state project. Within the limits set by the economic structure, a historical bloc exercises a considerable autonomy in the pursuit of a project that, if rooted in the particular interests of one narrow 'corporate' group, can be made to appeal to many others. Such a historical bloc struggles to achieve a more inclusive and dynamic language of politics, articulating a wide diversity of ideas, even potentially conflicting ones: it creates, one might say, a 'public sphere,' in which agreement on certain fundamentals (property, morality, respectability, progress, order) is the entry-ticket for debates over their implications (tariff policy, temperance, policing, workers' rights, diplomacy). It is not that these implications are of minor significance, but rather that they do not call into question the fundamental institutions and patterns established under the historical bloc's transformative aegis.

Of all these Gramscian concepts, it is 'passive revolution' that seems to hold the most promise for the ongoing Canadian elaboration of the liberal order framework. Gramsci developed this concept when writing about the multiple historic failures of Italian liberalism – first to genuinely unify the country, second to create a state capable of educating the masses and democratizing political life, and third to address Italy's perennial social and economic contradictions, especially its famous 'Southern Question.' From the outset in the first of the *Prison Notebooks*, the idea involves a political contrast between changes imposed from above and authentically democratic revolutions. Gramsci wants to construct a concept that allows us to understand (in Anne Showstack Sassoon's words) 'historical changes ... [that] take place without widespread popular initiative, from "on high."' She adds: 'Gramsci uses the term passive revolution to indicate the constant reorganization of state power and its relationship to society to preserve control by the few over the many and maintain a traditional lack of real control by the mass of the population over the political and economic realms.'[75]

3. The Canadian Project as Passive Revolution

Of Gramsci's different senses of 'passive revolution,' three can be reconstructed as successive moments of liberal order in Canada, to designate the order's formation, maintenance, and crisis. First, there was the passive revolution inherent in the nineteenth-century geohistorical patterns of Canadian state formation, lasting in essence from the 1840s to 1914. As was the case with its Italian counterpart, the new Canadian state relied upon the imposition of new state forms from above. The emergent historical bloc saw in the new Dominion a more ample scope for its economic and political ambitions.[76] What was 'passive' about this revolution – which admittedly did draw support from important social strata within civil society – was that, in contrast with the many republican and democratic movements in the colonies that had flourished from the 1820s to the 1840s, and which were then displaced by the new formulas of institutionalized parties and responsible government, its emergent governing formula of 'Peace, Order and good Government' systematically minimized the efficacy of popular power. As was also the case in Italy, the new state was not so much an independent country, whose sovereignty rested upon a free and active citizenry – of the sort that the radical democrat Gramsci hoped to create – but rather a liminal entity, caught between the interests of much stronger great powers.[77]

Passive revolution in a second sense – the routine maintenance of this regime – brought to bear many processes that worked to institutionalize its categories and bind people to its rule. Specifically, one thinks of the absorption of actual or potential opposition through the application of such measures as patronage, corruption, and *trasformismo*. In Canada, throughout much of the classical liberal century that began in the 1840s, this captures the pervasive 'small change' of hegemony-maintenance, the routine 'molecular' measures through which particular real or potential opponents were co-opted by the political order.[78] That is, the liberal order framework would place particular weight on the ways in which the ruling regime perennially brought over to its side many of its most serious critics – such as the 'Labour' MPs elected before 1921, the majority of the Progressive Party members who were absorbed one by one by Mackenzie King's Liberals through the 1920s, or the trade unionists throughout the entire period who found themselves drawn into state bureaucracies, legislative councils, and even into the federal cabinet. One might even venture the suggestion (following in Gramsci's footsteps) that these 'transformist' *techniques* came to be glorified in a veritable *philosophy of rule* – that in the humdrum material of patronage machines, parliamentary horse-trading, and outright corruption characteristic of much Canadian politics, liberals have somehow evolved an entire myth-symbol complex predicated on *compromise* as the true Canadian's categorical imperative. We could describe this historico-philosophical romance as an *'abstract trasformismo.'* The *passive revolutionary* (and, by implication, 'truly Canadian') thinker abhors conflict. The essence of his or her philosophy is that of obscuring the real (contradictory) possibilities presented by an (actual) situation, and blunting the hard edges and difficult questions posed by any historical contradiction. The *passive revolutionary* style proceeds, not by the dialectical engagement with the adversary's position, but rather through the highly selective conscription of only certain of his or her themes and arguments, which are then, in their edited form, made over to be those that all sane and sensible people believed all along. The unmistakable intent is to rob antithetical positions of their sharpness – and, more generally, to abolish any sense of history as an unfolding of contradictory social and political relations.[79]

Passive revolution in the third sense is the transformation of these first two patterns into strategies and tactics for the management of the acute, systemic – Gramsci would say, 'organic' – crisis. The 1840s could be reconstructed as one such crisis, punctuated by such moments as the highly violent repressions attending elections to the new Canadian parliament and by the burning-down of Parliament by Tory rioters in 1849. Another such moment of organic crisis was provided by the interwar period, during which many people believed that the political and social order was on the brink of dissolution. In both contexts, passive revolution refers to the liberals' recognition of the grave challenges confronting their order and the necessity of instituting fundamental and far-reaching changes to it – indeed, the infinitely delicate task of transforming the order in order to preserve it. What the historical bloc was called upon to do was to transpose well-established elements and principles of liberal political economy (such as private ownership of the means of production) into novel structures and relationships (such as state planning, accelerated technological change, and industrial legality) that were meant to preserve and even enhance them. In contrast with the two first senses of passive revolution, in this one the ruling bloc necessarily paid detailed attention to the 'basic structurality' of hegemony itself, 'organizing and reorganizing social relations as well as social groups.'[80] In this third form of passive revolution, the state's activism took the unmistakable form of a pre-emptive strike against an alarmingly effective counter-hegemony.[81]

Paradoxically, then, in this third form, 'passive revolution' often appears anything *but* passive. What was 'passive' about this 'revolution from above' was the ultimately pacifying, atomizing, and disorienting effects of liberal policies on subaltern forces – as given rulers, building on generations of experience with the techniques of routine maintenance, now adapted these methods to the far more serious business of disarticulating their counter-hegemonic opposition. In the Canadian context, one would think of new forms of liberalism in the mid-1930s – in Alberta, Ontario, and particularly in Duplessist Québec – that all entailed novel transpositions of liberal doctrines into new state forms; of the first advent of unemployment insurance in 1940, which came only after a protracted political and constitutional crisis; of the halting admission of organized labour into stable and legalized relationships with the state in 1944; and of the adroit federal management of Québec nationalism, exemplified above all by Mackenzie King's accomplished handling of the conscription crisis in the Second World War. In order to preserve liberal order, to echo the discerning diagnosis of R. Craig Brown and Ramsay Cook of the Great War of 1914–18, it was necessary, in both the late 1840s and the early 1940s, to reinvent it.[82]

As historians often forget, to periodize is also, at least implicitly, to theorize. The periodization 1840s–1940s is one that opens and ends in moments of profound *organic crisis*, and in transformative processes of passive revolution, whereby the ruling bloc sought to safeguard its position by pursuing systemic changes across the political, economic, and cultural spheres, whose consequence was the reform of both struc-ture and superstructure, civil society and the society. In both cases, then, this term describes not so much a 'passive' response to inherited conditions, as an 'active' struggle to transform them, and at a quite fun-damental level – but with the ultimate 'pacifying' outcome of sidelining actually existing radical alternatives: in the 1840s, that of the republi-cans and democrats of 1837, and in the 1930s and 1940s, that of the industrial unionists, socialists, and communists.

As Esteve Morera argues, in a ground-breaking study, the point of Gramsci's realist historicism is not to deny the efficacy of structures but rather to produce a concept of them appropriate for the complexities of history and its open character.[83] 'Hegemony,' 'historical bloc,' and 'pas-sive revolution' do not sustain all-encompassing theories of history. They function best as bridging concepts, which make visible connec-tions between seemingly disparate phenomena – connections the work-ing historian must then test against archival and other evidence. As is perhaps obvious, more of the Marxist framework survives in this way of reasoning than might at first be thought conventional or prudent in a neo-liberal epoch – but it is a Marxism of a specific type, a non-ortho-dox, non-teleological, problem-centred, and realist Marxism. It takes from historical materialism not any drive to scientific mastery of a 'closed system,' but the quest for determinate abstractions useful in the critical-realist exploration of an open one.

4. Property and Liberal Order

Critics of the liberal order framework have legitimately highlighted the relationship it proposes between the political regime and property relations. The liberal order framework maintains that 'property' – as, *inter alia*, a historically specific set of social practices, an evolving institutional framework, a political economic strategy, and a sine qua non for most claims to the status of 'individual' – was a fundamental aspect of the classical liberal order from the 1840s to the 1940s. Building on the foundational work of C.B. Macpherson – who defined a property right as 'an enforceable claim to some use or benefit of something'[84] – the framework argues that one of the most significant and tangible elements of the liberal revolution was to be found in the rapid extension of the 'moral economy' of liberalism both on the land (in the growth of freehold tenure) and in the commodification of social relations more generally. As in the work of Marx, 'property' in the liberal order framework is not a thing but a complex series of relationships – between humanity and the rest of the natural world, among different human societies, and within the ruling blocs of the 'neo-Europes' that from 1750 to 1900 transformed much of the world.[85] The concepts of John Locke, often filtered in part through the commentaries on the law of William Blackstone, served as an important (if understudied) resource for many Canadian liberals.[86] It is important to grasp precisely what is *not* at stake in this position. It does not involve the reductionist claim that the political can be reduced to the economic. All such metaphysical claims merit a sceptical reception. And in Canada they incur the additional charge of oversimplifying the Dominion's geohistorical position. In the context of a nineteenth-century Canada economically dependent upon the international market and politically subservient to the British Empire, it would be simplistic to deduce power relations straightforwardly from endogenous economic and social structures. Among the great liberal visionaries of the Canadian project, from Lord Durham through to Mackenzie King, we encounter thinkers who were not only 'Canadian' but also 'North Atlantic' intellectuals, proud contributors to a vast transatlantic liberal persuasion.

The *historical bloc* of Canadian state-builders was, as we have already anticipated in our excursus into Gramscian theory, precisely preoccupied with transcending the narrowly 'corporative' interests to encompass a much more far-ranging commitment to the new State and the old Empire. To the very considerable extent that they were indeed committed to capitalist development, which they demonstrated so eloquently with tariff policies, railway schemes, and the encouragement of mass immigration, they were not so much passively reflecting a pre-existing 'structure' as actively pursuing a comprehensive reconstruction of social and economic life, with the British model of industrial and cultural success before them.

Nor does it mean that those within the historical bloc could simply apply a uniform formula for property relations throughout the Dominion or even calculate to a nicety the consequences of applying their own policies. They were struggling to transform a markedly heterogeneous terrain whose many different social formations and property traditions posed a series of vexing politico-ethical paradoxes.[87] Nor, finally, does it mean that those resisting such formulae were powerless in the face of them, since the century was crowded with experiments, from such utopian communist communities as British Columbia's Finnish settlement at Sointula to state-assisted back-to-the-land movements in the 1920s and 1930s, that sought revolutionary and reformist alternatives to the rule of liberal political economy.[88]

What this position on property does mean is that, overall and in general, one can nonetheless discern an overwhelming specific tendency towards freehold tenure in land and individualized forms of ownership more generally, both in the long-settled neo-Europes of the Canadian South and the new neo-Europes of the Canadian North and West. Ownership came to be considered more and more an absolute right to the use of something – a 'despotic dominion' unconditioned by a multitude of other social considerations. Moreover, this was accompanied by a transition to contractual rather than customary forms in law. Processes that were once considered in a very different light, labour most obviously, took on the attributes of commodities for sale in the market.

As Philip Girard so sagely remarks, 'Liberal societies are made, not born. One of the tools for imagining and constructing them is the law, and within the law's toolkit the law of property and of contract are essential.' As Girard goes on to show, via an illuminating discussion of dower, conditional estates, and mortgages in Ontario and the Maritimes, this 'making' of a liberal society entailed a complex dialectic between a 'facilitative liberalism,' on the one hand, which posited an ideal that divorced land ownership from social function, privileged 'the

will of the owner over other interests,' and sought 'maximum exposure
of property to the market,' and an 'embedded liberalism,' on the other
hand, that recognized 'that landowners have families, live in communities, and participate in societies, and that these other entities may have
claims upon land resources held formally by individual owners.'[89]
Girard does not argue against the compelling evidence suggesting
the growing power of facilitative liberalism – he notes the tendency in
the Supreme Court to strike down clauses that imposed restraints on the
alienation of land – but he does resist any unilinear narrative of its predetermined triumph.

As both Rusty Bittermann and Margaret McCallum have so vividly
demonstrated, Prince Edward Island, with its famous land question,
exemplified the contradictions of those seeking to 'liberalize' an *ancien
régime* of property. As McCallum has eloquently argued, property is
best regarded, not as a thing, but as a multiplicity of relationships: 'The
possibility for renegotiating the exercise of power imports some fluidity into the property relationship. Thus, the meaning of property is not
immutable in all times and places, but can be redefined as individuals
and the state redefine the relationships encompassed by property
rights.' And as she goes on to show, in the mid-nineteenth-century context of the celebrated Prince Edward Island land question, the arguments of contemporaries could be grouped together in four great
themes: property as that almost magical quality that could transform a
dependent leaseholder into a virtuous freeholder; as that which, min-
gled with the labour of men, properly belong to them and not to mere
investors; as something contingent and historical, to be reconceptual-
ized according to circumstance; and as the indirect manifestation of
state power, 'involving a delegation of power from the state to the person whose private property rights the state will enforce.'[90] The fascinating paradox of the Prince Edward Island case was that the 'rights
of property' could be passionately invoked on either side: in defence
of the absentee landlords, whose long-standing interests must be defended; and on the side of their critics, who could and did invoke the
labour theory of property developed in Locke's *Second Treatise of Government* to support their calls for land reform.[91]

In short, from the 1840s to the 1940s, 'Canada' resounded with debates over property, many of them with overtones of Locke. Many
Canadians evidently thought they had found in liberal theory the firm
ground on which to plant the flag of property rights.[92] It was the era
in which Nova Scotia struggled to release its mining and mineral

resources from the monopolizing clutches of the General Mining Association, that wayward by-product of the royal prerogative;[93] in which, from the Red River to Vancouver Island, real and apprehended popular insurrections were sparked by aggressive land surveyors, correctly perceived to be the vanguard party of a freehold revolution that placed other ways of conceptualizing property at risk;[94] and one that laid to rest most of Quebéc's venerable seigneurial system.[95] In law, important innovations in the mid-nineteenth century – such as the abolition of entails in New Brunswick and Nova Scotia, the end of primogeniture in Ontario, the emergence of full-time police forces, and (most ambitiously) the Civil Code and Code of Civil Procedure in Lower Canada (1866 and 1867) – were all legal aspects of a transformation whereby, in Brian Young's words, 'the autonomy, custom, and privilege of feudal relations' gave way to 'strong central government,' to 'universal institutions,' and to a system that 'buttressed individual rights, freedom of contract, and equality before the law.'[96]

None of these struggles over property was predetermined in advance. Both in general and in specific cases, there were many pitched battles, as members of contesting social groups defended their particular interests, often with recourse to more general principles of rights and privileges. Even among those seemingly in the vanguard of the new regime on the land, we find a certain ideological fluidity and even uneasiness – as so suggestively shown by Cole Harris in his sympathetic portrait of G.M. Sproat, that conscience-stricken surveyor of the new order of reservations in British Columbia.[97] Even in the Nova Scotia coal mines, there could be strenuous debates, and even a sense of 'popular ownership,' over the coal resource itself – which could be said to be the property of the mine owners, the provincial government, *and* even the miners, all at the same time.[98] And even within the ever-expanding boundaries of the Dominion between the 1840s and 1940s, there was a remarkable diversity in forms of ownership – as producer and consumer cooperatives, crown corporations, public utilities, and federal parks revealed so plainly.

The laconic declaration in the Constitution Act (1867), formerly known as the British North America Act, that the constitution of the Dominion and each of its provinces was 'similar in Principle to that of the United Kingdom' would have been understood by every lawyer, R.C.B. Risk remarks, as enshrining common-law rights along with parliamentary supremacy and responsible government – which is why *Blackstone's Commentaries* on the common law, which many take to be profoundly Lockean in orientation, had such an enormous impact.[99] Against those who would minimize the extent to which property rights were central to the 'Founders' of Canada, Janet Ajzenstat convincingly argues that section 53 of the Constitution Act (1867) – which says that the House of Commons must approve taxing measures – effectively guarantees property rights, and would (she imagines) receive the imprimatur of John Locke himself. '[W]e have seen enough of the Confederation debates,' she declares, 'to know that most or all believed that security for the individual – the right to life, liberty, and property to use Locke's phrase – is Parliament's original and primary purpose.'[100] A language of property came to be deeply ingrained in the thoughts of the colonizers – it was, argues John Weaver, 'so persistently stated in letters, petitions, treaties, court judgments, and statutes, that even the most enlightened colonizers could engage only in narrow discussions about land with first peoples, because they were culturally bound and in a hurry.'[101] Much of the 'Labour Question' upon which Mackenzie King wrote so perceptively as twentieth-century Canadian liberalism's great organic intellectual came down to a fierce debate over the conditions workers could rightfully attach to the sale of their labour power. More controversially, one might also say of the many craftsmen and colliers who argued for the collective and individual 'rights' denied them by a liberal order suspicious of their conspiracies in restraint of trade, that they often did so with Lockean arguments about the inherent property rights of workers to the products of their labour.[102]

Thus, it seems from the standpoint of the liberal order framework that, with contradictions, complications, and conflicts duly noted and indeed applauded, there was a tendency in Canada from 1840 to 1950 for more and more aspects of life – land, goods, labour – to be construed in terms of individualized and clearly defined claims to 'private property' and to 'commodities.' And it seems equally evident that this placed the many and expanding Canadian neo-Europes in potential conflict with the First Nations societies that still occupied the vast majority of the land mass over which the Canadian state claimed a spatially extensive *and* an increasingly socially intensive sovereignty. In general, the First Nations had developed conceptions of land specifically and the material world more generally that could not be easily accommodated within Western legal and political systems. In the eloquent words of Bradley Bryan, 'Aboriginal property is thus a conundrum for the Western legal system because as soon as we begin our study in a truthful way, the terms revolt.'[103] Often combining liberal political economy with evangelical religion – John Locke with John Wesley, so to speak – the liberal order extended its effective boundaries outwards, through residential schools, treaties, Indian agents, and the remarkably intrusive Indian Act itself – into once autonomous aboriginal territories. To fly over southern Canada today, with its countless fenced farm lots and tidy suburbs, is to witness the scale of the triumph of the program. It would seem the liberal revolution in property, which left Aboriginal peoples with only pockets of their ancestral homelands, with millions of freehold property-holders in their place, was an unqualified success story.

Yet appearances can be deceiving, even when they take the irrefutably material form of fences and farm lots. The appearance of a unilinear process of Aboriginal displacement concealed the extent of persistent Aboriginal resistance. Astute liberal theorists of the Native Question – the brilliant *fin-de-siècle* poet-administrator Duncan Campbell Scott can be fairly placed within this category – intuited that the very one-sided treaties they had engineered with First Nations peoples carried within them serious challenges, at once cultural, economic, moral, and diplomatic, to the project of Canada itself. By combining Spencer and Locke, a racialized liberalism could construct the indigenous peoples as the Absolute Others of the Canadian project – the incomprehensible 'savages' and 'primitives' so pointedly singled out by John Stuart Mill as the fit objects of an improving liberalism. Yet Mill's logic carried within itself profound political and cultural contradictions that have survived into our own time. The liberal revolution would bequeath to its inheritors a vast landscape that looked like so much tranquil rural 'real estate,' but has in fact turned out to be a symbolic and political minefield – as subaltern land struggles from Oka to Caledonia have revealed so clearly.[104] The almost infinite contradictions of liberal order on the land, combined with Canadian state claims to sovereignty over the north, are the stuff of contemporary politics.

In short, anyone who says 'property' also says 'complexity' –and also conflict. Construing property as a thing and not a relationship, and imagining that this 'thing' provides us with an access to an all-explaining 'material base,' misreads the subtlety and originality, the *grounded* cultural revolution, entailed in the project of Canada. Throughout the colonies and then the Dominion, property debates mobilized passions not normally found in Canadian politics. How, for instance, married women should be conceptualized within the system – as incipient individuals, capable within some spheres of autonomous self-regarding behaviour, or as embedded family members, whose interests should always be articulated within a community or familial context – was a live question throughout the period.[105] It was a matter of high and infinitely complex politics – of the sort attending the abolition of the seigneurial system and treaty negotiations with the First Nations – and of mundane, everyday life. William Lyon Mackenzie King can be glimpsed at both ends of this propertied spectrum: as one of the great theorists of the Canadian liberal order with respect to race, who transposed into the vexed question of Asian immigration his exceptionally alert understanding of the imperatives of a propertied individualism, and as one of the anxious property-holders near Kingsmere, seeking to protect 'his lake' from the supposed dangers represented by property-seeking Jews.[106] The everyday world and the high ideals of liberal order mutually constructed each other.

With such liberal order themes in mind, one can put forward a number of testable hypotheses with respect to property:

(a) that from the 1840s to the 1940s, property rights in land became increasingly individualized, exclusive, and formalized, with a growing tendency to state-regulated freehold tenure. Owners increasingly came to be seen as enjoying exclusive rights to use and manage their properties, to transfer them to others, to capture the capital value of land by sale, operating without a term limiting the possession of such rights and normally without fear of expropriation by the state;[107]

(b) conversely, that other strategies with respect to property with substantial roots in European experience, based upon venerable concepts of social hierarchy and conveyed to northern North America in the expectation of their functionality in the New World, and all of them representing barriers to the alienability and unencumbered sale of land – such as seigneurialism in Lower Canada, clergy reserves in Upper Canada, absentee landlordism in Prince Edward Island, royal coal mines in Nova Scotia, and the vast monopoly claims of Her Majesty's Company of Adventurers, the Hudson's Bay Company – were, particularly in the period 1840–1940, progressively undermined and replaced by more individualistic forms of property-holding;

(c) that, even more radically, indigenous systems of laws and custom and those peoples who had upheld them for millennia 'were progressively dislodged from their lands and barred access to resources of both land and water in the settler territories of the British Empire,' sometimes through (overt or implied) armed violence, or through the seemingly unstoppable tide of squatters riding the global land rush, or through a wide diversity of one-sided negotiations, treaties, and so on – in essence the forceful substitution of systems of thought and custom within which 'rights' over things had been inclusively and reciprocally defined, to a more uniform system in which owners of things and land tended to enjoyed exclusive rights to them;[108]

(d) that far from constituting 'economic patterns' that can be relegated to the periphery of discussions of the political and social order, this revolution in property was rooted in deep-seated epistemological and ontological propositions about humanity, not only in the ever-debatable work of Locke, and more influentially in the more down-to-earth precepts of William Blackstone in his *Commentaries*; but also diffused through an immensely powerful imperative to 'improvement,' which ideal of land was taken up and sustained in the law and strengthened by the surveying, cartographic, and record-keeping apparatuses of a reformed administrative state;

(e) finally, that such landed property rights were then increasingly abstracted from the 1840s to the 1940s into (to cite Weaver once more) 'statements on documents, reduced to ciphers, and these texts and codes traveled, enabling interests in land to be traded or pledged for security against loans': and through this 'astonishing conceptual revolution, worked out in both old- and new-world settings, the most tangible and non-moveable property conceivable was organized into interests and condensed into paper assets that, in good market conditions, could be cycled quickly from persons to person, person to corporation, corporation to corporation, and so on.' The 'representation of land on documents participated in a metaphysical revolution by which words and numbers could stand in for something larger and concrete'[109] – or, in liberal-order language, the liberal consolidation of a coherent regime of property was, simultaneously, a *material reality*, a *complex of social relations*, a *philosophical problem*, the nucleus of a *vast cultural system*, and the *seedbed of profound contradictions for any twentieth-century Canadian nationalism*. Donald Creighton paralleled this neo-Marxist point brilliantly in his fine *précis* of John A. Macdonald's views of 1845: '[S]erious change in the established law of private property implied, without any question, the utter subversion of the existing social and political order.'[110]

Thus, as Creighton's observation suggests, for those closely identified with the project of Canada, questions of property went to the heart of the emergent political order. And we should remember that the propertied freeholder was just one of a whole new population of self-contained individuals – self-employed professionals, self-possessed debaters in the House of Commons, self-disciplined and temperate heads of household, self-improving businessmen, indeed a veritable army of self-made men – whose status and power were simultaneously produced and confirmed by their command over property, both movable and immovable. In bewhiskered plentitude, they crowd the pages of *Canadian Men and Women of Their Time*. Their cenotaphs and mausoleums tower over the anonymous paupers' graves in the city cemeteries (on the understanding that, even in the face of their Maker, individuals were only *formally* equal in a liberal order). Across big-city and even small-town Canada they would erect vast castles – one thinks of Craigdarroch in Victoria, Casa Loma in Toronto – which *seemed* to be confident representations of their own propertied status, and hence their claim to authority and power in the system – and yet which also suggested, by their very appeal to the romance of a pre-liberal feudal age, a fretful nostalgia for a time when property was not so fluid, so distressingly 'intangible.'[111]

Paradoxically, the liberal revolution, in so 'liquefying' property – in cleansing it of any seventeenth-century ('Lockean') preoccupation with any *direct* need to 'mix' labour into that over which one claimed ownership – also intensified its contradictions. As property became ever more alienable, transferable, and reified, it also became more abstract and 'metaphysical,' transcending the merely physical world of farms and ships to a more exalted realm of joint stock companies, conglomerates, and exchanges. Thus he who says 'liberalism' also implies, in the twentieth century at any rate, 'capitalist modernity' – as these temporally and analytically distinct projects came to be closely articulated to each other.

In the liberal gospel of improvement, seemingly contradictory dualisms – equality and accumulation, self-government and empire, wealth and poverty – could be reconciled. Propertyless individuals, peoples, or countries could be 'objectively' grasped as those who were merely as yet 'unimproved' and consequently incapable of self-government. As Uday Singh Mehta remarks (a propos of Bentham, Macaulay, and the Mills, *père et fils*), when confronted with the unfamiliar, such liberal theorists did little more than '"repeat," presume on, and assert ... the familiar structures of the generalities that inform the reasonable, the useful, the knowledgeable, and the progressive.' Without having *experienced* a moment of a colony's existence, they were able 'to compare and classify the world.' (It is difficult for a Canadian reading this critique not to think of Lord Durham, in his striking assessment of the 'barbarous' French Canadians, which provided the foundation upon which he could so authoritatively pronounce on their supposed lack of a history or a literature.)[112] Yet this knowledge was 'braided with the urge to dominate the world because the language of those comparisons is not neutral and cannot avoid notions of superiority and inferiority, backward and progressive, and higher and lower.'[113] In the distorted mirrors of the various nationalist myth-symbol complexes constructed in the second and third quarters of the twentieth century to help 'explain' Canadians to themselves, what has been systematically obscured is the extent to which the Canadian project extended and intensified this British colonizing gaze.

Property – as a coherent complex of claims, things, rights, traditions, and even people – is also the interface between liberalism and capitalism. Liberal order and capitalism cannot be conflated. Yet, after the 1840s, they also could not be easily separated. Crises in the latter – and the business cycles already evident in the 1830s would become sharply experienced catastrophes in the 1870s, on the eve of the Great War, and most famously in the interwar period – strongly affected the former. What was remarkable – as James Struthers's foundational work on less eligibility, along with much other work, has revealed – was how stubbornly the categories of classical liberalism persisted, even in the face of socio-economic structures that seemingly proved them obsolete.[114] On the level of the individual, property functioned as both the tangible manifestation of success and a more abstract measure of political and social worthiness – not only providing the legal qualification for formal participation in many political activities but also generating many of the core terms – respectability, propriety, prosperity, initiative, improvement, 'free enterprise' – of social and political debate. The lines between the propertied and the propertyless, the competent and the indigent, the self-supporting and the dependent, the public and the private were emphatically drawn in classical liberalism. They were not to be casually blurred. And they cannot be marginalized in any responsible historical account.

As Liberal Party leader Edward Blake put it so well in 1881: '[A]mongst the most valuable liberties in connection with property is freedom to sell or exchange it to the best advantage, freedom to dispose of it where you will, to whom you will upon the best terms you can ... We think that a free and voluntary exchange is to the mutual benefit of both parties who effect the exchange, and we believe that that position is established by the mere fact that it is a voluntary exchange, because if it had not been suitable to both parties it would not have taken place at all.' 'Here,' legal historian R.C.B. Risk astutely remarks, 'liberty was liberty from regulation by the state to participate in a private market, not the liberty to participate in the public life of the community.'[115]

5. Was Canada a 'Liberal Democracy' from 1840 to 1940?

Yet those critics of the liberal order framework who have so staunchly attacked its emphasis on property might quite justifiably point out that in this quotation Blake did *not* in fact place property at the centre of his ideological framework. Property rights were the third of the great 'liberties' to which he declared allegiance; prior to them, in his own mind, were 'political liberties,' the rights of the people 'to influence their government, especially the right to make government responsible to them,' and 'civil liberties,' the rights of individuals about their own conduct, 'especially their rights to liberty from restraint by government.'[116] As his case suggests, the useful heuristic device of imagining a 'hierarchy' of liberal values, with property trumping liberty and equality, cannot be interpreted mechanically: we are unlikely to find many documented instances of actually existing liberals consciously weighing such abstractions in their minds. Rather, it is a way of conceptualizing the *implicit* valuations permeating a liberal order – one that might not have completely accorded with a classical liberal's own sense of the social and political world. The conflation of worthiness with prosperity may simply have been part of Blake's common sense – as self-evident and obvious a reality as, say, the inherent 'independence' of adult male individuals when compared with 'dependent' women and children. Let us take up these *other* liberties extolled by Blake in turn.

With respect to political liberties, a recurrent pattern in liberal rejoinders to the liberal order framework is to argue that Blake's 'rights of the people' were *democratic* rights. The coming of Canadian liberal order meant the planting of an ideal of *deliberative democracy*. 'By 1854,' Jeff McNairn argues, in his immensely stimulating study, 'a liberal public sphere existed in Upper Canada. Its ideals and claims were integrated into the province's constitutional and social self-understanding. The acceptance of public opinion and deliberative democracy was something of a revolution. Pre-democratic concepts and assumptions were exploded in ways that remind us why contemporaries expended so much effort in public debate and why they sought to invest it with more authority.'[117] Since few today, and certainly no Gramscians, would dispute the value and significance of democratic deliberation, the argument that Canadian liberals were also democrats would seem to weigh heavily in their favour and creates a disposition to overlook contrary evidence. If we grow impatient with George Brown's anti-Catholicism, Wilfrid Laurier's stern warnings against the 'virus of democracy,' or the anti-Semitism of Goldwin Smith and J.W. Bengough,[118] we need merely fast-forward, in these liberal teleologies, to that postmodern age of democratic enlightenment and liberal tolerance that we ourselves apparently inhabit. Yet the impact of such polemically useful but analytically unsatisfying approaches is to undercut the possibility of a sober and realistic assessment of actually existing liberalism as a phenomenon in Canadian history from the 1840s to the 1950s, that is, when the country attained and developed the political institutions that still govern it.

True belief can thus be fortified against any and all empirical or logical objections. Such ideological blinkers raise the question, as Mehta remarks, of whether the 'exclusionary thrust of liberal history stems from the misapprehension of the generative basis of liberal universalism or whether, in contrast, liberal history projects with greater focus and onto a larger canvas the theoretically veiled and qualified truth of liberal universalism.' Through a close analysis of Locke, Mehta notes that behind the capacities ascribed to all human beings exists 'a thicker set of social credentials that constitute the real bases of political inclusion.' By specifying the capacities sufficient for an individual's political inclusion, Lockean liberalism conceals the specific cultural and psychological conditions that are the preconditions of these capacities. 'Liberal exclusion works,' Mehta concludes, 'by modulating the distance between the interstices of human capacities and the conditions for their political effectivity.' The distinction between universal capacities and the conditions for their actualization 'points to a space in which the liberal theorist can, as it were, raise the ante for political inclusion.' Through largely unadmitted conventions and cultural presumptions, one is thus able to define the 'individual' to exclude many categories of people from the supposedly universal capacity to reason. With respect to J.S. Mill's *On Liberty*, for example, Mehta notices the centrality of the three pivotal restrictions Mill attaches to the universal application of the principle of liberty: 'First, it applies only to mature adults ... Second, ... the principle of liberty has no application to backward societies. And finally, it requires that society not be in a state of war or severe internal turmoil.'[119] In short, the utopianism of the liberal vision can always be rescued by noting the exceptional circumstances that impeded its full real-world realization. This pattern of ideological defensiveness is repeatedly evident in the present volume.

Following Mehta's lead, what may seem to be 'betrayals' of liberalism with respect to how the Canadian architects of liberal order treated the First Nations were, on the contrary, fully in accord with both the *Second Treatise of Government* and *On Liberty*. In the first instance, not only was the general exclusion of 'Indians' from full-membership in the liberal order fully warranted by Locke's labour theory of property, but also – as Barbara Arneil has so convincingly demonstrated – the Amerindian case actually provided the factual basis for Locke's 'state of nature,' which was not (as many had previously believed) a merely speculative device, but rather an abstraction based on a reading of pre-contact North American history.[120] And in the second instance, Mill's three significant preconditions of liberty – that is, mature adulthood, advanced social institutions, peace – could easily be used to categorize the inhabitants of the immense territories outside southern cities and their agrarian hinterlands. Many of these territories were, throughout the period 1840–1940, populated by (to take Mill's *On Representative Government* as our guide) 'savages' whose 'improvement cannot come from themselves, but must be superinduced from without.'[121] Mill might have raised his eyebrows at the church/state alliance and the multifaceted regimes of discipline and punishment in the residential schools through which the liberal state established pedagogical authority over Native children. Yet it is difficult to find grounds in his work for a wholehearted rejection of these liberal re-education camps, since they seem obviously aligned with his own vision of improvement.

Individualism and improvement were thus both *positive* and *negative* concepts. They were the *positive* results of the wise policies of Canada, as it nurtured a consensus among those imagined to be uneducated and the childlike. They were the *negative* criteria by which to exclude the objects of policy from any participation in its formulation. Ironically, though 'human nature' in some settings is a liberal abstraction that supposedly sustains individuality and freedom, in the perpetual 'exceptional states' on the spatial edges of Canada's liberal empire, it functioned more as an argument for the exclusion and subjugation of the colonized. A more realistic, and arguably more respectful, treatment would probe both the 'negative' strengths and 'positive' limits of the Canadian liberal order as a political experiment.

And within the social and regional nucleus of the project, these strengths were many. As Jeff McNairn has argued so well and so eloquently, by the 1840s, operating against a backdrop of 'relatively similar assumptions and values,' 'the public sphere had overcome several older assumptions about difference and inequality,' although how it '[might] fare under conditions of deeper moral and epistemic pluralism' remained a question. 'Public opinion,' as it was understood in Upper Canada, had 'vanquished its original foes' and was 'full of revolutionary promise,' yet 'its ideals of inclusion and reason' were often betrayed and 'some of its internal tensions and potential pitfalls unforeseen.'[122] In this he is surely partly right. No historian of the nineteenth century can avoid evidence that many white male Canadians felt, deeply, that they were fully empowered participants in the political order. A language of liberty appealed deeply to them. If in the United States many of the great debates about freedom and citizenship centred on the Supreme Court, in the Canadian setting they were often (as Paul Romney and Robert Vipond have shown in the case of Ontario) shaped by traditions of provincial autonomy and grassroots political activism.[123] No one today can read the impassioned speeches of Joseph Howe, the editorials of George Brown's *Globe*, or the in-depth and detailed polemics surrounding Confederation itself without coming away with a greatly enhanced sense of the dignity and potential of public debate. Moreover, as McNairn so sagely observes, close attention to the liberal public sphere mitigates any exaggerated notion of atomism: one discovered in such debates 'individuals [who] were ... largely the product of their relations with others. Prejudices were worn off, manners polished, the value of tolerance learned, the desire to know stimulated, and the tools with which to listen, participate, and evaluate fashioned through interactions with others.'[124]

And yet, an unmistakable note of elegy enters into his eloquent celebration of the liberal Enlightenment's subsequent Ontario career. Pondering several of the emergent limitations of this supposed mid-nineteenth-century liberal 'deliberative democracy' – such as the degeneration of parliamentary debate or the new 'marketing and advertising tools' that could potentially 'manipulate a mass market,' McNairn echoes John Stuart Mill when he argues that the 'process of intellectual maturation' was still unconcluded.[125]

Janet Ajzenstat, although differing fundamentally with McNairn on the question of property, nonetheless takes his arguments for mid-nineteenth-century deliberative democracy even further in *The Canadian Founding* (2007). She in essence argues that a passionate commitment to deliberative democracy animated both the Fathers of Confederation (i.e., the famous thirty-three men who drafted the key resolution at Quebec in 1864) and the Founders of Confederation (i.e., those provincial legislators who debated Confederation in 'ratification debates' from 1865 to 1873). Underneath the seemingly prosaic provisions of the Constitution Act (1867), she argues, can be found the radical doctrines of John Locke. Specifically, both Founders and Fathers supported Locke's doctrine, outlined in the *Second Treatise of Government*, that legitimate government requires the consent of the people: 'All argued that there is no legitimate government without the people's consent. They disagreed only about the means to obtain this consent.'[126] All of them, that is, subscribed to Locke's view that 'no Government can have a right to obedience from a people who have not freely consented to it.'[127] Both Fathers and Founders believed that Parliament would secure key political values – 'equality, nondiscrimination, the rule of law, and the mores of representative government. Everyone in the union would be equally subject to Parliament's laws; every individual would be equally entitled to the benefits of "peace, order and good government."'[128] Convinced they were founding a new nation, they were just as certain that its people must be sovereign. They viewed Parliament as 'the institution that embodies the sense of nationhood because it represents equally everyone in the country and because, as they supposed, parliamentary deliberation gives everyone an equal voice in national affairs.'[129] In their minds, 'Parliament represents all subject to the law. And, even more foreign to our present-day way of thinking, they argued that Parliament secures the rights of all.' The essential political structure of the country, as they imagined it, would thus rest upon 'popular sovereignty, parliamentary sovereignty, and the rule of law.' Although all the parliamentarians were male and elected on a limited franchise, 'they were charged with the task of representing everyone within the country's boundaries, regardless of gender, class, minority nationality, and similar distinctions. This was the understanding in constitutional law at the time: Parliament represents and speaks for everyone who is compelled to obey its measures; it does not represent only the party winning a plurality of seats in the lower chamber, or only the electorate, or indeed, only men.' They intended to 'make of the new union a country among the countries of the world and to express Canadian nationhood,' and a core attribute of this new nation was deliberate democracy, as exemplified in Parliament. For here one found, at least in the Fathers' own conceptions of it, an institution that would provide 'a good and sufficient guarantee of national identity in the "civic" sense because – as they supposed – it excludes no one. There is no admission ticket, so to speak. No one is required to show proof of agreement with the majority on the interpretation of Canadian history, the importance of economics, Canada-America relations, or the proper role of Canadians on the world stage ... Being subject to Parliament's edicts suffices to make one a fully fledged Canadian, equally subordinate to the law and equally entitled to the law's benefits. And ... equally entitled to voice one's opinions.' Even if, at times, Canadian practices have 'often fallen short,' it is in Locke's *Second Treatise* and in the dreams of deliberative democracy in the 1860s that we find 'the founders' hopes.'[130]

Thus, Fathers and Founders were Lockean revolutionaries, intent upon founding a new nation on the principles of deliberative democracy and popular sovereignty. Even John A. Macdonald, not conventionally associated with subaltern radicalism, emerges on this reading as a 'proponent of popular sovereignty, an equalitarian, and a defender of parliamentary free speech.' Ajzenstat goes so far as to suggest that, in endorsing popular sovereignty, the Fathers and the Founders were even implicitly supporting the people's right of revolution: '[T]he doctrine of popular sovereignty that underpins our modern rights doctrines rests on – is derived from, necessarily entails – the right of revolution.' They were following a political philosophy that taught that 'there are no natural kings and no natural slaves. Kings *may* rule but only with the sovereign people's consent. One person may serve another but does not relinquish – indeed, cannot relinquish – the right to walk away from servitude.'[131]

Although they might disagree with one another over the ways in which popular sovereignty should be expressed – that is, over referring the Confederation question to legislatures or to a popular referendum – both Fathers and Founders supposedly believed that they were placing their scheme before a sovereign people. And in many respects, Ajzenstat hints, those who preferred to put the scheme to parliaments were more attuned to deliberative democracy: 'The legislators in the referendum camp think of the people, or come close to thinking of the people, as a homogeneous entity, a sort of single-minded giant who will announce its "yea" or "nay" with one strong voice. Adherents of the parliamentary camp regard "the people" as a heterogeneous mass of irreconcilable interests. Where political freedom prevails, disagreement, complaint, and opposition are the norm.' The heart of the case for entrusting Parliament with constitution-making is that, in 'law and tradition, Parliament is understood to represent the whole population in all its diversity. It represents equally all individuals subject to the law ... Parliament represents all and hears all and has necessarily developed a process of political deliberation that respects political minorities. A parliamentary majority, a deliberative majority, is more inclusive than the raw majority of a referendum, and because more inclusive, it has more legitimacy.'[132]

Thus, argues Ajzenstat, we have sorely misjudged the Canadian Fathers' handiwork, for what they forged was no mere 'second-rate thing of its kind,' but 'an excellent example of an Enlightenment constitution.' Such frameworks have proved durable, she remarks. 'Their record in protecting the equal right to life and liberty is unexcelled. It may be objected that the record is not perfect. I would agree that it is not. But there is none better.' 'The founders sought to secure the individual against the arbitrary and self-interested acts of autocratic rulers, bullies, and demagogues. They were very clear about the fact that governments and majorities can be oppressive.' For in this 'democratic Constitution' lies the best protection of our right *'to life, liberty, and property'* and the best guarantee of a Parliament whose very inclusiveness and freedom of deliberation 'protect dissent, political opposition, political minorities, and thus our political and legal equality.'[133]

Ajzenstat thus builds upon McNairn's thesis of a deliberative democracy in Upper Canada to mount a spirited defence of the democratic sensibilities of the founders of Canada as a whole – or, in Gramscian terms, the organic intellectuals of the new historical bloc through which Canada as a liberal project was consolidated. There is much to commend in these New Whig interpretations of Canadian history. Along with the equally innovative work of Romney and Vipond, they do much to lay the groundwork for the concept of a mid-nineteenth-century liberal revolution. At the same time, and most acutely in Ajzenstat's dramatically revisionist account, one is forcibly reminded of Gramsci's critique of Benedetto Croce's liberal historiography – that it was a form of idealistic utopianism, one that claimed to be a 'disinterested contemplation of the eternal becoming of human history,' but in fact rendered impossible an engagement with actually existing liberalism.[134] The upshot of this utopianism, Gramsci argued, was to produce an intensely abstract and speculative history incapable of a sustained and rigorous engagement with actual events. In the Canadian case, even if one overlooks the powerful empirical counter-evidence against the claims for 'deliberative democracy' as a constituent part of 'Canada's Founding' – such as the *explicit renunciations* of any such doctrine on the part of certain prominent Fathers, the glaring case of the Imperial overriding of the plain wishes of the Nova Scotia electorate to resist Confederation and subsequently to repeal it,[135] and the absence of any such 'Founding Debates' in the vast stretches of the lands claimed by the Hudson's Bay Company absorbed by the new Canadian state as so much uninhabited 'real estate' – one still comes up against the more formidable problem of essentialist idealism. In this school, any phenomena that do not correspond to the idealized 'liberalism' can be dealt with, not by accounting for them, but by 'cancelling them' by pointing out that, years later, such anomalies would come to be seen as exceptions to a unilinear, 'onwards and upwards' path of liberal reform and improvement.[136] Much of the New Whig interpretation of Canadian history works through an aggressive 'reading in' of political and philosophical positions, construed as transcendental essences, rather than by providing convincing evidence that either Fathers or Founders clearly defended them in theory or instantiated them in practice. If Macdonald, Cartier, and their comrades-in-arms in Confederation were indeed revolutionary equalitarians intent upon establishing a democratic public sphere, they were remarkably circumspect, not to say self-contradictory, in their selection of strategies. A non-elected senate with substantial property qualifications? A potent Crown? The imperial honours system?[137] A gender-specific, property-conscious franchise? The exclusion of ('non-civilized') Natives? Only under duress can the Constitution Act (1867) be made to sound like the U.S. Constitution and the Declaration of Independence or the Indian Act (1876) be made to read like the Charter of Rights and Freedoms (1982) and the Canadian Multiculturalism Act (1988). Moreover, on many crucial questions of policy – war and peace, the constitution itself – the British sovereign as instructed by the Imperial Parliament was *still the sovereign*. It seems curious to leave out of the discussion of supposedly influential doctrines of popular sovereignty any conception of the actually existing sovereign.[138] This *colonial* 'deliberative democracy' was precluded from deliberation, democratic or otherwise, not only upon certain 'exceptional' or 'unusual' issues, but also upon such seemingly basic questions as its own constitution, foreign policy, and head of state.

Thus, for all their imagination, iconoclasm, and emergent influence, the new school of Whig historians may be offering us a rather naive and simplistic master narrative, one that too readily abolishes historical evidence in the pursuit of conformity to a rigid ideology. They might usefully complicate their single-minded and unilinear approach through a critical dialogue with its liberal-order alternative. The Whigs' 'Story of Canadian Liberty' might be made more interesting and more accurate by noticing counter-currents and nuances. The concepts of historical bloc and hegemony lead us, not on such utopian quests for philosophical essences and pure origins, but to practical politics as influenced in complex and continuing ways by socially embodied theoretical frameworks. On the basis of this very different approach to historical inquiry, an alternative way of looking at the mid-nineteenth-century liberal revolution would be one that interprets its politico-ethical 'strengths' and 'limits' as two mutually constitutive aspects of the same hegemonic process of liberal state formation.[139] The strengths of deliberative debate (especially as the ruling group expanded its position, with the encouragement of Sydenham's revolutionary dictatorship and the regimes established by his successors, to embrace more and more social strata) were equally those that figure as its limits (as this expanded historical bloc also exerted itself mightily to contain and repress those who, by long-lasting liberal definitions, were characterized by what we might call their enforced *incapacity to judge*.)[140] The very first years of 'deliberative democracy' as instituted by the Canadian project's organic intellectuals were *necessarily* those of 'imposed cultural change' for many outside this core: for the First Nations, subjected under liberal order to the first consistent application of double-edged enfranchisement legislation aimed at 'civilizing' them out of existence;[141] for workers, whose attempts to develop their own capacity to judge on questions of political economy were forcefully contained, down to the 1940s, by their employers' far more developed capacity to fire them; for women, whose rudimentary pre-1840s voting rights were actually repealed by liberals, who moreover exerted themselves to tighten the bonds of moral regulation over them.[142]

So – in fact, *was* Canada a 'liberal democracy' from 1840 to 1950? One reasonable if unambitious definition of a democracy is a country with a political system that features, to cite Geoff Eley's sensible list, free, universal, secret, adult, and equal suffrage.[143] On this rather minimal basis, it would be difficult to make much of a convincing case for Canadian democracy from 1840 to 1950. First, it was a country that habitually denied the vote in federal and provincial elections to the majority of its adult inhabitants.[144] Second, it was a country that, well past the 1940s, relied (implicitly and often explicitly) on racial criteria for determining who could enter the country, vote in its elections, and receive equal treatment in its courts of law.[145] Third, and perhaps even more basically, if a qualification of a democracy is that 'the people,' however defined and however represented, should be able (as Blake urged) 'to influence their government, especially the right to make government responsible to them,' the obvious fact of the matter is that in colonial Canada, whose constitution, foreign policy, ultimate court of legal appeal, head of state, and so on were all well beyond the scope of 'the people,' many quite fundamental issues were by definition outside the realm of public debate altogether. In fact, down to 1947, there were, legally speaking, no Canadian citizens to whom the Crown or Parliament were answerable.[146] Indeed, as Peter Russell has so powerfully urged, making a case that to my eye Ajzenstat has not effectively answered, it is not at all clear that nineteenth-century Canadians constituted 'a people' or a 'political community' in any meaningful political sense[147] – hence the complex trauma of the Forty Years War on the constitution that continues to mark post-1967 politics, down to our own time.

These aspects of actually existing liberal order tell decisively against seeing Canada from 1840 to 1940 as a 'liberal democracy' – *pace* the many Whig writers who simply run 'liberalism' and 'democracy' together, as though the terms essentially mean the same things. Such restrictions were, at least for the majority outside the liberal historical bloc, something more serious than 'oversights' or 'imperfections.' In an expansive project of colonial liberal order, the capacity to judge of some was dialectically related to the marked political incapacity of many others. This was the profound contradiction of colonialism. Rather than the mere enumeration of mistakes and omissions – they were so benighted back then, we twenty-first-century Canadians tell ourselves so contentedly! – which so easily leads to an ahistorical projection into the past of our own presumed purity, this line of inquiry takes us into more analytically interesting and complicated territory, that of understanding the Canadian project as both enlightenment *and* enslavement, assertion *and* subjugation – and of present-day Canadians as, inextricably and unavoidably, the inheritors of the results of this process. What are conceptualized in the 'Heritage Moments' version of Canadian history (now massively disseminated by a liberal mnemonic apparatus preternaturally alert to the mines buried beneath the tranquil fields of the Peaceable Kingdom) as regrettable (but happily superceded) *exceptions* are interpreted afresh as profound and lasting *contradictions*. They have been buried, not resolved, in the liberal theory and practice of 'Canada.'

Herein lies, perhaps, the logic of some of the contrasting contemporary critiques of the framework, simultaneously taken to task for its traditionalism and its iconoclasm. What is really objectionable about it for liberals, one suspects, is its coolly realistic appraisal of the project of Canada, interpreted afresh as a white settler British dominion embarked upon a transcontinental project of liberal rule entailing coercion, consent, and corruption. It is quite accurate to charge that the liberal order framework takes seriously the generations of political historiography in Canada that it has become fashionable to neglect. Yet it rereads this historiography against its nationalist grain. Against a quasi-official narrative, in which 'liberal democracy' is read back into the words and deeds of Macdonald and Laurier, and a 'liberal nationalism' back into the unpromising text of the Constitution Act (1867) itself – both gestures that, as in the United States, serve as 'noble lies' or 'royal fictions' that work to rebaptize colonial liberals as Canadian democrats[148] – the liberal order framework offers a more analytical approach. It argues that we should go beyond mere lamentations about exclusions and celebrations of inclusions to strive for a logico-historical understanding of their mutual implication and necessary co-dependence within a coherent and contestable political paradigm. Rather than merely reducing to parenthetical exceptions the demographic majority of the population who were (as a matter of fact) *actually* excluded for much of this period, or conversely wringing our hands in academic anguish over the blindness of our liberal forebears, we could grasp their project more interestingly and rigorously as one that required inclusion and exclusion simultaneously, in the rigorous fulfilment of its underlying precepts and its evolving objectives. This would enable us to interpret with greater sensitivity and understanding such related phenomena as the racially segregated schools of liberal Nova Scotia, the political disenfranchisement and social marginalization of the vast armies of immigrant labourers who constructed the country's railways, the deportation of Eastern European dissidents back to tyrannical regimes in Europe, and the Canadian deployment of labour camps, secret trials, and even torture – all of which could be positioned, not as inexplicable departures from the script of liberal order, but rather as tactical fulfilments of its complex imperatives. It would push beyond the Whig Interpretation's mere cataloguing of exceptions, omissions, 'mistakes,' and limits – with its perhaps unintentional overtones of ideological apology – towards a rigorous understanding of the complex underlying contradictions that generated them.

Under the profoundly contradictory conditions of colonialism, the capacity to judge of some, in other words, coexisted with, and was conditioned by, the necessary *incapacity to judge* of many others. If *some* of the country – along its southern borders, in the cities, and within select groups – were living in a political order influenced (at least to some degree) by Locke and Mill, *most* of the country – including almost everyone in most of the subcontinent's north – were living in the rather different land of Hobbes and Schmitt. And sovereign was the regime that ruled upon this decisive distinction – that is, policed the line of exception that separated the entitled minority from the disenfranchised, colonized, and inferiorized majority.[149] This pattern whereby a reasonably coherent and legally enforceable program of property, politics, and personhood was extended across northern North America was racialized, gendered, and regionalized. The result was not an inexplicable series of paradoxes, anomalies, accidents, imperfections, and aporia – but a series of contradictory social and political relations, without which *actually existing liberalism* was unimaginable in Canada.[150]

Thus, one Gramscian position on the project of Canada insists that there was a logic in the proliferation, throughout the interstices of the liberal empire and especially on its geographical and social edges, of harshly authoritarian regimes – of pass laws that anticipated those of South Africa, of harsh religious intolerance with respect to expressions of Aboriginal and other communitarian forms of spirituality, and of dehumanizing and 'individualizing' enumerations of whole populations that ran roughshod over their own collectivist traditions.[151] In this Canada, liberal order arrived with the Indian agents, the residential schools, and the forced relocations. These were not the incidental 'imperfections' of liberal order. They were the 'margins' that defined its 'centre.' They were the logical consequences of its underlying commitment – discernible in Locke and Mill, not to mention George Brown, John A. Macdonald, Oliver Mowat, and Goldwin Smith – to propertied improvement and developmental perfectibility. To grasp liberal order as both a utopian project of individual liberation *and* one of colonialism and subordination – and as both processes *simultaneously* – is to begin to decipher the complexity and the contradictions of the political *and* cultural revolution called 'Canada.'

And, having discussed property and political rights, what of the third of Edward Blake's three great principles of liberal rule – those civil liberties that allowed individuals to express opinions, form associations, freely move about the country, publish books and newspapers, engage in academic and other research without fear of punishment, and, if accused of crimes, confront the case against them in an open court of law, without fear of arbitrary punishment or torture? Since in our own day and age, many of these freedoms, particularly the latter, have been placed under pressure, in large part by accredited liberals themselves,[152] it is refreshing to be reminded of the extent to which the past architects of our political order revered habeas corpus and other pre-liberal conventions. These rights, many of them given new salience by the great eighteenth-century revolutions, were indeed ably defended by some nineteenth-century liberals, and – as Jeff McNairn has eloquently remarked, 'state formation did not occur in spite of liberalization; it was part of the same process.' '[E]ven with its imperfections and contradictions,' he adds, 'public deliberation, rooted in expansive definitions of the rights of free speech and assembly, seemed the best means available to respect individuals as capable, equal agents while empowering strong, effective government to coordinate their collective endeavours.'[153] Here McNairn deftly captures much of the attractiveness of the theory of local grass-roots democracy, as developed in various ways by theorists extending from Rousseau to Marx, whose *The Civil War in France* is perhaps the nineteenth century's most eloquent tribute to grass-roots power and the possibilities of living otherwise.[154] Many Victorian Canadians believed that their basic civil freedoms were guaranteed by the British constitution – so discretely but unmistakably present in the BNA Act itself. Even before the Saskatchewan socialists introduced into Canada its first written bill of rights in 1947, Canadians might still believe they enjoyed substantial British liberties, such as freedom of expression, under their largely unwritten constitution.

Many Canadians were indeed free to express themselves on many issues. Their newspapers and assemblies from the 1840s to the 1940s prove the point. The British tradition was widely seen on the left as one that created more space for meaningful dissent than was found in the twentieth-century United States – as suggested, for instance, by Emma Goldman's ability to operate in Toronto as a public anarchist in the 1920s and 1930s, in marked contrast to her treatment in the United States; or by the august Toronto *Mail and Empire*'s reprinting in 1918 of Trotsky's *The Bolsheviki and Peace*, complete with footnotes; or by the circles of Ukrainian dissidents in Winnipeg who, in a nice moment of left multiculturalism, brought out a Ukrainian-language edition of Anton Pannekoek's *Darwinism and Marxism*, translated from the Dutch.[155] Certainly no freedom-loving radical, and certainly no knowledgeable student of Marx – whose radical-democratic animosity towards officious and meddlesome censorship and repression was a leitmotif of a long career – would cavil at these achievements. For many of these years, Canada was a substantially freer place for left-wing critics of the established order than the United States, France, or Germany. Liberal Canada was not Czarist Russia.

And yet. The pattern from the 1840s to the 1940s actually disallows any such whole-hearted celebration of Canada, Land of the Free. Once again, if even more complexly, the freedom of some coexisted with the marked unfreedom of many others. Basic freedoms – of expression, assembly, conscience – could not in fact be predictably counted upon within the borders of the Liberal Dominion. In the very period that the *Mail and Empire* was reprinting Leon Trotsky, Isaac Bainbridge of the Social Democratic Party of Canada would go to jail repeatedly for reprinting materials in the *Canadian Forward* that were ostensibly far less revolutionary.[156] Moreover, in many ways such freedoms of expression were more radically endangered in the 1910s to 1940s – with their banned political parties, coerced labour camps, a massive apparatus of state surveillance, police shootings and deportations, even officially proscribed *languages* – than in the 1840s. Twentieth-century academic freedom of discussion was (and to a lesser degree remains) precariously positioned within a liberal order – as numerous firings, often on the flimsiest grounds, suggested.[157] Those who were by the order's racialized definitions not fully-fledged individuals – the First Nations most obviously – were explicitly denied civil rights, including the rights to the exercise of their religious beliefs, to assembly, to free movement – even to secure legal assistance to contest such abrogations of their rights.[158]

In essence, whenever and wherever liberal order seemed fundamentally challenged, and especially in those moments of organic crisis when the rights of property were at issue, its rulers would move with awe-inspiring efficiency to contain or, if necessary, deport its opposition.[159] In such periods of organic crisis – that is, ones that put both the socio-economic structure and the historical bloc at risk[160] – liberal freedoms were largely reserved for liberals themselves. Outside the liberal pale, in the vast realm of the 'exception,' other rules applied. Whatever the values of equality and liberty, the 'trump card' of the rights of property was played repeatedly throughout the 1930s and 1940s – as a tocsin for individuals whose property was threatened, as a commanding politico-ethical ideal of 'Free Enterprise,' and as a fundamental principle of the order to which both Prime Ministers Bennett and King were loyal.

The liberal order was born of the passive revolution of the 1840s–

1860s, wherein, seeking to restore normal conditions of law and order after the Rebellions of 1837, and confronting a transnational crisis of enormous proportions (the crisis of the slave republic and the U.S. Civil War, a looming U.S./British conflict punctuated with armed raids on Canadian soil, the abrogation of the Reciprocity Treaty in 1866), a revolutionary regime engineered a far-reaching hegemonic compromise between Tories and Radicals out of which could emerge a new Canadian historical bloc, one eventually capable of undertaking far-ranging economic and social initiatives. Gradually, coercion – mass arrests, executions, deportations, and special councils of the early period of the late 1830s / early 1840s – could be supplemented with consent and corruption, as the state perfected the arts of *trasformismo* and gradually widened its sphere of popular influence. A century later, from the 1920s to the 1940s, the Canadian project entered a second period of organic crisis and initiated a second passive revolution. This moment was characterized by government by order-in-council under the War Measures Act, the outlawing of entire parties, mass arrests and detentions in camps, and the deportation of the Japanese in the 1940s – in essence a vast liberal experiment in racialized social engineering.[161] In this second instance as well, coercion was gradually supplemented by consent, in the form of the unemployment insurance and the calculated inclusion of dissident intellectuals within the state apparatus, and ultimately through a powerful articulation of Canadian nationalism. At both ends of the liberal revolution, the state was vested with extraordinary powers, largely insulated from the burdens of parliamentary democracy, and empowered to act as a decisive and coherent force within civil society without being required to worry very much about the 'rights of the individual.' The undoubted freedoms enjoyed by some between these two book-end passive revolutions were always contingent upon the state's well-demonstrated capacity to suspend them, retroactively and even for decades, if it perceived its fundamental project was in danger. Again and again, the exercise of freedoms of speech and assembly was curtailed by the prior claims of property and public order. Even crimes of sedition and seditious conspiracy, imagined to be relics of the distant past, came back into vogue.[162] Winnipeg activist Fred Dixon was only being slightly facetious when he told the jury sitting on his case in 1920 that, under these conditions, anyone who wrote a letter to the press criticizing the local weed inspector ran the risk of being charged with publishing seditious libel.[163]

Both spatially and temporally, liberal order necessarily entailed the generation of officially demarcated 'exceptional states,' special periods and special spaces, within which foes were marked with precision and punished with an implacable enthusiasm. The passage of the War Measures Act in 1914 provided Canadian proof of the adage 'C'est seulement le provisoire qui dure' – in that its extraordinary provisions for cabinet dictatorship, arrests without trial, and so on, would remain as a weapon in the arsenal of liberal order for a further seventy-four years.[164] The political party one joined in 1911, in the carefree expectation of its free participation in the cut and thrust of open debates in the liberal public sphere, might well be ruled illegal in 1918 – and one's once perfectly legal membership could now become a retroactively applied pretext for arrest, imprisonment, and deportation. Both the main socialist parties of the pre-war era were harried out of effective existence after 1918 – in part because of their own schisms, but in larger part because of the weight of official repression. The condition of civil liberties was such in the 1930s that many astute intellectuals, the level-headed Frank Scott among them, worried that the country was moving towards its own idiosyncratic forms of fascism.[165]

Conventional liberal historiography remembers some of these moments, without doing much with them. The official mnemonic apparatus encourages us to lament the influence of the few 'bad apples' – Hepburn, Aberhart, Duplessis – and the odd 'unfortunate mistake' – the 1937–57 Quebec Padlock Law,[166] the Head Tax, the internment and subsequent disenfranchisement of Japanese Canadians by the Liberal government in the 1940s, the War Measures Act. A critical-realist approach, on the other hand, would zero in on such exceptional periods and spaces as fascinating indications of underlying organic tensions within the liberal project itself.

As John Gray has suggested, in his brave reflections on the core incoherence of contemporary liberal theory, within any *actually existing liberalism* under conditions of value pluralism, liberal freedoms may not only coexist with difficulty but may, in fact, undermine each other.[167] In the Canadian case, and repeatedly, liberty and equality were undermined by property and the imperatives of the security state. For example, in the Canadian case, the achievement of the mid-nineteenth-century historic compromise required the conciliation of the Catholic Church in Québec, which thereby became, ironically enough, a constituent part of a project associated with the very liberalism it so staunchly critiqued. The church enjoyed far-ranging quasi-state powers in education, social services, and northern colonization (among other things).

With respect to 'freedom of conscience,' it was able to impose some substantial limitations on the actual exercise of any such freedom – as evidence by its successful elimination of the liberal-democratic Institut Canadien, the denial of a Catholic burial to the freethinking Guibord in the 1870s, and its even more extraordinary ability to curtail so dangerous a project to order and good government as the construction of Montreal's first public library.[168] The 'freedom of conscience' beloved of liberal theory was thus, in this instance, subordinated to the pragmatics of liberal order. Even more striking on a Dominion-wide level was the church/state alliance in constructing the liberal order's most imposing and imaginative disciplinary apparatus, the residential schools, wherein its precepts of hard work, individualism, and property frequently coexisted with seemingly 'illiberal' proscriptions on the use of native languages and the rights of native parents to raise their own children. Freedom of conscience was deeply compromised in institutions designed to effect a top-down cultural revolution.

From 1840 to 1950, with respect to the related freedoms of association and assembly, one notes some equally interesting contradictions. Certainly, at the social and cultural core of the project – among the Euro-Canadian propertied individuals and their kin – there was a great and largely unregulated flourishing of voluntary societies and clubs, fraternal orders and charitable societies.[169] Yet subaltern associations that, by design or implication, placed liberal property rights at risk were far more embattled. The deeply ambiguous status of trade unions is a case in point. As J.M.S. Careless so discerningly wrote in the case of George Brown, 'An adherent of British mid-Victorian liberalism could hardly deny the principle of the freedom of association. But – and it was a large *but* – labour associations could not infringe on another basic liberal principle, freedom of contract ... [H]is attitude was based on more than self-interest and natural class bias; *it reflected an intellectually consistent set of doctrines regarding economic freedom and natural laws that he ardently believed were right and almost divinely revealed.*'[170]

As Careless so powerfully argued, in this case there *was* a hierarchy of values – and freedom of association was trumped by the claims of property. Within what he so eloquently describes as a 'consistent set of doctrines,' workers' associations became highly questionable at the precise moment they called into question the free-standing individual's right to manage his own affairs. It would take almost a century – from the 1850s to the 1940s – to reach a radically different understanding of the rights of labour, through a system of industrial legality that in essence legitimized unions, with the understanding that they actively edit out those dissidents who most strenuously contested the 'rights of property.'[171] William Lyon Mackenzie King, so strangely disregarded by so many of the new Whigs yet so obviously one of the pivotal organic intellectuals of the twentieth-century liberal state, was working entirely within the framework he had inherited from the nineteenth century when he developed his finely honed distinctions between the 'deserving' and the 'undeserving' labour movements. The first were distinguished by their acceptance, and the latter by their critique, of liberal concepts of private property. The former would receive the state's consideration and even patronage. The latter would be restricted and, if necessary, forcibly crushed.[172] For many Canadians, in short, Anthony Arblaster's pithy observation would have had the ring of truth: in the expression 'Liberal democracy,' the 'adjective "Liberal" has the force of a qualification.'[173]

6. Reconnaissance and Immanent Critique

Neither 'hegemony,' 'historical bloc,' nor 'passive revolution' lend themselves to master narratives or unilinear theories of history. They provide us, not with grand theories of everything, but with useful ways of generalizing about specific situations. They function best as bridging concepts, which make visible connections between seemingly disparate phenomena – connections the working historian must obviously then test against archival and other evidence.

'Reconnaissance' is a more succinct term to describe this quest – that is, the challenge of producing a critical and realistic knowledge about the world under conditions of postmodernity. The metaphor implies that historical knowledge is both possible and necessary. That is, it argues, against the currents of radical nominalism that were especially popular within the liberal academy in the last quarter of the twentieth century, that it is possible to acquire knowledge about historical processes, whose necessary preconditions – or underlying 'generative mechanisms' – are susceptible to logical and empirical investigation. It holds that while many stories about these processes should be told, some stories are better – that is, more coherent, evidence-based, and comprehensive – than others.[174] At the same time, the very metaphor of reconnaissance – a scout's report from the terrain, in all its inevitable incompleteness – is meant to draw out both the urgency of the struggle for historical knowledge and its precariousness. Even on so small a topic as Canadian liberal order, no human being today could read more than a fraction of the pertinent books and articles (especially if one attempted to trace actually existing liberal institutions back to their intellectual origins in early modern Europe or to work forward to contemporary theoretical reflections on their implications). Reconnaissance is not synthesis, a scout is not a guru, and, under conditions of postmodernity, totalizing claims to the completeness and closure associated with 'master narratives' (such as those now put forward by neo-liberals) are not credible.

A final implication of reconnaissance should be mentioned here: its radical break with individualistic styles of scholarship. It metaphorically suggests that any particular scout's report is meaningful only within a collective context. At least as one might imagine it – actually existing academic life works rather differently – the intellectual context within which such projects of reconnaissance would flourish would be a radically post-individualist one. Reconnaissance assumes a willingness to take risks, make errors, and unsettle conventional knowledge. It places a premium on the generation of falsifiable claims. Metaphorically, at least, it is not the scout's individual capacities or subjective desires that are centrally at issue in the reception of a report, but the accuracy and usefulness of the report itself – that is, not merely as a plausible *depiction* of a field, but also as a realistic prescription for *re-occupying* it. Critical realism urges us to ask, what elements were *necessarily* in place for a given historical development? And what are the concepts we need to grasp them? The scout who undertakes a political act of research does not do so with the aim of dampening critiques but of arousing them – since the successful occupation of the new terrain requires the calibration of many such reports.

In this spirit, one turns to the framework's often very thoughtful and insightful critics. In addition to raising the question of property, which we have already discussed, critics have focused on periodization, place, definition, reductionism, and ideology.

One might first self-critically wonder about the framework's strict parameters of time and place. Does the frame of the 'long liberal revolution' from the 1840s to the 1940s actually encompass the decisive moments in the history of liberal order in northern North America? As we see in so much exciting new work on the history of British North America from 1710 to 1840, many issues important to the liberal order framework were first debated then. Such a long revolution surely had deep roots – as evident, for instance, in policies with respect to the accommodation of Catholicism within the British Empire after the Conquest of Acadia in 1710,[175] or regarding the rights of the First Nations in the Royal Proclamation of 1763.

Yet there are real risks in reading liberal order back into periods before the term or many of the ideas associated with it were clearly in general circulation. It is all too easy to slip into the Eurocentric patterns so tellingly analysed by post-colonial theory, in which (as Frantz Fanon suggested) the colonizers arrive with a heroic narrative, which then overpowers and even destroys any pre-existing sense of history.[176] The First Nations formed the majority over most of the land mass claimed by the Dominion of Canada. Even if we focus only on the 'neo-Europes' that arose as the decisive nuclei of liberal order in the south, and pay close attention to the emergence of liberal themes – for instance, de facto freehold tenure and mercantile independence in Acadia in the early seventeenth century[177] and the much-more-extensively celebrated emergence of representative government in Nova Scotia in the eighteenth century – we run the risk of overlooking the Aboriginal context within which all such developments necessarily occurred.[178] Moreover, attributing a quasi-hegemonic status to certain highly visible minorities (such as the Loyalists) may unduly homogenize and elevate a notoriously amorphous group into a ruling status they did not generally enjoy. It might also lead us to oversimplify the United States as the stably demonized revolutionary 'counter-example,' without due regard for the extent to which both British North American 'civic humanists' in the 1830s and Canadian Liberals in the 1870s and 1880s adopted U.S. ideas, notwithstanding their supposed republican taint.[179]

In the many neo-Europes of northern North America before their consolidation in a Dominion-wide liberal order, we also find a host of European-derived aliberal social formations. In some cases there were undoubtedly processes that 'cleared the slate' for eventual liberal ordering: here one would think, on Jerry Bannister's useful suggestion, of the deportation of the Acadians in 1755 as a prelude to the more clearly individualized and state-organized property-holding patterns of the New Englanders succeeding them. Yet against such moments of precocious 'individualization,' one would also want to place equally glaring instances in which the imperial tie led to the attempted reinvention in North America of various *ancien régime* customs and institutions – from the unusual use of the royal prerogative in Nova Scotia's coalfields to settle royal jewellery debts, to the reinvigoration of the seigneurial system under the British regime in Québec from the 1760s to the 1850s, to the Anglican design in Upper Canada, in which the clergy reserves and other privileges of a semi-established church were only gradually forced to cede before the colony's stubbornly non-conforming demographic and religious realities.

There would seem to be fewer risks in reading liberal order *forward*, but in fact this may also pose significant interpretive challenges. A significant theme within international liberalism was the 'discovery of the social' in the *fin de siècle* – essentially, an attempt to reconcile individualism with the evident non-individualistic processes documented by students of social evolution, institutional economics, and social history. A host of British writers developed the 'new liberalism,' which sought to integrate social evolutionary themes into political theory.[180] Somewhat similar patterns have been found in Canada, especially with regard to the 'Queensian' liberals who would eventually migrate in some numbers to the interwar federal civil service.[181] Intellectuals of this persuasion were also significant within the first substantial academic left, which emerged in the 1920s and 1930s.[182] Much of this 'new liberalism,' diffused through a gradual process of permeation, had become plainly a force to reckon with in the coming of the welfare state in the 1940s. Nonetheless, one can make the argument that, in terms of actually existing liberal governance, until that decade the 'new liberals' modified but did not fundamentally rework the structures of liberal order.[183]

Since the late 1970s, 'new liberalism' has been largely superseded by 'neo-liberalism.' (It is interesting that both the major 'left' and 'right' twentieth-century developments of the classical paradigm nonetheless preserved the term 'liberalism' itself). Its key theorists, most notably the enormously influential F.A. Hayek, have insisted they *are* truer believers than the true believers – as evidenced by their reverence for property rights and market freedoms.[184] Many consider their movement to be the revival of classical liberalism – as John Gray explains, '[W]e find in Hayek a restatement of classical liberalism in which it is purified of [its] errors.'[185] As Chandran Kukathas observes, F.A. Hayek's influence in the history of twentieth-century liberalism 'has ... been enormous.' He inspired many of the classical liberal think tanks that have changed the policy-making agenda around the world.[186] At the same time, the 'left' opponents of neo-liberalism, confusingly known in the United States as 'liberals,' attack its very theoretical credentials, note its under-theorized reliance on Darwinistic ideas, and argue that its 'libertarianism' constitutes a departure from the more socially grounded liberalism of the nineteenth century.[187] It might be presumptuous for a non-liberal radical democrat to pronounce upon such questions of doctrine, yet it does seem, to this historian at any rate, that there is very much in contemporary neo-liberalism that George Brown and the middle-class readership of the *Family Herald* would have recognized at a hundred paces.[188] What seems different is not the doctrine so much as the wider context within which it functions. As Girard suggests, nineteenth-century liberal individualism was often 'embedded' in restraining contexts – familial, religious, national, or merely ethical. Free of many such constraints, twenty-first-century neo-liberalism seems freer to totalize the social world. Both 'new liberalism' and 'neo-liberalism' suggest the enduring capacity of the ideology to generate debates that routinely extend right to its doctrinal fundamentals. How this field of forces will eventually be understood is unclear, but it does seem probable that a firm grasp on the patterns of liberal order from the 1840s to the 1940s will provide some useful benchmarks for studies of the contemporary period.

Others wonder why the liberal order framework should be so focused on Canada, when colonialism functioned in similar ways throughout the world – as the new imperial historians have demonstrated. In theory, there is no reason why the framework should be confined to the borders of a particular nation-state, and in fact one of the arguments it has raised against the New Whigs targets their anachronistic 'reading back' of conceptions of Canadian national sovereignty that do not fully apply in a colonial context. Here one remembers Gramsci's own highly internationalist conception of passive revolution, which (as we have seen) explains the Italian state's distinctive political trajectory in terms of its geohistorical dilemmas. Rather than treating 'Canada' as a 'case,' then, one might rather conceptualize it as a 'node' within a global process, generating social phenomena comparable to those of other 'nodes,' because they are all the *outcomes* or *moments* of an historically integrated process.'[189] The Canadian processes of passive revolution and liberal ordering thus merit exploration in their own right, yet also provide rich materials for more global analyses of such processes worldwide. The reconnaissance of Canadian liberal order has everything to gain from rigorous comparative history – a precondition of which is a more accurate and analytical understanding of the project of Canada itself, one that was, one might say, always already transnational.

In addition to these temporal and spatial critiques, we find those that, accepting the centrality of liberal order, seek to revisit liberalism's definition, in the interests of paying due attention to an important principle seemingly overlooked in its minimalist triune formulation. Looking at liberalism from various points of view – feminism, critical race theory, environmentalism, to cite three strong contenders; or queer theory, religious history, and the critical history of nationalism, others might quite rightly add – often leads to calls to expand the definition of liberalism itself. Modifying the ideal type of the classical liberal – the person who, in his calculation of true individuals and genuine individualism, implicitly or explicitly conjugates values of liberty, equality, and property – these friendly critics would often add to the definition a commitment to patriarchy, racialism, heteronormativity, environmental domination, and administrative rationality – and so on.

These may be, one and all, valid extensions of the concept of liberal order. Yet a useful distinction can be drawn between the core definition of a political paradigm and its many theoretical and practical implications. Seeking to pack more and more into liberal order risks undermining its heuristic usefulness, both as a concept that can illuminate different periods and one that can suggest parallels and contrasts between widely different spheres.[190] Some serious political theorists have, conversely, urged that the term simply be abandoned. Like John Gray in *Post-Liberalism*, they believe it has collapsed under the historic weight of its internal contradictions.[191] Although one might abstractly sympathize with such sceptics, the working historian is left with the quandary that, from the 1840s to the 1940s, a multitude of Canadians did, as a matter of fact, identify themselves as liberals. Liberalism was a central part of their lives. They wrote hundreds of articles, pamphlets, editorials, books, and acts of parliament professing their attachment to what they believed was a coherent set of beliefs. And since these Canadians were often prime ministers, premiers, and leading businessmen, no adequate account of the country's history could possibly neglect the ideology that they themselves so often referenced when they sought to understand and to shape their pragmatic decisions in grander, more abstract terms. Hence the need for a usable definition that encapsulates, as best one can, the leading principles of their faith and practice.

Here one should remember the distinction between reconnaissance and synthesis. Were one attempting to write a master narrative of all of Canadian history, it would make sense to demand a far more all-embracing list of attributes, especially if one purported to be 'summing up' and 'defining' subaltern lives and struggles. Reconnaissance does not aim to speak for others. It aims to provide tools of analysis that may help others speak. It does not aim for ideological closure. It merely aims to provide tools of analysis that may be useful to others engaged in the intellectual and political task of understanding Canada as a project of rule.[192] It is entirely likely that the liberal order framework will be useful in some such contexts and not in others.

Hence, the liberal order hypothesis would not be that, everywhere and always, we can find the 'master key' to a period, problem, or person in 'liberalism.' Rather, the core hypothesis put forward by the framework is that powerful people, acting in many different spheres and with enduring effects, transposed 'the individual' and the triune formula of liberty, equality, and property from one field to another. The liberalism so transposed was subtly changed in the process, yet not so radically altered that a researcher can detect no 'family resemblances' among its variants. Moreover, since these structures intersected, a transformation within one would have widely ramifying effects upon them all. A minimalist but workable definition of liberalism may well prove a more serviceable tool for the exploration of this open-ended and complex process than a seemingly all-encompassing attempt at a comprehensive description.[193] Such a minimalist definition potentially allows for many more links between hitherto-separated areas, and, ironically, for a much more open field in which subaltern scholars and groups can put the framework to whatever uses they find illuminating and appropriate. In short, the 'narrowness' of the concept of liberal order – in terms of period, spatial impact, and its definitional core – may well be the key to the future breadth of its application across many now-separated fields of historical enquiry and subaltern struggle.

This relates to another potential critique, which is the extent to which the liberal order framework might work to homogenize and oversimplify the past – to steamroll over such interesting and vital traditions as republicanism, conservatism, and ultramontanism, and to impose a misleadingly 'totalizing' perspective on a far more variegated world. For conservatism, for example, one would want to ponder the distinctive patterns of patron/client relationships so richly developed by S.J.R. Noel and Paul Maroney in Ontario.[194] By reducing the entire Canadian past to a master narrative of the rise of liberalism, it might be argued, the framework has simply recast in deceptively 'radical' garb the age-old Whig Interpretation of History.

Perhaps we can draw valuable lessons here from the debate that engulfed late-twentieth-century American political history in response to the work of Pocock and Skinner on republicanism. In Louis Hartz and Carl Becker one found claims that Lockean liberalism – meaning individualism, economic self-interest, and materialism – constituted the primary intellectual impetus behind the Revolution, and even, by a somewhat daunting leap of faith, of the entire history of the United States. Among such 'republican revisionists' as Gordon Wood and Bernard Bailyn, often inspired by J.G.A. Pocock's magisterial *The Machiavellian Moment*, one found a contradictory emphasis on classical republicanism. Subsequent scholars such as Isaac Kramnick, Steven Dworetz, and Thomas L. Pangle then partially reinstated Locke as the Revolution's founding father, although they placed different emphases on which version of the ever-interpretable Locke was operative in the U.S. context. There would seem to be an emergent consensus among scholars that interpreting liberalism and republicanism as *entirely* antithetical traditions was 'neither historically nor theoretically sound.'[195]

The cautionary tale for historians of another time and place (although one obviously affected by and reactive to trends in the United States) is that the utmost caution must be exercised in treating any given thinker as the fixed origin or stable essence of a complex political paradigm. Citation-hunting and quotation-counting may be valuable as elements within a wider argument, but hazardous if they are asked to carry the burden of proof for arguments about an entire ideological formation. On its own, political theory applied to history entails the hazard – or so it would seem from this example – of reductionist interpretations that risk reifying and oversimplifying the past. This does not mean that we must not struggle to find coherent intellectual patterns, but rather that we should be cautious about an over-reliance on intellectual history alone. The hypothesis of liberal order does not require that everyone in the Dominion be a liberal, and in fact evidence of conscious rejections of liberal social and political relations provides plausible indications that the order impinged even upon those who wished to reject it. Rather, it maintains that a liberal logic can be deciphered in the activities of the state, the interpretation of the law, the orchestration of popular opinion, and the structures of everyday life. The more clearly we specify what this liberal logic was – with reference, for instance, to the formula of liberty, equality, and property – the more clearly will we be able to say when and how it was at work and when it was not.

Returning to the hypothesis of a long liberal revolution from the 1840s to the 1940s, we might argue that it can accommodate, and indeed requires, the coexistence within an overall liberal order of contrasting ideological formations. It interestingly complicates but does not to my mind refute the liberal order framework, for instance, that on S.J.R. Noel's reading, Macdonald's Liberal Conservatives carried into the 1870s rather different, more paternalistic styles of patron/client relations than their Grit rivals in Ontario.[196] Similarly, the strength of Catholic ultramontanism in Québec calls into radical question any 'liberal' separation between church and state. Yet, to cite an interesting passage from Jean-Marie Fecteau's immensely suggestive work, the Church was in fact caught up in 'a complex dialectic by which the proclaimed refusal of the new' was combined 'with an often unconscious acceptance of it.'[197] Never as monolithic as it appeared to outsiders, the late-nineteenth-century Church was necessarily responsive to moderating counsel from the Vatican and to the transforming ideological and social world surrounding it.[198] With respect to property, as Brian Young's splendid work reveals, elements within the Church were often enthusiastic participants in the post-feudal commercialization of real estate.[199] Religious nuns and brothers brought to the expanding state institutions of liberal order a low-wage workforce; liberal political economy could use their low wages to free up provincial monies for other expenditures – railways, for instance.[200] Rather than minimizing all such countercurrents, the judicious use of the liberal order framework seems able to lead to a fuller and more sympathetic appreciation of them.

Revolutions are not straightforward, especially when they are projected into vast subcontinents made up of a myriad different societies and cultures. To use the phrase 'the Revolutionary period' to cover U.S. history from 1774 to 1800 or Russian history from 1917 to 1935 by no means implies a homogeneous attachment of the many peoples and nations to the regimes governing in their name. Nor does it imply that each and every topic in U.S. or Russian history – the intricacies of evangelical Protestantism or of Russian Orthodox theology, or kinship patterns among the Cherokee or the Yakut – can all be traced back to 'the Revolution.' Nor can we even say that, notwithstanding their best efforts, the ruling regimes were monolithic forces – since in both cases, they were plainly internally divided on a number of fundamental issues, including those relating rival conceptions of property, equality, and liberty. At the same time, it would seem obtuse to deny that many developments in the United States from 1776 to 1800 or in Russia from

1917 to 1935 are best understood by keeping the revolutionary context in mind. It would seem possible to retain these 'Revolutions' as powerful moments in history, around which many different social and political structures were articulated, without making them steamrolling 'juggernauts' that flatten every topic they approach.

In the case of the two passive revolutions in Canada – which respectively initiated and transformed the liberal order – maintaining the same interpretive balance seems both possible and advisable. The liberal order framework consolidates and builds on the findings of recent innovative historiography – notably, although not exclusively, in such fields as legal history, the history of political thought, and the study of state formation – by proposing a new general approach, focused on the critical exploration of the new Canadian state's logical and historical conditions of possibility as a specific project of rule in a particular time and place. Rather than proposing a master synthesis or narrative in which all subaltern identities are submerged or integrated, it is based upon a strategy of 'reconnaissance' – that is, a 'knowing again,' facilitated by 'bridging concepts,' of which liberal order is but one, that might provide useful hints for the critical-realist interrogation of power relations. Rather than aiming at closure, which is arguably the aim of much academic synthesis and almost all ideological polemic, reconnaissance sets itself the more modest objective of offering helpful suggestions for those interested in exploring power relations in northern North America.

A related criticism might be that the liberalism invoked by liberal order often seems an immobile and exclusively bourgeois affair – one whose vulgar triptych of 'liberty-equality-property,' evident in the pared-down petit-bourgeois formulations of chambers of commerce and boards of trade, actually traduced a much more expansive and long-lasting drive for liberty in the nineteenth century.[201] As Robert McDonald so well observes in his contribution to this volume, working-class liberalism was a substantial force to contend with in Canada, and any attempt to map liberal hegemony must include, as a central topic, the deep penetration of the subaltern classes by liberal doctrines. Much recent suggestive work has been done on popular liberalism in Britain that demonstrates how powerfully Gladstonian liberal ideals influenced the working class.[202] In Canada, although it was not explicitly theorized in this way, some interesting work has focused on the 'producers' ideology' that valorized the dignity of the labour of the worker and the manufacturer in implicitly Lockean terms.[203] Moreover, one might point to work on the Provincial Workmen's Association in Nova Scotia, the most durable coal miners' union in Victorian Canada, which named one of its lodges after William Gladstone, and whose leader, Robert Drummond, was a liberal organic intellectual of the rapidly industrializing coalfields.[204] The notion of collective subaltern deafness to the call of propertied independence, implicit as an unspoken assumption in much left labour historiography of the 1970s and 1980s, my own included, thus stands in need of revisionist work exploring the ways workers experienced liberal social and political relations – including those regarding property and the price of their own labour-power. Explorations of the role of workers within the liberal historical bloc would entail looking at the manifold faces of property, even in places, like coal mines, that are generally if misleadingly considered to be the workplaces of the archetypically 'propertyless' proletarians.[205]

In addition, a more developed hypothesis of liberal order would entail exploration of a vast cultural system through which understandings about individualism and property were disseminated very generally – in bestselling novels about 'self-made' men and an extensive therapeutic literature advising how to become one, in a culture of advertising increasingly based upon the almost magical transformations particular commodities could make in one's own life, in widespread admiration for the 'improvement' of nature by 'free enterprise,' in a general recourse to conspicuous displays of wealth to sustain claims to status and prestige, in an honours system that rewarded outstanding individuals, in forms of domestic architecture that vaunted the individuals who owned them: all contributing to what Stephen Leacock so tellingly and critically diagnosed as his own society's 'elephantiasis of individualism.'[206] We are only beginning to explore the everyday world of a liberal order.

Liberalism was a popular faith in much of working-class and agrarian Canada from 1840 to 1940. Its beliefs were written not only in words but in the material world. It not only preached the honest, straightforward values of the yeoman farmer, the honest exemplar of free-standing independence, but it gave him the glowing prospect of western farms for his sons – lands to be divvied up according to the most advanced forms of land tenure. It not only offered economic benefits to investors and patronage positions to its supporters, erecting rival party machines of Liberals and Liberal Conservatives across the land, but –

much more – it articulated an inspiring philosophy of improvement, which tied the humdrum brokerage politics of favours and contracts to a heroic vision of continental progress.[207] It developed a concept of the individual with elective affinities with the Christian concept of the soul – and in Gladstone and Brown it found politicians who could easily combine the ideals of free-standing independence with an evangelical emphasis on spiritual salvation. It not only spoke the language of crass economic advantage, but, over time, that of science and the Enlightenment itself – bringing rational order to the wheatfields, the forests, and the fisheries. It not only coexisted with and provided an ideological rationalization of the extraction of surplus value from the working class, but gave many workers the firm conviction that, especially in the turn-of-the-century conservative Liberals, one could find the truest friends of the 'masses' against the 'classes,' the honest brokers and straight shooters of Canadian politics – a populist formula the rival Liberal Conservatives struggled to adopt as their own. To those within its slowly expanding circle, it offered acknowledgment not only of their 'capacity to judge' on political issues but also of their freedom to enjoy the fruits of their hard work and rugged enterprise. It also provided a liberal language of labour – not 'class' per se – that allowed those who had attained the status of respectable individual workingmen to demarcate themselves from those who, on grounds of race, class, gender, sexuality, or skill, were prohibited from doing so.

Yet, in another sense – and to amend the 'static impression' created by any over-reliance on too stable an interpretation of the triune formula of liberal values – when we watch the transposition of liberal categories into such contexts as coal mines, we are also placing ourselves in contexts in which those categories will be severely tested and ultimately transformed. Over time we will witness a multitude of liberalisms within the overall framework of liberal order, which 'share a definitional family resemblance, but not an essential identity.'[208] As Nadia Urbinati remarks, 'A market economy invariably generates, or at least is not able to impede the growth of, social inequality. As a consequence, the justice, equality, and liberty called for by liberalism will become the legitimate opponents of the effects of a market economy, as will the principles nurturing the growth of common interests and alternative visions of the just society.'[209]

If we focus tightly on a given moment – that of 'achieved liberal rule,' for example – we may be tempted to minimize both the precariousness and volatility of that rule, the sheer difficulty of managing the intrinsic conflicts between various readings of liberal faith. We may be tempted to overlook the complexities and subtleties of state/civil society relationships, reshaped in each area by pre-existing communities and groups, so that any discussion of the local lived experience of 'liberal state formation,' although trackable through statutes and inspectors' reports and census returns, must attend carefully to the pre-existing structures, and not assume the state's ability to suddenly impose a 'new order of things.'[210] Moreover, the exploration of the process of hegemony in any of its overlapping moments requires (to an extent generally overlooked in Anglo-American appropriations of the concept in the 1970s and 1980s) a critical-realist emphasis on the *materiality* of human relations, economic, political, and cultural. Thus, the critical-realist strategy of researching 'hegemony' sees it as an *eventful historical process*, through which a given group comes to exercise leadership over a society. It calls upon us to *problematize* events – to ask, 'What is *necessarily* in place for these events to occur?' If it will often include economic and social structures among these necessarily present conditions, it will do so, not on the basis of a prior metaphysical commitment to 'materialism,' but because of its interest in a realist reconstruction of actually existing conjunctures.

Finally, it would be naive to overlook the present-day *political* dimensions of the liberal order framework, even if, as this piece has insisted, it is most suited to the exploration of the years from the 1840s to the 1940s. There is an ideological intensity to some critiques that seems suggestive of an underlying ethical and political unease. Since the institutional and cultural contradictions bequeathed by this 'long Confederation' remain painfully unresolved to this day, to raise critical questions about it – about colonialism, cultural repression, economic exploitations, and social exclusion, among other things – is, by implication, to raise questions about Canada itself. Any problematization of the official liberal history of the inevitability and goodness of Canada, and any critical-realist discussion of its actually existing liberalisms, is bound to strike a nerve in a country whose immense state mnemonic apparatus seems designed to celebrate its own achievements and, one might also say, to obscure its origins as an experiment in liberal colonialism. Moreover, Canada has for the last half-century been undergoing a complex crisis of decolonization – one that has simultaneously robbed 'British Liberty' of its commonsensical obviousness, aroused different and challenging forms of national liberalism in Québec, and generated debates over Aboriginal sovereignty with the potential to transform power relations

over vast stretches of the liberal Dominion. It is perhaps this post-colonial context that has both allowed for the construction of a new theorization of Canada and also intensifies the often somewhat emotional
responses to it – often taking the forms of denial (most frequently by
omission or selection, such as the 'evaporation' from the record of
labour camps, deportations, and abuses of the First Nations), deferral
(the full fruits of liberalism were/are yet to appear – i.e., liberalism as
the perpetually distant future anticipated by today's 'work in progress'); distanciation (our Canadian problems are all the fault of the
'British' or the 'Americans') or temporal distancing (everything pre-
1982 is cordoned off as ancient history, and consequently of no real
bearing on today's purer and better post-Charter and 'multicultural'
Canada).

Those who truly believe in a given ideological framework often mistake immanent critiques for hostile attacks. An immanent critique, such
as the one Antonio Gramsci directed against the liberalism of Benedetto
Croce, is 'a form of theorizing that seeks standards of rationality within
existing systems of thought and forms of life.'[211] The struggle in which
reconnaissance is implicated entails not an 'attack' upon an external
enemy but an 'immanent critique' of a framework and a way of life
from which no Canadian can simply stand apart. A *radical democratic*
immanent critique of liberal order would argue that, in its actually
existing historical forms, much of Canadian liberalism has historically
been premised on a very impoverished, unrealistic, abstract, ahistorical, and even inhuman concept of 'the individual.' Liberal order in Canada has historically elevated the 'haggling, fractious competition of
economic action into a higher abstraction, the market, stripped it of its
relationship to other activities, and reimagined it as a special realm of
natural, autonomous, and automatically self-regulating processes.'[212]
This market liberalism was, and remains, a central principle of our economic and social order. Contemporary neo-liberalism merely puts a
more totalizing Spencerian spin on a long-standing pattern of liberal
belief.[213] State action in order to achieve *non-market* objectives has
been persistently rendered since the nineteenth century as 'intervention,' and juxtaposed with the supposed rationality of the market. This
creed could and did easily survive the emergency twentieth-century
measures aimed at surmounting the periodic crises generated by the
business cycle. If its more radical and quasi-totalitarian form as an
anticipatory 'abolition of society' (*à la* Thatcher) sounds new, it in fact
merely recapitulates a standard common sense of the early-nineteenth-

century Benthamites and some late-nineteenth-century Spencerians.[214]

A *radical democratic* critique of liberal order would press it on its inconsistencies and aporias and remember well the 'enormities' (in the original definition of the word) committed in its name. Yet in its struggle to transcend liberalism, it would not take a cavalier attitude towards the liberties to which liberals have, admittedly inconsistently and partially, at times pledged their sincere allegiance.

In essence, the liberal order framework is invested in a post-nationalist defamiliarization of the official story of the inevitability and goodness of the project of Canada. Like Gramsci in his analysis of the *Risorgimento*, it is involved not in the celebration of the supposed nation, nor conversely in a callow and shallow denunciation of it – but in a re/connaissance, a knowing again, of this project of rule and of the liberal state that is one of its outcomes. If the liberal order framework works with many topics that are quite conventional among historians, such as responsible government or the coming of the welfare state, and doubtless evinces an unusual respect and affection for the achievements of earlier generations of political historians, it aims to access this historiography in an unconventional way. It keeps an eye on the necessary preconditions of past political and social forms. It sets itself apart from dominant nation-building narratives, both old (colony-to-nation) and new (the triumph of multiculturalism and so-called 'people's history'), many of which simply naturalize Canada, whether by reifying it as merely one nation among nations, whose emergence holds no particular analytical interest, or conversely by talking about it as though its consolidation were pure happenstance, contingency, or even a 'miracle' – logically exclusive interpretations that are imaginatively combined in much nationalist historiography. Radically non-teleological and non-fatalistic, reconnaissance frontally assaults the 'noble lie' of the inevitability and goodness of Canada itself.

A present-day implication of the liberal order framework is that many of the most pressing political issues of our own day – the national oppression of racialized minorities, the erosion of the welfare state and the return of 'less eligibility,' the looming environmental catastrophe – can only be accurately grasped if we bear in mind the heavy legacies of classical liberalism.[215] Yet it also points out – and this returns us to the initial point about periodization with which we began – that with the rise of a much more organized social democratic opposition, particularly in the second quarter of the twentieth century, those most invested in liberal order concluded that only through an extensive 'revolution from above,' encompassing social and economic institutions as well as political life, could the liberal order surmount the organic crises that seemingly threatened its very existence. Far from denigrating the achievements of subaltern groups in achieving important rights and freedoms under the liberal order, this immanent critique highlights the economic and social contradictions that have limited their extension and preservation. Canada as a liberal project was aligned with other projects of western colonialism. The extension of this political project from coast to coast to coast – to cite the sadly banal slogan of contemporary Canadian Manifest Destiny – was an act of political will on the part of relatively few Europeans who as white settlers saw the project of Canada as a way of fulfilling the individualistic ideals of British liberalism – liberty, equality, and property. As contemporary Native land debates reveal only too clearly, the legacies of liberal colonialism do not evaporate merely because the colonizers have forgotten the history of their actually existing political order. As Cole Harris remarks, although this story seems so fundamental and obvious that it should be general knowledge, it is in fact widely disregarded: 'I suspect that it may be some measure of the thinness of our understanding of ourselves – and of our disinclination to admit how enmeshed our lives have been and remain in the strategies and tactics of colonialism – that considerable parts have not been told before.'[216]

To identify the liberal order framework with the radical democracy espoused by the left is, then, not unreasonable. Yet it may be too limiting, especially since, under twenty-first-century conditions of severe environmental crisis, 'left' and 'right' are undergoing profound shifts, reminiscent in many respects of their mutations in the interwar years of the twentieth century. Both 'liberals' and 'socialists,' when they think through the global environmental crisis, will necessarily be driven to reappraisals of their own traditions, which have often shared promethean ideals of domination over nature. They will be, above all, driven to think about their underlying values, and particularly the place of property rights within them. As the economist Adolph Wagner told the new liberals of an earlier time: '[T]he legal privileges of property have to be rethought, down to their social core.'[217] The confiscation of private property, and not necessarily with compensation, can be seen as an aspect of liberalism when it unselfconsciously spoke a language of equality and liberty; it can find forerunners, among liberals, in such classic nineteenth-century movements as those of abolitionism and temperance. At the same time, socialists also need to be reminded of the

very mixed environmental record of post-capitalist state enterprises,
which often differed little in their ideals and behaviours from those of
the private sector. Both traditions confront the fundamental challenge of
thinking in a far more revolutionary way about the abolition of private
and state property, as a precondition to any conceivable resolution of the
looming organic crisis of the planetary political order. In the face of this
crisis, we confront the necessity of deconstructing and superseding the
very concept of 'ownership,' which will be progressively seen not as
conferring absolute and inter-generational, but highly contingent and
personally limited, claims to the use of things and relations in the world.
And this rethinking will apply not only to individual and capitalist
ownership, but also to the claims of 'ownership' and 'dominion' made
by sovereign states.

One is tempted, in short, to read into the various refusals of any link
between liberalism and property not claims about the past – for they
would seem on balance to be very implausible – but utopian projections
of the future. Liberated from the ethical quagmire of justifying the enormities of capitalism, and from mystifying their own past in the interests
of Canadian nationalism, liberals can re-engage with what is authentically radical in their own tradition.[218] In a popular front against planetary environmental devastation, liberals, Marxists, anarchists, and
indigenous activists can draw upon the respective analytical and political strengths of their traditions to create a revolutionary post-capitalist
historical bloc, integrating science and social justice in a new transcendence of 'merely corporative' interests. Such a new political formation
will necessarily entail a searching defamiliarization of many accepted
categories – society, individual, property, freedom, equality, and Canada, for instance – which have become the common sense of conventional politics, and the recovery of Locke's and Marx's principle of the
right of revolution. Embarking upon this venture will require of both
liberals and socialists the 'strength of consequences,' that is, a willingness to confront each other in meaningful debates that place their fundamental categories at risk. It will also demand the tabling of shallow
polemics and the beginnings of serious critical-realist analysis.[219]

'I set out on this ground, which I suppose to be self-evident, "that the
earth belongs in usufruct to the living": that the dead have neither powers nor rights over it.' So wrote Thomas Jefferson in 1789. In this conception of human history, each generation has the right to be 'free from
the burdens assumed by the past generation and the concomitant duty
to respect the same right of its successor.'[220] Many of the moral and

political contradictions of liberal order, in Canada as around the world, and much of the looming tragedy of planetary environmental devastation, stem from this belief that living individuals, liberated from the ties that bind them to past generations, present communities, or future citizens, let alone to other species, enjoy rights of ownership over the earth. If an 'inconvenient truth' of our own time is the inescapable evidence of global environmental crisis, an even *more* inconvenient truth is that human survival will require an unprecedented capacity to imagine a radically post-individualist politics, in which the categories of liberal order are simultaneously preserved in the scope they provide for rational debate, cancelled insofar as they have functioned historically as transcendental justifications of private property and cultural oppression, and transcended in new, more generous, and more realistic concepts of human freedom.

NOTES

1 I would like to thank participants at the Liberal Order workshop at McGill University in Montreal, the Gramsci and Historical Research workshop at the University of East Anglia in Norwich, and the International Gramsci Society sessions at the Rethinking Marxism Conference in Amherst, MA, all in 2006, for their many helpful comments and suggestions on sections of this paper. Following international convention, the notebook (Q) and section (§) numbers accompany citations from Gramsci's *Prison Notebooks*, to enable readers to find them more readily in their own sources. For a most helpful research tool, see the International Gramsci Society concordance to Gramsci's writings as compiled by Marcus Green, which can be found at http://www.internationalgramscisociety.org/resources.

2 The very way that 'Canadian history' is organized as a subject implies just such a naturalization of the country. Typically, textbooks read back into the past the country's present-day spatial boundaries and treat as definitional its supposed birth dates (hence, the increasingly problematic 'pre-Confederation' and 'post-Confederation' boundary, which silently places an Act of the Imperial Parliament in London at the epicentre of the history of all of northern North America).

3 For fascinating discussions of Benedict Anderson's concept of 'imagined community,' see Jonathan Culler and Pheng Cheah, eds., *Grounds of Comparison: Around the Work of Benedict Anderson* (New York and London: Routledge, 2003).

4 From the Act of Union in 1841, successive acts, generally initiated in central Canada and confirmed by the British – Confederation of the Province of Canada, New Brunswick, and Nova Scotia in 1867, the acquisition of the Hudson's Bay Company's vast empire in 1870, the entry of Manitoba, British Columbia, and Prince Edward Island in the 1870s, the designation of Alberta and Saskatchewan in 1905, and the Canadian claim since 1925 to all the islands and waters of the Arctic between 60°W and 141°W longitude, all the way to the North Pole – transformed an unimposing set of seven British colonies and assorted possessions, with their European populations concentrated in the St Lawrence Valley and on the Atlantic coasts, into a transcontinental realm entailing a claim to sovereignty over a vast array of different indigenous nations, territories, and societies. Canada as a sovereign state now encompasses territories most Canadians will never see, yet which, in some sense, they collectively feel they 'own.'

5 For example, in today's world, many liberals evidently do not believe that, under the seemingly permanent emergency conditions of the 'war on terror,' all persons accused of a crime have the right to confront the charges against them in an open court of law – as evidenced by the support given to security certificates and other 'anti-terrorism' measures by the country's two mainstream political parties. Other liberals would join social democrats and other leftists in condemning such measures as cruel violations of human rights and wonder about the logic of racialization underlying them.

6 That these 'true individuals' could only be created within particular contexts was a truism contested, to my knowledge, by very few nineteenth-century Canadian liberals.

7 Important new work calls out to be done on the 'individual' as he or she was represented in various cultural settings – in newspaper obituaries, local histories, cemeteries and church memorials, even county atlases (which in the 1870s were often beautifully illustrated with representations of the mansions and properties of the local notability). A hypothesis: in much of Canada from 1840 to 1940, much 'history' was apprehended through an individualistic lens – not only with respect to the 'great men' of Canadian history, but also to the many local notabilities making up the 'commonsense world.' For interesting reflections on the category 'individual,' see Thomas C. Heller, Morton Sosan, and David E. Wellbery, eds., *Reconstructing Individualism: Autonomy, Individuality and the Self in Western Thought* (Stanford: Stanford University Press, 1986). For exciting new work on local commemoration of individuals as moral exemplars, see Bridget Fowler, *The Obituary as Collective Memory* (London: Routledge, 2005).

8 A major transformation effected by the Great War of 1914–18 was the partial

disruption of the two-party system, with the rise of the Progressives to become the second largest group in the House of Commons in 1921. Interestingly, however, the political system was shaken but not transformed (as it would be in Great Britain). At the provincial level, one should note significant political experiments that at the time seemed pregnant with post-liberal possibilities: the reign of United Farmers parties in Ontario and the West from 1919–35; the 1935 triumph of Maurice Duplessis and the Union Nationale (made up of an alliance between the Action libérale nationale and the Conservative Party); the victory of Social Credit in Alberta in 1935; and the slower rise and consolidation of the socialist Co-operative Commonwealth Federation, which came to power in 1944 in Saskatchewan.

9   The classic discussion of 'less eligibility' remains James Struthers, *No Fault of Their Own: Unemployment and the Canadian Welfare State 1914–1941* (Toronto: University of Toronto Press, 1983); note also his *The Limits of Affluence: Welfare in Ontario, 1920–1970* (Toronto: University of Toronto Press, Ontario Historical Studies Series for the Government of Ontario, 1994), which concludes with a persuasive critique of the notion of a 'Red Tory' Ontario: 'Certainly, there is no evidence that conservative traditions led to more activist state leadership within the welfare field in Ontario, relative to other provinces or adjacent American states' (262). See also his 'Unequal Citizenship: The Residualist Legacy in the Canadian Welfare State,' in *Mackenzie King: Citizenship and Community,* ed. John English, Kenneth McLaughlin, and P. Whitney Lackenbaur (Toronto: Robin Brass Studio, 2002), 169–85. One major reservation about the 'universal applicability' of less eligibility can be found in Jean-Marie Fecteau, *La liberté du pauvre: Crime et pauvreté au XIXe siècle québécois* (Montreal: VLB Éditeur, 2004), 262.

10 For a provocative discussion of 'improvement,' see John Weaver, 'Concepts of Economic Improvement and the Social Construction of Property Rights: Highlights from the English-Speaking World,' in *Despotic Dominion: Property Rights in British Settler Societies,* ed. John McLaren, A.R. Buck, and Nancy E. Wright (Vancouver and Toronto: UBC Press, 2005), 79–102, and the same author's *The Great Land Rush and the Making of the Modern World, 1650–1900* (Montreal and Kingston: McGill-Queen's University Press, 2003): 'Improvement and its synonyms and antonyms – terms such as betterment and advancement; negligence and waste – were intrinsic to formal and informal practices of taking and allocating land. The rationalizations and rhetoric of legislators and administrators incorporated these almighty words when they justified formal schemes to take land from indigenous peoples or drafted regulations for distributing land to settlers' (5). For a masterful and multidimensional analysis of the theory and practice of improvement in

Nova Scotia, see Daniel Samson, *The Spirit of Industry and Improvement: Liberal Government and Rural-Industrial Soiety, 1790–1862* (Montreal and Kingston: McGill-Queen's University Press, 2008).

11 William H. Sewell, Jr, *Logics of History: Social Theory and Social Transformation* (Chicago and London: University of Chicago Press, 2005), 9–10. Sewell also remarks that 'social life is fundamentally constituted by culture,' which (in my view) introduces an extraneous and problematic term into his otherwise illuminating discussion. See Robert J.C. Young, *Colonial Desire: Hybridity in Theory, Culture and Race* (London: Routledge, 1995), chaps. 2 and 3, for an important postcolonial critical genealogy of the concept of 'culture.'

12 Although it arose in Europe in the first quarter of the nineteenth century, liberalism characteristically entailed a claim to ownership over the entire Enlightenment tradition. This often meant an aggressive rereading and recontextualization of such earlier figures as John Locke, Immanuel Kant, Adam Smith, David Ricardo, and David Hume, to name but five re-baptized 'founders' of the tradition – a retroactive conscription of imagined founding fathers that has stoked the true believers' exegetical fires for generations. Canadian liberalism could be fascinatingly approached as a transgenerational and transnational 'imagined community,' one sanctified by heroic events (Responsible Government, the Charter of Rights and Freedoms), sacred landscapes (Parliament Hill, not to mention Laurier House and Kingsmere), and fearsome villains (in the present volume, often conveyed by embarrassingly dated Cold War evocations of the very Soviet bloc to which so many Canadian liberals – one thinks only of P.-E. Trudeau and Joseph Smallwood – travelled as credulous hopeful travellers from the 1930s to the 1970s).

13 To expand on this point: it is useful and important to read as much as possible about liberalism-in-general as a vast international current, formidably complex, with its vast galaxy of real and imagined ancestors. It is perhaps even more useful to consider figures closer in time to the Canadian liberal revolution – Alexis de Tocqueville, whose aristocratic reflections on the gaucheries of North American politics and colonizing enthusiasms in Africa undermine any credulous belief that liberals were necessarily or perhaps even tendentially 'democrats,' or John Stuart Mill, who commented explicitly and favourably on the revolutionary dictatorships of Durham and Sydenham, with their utilitarian drive for a new political order, or – to reference one of the most widely cited and revered figures of the entire tradition – Herbert Spencer, that brilliant liberal meteor who dazzled his generation, and who must be included in any level-headed description of the liberal pantheon, especially as it was understood by many nineteenth-century

Canadians. There remains to be written a complete account of Spencer's role
as an immense force upon nineteenth-century Canadian liberals (and, although his ideas are rarely explicitly referenced, an important inspiration
for contemporary Hayekian neo-liberals as well). As the *Manitoba Free Press*
put it so eloquently upon Spencer's death in 1903: 'The death of Herbert
Spencer removes "from out our bourne of time and place" a great intellect,
whose achievement in the field of philosophy ranks among the most important of the things accomplished during the nineteenth century.' Goldwin
Smith remarked: 'No one ever was more thoroughly dedicated to the pursuit of truth. For some years he was not only dedicated, but self-sacrificed to
it. Spencer is entitled to rank among the discoverers. He was a thorough-
going free-thinker, but was not destructive. On the contrary, he was a
builder of morality and society on a biological foundation, and his work,
if it is not destined to be final, will certainly be lasting.' *Manitoba Free Press*,
9 December 1903; *Montreal Star*, 9 December 1903.

14 For a fascinating discussion of Mill, in the context of a particularly 'aristocratic' strain of mid-nineteenth-century liberalism, see Alan S. Kahan, *Aristocratic Liberalism: The Social and Political Thought of Jacob Burckhardt, John
Stuart Mill, and Alexis de Tocqueville* (New Brunswick and London: Tavistock,
2001). Mill's 'aristocratic liberalism,' was that of a 'fringe group,' one that
drew massively upon classical humanism in its disparagement of commercial society, and of the middle and working classes, and critiqued
'individualism' as opposed to 'individuality.' Rather than relying upon
decontextualized quotations from *On Liberty* or *Considerations on Representative Government*, Kahan's work suggests the importance of reading Mill
more carefully and in context. How did Canadian contemporaries use Mill,
and to what purpose? How did they balance the Mill of *On Liberty* with that
of *Principles of Political Economy*? For Mill's mid-nineteenth-century views
on slavery, see John Stuart Mill, *Considerations on Representative Government*,
2nd ed. (London: Parker, Son, and Bourn, 1861): 'Hence even personal slavery, by giving a commencement to industrial life, and enforcing it as the
exclusive occupation of the most numerous portion of the community, may
accelerate the transition to a better freedom than that of fighting and rapine.
It is almost needless to say that this excuse for slavery is only available in
a very early state of society. A civilized people have far other means of im-
parting civilization to those under their influence; and slavery is, in all its
details, so repugnant to that government of law, which is the foundation of
all modern life, and so corrupting to the master-class when they have once
come under civilized influences, that its adoption under any circumstances
whatever in modern society is a relapse into worse than barbarism' (37–8).

15 Rudolf Bahro in *The Alternative in Eastern Europe*, trans. David Fernbach (London: Verso, 1982).

16 That is, thinkers who were directly involved in underlying and emerging structures in economy and society, as opposed to those 'traditional' intellectuals who were merely the legatees of superseded social forms, or others whose interests had no relationship to underlying social processes. In general, Gramsci juxtaposes 'organic' (of or pertaining to long-term, permanent changes) and 'conjunctural' (relating to short-term and less permanent processes). In many respects, he paralleled the *Annales* school in his quest for a stratified conception of temporality – although, obviously, not pronouncing the last word on the subject.

17 One thinks of the *Eaton's Catalogue* and the *Family Herald* as Canada's homegrown equivalent of the countless Enlightenment pamphlets and plays that 'moved like a spark along the lines that were already stretched between state and state, between region and region, and found the same supporters and the same opponents everywhere and every time,' so that the 'bayonets of Napoleon's armies found their road already smoothed by an invisible army of books and pamphlets that had swarmed out of Paris from the first half of the eighteenth century and had prepared both men and institutions for the necessary renewal.' Antonio Gramsci, *Selections from the Political Writings, 1910–1920*, ed. Quentin Hoare, trans. John Mathews (London: Lawrence and Wishart, 1977), 12. For a fascinating reading of the *Family Herald* as a force for liberalization, see Jennifer Marotta, 'A Moral Messenger to the Canadian Middlemost: A Reading of The Family Herald and Weekly Star, 1874–1914' (PhD diss., Queen's University, 2006). I owe the point about the *Eaton's Catalogue* to an anonymous reviewer of this essay.

18 Daniel T. Rodgers, *Atlantic Crossings: Social Politics in a Progressive Age* (Cambridge, MA, and London: The Belknap Press of Harvard University Press, 1998), 78.

19 See Jürgen Habermas, *The Structural Transformation of the Public Sphere: An Inquiry into a Category of Bourgeois Society*, trans. Thomas Burger (Cambridge, MA: MIT Press, 1989); for a forceful critique of how historians have 'liberalized' Habermas, see Harold Mah, 'Phantasies of the Public Sphere: Rethinking the Habermas of Historians,' *Journal of Modern History* 72, 1 (March 2000): 153–82. North Americans easily overlooked Habermas's declared intention of providing critique and retrieval from the perspective of social democracy of a 'category of bourgeois society' (*Structural Transformation*, 4).

20 J.S. McClelland, *A History of Western Political Thought* (London and New York: Routledge, 1996), chap. 19, citations at 430, 436, 444, and 446. It should

426   Ian McKay

be noted that, with respect to 'moral' economy, McClelland also stresses classical liberalism's significant division into utilitarian and natural-rights traditions.

21 This would be my reservation about David F. Ericson's deeply interesting typology of republican ideas in his *The Shaping of American Liberalism* (Chicago and London: University of Chicago Press, 1993).

22 See Fernande Roy, *Progrès, harmonie, liberté: Le libéralisme des milieux d'affaires francophones de Montréal au tournant du siècle* (Montreal: Boréal, 1988). Roy's invaluable work is unusual in its unequivocal confrontation with the combined 'semantic overabundance' and 'semantic poverty' of liberalism, so often confounded with the 'economic-social system that it has well served, capitalism,' and with the 'political system that has often accompanied it, democracy.' To be a liberal, for Roy, means to adhere to a general perspective on progress, liberty, equality, and property (which is, implicitly or explicitly, the central value), and to subordinate the public realm to the private in the interests of possessive individualism (58). Roy's definition helps us understand that liberalism was not then inherently opposed to 'conservatism' nor to 'Catholicism' or any other religion – and why, in the 1930s, so many liberals flocked first to the Action libérale nationale, and then to Duplessisme. For a superb account of liberal themes within Duplessist political discourse, see Gilles Bourque and Jules Duchastel, *Restons traditionnels et progressifs. Pour une nouvelle analyse du discours politique: Le cas du régime Duplessis au Québec* (Montreal: Boréal, 1988) and its even more persuasive sequel: Gilles Bourque, Jules Duchastel, and Jacques Beauchemin, *La société libérale duplessiste* (Montreal: Les Presses de l'Université de Montréal, 1994).

23 The point of this obviously metaphorical conception of a hierarchy of values is that liberals from 1840 to 1940 would agonize long and hard before they intruded upon what they deemed to be the private realm of the individual – only very rarely, and in unusual circumstances, would they act in ways that impeded that marriage of equality, liberty, and property that would eventually take the richly evocative name of 'Free Enterprise.' The liberal order framework would certainly sustain serious damage if it could be shown that, within both central political institutions and everyday life, actually existing 'free enterprise' and 'rights of property' were dead letters from the 1840s to the 1940s, or that the language of 'individual initiative' was confined to an elite, and had no capacity to mobilize enthusiasm or concern outside their rarefied and uninfluential world of opinion.

24 The prohibition movement – which entailed the closing down of an entire market and the seizure without compensation of private property – could perhaps be viewed this way, if one judged its goals to be liberty and equal-

ity, as some of its proponents did (although one would suspect that as strong a liberal argument for it was that drunkenness placed an economic burden on society, thereby imposing an unfair burden on the prosperity of the middle-class public). It was perhaps because it flew in the face of widespread social and cultural expectations with respect to property rights that this revolutionary measure proved so difficult to enforce and so fleeting in its duration. Moreover, it provided an instance in which liberal arguments could be effectively deployed on either side of the debate. An earlier example of a successful campaign to seize property without compensation was constituted by the abolition of slavery in the British Empire and in North America – a development that was widely and coherently denounced on orthodox Lockean liberal grounds by slave-holders themselves.

25 For a classic exposition of such debates, and one profoundly influential in the construction of the framework, see Karl Polanyi, *The Great Transformation: The Political and Economic Origins of Our Time* (1944; Boston: Beacon Press, 1971).

26 The great liberal historian J.B. Brebner aptly distilled Canadian nineteenth-century life as follows: 'The prevailing social tone in Canada was that of a middle-class, businessman's civilization (with all the great merits and defects that that implied). If old wealth and family found it crass and distasteful, they could put their money in land, mortgages, or impersonal bonds and stocks, and insulate themselves in exclusive associations and clubs. The materially successful and undiscriminating could afford to laugh at the old leaders and often did, in their confidence of present well-being and future improvement.' J. Bartlet Brebner, *Canada: A Modern History* (Ann Arbor: University of Michigan Press, 1960), 353.

27 For one attempt to measure the 'size of the state,' see Nicole Morgan, *Implosion: An Analysis of the Growth of the Federal Public Service in Canada (1945–1985)* (Montreal: Institute for Research on Public Policy, 1986). She notes that the number of federal employees c. 1940 – 49,739 – would rise to 131,646 by 1952. It would be interesting if difficult to extend her exercise in counting state functionaries throughout the entire period 1840–1940 at all three levels of government.

28 William Gladstone most particularly (who was as much a hero in Canada as he was in Britain: William Lyon Mackenzie King, the country's most significant early-twentieth-century liberal theorist and politician, cultivated a deep relationship with the legacy of Gladstone, through reading and rereading his biography, visiting his stomping grounds in England, and (more eccentrically) posthumously conversing with the revered British prime minister in séances. For ground-breaking revisionist work on the Gladstone/

King relationship, see Margaret Bedore, 'The Reading of Mackenzie King' (PhD diss., Queen's University, 2008).

29 For an imaginative exploration of the new logic of the state, see Michel Ducharme, 'Aux fondements de l'État canadien: La liberté au Canada de 1776 à 1841' (PhD diss., McGill University, 2005).

30 One thinks especially here of Phillip A. Buckner, *The Transition to Responsible Government: British Policy in British North America, 1815–1850* (Westport, CT, and London: Greenwood Press, 1985) and Janet Ajzenstat, *The Political Thought of Lord Durham* (Montreal and Kingston: McGill-Queen's University Press, 1988).

31 On Sydenham, see Ian Radforth, 'Sydenham and Utilitarian Reform,' in *Colonial Leviathan: State Formation in Mid-Nineteenth-Century Canada,* eds. Alan Greer and Ian Radforth (Toronto: University of Toronto Press, 1992); and, of course, Adam Shortt's venerable *Lord Sydenham* (Toronto: Morang, 1908), which is perhaps as interesting for what it tells us about its early-twentieth-century liberal author. Irving Abella, 'The Sydenham Election of 1841,' *Canadian Historical Review* 27, 4 (December 1966): 326–43, introduces some fascinating materials and perhaps opened up some interesting interpretive territory with his association between Sydenham and Machiavelli. See Phillip Buckner, 'Charles Edward Poulett Thomson,' *Dictionary of Canadian Biography,* vol. 7 (Toronto: University of Toronto Press and Les Presses de l'Université Laval, 1988), 855–62. For very interesting neo-Pocockian reflections on the patronage system, see Gordon T. Stewart, *The Origins of Canadian Politics: A Comparative Approach* (Vancouver: UBC Press, 1986).

32 Gerald M. Craig, *Upper Canada: The Formative Years, 1784–1841* (Toronto: McClelland and Stewart, 1963), 275.

33 On this third path, too often neglected in distillations of Gramsci's approach to hegemony, see the astute analysis of Lafontaine and the strategy of 'multiplying the vendus' in Jacques Monet, *The Last Cannon Shot: A Study of French-Canadian Nationalism* (Toronto: University of Toronto Press, 1976 [1969]).

34 For a deft formulation of this compromise, see Michel Ducharme, 'Penser le Canada: La mise en place des assises intellectuelles de l'État canadien moderne (1838–1840),' *Revue d'histoire de l'Amérique française* 56, 3 (Winter 2003): 374–6.

35 It would make for a fascinating and instructive exercise in transnational comparative history to construct a general history of the hemisphere's many mid-nineteenth-century 'liberal revolutions.' For example, the success of the Canadian liberals in the 1840s–1860s might be interestingly contrasted with their fellow-travellers' much less successful outing in Central America,

where the legacy of Spanish colonialism seemingly did not allow for the
success of a similar project of liberalization, secularization, and federal
state-formation.

36 The St Lawrence Valley was, then, in essence, the 'Canadian Piedmont.'
Note, however, that in the early years of Confederation, the Maritime Provinces, particularly Nova Scotia, also contributed essential ideas and pivotal
figures (Tilley, Howe, Tupper, Thompson, Borden, to name just five) to the
new Confederation – and, as diplomatically and militarily decisive links to
the British metropole, were by no means initially regarded as political back-
waters. This notion of a 'nucleus' – which is not drawn from dependency
theory, except insofar as it too shares an ancestor in Gramsci – admittedly
needs more theoretical and empirical work. It also calls out for comparative
application to everyday spheres outside formal politics.

37 Although it should also be remembered that the boundaries of the Canadian
state were later ambiguously extended over an even vaster area of the
planet (roughly two million square kilometres) under the United Nations
Convention on the Law of the Sea in 1982.

38 Here one thinks of the work of Bruce Curtis, *The Politics of Population: State
Formation, Statistics, and the Census of Canada, 1840–1875* (Toronto: University
of Toronto Press, 2001), who argues for the significance of census-making as
a process of centralizing knowledge that served to 'increase the possibilities
for intensive administration' (3), and of John Varty, 'Growing Bread: Tech-
noscience, Environment, and Modern Wheat at the Dominion Grain Research Laboratory, Canada, 1912–1960' (PhD diss., Queen's University,
2005), who remarks: 'Modernity as we know it is, in general, the historically
distinct form of existence created at the nexus of deliberate distance creation
and restless distance negotiation' (370).

39 For the *locus classicus* of the opposing viewpoint, see Janet Ajzenstat, *The
Canadian Founding: John Locke and Parliament* (Montreal and Kingston:
McGill-Queen's University Press, 2007).

40 See Anthony D. Smith, *The Ethnic Origins of Nations* (Oxford: Blackwell,
1986), who uses the term to denote the myths, symbols, historical memories,
and central values of ethnic communities (15).

41 See Gad Horowitz, *Canadian Labour in Politics* (Toronto: University of Toronto Press, 1967), chap.1; for a critique, see Rod Preece, 'The Myth of the Red
Tory,' *Canadian Journal of Political and Social Theory* 1, 2 (Spring/Summer
1977): 3–88.

42 To repeat a passage from the original 'Liberal Order' article: 'Long-established and once militarily powerful, Aboriginals, the demographic majority
in most of the territory eventually to be claimed by the liberal dominion,

were people whose conceptions of property, politics, and the individual were scandalously not derived from the universe of Locke, Smith, Bentham, or Lord Durham. The containment of these alternative logics was an ideological imperative of the liberal order without which it could not exist as a transcontinental project.' Ian McKay, 'The Liberal Order Framework: A Prospectus for a Reconnaissance of Canadian History,' *Canadian Historical Review* 81 (2000): 636. The First Nations were initially and by definition outside liberal order, insofar as they were defined as the 'others' upon whom the liberal order necessarily had to act in order to attain its transcontinental dimensions (and, as we shall see, there were venerable Lockean texts that directly justified this mission).

43 David E. Smith, *The Invisible Crown: The First Principle of Canadian Government* (Toronto: University of Toronto Press, 1995). Smith provocatively defines Canadian federalism as a 'system of compound monarchies,' and remarks: '[T]he Crown is the organizing force behind the executive, legislature, administration, and judiciary in both the federal and provincial spheres of government. Moreover, because of this dual presence, the Crown exercises determinative influence over the conduct of intergovernmental relations' (x). Smith's fascinating work could be brought into fruitful conversation with other scholarship, such as Kahan's, on 'aristocratic liberalism.'

44 For an overview, see Maris A. Vinouskis, 'Stalking the Elusive Middle Class in Nineteenth-Century America: A Review,' *Comparative Studies in Society and History* 33, 3 (July 1991): 582–7. For highly suggestive recent Canadian work influenced by Gramsci, see Stephen Cole, 'Managing Consent: The Royal Commission on the Relations of Capital and Labour in Canada, 1886–1889' (Ph.D. diss., Queen's University, 2007).

45 A most useful text here is Greer and Radforth, eds., *Colonial Leviathan*.

46 For a superb exploration of this phenomenon with respect to Native peoples, see Frank J. Tester and Peter Kulchyski, *Tammarniit (Mistakes): Inuit Relocation in the Eastern Arctic, 1939–63* (Vancouver: UBC Press, 1994).

47 As of 2007, only three volumes of the complete *Prison Notebooks* have been published in English.

48 Roger Simon, *Gramsci's Political Thought: An Introduction*, rev. ed. (London: Lawrence & Wishart, 1991), 22, 24, 38.

49 Denis Forgacs, 'Hegemony,' in *The Antonio Gramsci Reader: Selected Writings 1916–1935*, ed. Forgacs (New York: New York University Press, 2000), 422–3.

50 Simon Gunn, 'From Hegemony to Governmentality,' *Journal of Social History* (Spring 2006): 705–20.

51 Peter Ives, *Gramsci's Politics of Language: Engaging the Bakhtin Circle and The Frankfurt School* (Toronto: University of Toronto Press, 2004), 11.

52 Leo Panitch and Sam Gindin, 'Superintending Global Capital,' *New Left Review*, 2nd ser., 35 (2005): 121.

53 Antonio Gramsci, *Selections from the Prison Notebooks*, ed. and trans. Quentin Hoare and G. Nowell-Smith (London: Lawrence & Wishart, 1971) [hereafter *SPN*], 161 [Q13§18].

54 Adam David Morton, *Unravelling Gramsci: Hegemony and Passive Revolution in the Global Economy* (London and Ann Arbor: Pluto, 2007), 115 (emphasis in original).

55 Kate Crehan, *Gramsci, Culture and Anthropology* (Berkeley and Los Angeles: University of California Press, 2002).

56 Jonathan Joseph, *Hegemony: A Realist Analysis* (London and New York: Routledge, 2002), 39.

57 Robert Cox, 'Social Forces, States and World Orders: Beyond International Relations Theory,' *Millennium: Journal of International Studies* 10, 2 (1981): 139, as cited in Morton, *Unravelling Gramsci*, 113.

58 A good example can be found in Foucauldian critiques of Gramsci for supposedly restricting himself to the 'manifest' politics of parties and policies, to the neglect of the everyday, 'capillary' politics of bodies, pleasures, discipline, etc. That the latter term was in fact used extensively by Gramsci suggests some of the ways in which he has been persistently misread in contemporary critical theory in North America. For a refreshing sign that some Foucauldians are reconsidering the rift with Marx, one that was only partially supported by Foucault himself, see Alan Hunt, 'Getting Marx and Foucault into Bed Together!' *Journal of Law and Society* 31,4 (December 2004): 592–609. Gramsci was keenly alert to that 'diffused and capillary form of indirect pressure' a realized hegemonic order could bring to bear upon the average person. In a fully realized hegemony, street names and daily newspaper articles, television advertisements and web pages, architecture and church services all function as so many 'social infusoria,' the 'material structure of ideology,' generating a vivid, lived, and generally compulsory experience of a particular interpretation of reality, the refusal of which entails far-reaching cultural and economic costs. See Morton, *Unravelling Gramsci*, 92–3; Gramsci, *SPN*, 110 [Q15§11]. Conversely, although some orthodox Marxist critics have alleged that Gramsci substitutes a 'soft politics of pleasure' and an excessive emphasis on consent for a more realistic and revolutionary grasp of the role of force in history and for the brute power of economic realities, in fact he conceives of the normal exercise of hegemony as one involving a reciprocal balance of force and consent, with corruption looming as a valid possibility when neither of these two options can be easily or safely pursued.

59 See Gramsci, *SPN* 405 [Q11§62].

60 John Gitling, *Capital and Power: Political Economy and Social Transformation* (London, New York, and Sydney: Croom Helm, 1987), [v].

61 Sewell, *Logics of History*, 101.

62 That is to say, Gramsci develops a critical-realist narrative that grasps this 'hegemony' at various points of its development. It probes its preconditions – such as the forces and relations of production, the existence of a widely shared language, the generation through that shared language of a concept of the 'people-nation,' the development by organic and traditional intellectuals of historical blocs that can transcend the economic-corporate limitations of specific economic and social groups, and so on. When we 'freeze' this evolution at a particular moment, and then hypostatize this moment as definitional of the whole process, we inevitably run the risk of reducing the whole to a part. Herein lies one reason why an Italian 'absolute historicist' has so often been mistaken as a banal structural functionalist in North America.

63 Using the concept of 'neo-liberalism' to describe twenty-first-century politics, for instance, may be a useful way of hypothesizing links between market-driven policies – ones that have been transposed from business to an immense diversity of spheres, from international relations to academic life – and other spheres. Is neo-liberalism 'hegemonic?' Or are neo-liberals faltering in their grasp of the fundamentals of wielding power in a newly globalized situation? The theory of hegemony helps us ask the question; it does not predetermine the answer.

64 '*Blocco storico*' was also earlier translated as 'historic bloc,' but, as Adam David Morton observes, this convention may misleadingly place 'too much emphasis on the momentous, one-off, or literally "historic" formation of such a bloc,' rather than on its capacity to interpret and reshape historical processes. See Morton, *Unravelling Gramsci*, 218n8, who in turn draws upon Derek Boothman, 'Introduction,' to Antonio Gramsci, *Further Selections from the Prison Notebooks*, ed. and trans. D. Boothman (London: Lawrence and Wishart, 1995), xi–xii; Wolfgang Fritz Haug, 'Rethinking Gramsci's Philosophy of Praxis from One Century to the Next,' *Boundary 2* 26, 2 (1999): 111.

65 Gramsci, *SPN*, 418 [Q11§67].

66 Some would go so far as to suggest Gramsci is of primary interest only as a (flawed) interpreter of Italian political and cultural history. See R. Bellamy, 'Introduction,' to Antonio Gramsci, *Pre-Prison Writings*, trans. V. Cox (Cambridge: Cambridge University Press, 1994).

67 Gramsci, *Further Selections from the Prison Notebooks*, 156–7 [Q1oII§44] cited in Morton, *Unravelling Gramsci*, 98–9.

68 Morton, *Unravelling Gramsci*, 122.

69 For example, a phenomenon like contemporary global neo-liberalism can be explored and resisted on the local level (the culture of consumption in the local shopping mall or layoffs at the plant), at the national level (the triumph of market ideology in country-wide think tanks and the erosion of the welfare state in government budgets), and at the transnational level (the global energy crisis, the militarization of the planet under the guise of a war on terror, and the interventionist strategies of the World Bank).

70 Morton, *Unravelling Gramsci*, 115.

71 Ibid., 58.

72 Ibid., 70–1; the first passage is a quotation from Phillip McMichael, 'Incorporating Comparison within a World-Historical Perspective: An Alternative Comparative Method,' *American Sociological Review* 55, 3 (1990): 385–97.

73 See Morton, *Unravelling Gramsci*, 101. Morton's analysis has shaped this discussion of passive revolution throughout.

74 Gramsci, *SPN*, 58 [Q19§24].

75 Anne Showstack Sassoon, ed., *Approaches to Gramsci* (London: Writers and Readers Publishing Co-operative, 1982), 129.

76 As revealingly documented in Janet Ajzenstat, Paul Romney, Ian Gentles, and William D. Gairdner, eds., *Canada's Founding Debates* (Toronto: Stoddart, 1999), chap. 5.

77 A geopolitical point best developed by Brebner, who can be retroactively drawn upon as the irreplaceable *fons* and *origo* of the liberal order framework: John Bartlet Brebner, *North Atlantic Triangle: The Interplay of Canada, the United States, and Great Britain* (Toronto: McClelland and Stewart, 1966 [first published New Haven: Yale University Press and Toronto: Ryerson Press, 1945]), 252.

78 On the patronage system, see Stewart, *Origins of Canadian Politics*.

79 Herein lies the crucial underlying difference between the 'war of position' that Gramsci urges the left to adopt in the West and 'passive revolution': in the first one seeks to sharpen and develop the dialectical struggle between rulers and ruled, whereas in the second one aims to freeze the social struggle as much as possible, to isolate and contain its dynamism, to preserve almost at any cost the identities and categories called into question by modernity itself, to equilibrate social and political forces even at the cost of the overall rationality and coherence of the system as a whole, and to evade even the appearance of a coherent ideological orientation.

80 Joseph, *Hegemony*, 31.

81 For an interesting discussion, see Robert Fatton, 'Gramsci and the Legiti-

mization of the State: The Case of the Senegalese Passive Revolution,' in *Antonio Gramsci: Critical Assessments of Leading Political Philosophers*, vol. 4, *Contemporary Applications*, ed. James Martin (London and New York: Routledge, 2002), 259.

82 See R. Craig Brown and Ramsay Cook, *Canada, 1896–1921: A Nation Transformed* (Toronto: McClelland and Stewart, 1974), 249. Although there were some permanent changes ushered in by the Great War, such as income tax and fiscal reliance upon the United States, the hypothesis here is that the 'new liberalism' seemingly foreshadowed by such measures was successfully staved off until the 1940s.

83 Esteve Morera, *Gramsci's Historicism: A Realist Interpretation* (London and New York: Routledge, 1990).

84 C.B. Macpherson, *Property: Mainstream and Critical Positions* (Toronto: University of Toronto Pres, 1978), 202.

85 Alfred W. Crosby, *Ecological Imperialism: The Biological Expansion of Europe, 900–1900* (Cambridge: Cambridge University Press, 1986). According to John Weaver, between 1.5 billion and 2 billion acres of arable land and productive pastures were newly exploited from 1750 to 1900 (*The Great Land Rush*, 89).

86 In *The Canadian Founding*, Janet Ajzenstat suggests Lockean overtones to some of the statements made by prominent politicians in the 1860s, although the implication that Locke is an unacknowledged Father of Confederation seems overstated, and her emphasis is resolutely on Locke as a theorist of the state. For more far-ranging observations, see Jerry Bannister, *The Rule of the Admirals: Law, Custom, and Naval Government in Newfoundland, 1699–1832* (Toronto: University of Toronto Press, 2003) as well as his contribution to this volume; see also John McLaren, A.R.Buck, and Nancy E. Wright, eds., *Despotic Dominion: Property Rights in British Settler Societies* (Vancouver and Toronto: UBC Press, 2005). The American literature on Locke is enormous: for some suggestive discussions, see John R. Nelson, *Liberty and Property: Political Economy and Policymaking in the New Nation, 1789–1812* (Baltimore and London: Johns Hopkins University Press, 1987); Joyce Appleby, *Liberalism and Republicanism in the Historical Imagination* (Cambridge, MA, and London: Harvard University Press, 1992), esp. chap. 2, 'Locke, Liberalism and the Natural Law of Money'; Gregory S. Alexander, *Commodity & Property: Competing Visions of Property in American Legal Thought 1776–1970* (Chicago: University of Chicago Press, 1997). C.B. Macpherson, *The Political Theory of Possessive Individualism: Hobbes to Locke* (Oxford: Oxford University Press, 1962) has been attacked and defended for over forty years (with his suggestion that Locke was responding to an emer-

gent capitalism proving far more vulnerable to empirical critique than his general point that Lockean doctrines have been instrumental in the generation of 'possessive individualism'). Of the more recent work on Lockean liberalism, I have found Gopal Sreenivasan, *The Limits of Lockean Rights in Property* (New York and Oxford: Oxford University Press, 1995) and Barbara Arneil, *John Locke and America: The Defence of English Colonialism* (Oxford: Clarendon Press, 1996) particularly useful. The first suggests that, since within a Lockean theory of property 'the only justification that can be provided for the legitimacy of the potential owner's right of acquisition is the justification provided by her labouring,' the logic of Locke's argument leads unmistakably to a substantially egalitarian regime of property (151–2); the second shows that 'the world known as America is, in the Two Treatises of Government, the same world as that inhabited by natural man,' with the consequence that the very existence of aboriginal peoples undermines a duality inherent in liberal thought 'between nature and culture, between passion and reason, between wasteland and private property' (201, 210). Locke the incipient capitalist recedes in these more contemporary readings – but if anything Locke as an apostle of Macpherson's 'possessive individualism' is even more emphatically present. For an excellent discussion of Blackstone and common law, see Bruce Ziff, 'Warm Reception in a Cold Climate: English Property Law and the Suppression of the Canadian Legal Identity,' in *Despotic Dominion* 103–19.

87 In fact, one of the most fascinating aspects of the Canadian liberals was that, like revolutionaries in quite different settings, they might resort to seemingly inharmonious tactics in order to achieve the ultimate ends of their project. An obvious and fascinating example here would be the recruitment of such collectivists as Hutterites and Doukhobors to settle in the West. See Alvin J. Esau, 'The Establishment and Preservation of Hutterite Communalism in North America, 1870–1925,' and John McLaren, 'The Failed Experiments: The Demise of Doukhobor Systems of Communal Property Landholding in Saskatchewan and British Columbia, 1899–1999,' both in *Despotic Dominion*, 207–21 and 222–47. As McLaren suggestively concludes, with respect to the contrasting fates of the two experiments in communalism: 'It may be that the Doukhobors suffered in part because of their reluctance to engage with the Weberian rationalism of the liberal democratic state on its own terms and in its own language. Misunderstanding, however, might have been less of a problem had a spirit of accommodation and greater cultural sensitivity been demonstrated by government. In this, the official representatives of the dominant legal culture typically displayed an aggressive posture of cultural superiority that branded Doukhobor commu-

nalism in particular as anachronistic, otherworldly, and unlikely to contribute to responsible nation building. Land settlement, as a process within the
dominant culture, was closely related to that blend of order, individualism,
and deference that has marked the history of colonialism in Canada and
was seen as essential to nation building and the progressive development of
a commercial and industrial economy' (242).

88 On the latter, see particularly the highly original work of James Murton,
'Constructing a Countryside in British Columbia' (PhD diss., Queen's
University, 2002).

89 Philip Girard, 'Land Law, Liberalism, and the Agrarian Ideal: British North
America, 1750–1920,' in *Despotic Dominion*, 120, 122.

90 Margaret E. McCallum, 'The Sacred Rights of Property: Title, Entitlement,
and the Land Question in Nineteenth-Century Prince Edward Island,' in
Essays in the History of Canadian Law in Honour of R.C.B. Risk, ed. G. Blaine
Baker and Jim Phillips (Toronto: University of Toronto Press, 1999), 358, 367.

91 See in general Rusty Bittermann, *Rural Protest on Prince Edward Island: From
British Colonization to the Escheat Movement* (Toronto: University of Toronto
Press, 2006). For the explicit use of Locke in debates in Prince Edward
Island, see McCallum, 'Sacred Rights of Property,' 372. For Québec parallels,
note Brian Young, *The Politics of Codification: The Lower Canadian Civil Code
of 1866* (Kingston and Montreal: McGill-Queen's University Press, 1994).

92 That this actually was a striking departure from Locke's theory of property,
properly construed, is the gist of Sreenivasan's timely study (see n. 86
above).

93 See Daniel Samson, 'Industrial Colonization: The Colonial Context of the
General Mining Association, Nova Scotia, 1824–1842,' *Acadiensis* 29, 1
(1999).

94 As Cole Harris remarks, drawing upon the work of Patricia Seed: 'No other
colonists, ... made such use of surveyors, or wrote so much about gardens.
For English colonists, planting a garden and, in the process, subduing the
land, was much more than a horticultural experience. A properly fenced
garden was property. It followed from this that those who did not plant gardens, or did not fence them, or did not create landscapes that bore imprints
familiar to the English, did not possess the land and could not have property rights to it. English settlers in early colonial America considered that
even a Native garden, unfenced, was an inadequate measure of property.' R.
Cole Harris, *Making Native Space: Colonialism, Resistance, and Reserves in British Columbia* (Vancouver: UBC Press, 2002) 48.

95 For which see the superb monographs of Brian Young: *The Politics of Codification* and *In Its Corporate Capacity: The Seminary of Montreal as a Business*

Institution, 1816–1876 (Kingston and Montreal: McGill-Queen's University Press, 1986). Of course, important legacies of seigneurialism, such as a prodigiously powerful and wealthy Catholic Church, were hardly effaced by its formal (and protracted) abolition.

96 Young, *Politics of Codification*, xiii–xiv.

97 Harris, *Making Native Space*, chap. 6.

98 For an insightful analysis, see Jon Spira, 'Regulating the "Treasures of the Earth": The Liberal State and the Regulation of Nova Scotia's Coal Industry, 1858–1893' (MA thesis, Queen's University, 1995).

99 R.C.B. Risk, *A History of Canadian Legal Thought: Collected Essays* (Toronto: University of Toronto Press, 2006), 97.

100 jzenstat, *The Canadian Founding*, 59–60, 50.

101 Weaver, *Great Land Rush*, 95:

102 See esp. Gregory S. Kealey, *Toronto Workers Respond to Industrial Capitalism 1867–1892* (Toronto: University of Toronto Press, 1980), chaps. 8 and 9. In Kealey's account, even proponents of the National Policy – and critics of 'Manchester Liberalism' – nonetheless speak in favour of a 'liberal' tariff policy (156). Reading his fine study against the grain, it might be said that the Toronto Tories prevailed to the extent that they learned to speak a Lockean-liberal language of the 'producers' ideology.'

103 Cited in Richard Overstall, 'Encountering the Spirit in the Land: "Property" in a Kinship-Based Legal Order,' in *Despotic Dominion*, 23.

104 For an interesting scholarly collection about one such moment, see Bruce W. Hodgins, Ute Lischke, and David McNab, eds., *Blockades and Resistance: Studies in Actions of Peace and the Temagami Blockades of 1988–89* (Waterloo: Wilfrid Laurier University Press, 2003).

105 See esp. Girard, 'Land Law, Liberalism,' 120–43; and Peter Karsten, *Between Law and Custom: 'High' and 'Low' Legal Cultures in the Lands of the British Diaspora – The United States, Canada, Australia, and New Zealand, 1600–1900* (Cambridge: Cambridge University Press, 2002).

106 See Edwinna von Baeyer, *Garden of Dreams: Kingsmere and Mackenzie King* (Toronto and Oxford: Dundurn Press, 1990), 60–1.

107 To paraphase Weaver, *Great Land Rush*, 49.

108 Overstall, 'Encountering the Spirit in the Land,' 46.

109 Weaver, *Great Land Rush*, 93.

110 Donald Creighton, *John A. Macdonald: The Young Politician* (Toronto: Macmillan of Canada, 1952), 107.

111 If one seeks evidence of this deep liberal disquiet, one can find it in both Duncan Campbell Scott's recourse to repressive measures against the Six Nations and other Native dissidents in the 1920s, but perhaps even more

emphatically in his extraordinary poetry – one thinks especially of the 'Onandoga Madonna' – which combines liberal Spencerian themes of inevitable development with gothic fears of racial contamination and degeneration, violence and vampirism. He writes with the panic of a white liberal and colonizer whose fundamental ontological and epistemological understandings have been placed at radical risk through his traumatic encounter with the colonized Other. See E. Brian Titley, *A Narrow Vision: Duncan Campbell Scott and the Administration of Indian Affairs in Canada* (Vancouver: UBC Press, 1986), which should now be supplemented with Stan Dragland, *Floating Voice: Duncan Campbell Scott and the Literature of Treaty 9* (Concord, ON: Anansi, 1994).

112 On Durham's attribution of 'barbarism' to the French Canadians, see Ducharme, 'Penser le Canada,' 381.

113 Uday Singh Mehta, *Liberalism and Empire: A Study in Nineteenth-Century British Liberal Thought* (Chicago and London: University of Chicago Press, 1999), 20–1.

114 In addition to Struthers, *No Fault of Their Own*, see Hugh Shewell, *'Enough to Keep Them Alive': Indian Welfare in Canada, 1873–1965* (Toronto: University of Toronto Press, 2004), which shows in compelling detail how 'less eligibility' was brutally applied in the case of Native famines.

115 Citation from Edward Blake and discussion in Risk, *History of Canadian Legal Thought*, 139. This volume of essays, from a foremost legal scholar, is a wonderful resource for the study of the legal aspects of the Canadian liberal revolution, although it unaccountably leaves out some of his most interesting legal-history articles from the 1970s on property and markets.

116 Ibid., 131–2.

117 See esp. Jeffrey L. McNairn, *The Capacity to Judge: Public Opinion and Deliberative Democracy in Upper Canada 1791–1854* (Toronto: University of Toronto Press, 2000), 436.

118 For which see the fascinating new work of Alan Mendelson: 'Grip Magazine and "the Other": The Genteel Antisemitism of J.W. Bengough,' *Histoire sociale / Social History* 60, 79 (May 2007): 1–44, who builds in part on Gerald Tulchinsky, 'Goldwin Smith: Victorian Canadian Antisemite,' in *Antisemitism in Canada: History and Interpretation*, ed. Alan Davies (Waterloo: Wilfrid Laurier University Press, 1992), 67–91.

119 Mehta, *Liberalism and Empire*, chap. 2, 'Strategies: Liberal Conventions and Imperial Exclusions,' citations at 46–7, 49, 70.

120 Arneil, *John Locke and America*, especially chaps. 6 and 7.

121 Mill, *Considerations on Representative Government*, 39.

122 McNairn, *Capacity to Judge*, 425, 433.

123 Paul Romney, *Getting It Wrong: How Canadians Forgot Their Past and Imperilled Confederation* (Toronto: University of Toronto Press, 1999); Robert C. Vipond, *Liberty and Community: Canadian Federalism and the Failure of the Constitution* (Albany: State University of New York, 1991).
124 McNairn, *Capacity to Judge*, 418.
125 Ibid., 434, 436.
126 Ajzenstat, *The Canadian Founding*, xiii.
127 See John Locke, *Second Treatise of Government*, ed. C.B. Macpherson (Indianapolis and Cambridge: Hackett, 1980), 98 [§192]. It is interesting to remark that the full paragraph concerns the right of 'every man' to 'inherit with his brethren his father's goods,' and focuses on the rights of people, such as 'Grecian christians,' who have been forced under the 'Turkish yoke,' and owe no obedience to that government because they had not consented to it. Whether this same characterization could be applied to indigenous Canadian peoples under the 'British yoke' is an issue best left to Lockeans.
128 Ajzenstat, *The Canadian Founding*, 8.
129 Ibid., 11.
130 Ibid., 11, 16, 17.
131 Ibid., 42, 34, 26. Of course, many North American Lockeans before the Civil War would have argued against any notion that there were no natural slaves.
132 Ibid., 41, 43.
133 Ibid., 47, 64, 65 (emphasis added).
134 Peter Thomas, 'Historicism, Absolute,' *Historical Materialism* 15 (2007): 251, citing Gramsci, Q8§39.
135 The Nova Scotia case is in my view highly significant, but it is perhaps revealing that it has not been intensively studied for thirty years. It merits reconsideration in view of the case the New Whigs have made for deliberative democracy and the 'right of revolution' in mid-nineteenth-century Canada. At first sight, it would seem that the Nova Scotians had every right to debate Confederation, and exercised that right with the moving conviction that their opinions really mattered. It then would seem that their unmistakable democratic decision *not* to join Confederation was overruled by the key colonial decision-makers in Britain. So emphatic and massive a public debate over the constitution merits a detailed examination, and would permit the two emergent schools of interpretation to test their theses against actual Canadian political history. It is interesting and ironic to note that many of the most eloquent voices Ajzenstat has uncovered for the doctrine of popular sovereignty were precisely those of Nova

Scotians who were *opposed* to Confederation. One might add that one of the most eloquent defences of the 'right of revolution' came from Joseph Howe, who threatened to take up arms against the iniquitous new constitution.

136 This is the path followed by Ajzenstat, *The Canadian Founding*, 71, when after implicitly conceding Peter Russell's point that the exclusion of the Rouges from the Quebec Conference damaged the representativeness of the Confederation deal, she then redeems the Fathers by citing much later political events: 'We have the benefit of hindsight today. We know that parties akin in respects to the Rouges of the Confederation period have competed for seats in national and provincial legislatures with success; the Progressives, the United Farmers, the Cooperative Commonwealth Federation, the Reform and Alliance Parties. We know that individuals excluded from the franchise at the time of Confederation now enjoy the vote: aboriginals, women. It proved possible to loosen the guy ropes without moving out of the parliamentary tent. Indeed, the Parliament of Canada is a remarkably tolerant institution.' The upshot of this teleology is to rebut any critical realist analysis of an actually existing liberal order by fast-forwarding to utopian depictions of the glowing future that lay beyond the time period under discussion.

137 For a fascinating insight into the centrality of honours to Victorian-Canadian politicians, see Christopher McCreery, 'Honour, Nation and Citizenship in a Multicultural Polity: The Foundations of Canada's Federal Honours System' (PhD diss., Queen's University, 2003).

138 It is striking that so little attention is paid to Smith's invaluable *The Invisible Crown* (1995).

139 As Brian Young observes, even so foundational a Liberal Conservative as George-Étienne Cartier was actively involved in both the *positive* construction of subjects of liberal order – as evidenced by his 'role in the transformation of the elementary school system, the provision of provincial police, regional courthouses and jails, the tightening of parish record-keeping systems, the growth of savings banks, and the neutralization of national societies' – and its seemingly opposed *negative* and coercive activities: 'He modelled the St. Jean Baptiste Society on the Roman legion and encouraged companies like the Grand Trunk Railway to form company militia units; his militia bill of 1868 gave military authorities the right to search houses arbitrarily and force citizens to perform military service.' Brian Young, *George-Etienne Cartier, Montreal Bourgeois* (Kingston and Montreal: McGill-Queen's University Press, 1981), 133–4.

140 In addition to the formal restriction of the adult majority from voting

rights, one might also look at the extent to which the 'public debates of private persons' more subtly established a hierarchy of opinion. For a thoughtful feminist critique of Habermasian historiography, see Carmen Nielson Varty, '"A Career in Christian Charity": Women's Benevolence and the Public Sphere in a Mid-Nineteenth-Century Canadian City,' *Women's History Review* 14, 2 (2005): 243–64. As she remarks: 'A patriarchal public sphere occluded the development of a unique, female identity in charitable work. Domesticity and motherhood were notions that referred to the "particularity" of womanhood and were, thereby, antithetical to the principles of the public sphere, which had to (appear to) operate as an objective, unitary subject that represented a universal, common good' (254). In other words, an indication of one's obvious *incapacity to judge* was one's visible or invisible attachment to non-universalizable attributes.

141 Even in *The Capacity to Judge*, which so memorably celebrates the achievement of the liberal public sphere in parts of Upper Canada, one discerns a certain uneasiness when the text comes to ponder those who, on both Lockean or Millian grounds, could only be the objects rather than the subjects of state policy. With respect to the epochal 1857 Act to 'encourage the gradual civilization of the Indian tribes,' McNairn, after candidly describing the apparent 'brutal trade-off' between distinctiveness and inequality entailed in this act – which defined the Indian tribes as minors in need of 'protection' – concludes that the '"uncivilized," traditional forms of native self-government and landownership were beyond the pale' (347).

142 See esp. Constance Backhouse, *Petticoats and Prejudice: Women and Law in Nineteenth-Century Canada* (Toronto: Women's Press, 1991). One might add that liberal order might conceivably add new dimensions to the study of sexuality and gender politics, as suggested in the Latin American case by Christine Hunefeldt, *Liberalism in the Bedroom: Quarreling Spouses in Nineteenth-Century Lima* (University Park: Pennsylvania State University Press, 2000). For example, the increasing emphasis on the policing of homosexuality within a liberal order might be closely correlated, not so much with a pervasive post-Enlightenment drive to moral regulation, as with a more clearly focused need to shore up the eroding boundaries of the liberal individual in *fin-de-siècle* urban communities.

143 Geoff Eley, *Forging Democracy: The History of the Left in Europe, 1850–2000* (Oxford: Oxford University Press, 2002), 3. 'By this standard,' Eley adds, 'democracy was achieved nowhere in the world during the nineteenth century and arrived in only four states before 1914 – New Zealand (1893), Australia (1903), Finland (1906), and Norway (1913). If we relax our definition by ignoring women's suffrage, then the male democracies of France and

442   Ian McKay

Switzerland may also be added.' One might want to amend Eley's minimalist definition slightly to add the provision that political parties should
be allowed to freely contest such elections and publicize their points of
view – once again, a provision only partially followed in Canada down to
1940.

144 See John Garner, *The Franchise and Politics in British North America, 1755–
1867* (Toronto: University of Toronto Press, 1969). I think there is room for
more studies on the franchise in British North America and Canada, especially ones that would draw upon contemporary theory to illuminate debates over the exclusion of Asian immigrants from the vote, the removal
of the vote from women, and the gradual winning of a full franchise by
coal miners living in company housing. The general impression that Canadians did not hotly debate franchise issues may be a somewhat misleading
one.

145 See, among many excellent titles, James Mosher, *Discrimination and Denial:
Systemic Racism in Ontario's Legal and Criminal Justice Systems, 1892–1961*
(Toronto: University of Toronto Press, 1998); James St. G. Walker, *'Race,'
Rights and the Law in the Supreme Court of Canada: Historical Case Studies*
(Waterloo: Wilfrid Laurier University Press, 1997); Constance Backhouse,
Colour-Coded: A Legal History of Racism in Canada, 1900–1950 (Toronto: Uni-
versity of Toronto Press, 1999); and Patricia E. Roy, *The Oriental Question:
Consolidating a White Man's Province, 1914–41* (Vancouver: UBC Press,
2003).

146 At the same time, it is obvious that many Canadians from 1840 to 1940
did think of themselves as 'citizens,' as suggested by the name defiantly
selected by one of its first left-wing publications: *Citizen and Country.* There
are some interesting details in William Kaplan, ed., *Belonging: The Meaning
and Future of Canadian Citizenship* (Montreal and Kingston: McGill-Queen's
University Press, 1993), although it by no means can stand in for a major
historical monograph.

147 Peter H. Russell, *Constitutional Odyssey: Can Canadians Be a Sovereign People?* (Toronto: University of Toronto Press, 1992).

148 See the fascinating discussion of liberalism and legitimacy in Steven M.
Dworetz, *The Unvarnished Doctrine: Locke, Liberalism and the American Revolution* (Durham and London: Duke University Press, 1994), 187.

149 With respect to Edward Blake, R.C.B. Risk very powerfully remarks: 'The
vote was fundamental to this liberty: it was "the crowning badge" and the
"flower" of freedom. His faith in democracy meant a preference for a wide
franchise, although his campaign for provincial rights imposed the overriding principle that the franchise should be settled by the provinces. "The

true tests to my mind are citizenship and intelligence." There were, though, limits: faced with the question of giving the franchise to women, he took refuge behind the principle of provincial choice, but waffled long enough to seem to be unwilling; most native persons were not free enough or educated enough to be worthy; and Chinese were beyond consideration.' Risk, *History of Canadian Legal Thought*, 137. One notes that these 'limits' – by no means an exhaustive list – excluded the majority of the adult population inhabiting the territories claimed by 'Canada.'

150   A concrete instance of such contradictions would emerge with the drive among Maritimers and Upper Canadians, the latter inspired by George Brown and by the Clear Grits, to acquire land in the prairie west – a 'Promise of Eden' for some that logically entailed an extensive and rigorously enforced 'Policy of Purgatory' for its indigenous inhabitants, who would be variously classified as children, disorderly elements, barriers to development, inevitably failing races, or simply 'inscrutable' – but almost never, from the 1840s to the 1940s, as individuals endowed with the capacity to judge or collectivities vested with rights of self-determination. For an illuminating discussion, see Doug Owram, *Promise of Eden: The Canadian Expansionist Movement and the Idea of the West, 1856–1900* (Toronto: University of Toronto Press, 1981). It is striking that the 'historic treaties' of the 1720s-1760s that now preoccupy the courts were virtually unknown to most Canadians of the 1840s-1940s – indeed, they were generally neglected by most members of 'the public' until the 1970s.

151   For one striking example, see Derek G. Smith, 'The Emergence of "Eskimo Status": An Examination of the Eskimo Disk List System and Its Social Consequences, 1925–1970,' in *Anthropology, Public Policy and Native Peoples in Canada*, ed. Noel Dyck and James B. Waldram (Montreal and Kingston: McGill-Queen's University Press, 1993), 41–66. For an important legal-history overview, see Sidney L. Harring, *White Man's Law: Native People in Nineteenth-Century Canadian Jurisprudence* (Toronto: University of Toronto Press, 1998). See also Robert A. Williams, *The American Indian in Western Legal Thought: The Discourses of Conquest* (New York and Oxford: Oxford University Press, 1990). On the residential schools, see J.R. Miller, *Shingwauk's Vision: A History of Native Residential Schools* (Toronto: University of Toronto Press, 1996) and John S. Milloy, *A National Crime: The Canadian Government and the Residential School System, 1879 to 1986* (Winnipeg: University of Manitoba Press, 1999).

152   Both the mainstream political parties in contemporary Canada, the Liberals and the Conservatives, have recently supported the detention without public trial of persons denied the right to confront the full case against

them. Under the conditions of the twenty-first-century 'war on terror,' in Canada and elsewhere, the principle of the presumption of innocence, once considered an axiomatic element of the decent treatment of those accused of crimes, has been effectively suspended.

153 McNairn, *Capacity to Judge*, 418–19.

154 As Marx explained so well, the radical democracy of the Paris Commune at the top was dialectically related to freedom of discussion and assembly at the bottom: indeed, the whole libertarian logic of the great revolution was to progressively blur the boundaries between the 'top' and 'bottom,' the rulers and the ruled. See Karl Marx, *The Civil War in France*, in Karl Marx and Frederick Engels, *Collected Works*, vol. 22 (New York: International Publishers, 1986), 307–59.

155 For an engaging portrait of Goldman in Toronto, see Theresa Moritz and Albert Moritz, *The World's Most Dangerous Woman: A New Biography of Emma Goldman* (Toronto: Subway Books, 2001). Leon Trotsky, 'The Bolsheviki and World Peace,' *Mail and Empire* (Toronto), 12, 14, 16, 24, 26, 28 January 1918.

156 For a fascinating discussion, see Ian Milligan, '"Seemingly Onerous Restrictions": Sedition in Ontario, 1914–1919,' unpublished paper, York University, 2007.

157 As Michiel Horn astutely observes, the 1930s eroded an already fragile tradition of academic freedom, and 'those professors [who] claimed the "rights" of academic freedom and free speech in order to criticize the capitalist order and the British connection' provoked powerful movements for their dismissal. See Michiel Horn, *Academic Freedom in Canada: A History* (Toronto: University of Toronto Press, 1999), 350.

158 Duncan Campbell Scott, perhaps the most influential and imaginative liberal organic intellectual of Ottawa's First Nations policy, even arrived at the point of making it illegal for individual Native activists to legally challenge aspects of the Indian Act. See Titley, *A Narrow Vision*, 59.

159 See Barbara Roberts, *Whence They Came: Deportation from Canada 1900–1935* (Ottawa: University of Ottawa Press, 1988).

160 See Joseph, *Hegemony*, 33. In such a crisis, classes become detached from their traditional parties, and there is a pervasive sense of a crisis of leadership. In Canada, evidence of such an organic crisis in the 1920s and 1930s would include the growing chasm between the two traditional parties and many subaltern classes and groups, the growth of a large extra-parliamentary left with the capacity to stage massive demonstrations, and the emergence of new, more collectivist forms of trade unionism.

161 See Ann Gomer Sunahara, *The Politics of Racism: The Uprooting of Japanese*

Canadians during the Second World War (Ottawa: The Author, 2000), available on-line at http://www.japanesecanadianhistory.ca/ (accessed January 2007).

162 The first was applied to 'all those practices, whether by word, deed or writing, which fall short of high treason, but directly tend to have for their object to excite discontent or dissatisfaction; to excite ill-will between different classes or the King's subjects; to create public disturbances, or lead to civil war, to bring into hatred or contempt the Sovereign or the government, the law or constitution of the realm ... [; or] to incite people to unlawful associations, assemblies, insurrections, breaches of the peace.' The second pertained to any parties, whether or not they had been in communication with each other, who could be described as having pursued this 'one common intention.' For a discussion, see J.M. Bumsted, *The Winnipeg General Strike of 1919: An Illustrated History* (n.p.: Watson Dwyer Publishing Ltd, 1994), 67.

163 Defence Committee for the Dominion Labor Party, *Dixon's Address to the Jury. An Argument for Liberty of Opinion* (Winnipeg: Israelite Press, 1920), 73. It should be noted, of course, that Dixon was acquitted (while many of his fellow accused were sent to penitentiary).

164 And one must say its spirit lives on today, as evidenced by the zeal with which liberals have defended security certificates, the suspension of habeas corpus, and even the 'aggressive questioning' of suspects.

165 For an outstanding discussion, see Sean Mills, 'When Democratic Socialists Discovered Democracy: The League for Social Reconstruction Confronts the Quebec Problem,' *Canadian Historical Review* 86, 1 (March 2005): 53–81.

166 It was never, suggestively, disallowed by the Liberals in Ottawa; rather, it was ultimately overturned by the Supreme Court of Canada as being outside Quebec's jurisdiction.

167 John Gray, *Post-Liberalism: Studies in Political Thought* (London and New York: Routledge, 1993).

168 For an excellent guide to the vicissitudes of liberalism in nineteenth-century Québec, see Yvan Lamonde, *Histoire sociale des idées au Québec*, vol. 1, *1760–1896* (Montreal: Fides, 2000); vol. 2, *1896–1929* (Montreal: Fides, 2004).

169 In many of these, the classical liberal equation of 'the individual' with the 'adult male' was evident in criteria for membership – as suggested by the very title of Darryl Newbury's nuanced study: 'No Atheist, Eunuch or Woman: Male Associational Culture and Working-Class Identity in Industrializing Ontario, 1840–1880' (MA thesis, Queen's University, 1992).

170 J.M.S. Careless, *Brown of the Globe*, vol. 2, *Statesman of Confederation 1860–1880* (Toronto: Macmillan, 1963), 189–90 (emphasis added).
171 For an important overview of the 1940s, see Peter S. McInnis, *Harnessing Labour Confrontation: Shaping the Postwar Settlement in Canada, 1943–1950* (Toronto: University of Toronto Press, 2002).
172 See Judy Fudge and Eric Tucker, *Labour before the Law: The Regulation of Workers' Collective Action in Canada, 1900–1948* (Toronto: University of Toronto Press, 2001).
173 Anthony Arblaster, *The Rise and Decline of Western Liberalism* (Oxford: Basil Blackwell, 1984), 78.
174 For interesting works on critical realism and historical inquiry, topics that can only be briefly hinted at here, see Martin Bunzl, *Real History: Reflections on Historical Practice* (London and New York: Routledge, 1999) and Sean Creaven, *Marxism and Realism: A Materialistic Application of Realism in the Social Sciences* (London and New York: Routledge, 2000).
175 John Bartlet Brebner, *New England's Outpost: Acadia before the Conquest of Canada* (1927; Hamden, CT: Archon Books, 1965), 157.
176 See Frantz Fanon, *The Wretched of the Earth*, trans. Richard Philcox (1961; New York: Grove Press, 2004). For a discussion, see Robert J.C. Young, *Postcolonialism: An Historical Introduction* (Malden, MA: Blackwell, 2001).
177 A point developed by Naomi Griffiths, *The Contexts of Acadian History 1686–1784* (Montreal and Kingston: McGill-Queen's University Press, 1992), 21.
178 See John G. Reid, 'Pax Britannica or Pax Indigena? Planter Nova Scotia (1760–1782) and Competing Strategies of Pacification,' *Canadian Historical Review* 85, 4 (December 2004): 669–92, for an important revision of Brebner in this respect.
179 For 'civic humanism' and the Patriotes' impressions of the United States, see Louis-Georges Harvey, *Le printemps de l'Amérique française: Américanité, anticolonialisme et républicanisme dans le discours politique québécois, 1805–1837* (Montreal: Boréal, 2004); for Canadian Liberals and the U.S. constitutional counter-example in the 1870s–1890s, see Vipond, *Liberty and Community.*
180 For an interesting overview, see Michael Freeden, *Liberalism Divided: A Study in British Political Thought 1914–1939* (Oxford: Clarendon Press, 1986). For a classic statement of new liberalism, see L.T. Hobhouse, *Liberalism* (1911; New York: Oxford University Press, 1964).
181 See Doug Owram, *The Government Generation: Canadian Intellectuals and the State 1900–1945* (Toronto: University of Toronto Press, 1986) and Barry

Ferguson, *Remaking Liberalism: The Intellectual Legacy of Adam Shortt, O.D. Skelton, W.C. Clark, and W.A. Macintosh, 1890–1925* (Montreal and Kingston: McGill-Queen's University Press, 1993).

182 See R. Douglas Francis, *Frank H. Underhill: Intellectual Provocateur* (Toronto: University of Toronto Press, 1986) and Michiel Horn, *The League for Social Reconstruction: Intellectual Origins of the Democratic Left in Canada 1930–1942* (Toronto: University of Toronto Press, 1980).

183 As Nancy Christie, *Engendering the State: Family, Work, and Welfare in Canada* (Toronto: University of Toronto Press, 2000), sceptically observes: 'From the Liberals' point of view, family allowances were but a temporary cash bonus. While they promised access to postwar abundance, they were in fact yet another defence of the old Victorian work ethic' (309).

184 See F.A. Hayek, 'The Principles of a Liberal Social Order,' in *Liberalism: Critical Concepts in Political Theory*, vol. 1, ed. G.W. Smith (London and New York: Routledge, 2002), 41–56.

185 John Gray, *Hayek on Liberty* (Oxford: Martin Robertson, 1986), ix; see also David Graham and Peter Clarke, *The New Enlightenment: The Rebirth of Liberalism* (London: Macmillan, 1986).

186 Chandran Kukathas, 'Hayek and Liberalism,' in *The Cambridge Companion to Hayek*, ed. Edward Feser (Cambridge: Cambridge University Press, 2006), 182.

187 See Murray Forsyth, 'Hayek's Bizarre Liberalism,' *Political Studies* 36 (1988): 235–50.

188 See Nikolas Rose, *Powers of Freedom: Reframing Political Thought* (Cambridge: Cambridge University Press, 1999), chap. 4, 'Advanced Liberalism,' 137–66 for some shrewd insights into the implications of 'advanced' (or Hayekian) liberalism for the concept of the 'citizen.'

189 Morton, *Unravelling Gramsci*, 70–1, citing Philip McMichael.

190 Here I differ with Anthony Arblaster, whose work on liberalism I have found generally helpful, but whose fourteen-part definition encompasses not only the (relatively uncontroversial) concept of the primacy of the individual, but also the much more contentious attributions of atomism, the sovereignty of desires, and so on – some of which fit Canadian liberalism awkwardly at best. See Arblaster, *Rise and Decline of Western Liberalism*, chap. 1.

191 John Gray, *Post-Liberalism: Studies in Political Thought* (London and New York: Routledge, 1993).

192 In this respect, reconnaissance has tried to absorb some post-structuralist insights and lessons, while humbly differing on critical-realist grounds with the nominalist positions attributed to certain post-structuralists. It

seems to me that much of the work Foucauldians have undertaken on the formation of the administrative state complements rather than competes with Gramscian concepts of hegemony, if the former are taken as observations about historical phenomena amenable to empirical investigation, and the latter as observations about the specific modalities of rule rather than as deterministic master narratives. At least among its foremost Canadian practitioners – here one thinks especially of the work of Bruce Curtis – their framework does not seem to demand either a consistent nominalism or the idealistic dematerialization of the state: see, for instance Bruce Curtis, 'Taking the State Back Out: Rose and Miller on Political Power,' *British Journal of Sociology* 46, 4 (1995): 575–89.

193 As Nikolas Rose remarks: 'To individuate a rationality is not to construct an ideal type against which a non-ideal reality can be calibrated, but to diagnose the moral, epistemological and linguistic regularities that make it possible to think and say certain things truthfully – and hence to conceive and do certain things politically. Undoubtedly the naming is a creative act, individuating problems, objects, explanations, strategies and justifications in a new way. But the proper name is also an operative element in political thought itself, which troubles itself "reflexively" over what it is, for example, to govern in a "liberal" way.' Rose, *Powers of Freedom*, 275. Earlier, Rose provided an example in his discussion of the much-contested concept of 'neoliberalism': '[T]he various tactics enacted by the British Conservative government under Margaret Thatcher in the 1980s were not realizations of any philosophy – whether it was Keith Joseph reading Adam Smith or one of his advisers reading Hayek. They were, rather, contingent lash-ups of thought and action, in which various problems of governing were resolved through drawing upon instruments and procedures that happened to be available, in which new ways of governing were invented in a rather ad hoc way, as practical attempts to think about and act upon specific problems in particular locales, and various other existing techniques and practices were merely dressed up in new clothes. But, in the course of this process, a certain rationality, call it neo-liberalism, came to provide a way of linking up these various tactics, integrating them in thought so that they appeared to partake in a coherent logic. And once they did so, once a kind of rationality could be extracted from them, made to be translatable with them, it could be redirected towards both them and other things, which could now be thought of in the same way – as, for example, in the various deployments in the notion of entrepreneurship. And such rationalities were then embodied in, or came to infuse, a whole variety of practices and assemblages for regulating economic life, medical care, welfare benefits,

professional activity and so forth' (27). This is a fine Foucauldian rendition, it seems to me, of the Gramscian logic of hegemony and transposition – an indication, perhaps, that these two frameworks of analysis, so often placed in stark contrast with each other, may be capable of a mutually beneficial conversation.

194 S.J.R. Noel, *Patrons, Clients, Brokers: Ontario Society and Politics, 1791–1896* (Toronto: University of Toronto Press, 1990); Paul Maroney, 'The Peaceable Kingdom Reconsidered: Attitudes toward War in English Canada, 1885–1914,' (Ph.D. diss., Queen's University, 1995).

195 Dworetz, *Unvarnished Doctrine*, 191. The thesis that civic humanism and liberalism were completely separate traditions is also powerfully critiqued by Vickie B. Sullivan, *Machiavelli, Hobbes, and the Formation of a Liberal Republicanism in England* (Cambridge: Cambridge University Press, 2004).

196 Noel, *Patrons, Clients, Brokers*, chap. 13.

197 Fecteau, *La liberté du pauvre*, 273 (my translation).

198 Note the superb description of Vatican diplomacy with respect to Canada in Roberto Perin, *Rome in Canada: The Vatican and Canadian Affairs in the Late Victorian Era* (Toronto: University of Toronto Press, 1990).

199 Young, *In Its Corporate Capacity*; see also his intriguing study of clerical nationalism, railway promotion, and inter-city rivalry in *Promoters and Politicians: The North-Shore Railways in the History of Quebec, 1854–85* (Toronto: University of Toronto Press, 1978).

200 As Marta Danylewycz remarks, in *Taking the Veil: An Alternative to Marriage, Motherhood, and Spinsterhood in Quebec, 1840–1920* (Toronto: McClelland and Stewart, 1987), 26: '[C]onservative politicians, who played a leading role in the Assembly in these crucial years of building the school system, acquiesced in religious involvement, leaving educational affairs in the hands of the overly zealous priests. Such an arrangement freed a greater share of public money and time for investment in lucrative enterprises such as the railway' (26). As she goes on to demonstrate, even many supporters of the Liberal Party were swayed by the argument that the Church, unlike the state, was immune to the 'evils of nepotism and patronage and would not compromise education in partisan politics' (28).

201 I paraphrase Fecteau, *La liberté du pauvre*, 9. It is not altogether clear to me whether Fecteau is objecting as much to the historians who have drawn attention to the actual potency of this petit-bourgeois 'triptych' as he is to its actually-existing effect of reducing the emancipatory potential of 'liberty.'

202 See esp. Eugenio F. Biagini and Alastair J. Reid, eds., *Currents of Radicalism: Popular Radicalism, Organized Labour and Party Politics in Britain 1850–1914*

(Cambridge: Cambridge University Press, 1991) and Eugenio F. Biagini, *Liberty, Retrenchment and Reform: Popular Liberalism in the Age of Gladstone, 1860–1880* (Cambridge: Cambridge University Press, 1992).

203 As Fecteau remarks, 'liberal charity' rests on the principle 'that poverty is a private affair, that nothing at all justifies state interference in the liberty of the rich and the poor.' It hence depoliticizes the question of poverty. Many workers' associations, he goes on to say, fully accepted the logic of this position, 'to the extent that they valorized the organizational capacity of the workers and their liberty in the face of the bourgeois state. The development of associations of mutual aid and of cooperativism thus appeared as an ambiguous response to this liberal ethic, translated into the language of solidarity of the working class.' Fecteau, *La liberté du pauvre*, 249 (my translation).

204 Ian McKay, 'By Wisdom, Wile or War: The Provincial Workmen's Association and the Struggle for Working-Class Independence in Nova Scotia, 1879–97,' *Labour/Le Travail*, 18 (Fall 1986): 13–62; McKay, 'Robert Drummond,' in *Dictionary of Canadian Biography*, vol. 15 (Toronto: University of Toronto Press, 2006).

205 For an outstanding work of revisionist labour history that calls this archetype into question, see John Belshaw, *Colonization and Community: The Vancouver Island Coalfield and the Making of the British Columbian Working Class* (Montreal and Kingston: McGill-Queen's University Press, 2002).

206 Stephen Leacock, *The Unsolved Riddle of Social Justice and Other Essays: The Social Criticism of Stephen Leacock*, ed. and intro. Alan Bowker (1920; Toronto: University of Toronto Press, 1973), 130.

207 See A.A. den Otter, *The Philosophy of Railways: The Transcontinental Idea in British North America* (Toronto: University of Toronto Press, 1997), who undermines the nationalist myth of the Canadian Pacific Railway (but not the notion that contemporaries identified connection with the railway with their own economic and social improvement).

208 McKay, 'Liberal Order Framework,' 627.

209 Nadia Urbinati, Foreword to Piero Gobetti, *On Liberal Revolution*, ed. Nadia Urbinati, trans. William McCuaig (New Haven and London: Yale University Press, 2000), xxii.

210 See, for instance, J.I. Little, *Society and State in Transition: The Politics of Institutional Reform in the Eastern Townships, 1838–1852* (Montreal and Kingston: McGill-Queen's University Press, 1997). This approach is much closer to Gramsci's concept of hegemony than a narrow focus on one-sided 'state control' or 'moral regulation.' See also Gilbert M. Joseph and Daniel Nugent, eds., *Everyday Forms of State Formation: Revolution and the Negotia-*

tion of Rule in Modern Mexico (Durham and London: Duke University Press, 1994), esp. Derek Seyer, 'Everyday Forms of State Formation: Some Dissident Remarks on "Hegemony,"' 367–77: '[T]o abstract out, reify, and monolithically counterpose "hegemony" and "resistance" is to misunderstand both' (377).

211 Steven B. Smith, *Hegel's Critique of Liberalism: Rights in Context* (Chicago and London: University of Chicago Press, 1989 [1991 edition]), 10.

212 Rodgers, *Atlantic Crossings*, 78.

213 The relationship between classical nineteenth-century liberalism and contemporary neo-liberalism merits much further work by Canadian political historians and theorists. For interesting international work that documents linkages between the two, see Norman P. Berry, 'The New Liberalism,' *British Journal of Political Science* 13 (1983): 93–123; Ellen Frankel Paul, 'Liberalism, Unintended Orders and Evolutionism,' *Political Studies* 36 (1988): 251–72, which invaluably explores the relationship between Herbert Spencer and F.A. Hayek; and Edna Ullmann-Margalit, 'The Invisible Hand and the Cunning of Reason,' *Social Research* 64 (1997): 181–98, which documents the continuity of Adam Smith's 'hidden hand' motif from the eighteenth to the twentieth centuries: all three are included in *Liberalism: Critical Concepts in Political Theory*, vol. 2, *Rights, Property and Markets*, ed. G.W. Smith (London and New York: Routledge, 2002). The ideals of neo-liberalism are amusingly summarized by Steven Lukes, *Liberals and Cannibals: The Implications of Diversity* (London and New York: Verso, 2003), chap. 12. On the face of it, Lukes's fabled 'Utilitaria' and 'Libertaria,' i.e., utopia as imagined by utilitarians and libertarians respectively, would, combined, seem to capture much of the underlying political landscape of Canada, 1840–1940. For an important argument on the links between classical liberalism and contemporary neo-liberalism, see Daniel Shapiro, 'Liberalism and Libertarianism: Narrowing the Gap,' in *Liberty in the 21st Century: Contemporary Libertarian Thought*, ed. T. Machan and D.B. Rasmussen (Lanham, MD: Rowman and Littlefield, 1995), 298–304.

214 See especially Jennifer Pitts, *A Turn to Empire: The Rise of Imperial Liberalism in Britain and France* (Princeton and Oxford: Princeton University Press, 2005), chap. 4; David Wiltshire, *The Social and Political Thought of Herbert Spencer* (Oxford: Oxford University Press, 1978); Daniel Becquemont and Laurent Mucchielli, *Le cas Spencer: Religion, science et politique* (Paris: Presses Universitaires de France, 1998).

215 Much of the best historiography on the welfare state has developed in this context, and productive exchanges between the liberal order framework and environmental history are already well under way. See, for example,

James R. Allum, 'Smoke across the Border: The Environmental Politics of
the Trail Smelter Dispute' (PhD diss., Queen's University, 1995).
216 Harris, *Making Native Space*, xxviii. This is perhaps a good place to indicate
that British Columbia historiography is currently in the vanguard of the
new political and social history in Canada: in essence, it has become the
site wherein many major debates over theory and evidence are first elaborated.
217 Rodgers, *Atlantic Crossings*, 91, paraphrasing the views of Wagner.
218 They can rejoin a properly understood Locke, for instance, in appreciating
the very narrow limits of rights over property. See Sreenivasan, *Limits of
Lockean Rights in Property*, passim.
219 And here we may find especially interesting the particular forms of 'revolutionary liberalism' developed in Italy, and associated with such figures
as Carlo Rosselli and Piero Gobetti, who can both be considered exponents
of Gramsci-like currents of radical immanentism and critical realism.
Within this tradition, conflict between ideas and interests is viewed posi-
tively – not in the sense of the liberal public sphere, geared to produce premature harmonies based upon a homogenization of 'Opinion,' but rather
because, in the midst of revolutionary dissent, people acquire the opportunity to develop self-reliance and a dialectical appreciation of historical
choices. See Carlo Rosselli, *Liberal Socialism*, ed. Nadia Urbinati, trans. William McCuaig (Princeton: Princeton University Press, 1994); Gobetti, *On
Liberal Revolution*. Gobetti brought to the study of the Risorgimento and its
passive revolution a critical realist mode of analysis strongly reminiscent
of that of Gramsci (with whom he was a collaborator at *L'Ordine Nuovo*).
220 For the citation and discussion, see Alexander, *Commodity & Propriety*, 26–7.

Contributors

Jerry Bannister is Associate Professor of History at Dalhousie University. He is the author of *The Rule of the Admirals: Law, Custom, and Naval Government in Newfoundland, 1699–1832* (University of Toronto Press and the Osgoode Society, 2003), which won the Sir John A. Macdonald Prize.

Robin Jarvis Brownlie teaches in the History Department at the University of Manitoba and is the author of *A Fatherly Eye: Indian Agents, Government Power, and Aboriginal Resistance in Ontario, 1918–1939* (Oxford University Press, 2003).

Stéphane Castonguay is Canada Research Chair in Environmental History, and a member of the Centre interuniversitaire d'études québécoises at the Université du Québec à Trois-Rivières. He has published books and articles in the history of science. In 2006 he edited two special editions on the environmental history of Quebec, in the *Revue d'histoire de l'Amérique française* (60, 1–2, pp. 3–203) and in *Globe: La revue internationale d'études québécoises* (9, 1, pp. 11–255). An abridged version of the latter appeared in English in the collection *New Perspectives in Quebec Studies* (Nota Bene, 2007).

Jean-François Constant is a doctoral candidate in the department of history at McGill University and a member of the Montreal History Group. His research explores the social and cultural origins of the modern consumer society through the interactions of liberalism and the market economy.

Bruce Curtis teaches in the Department of Sociology and Anthropology at Carleton University. His most recent book is *The Politics of Population: State Formation, Statistics, and the Census of Canada, 1840–1875*. In addition to making contributions to the literatures on scientific discovery, the government of sexuality, and the history of the human sensorium, his main ongoing project is on literacy, schooling, and politics in Lower Canada.

Michèle Dagenais is Professor of History at the Université de Montréal. Her research focuses on comparative political and environmental history in urban areas. She is the author of *Faire et fuir la ville: Espaces publics de culture et de loisirs à Montréal et Toronto aux XIXe et XXe siècles* (Les Presses de l'Université Laval, 2006) and *Des pouvoirs et des hommes: L'administration municipale de Montréal, 1900–1950* (McGill-Queen's University Press, 2000).

Michel Ducharme was educated at the Université de Montréal and McGill University. He is an Assistant Professor in the History Department at the University of British Columbia. His research focuses on the intellectual, cultural, and political debates between 1760 and 1867 and examines the discursive foundations on which the development of the Canadian state rests.

E.A. Heaman is Associate Professor of History and Canada Research Chair at McGill University. She is the author of *The Inglorious Arts of Peace: Exhibitions in Canadian Society during the 19th Century* (University of Toronto Press, 1999) and *St Mary's: The History of a London Teaching Hospital* (McGill-Queen's University Press, 2003).

Darin Kinsey is a postdoctoral fellow at the Université Laval, where he is specializing in the geographical and environmental dimensions of Québec's eel fishery. He earned a PhD at the Université du Québec à Trois-Rivières in 2008 with a dissertation entitled 'Fashioning a Freshwater Eden: Elite Anglers, Fish Culture, and State Development of Quebec's Sport Fishery.' He is also the author of '"Seeding the Water as the Earth": The Epicenter and Peripheries of a Western Aquacultural Revolution,' *Environmental History* 11, 3 (2006): 527–66.

Robert McDonald is an Associate Professor of History at the University of British Columbia, where he teaches British Columbia history and Canadian social history. In *Making Vancouver* (1996) he explored the role of class and status in structuring social relations in the early history of the city of Vancouver. Currently he is writing a book on modernity, liberalism, and the populist impulse in British Columbia politics to the 1970s.

Ian McKay, educated at Dalhousie University and the University of Warwick, teaches history at Queen's University. His books include *Quest of the Folk: Antimodernism and Cultural Selection in Twentieth-Century Nova Scotia* and *Rebels, Reds, Radicals: Rethinking Canada's Left History.* His present project is a multi-volume history of the Canadian Left.

Jeffrey L. McNairn is a member of the Department of History at Queen's University. He is particularly interested in state–civil society relations, the public sphere and print culture, British imperialism and the development of neo-British settler colonies, and the history of political and economic liberalism. He is currently working on a project tentatively entitled 'Insolvent, Imprisoned, Bankrupt: Failure and the Law in Common-Law British North America, 1752–1869.'

Adele Perry teaches at the University of Manitoba, where she is Canada Research Chair in Western Canadian Social History. She is working on a project on kinship, migration, and transnationalism in the nineteenth-century British empire.

R.W. Sandwell teaches in the history and teacher education programs at the Ontario Institute for Studies in Education of the University of Toronto. In addition to being a historian of rural Canada, education, and the family, she is interested in the intersection of history education and public memory in contemporary Canada. Her most recent book is *Contesting Rural Space: Land Policy and Practices of Resettlement on Saltspring Island, 1859–1891* (McGill Queen's University Press, 2005). She is editor of two collections of essays, *Beyond the City Limit: Rural History in British Columbia* (UBC Press, 1999) and *To the Past: History Education, Public Memory, and Citizenship in Canada* (University of Toronto Press, 2006).

Index

Note: Page numbers in italics refer to the original pagination of Ian McKay's 'The Liberal Order Framework: A Prospectus for a Reconnaissance of Canadian History,' *Canadian Historical Review* 81 (2000): 617–45. This article is reprinted here as chapter 2 (pp. 35–63).

Aberhart, William, 335, 401

Aboriginal peoples: and Christian churches, 281, 302–4, 310, 402 (*see also* missionaries *and* residential schools); enfranchisement of, 301–2, 308, 310–12, 314, *625* (*see also* citizenship *and* suffrage); and government policy, 8, 67, 168, 298–302, 304–5, 308, 312–14, 316; legal status of, 20, 275, 280–1, 311–12 (*see also* Indian Act [1876]); and the liberal order, 8, 103, 164, 181, 234–5, 257–8, 263, 279–81, 298–300, 305, 307–8, 311–12, 325, 361–2, 381, *626, 636–7* (*see also* liberal order, resistance to); regulation of, 276, 285; rights of, 12, 154, 159–60, 167–8, 258, 289, 298, 301, 309–12, 316, 362, 405

Aborigines Protection Society, 300

Acadians, deportation of (1755), 103, 405

Acton, Lord, 13

Act for the Protection of Fisheries (1855), 233

Act of Union (1841), 207, *632*

African-Canadians, 282; discrimination against, 279, 282–3, 285. *See also* immigration policy

Ajzenstat, Janet, 9, 125, 380, 389, 391–2, 395

a-liberalism, 76, 214, 246–7, 250–2, 259, 261–3, 266–7n28, 316, 325, 405, *629–30, 640*

American Revolution, and loyalist order, 99, 104, 127

Amerindians. *See* Aboriginal peoples

analytical philosophy, 65

anarchism, 8, 25n23, 354, 398, 419

Anderson, Kay, 282

Anderson, Warwick, 190

anglers. *See* sport fishery

Angus, Ian, 277

animals, cruelty towards, 227

anti-Americanism, 104, 128–9

anti-communitarianism, 250
antiliberalism, 144n172
Appiah, Kwame Anthony, 76
Arblaster, Anthony, 403
Armitage, David, 100
Arneil, Barbara, 388
Arthur, George, 112–18
Asians: discrimination against, 282, 285, 290, 382; and the liberal order, 325. *See also* head tax *and* immigration policy
Atlantic history, 100, 153
autonomy. *See* liberalism, and autonomy

Backhouse, Constance, 282
Bagot, Charles, 159
Bahro, Rudolf, 353
Bailyn, Bernard, 410
Bainbridge, Isaac, 399
Baldwin, Robert, 112, 353
Bannister, Jerry, 12, 17, 19, 74, 152, 160, 165, 246, 249
Baron, Hal, 262
Baskerville, Peter, 326
Beard, Charles, 152
Becker, Carl, 410
Bell, David, 104
Bellamy, Richard, 76, 327–8
Belshaw, John, 333
Bengough, J.W., 387
Bennett, R.B., 283–4, 353, 399
Bennett, W.A.C., 330
Bentham, Jeremy, 181, 183, 190, 352–3, 384, 416, 632, 636
Benthamites. *See* Bentham, Jeremy
Benton, Lauren, 104
Berger, Carl, 65–6, 100
Beveridge, William, 330
Biagini, Eugenio F., 182, 328–31

Bill of Rights (1689), 156
Binnema, Theodore, 306
biopolitics, 178, 190, 227
biopower, 227
Bittermann, Rusty, 378
Blackstone, William, 156, 376, 383
Blackstone's Commentaries (Blackstone), 379, 383
Blake, Edward, 151–2, 385–6, 395, 397
Bliss, Michael, 3
Bolsheviki and Peace, The (Trotsky), 398
Bolshevism, 194
Bourassa, Henri, 640
Bourdieu, Pierre, 194
Bourget, Ignace, 163
Bradburn, Douglas, 125
Bradbury, Bettina, 286–8
Brant, John, 289
Brewer, John, 103
Brinton, Crane, 99
British North America Act (1867), 127, 169, 379–80, 390, 393, 396, 635
British North American Land Company, 184
Brebner, J.B., 622n11
Brode, Patrick, 118
Brougham, Lord, 111
Brown, George, 66, 353, 387, 389, 397, 402, 407, 414
Brown, R. Craig, 375
Brown, Wendy, 276, 278, 291
Brownlie, Robin Jarvis, 8, 22, 84, 281
Bryan, Bradley, 380
Buller, Charles, 184, 207
Bumsted, J.M., 126
Burke, Edmund, 112, 122, 127, 150–1, 156

Cahill, Barry, 106

Cail, Robert, 332
Cairns, Alan, 311
Calder decision (1973), 314
Caldwell, Boyd, 151
Campbell, Robert, 283
Canada's Origins: Liberal, Tory, or Republican? (Ajzenstat et al.), 125
Canadian Forward, 399
Canadian Men and Women of Their Time, 384
Canadian Multiculturalism Act (1988), 393
Canovan, Margaret, 334, 336
capitalism, 4, 9, 65, 81, 85, 253, 257, 262, 270–1n50, 283, 304, 308, 331, 337, 339, 369–71, 419, *622, 629, 633*. *See also* liberalism, and capitalism
Careless, J.M.S., 402
Carson, William, 105
Carter, Sarah, 303
Cartier, George-Étienne, 393
Castonguay, Stéphane, 15, 17
Catholic Church, in Québec, 14, 162–4, 411, *633*. *See also* liberal order, and Catholic Church
Chadwick, Edwin, 181
Champlain, Samuel de, 164
Chapais, Jean-Charles, 230
Charter of Rights and Freedoms (1982), 127, 170, 311, 393, 416
Chartier, Roger, 79
Chartist movement, 329
Château Clique, 125
Chinatown, 282
Chinese-Canadians, discrimination against, 275, 279, 282–5, 289–90, *625*. *See also* Asians, discrimination against
Chinese Immigration Act (1885), 284. *See also* head tax *and* Royal Com-

mission on Chinese Immigration (1884–5)
Chinese Immigration Act (1923), 284. *See also* head tax
Chrétien, Jean, 128
Christie, Gordon, 307
church, relations with the state, 67, 388, 402, 411. *See also* liberalism, and religion
citizenship, 151, 182, 192, 246–8, 256–8, 278–81, 284, 302, 308, 310–12, 314, 325, 360, 363, *641*. *See also* suffrage
civic humanism, 66, 69, 82, 101, 154, 182, 329, 405, *618, 633–4, 640*; and socialism, 76
civic republicanism. *See* republicanism, civic
Civil Code (1866), 19, 379
civil law, 332, *633*
civil liberties, 7, 9, 12–13, 126, 148–9, 324, 386, 397–8, 401
Civil War in France, The (Marx), 398
Clarkson, Christopher, 262
class, 7–8, 66, 68, 71, 82, 105, 108, 112, 116, 176–8, 185, 187, 192–3, 207, 248, 251, 254, 259, 279, 326, 328–31, 337, 351, 356, 362, 390, 402, 407, 412–14, *627*; and hegemony, 16, 20, 84–5, 117, 177, 179–80, 323, 363–4, 369–71
Clear Grits. *See* Grits
clergy reserves, 161, 382, 406
Code of Civil Procedure (1867), 379
collectivism, 82, 84, 124, 152, 170, 181, 305–6, 329, 331–3, 397, *625*; agrarian, 182
Colonial Leviathan (Greer and Radforth), 164, 274
colonialism, 190, 247–8, 258, 263,

264n4, 286, 291, 298, 303–4, 309,
388, 395–7, 407, 415, 418
colonization, 166, 184, 302, 308–10,
315, 332, 361, 380, 401, 405, 415
Commentaries on the Laws of England
(Blackstone), 156–7
Communist Party, *643–4*
Confederation, 19, 122, 124, 150, 168,
177, 192, 358, 360, 367, 380, 389–91,
393, *633–4. See also* British North
America Act (1867)
Connell, Robert, 338
Conquest (1760), 101, 103, 162
Conquest of Acadia (1710), 405
conservationism, 222, 229–31, 233–4,
236
conservationist movement. *See* conservationism
conservative rights talk. *See* rights
talk
conservatism, 7, 66, 147, 150 (*see also*
liberalism, and conservatism); definition of, 11, 149; and the liberal
order framework, 11–12, 18, 153,
358, 409; and neo-liberalism, 11, 80,
128, 331, 406–7, 416, *624, 645*; and
socialism, 11, 124, 330
*Considerations on Representative Gov-
ernment* (Mill), 13
Constant, Benjamin, 72
Constitution Act (1791), 103
Constitution Act (1867). *See* British
North America Act
Constitution Act (1982), 127–8
Continuous Passage Act (1908), 285
contractualism, *640*
Cook, Jane. *See* Gah-uk-sta-lus
Cook, Ramsay, 101, 375
Co-operative Commonwealth Feder-
ation (CCF), *643–4*; in British

Columbia, 327, 335–9; Regina
Manifesto (1933), 337
Cosgrove, Jack, 284
Coutume de Paris, 286
Cox, Robert, 365
Craig, Gerald, 358
Crehen, Kate, 364
Creighton, Donald, 383
Criminal Code, 19, 177, 359–60, *629,*
633
criminal law, 110, 116, *633*
critical race theory, 408
Croce, Benedetto, 366, 392, 416
Curtis, Bruce, 7, 17, 206, 226, 249, 262,
274, 324, 369

Dafoe, J.W., *641*
Dagenais, Michèle, 15, 17, 178, 226
Darwinism and Marxism (Pannekoek),
398
Declaration of Independence (1838),
154, 156, 161
Declaration of Independence, Amer-
ican, 291
Declaration of the People of Rupert's
Land and of the Norhtwest (1869),
165–7, 174n56
Declaratory Act (1778), 109–10
decolonization. *See* colonization
Demerson, Velma, 279
democracy, definition of, 86–7n1. *See*
also liberalism, and democracy
Department of Indian Affairs. *See*
Aboriginal peoples, and govern-
ment policy
Desmond, Viola, 279
Dickinson, H.T., 156
Diefenbaker, John, 170
DiGaetano, Alan, 205
Dixon, Fred, 400

Dominion Lands Act (1872), 287
Dorion, Antoine-Aimé, *634*
Douglas, Mary, 224
Drummond, Robert, 413
Ducharme, Michel, 154
Dunsmuir, Robert, 332–3
Duplessis, Maurice, 353, 401
Durham, Lord, 104–5, 108, 125, 161, 205, 207–8, 351, 353, 376, 385, *636*
Durham report, 101, 114, 124, 177, 201, 210, *632*
Durhamites. *See* Durham, Lord
Durkheim, Émile, 183
Dworetz, Steven, 410

East India Company, 304
economic determinism, 177
Economic Interpretation of the Constitution of the United States, An (Beard), 152
economics, 65, 153, 252, 305, 391, 406; and religion, 66
Eley, Geoff, 394
Elias, Norbert, 190
elites, 20–1, 77, 105, 122, 124, 204, 213, 226, 229, 233–6, 326, 328–9, 332, 334, 339, 361; political, 4, 18–19, 105, 204, 325
Elkins, David, 334
enfranchisement. *See* citizenship *and* suffrage
Enfranchisement Act (1869), 302
environmentalism, 229, 408
equal rights. *See* rights
equality. *See* liberalism, and equality
Escheaters, 357. *See also* Prince Edward Island land question
ethnicity, 13, 17, 159, 162, 167, 187, 207, 247, 256–7, 279, 347, 351, 356, *627*

Evans, Arthur 'Slim,' 283

Family Compact, 110, 113, 122, 125, 161, 288, 309–10
Family Herald, 407
Fanon, Frantz, 405
Faragher, John Mack, 103
fascism, 7, 253, 401
Febvre, Lucien, 79
Fecteau, Jean-Marie, 12, 14, 155, 163–4, 169, 274, 411
federal disallowance, 151–2
feminism, first-wave, 82, 84, 278, 286–7, 293n15, *634–5*
feminism, maternal. *See* feminism, first wave
feminist theory, 177, 274, 276–7, 408
Fierlbeck, Katherine, 125
First Nations. *See* Aboriginal peoples
fish and game clubs. *See* sport fishery
Fordism, 180
forestry, 228–32
Forgacs, Denis, 363–4
Foucault, Michel, 17, 164, 179–80, 186–8, 190–4, 203, 210, 226, 240n24, 431n58, *619*
Founding of New Societies, The (Hartz), 123
Frank, Thomas, 153
Free Trade Agreement, 128
Freeden, Michael, 71–2, 325, 330, 336
freedom. *See* liberty
French Revolution, 127, 150, 156–7, 161, 328
Friedman, Harriet, 262
Fyson, Donald, 205

Gah-uk-sta-lus (Jane Cook), 83–4
Gardiner, Michael, 254
Gazette (Quebec), 158

gender, 7–8, 82, 112, 177, 187, 189, 207, 254, 256–7, 275–80, 282–3, 288, 291, 325–6, 351, 390, 393, 397, *627. See also* liberalism, and gender; liberal order, and gender; *and* liberal order framework, and gender

General Mining Association. *See* royal prerogative, in coalfields of Nova Scotia

Gentlemen's Agreement (1907), 285

Gindin, Sam, 364

Girard, Philip, 377–8

Gladstone, William, 329, 333, 412–13

Glenelg, Lord, 113–15

Globe, 67, 389

Glorious Revolution, 150, 160

Goldman, Emma, 398

Gould, Eliga, 104

governmentality, 17, 179, 186–7, 194, 203, 207, 222, 226–7, 247, 249, 255, 263–4, 264n4, *619;* Anglo-Australian school of, 188

governmentalization of the state, 193–4

Gradual Civilization Act (1857), 299, 308

Gramsci, Antonio, 5, 15–16, 65–6, 68–9, 77, 80–1, 84, 86, 170, 176–7, 179–80, 184, 194, 323, 326, 349, 363–75, 387, 392, 397, 407, 416–17, *619, 627–9, 638*

Gramsci's Political Thought (Simon), 363

Gramsci Reader (Forgacs), 363

Granatstein, Jack, 3, 123

Grant, George, 68

Gray, John, 70–1, 401, 406, 408

Green, T.H., 329

Greenwood, Murray, 108

Greer, Allan, 82, 108, 274–5

Grits, 10, 357

Grote, George, 182

Guerre des éteignoirs, 214

Guibord, Joseph, 402

Guide illustré du sylviculteur canadien (Chapais), 230

Gunn, Simon, 364

Guthrie, Sam, 337

Habeas Corpus Act (1679), 147

Habermas, Jürgen, 354

Hagerman, Christopher, 114–15

Hak, Gordon, 335–6

Halifax, as imperial outpost, 102–3

Hall, Catherine, 277

Hall, John, 149

Hall, Stuart, 10, 326, 328–31, 336

Harper, Stephen, 128

Harring, Sidney, 159

Harris, Cole, 379, 418

Harris, José, 331

Hartz, Louis, 123–4, 153, 409, *626–7*

Hartz-Horowitz, framework or thesis, 107, 125, 360

Harvey, Louis-Georges, 101, 182

Hay, Douglas, 116

Hayek, F.A., 183, 406

Head, Francis Bond, 112–16

head tax, 128, 284, 401. *See also* immigration policy

Heaman, E.A., 9, 17, 21, 71, 99, 249, 277, 315, 324

hegemony, 5, 15–17, 117, 134n42, 169–70, 194, 203, 323, 339, 340n5, 363–72, 394, 415, *627–8 (see also* liberalism, and hegemony); and historical bloc, 368–9, 372, 376–7, 394, *628;* and Italian Risorgimento, 366–7, 417; limits to theory of, 83, 184; Lockean, 124; and passive revolution, 5, 18, 99, 358, 370–5, 407, 642–3 (*see also* liberal order, and passive revolution); transnational character of, 369–70

Hemings, Sally, 291

Hepburn, Mitch, 353, 401

Hexter, J.M., 149

Hilton, Boyd, 78–9

historical bloc. *See* hegemony, and historical bloc

historiography: Canada, 3–6, 66, 123–4, 129, 176–7, 179, 204, 223, 257, 274, 347–8, 389–94, 396, 403, 407, 420n2, 617–20; Québec, 4, 14, 182, 347

Hitler, Adolf, 179

Hobbes, Thomas, 149, 164, 166, 182, 397

Hobhouse, L.T., 74, 330

Horowitz, Gad, 11, 124

Howe, Joseph, 106–8, 110, 353, 389, 637

Hudson's Bay Company, 166, 633

human rights, 154–6, 159, 161–2, 165, 170, 258, 324. *See also* rights

Hume, David, 149

Humphrey, John, 170

Ignatieff, George, 170

immigration, racialization of, 276

Immigration Act (1910), 285

immigration policy, 275, 284–5, 377, 628

imperialism, 101–5, 126, 167, 275, 282

improvement. *See* liberalism, and improvement

Indian Act (1876), 280–1, 298, 301–2, 304, 310–12, 314, 316, 393

Indian Affairs system. *See* Aboriginal peoples, and government policies

Indigenous peoples. *See* Aboriginal peoples

individual: as abstract principle and category, 7, 350–1, 355, 421n7, 623–5; categories of, 82–4, 192, 362; humanity of, 276–7; and liberalism, 7, 70, 248, 250, 630–1 (*see also* individualism); rational and self-governing, 178, 181, 223–4

individualism, 8, 73, 128, 148–9, 152–3, 163, 169, 181–2, 250, 255, 276, 286, 303, 306, 316, 323, 329, 332–3, 337, 350, 406, 624–5, 644–5. *See also* possessive individualism

individuality. *See* individualism

individual rights. *See* rights

Institut Canadien, 402

Isin, Engin, 203–4

Ives, Peter, 364

James II, 156

Japanese Canadians, 401, 625. *See also* Asians, discrimination against

Jefferson, Thomas, 119, 181, 291, 419

Joly de Lotbinière, Henri-Gustave, 230

Jones, Gareth Stedman, 78

Jones, Peter, 159, 308

Joseph, Jonathan, 365

Joyce, Patrick, 211

Kant, Immanuel, 98

Keynes, John Maynard, 330, 643

King, William Lyon Mackenzie, 330, 351, 353, 373, 375–6, 380, 382, 399, 403, 642

Kingwell, Mark, 128

Kinsey, Darin, 15, 17

Knights of Labor, Nanaimo Lodge of, 333

Komagata Maru, 285
Kramnick, Isaac, 410
Kukathas, Chandran, 406
Kymlicka, Will, 311

labour associations. *See* trade unions
labour camps, 396, 399, 416
labour movement, 333, 338, 375, 403, 634–5
Laclau, Ernest, 336
Laflèche, Louis-François, 82
La Fontaine, Louis-Hippolyte, 124
Lambton, John George. *See* Durham, Lord
Lamonde, Yvan, 154, 162
LaRocque, Emma, 306, 312
Last Cannon Shot, The (Monet), 124
late modernity, 276. *See also* modernity
Laurier, Wilfrid, 81, 162, 387, 396, *640*
Lawrence, Jon, 330
Laycock, David, 334
Leacock, Stephen, 413
League for Social Reconstruction, 330, 339
Leca, Jean, 13
Lefeaux, Wallis, 337
Lehning, James, 253
Levi, Giovanni, 253–4, 257
liberal conservatism, 149–50, 331. *See also* liberalism, and conservatism
Liberal Conservatives, 18, 150, 350, 359, 411, 413–14, *643*
Liberal Era. *See* Liberal Revolution
liberal governance, 202, 209, 211, 236, 322–3
liberal governmentality. *See* governmentality
liberal hegemony. *See* liberalism, and hegemony

liberal individual. *See* individual
liberal individualism. *See* individualism
liberalism: and authority, 153, 298; and autonomy, 11, 120, 152, 178, 190, 278–80, 287; and capitalism, 75–6, 81, 182–3, 336, 339, 354, 356, 377, 384–5, *623*; and Catholicism, *625*; and Christian churches, 302, 310; and conservatism, 11–13, 21, 68, 124, 149–50, 154–6, 164, 168–9, 330; definitions of, 6–10, 69–76, 86, 92n40, 125, 147–8, 248–50, 349–50, 353–6, 408–9, *624*; and democracy, 9, 72–3, 80, 120, 124, 126, 154, 164, 183, 316, 328–31, 339, 352, *623*; economic definition of, 4, 9; and equality, 7, 9–13, 21, 70–4, 80, 127–8, 148, 176, 180, 185–6, 206, 223, 225, 245, 248–9, 257, 259, 263, 276–8, 290, 300, 302–5, 308, 311–12, 315–16, 323, 325, 331, 355–6, 379, 384, 386, 392–3, 399, 401, 408–12, 414, 418–19, *624*; and everyday life, 253–5; and exclusion, 8, 21, 178, 185–6, 263, 276, 279; and gender, 277, 351, 414; and governmentality, 226–7; and hegemony, 126, 129, 147–9, 152, 154–5, 163, 167, 169, 176, 247, 251, 256–7, 260, 263, 316, 323, 326; historicization of, 65; as ideology, 5, 6, 7, 123, 147, 177, 186, 256, 326; and improvement, 76, 224–5, 255, 263, 325, 333, 335, 350, 353, 362, 383–4, 388, 393, 397, 414, 422n10 (*see also* liberalism, and progress); leftist critique of, 164; libertarian, 180, 183; and liberty, 147, *624*; limits of, 186; Lockean, *see* Locke, John; as a mode of gov-

ernment, 178–9, 181–2, 186; and 'new,' in Britain, 329–30; 'new,' in Canada, 406; origins of, 155, 276; political culture, 327–31; political definition of, 9, 71; and political liberties, 148; popular vs classical, in Britain, 328–9; and populism, 333–6; and progress, 71, 213, 221, 224, 227, 246, 254, 256, 263, 372, 385, 426n22; and race, 7–8, 189, 254, 257, 276–7, 414; and religion, 71, 162–4, 411; and republicanism, 182; and responsible government, 107–8; revolutionary character of, 65; and security, 180–1; and social-ism, 78, 80, 183, 329–31, 334, 335–9; and state authority, 122; varieties of, 184, 246, 249, 251, 278, 324–5, 330–1, 336, 340, 627; and violence, 178, 180. *See also* liberal order *and* liberal order framework

Liberalism (Hobhouse), 74

Liberalism and Modern Society (Bel-lamy), 327–8

liberalisms, multiplicity of. *See* liber-alism, varieties of

liberal order, 4, 5, 8, 150, 181, 222, 248, 356–7, 623–5; in British Columbia, 20, 324–7, 330–9; and British Empire, 351; and Catholic Church, 12, 14, 82, 162–4, 169, 401–2; and democracy, 213, 327, 356, 386–403; difference with liberal-ism, 6–7, 148 (*see also* a-liberalism *and* liberalism, varieties of); estab-lishment of, 202, 206, 214, 227, 286, 323, 332, 358–9; and exclusion, 224–5, 247, 251–2, 257, 268–9n39, 275, 278–9, 281, 285, 287–8, 325, 362–3, 626; and the family, 259,

261–3; and gender, 276, 356; illib-eral characteristics of, 116, 126, 281, 312–14 (*see also* a-liberalism); immanent or radical democratic critique of, 416–18; landscape of, 229, 236; masculinity of, 278; and non-human actors, 222–5, 233, 236; organic crises of, 369, 374–5, 399–401, 418, 444n160; organic intellec-tuals of, 85, 353, 355, 371, 380, 392, 394, 403, 413, *641*; origins of, 126, 166; resistance to, 21, 164–9, 213, 222, 247, 255–6, 298–301, 314–16, 326, 336–7, 339, 399, *634–7* (*see also* a-liberalism); and passive revolu-tion, 372–5, 400, 407, 412; and property, 376–86, *627*; in Québec, 14, *633*, *635–6*; and race, 276, 279, 282–3, 289, 356, 382; and residen-tial schools, 303, *637*; revolution-ary aspect of, 350, 357, *630–1*; and rural people, 260–3; transforma-tion of, 322; and women, 325–6, *626*. *See also* liberal order frame-work *and* liberalism

'Liberal Order in Canadian History' (2006 symposium), 6, 98, 265n14, 322–3

liberal order framework: and aborig-inal history, 257; definition of, 347–53; and democracy, 6, 65, 81, 418; and environmental history, 221–3, 225–6, 237; and feminist scholar-ship, 274; and gender, 275; and hegemony, 363, *638*; historiograph-ical influences in, 412; and intellec-tual history, 64–9, 85–6; and methodology, 77–82, 128, *627–8*; and microhistory, 254, 261; as par-adigm, 5, 7, 9, 79, 98, 123, 125, 147,

176, 184, 246, 274, 359–60, 396, *620–1*; and political history, 322; and postcolonial scholarship, 274; political implications of, 5, 415–16; and race, 258–9, 269–70n47, 275, 374; regional approach to, 324; and religion, 14; religious dimension of, 14; tautological aspect of, 79–80; and women, 275. *See also* liberal order *and* liberalism)

'The Liberal Order Framework: A Prospectus for a Reconnaissance of Canadian History.' *See* McKay, Ian

Liberal Revolution (c. 1840 to c. 1950), 4, 8, 358, 360–1, 404–5, 411, *632*

liberal revolution, 180, 348, 354, 357–9, 381, *637*; as counter-revolution, 122

Liberals, 10, 18, 124–5, 151, 155, 359, 373, 413–14, *633–4, 640, 643*

liberal theory, 185, 257, 276–7, 291, 378, 395, 401–2

libertarianism, 8, 25n23

libertarian liberalism. *See* liberalism, libertarian

liberties, 147, 149, 157, 159, 161. *See also* civil liberties

liberty, 148, 155, 163, 176, 180–1, 185, 208, 211, 223, 278, 300, 305, 323–4, 352, 355, *630* (*see also* liberalism, and liberty); liberal vs republican, 154

Lipset, Seymour Martin, 99, 107

Little, J.I., 204–5

Locke, John, 9, 26n24, 74–5, 78, 118–22, 127, 149, 152–4, 164, 166, 168, 182, 353, 376, 378, 380–1, 383–4, 387–8, 390–1, 397, 410, 419, *626, 636*

Loewen, Royden, 262

London Debating Society, 182

'long liberal revolution.' *See* Liberal Revolution

Loo, Tina, 83, 166

Lount, Samuel, 112–22, 160

Lowe, Lisa, 285

Lower, Arthur, 203, *641–2*

loyalism, 101, 124–8; and democracy, 105, 126

Loyalists, 19, 103–4, 118, 125–6, 153, 160, 283, 405

loyalist ethos, 127

loyalist order, 19, 99, 102–3, 105, 108, 112, 118, 126, 128

Lynch, William, 231

McCallum, Margaret, 378

McCallum, Todd, 256

McCarthy, D'Alton, 152

Macaulay, Thomas, 384

McClelland, J.S., 353–5

Macdonald, Angus L., 353

Macdonald, John A., 81, 150–1, 168–9, 281, 383, 391, 393, 396–7, 411, *637–8*

MacDonald, Norbert, 327

McDonald, Robert A.J., 7, 10, 17, 20, 249–50, 266–7n28, 412

McDougall, William, 167

McEachern, Allan, 258

Machiavelli, Niccolo, 154

Machiavellian Moment, The (Pocock), 410

McKay, Ian, 3–10, 12–13, 15–16, 17–22, 30n52, 64–5, 67–77, 79–82, 86, 98–103, 111, 117, 122–3, 126, 128–9, 147–9, 152–3, 158, 164, 169–70, 176–82, 184, 188, 192, 194, 202–3, 208, 214, 221, 223, 225, 246, 248–53, 263, 274–9, 285, 291, 298, 301, 303, 322–6, 329, 331, 339

Mackenzie, William Lyon, 108, 110–11, 121, 161, *634*

McLaren, Peter, 151

MacMahon, D.J., 121

McNairn, Jeffrey L., 7, 9–10, 17, 99, 105, 149, 179, 187, 323–4, 363, 386, 389, 392, 398

McNaught, Kenneth, 117–18

Macpherson, C.B., 9, 74, 120, 149, 163, 188, 306, 376

McRae, A.D., 335

McVety, James H., 337

Magna Carta, 159

Mail and Empire, 398–9

Makus, Ingrid, 278

Mandeville, Bernard, 76

Manitoba Act (1870), 169, *635*

Manitoba Free Press, *641*

Manning, D.J., 78

Manning, Preston, 330

marginalized peoples. *See* liberal order, and exclusion

market economy, 80, 149, 182, 191, 231, 261, 263, 268–9n39, 271–2n54, 332, 354, 356, 377–8, 414, 416

marketplace. *See* market economy

market relations. *See* market economy

market revolution, 66

Maroney, Paul, 409

marriage, women's rights in. *See* women, legal status of

Marsh, Leonard, 330

Martin, Clara Brett, 286

Marx, Karl, 153, 164, 181, 376, 398, 419, *622*

Marxism, 75, 85, 188, 195n3, 366, 368, 375, 403, *628–9*

Marxist analysis or framework, 84, 176–7, 403, *619*, *628*

Marxists, 152

Matthews, Peter, 112–22, 160

Mawani, Renisa, 280

Meighen, Arthur, 353

Metha, Uday Singh, 185, 279, 384, 387–8

Métis people, 165–9, 277, 306

Midgley, Victor, 338

middle-class. *See* class

Military Voters Act (1917), 290

Mill, James, 183–4, 384

Mill, John Stuart, 8, 9, 73, 82, 181–5, 193, 304, 329, 352–3, 381, 384, 387–9, 397, 423n13, 424n14

Miller, J.R., 281

Milloy, John, 299, 302

Mills, Charles, 276–7

Mills, David, 353

Miners' and Mine Labourers' Protective Association, 333

Mirror, 121

missionaries, 302–4, 310

Mitchell, David, 335

modernity, 65, 126, 255, 258, 264, 264n4, 269–70n47, 336, 369–70, 384

Monet, Jacques, 124

Mongia, Radhika Viyas, 285

Montesquieu, Charles-Louis de Secondat, baron de, 26n24

Morera, Esteve, 375

Morgan, Jennifer, 291

Morton, Adam David, 364, 370

Mountain, Jacob, 160

Mowat, Oliver, 397

multiculturalism, 128

municipal government, 183, 201–3, 206–12; opposition to, 213–14

Murray, James, 157–8

Nanaimo Free Press, 333

nation: as historical category, 274–5; and race, 282–4, 288–9, 291

nationalism, 7; definition of, 28–9n40; English Canadian, 128, *641*; in the liberal order framework, 13–14; in Québec, 124

National Policy, 19, 123, 177, *633*, *638*, *640*

Native peoples. *See* Aboriginal peoples

Natural Right and History (Strauss), 156

Nelson, Robert, 154, 156, 161, 167

Nelson, Wendie, 214

Neocleous, Mark, 194

neo-conservatism. *See* conservatism, and neo-liberalism

neo-Gramscianism, 191

neo-liberalism. *See* conservatism, and neo-liberalism

neo-Marxism, 187, 323, 383, *629*. *See also* Gramsci, Antonio

New Brunswick school question, 152

New Democratic Party (NDP), 338

Newfoundland, naval government in, 102, 105–6

Newfoundlander, 106

new Whig historiography. *See* historiography, Canada

Ninety-Two Resolutions, 108–9

Noel, S.J.R., 409, 411

non-individuals, 7, 356

non-Western peoples, 275, 291

northern North America, 275, 279, 282, 286, 288, 290–1, 353, 360, 397, *622*, *634*

North-west expansion, 177, *633*

North-West Rebellion (1885), 277

Nouvel ordre des choses, Un (Fecteau), 274

Novascotian, 106

Oliphant, Lawrence, 308–9

Oliver, John, 335

Oliver, Peter, 110

On Liberty (Mill), 13, 387–8

On-to-Ottawa Trek (1935), 283–4

On Representative Government (Mill), 388

organic intellectuals. *See* liberal order, organic intellectuals of

Ormsby, Margaret, 327

Padlock Law (1935–7), 401

Pangle, Thomas L., 410

Panitch, Leo, 364

Pannekoek, Frits, 165, 398

Papineau, Louis-Joseph, 108, 161

Parry, J.H., 100

passive revolution. *See* hegemony, and passive revolution *and* liberal order, and passive revolution

Pateman, Carole, 277–8, 286

paternalism, 304–5

patriarchy, 275–6, 280, 291, 326

Patriotes, 18, 82, 357

Pattulo, Duff, 353

Pearson, Lester B., 170

peasant society, 252–3, 265n17

periodization, 18–20, 98, 102, 275, 349, 359, 404–5, *632–3*

Perry, Adele, 8, 22, 224

Pierson, Stuart, 122

pisciculture, 235

Plank, Geoffrey, 103

Plan of Parliamentary Reform (Bentham), 183

poaching, 234

Pocock, J.G.A., 66, 125, 153, 409, 410

POGG (peace, order, and good government), 127, 145n177, *645*
political economy, 75, 77–8, 180, 190–1, 252, 261, 263, 354, 374, 377, 380, 394, 411, *639*
Political Theory of Possessive Individualism, The (Macpherson), 74
Politics of Population, The (Curtis), 274
population: as category, 178, 191–2; government of, 227, 229
Populism and Democratic Thought in the Canadian Prairies, 1910 to 1945 (Laycock), 334
Porter, John, 126
possessive individualism, 9, 100, 188, 300, 306, 308. *See also* individualism
postcolonial theory, 274, 276, 405
Post-Liberalism (Gray), 408
postmodernity, 369, 403–4, *617–18*
post-structuralism, 179, 186, 191, 254
potlatch, criminalization of, 83
praxis, philosophy of, 366
Prince Edward Island land question, 378
Prison Notebooks (Gramsci), 363, 365–6, 372
Pritchard, W.A., 338
private property. *See* property *and* property rights
Problem of Canada, 348–9, *622*
Programme catholique (1871), 163
Progrès, harmonie, liberté (Roy), 7
progress. *See* liberalism, and progress
Progressive Conservatives, 350
prohibition movement, 426–7n24
property, 74, 117–22, 148–52, 160, 164, 168, 186, 231, 276, 309, 312–13, 323–4, 402–3, *624, 638*; rights, 7, 9–13, 16, 151–3, 168–9, 176, 180, 208, 223, 286, 326, 355, 402–3, *624*. *See also* liberal order, and property
Provencher, Joseph-Alfred-Norbert, 167
Provincial Workmen's Association (Nova Scotia), 412

Quebec Act (1774), 103
Quebec Revenues Act (1774), 109–10
queer theory, 177, 408
Quelques considérations sur les rapports de la société civile avec la religion et la famille (Laflèche), 82
Quiet Revolution, 14, *621*

race. *See* liberalism, and race; liberal order, and race; liberal order framework, and race; *and* nation, and race
racial contract, 286
racism, 248, 257, 282, 291, 303
Radforth, Ian, 274
Radicals, 18–19, 400, *632*; in Britain, 74, 78, 111, 182, 184; Pictou, 357
rational-choice theory, 65
Razack, Sherene, 282
Read, Colin, 111
reading instruction, in Canada West and Ontario, 189–90
Reagan, Ronald, 11
Rebellion (1837–8). *See* rebellions (1837–8)
rebellions: (1837–8), 18, 101–2, 108, 111–12, 122, 127, 178, 205, 400, *632*; in Lower Canada, 108, 110, 121, 124, 207, 209; (1837), in Upper Canada, 113–14, 117
Rebels, Reds, Radicals (McKay), 5, 15, 339

reconnaissance, 4, 83, 85, 99, 176, 202, 225–6, 263, 298, 322–3, 361, 403–4, 407–9, 412, *620–1, 624, 627, 630*; and Atlantic history, 100; and hegemony, 15–16, 80, 366, 403, 416–77; political implications of, 69, 90n27, 404

Red River Rebellion (1869–70), 165–7, 178, 277

Reddy, William, 75–6, 248, 250, 254

Reflections on the Revolution in France (Burke), 150

reforestation. *See* forestry

Reformers, 72, 104–5, 110–11, 113, 121–2, 161, 350

Reid, Alastair, 328, 330–1

Reid, Escott, 170

Reid, John, 100, 103

religion, 160–3, *627. See also* liberal order framework, and religion *and* liberalism, and religion

'Report on the Affairs of the Indians in Canada,' 159

republicanism, 7, 112, 126, 153, 410; civic, 125, 182; classical, 183; patriot, 182

reserves, 299–302, 304, 309, 312–14, 316, 332

residential schools, 74, 281, 303, 315, 361, 381, 388, 397, 402. *See also* liberal order, and residential schools

responsible government, 18, 106, 111, 177, *632. See also* liberalism, and responsible government

R. v. Howe, 106

Ridington, Robin, 258

Riel, Louis, 165–7, 169, 277

Riel Rebellion. *See* Red River Rebellion

rights, 7, 148–50, 152–7, 161–3, 166–9, 186, 223, 278, 298, 309; British, 155–62, 167–8; Catholic, 162–3

rights-speak. *See* rights talk

rights talk, 148–9, 153–8, 160, 162–3, 165–6, 169–70, 250, 311, 315

Risk, R.C.B., 379, 386

'Rivers and Streams' controversy, 151

Robinson, John Beverley, 12, 112–22, 126, 128–9, 165

Rodgers, Daniel T., 354

Roebuck, J.A., 184

Romney, Paul, 110, 389, 392, *633*

Rose, Nikolas, 188

Rouges, 10, 19, 154, 162, 357

Rousseau, Jean-Jacques, 82, 154, 398

Roy, Fernande, 7, 70, 426n22, *623–4*

Royal Commission on Chinese Immigration (1884–5), 284, 333

royal prerogative, in coalfields of Nova Scotia, 379, 406

Royal Proclamation (1763), 168, 286, 301, 310, 316, 319–20n34, 405

Rudy, Jarrett, 14, 17

rule, Canada as project of, 4, 64, 98–100, 112, 184, 215n5, 249, 322, 348–9, 357–8, 360–1, 396, 409, 412, *620–1, 623, 627, 640*

rule of law, 10, 12, 110, 116–17, 120, 127, 151, 156, 166, 326, 330, 390, *636*

Russell, John, 109–10, 201

Russell, Peter, 395

Ryerson, Egerton, 72, 125

Ryerson, John, 114

Samson, Daniel, 262

Sandwell, Ruth, 17, 20, 75–6, 287, 325–6

Sassoon, Anne Showstack, 372
Scatzki, Theodore R., 253
Schabas, William A., 170
Schmitt, Carl, 397
school toilets, 189–90
Schools for All (Mill), 183
Scott, Duncan Campbell, 353, 381
Scott, Frank, 401
Scott, James, 228
Scott, Thomas, 166
Second Treatise of Government (Locke),
    118, 378, 388, 390–1
segregation, 282–3
seigneurial system, 379, 382, 406
self: modern notion of, 66; technolo-
    gies of the, 187–90. *See also* individ-
    ualism
self-determination, right to, 185, 299
self-government, 151, 157, 178, 185,
    203, 207–9, 212, 226, 229, 316, 329,
    384
self-interest, 68, 73, 76, 149, 153, 249,
    255, 257, 260, 263, 278, 402, 410
self-possession, 7, 74–5, 189, 350, 384,
    623–5
separate schooling, 282
Sewell, William, 351, 367
sexual contract, 278, 286–7
Sexual Contract, The (Pateman), 278
Shanin, Teodore, 253
Sifton, Clifford, *641*
Simon, Roger, 363
Sketch of the North-West of America
    (Taché), 165
Skinner, Quentin, 79, 409
slavery, 71, 161, 275, 282, 352
Smith, Adam, 9, 26n24, 75–6, 78,
    171n8, *636*
Smith, Goldwin, 353, 387, 397

social control theory, 367
Social Credit: in Alberta, 335; in Brit-
    ish Columbia, 330, 334–6, 339
Social Gospel, *642, 644*
socialism, 7, 86, 365, 398, 401, 418–19,
    642 (*see also* civic humanism, and
    socialism; conservatism, and
    socialism; *and* liberalism, and
    socialism); Fabian, 338
social regulation, 4, 332
Société pour le reboisement de la
    province de Québec, 230
Spencer, Herbert, 353, 381, 416, 423–
    4n13
sport fishery, 233–6
Sproat, G.M., 379
Spry, Irene, 301
Stagg, Ronald, 111
Stamp Act, 159
state formation, 4, 15, 101, 122–3, 164,
    178, 186, 191–2, 194, 204–5, 222,
    225–7, 236, 275, 348, 358, 368, 370–
    3, 394, 398, 415, *619, 642*
state formation, historiography. *See*
    historiography, Canada
state science, 227–9
States of Injury (Brown), 278
Status Indians. *See* Aboriginal peo-
    ples, legal status of
Steeves, Dorothy, 337
Strachan, John, 160–1
Strauss, Leo, 156
Struthers, James, 385
subjectivity: constitution of, 180,
    187–8, 249; government of, 189
suffrage: female, 82, 288–90, 326,
    625, 635; rights, 209, 276, 278, 287–
    9, 362, *625, 641*; universal, 183,
    290

Sydenham, Lord, 183, 201, 207–8, 210, 353, 358, 394, *632*

Sylvester, Kenneth, 262

Taché, A.A., 165–9

tacit consent, 121–2, 160

tariffs, 67, 362, 370, 372, *628–9*; protective, 81, 362, 377 (*see also* National Policy)

taxation, 82, 105–11, 208–9, 253, 267, 304, 310–11, 313, 380; opposition to, 212–14, 309–10

Taylor, Harriet, 82

technologies of power, 186–8, 207, 228

Test Act, 162

Thatcher, Margaret, 11, 80, 179–80, 416, *624*

Thatcherism. *See* Thatcher, Margaret

Thevet, André, 164

This Is Not a Peace Pipe (Turner), 310

Thom, Adam, 212

Thompson, E.P., 116, 164

Thomson, Charles Edward Poulett. *See* Sydenham, Lord

Tocqueville, Alexis de, 423n13

toilets. *See* school toilets

Tories, 10, 110, 125–6, 151, 156, 304–5, 309–10, 358–9, 400, *632*

Tory touch, 123–5, 360, *639*

trade unions, 373, 402–3, *643*

trasformismo. *See* hegemony, and passive revolution

treaties, First Nations, 299–300, 302, 309–10, 312–13, 316

Trotsky, Leon, 371, 398–9

Trudeau, Pierre-Elliott, 170, 313

Trudel, F.-X.-A., 163

Turner, Dale, 310–11

Two Treatises of Government (Locke), 74

ultramontanes, 162–3, 167, 169, 411, *640*

Underground Railroad, 282

Underhill, Frank, 152–3

United Empire Loyalists. *See* Loyalists

Universal Declaration of Human Rights (1948), 170

Urbinati, Nadia, 414

utilitarianism, *640*

Van Arnam, John, 121

variants of liberalism. *See* liberalism, varieties of

Vipond, Robert, 152, 389, 392

voting. *See* suffrage

Wagner, Adolph, 418

Wakefield, Edward Gibbon, 73, 184

Walker, Thomas, 157

Wal-Mart stores, 193

Walrus, The, 128

War Measures Act, 178, 401

Wartime Elections Act (1917), 290

Watson, John, *642*

Weaver, John, 380, 383

Wesley, John, 381

Western Clarion, 337

What's the Matter with Kansas? (Frank), 153

Who Killed Canadian History? (Granatstein), 123

Wilson, Kathleen, 101

Winnipeg General Strike (1919), 284

Wise, S.F., 65, 123–4, 161

women: humanity of, 276; legal sta-

tus of, 19, 275, 286–7 (*see also* citizenship)
Women's Franchise Act (1918), 290. *See also* suffrage
Wood, Gordon, 125, 410
working class. *See* class

Wright, Barry, 108, 110

Yip, Harry, 279
Young, Brian, 379, *627–8n22*
Young, Walter, 339, 411